Gospel & Culture

THE WILLIAM CAREY LIBRARY SERIES ON
APPLIED CULTURAL ANTHROPOLOGY
William A. Smalley, Editor

Becoming Bilingual: A Guide to Language Learning by Donald N. Larson and William A. Smalley, 425 pp., $5.95x

Christopaganism or Indigenous Christianity? edited by Tetsunao Yamamori and Charles R. Taber, 264 pp., $5.95

The Church and Cultures: An Applied Anthropology for the Religious Worker by Louis J. Luzbetak, 448 pp., $5.95

Culture and Human Values: Christian Intervention in Anthropological Perspective, articles by Jacob A. Loewen, edited by William A. Smalley, 464 pp., $5.95x

Customs and Cultures: Anthropology for Christian Missions by Eugene A. Nida, 320 pp., $3.95x

Gospel and Culture edited by John Stott and Robert T. Coote, 480 pp., $6.95x

Manual of Articulatory Phonetics by William A. Smalley, 522 pp., $5.95x

Message and Mission: The Communication of the Christian Faith by Eugene A. Nida, 272 pp., $3.95x

Readings in Missionary Anthropology II edited by William A. Smalley, 944 pp., $9.95x

Religion Across Cultures by Eugene A. Nida, 128 pp., $3.95x

Solomon Islands Christianity: A Study in Growth and Obstruction by Alan R. Tippett, 428 pp., $5.95

Tips on Taping: Language Recording in the Social Sciences by Wayne and Lonna Dickerson, 208 pp., $5.95

Understanding Latin Americans with Special Reference to Religious Values and Movements by Eugene A. Nida, 176 pp., $3.95

Worldview and the Communication of the Gospel: A Nigerian Case Study by Marguerite G. Kraft, 240 pp., $7.95

Gospel&Culture

THE PAPERS OF A CONSULTATION ON
THE GOSPEL AND CULTURE, CONVENED
BY THE LAUSANNE COMMITTEE'S
THEOLOGY AND EDUCATION GROUP

JOHN STOTT

ROBERT T. COOTE

editors

William Carey Library

1705 N. SIERRA BONITA AVE • PASADENA, CALIFORNIA 91104

Library of Congress Cataloging in Publication Data
Main entry under title:

Gospel and culture.

   "Sponsored by the Theology and Education Group and
the Strategy Working Group of the Lausanne Committee for
World Evangelization."
   Includes bibliographical references.
   1. Christianity and culture--Congresses. I. Stott,
John R. W. II. Coote, Robert T., 1932-   III. Laus-
anne Committee for World Evangelization. Theology and
Education Group. IV. Lausanne Committee for World
Evangelization. Strategy Working Group.
BR115.C8G67 1979   261   79-15739
ISBN 0-87808-166-6

In encouraging the publication and study of this paper, the
Lausanne Committee for World Evangelization does not neces-
sarily endorse every viewpoint expressed in it.

Published by William Carey Library
1705 N. Sierra Bonita Avenue
Pasadena, California 91104
Telephone (213) 798-0819

In accord with some of the most recent thinking of the academic press, the William Carey Library is pleased to present
this scholarly book which has been prepared from an author-
edited and author-prepared camera ready copy.

PRINTED IN THE UNITED STATES OF AMERICA

Contents

v

Foreword

In January 1978 a group of 33 theologians, anthropologists, linguists, missionaries and pastors representing six continents met to study issues related to the question of "Gospel and Culture." The meeting, sponsored by the Theology and Education Group and the Strategy Working Group of the Lausanne Committee for World Evangelization, was an outgrowth of the Lausanne Congress on World Evangelization held in 1974.

The goals of the meeting, as stated in its report,[1] were:

1. To develop our understanding of the interrelation of the Gospel and culture with special reference to God's revelation, to our interpretation and communication of it, and to the response of the hearers in their conversion, and their churches and their life style.

2. To reflect critically on the implications of the communication of the Gospel cross-culturally.

3. To identify the tools required for more adequate communication of the Gospel.

4. To share the fruits of the consultation with Christian leaders in church and mission.

This volume contains the original papers for the conference, published here for those missiologists and other scholars who want to study the issues raised at the conference more fully.[2]

Some of the papers are general, others case studies of individual situations. Some are biblical or theological in their primary perspective, others anthropological or sociological. They treat issues as varied as revelation and Christian life-style, all from the standpoint of the relation of that aspect of the Gospel to the culture which carries it.

The issue of the relation between Gospel and culture has moved to the center of missiological concerns in recent years, and opinions are hotly debated.[3] These papers mark an important step in the recognition of the centrality of the issue, and contribute to the debate.

William A. Smalley

<hr>

1. *The Willowbank Report: Report of a Consultation on Gospel and Culture,* 1978, Wheaton, Illinois: Lausanne Committee for World Evangelization. (See Appendix, p. 429.)

2. In addition to the brief 36 page report (*Ibid.*) and this present complete set of papers, there is being published a condensation of the papers, under the title *The Gospel and Culture* (Eerdmans: Grand Rapids, 1979; Hodder and Stoughton: London, 1979).

3. An inside view on some of the serious differences which came up in the discussion of these papers and the preparation of the report of the Consultation may be seen in the editorial by Charles R. Taber and the comments by Orlando E. Costas in *Gospel in Context,* 1.2 (April 1978):2,16.

Preface

"Culture" has been on the agenda of communication theorists for a very long time. And recent well-known books like Richard Niebuhr's *Christ and Culture* (1952) and Eugene Nida's *Customs and Cultures* (1954), *Message and Mission* (1960) and *Religion Across Cultures* (1968) have introduced the topic to a wider public. Yet only, I suspect, as a result of the Lausanne Congress on World Evangelization in 1974 has the evangelical constituency as a whole come to acknowledge the central importance of culture for the effective communication of the Gospel. At Lausanne Rene Padilla startled his listeners by describing some missionaries as exporters of a "culture Christianity" rather than of the authentic Gospel. Paragraph 10 of the Lausanne Covenant is entitled "Evangelism and Culture." No responsible messenger of the Gospel can ignore the subject any longer.

"Gospel and Culture" is not a topic of purely academic interest. On the contrary, it is the burning practical concern of every missionary, every preacher, every Christian witness. For it is literally impossible to evangelize in a cultural vacuum. Nobody can reduce the biblical Gospel to a few culture-free axioms which are universally intelligible. This is because the mind-set of all human beings has been formed by the culture in which they have been brought up. Their presuppositions, their value system, the ways in which they think, and the degree of their receptivity or resistance to new ideas, are all largely determined by their cultural inheritance and are filters through which they listen and evaluate.

The overriding reason why we should take other people's cultures seriously is that God has taken ours seriously. God is the supreme communicator. And his Word has come to us in an

extremely particularized form. Whether spoken or written, it
was addressed to particular people in particular cultures using
the particular thought forms, syntax and vocabulary with which
they were familiar. Then when God's Word actually "became
flesh," the "flesh" he became was that of a first-century, male,
Palestinian Jew. Thus both Inspiration and Incarnation—two
fundamental evangelical truths—are models of sensitive cross-
cultural communication, and summon us to follow suit.

To Christian obedience we add Christian strategy. Church
growth statistics in large areas of the Third World are thril-
ling to read. Yet the great mass movements into the church
have, generally speaking, involved people of broadly "animistic"
background. By comparison very few of those who have inherited
one of the major "culture-religions"—Hindus, Buddhists, Jews,
Moslems and Marxists—have been won to Christ. As a historical
example I mention Adoniram Judson of Burma. When he died in
1850, after 37 years of devoted and sacrificial labor, during
which he returned home to the United States only once, he left
about 7,000 converts from the animistic Karens, but a mere 100
Burmese converts from Buddhism. Why was this? What are the
reasons for people's resistance to the Gospel? How are we to explain the pitifully small "dent" which has been made, for instance, on the 600 million Hindus of India or the 700 million
Moslems of the Islamic block? Although different answers are
given to these questions, they are all basically cultural. The
major challenge to the worldwide Christian mission today is
whether we are willing for the cost of following in the footsteps of our incarnate Lord, in order to contextualize the
Gospel. Our failure of communication is a failure of contextualization.

The problem facing every cross-cultural messenger of the
Gospel can be simply stated. It is this: "How can I, who was
born and brought up in one culture, take truth out of the Bible
which was addressed to people in a second culture, and communicate it to people who belong to a third culture, without either
falsifying the message or rendering it unintelligible?" It is
this interaction between three cultures which constitutes the
exciting challenge of cross-cultural communication. And then,
when the message has been understood and received by the hearers,
further questions arise. How should they relate to their own
culture in their conversion, in their ethical lifestyle and in
their church life?

Culture in revelation and in hermeneutics (i.e., in the
writing and the reading of the Bible), in evangelism and in conversion, in ethics and in churches: these were the six aspects
of "Gospel and Culture" which brought 33 of us to Willowbank in
Bermuda in January 1978, under Lausanne auspices, for six

strenuous days of thought and debate. Our Consultation was not lacking in cultural drama. The theologians and the anthropologists, having different starting points, did not always reach the same destination. Africans and Asians had to complain of Euro-American dominance, while an uninhibited Latin American brother protested in uninhibited Latin American style against the oppressive behavior of the Anglo-Saxon moderator who sought to impose on the proceedings a Westminster parliamentary model, and who now penitently confesses the error of his ways!

At the end of our Consultation the *Willowbank Report* was issued and may be found on pages 429 ff. This volume contains the 17 papers submitted to the Consultation, some having been revised by the authors subsequent to the Consultation. To Peter Savage who coordinated the Consultation so efficiently, and to Robert Coote and their agency Partnership in Mission who supervised the compilation of the papers for this volume, we express our heartfelt thanks.

John Stott

1

Religion and Culture:
A Historical Introduction

Stephen Neill

Throughout human history religion and culture have been in-
dissociably connected. There has never yet been a great religion
which did not find its expression in a great culture. There has
never yet been a great culture which did not have deep roots in
a religion. When religion is separated from culture, it becomes
anemic -- religion cannot feed on religion, it has to feed on
life. Whenever a culture is set loose from religion, it becomes
demonic. The Russians set out to develop a culture free from
every religious connection; we have seen the result in Stalin.
In western Europe the Christian substance underlying the culture
is diminished; we have seen the demonic possibilities in Hitler.

We can speak of religion and culture as separate entities; but
in actual living they are very closely entwined. The influence
of religion can be clearly seen in three central areas of human
experience, which are generally regarded as cultural rather than
as specifically religious: language, social custom, art.

The influence of religion in all these three areas can be seen
more clearly in Islam than in most other religious systems.
Islam claims that in the Koran a revelation has been given not
only for the spiritual and liturgical aspects of human life, but
for the social, the political, the economic and the personal as
well.

So Islam has consecrated one language as the language of
worship and of religious expression. The set prayers must be
said in Arabic and not in any other language. The Koran cannot
be translated into any other language, since the language is an
essential part of the revelation. In the early days of Islam a
serious attempt was made to eliminate every other language and
to make Arabic the sole medium of communication. The success
attained by Islam, though not complete, is very remarkable. In
Egypt, Greek totally disappeared, and Coptic was rescued to serve
as the liturgical language of a minority. In North Africa no
other language is spoken, until we come to the Tuareg and other
independent people of the Sahara. But success had its limits.
The Turks insisted on speaking Turkish, the Persians on speaking
Persian. India has produced the elegant hybrid Urdu, East Africa
the elegant hybrid Swahili. Malaya and Indonesia speak Malay in
various forms. Each of these languages had been profoundly
influenced by Arabic; but the familiar forms of speech, and the
older traditions of culture have in a measure managed to maintain
themselves against the unifying influence of Islam.

Social custom tends to be uniform throughout the Islamic world.
Male circumcision, though not actually required by the Koran, is
everywhere accepted as obligatory. Both men and women are expected to observe a great many prescriptions with regard to dress,
nomenclature, sanitary habits and so forth, which have in one way
or another become part of the Islamic tradition.

The strict prohibition of any representation of the human form,
though comprehensively disregarded by the Moguls in India, has
laid its heavy hand in most areas on the development of Islamic
art. Architecture and calligraphy have been the two forms of art
in which the Islamic world has excelled.

This Islamic totalitarianism is not a thing of the past; it is
possible to observe it in operation in any part of the world in
which Islamic propaganda is intense and has the support of the
ruling powers. In Sabah, for example, it is the declared policy
of the government to make Malay, the language of the Muslim
minority, the sole official language, in the hope that the non-
Muslim languages, Chinese and English, will be relegated to the
areas of purely private discourse. Any Chinese who accepts Islam
is expected at the same time to adopt a Muslim name, to accept
the use of Islamic dress, and to conform to many of the social
usages demanded by the Islamic tradition. It is true that in
many parts of the world a good deal of the old way of looking at
the universe persists, and that much which Islamic orthodoxy
would condemn as pre-Islamic superstition continues to flourish
underground, and in some areas not far underground. But the
supremacy of Islam is nowhere in question: the Muslim speaks no
more than the truth, when he claims that there is an Islamic

unity, which stretches from Morocco to Java, and from Cape Town
to Albania.

Hinduism can be seen operating in a rather similar fashion.
As Hinduism spreads among the peoples of non-Aryan origin, these
peoples are absorbed into the caste system, which is wholly alien
to them. More freedom for caste-variation is permitted than
would be the case under absorption into the world of Islam; but,
with government policy to make Hindi the national language, the
old tribal languages are reduced to a status of inferiority, and
it seems probable that some, at least, of them will disappear.

When Christian missions began again to be actively developed
at the beginning of the sixteenth century, they were in the hands
of the two western nations that had been most profoundly influenced by Islam, and this must be regarded, from the Christian
point of view, as having been in many ways a misfortune.

It is often forgotten that the period of Islamic colonial rule
in the Iberian peninsula lasted for more than six centuries, and
did not reach its final end, with the capture of Granada, until
1495, three years after the discovery of America by Columbus,
and three years before the opening up of the sea-route to India
by Vasco da Gama. It is true that Islamic domination had begun
to break up considerably earlier, especially in Portugal. And
Iberian resistance had never entirely ceased during these six
centuries. The Spanish and Portuguese languages had never been
submerged by Arabic; and the Christian faith had managed, with
some difficulty, to maintain itself against all the prosely-
tizing efforts of the Muslims. But the Muslim influence had
penetrated everywhere, and continued to be felt long after the
colonial period had come to an end.

After the completion of the liberation, the two groups of
peoples, Christian and Islamic, found themselves in a curious
love-hate relationship which lasted for centuries.

Naturally, after so long a period of colonial subjection,
hatred of the oppressors was intense. The Portuguese carried
over into their Asiatic wars a ferocity which accorded ill with
the ideals of Christian chivalry. To Indian Muslims they were
prepared to permit a considerable measure of tolerance; but for
the Arabs there could be nothing but extermination, at least in
the correct and more moderate understanding of that term.

On the other hand, having been so long accustomed to Muslim
totalitarianism, both races, Spanish and Portuguese alike, took
over in their missionary work, almost unaltered, the methods with
which they had become familiar in the Muslim propagation of the
Islamic faith, though neither was quite as thorough in the

execution of their purpose as the Muslim had been, and there was
more flexibility in their methods.

Over large areas of the western world, Spanish came to be
accepted as the sole medium of educated intercourse. The one
notable exception was the famous Jesuit "reduction" in Paraguay.
The dominance of the Jesuits was absolute, and the law of Christ,
as understood by Roman Catholics of that period, was to be the
law of the communities. And yet the language of the people,
and to a considerable extent their traditional customs, were to
be preserved. Christian literature was developed in Guarani,
the books being printed on presses developed by the mission.
This was a matter of policy rather than of philosophy; the aim
of the Jesuits was to preserve their garden of Eden intact, and
knowledge of Spanish on the part of the Indians might make a
fatal breach in the hedge. With the withdrawal of the Jesuits
the experiment came to an end, and was never repeated in the
same form. But the existence at the present time of hundreds
of Amerindian languages indicates the limits of Spanish
penetration and of the Hispanization of the populations.

In the East, the Portuguese followed much the same pattern,
but with perhaps an ever closer approximation to the Islamic
ideal.

In a strictly Muslim country, no Christian symbol, not even
the cross on a church, might be displayed. This is the case in
Saudi Arabia at the present time. In exactly the same way, it
was felt that a Christian king could not tolerate the display of
any Hindu symbol in any territories which he controlled. Hindus
in Portuguese possessions were not compelled (though they were
warmly encouraged) to become Christians; but if they continued
to observe Hindu rites and ceremonies, this must be done only
in the strictest privacy.

Any Hindu who became a Christian was given a Christian name,
i.e. a Portuguese name, to the confusion of the historian, who
is constantly in doubt as to whether persons referred to in the
records were of European or of Indian nationality.

Candidates for baptism were given a robe of European fashion
to indicate the passage from one community to the other. This
was regarded by the candidates as so important a part of the
ceremony that on occasion they refused to be baptized if the
robe was not provided, and at times baptism had to be postponed,
because there just were not enough robes to go around. The
wearing of Christian, i.e. western dress by Hindus was strictly
forbidden.

Latin was the sole liturgical language; it never occurred to a Portuguese that any other could be used than that which was familiar to him as the universal language of the Catholic Church (as we shall see in a moment, he had to learn otherwise). Portuguese was the basis of education, with the odd result that children could read their own language Konkani in Roman letters but could not read it in its own Devanagari script. There was even at one time an attempt to follow up the Islamic precedent by suppressing the Konkani language in favor of Portuguese; but the steady resistance of the people was too strong, and this foolish enterprise was soon given up. But it was an English Jesuit, Thomas Stephens, and not a Portuguese, who was the pioneer in the creation of Christian literature in Konkani.

So far we have been considering Portuguese methods in areas which had been conquered and were controlled by them. They showed considerably more flexibility in areas which were under their influence but not under their control. The ancient church of the Thomas Christians in Kerala, was more or less forcibly brought into union with the church of Rome at the Synod of Diamper in 1599. But the Portuguese, compelled at length to recognize the intense loyalty of these people to their ancient traditions, in the end allowed them to keep Syriac as their liturgical language, and made no attempt to insist on western dress as a condition for being recognized as a Christian. At a rather earlier date, when the whole community of the fisher folk of the Coast of Cornandel became Christian, their traditional organization was left almost intact, and no attempt was made to interfere with their traditional way of living, except that fishing on Sunday was forbidden. Four centuries of Roman Catholic influence have left the Bharathas as an unmistakably Indian community. In 1606 the redoubtable Italian Robert de Nobili appeared on the scene, and made the first attempt to create an Indian church, with the fewest possible changes in the traditional Indian way of living. His method of accommodation gave rise to a notable and long-lasting controversy, which unfortunately was decided by Rome in the sense that everything in India was to be done after the high Roman fashion, and that no changes whatever were to be made in the western way of doing things.

When the Protestant missions appeared on the scene, their policies were in many ways different from their Roman Catholic predecessors. They came from countries which had never been under the Muslim yoke and they were unfamiliar with Muslim methods. At many points they deliberately departed from the methods followed by the Roman Catholics. For the most part their purpose was to Christianize and not to westernize.

Once again language was the crucial test. It was the aim of
the Protestants that the people should, as soon as possible,
have the Word of God in their own language, and should be able
to read it for themselves. Therefore education must be in a
local and not a European language, and missionaries, unlike the
great majority of those of the Roman tradition, must be well
acquainted with the language of the people. For this there were
two reasons. In the first place this was one of the major
principles of the Reformation; Luther and Tyndale had not
labored in vain; Bible reading and worship in a language understood by the people was a cardinal Reformation principle.
Secondly, the missionaries seem to have felt that the curse of
Babel and the multiplicity of languages were a part of the human
situation, which must endure until the second coming of Christ.
The motto of Bagsters, the publishers, *Multae terricolis
linguae, caelestibus una,* many languages to those upon earth,
but to those in heaven one ·only, would seem to express this
point of view. In many areas there was a strong prejudice
against introducing converts to any western language, since this
was likely to expose them to undesirable western influences, and
to hinder the development of a robust and independent Christian
faith on the lines which God had indicated for the various races.

It is impossible to overestimate the services rendered by the
Protestant missions in the field of language study. Literally
hundreds of languages have been for the first time reduced to
writing, and in each of these through the translation of the
Bible the foundations have been laid for an indigenous literature.
It may be interesting to read the testimony of an Indian scholar,
Sri Sargunar, to the services rendered by Europeans, many of
them missionaries (and not all Protestants) to the development
of Tamil, one of the most ancient languages in the world:

> *They were the first to print Tamil tracts, books and
> papers. They were the first to introduce the study
> of Tamil into the civilised countries of the World.
> They were the first to make Tamil translastions into
> European languages. They were the first to show us
> how to make a critical study of our languages,
> literature and grammar. And they also taught us to
> write 'modern Tamil prose' and created the reading
> habit among us.*

The service rendered by the missionaries in the conservation
of ancient cultures has often been overlooked. But it has to be
recognized that this is only one side of the medal. The introduction of a new religion, or of a new religious principle inevitably involves far-reaching cultural and social changes,
with the destruction of much that was old.

This is as true of Christianity as of any other religious
faith. Jesus came as Savior, but he also came as destroyer.
Loyal as he was to his Jewish inheritance, he was critical as
well as faithful. In a single pungent saying, he abolished the
distinction between clean and unclean meats -- it is what comes
forth from a man that defiles him and not what enters into him
from outside. His teaching has made a clean sweep of the
entire ritual and ceremonial law of the Jews. Circumcision,
central in the old Jewish law, is now nothing in the world,
and uncircumcision is nothing in the world. Christians may have
their children circumcised, if they wish to do so; but this has
nothing to do with the new covenant in Christ; it adds nothing
to the perfect salvation given through Him. The old law of
sacrifices has been completely abrogated. The Epistle to the
Hebrews tells us why; when the one perfect sacrifice has been
offered, there is no place for any further sacrifice. The
church has done well to keep the Old Testament in its canon; but
we can read it only because we are not Jews.

The radical character of what Jesus has done was not
immediately evident even to believers. The first great controversy in the infant church related to the status of Gentile believers in the church. The progress of the debate is clearly
seen in the contrast between the Epistle to the Galatians and
that to the Romans. In Galatians, circumcision is a burning
issue; the whole nature of salvation is at stake; when Romans is
written, it has become no more than a question relating to the
peaceful co-existence of different groups within the church.
There must always be a place for differing customs, and for
mutual concessions. If Jews and Gentiles are to meet at the
Lord's table, Gentiles must have respect for the age-long
traditions, even if they regard them as prejudices of the Jews,
and must not insist on their way of doing things. Similar
problems arise today. Some missionaries in India have become
vegetarians, out of respect for the traditions of the high-caste
Hindu. Others eat neither beef nor pork, because of the intense
repugnance felt by Hindus and Muslims for parts of European
practice.

Some religions have been modified by the Christian impact;
others have died out. The dying out of religions is a subject
to which perhaps inadequate study has been directed.

There were rivals to Christianity in the early days of the
Church. It seemed at one time that Gnosticism, or the special
form of it called Manicheanism might win the world. Nowhere in
the world today are there either Gnostics or Manicheans (though
there are still strange survivals of both in remote corners of
the world, and in the underground of the great religions). The
dualism of matter and spirit which they offered has not commended

itself to the minds of men in later ages. Mithraism was widespread in the ancient world; it has disappeared with the world
in which it prospered. The mystery religions, of which
Mithraism was one, had no very long career. They could not in
reality provide that which they promised -- assurance of immortality and inner transformation. They were undone by their
lack of factual content, and of a serious and consistent theology.
The Church triumphed because it offered the reality, where these
others gave only the shadow.

The fate of the ancient Greek and Roman gods was rather
different. No one today worships Zeus or Hera or Apollo, not so
much because they were not entirely edifying figures as because
they represented a world outlook which, in the days of Paul and
John, were already passing away. These were the gods of city
states, to be worshipped as a matter of civic duty by the
citizens of those states. With the immense extension of the
Roman empire and of the field of Greek culture, there was no
particular purpose that they could serve. The Greek cities
which stretched from Marseilles to the Hindu Kush found a certain
unity in the quasi-religious teaching of the later Stoicism with
its noble ideal of the universal city of man. The Roman empire
was held together by the cult of the emperor, a political form
of religion with little spiritual content. Neither of these had
staying power. Man yearned for something other than these
substitutes. Philosophy was too cold a mistress. One could not
really worship the Roman emperor. Men found in the warmth of the
Gospel what they could not find in the old ways.

Yet the Gospel was not only destroyer, it was also preserver.
It is easy to find fault with the synthesis resulting from the
Constantinian fusion of church and state, and with the secularization suffered by the western church, as it took over so many
of the functions of the disappearing Roman empire. It should
not be forgotten that for eight centuries the eastern empire
was the bulwark of the west against Islam, and saved Europe until Europe was strong enough to save itself. When at last it
fell, it passed on to the west many of the treasures of the
ancient world, and these the west in its turn has preserved
and passed on to us, who would have been immeasurably poorer
if all this had been lost.

Through all the centuries of conflict and weakness, neither
branch of the church, eastern or western, forgot the vocation
of the church to be universal home of all the nations, and so
to be, though this was not the primary purpose of its preaching,
not only the preserver of ancient cultures, but the creator of
new worlds of culture. Thus Byzantium reached out to Russia,
and laid the foundations of the great cultures of the Slavic
races. Gregory the Great with prophetic insight saw that a new

world must be called in to redress the balance of the old. His
mission to the Angles, was far more than a sentimental gesture
to a people he so mistakenly associated with angels; it was also
a great strategic concept. As Professor Ullmann puts it,
"Gregory made the revolutionary breakthrough to the Germanic
peoples. It was to be the union of Latin Rome with the un-
sophisticated Germanic nations which was to yield that Europe
of which the spiritual parent was Gregory the Great" (*A Short
History of the Papacy in the Middle Ages*, p. 38).

Unlike the eastern church, which recognized variety of
liturgical use and language, Rome imposed on northern Europe a
single liturgical language, and Latin became the common language
of all educated men from Iceland to Sicily, a factor of unity
which was not lost until the end of the eighteenth century. But
the vigor of the northern nations resisted total assimilation.
In spite of the steady influence of the Latin of the church, in
spite of conquest by Danes and Normans, the English still
obstinately speak a language the basis of which is of Teutonic
and not of Romance origin.

In the field of religion the story is very different. The
victory of Christianity was complete. Lord Bryce once commented
on our misfortune in that the Romans were not interested in the
culture and religion of the peoples they conquered, and never
set out to record systematically their ideas and usages. In
consequence we know sadly little of the religion of the Britons
and other Celtic peoples. The Germans are in rather a better
case, since Tacitus wrote a highly imaginative account of them.
The Scandinavians alone are the exception, since the Gospel came
to them so late in time (from the eleventh century on), there
alone an extensive pre-Christian literature has survived. The
Icelandic language has undergone so little change in a thousand
years that the Icelandic school child today can begin to read the
Edda in a way that it is impossible for the English student
faced with Beowulf. I do not think that anyone would seriously
wish to return to the world which the Eddas depict. We may
regret our isolation from our cultural past; but to attempt to
reconstruct it would be no more than an archaizing fantasy. Our
roots are Christian. When the first renaissance dawned in the
eleventh century, and the great languages of modern Europe began
to emerge from the dominance of Latin, they were unashamedly
the expression of a great Christian culture, varied within its
Christian unity, which found its creative outlet in such
glorious achievements as the *Divina Comedia*, Chaucer's
Canterbury Tales, Lincoln Cathedral, Giotto and the beginning of
modern music. Many factors contributed to this splendid outburst of genius; the most creative factor of all was the Christian Gospel transmitted through the Christian church.

We have seen then that the Gospel can serve as the destroyer,
the preserver and the creator of cultures. We must now turn the
clock back and look more closely at the fortunes of the church
in its first cultural environment, the world of Greece and Rome.
The story can be summed up in a sentence -- the church entered
into easy relations with that culture only when the religion
which underlay it had ceased to be a living force.

In the earliest days, Paul found it possible to adopt an attitude of reasonable tolerance. There must be no compromise; yet
for people who had realized that an idol is nothing in the world,
the eating of meats offered to idols need cause no unbearable
scruples of conscience. Persecution was on the horizon; but the
empire had not yet become the great persecuting power. The
change is already apparent in the book of Revelation. By the
third century the world outside the Church has become the world
of the persecutors and of the evil spirits by whom the persecutors are inspired. Tertullian the lawyer had come into the
church as an adult convert, and brought with him an intimate
knowledge of the world from which he had come. As is well known
he had an almost pathological dislike of it. He realized, as
so many converts do today, that every part of that old life is
linked to non-Christian ideas and non-Christian worship; how can
there be any fellowship between Christ and idols, between
Jerusalem and Athens? Tertullian represents an extreme point of
view, but it was without doubt shared by a great many people in
his day and for a hundred years after his time. It was difficult
for Christians to make use of the public baths, not so much
because of the notorious immorality of which they might be the
scene, as because of the worship of local spirits of fountains
and streams which was regularly practiced there. Hence the
association of godliness with dirt which lasted for many
centuries. A Christian could not serve as a magistrate, since
as such he would be required to take part in civic worship such
as was not permitted by the Christian conscience. A Christian
could not serve as a soldier, not so much because that trade
might involve him in the taking of life (the early Christians
were not pacifists), as because the soldier was required to
worship the standards of his regiment, and this the Christian
could not do. A change in religious allegiance could not but
have consequences in the world of social custom and public order.

The change in attitude was slow in coming. When the
Alexandrians began to encourage the study of pagan literature
and philosophy, they encountered strong opposition in the Church.
Clement of Alexandria defended his view of Greek philosophy as
a *praeparatio evangelica* by the curious argument that the Greeks
had derived the best of their philosophy from Moses, so that
this philosophy was in essence only part of the revelation given

by the one and true and only God. Origen, as we are told by
Gregory Thaumaturgus, put his students through a rigorous course
of Greek philosophy, but this was only to sharpen their minds
for the serious studies which were to follow, namely the study
of Scripture and of Christian theology. In neither of these
great thinkers is there any hint that Greek thought can be regarded as an independent source of truth; Scripture is supreme,
and all other studies are auxiliary to the study of it.

Only when the religions of Greece and Rome ceased to be living
realities did the church feel free to take into itself the
treasures of the ancient culture. When Christians obtained
liberty to build churches they naturally followed the best model
that they knew, and the Christian Church looked just like a
Roman basilica. In the same way, the Christian scholar roamed
through the broad fields of ancient literature. Augustine had
been a professor of rhetoric before he became a Christian,
Jerome had to blame himself for preferring Cicero to the Latin
version of the Scriptures. It is fairly easy to discover what
the Fathers had read. Virgil was, of course, the favorite of
Latins and was treated almost as though he had been a Christian
poet. The Greeks were thoroughly familiar with Homer, whom
every Greek schoolboy knew almost by heart. They read Plato,
especially Timaeus because of their interest in the doctrine of
creation. The later Stoicism was still an influence. Plotinus
was known but exercised less influence than might have been expected. But in every one of the Christian writers of the third
and fourth centuries, Scripture is supreme, and the scriptural
reference is constant. Some of the Greek Fathers write Greek
with considerable elegance; in Augustine patristic Latin rises
to magnificance. But the ancient culture is never more than a
tool for the elucidation of Scripture and for the expression of
biblical truth. Nowhere is there any suggestion, as we have
already said, that the ancient culture can in any way serve as
an independent source of revelation. The Fathers may not always
have been successful in doing what they set out to do; there
can be no doubt as to their aim. The Bible is always text; other
writings can never be anything more than commentary.

The first writer in whom a change can be detected is the
anonymous monk of the sixth century who wrote under the name of
Dionysius the Aeropagite, and whose writings unfortunately were
very widely accepted as a document of the first century and as
coming from the pen of the convert of Paul at Athens. Here we
can for the first time speak of a deep influence of neo-platonism
on Christian thought. Neo-platonic ideas seem already to have
entered into Jewish speculation, and may have returned to
pseudo-Dionysius from that source. He seems to have been influenced rather by Proclus and the later neo-platonism than by
Plotinus himself. But here we begin to see what can happen when

the supremacy of Scripture is threatened, and other words and
voices are allowed to acquire authority in the field of Christian
thought and doctrine.

How did ordinary Christians settle down to live in the midst
of a non-Christian culture from which they could not entirely
segregate themselves? To some extent they did separate themselves from the world around them, but it was not possible to go
and live on a desert island. Some measure of adaptation, and
of discrimination, was necessary. The story is paradigmatic
for every Christian community faced by a similar situation.

The Christians found it necessary to distinguish between those
things which must immediately and totally be forbidden; those
which were undesirable, and which it was hoped would gradually
die out; and those which were merely cultural, and represented
no more than differences of habit and tradition. The Romans,
like the highlanders in Scotland, regarded the wearing of breeches
as a barbarous habit; but if Christians of barbarian origin
wished in such matters to follow the customs of their ancestors,
there was no need to forbid them to do so.

It is self-evident that, if a religion is to win credit as a
potentially universal religion, it must show itself capable of
adaptation to a great variety of situations. It is equally
evident that no other religion so far can compare with Christianity in its capacity for just this kind of adaptability. Christians do not always realize how fortunate they are in that Jesus
Christ gave us so few specific or precise commandments, and that
those which he did give are not time or situation conditioned.
This becomes plain at once, if a comparison is made between
Christianity and Islam. The rules governing the fast of Ramadan
are quite clearly laid down. These rules can quite well be
observed in Arabia. If Ramadan happens to fall in June or July,
they cannot be observed north of the Arctic circle, because there
the sun never sets at all. But, even in a less extreme situation
sincere and devout Muslims are asking whether the fast can be
observed in accordance with the traditional rules, under the
conditions of work demanded in an industrial situation. For the
Christian such problems do not exist; we are less tied to
locality and to exact regulations.

There are, however, limits to adaptability. Christians now as
then, have to ask whether there are certain customs and social
usages which are wholly incompatible with the Christian Gospel,
and whether there are others which may be tolerated, for a time
or for any foreseeable future. On many issues there may be
differences of opinion among Christians; in certain areas there
is likely to be near unanimity of judgment.

1. It is probable that there would be agreement among Christians
of all persuasions that the following practices must be given up
by all those who wish to call themselves Christians:

> Idolatry; that is the observance of customs and
> ceremonies, including those associated with birth,
> marriage and death, which imply the existence and
> claims of deities other than the one true God, to
> whom alone worship and adoration may be paid.

> Witchcraft and sorcery in their evil forms, in
> which alien powers of darkness are called in to
> injure human beings.

> Female infanticide, defended by some peoples as
> the best means of preventing the increase of
> population beyond the capacity of the land to
> support it, but condemned by Christians in light
> of Christian doctrine of the sacredness of all life.

> Twin-murder, especially when it is supposed that
> one of the twins is the child of an evil spirit.

> Cannibalism, as involving disrespect to the person
> of another human being even where murder is not
> involved.

> Head-hunting; although this is so central in the life
> of some people that the abolition of it causes
> very grave disruption of the entire social structure.

> Private vengeance and the blood feud, as practiced
> among many peoples of Arabia until recent times,
> and perhaps even at the present time.

> Physical mutilation as a legal penalty, as recently
> reintroduced in Pakistan, in accordance with Islamic
> law.

> Cattle-raiding; this comes hard on the Masai, who
> believe that at the creation God gave all the
> cattle to the Masai, and that cattle-raiding is
> simply the recovery of stolen property.

> Ritual prostitution, as familiar to Paul in Ephesus
> and Corinth and in many other cities of the Levant,
> and as widely practiced in India until recent times,
> and even perhaps at the present time in certain
> places.

There would, I think, be general agreement that the abandon-
ment of such practices must be required as a condition for
baptism.

2. There is a second class of customs, which it may be impossible
to abolish, though Christians must desire that these customs
should in time disappear. We may give the following as examples:

> Slavery, which is permitted by Islamic law, and is
> still practiced in some Islamic countries. The
> British put down the slave-trade, but in Tanzania,
> wisely, did not abolish the status of slave until
> 1922. The situation may be more complex than is
> imagined by those who have not studied the subject
> closely. In the U.S.A. a man might find himself a
> slave-owner by inheritance, in a state in which the
> emancipation of slaves was forbidden by law.

> The caste system. A system which condemns eighty
> million people, with religious sanctions, to a
> status of permanent social and economic inferiority,
> is clearly contrary to the law of God and the
> principles of Christ. The church could do no
> more than point to the evils of the system and to
> work quietly for its disappearance. The independent
> government of India has legally abolished untouch-
> ability, without touching the religious claims on
> which the system is based. More generally, the
> demand that Christians should totally cut them-
> selves off from all caste connections has not
> proved workable. If put into effect, it would have
> meant simply that the Christian church become a new
> caste among the many; this is what happened to the
> Thomas-Christians in Kerala, and resulted in their
> ceasing to be a witnessing and expanding community.
> And where a mass movement takes place, the new
> community is bound to reflect a good many of the
> features of the old.

> Tribalism. This cannot but be modified by in-
> corporation into the wider fellowship of the
> church. But it is still a great power in many
> parts of the world. Whether it can be allowed to
> survive in any form within the church is one of the
> major problems faced by the churches today.

> Polygamy. Every polygamous marriage means that
> one young man will not be able to marry at the
> normal age. The presence of a large number of
> marriageable but unmarried young men produces

very grave social disruption. Almost all
Christians agree that this form of the family
must disappear; not all are agreed as to the
rate and manner of its disappearance.

3. A third set of problems arises in connection with marriage
rules and regulations. The traditions of the Christian churches
are based on Jewish and Roman views of family life, but these
are not everywhere applicable. For example, in the west marriage
between cousins, though not encouraged, is not prohibited. But
in India marriage between cousins in the male line is absolutely
prohibited. Where the joint family system still prevails, and
all children living on the same compound are regarded as brothers
and sisters, this would seem to be necessary. Marriage between
uncle and niece is generally disallowed by the Christian tradition.
But in some castes in India marriage of a man with his elder
sister's daughter is almost obligatory. This is open to grave
objections, not only on the ground of propinquity of blood but
also because of the disparity in age, with the long period of
compulsory celibacy imposed on the young man, not always to the
advantage of society. The churches are divided in their
attitude to marriages within this degree of consanguinity.

The admirably sensible report on this subject of a committee
of the Lambeth Conference seems to have attracted less attention
than it deserved. It is clear that there is a place both for
Christian principle and for flexibility in application.

4. Outside such areas in which Christian principles may be involved, there is a vast range of customs and traditions which
deal only with *adiaphora,* customs which differ, but of which it
is impossible to say categorically that one is in all circumstances better than another.

In India in almost all churches men and women sit separately
on opposite sides of the church. Westerners prefer the custom
of members of the same family sitting together. In India it is
the custom for men and women to eat separately. A few missionaries tried to change the custom; the vast majority felt that
this was a matter which must be left to the Indian Christians
themselves to decide. Today in some westernized families the
western custom of men and women eating together has been adopted,
but it cannot be said that the change has become general. In
India for any man to touch any woman in public is still in many
areas a grave social solecism. When African girl students came
up to me with outstretched hand expecting to be shaken hands
with, I experienced a frisson of horror, and had to remind myself sharply that I must not expect to behave in Africa just
as I had been accustomed to behave in India.

In Kerala men when bathing will remove all their clothing under the water, no Tamil is likely ever to do such a thing. Westerners use both hands in eating. In India the strict rule was that the right hand only was used for eating and the left for drinking. The Chinese eat with chopsticks, and regard with distaste the Indian habit of eating with the right hand.

It would be possible to go on endlessly. There seems no particular reason why such customs should be changed, or the customs of one community imposed upon another. The important thing is that when Christians move from one cultural area to another, they should try to understand and respect the customs of those among whom they have come to live. A good many changes are likely to take place simply on the grounds of convenience. A great many men in India now have their hair cut short ("the Christian crop" in local parlance) and wear trousers for no reason other than they find the European way of doing things more convenient than the old. When two communities live in close propinquity, many changes and exchanges are to be expected. It is said that today even in Russia young people listen to pop music on the radio and like to wear blue jeans (note that only those imported from America will do!). To changes of this kind no objections can be taken, provided that some attention is paid to the rules of decency and the expectations of each of the communities concerned. It would be very dull, if we all did everything in the same way. It seems that God likes us to be all different, and that it is only the media which wishes to re-duce us all to a dead level of monotonous mediocrity.

We must come back, however, to the world of principle. All that has been said in this article can be related to a single principle, which can be expressed in a single brief phrase. Christ is the Lord of all life. Everything in the life of the individual, of the family, of the church, of the community must constantly be referred back to him for judgment. No culture, no civilization, no ordering of society, is sacrosanct since all are imperfect. Christ through the Holy Spirit is the continual critic of all churches and all societies, demanding sometimes that what had seemed good should be thrown away, at other times that what had once seemed menacing as undermining the stability of society should be accepted as good and right. Immense changes have been recorded in historic times. Western society was remarkably slow to realize that slavery is an abomination, wholly incompatible with the doctrine of Christian freedom. But the lesson, once learned, seems to have been learned for good; it is unlikely that it will ever be forgotten. Even a century ago there was strong opposition in India to the education of girls; the missionaries had literally to bribe the parents into sending their daughters to school. Since independence thirty years ago, women have served as cabinet ministers, as governors of provinces and finally as prime minister.

The list of changes is endless; a whole book could be written
about them. The lesson is simply that societies are much less
static than is often supposed, that cultures are living and growing things, in a perpetual process of change. A special responsibility rests on Christians to be sensitive to the movement
of history, to discern the signs of the times, to distinguish
between that which is of real advantage and that which has a
merely deceptive attractiveness, to ensure that the will of God
becomes criterion of change, and that the whole life of man is
conformed to the likeness of Christ, and renewed according to
the pattern which God himself has revealed to us in the life
of the Lord Jesus Christ himself.

PART I

Culture
and the Bible

2

Culture and
the New Testament
I. Howard Marshall

Many of the difficulties which arise in the course of a discussion of "The Gospel and Culture" stem from our varied understandings of the terms used in the title. While we may think
that we have a clear idea of what is meant by the "Gospel," the
problem before us is the way in which our understandings of this
term may need to undergo alteration in order that we may communicate the Gospel effectively in different cultural settings.
In other words, although we may think that we understand clearly
what we mean by the Gospel, we may come to realize that this
term is more slippery than we realized, and that in other cultural situations than our own the form and perhaps even the content of "the Gospel" may be open to modification; we should then
be faced with the problem of whether there is a central, un-
changeable core to "the Gospel."

I. THE DEFINITION OF "CULTURE"

So far, however, as "culture" is concerned, it is more
likely that we begin with the consciousness that this is a slippery concept with a variety of meanings. There is no agreed
definition of what it means, and therefore we may find ourselves
trying to work towards one. In this situation it seems advisable
that I should lay my cards on the table at the outset by indicating what I mean by the term in order that misunderstanding

may not be caused simply through unrecognized differences in the use of key terms.

The problem is especially acute for the present paper. In the case of a study of, let us say, "The New Testament View of the Gospel," it is comparatively easy for the student to lay aside his own understanding of the term and to interrogate the NT documents in order to discover what the term means there. Such a task may not in fact be all that easy, since it is impossible for the student not to see the documents from his own particular angle and this will color his understanding of what the documents teach; he is in fact a prisoner of his own culture, and the task of achieving an objective stance outside it faces insuperable difficulties.[1]

The difficulties, however, are all the greater in the present situation where we are not dealing with a term actually found in the NT like "gospel" or "repentance" or "soul" but with a general concept that is not tied to any particular set of vocabulary items; and indeed the problem is perhaps greater still, since we may well have to ask whether the NT possesses a concept of "culture" as such, so that we can talk about something which was in fact a preoccupation of the NT writers themselves. We may in other words be trying to shed light from the NT on a concept which is not itself present in the NT, just as a Christian moralist, for example, might try to assemble biblical teaching relevant to the problem of abortion, although this particular problem was simply not present to the consciousness of the biblical writers.

It seems advisable, therefore, that I should begin by attempting to understand what is meant by culture before I try to assess what the NT may have to say that is relevant to this topic.[2] We shall bear in mind that the word may have a number of meanings, and that we are describing how the word is actually used rather than laying down a definition of what it ought to mean.

1. When we go back in time to a comparatively simple state of affairs and distinguish between, say, "Stone Age Culture" and "Iron Age Culture," it is clear that we are referring to two total types of human response to the environment, and the historian attempts to describe the whole life of the people of these particular ages insofar as it can be deduced from the surviving evidence. But it seems clear that these two particular "cultures" are distinguished by the different levels of technical knowledge and skill that dictated the way of life of the peoples, iron age man having discovered ways of dealing with natural resources that enabled him to do various things that were not possible for stone age man and which we, from the

point of view of a culture that values such things, would regard as constituting progress in the control of environment and an advance in the resulting standard of living. Culture, then, can refer to *the whole activity of man in his ability to control and utilize the environment*.

2. More particularly, the term can be used to describe *those powers of man which go beyond the mere ability to survive and which are concerned with the production of things or activities which are aesthetically pleasing*. Stone age man may make a rough cooking pot, adequate for its task, or a more polished and decorative one, no more adequate for its purpose of cooking but having the additional virtue of being pleasing to the eye and a delight to handle. We speak, therefore, of one man as being more cultured than another, in the sense that he is more concerned with, or more capable of, aesthetic effects. Culture in this sense presupposes in man the leisure and the ability to do things other than those required for mere survival.

It is in this sort of sense that we might regard the Greeks as more cultured than the Romans and the Romans as more cultured than the Vandals. This same illustration, incidentally, demonstrates that the progress of culture is not always in the direction of greater culture: "captive Greece took her conquerors captive" in the sense that the Greeks passed on to the Romans their artistic ideals and thereby imparted a new dimension to a people which had hitherto lived a rougher life, but on the other hand the Vandals failed to appreciate the culture of the Romans and simply destroyed it without replacing it by anything comparable to their own.

3. We have spoken so far of the technical skills which may characterize a given culture. But a culture is surely also *a set of values*. The Greeks valued the dramatic and plastic arts, and they passed on these values to the Romans who in turn accepted them and gave drama and sculpture a place in their own life. The Vandals did not value these things and therefore did not practice them. There was, therefore, in each case a set of values recognized, whether consciously or unconsciously, by the community. Such a set of values could be upheld by some kind of philosophical or religious ideology which gave a status to the values of society. A culture, therefore, represents a definite attitude to human life and is characterized by the adoption of a set of values. It is from the point of view of our own set of values that we tend to judge the values of other cultural groups and to offer some kind of assessment of them. For example, a modern historian of art would probably accord high praise to the cultural achievements of Greek civilization, and might well want to speak of the Greek achievement in absolute terms. This

verdict would apply to many areas of Greek life, the theatre,
poetry and philosophy, sculpture, and architecture, and so on.
Somebody else, who might or might not have the same high esti-
mation of the Greek achievement within these particular areas,
might, however, draw attention to the fact that this achievement
was possible only at the price of the enslavement of a considerable proportion of the Greek population who were denied the
privileges enjoyed by their masters. The Egyptian pyramids may
be monuments to the magnificent designs of their rulers, but
they also represent the terrible labor of thousands of forgotten
workers who slaved in the atrocious conditions of the desert to
make them. A view of culture which attaches high value to the
freedom of the individual and to the right of all men to share
in the fruits of culture might well protest that measured by
this standard Greek and Egyptian culture was of a woefully low
standard; a society which inflicted such suffering on so many of
its people was not a cultured society and the value of the
artistic achievements of these peoples, high though it may have
been, becomes very hollow when placed in the context of human
suffering. Yet it is improbable that thoughts such as these
entered the minds of the Greeks; they were not within their
mental horizon. Their cultural ideology did not include them.
The question then arises as to how we justify our set of values,
which condemns the slavery of ancient Greece and Egypt.

4. From what has been said it emerges that culture is *a
social phenomenon*. In the extreme case a man may make a beautiful object simply because it brings pleasure to himself, but
ordinarily speaking such objects are made for the benefit of
people at large, and the standards by which they are evaluated
are those of the group as a whole. A cultured man is one who is
recognized as such by other people. It follows too that the
standard of culture in a given group is not necessarily the
standard of each individual but is a characteristic of the
society as a whole. Not all Scots are footballers, and not all
Scottish footballers are good footballers, but nevertheless one
can broadly speak of Scotland as a great footballing nation in
a way in which it is certainly not possible to speak of it as
a great cricketing nation. Further, there can be different
cultures associated with different groups in the same country,
according as different groups have different sets of values and
ways of life: one often distinguishes between working class
and middle class cultures, although the characteristics and
differences are extremely hard to pinpoint.

5. Along with all these things there is the further point,
important for our present purpose, that a culture may be
characterized by *a specific way of thinking*. We have already
observed that different cultures may have different sets of
values. A Scottish boy may place high value on learning to play

football, whereas his American counterpart will favor baseball. Clearly these differences in aim will lead to somewhat different ways of life, the acquisition of different skills, and so on. Yet fundamentally there is no obvious difference in the *method* of thinking that accompanies these differences in aim. Both are types of sport, and we might find a more important difference between these sportsmen and people who attach no value to sport whatever. Yet even this difference within sport may be associated with other cultural differences.

One thinks of the standards of fair play associated with cricket, such that (at least until recently) certain types of conduct in ordinary life could be condemned by the comment "that's not cricket," whereas one would not say "that's not football." Here we have a set of ethical values somehow associated with a particular sport in a way that is not found in the same way in other sports, and it is an interesting question whether the ethical values were somehow stimulated by the game itself or where characteristic of the type of people who played cricket, or became associated with cricket in some other way. Here, then, we have a difference in ways of thinking that may be regarded as cultural and which goes down to the roots of human behavior.

Perhaps more important is the way in which a people may develop different methods of thinking, as opposed to different values. One may note how certain peoples developed mathematical ways of thinking which enabled them to solve practical problems not soluble by people without these skills, or certain peoples were more prone to tackle problems by means of philosophical analysis and thus to arrive at a different view of the world from people who did not have these powers of thinking. The development, however adventitiously, of different philosophical outlooks and religious systems means that people come to problems with different presuppositions and different methods of thinking, and some of these may be better suited to solving certain problems than others.

Thus it is arguable that the development of modern science in western European civilization was possible only because of the Christian world view which de-sacralized nature and made it an object for scientific study in terms of natural law instead of a mysterious entity inhabited and controlled by unknown supernatural powers that were in principle beyond the reach of human scientific investigation. One might also contrast the difference between the so-called armchair approach to investigation of phenomena in the natural world with the empirical method of scientific experiment, and note that while the former approach is the appropriate one for certain types of study, adherence to it alone will prevent attainment of the insights discovered by

the latter. Where a person is culturally conditioned to the
former approach and it never enters his head to attempt a
scientific experiment, he will never make any real progress in
physics or chemistry. Our ways of thinking and investigating
may thus be part of our culture.

   The same thing is to some extent true of language. Although
theories that language influences the way in which we think are
heavily discounted, there is nevertheless something important
that should be retained from them. The vocabulary of one
language, as compared with another, may indicate the existence
of a different culture. The technical terms for occurrences
in the game of cricket do not exist in the languages of countries
that do not play cricket and can be expressed only by clumsy
circumlocutions. A person would find it difficult to explain
the game of cricket in detail (with reference to yorkers,
silly mid on, caught in the gully, and so on) to a person speaking some tribal language. The tribal person's culture prevents
him from assimilating this new sport without considerable, though
not insuperable difficulty. The point is, not that he cannot
learn about cricket, but that the existing state of his language
reflects the absence of this dimension from his culture. On the
other hand, the existence of particular linguistic items may
positively help forward the development of certain ideas. One
may instance the way in which Paul was able to formulate his
doctrine of the church as the body of Christ, thanks to the
existence of the Greek word *soma*, in a way that would have been
difficult, if not impossible, had he been confined to a Hebrew
vocabulary. Language is a part of culture, both reflecting the
character of culture and to some extent helping to shape it.

   6. A final point to be observed is that *a culture may consist
of various separable parts or aspects*. We tend to talk of
"western culture" as it were a coherent whole, each part fitting
logically and coherently into one grand system. But we should
remind ourselves that the different individuals or groups will
be affected by the culture of their society to varying extents,
and also that the various elements which go to make it up will
have grown up piecemeal and do not necessarily stand in organic
relationship to one another. We should beware of the tendency
to speak of culture as a monolithic phenomenon, so that the
various parts stand or fall together.

   To summarize: the word "culture" can refer variously to the
particular ways in which man learns to control his environment,
to develop intellectual and aesthetic values and expressions
of them, and to produce an ideology which expresses and upholds
these values. Culture is a social phenomenon, and can have
various, separable parts. Culture means a way of thinking, an
approach to life in the world, which opens up possibilities for

those who hold to it, and at the same time may impose limits on
their understanding and ability.

II. THE BACKGROUND: JEWISH AND HELLENISTIC CULTURE

In turning now to the problem of culture in the NT, we must
first of all consider the environment in which the NT writings
were created. Here I want to make the point that *the world of
the New Testament was a world in which different cultures or
ways of life were in contact with one another, leading to
assimilation between them as well as to sharp collision.* The
most significant case is Palestine itself. At the end of the
OT period we find a small group of Jews returned from exile and
settled in and around Jerusalem. Their leaders, such as Nehemiah,
imposed on them a policy of rigid segregation from the surrounding peoples so that they might keep their religion pure from de-
filement with paganism. We have always known that there were
strong temptations for them to compromise with the life of the
neighboring peoples or the various foreign rulers who gained
domination over Palestine, and that while a certain element in
the people succumbed to the attractions of a non-Jewish way of
life, the rest of the people fought with determination for
their ancestral faith and remained true to it in their way of
life. The tendency has therefore been to think in terms of a
Palestinian Judaism which was intensely loyal to the Jewish law
and highly traditional in its way of life. It was recognized
that Jews who lived in the Dispersion were more influenced by
their pagan environment and had adapted their way of life and
thought to it in various ways, so that the Judaism of the
Dispersion could be broadly labeled Hellenistic Judaism.

What has become increasingly clear in the course of the last
half a dozen years or so is that this picture is a misleading
simplification of the situation. The credit for developing fresh
insights here goes to M. Hengel in his survey of the character
of Palestinian Judaism in the third and second centuries BC.[3]
The effect of his minute study of the evidence is to show that
Hellenistic influences were powerfully at work in Palestine
throughout this period and that they had a very deep effect on
the thought and life of the Jews, including those who were most
resistant to change. In the period preceding the Maccabean
revolt there was a strongly pro-Hellenistic party in Palestine,
mostly among the upper-classes including the priestly hierarchy.
They were extremely hospitable to the Hellenistic way of life,
and they cooperated with the Seleucid rulers in giving Jerusalem
the status of a Greek city with a Hellenistic "democratic"
constitution, and in promoting the spread of Greek education,
including Greek literature and Greek forms of sport. The
experiment was shortlived, owing to the strong resistance which
it provoked. The efforts of Antiochus Epiphanes to speed up the

process of Hellenization led to armed revolt and eventual defeat.
But then the leaders of the traditionalist revolt themselves became infected by the Hellenistic life-style and completely
alienated their supporters. The rulers and priests became increasingly worldly, living in luxury and wealth, and ignoring
the demands of the Law, and were cordially hated by the pious
groups. Various groups became disillusioned with the situation,
and some retreated from communal life to set up their own communities in the desert. Yet even these groups were affected by
Hellenistic ideas in the way in which they organized themselves,
and were evidently unaware how deeply the infection had spread.

The evidence for this development of a Hellenistic Judaism in
Palestine is considerable. It can be seen in the way in which
Greek came to be used as a language in Palestine. We can find
plenty of perfectly orthodox Jews who bore Greek names. The
possibility that Jesus understood and on occasion spoke Greek
can certainly not be dismissed. There was, too, much trade in
foreign wares which were bound to affect the lifestyle of those
who could afford them. There was considerable movement of
foreign troops in Palestine; the first impact of Hellenism was
perhaps in the coming of Hellenistic armies and Hellenistic
methods of warfare to Palestine, and many Jews served as
mercenaries in Hellenistic armies. Nor should we forget that
there was a very large non-Jewish population in Palestine, to
such an extent in fact that the Jews were a minority people in
their own land. Our familiar Bible maps are often seriously misleading in that they only print the Jewish towns actually named
in the NT and ignore the many Gentile towns that were scattered
up and down the land.[4]

Along with all these tangible influences there came inevitably
the influence of Greek literature and Greek ideas. The result
is that we find Jews writing works in the Greek language and
expressing themselves in Greek styles of work. And what they
write shows the influence of Greek ideas. A cultural revolution
was taking place during the period before Jesus and right on
throughout the NT period.

This revolution in Palestine was but part of a process that
had been going on in the ancient world since the end of the
fourth century BC. The policy of Alexander the Great and his
successors throughout their extensive dominions was to spread a
Greek way of life, a way of life that has come to be called
Hellenistic, since it was not purely Greek but represented an
amalgam of the Greek way of life with the local cultures onto
which it was grafted. It was characterized by the use of the
Greek language as a universal means of communication, the spread
of trade, the setting up of a Greek type of political system,
seen especially in the growth of cities each with self-government,

and along with this the spread of Greek thinking, literature
and art. In some cases this led to the stifling of native
ways of life, but more often it produced a mixture of the old
and the new, so that while there was a uniform Greek element
the local manifestations of Hellenistic culture could vary considerably.

As an example of the effect one might cite the admittedly not
altogether typical case of Philo. This man was a Jew, brother
of the Roman governor of Palestine, living the life of a rich
man, and spending his life in the cultured occupation of a
philosopher, producing a remarkable eclectic system in which
Plato, the Stoa and Moses were joined to one another. The most
famous Jewish scholar of his day wrote throughout in Greek,
and was unable to read the Pentateuch in Hebrew. Philo remained
a loyal Jew, but he well illustrates the syncretistic character
of the age in which ideas of all kinds were being thrown together. Nor must one forget the other influences. There was
also the effect of Roman culture, itself strongly indebted to
Greece, which imposed its distinctive work throughout the
ancient world, and in addition there was a powerful current of
influence from the Orient as a result of the extension of the
borders of the Roman Empire towards the east.

To summarize: It is important to bear in mind that the
cultural relationships of Christianity were part of a broader
process of cultural assimilation in Palestine which was still
going on in the first century, and which also provides a background against which we can assess the nature of what was going
on in the early church.

III.   THE EFFECT OF CULTURE ON THE FORM OF THE GOSPEL

The relation of Christianity to culture in the NT has a number
of aspects which it is hard to arrange in a logical sequence.
We shall begin by considering the vocabulary and thought-forms
in which the Gospel was expressed. It has long been obvious
to scholars that the NT is written in the Greek of the time
rather than in any special "language of the Holy Ghost"; any
words in the NT which have not been found in other contemporary,
secular sources are unimportant, and their absence is a purely
chance phenomenon due to the fragmentary nature of our sources.
The language used to express the Gospel was the language used at
the time.

Moreover, the decisive words and concepts which were used
both in the teaching of Jesus and in the preaching and teaching
of the early Christians were drawn from the OT. A knowledge of
the OT is the indispensable key for understanding the thought of
the NT. We can, therefore, say that *the Gospel is expressed in*

*the language and thought-forms of a particular culture (or group
of cultures), and that in the form in which we have it, it is
tied to this particular culture.* The point may be put even more
sharply by observing that God did not simply become man, as if
the incarnation could take place in "man in general" rather than
in "man as belonging to a particular culture": he became man in
Jesus, who was a Jew, not a Samaritan, nor a Greek, nor a Scot,
nor an American, nor anyone else.

This leads to the question whether the content of the revelation can be separated from the form in which it is expressed.
We can, of course, translate the Gospel out of one language into
another, and this can bring some shifts in meaning, since the
corresponding words in the receptor language may have different
constellations of meaning from the original words, but it is
doubtful whether the central content of the message is going to
be seriously disturbed. Basically, it remains tied to the
Jewish OT categories in which it was originally expressed.

Now it is well-known that an attempt to do a translation of
this kind was made by R. Bultmann in his program of demythologi-
zation. He argued that certain aspects of the Gospel were expressed in the form of myths which no longer spoke to modern
man; his proposal was that these myths should be demythologized
to lay bare their essential message, and that this should then
be expressed for modern people in a re-mythologized form, the
categories for which he found in the philosophical concepts of
Heidegger. In other words, just as the biblical message must be
translated out of an ancient language into a modern one, so too
the ancient "mythical" form of the message must be "translated"
into a corresponding modern form. Behind Bultmann's concern lay
not simply the fact that the ancient "myths" might be unintelligible to modern man, but also his claim that the worldview which they presupposed (especially its acceptance of the
supernatural) was unacceptable to modern people with their
scientific outlook.

While Bultmann's desire to make the Gospel intelligible in
the modern world is praiseworthy, it is regrettable that his
actual performance is so unsatisfactory. He operates with a
very loose and inadequate understanding of "myth"; he assigns
much that should be regarded as historical (e.g. the physical
resurrection of Jesus) to the category of "myth"; he fails to
reckon with the fact that our modern worldview with its rejection of the supernatural may need to be corrected by the
biblical revelation; and in the course of his "translation" of
the biblical message into modern terms a good deal of the
original content appears to get lost on the way.

There is clearly no easy solution to the problem of separating

the content of the Gospel from the cultural forms in which it has
been expressed. What is certain is that the Gospel cannot be expressed apart from the categories of *some* culture; there is no
such thing as a Gospel detachable from some cultural expression.
Granted this fact, we may suggest that the analogy of translation
from one language to another provides a clue. The accuracy of a
translation is tested not only by its own inner consistency but
above all by its correspondence with the original text. The decisive test is: if the translation is turned back into the original language, will the resulting retranslation express the same
thoughts as the original text? So too the test of the accuracy
of our expression of the Gospel in new cultural categories will
be whether the new form of the message conveys the same truth as
in the Bible. We must constantly check the modern form of the
message against the original revelation.

In saying this I am assuming the finality of the original
revelation given in its cultural setting. The translation of
the message into any new form does not produce a new revelation
which can be assessed by some other standard than its fidelity
as a translation. Nevertheless, it must be allowed that new insights can be developed in the progress of Christian doctrine,
although we would claim that these were always latent in the
original revelation.

So my first point is that the Gospel was given in a particular cultural setting and inevitably made use of the available
categories. There is a sense in which it cannot be separated
from that setting.[6]

Second, it must be noted *that the original revelation transcended the categories available for its expression.* Here I am
thinking of the way in which a term like "Messiah" was available
for use to express the significance of Jesus and was in fact
used to do so. But it is obvious that once the existing term
was applied to Jesus it began to shift in meaning and was filled
with new content so that henceforth it came to be used in a new
way. Jesus himself was reticent about applying the term to himself precisely because the popular usage of the term (and
popular usage *is* the meaning of the word) did not express what
he conceived to be his own mission and destiny. As the term
came into Christian usage, it took on a new meaning which corre-
sponded to Jesus' understanding of how the word might be used.[7]
Thus it is possible to be creative within the bounds of a particular culture and to produce something which transcends the
original cultural elements. The existing culture need not tie
the Gospel down to its own particular form, but the Gospel has
the power to change the terms and so eventually to change the
culture itself. One can produce other illustrations of this

phenomenon not only by examining the vocabulary of the NT, but
also by examining the vocabulary of the OT, especially in its
Greek form, which shows important differences from the secular
Greek of the time.

Third, as the church developed and spread, *the Gospel had to
be expressed in new ways in order to be comprehensible by more
people*. It had to be expressed in Greek rather than Hebrew or
Aramaic, although it must be insisted that the use of Greek in
the church must be almost as old as the church itself, and that
the influence was not solely in the one direction, from Hebrew
to Greek, but rather the two languages exercised a mutual
influence; consider how in the case of a bilingual thinker like
Paul (and he was not alone) both forms of expression must have
worked together in his mind.

At the same time, new categories of understanding could be
pressed into service. Older ones may have been less comprehensible and needed to be replaced by others. The title "Son of
Man," for instance, had no pre-history outside Jewish circles
and even the Greek form of the phrase was grotesque; it is not
surprising that the title totally disappeared from use outside
the traditions of the teaching of Jesus. Other ways of expressing the significance of Jesus had to be found. A title
such as "Lord" came into more frequent use, and while this had
been used in Jewish Christianity, it probably developed in
meaning through the influences of secular Greek usage, such as
its use as a title of dignity by the Roman emperors. A term
like "redemption" which is used in a rather vague way in early
Christianity against an OT background of Yahweh's deliverance
of his people assumed much more definite contours when it was
understood against the background of its use in Greek society
in the context of sacral manumission. Here we have good
examples of the cultural stock of the Greco-Roman world being
put to the service of expressing the Gospel.

This process could be taken to a surprising extent, as two
types of example will show. In Acts 17:28 Paul describes the
character of God by means of two quotations: "In him we live
and move and have our being," and "For we are indeed his offspring." Not only are these quotations from pagan poets, but
also they referred unequivocally to Zeus, the chief god in the
Greek pantheon. And yet Paul uses them to depict the character
of the Christian God. Indeed, the whole of the Areopagus speech
is a striking example of the way in which Christian truth could
be expressed with the categories of paganism. Now there was
danger here. M. Dibelius could argue that the Areopagus
speech was an erratic block in the NT, certainly not Pauline in
character, since it depicted a Hellenistic type of God rather
than the God of the OT.[8] The garb used by Paul to clothe God

here could lead to doubts about his identity. No doubt Dibelius'
estimate of the speech was wrong: B. Gärtner has shown con-
vincingly that the basic ideas of the speech stem from the OT,
although the language used to express them is Hellenistic.[9] But
the fact that Dibelius could be taken in by the speech is
significant. It shows how easily the use of non-Christian
language can be understood to convey non-Christian ideas. We
should also want to raise the question of precisely what was
going on when Paul took pagan quotations about Zeus and said,
"Yes, they are true, but they apply to Yahweh." Evidently he
was prepared to allow their truth, but only if Zeus was recognized as somehow depicting Yahweh; yet it is obvious that much of
what pagans said about Zeus certainly could not be applied to
Yahweh. Only where it was in agreement with the OT and Christian
revelation in Jesus was Paul prepared to take the step. The
risks that attach to our attempts to take over pagan deities and
syncretize them with Yahweh stand out vividly.

The other type of example is where Paul was in debate with
Christian heretics and was prepared to take over their vocabulary
and to apply it to Jesus in what H. Chadwick has described in a
well-known phrase as a "disinfected" use.[10] This seems to be
the case with some of the expressions used by Paul in Colossians,
where the terms "fulness" and "head" may have been used by
gnosticizing teachers in their own way, but Paul was quite prepared to take them over and reapply them to Christ in his own way.
And if the gnosticizing teachers spoke of the existence of
"principalities and powers" Paul was prepared to admit their
existence, but to say, "Yes, but Christ created them all and he
is superior to them in every way." Here it may be claimed, we
can see how Paul's thought about Jesus was deepened by his
encounter with gnosticizing tendencies, and it may be that he
actually took over some ideas first expressed by gnosticizing
teachers, just as we saw that even orthodox Jewish groups were
partly affected by the very Hellenism that they so rigorously
opposed.

In these various ways we can find examples of the development
of the Christian Gospel through the use of categories drawn from
other sources, pagan and heretical. It should not need to be
said here that the truth of ideas is independent of their origin,
and that to assert the Hellenistic origin of a concept rather
than an OT origin is not to declare it false; fears that the
discovery of a non-Jewish background for NT concepts renders
their truth suspect are false, although sometimes scholars have
argued in this way.[11]

To summarize: we have considered the way in which the
surrounding culture has conditioned the expression of the Gospel
message, and seen how the message is necessarily expressed in

the categories of particular cultures, how it breaks through the
limits of existing cultural categories of expression, and how it
can be re-expressed in terms of fresh cultural categories which
may lead to its enrichment.

IV. THE EFFECT OF THE GOSPEL ON CULTURE

We turn next to the question of how the Gospel can affect the
surrounding culture. This is most obvious in the NT in the case
of behavior and style of life. The followers of Jesus were pious
Jews like their Master and followed a way of life typical of
Palestinian Jews. It involved adherence to the Jewish law which
was concerned with every aspect of life and legislated for it.
It can be assumed that for the most part they lived according
to the law, since this was the way in which they were brought up
and it probably did not occur to them to do otherwise. Yet even
in the Gospels we have accounts of the critical questions that
arose when Jesus and the disciples failed to observe the accepted
mores. Why did they not keep the Sabbath in the prescribed
manner? Why did they ignore the ritual rules of cleanliness,
both in their habits of eating and in their association with
sinful people? To be sure, the rules which they broke were
perhaps more the rules of the Pharisees than of the OT itself,
but the Pharisees were in a position to dictate the character of
normative Judaism, so that Jesus and his disciples would certainly stand out as being different from the generality of the people.
What was happening was that Jesus was criticizing the character
of the surrounding culture, or the character of certain aspects
of it, in the light of the principles of the religion which he
taught; this religion cut clean against the tedious legalism of
the Pharisaic way of life. It could be argued that Jesus merely
represented one particular type of Judaism over against
Pharisaic Judaism. But there were latent trends in his teaching
which were to lead to further criticisms of the whole Jewish way
of life.

The most important of these was undoubtedly the accession of
Gentiles into the church which raised the twin questions of
whether they needed to embrace Jewish practices in order to be
saved, and whether Jews could have fellowship with them other
than on the terms allowed by the Jewish law. Gentiles ranked as
"unclean" in contemporary Jewish understanding (though not
according to the OT), and circumcision and observance of the
law of Moses were regarded as necessary for salvation. It cost
the early church a tremendous struggle but two essential points
were recognized. It was recognized that Gentiles did not need
to be circumcised or keep the law of Moses but only to believe
in Christ (with all that that involved) in order to be saved.
At the same time, it was recognized that in the Christian church
Jew and Gentile stood on an equal footing, so that Gentiles no

longer ranked as "unclean" in relation to Jews. To be sure, Jewish Christians did not cease at once to be circumcised or keep the law of Moses, and Gentile Christians were asked to keep certain rules to avoid offending the susceptibilities of Jews. But in course of time these half-measures were forgotten. The result was the development of a new life style in which it was no longer characteristic of Christians to live according to the law of Moses in respect of circumcision, the observance of Jewish festivals, and treating Gentiles as "unclean."

Two other changes in way of life developed at the same time. The one concerned worship. The temple ceased to have any significance for Christians, a change that was accelerated in any case by its destruction so that it could no longer figure even in Jewish religion. It would be interesting to compare the different effects of AD 70 on Jews and Christians. Synagogue worship also ceased for Christians, although since the synagogue was more than a building for Jewish worship and acted as the focus of Jewish community life, it is likely that Christians continued to associate with it so far as they were able; the *Birkath ha-Minim* probably made them depart more quickly than they otherwise would have done.

The other change was that the teaching of Jesus on things clean and unclean was recognized as destroying the whole distinction between clean and unclean foods, and thereby a drastic change in Jewish eating habits must have taken place.

These developments thus led to the development of a quite new life-style for Christian Jews, and we would be justified in talking of the development of a new culture alongside Jewish culture, using "culture" in the same sense of a general way of life, closely associated with moral and religious attitudes.[12]

The attitude of the church to pagan ways of life at first sight produced less spectacular changes. Outside Judaism there was a much greater range of ways of life within the general gamut of Hellenistic civilization. There were so many different religions, each with their own group of adherents, that the development of a fresh one was not particularly note-worthy, and there was nothing culturally odd about belonging to the Christian church rather than to some mystery sect. Within a pluralistic culture it is hard to produce a lifestyle that cuts clean against the general way of life of the culture. But although the Gospel did not create a headlong clash with Hellenistic civilization, simply because there was no one culture, it did produce a new way of life alongside the several existing ones, and it thus profoundly affected the lives of converts.

The point may be illustrated in the realm of ethics. The NT
writers certainly inveighed against the signs of paganism and
urged their readers not to continue in their old way of life
with its carousing, sexual immorality and general misbehavior.
There could be a very real change of life for people who had
lived immoral lives. But the new moral teaching offered by
Christianity did not offer a way of life so markedly different
from the ideals of certain areas of Hellenistic culture. This
can be seen in the example of the various "House tables" or
ethical codes for different classes in society which are found
in the Epistles. Some of the teaching in these is remarkably
close to pagan (and also to Jewish) moral teaching. It has been
Christianized, but in some cases it did not need a lot of change
to Christianize it. The fact is that Stoics and Epicureans both
recognized the existence of moral values, and their understanding
of these values in practical terms was not all that different
from the Christian understanding. I do not want to minimize the
extent of the differences, especially the significant difference
enshrined in the Christian new commandment of love, but the
fact remains that many pagans would have recognized Christian
ethics as being fairly similar in character to the ethical
teaching of the best philosophers of the time. The vital
difference lay in the way in which Christianity put a social
ethic of love into practice. The situation among Gentile
communities was thus to some extent different from that in a
Jewish environment, where, as we have seen, the Christian way of
life cut at the very roots of Jewish national and religious
practice. If Christian culture effected a revolution in the
lives of Jewish Christians, it is by no means obvious that it
demanded a similar revolution in the lives of Gentile Christians.
The historian of culture might regard the development of Jewish
Christians as being simply part of the Hellenizing process which
was affecting Judaism; it was, of course, much more than that,
but the question is worth raising whether Christian culture is
largely the product of Hellenism.

Nevertheless, there were occasions where Christians ran up
against pagan culture. We need to ask ourselves why Christians
were persecuted. D. R. A. Hare has suggested that a society can
tolerate a certain amount of deviation from its general way of
life, but once people start to question or attack the symbols of
cultural solidarity they go beyond the limit of toleration.[13]
So the Jews persecuted the Christians because they attacked
the temple and the law of Moses. The Romans persecuted the
Christians when they refused to take part in the worship of the
emperor which was the formal sign of loyalty and hence a
cultural solidarity. It was perhaps fortuitous that the symbol
was one which clashed with Christian loyalty to Christ, and
unfortunate that the Christians could not claim the same immunity
from the practice as the Jews had obtained, but this was how it

was, and the Christians suffered for it. Otherwise the Roman government did not find the Christians a problem at this period. The Christians also suffered at the hands of their neighbors, and this seems to have arisen out of dislike of their moral standards (1 Peter), but it was not on a large scale at this point. All this would confirm our suggestion that in the NT period the Gospel did not create a new culture over against the Hellenistic world as a whole; it simply created a new variant that might have existed fairly happily within Hellenism with its broad toleration of different ways of life. It was only when the symbols of national and imperial solidarity were challenged, and when the superior morality of Christianity touched uneasy pagan conscience that pagans turned to persecution.

To summarize: The effect of the Gospel was to challenge sharply the lifestyle of Judaism as a religious and national culture, and also to challenge the lifestyle of Gentiles by creating a new way of life in a pluralistic pagan setting. It was impossible to be a Christian and live as one had formerly lived. The new faith led to a new way of life.

V. THE NEW TESTAMENT ATTITUDE TO CULTURAL VALUES

We turn next to the particular question of the relation between the Gospel and culture in the sense of aesthetic values and the things associated with them.

This is a difficult subject to probe since the NT is primarily a book about religion, and not about the cultural life of Christians. Any information on the latter thus comes out incidentally and indirectly rather than explicitly.

But we can note that Jesus was evidently interested in the natural world around him and was impressed by the beauty of the flowers. He used them as an illustration of a religious point, but it is clear that he must have appreciated their beauty for its own sake. Similarly, the disciples were impressed by the magnificence of Herod's temple, although their comment on this became the occasion for a prophecy of its impending destruction. In general, it is clear that Jesus was a keen observer of the rural scene and drew many of his illustrations from it. It is difficult to be sure that his experience as a carpenter dictated his insights into the joy of an easy yoke for its bearer, since a similar metaphor was used in rabbinic teaching for the Torah. It is also evident that there were aspects of social life that Jesus simply took for granted without criticism. He described a world in which slaves were entirely at their master's disposal, and he portrayed oriental monarchs cruelly slaying their enemies without uttering any moral condemnation of them.

Jesus displayed considerable artistic power in the use of words, so that his parables and metaphorical sayings stand out for their literary power and effect. Although his literary skills were used in the service of his message, it is not the case that they were purely utilitarian, but rather their literary beauty was part of the message. We can conclude that Jesus himself enjoyed the world of nature and the pleasures of human society and friendship. Although he himself was not married, he approved of marriage and commended it. There was a positive attitude on the part of Jesus to the world around him, so that life in the world was a joy to him. If on occasions he adopted ascetic ways, these were for the sake of the kingdom of God, and we can say that he deprived himself of the joys of life as God intended it in order that other people might enjoy these pleasures.

The situation is basically the same when we consider the attitudes of the early Christians. The one text that is specifically on the issue is Phil. 4:8: "Whatever is true, whatever is honorable, whatever is just, whatever is pure, whatever is lovely, whatever is gracious, if there is any excellence, if there is anything worthy of praise, think about these things." Here we have a positive commendation of what is good in the world as being worthy of the attention of the Christians. A high value is placed on married love, and this extends to the joys of the physical side of marriage. Paul was made happy by the gifts of his friends and their fellowship with him. Feelings of human love and affections were nurtured in the spiritual life of the church so that he felt close human ties with his friends. Philemon was to welcome Onesimus, newly converted, as a beloved brother both from a human point of view and from a Christian point of view.

Where the NT writers condemn culture it is when it has become contaminated by sin and no longer achieves the divinely intended purpose. Commentators have noted that Paul was blind to the beauties of ancient Athens since he could not get beyond the fact that its beauty was in the service of idolatry; this is perhaps to read more into Paul's opening gambit in his speech there than is justified. The life of the world comes under strongest condemnation in Revelation in its description of the fate of Babylon with all its rich commercial and social life, but here again the point is that the city had become thoroughly tainted by sin. The writer to the Hebrews acknowledges that there are certainly pleasures in sin, otherwise nobody would bother to sin, but regards these as things that the Christian must forego. There is an enjoyment of God's creation which is free from sin. In a sense, however, the created world is infected by sin, and the problem of separating between what is sinful and what is sinless is a tricky one. Since sin is basically a question of human attitudes, Paul can declare that nothing is unclean in itself, but only if it is regarded as such. It is the attitude of selfishness and lack of love which makes the enjoyment of culture sinful.

This conclusion is confirmed by one of the few texts which is self-conscious of the problem of surrounding culture. The nearest thing that the NT has to a word for "culture" is "world" (*kosmos*) which expresses the organized life of mankind in the created world. *Kosmos* is not simply the created universe inhabited by man; it is much more human society itself as it inhabits the universe and stands over against God. 1 John 2:15 contains a warning not to love the world. As the immediately following verse makes clear, the world in this context means the sinfulness of human society, and the Christian is not to be attracted by what is sinful, by temptations to self-aggrandizement of whatever kind. Yet John also declares that God loved the world; the thought is primarily of his self-giving *agape* for the world, but behind this *agape* there must surely also stand the delight which the Creator took in his creation when he pronounced it "very good." This means that in the last analysis the Christian positive attitude to culture is based on the Creator's own delight in and approval of his creation, except insofar as it is tainted by sin; God continues to work in his creation.[14]

Alongside this view of God as being active in the continuing creation of the world (a point which will stand even if we think merely of God continuing to uphold the universe by his Word), we must also reckon with the question of whether the creation embraces human culture. Our evangelical doctrine of salvation tends to be intensely individualistic, in the sense that it is concerned with the redemption of individual persons, even though we recognize that these individuals form the new society called the church. Is there any sense in which human institutions and culture participate in the new creation? In Revelation the end result of the new creation is the manifestation of a "new Jerusalem," a new city of God which replaced sinful Babylon and in which God's people dwell. Is the significance of this imagery that the life of the new age represents a new creation of human culture? But if so, what elements of continuity, if any, are there between the old city and the new? We accept that the persons who will live in the new city are those who have come out of the old city, dead but resurrected and given heavenly, spiritual bodies suitable for their new environment. But is the new city a resurrected form of the old city? The language used does not suggest this. Heaven and earth flee away when he comes to reign; the new Jerusalem descends from above, from God, and this might suggest that it is entirely new and does not stand in continuity with the old city. Perhaps we

need to consider seriously the implications of Rev. 21:24,26
which allow the place of human culture in the city of God.
Otherwise we face two difficulties.

1. The whole human cultural enterprise seems doomed to destruction and is of no ultimate lasting value; it is therefore doubtful
whether it is worth pursuing. A world-denying attitude then
becomes intelligible. We are strangers and pilgrims here, not
citizens of this world, and the best that we can do is to
rescue as many brands as possible from the burning; the preservation of souls for heaven is all that we need be concerned
about, beyond the elementary tasks needed to preserve us alive
in the world to do this. Evangelical eschatology typically
works with a "complete break" type of future expectation in
which all human history and achievement is ultimately of no
significance; we brought nothing into this world and we can take
nothing out of it. But although we may hold this view in theory,
in practice we live otherwise -- are we being sinful in "living
otherwise"?

2. Culture is inextricably bound up with people; it is people
which form societies, and so if the people move over into the
next world, to some extent their societies and thus some
aspects of their culture go with them. It can be objected that
this is not so, that in heaven they neither marry nor are given
in marriage, and human society as we now know it no longer
exists and is replaced by a colossal individualism in which we
are all joined to God in fellowship but not to one another except
perhaps in a holistic, undifferentiated kind of way. But to
argue thus is to imply that the whole of human society-formation,
blessed in this life by God, passes away and the life of the
world to come is infinitely poorer than the life of this world.
Surely this is a ridiculous conclusion. The view of C.F.D.
Moule is altogether preferable, that there is, for example, no
marriage in heaven, not because the married are demoted to the
level of unmarried individuals, but because *all* human relationships are raised to a new level of fellowship and intimacy.[15]

These hints suggest that our traditional understanding of NT
teaching in terms of a sharp discontinuity of the End involving
the destruction and ultimate non-significance of human culture
and its replacement by a purely religious fellowship is wrong,
and it raises afresh the questions of the possibility of the
redemption of culture to take its place in the new world. I
am far from clear, however, how this question is to be answered,
and indeed whether the NT provides an answer to it. Perhaps one
might say that this is a question implicitly posed by the NT
revelation.

To summarize: The New Testament attitude to aesthetic values is a positive one. Christianity is not world-denying, for the world remains God's world in which he continues to be active, but it is sin-denying. Since the world of values embraces communities as well as individuals, a question mark is placed against our traditional evangelical eschatology which works in terms of the survival and transformation of individuals in the kingdom of God and has not faced up to the problems of the conservation and transformation of human culture and human society in the world to come.

VI. THE PROBLEM OF A CULTURE-BOUND REVELATION

This study has raised questions rather than answered them, and it has covered a topic with many different facets. This will also be true in this final section in which we consider briefly the problem raised by the fact that the Gospel was given in a particular cultural situation. We shall focus our attention on the problem raised by P.K. Jewett's controversial book *Man as Male and Female.*[16] Part of the thesis of this book is that the central teaching of the Bible, seen in its understanding of the image of God and in the attitude of Jesus, regards man and woman as equals with complementary functions. (The traditional understanding is that woman is subordinate to man and, though this is not always openly admitted, this subordination is based on an inferiority.) Jewett has no difficulty in establishing that this is the main thrust of biblical teaching. The problem is that there are passages in which the subordination of woman to man is also taught, culminating in the command that women should not be allowed to teach men, since this would call in question the authority of man. Faced by these two streams of thought, Jewett in effect suggests that the latter represents the thinking of Paul, as conditioned by a Jewish environment in which the inferiority of women was accepted, and that we ought to regard this line of thought as a hangover from the past and not be governed by it; in other words, we should distinguish between the attitude of Paul the apostle of Christian liberty and the attitude of Paul the Jewish Rabbi (two attitudes which remain unreconciled in his thinking) and we should be governed by the former and not by the latter. In support of this approach Jewett observes how the NT contains teaching on how slaves should obey their masters, and yet it also contains teaching (in Philemon especially) which implicitly shows that slavery is inconsistent with a Christian (i.e. biblical) view of man; Christians today recognize that we must perfectly implement this biblical view of man by abolishing slavery, and so go beyond the situation which Paul regarded as normal and compatible with the Gospel. If we are prepared to condemn slavery, logically we should also condemn the subordination of women and regard them as the equals of men.

Here is a good example of how the Gospel may be associated
with a particular outlook characteristic of a certain culture,
and the question is whether we are entitled to break this
association. How can it be done? The particular application of
Paul's remarks about the subordination of women was to their
praying and prophesying in church (allowed, if they are veiled)
and to their teaching in church (disallowed). Liberal advocates
of the ministry of women simply disregard Paul's teaching as
being of no authority, since we are not bound by the authority
of Scripture. Conservative scholars who wish to defend the
ministry of women will argue that Paul's particular application
of his principles in the culture of his day may be meaningless
and irrelevant in the culture of today, and that we may still
obey his principles while not following his detailed practice.
Thus a veil no longer has whatever significance it had in the
first century, and to make a woman today wear a garment which is
not in common use is no longer significant but rather ludicrous.
In the same way, it can be argued that today the fact of a woman
teaching or ministering is not regarded as a sign of insub-
ordination in our culture, and therefore a teaching ministry by
women today is quite compatible with an acceptance of the
principles that lay behind Paul's prohibition of this.

The conservative position is thus that we adhere to Paul's
principles, but the method of carrying them out in a changed
cultural situation may be different from what it was in the
first century and so we may feel at liberty to do today what
Paul specifically forbade.[17] By way of support we might note
that women undoubtedly did teach in the early church, so that it
looks as though even Paul's command was not universally obeyed.

But now, if I understand him aright, Jewett is claiming that
even some of Paul's underlying principles may require to be
amended in the light of the total biblical revelation. It is
not just a case of rejecting an imperfect implementation of a
Christian principle, since Paul backs up his practice with
points of principle which, in Jewett's view, are incompatible
with other major biblical principles. Jewett argues that we
ourselves silently lay aside other biblical principles, such as
the command that slaves should give their masters unquestioning
obedience in the Lord, which was valid enough within the
situation of slavery, but is ultimately based on the unchristian
view that one man can have the right to total obedience from
another.

The cynic may be tempted to observe that the view of man and
woman held by Jewett is not unlike that found in modern western
culture with its emphasis on the emancipation of women, and he
may go on to wonder whether Jewett has been led to identify as
central in the biblical revelation that element which is most

congenial to modern western society; in other words, is Jewett
simply interpreting the Bible for his own (time-bound) cultural
setting and discarding what doesn't fit in with it? On the other
hand, however, it might be said more positively that it is precisely the high view of woman in contemporary culture which has
given Jewett the insight to recognize that some of the biblical
teaching on this matter is obsolete and time-bound.

The problem raised is akin to the question of progressive
revelation, the NT forbidding actions that were permissible in
the OT, and even God being represented in the OT as acting in
ways that are no longer permissible for him in the light of the
NT (e.g. God sends fire from heaven to consume Elijah's
opponents, 2 Kings 1:12, but Jesus' disciples must not even
think of asking God to do the same, Luke 9:54f). Similarly, it
is being suggested that some of Paul's thinking is a carry-over
from earlier ideas, we must discard it in the light of Paul's
Christian insights (although it must sadly be admitted that Paul
himself failed to detect the inconsistency).

Jewett's approach, however, raises difficulties. It can be
argued that it leads to subjectivism (how shall we differentiate
between biblical principles?), and, even if there is room for
subjective difference of opinion on many points of biblical
interpretation, there is some force in this argument; the task
of exegesis is surely to move on beyond mere subjectivity. More
strongly, it may be claimed that he is simply replacing one
cultural relativism (divinely sanctioned by inscripturation) by
a new relativism in which we assess Scripture by the standards
of our culture. Jewett would perhaps claim that he is assessing
Scripture by Scripture, but this still leaves him open to the
charge that he is establishing a canon within the canon and de-
priving certain passages of the NT of their authority; in short,
he is practicing the *Sachkritik* which we are so ready to condemn
in Bultmann and his school.

In the present case the difficulty is that Paul's teaching
goes back to the teaching in Genesis about the place of man and
woman in creation, and it is hard to believe that this is over-
turned by the Christian revelation. Here it stands in contrast
with Paul's teaching about slaves which is not based on such
fundamental principles but rather prescribes how slaves should
behave on the basis of existing society. Further, Paul's own
teaching on the equality of men and women (e.g. 1 Cor. 7:3;
11:11; Gal. 3:28) suggests that he was not teaching the
inferiority of the wife to her husband (still less a general
inferiority of woman to man), but rather the divine ordering of
society which ascribes a certain "headship" to the man. This
"headship" issues in the command to husbands to love their wives
and treat them with understanding while wives are to be sub-

missive to their husbands. It may well be that this biblical teaching stands over against the contemporary understanding of the marriage relationship and warns against possible inherent dangers in a society which dislikes the idea of law and order in human relationships generally.

Even though Jewett's solution is thus open to criticism, the example discussed remains important in that it opens up the questions posed by applying biblical principles to contemporary cultural situations. It is probable that some of the difficulties faced by Paul at Corinth in particular were caused by the movement of the Gospel out of a purely Jewish environment into the wider world of Hellenism. The clue to our difficulties in relating the Gospel to contemporary culture may well lie in observing how Paul and other early Christians faced analogous problems in the Hellenistic world.

If this paper has given some insight into the process which was going on, it will have accomplished its purpose: the application must be left to others to take further.

To summarize: The example of man-woman relationships raises the problem of distinguishing between biblical principles and their culture-conditioned application. While most evangelical Christians would agree that the application will vary in different cultures, some would suggest that even the principles themselves may be in need of revision in the light of other biblical teaching. This suggestion is a dubious one, and it may be urged that the biblical principles remain valid for all cultures.

NOTES

1. The best approach in this situation might be to examine the views on the New Testament concept in question which have been expressed by a number of scholars from different cultural backgrounds, so that one can compare these, eliminate the elements which appear to be due to their individual cultural conditioning, and discover what elements in their understanding come from the New Testament itself rather than from their own contribution to the process of understanding. It is, however, one thing to state this principle and another to carry it out in practical instances.

2. See H.R. Niebuhr, *Christ and Culture*, London, 1952, pp. 44-52.

3. M. Hengel, *Judaism and Hellenism*, London, 1974.

4. A. Alt, *Where Jesus Worked*, London, 1961.

5. Here I am using Bultmann's own definition of a myth as "the use of imagery to express the other-worldly in terms of this world and the divine in terms of human life, the other side in terms of this side" (in H.W. Bartsch (ed.), *Kerygma and Myth*, London, 1953 I, 10). F.F. Bruce rightly contends that to give up this way of speaking is to give up "many (perhaps most) of the central affirmations of Christian doctrine" ("Myth and History," in C. Brown (ed.), *History, Criticism and Faith*, London, 1976, 87). See further J.D.C. Dunn, "Demythologizing the problem of myth in the New Testament," in I.H. Marshall (ed.), *New Testament Interpretation*, Exeter, 1977, 285-307.

6. On the difficulty of separating the revelation from the form in which it is given see L.S. Thornton, *Revelation and the Modern World*, London, 1950.

7. I. H. Marshall, *The Origins of New Testament Christology*, Leicester, 1976.

8. M. Dibelius, *Studies in the Acts of the Apostles*, London, 1956, ch. 2.

9. B. Gärtner, *The Areopagus Speech and Natural Revelation*, Uppsala, 1955.

10. H. Chadwick, "All things to all men," *New Testament Studies* 1, 1954-55, 261-272 (quotation).

11. I have spoken above of concepts. It is more difficult to deal with the taking over of methods of thinking. The sort of thing that arises for instance, when Christian theology is practiced by people who think in a legal fashion, and see things in an inappropriate manner, perhaps getting the wrong answers out of a text which was not concerned with legal questions at all.

The question whether various cultural differences in thinking can be traced in the New Testament is too complicated to discuss here. One may compare the difficulties into which T. Boman got himself when he attempted to contrast Hebrew and Greek ways of thinking (T. Boman, *Hebrew Thought Compared with Greek*, Philadelphia, 1960).

12. We should note incidentally that the changes which have been described signalled the dethronement of the Old Testament law as the guide of life; if Jesus refused to follow the Pharisaic elaboration of the Old Testament, now the legal prescriptions of the Old Testament itself ceased to have validity, although the fundamental religious and moral principles remained in force. However, the question of how the Old Testament could be

regarded as Scripture, while its legal enactments were put on
one side, lies outside our present scope.

13. D.R.A. Hare, *The Theme of Jewish Persecution of Christians
in the Gospel According to St. Matthew*, Cambridge, 1967.

14. Our traditional doctrine of creation tends to be deistic.
We think of God creating the universe and then upholding it, to
be sure, but no longer active as creator. But surely it is
right to say that God continues to be active in every act of
creation. Who made me? In one sense the answer is "my parents,"
but at the same time surely God made me in and through their
creative act. It is one of the dangers inherent in our understanding of the creation story as a historical narrative of
what happened in the past that we have failed to see in it a
paradigm of what God is continuing to do (John 5:17). Admittedly
this concept of "continuing creation" raises the problem of the
relation between God's continuing goodness in creation, and the
sinfulness that taints the creation, but in principle this
problem is not different from that of the sinfulness of God's
original creation in the beginning. A further point is that on
this view the hand of God is present in the creations of human
culture, in music, art, landscaping, technology, and so on. A
theory developed in this way, which goes beyond my brief as a
New Testament student, would surely lead to a highly positive
evaluation of culture as God's creation, coupled with a critical
attitude to it insofar as it is tainted by sin.

15. C.F.D. Moule, *The Gospel According to Mark*, Cambridge, 1965,
on Mark 12:18-27.

16. Grand Rapids, 1975.

17. C. Brown, *The New International Dictionary of New Testament
Theology*, Exeter, 1976, II, 1959-162; I.H. Marshall, "Interpreting scripture today," *Third Way* 1:16, August 18, 1977, 7-9.

3

Culture and
the Old Testament

S. Ananda Kumar

Today we hear a great deal about the importance of culture in
the propagation of the Gospel. Certainly much damage can come
to the mission of the church if cultural factors are ignored.
Even though "culture" is not an explicit subject of the Old and
New Testaments, biblical studies have made it abundantly clear
that human cultures have played a far more significant role in
biblical history than we may at first be prepared to recognize.
Perhaps we can learn from the Bible itself neither to over-
emphasize nor underestimate the significance of culture. The
fact that culture forms an inseparable part of the content and
context of the Holy Scriptures, yet at the same time stays below
the surface, suggests both the value and the limitation of culture in the task of world evangelization.

The word "culture" comes from the Latin *colere*, meaning to cultivate. It indicates man's environment as shaped and patterned
by the whole of human activity.[1] Culture is the core and driving
force of civilization both ancient and modern. It is seen in the
works of man and in human creative activity as a reflection of
mankind's striving after higher things.[2] Culture is essentially
a social phenomenon and can be realized in the individual
through encounters with other members of society. History witnesses to the fact that religion is a chief source of culture;
in the ancient world, especially, religion and culture were in-

separably bound together.[3] This is still the case today in many
societies, including India.

Culture, with all its merits and limitations, has played a
fundamental role in God's self-disclosure in human history. Divine revelation does not come in a vacuum. It can only come
with reference to culture—i.e., in relation to the religious
environment, language and understanding of man; otherwise we
could not understand it. It is the greatness of God's mercy
that he voluntarily limits himself to the vehicles of human culture to make himself known.

Christians have accepted the Bible as a reliable record of
God's dealing with mankind in history. Further, it is an inspired record, so that, in the words of J.I. Packer, "The biblical record of God's self-disclosure in redemptive history is
not merely human testimony to revelation, but is itself revelation."[4] This revelation has come to us in two stages which can
be distinguished but not separated. The first of these, with
which we are now mainly concerned, belongs to the pre-Christian
period and forms the basis of the second and final stage in
Christ. Our Lord, his apostles, and the early church looked
upon the Old Testament record as authoritative Scripture.[5]
Their testimony as to its divine inspiration witnesses to the
fact that inspiration did not come in a cultural vacuum. Divine inspiration did not despise culture but accepted it to the
extent that it could be employed as the vehicle of divine self-
disclosure.

To do justice to our theme we have to wrestle with a number
of questions and problems that have come to light during the
last few decades in Old Testament studies and scientific research. In the case of some issues it is impossible to draw absolutely firm conclusions, and we have to be content to speak in
terms of "probabilities." In other cases we can be more definite. Whether our understanding of these matters is correct or
not, the Bible remains the Word of God. Our scholarly efforts
must not be permitted to dull our vision of our Lord and his
mission. Rather we desire to be strengthened in our faith and
enriched in our understanding of how God speaks through his Word
and calls us within culture to glorify his name. It is in this
spirit that we now turn to several examples of cultural influence
as perceived in the Old Testament. Our examples have been chosen
to be representative of the areas of doctrine, religious ritual,
social institutions, and ethics.

DOCTRINE: THE CREATION ACCOUNT IN GENESIS 1

The similarities and parallels between ancient Near Eastern
creation cosmogonies and the Genesis account of Creation are

well known.[6] Of course, many key differences mark the Genesis
record; these are not difficult to explain in light of the divine
purpose, as we shall see shortly. But justice cannot be done
to our subject by overemphasizing the differences and ignoring
the parallels. However exalted our theory of inspiration of the
Holy Scriptures, we have to take account of the similarities.
The most striking similarities with the Genesis account are
found in the Babylonian Creation Epic:[7]

1. In both accounts, in the beginning the world consists of
water, darkness and chaos.

2. The Tehom of Gen. 1:2 ("the deep" in A.V. and "the raging
ocean" in the Good News Bible;[8] LXX has *abussou*) is the Babylonian Tiamat, which is used like a proper name without the article. Tiamat was "the Goddess of the Great Deep" with a
dragon's body.

3. God divides the primeval waters by means of the firmament
(GNB has "dome" in Gen. 1:6-8). This corresponds to the episode
in the fourth of the seven tablets of the Creation Epic of Babylonia:

>He [Marduk, the supreme deity] split her [Tiamat]
>like a fish...in two halves,
>From the one half he made and covered the heaven:
>He drew a barrier, placed sentinels,
>Commanded them not to let its water through (11. 137-140).

4. In Gen. 1:3 light appears before the creation of the heavenly bodies. In the Babylonian Epic light appears before the
coming of Marduk, the youngest of the gods,[9] since light belongs
to the essence of the "upper gods."

5. The creation of sun, moon and stars on the fourth day
(Gen. 1:14-19) is parallel to the creation of the heavenly bodies
by Marduk, recorded in the Fifth Creation Tablet; special mention is made of the moon-god (Nannaru) as ruler of the night
(11. 12 ff.).

6. Creation of the beasts of the field, wild animals and
creeping things is also found on a fragment, but it is not certain whether it belongs to the same Creation Epic series (Sixth
Tablet, 11. 22 ff.).

7. Creation of man to inhabit the earth is mentioned (Sixth
Tablet, 11. 4 ff.). "I will make man...I will create man, who
shall inhabit the earth" (11. 6-7). This is parallel to God's
declaration in Gen. 1:26: "Let us make man in our image." The
relation between man and the Creator is expressed here in the

Genesis account; the same is found in the Babylonian Creation
Epic: "My blood will I take, and bone will I [fashion], I will
make man..." (Sixth Tablet, 11. 5-6). Such a relation is not
expressed with reference to the creation of other things and
animals both in Genesis and in the Babylonian Creation Epic.

8.   In Genesis, God beholds all that has been created by the
Word of his mouth and calls it good. With this the hymn of
praise to Marduk should be compared: "God of pure life, God of
kindly breath, Lord of hearing and grace, creator of fulness,
maker of abundance, God of the pure crown, raiser of the dead,...
May one rejoice over the Lord of Gods, Marduk, cause one's land
to abound, himself enjoy peace. Firm abideth His word. His
command changeth not. No god hath caused the utterance of His
mouth to fail" (Sixth Tablet, conclusion).

9.   Finally, the seventh day or the Sabbath of divine rest
is essentially of Babylonian origin.[10]

It should be observed that, except for the exchange in the
position of the creation of the plant world and the heavenly
bodies,[11] the order followed in the Genesis account is the same
as in the Babylonian Creation Epic. This cannot be mere coinci-
dence. Four responses are offered by biblical scholars:

1.   The Babylonian cosmogony is just a "pagan" or "heathen"
myth which has nothing to do with the divinely inspired record
of creation. But this simply ignores the question under consideration.

2.   Both accounts have a common origin.[12] This is a possibility, but thus far there has been found no trace of a document
more ancient than that of the Babylonian Creation Epic.

3.   "The view now increasingly favored is that Gen. 1-11, and
especially 1-3, were from the start aetiological prophecy, oriented to the past."[13] We agree with Heinrich Gross in this
judgment. Yet we see other factors as well.

4.   The most obvious and satisfactory explanation seems to be
that the Babylonian Creation Epic has had an "influence" on the
Genesis account.[14] H. Gunkel has forcibly argued that the Babylonian Creation Epic, involving a conflict between Tiamat, the
dragon of chaotic darkness, and Marduk, the god of light and
order, had influenced Israel long before the Exile period.[15]
Owen C. Whitehouse seems correct in saying, "It is to Babylonia,
the land of the highest and most ancient Semitic culture, we
must look for the most fruitful clues to ancient Hebrew thought
and life."[16] Still, as J.A. Thompson points out, the fact that
Babylonian influence can be seen does not necessarily mean that

the Genesis account was borrowed directly.[17] We shall see the implications of this in a moment.

Accepting the hypothesis that the Genesis account did not totally ignore or reject the Babylonian Creation Epic, in spite of the latter's undesirable elements, the limits of its influence may be outlined as follows:

1. While there is affinity between the two, there are also differences and distance between them.

2. The Genesis account did not incorporate all the elements of the Babylonian account.

3. Some of the elements received from the Babylonian account are so modified that they can be recognized only in the background of the Genesis record.

In other words, the Babylonian account has been subjected to a thorough process of critical theological reflection, so that the biblical account is far more than a mere reproduction of the Babylonian Creation Epic.[18] S.H. Hooke's observation is apropos: "The point of the parallels is not, however, to emphasize the dependence of Hebrew symbolism upon Babylonian myths, but to emphasize the fact that the Hebrew writers, whether Yahwist or Priestly, did not invent a symbolism to express the various aspects of the divine activity, but took what lay ready to their hand, the material which they had inherited as part of their early cultural contacts, and transformed it into the vocabulary of the divine speech."[19]

Now we are ready to examine the process of elimination, adaptation and transformation by which the Genesis account distances itself from the Babylonian Creation Epic. In this process we see how divine inspiration uses culture to communicate along lines familiar to the audience, yet by virtue of new and refined content impresses upon its readers its divine authority. We begin with elements in the Babylonian account which have been virtually eliminated in the Genesis account:

1. The Genesis account rejects all polytheistic references in the Babylonian mythology as they are completely opposed to revealed monotheism. On the other hand, it begins with a solemnity which belongs to God alone and which is lacking in the Babylonian myth: "In the beginning God."

2. All references to fighting between the gods and their struggle to overcome the dragon of the chaos are omitted, as incompatible with the sovereignty and majesty of the one universal God.

3. Reference to idolatry or anything reminiscent of idolatrous practices has been totally eliminated. Thus, sun and moon, which were objects of worship both at the time of the inscription of the Babylonian tablets and at the time of the writing of the Genesis account, are deliberately called simply "the greater light" and "the lesser light" (Gen. 1:16).[20]

4. "The Genesis Cosmogony has dispensed with the grotesque and often unlovely and confusing details of the Babylonian mythology. For example, whereas man is made out of the compound of Marduk's blood and the dust of the earth, the truth, which underlies this crude representation, is stated by the Hebrew writers in the simple words, 'And God said, Let us make man in our image, after our likeness' (1:26)." [21]

Other elements have been adapted rather than eliminated:

5. In order to dramatize the fact that the Creator-God is the God of order and almighty power, both accounts begin with darkness and chaos. The Genesis account differs in that it is purified of the mythological details.

6. In both accounts light appears before the creation of heavenly bodies, emphasizing that the Creator-God is the God of Light. Again, the mythological details mentioned in the Babylonian Creation Epic have been omitted.

7. Both accounts note that the heavenly bodies are given to rule the day and night as well as to determine the seasons; but the Genesis account is stripped of all idolatrous implications.

Finally, there are significant elements which echo the Babylonian Creation Epic but which have undergone a thorough process of transformation:

8. Tehom (Gen. 1:2a) parallels the Babylonian Tiamat, but the mythological background has been ignored. Tehom conveys a new meaning, i.e., the depth of the dark sea or ocean. The reality of this physical feature of the sea can be experienced even today. (Cf. Pss. 33:7; 104:6).

9. It is possible to translate Gen. 1:2b, "a great wind swept over the deep" (so Goodspeed and von Rad), in which case we might have another echo of the Babylonian Epic of Creation where Marduk arms himself with the winds in order to overcome Tiamat.[22] But the biblical account clearly symbolizes the invisible operation and influence of the Almighty God.[23] The mythological idea has given way to the noble spiritual truth of God's action in bringing chaos into order by his own power.

10. The crude mythological element of splitting Tiamat in two gives way to God dividing the primeval chaos into heaven and earth. The reader is appealed to by the reality--which he experiences daily--of sky above and earth beneath. This is retained in the Genesis account without any contamination with mythological elements.

11. The fact that man has relation to God as well as to the world in which he lives has been brought out both in the Babylonian Epic and also in Genesis. But, as noted earlier, in the latter the mythological details of Marduk's blood being mixed with earth to create man have given way to the sublime language "Let us make man in our image, after our likeness."

One of the most striking differences in the two accounts is highlighted by Ryle: "The narrative begins with a statement assuming the Existence of the Deity. It is not a matter of discussion, argument, or doubt. The Israelite Cosmogony differs in this respect from that of the Babylonians, Phoenicians, Egyptians, etc. The Cosmogonies of the ancients were wont to be preceded by Theogonies. The existence and nativities of the creating divinities were accounted for in mythologies which were often highly complicated, and not seldom grotesque. The Hebrew narrator, by beginning with the Creation, emphasized his entire freedom from, and exclusion of, polytheistic thought."[24]

Whitehouse adds, "In the Babylonian epic we have wild, grotesque, tumultous mythology expressed in poetic form. In the biblical account we have serene majestic calm and sober prose. In the one, the gods rise into being in the course of the drama. In the other, God pre-exists and remains from the first the creative source and summons each new order of created things into existence."[25]

Concerning the beauty and the spirit of the Genesis account Thompson says, "It is a lofty, dignified statement devoid of those coarser elements that are to be found in the non-biblical creation stories. . . . The fact of inspiration preserved the writer of Genesis 1 from the language and crudities of contemporary polytheism, but the writer remained an ordinary man who used his eyes to good advantage as he sought to describe the way in which God brought this world into being . . . for there is depth and dignity in Genesis 1 that is not to be found in the Babylonian story."[26]

Eugene H. Maly says concerning the relation between the two accounts, "The primitive cosmology of the author's time is used to teach the creation of all things by God. The absolute power of the transcendent God is emphasized. Whereas the pagan epics depict creation as the result of a struggle between the gods

and forces of chaos, the biblical account stresses the effort-
less activity of the one God. The imagery borrowed from these
other accounts becomes material for the author's polemic
against the myths; it also helps to make the picture live for
his readers."[27]

Our own summary is as follows:

Inspiration with reference to creation, as recounted in
Genesis 1, made use of the non-Israelite culture of the ancient
world of the Near East. But great caution and care is obvious
in the inspired writer's use of already existing material (cf.
Luke 1:1-4). The divine revelation involved the elimination of
polytheistic and idolatrous elements as well as of undignified,
absurd and crude mythological factors which were directly contrary to the sovereignty, majesty and dignity of the Creator-
God, who revealed himself in the history of Israel. Inspiration also involved the incorporation and adaptation of certain
ideas or concepts within the framework of "heathen" or "pagan"
myths which were in harmony with the character of the Creator-
Savior God of Israel.

Some may think that there is a subtle syncretism in this
summary. But I suggest that syncretism, though often used
purely in its negative connotation, is capable of a positive
sense. When we study the Holy Scriptures against their cultural, religious and theological background, the fact of syncretism in this good sense becomes evident. The whole process
from beginning to end is a theocentric cultural contextualization. It is a process enlightened, guided, controlled and
sanctified by God himself, as the Israelite theologians were
struggling with the framework and content of the cultures in
which they lived, to make God's Word indigenous and theologically relevant to their own situation.

In the same way other Old Testament doctrines like the
Seventh-Day Sabbath, covenant, circumcision, etc., could be
dealt with in detail, and would yield further enlightenment on
the process of cultural contextualization or indigenization.
Such a study would correct traditional misunderstandings,
deepen our knowledge of the divine inspiration of the Scriptures, widen the horizon of our theological apprehension, enhance our ability to evaluate good and bad influences in our
own culture, broaden the vision of mission in its cultural context, deliver us from the paralyzing fear of syncretism, and
help us see the movement of the Spirit of God in a new light.

RELIGIOUS RITUAL: PROHIBITION RE COOKING
A KID IN ITS MOTHER'S MILK

"You shall not boil a kid in its mother's milk" (Exod. 23:19;
34:26; Deut. 14:21). This prohibition has puzzled commentators
for centuries.[28] J.B. Taylor calls it "the strange Mosaic prohibition," and says it "probably referred originally to a Canaanite ritual."[29] B.J. Roberts supports this connection without explaining it.[30] It was given, adds J.W. Jack, "to avoid
its heathen associations."[31]

But, as we have seen in regard to the creation account in
Genesis 1, cultural elements are not necessarily rejected simply because of their "heathen associations." Beliefs or practices rejected by Israel were always rejected on some solid
theological ground. Let us look at this prohibition more
closely, therefore, and see why it is that in this particular
example of contextualization the inspired writer called for the
complete rejection of a local practice.

In the two Exodus passages, the context deals with harvest
sacrifices and festivals. In Deuteronomy 14 the prohibition
appears at the end of a long passage on "clean" and "unclean"
animals, and therefore some commentators have seen it as part
of the Mosaic dietary code. (Jewish dietary laws, forbidding
the eating of meat and milk products at the same meal, are
based on this injunction.) A. Macalister recalls other interpretations: mother and offspring should not be killed at the
same time (cf. Lev. 22:28); an animal should not be killed before it is eight days old (cf. Lev. 22:27); and, meat should not
be drenched in butter, "milk" being read as an euphemism for
butter.[32]

It was the discovery and deciphering of the Ras Shamra Tablets in the 1930s, at the site of ancient Ugarit in northern
Syria, that lent weight to an explanation connected with
harvest-time. D.M.G. Stalker writes: "The significance of this
prohibition has now been made clear by the Ras Shamra texts.
According to the 'Birth of Gods,' 1. 14, a kid was cooked in
its mother's milk to procure the fertility of the fields, which
were sprinkled with the substance which results. In this case,
a Canaanite practice is rejected, no doubt because it savoured
of magic."[33] James M. Freeman supports this as follows:
"Cudworth says, on the authority of an ancient Karaite comment
on the Pentateuch, that it was an ancient heathen custom to
boil a kid in the dam's milk, and then besprinkle with it all
the trees, fields, gardens, and orchards. This was done at
the close of their harvests for the purpose of making trees
and fields more fruitful the following year."[34] Macalister
adds, " . . . the broth [was] sprinkled on the ground as a

sacrifice to propitiate the harvest gods and ensure fruitful-
ness."[35]

So the practice of boiling a young goat or sheep in its
mother's milk was an idolatrous, polytheistic Canaanite fertility ritual, with strong elements of cult magic. This practice
was performed by the Canaanites at their feast of harvest. The
comparable event in Israel, known as the Feast of Weeks,[36]
could easily become an occasion for assimilation of pagan influences. As John Gray indicates, the Ras Shamra Tablets "document very fully the Canaanite fertility-cult, by which the
Hebrews were influenced and against the grosser aspects of which
their leaders reacted."[37] The ritual ordinances of Israel, including the one under discussion, are designed to preserve the
distinctive character of the community of Yahweh, and to avoid
assimilation with the cultic practices of Israel's neighbors.[38]
Because idolatry, polytheism and magic[39] are all opposed to God,
his people should not make any compromise with them. (K.A.
Kitchen suggests that a New Testament injunction with "similar
implications" would be the prohibition regarding food offered to
idols; 1 Cor. 10:14-22).[40] Therefore, in this instance, there
was no question of modification or transformation of a local
practice but rather complete rejection of it.

SOCIAL INSTITUTIONS: KINGSHIP IN ISRAEL

The idea of kingship in Israel did not spring up spontane-
ously. Rather, as the Bible indicates, it arose in response to
the influences of the surrounding pagan peoples (1 Sam. 8:5 ff).
G.W. Anderson states, "A most important element borrowed by
Israel from Canaan was the monarchy. . . . It is probable that
the monarchy in Israel was not simply borrowed from Canaan but
was a fusion of Canaanite kingship with the Israelite tradition
of charismatic leadership exemplified in the judges."[41]

Indeed, the office of "king" was known among the Semitic
peoples of the Middle East long before the Hebrews settled in
the Promised Land, and the word for "king"--*melek*--was a common
Semitic word. Though its origin is uncertain, *melek* may be connected with an Assyrian and Aramaic word meaning counsel or advice, so that it signified "counselor" or "ruler." The title is
applied to the rulers of small city-states in Canaan and its
neighborhood, as well as to rulers of wider territories such as
Egypt, Moab, Syria, and in later times Assyria, Babylonia and
Persia.[42]

The monarchy arose in Israel in reaction to the political
power of the Philistines. Saul was in the first place a charismatic leader like others (i.e., the Judges) before him and was
later chosen to be king.[43] In the biblical data there appear to

be two versions or traditions about the origin of the monarchy
(1 Sam. 8:1-22; 10:17-27; 12:1-25, and 9:1-10,16; 11:1-15).
Most commentators recognize a fusion of anti-monarchy and pro-
monarchy sources in these passages. Though the two perspectives
are not readily reconciled, there is something to be said for
the view that the monarchy first willed by the people was later
allowed and willed by God, and eventually by Samuel himself, although at the outset he was opposed.

Now let us see to what extent the monarchy in Israel was borrowed unchanged from Israel's neighbors and to what extent it
developed along unique lines. The borrowed elements include the
following:

1. The very term *melek*.

2. The Canaanite kings were leaders in war and sometimes led
the troops to battle in person (cf. Gen. 14:1-12). This model
was followed in Israel as well: for instance, Saul on Mt. Gilboa
(1 Sam. 31:2) and Ahab at Ramoth Gilead (1 Kings 22:29 ff.).

3. The Canaanite kings were typically the supreme judges, to
whom final appeal might be made from the findings of local elders or professional judges[44] (cf. 1 Sam. 14:1-20 and 1 Kings
3:16-28).

4. They were also the chief persons from the cultic point of
view to offer sacrifice, to bless the people and to take the
lead in organizing the nation's worship (cf. 2 Sam. 6:13,17 and
24:25; 1 Kings 5-8; 8:14; 12:26-32). (Despite the evident similarities, we must note that in Israel the king was not necessarily the religious head of the nation.[45])

5. There was the idea of sacral kingship as the deity's
anointed. The king was regarded as sacrosanct[46] (cf. 1 Sam. 24:
10; 26:9; 2 Sam. 1:14,16).

6. The office of the king was thought to be hereditary like
that of the priest (cf. 1 Sam. 20:30 ff., and 1 Kings 2:15; 14:
21; 15:25; 16:29).

7. The sceptre was the sign of supreme authority[47] (cf. Pss.
45:6-7; 110:2; Gen. 49:10 and Esther 4:11).

8. The use of oriental courtly language, such as the extol-
ling of the king in exaggerated felicitations and songs, and
the development of a definite stock of stereotyped titles, comparisons, epithets and styles of address.[48] Israel, too, shared
these courtly forms of address, perhaps through the medium of
older traditions from Canaanite Jerusalem (cf. Ps. 110).

9. The idea of the divine sonship of the king, who is magnified as the one with whom a new era of peace and righteousness
dawns and to whom the ends of the earth are assured.[49] In this
connection, see the "Royal Psalms": 2, 20, 21, 45, 72, 101, 110
and 132.

10. The application of the term *melek* to the godhead or
deity.[50]

Among the elements in the Israelite kingship which are different than found in Canaan and surrounding areas, are these:

1. The Israelite monarchy did not develop simultaneously
alongside religion. By the time of Saul and David, the faith of
Israel had developed along its own original lines.[51]

2. The monarchy was not a basic element in the faith of
Israel.[52] Yahwism, in fact, brought to bear upon the monarchy
a certain degree of tension and pointed beyond the monarchy for
Israel's ultimate hope.

3. There is no hint whatsoever of the deification of the
Israelite or Jewish monarchy.[53]

4. The ideal in Israel set kingship apart from despotism and
dictatorship, in contrast to the typical oriental monarchies.[54]
(Jezebel's action in the Naboth affair was characteristic of
pagan notions of the power and privilege of the court, 1 Kings
21:5-15.) The presence and ministry of the prophets of Yahweh
challenged the kings' authority whenever they misused it (e.g.,
Nathan's rebuke of David, 2 Samuel 12). The idea was never lost
sight of that the office was instituted for the good of the nation and that it ought to be a help and not a burden to the
people. In the people's minds, law and custom superseded the
kingly authority. Of course, the king, who according to ancient
ideas embodied the people, was necessarily a prominent object of
gracious promises of Yahweh. Nevertheless, the Israelite religion remained stronger than the adopted forms of kingship.[55]

The list could be extended. But the above items are enough
to support our conclusion: In the religio-politico-social environment in which the people of God lived, they were guided to
incorporate those elements from the surrounding culture which
would be beneficial to the nation, while rejecting those elements which were outside the divine framework of social
righteousness and justice and contrary to human dignity and
welfare.

ETHICS: POLYGAMY AND CONCUBINAGE

Assuming that monogamy is God's ideal,[56] it is pertinent to ask why polygamy was practiced in ancient Israel and why the Old Testament fails to condemn it.[57] The inspired writers prohibited other undesirable social practices;[58] why not polygamy?

Polygamy and concubinage predate Israel by many centuries. Ancient codes of the Middle East recognize and seek to regulate polygamy as an established institution.[59] In addition to polygamy and concubinage--often associated with power and wealth-- there were instances of bigamy which indicate that even men of no particular prominence entered into plural marriages (e.g., Elkanah, 1 Sam. 1:2 ff.).[60]

To understand the Old Testament attitude toward polygamy, we must take into account the social causes of the practice. These include:

1. The desire for numerous offspring could not normally be fulfilled through monogamy.[61] This desire, which is still prevalent throughout eastern countries, was especially powerful among the Hebrews.[62]

2. The barrenness of a wife made the family atmosphere unhappy.[63] Abraham's case is directly ascribed to this, and among many peoples polygamy is permitted on this ground alone.[64]

3. When there was a disproportionate number of females, they could not be married in any other way except through polygamy. In the Orient, for a young girl to remain unmarried was an insult to her as well as to her family.

4. After the war, women captives accentuated the problem of the overpopulation of women. Polygamy helped provide a solution (cf. Deut. 21:10-14).[65]

5. In ancient society, where slavery was common, the master of a household had sexual rights over his female slaves.[66]

6. Polygamy was common among wealthy and influential men, who gained prestige and honor by having plural wives, the wives being part of the display of wealth.[67]

7. In a number of cases the wife or wives were willing to give their own servants, i.e., slave-girls, to the husband as concubines.[68] Sarah, Leah and Rachel are examples: Gen. 16:1-4; 30:9-13. Even when they had children this custom was not prohibited.

8. In ancient times people felt themselves insecure, and
their safety lay in numbers and joint-family system. This also
played a part in motivating polygamy.[69]

9. The position and importance offered by numerous alli-
ances, as for example in the case of Solomon, was a factor in
polygamy.[70]

"Marriage is the state in which men and women can live together in sexual relationship with the approval of their social
group. Adultery and fornication are sexual relationships that
society does not recognize as constituting marriage."[71] This
definition, when applied to ancient Israel, prohibits neither
polygamy nor concubinage.

In truth, however, polygamy was regulated by custom and legally maintained rather than successfully managed. In the Old
Testament, polygamy is seen as leading to quarrels, jealousies
and family troubles, and kings are clearly warned against it.[72]
If there were such evils and sorrows in polygamy and if monogamy is the ideal marriage relationship, why was it allowed in
the Old Covenant at all?

It has been suggested that (1) God had ordained monogamy at
the start but man in his sinfulness managed otherwise;[73] (2) the
Mosaic Law aimed at mitigating rather than removing evils which
were inherent in the state of society in that day;[74] and (3)
God left it to man to discover by experience that his original
institution of monogamy was the proper relationship.[75] (This is
borne out by the fact that by the time of the prophets, monogamy
is increasingly looked upon as the ideal[76]).

But perhaps the most satisfactory explanation is found in the
distinction between imperfection and corruption. Divine inspiration, while not countenancing corruption, makes allowances for
imperfection. The obvious example is in the matter of the prescribed sacrifices for sin, which though imperfect in the Old
Testament era, were allowed by God until the coming of the perfect sacrifice in Christ. Only then was the imperfect fully exposed and consequently abandoned. Polygamy and concubinage belong to the same category of imperfection in the realm of ethics.
It is in this sense that our Lord spoke of the weightier and
lighter matters of the Mosaic Law.   But it should be underlined that divine inspiration does not permit corruption either
in religion or ethics. Child-sacrifices and sacred prostitution
are examples; these were absolutely forbidden in the Old Covenant, though they were common among Israel's neighbors.   In regard to polygamy, however, providence made a concession for a
time to human imperfection, which was subject to greater light
at a later time. This points to the patience of God as he seeks

to bring us into harmony with his purpose. Likewise, a proper contextualization of the Gospel will take into account the imperfection of men and women in the present state of society, yet at the same time it will absolutely forbid that which is fundamentally counterposed to the will of God in Jesus Christ.

CONCLUSION

The results of our research are necessarily tentative. Our viewpoint itself may be defective in various areas, and the evidence available to us through archaeology and historical studies may be insufficient to arrive at ultimate conclusions. We are not to be blamed for ignorance of light that is still to come; we are responsible only for the light already received. In this spirit we offer our findings, grateful to know that our salvation is not affected by the defects and faulty conclusions that may be found in our work.

In this connection it may be useful to draw attention to the judgment of Norman H. Snaith.[77] He points out the limitations in any such attempt as ours in this paper, particularly the dangers involved in belaboring one viewpoint or another in the name of scholarship and broadmindedness. We should never cease to be critical of our own work and to resist the temptation to consider our conclusions correct and final.

The purpose of our study has been to see how and to what extent the Spirit of God used the cultural environment of the Old Testament writers as they contributed to the inspired record. It seems clear enough that God did indeed speak in the context and employed elements of the content of the surrounding cultures in order to convey his message to his ancient people and, through them, to us. As a corollary, it seems fair to say that God worked to some degree in other peoples and cultures apart from his work in the Jewish nation (Rom. 2:14,15; 3:29; Acts 14: 17). If this were not so, we would have to question whether the inspired writers could have "borrowed" anything at all from the surrounding pagan environment.

Regardless of the light we have received from extra-biblical sources, which have helped us arrive at our present understanding of the Bible, we should never lose sight of the fact that the latter is the Word of God. It is both timely and timeless. Whether our understanding of it is correct at all points, whether the insights gained through historical and cultural studies are entirely valid or not, the Bible remains the Word of God. To speak in terms of one of our examples, Genesis 1 is the Word of God for us, not the Babylonian Creation Epic, even though the former may be appreciated best when seen against the background of the latter.

So let us never lose sight of the fact that the Bible is God's Word, especially when we are engaged in investigating extra-biblical "evidences." We may be enriched through such scientific studies, but our ultimate Source is God, the Creator and Savior. At best our studies are *means*, while God is our Life and Goal. Beyond him is nothing, and in him is everything.

NOTES AND REFERENCES

1. Robert Scherer, Art.: "Culture," *Sacramentum Mundi (SM), An Encyclopedia of Theology,* Bangalore, India, 1975, Vol. 2, p. 45, col. 2. See also T.S. Eliot, *Notes Towards the Definition of Culture,* 1948.

2. *Ibid.,* p. 46, col. 1.

3. See C. Dawson, *Religion and Culture,* 1948.

4. J.I. Packer, Art.: " Inspiration," *New Bible Dictionary (NBD),* IVF, London, 1967, p. 565, col. 1. Also see Packer, Art.: "Revelation," *NBD,* pp. 1090-1.

5. See F.F. Bruce, Art.:"Bible," *NBD,* p. 149, col. 2.

6. "This P Account (Gen. 1:1-2,4a) has obvious parallels in the Babylonian creation and flood epics (cf. also Pss. 74:13-15; 89:10; Isa. 51:9). John H. Marks, "The Book of Genesis," *The Interpreter's One-Volume Commentary on the Bible (IOCB),* Charles M. Laymon, ed., Nashville and New York, 1971, p. 3, col. 2; "The . . . point we have to bear in mind is that, either by direct contact with Babylonian civilisation before their entry to Canaan, or indirectly through Canaanite civilisation after their entry into Canaan, the Hebrew people had taken over into their own body of traditions a number of these myths . . . but for the present it may suffice to point out that none of the myths in this section of Gen. has been shown to be of distinctively Hebrew origin, while most of them, the flood story in particular, are of Mesopotamian origin." S.H. Hooke, "Genesis," *Peake's Commentary on the Bible (PCB),* Matthew Black-H.H. Rowley, eds., London and Edinburgh, 1964, p. 177, col. 1; "Comparison of the biblical creation story with the Babylonian story does give a number of parallels, but the external relationship between the two is not clear." J.A. Thompson, Art.: "Creation," *NBD,* p. 270, col. 2; see also A. Heidel, *The Babylonian Genesis,* 1950, pp. 82-140; J.B. Pritchard, *Ancient Near Eastern Texts (ANET),* 1950, pp. 1-9; S.N. Kramer, *Mythologies of the Ancient World,* 1961 (especially for details of Sumerian and other traditions); H.E. Ryle, *The Book of Genesis,* Cambridge, 1921, pp. 42 ff. and 447-451; "Epics of creation, in various forms, on tablets which were in circulation before the

time of Abraham, have been found in recent years in the ruins of
Babylon, Ninevah, Nippur and Ashur, which are strikingly similar
to the 'Creation Hymn' of Genesis. . . ." Henry H. Halley,
Halley's Bible Handbook (HBH), 24th edition, Michigan, 1965, p.
62; see also Owen C. Whitehouse, Art.: "Cosmogony," *A Dictionary
of the Bible (HDB)*, James Hastings, ed., Edinburgh, Vol. 1, 1900,
pp. 503-505; similarities are found in the Hindu epic
Mahābhāratha of India, *Srīmanmahābhāratha*, Vol. 1, Chapter 1.

7. Compare with Whitehouse, *op. cit.* p. 505, col. 2 and *HBH*,
p. 60.

8. *Good News Bible, (GNB)*, American Bible Society, 1976.

9. The Third Tablet describes the gathering of the great gods
in council and the first part of the Fourth Tablet (11. 1-94)
describes the elevation of Marduk to supremacy over the gods.
See Ryle, *op. cit.*, p. 449.

10. See Schrader, *Cuneiform Inscriptions and the Old Testament*,
Vol. 1., pp. 18 ff.; Sayce, *The Expository Times*, Vol. 7, March
1896, p. 264; cf. J. Skinner-J. Muilenburg, Art.: "Sabbath," *Dictionary of the Bible (DBH)*, second edition, revised by F.C. Grant-
H.H. Rowley, Edinburgh, 1963, p. 866, col. 1; Cnana Robinson,
"The Origin and Development of the Old Testament Sabbath," unpublished doctoral dissertation, Hamburg, June 1975, pp. 208-
220; 314-377; 407.

11. Ryle, *op. cit.*, p. 43. In our list the creation of plants
(not found in our present text, but evidently an original element of the Epos, probably in the Fifth Tablet after the setting
up of the heavenly bodies) would become (5) and (6).

12. *HBH*, p. 62.

13. Heinrich Gross, Art.: "Creation," *SM*, Vol. 2, p. 29, col. 2.

14. Whitehouse, *op. cit.*, pp. 505-507.

15. *Schopfung and Chaos*, pp. 11 ff.

16. *Op. cit.*, pp. 506-507.

17. Thompson, *op. cit.*, p. 270, col. 2.

18. Ryle, *op. cit.*, p. 42.

19. Genesis, *PCB*, p. 170, col. 1.

20. Compare Ryle's comment on the same verse: *op. cit.*, p. 13.

21. *Ibid.*, p. 43.

22. Hooke, *op. cit.*, pp. 178-179.

23. Ryle, *Genesis*, p. 5.

24. *Ibid.*, pp. 1-2.

25. Whitehouse, *op. cit.*, p. 505.

26. *Op. cit.*, p. 270, cols. 1-2.

27. Eugene H. Maly, "Genesis," *The Jerome Biblical Commentary (JBC)*, Bangalore, India, 1968, Vol. 1, p. 11, col. 2.

28. John E. Huesman, Art.: "Exodus," *JBC*, Vol. 1, p. 61, col. 1.

29. Art.: "Milk," *NBD*, p. 822, col. 2.

30. A.R.S. Kennedy-B.J. Roberts, Art.: "Milk," *DBH*, p. 659, col.2

31. J.W. Jack, *The Ras Shamra Tablets*, p. 32.

32. A. Macalister, Art.: "Food," *HDB*, II, pp. 35-36.

33. D.M.G. Stalker, Art.: "Exodus," *PCB*, p. 232, col. 2 (comment on Exod. 23:19b).

34. James M. Freeman, *Manners and Customs of the Bible*, Logos, 1972, p. 73.

35. Macalister, *op. cit.* However, Joseph Blenkinsopp considers the Ugaritic reference "obscure" and says "the exact import of [the Deut. 14:21 prohibition] escapes us." Art.: "Deuteronomy," *JBC*, I, p. 111, col. 1. Cf. G.R. Driver, *Canaanite Myths and Legends*, Edinburgh, 1956, p. 121; and A. Casey, *Verbum Domini (VD)*, Vol. 16, 1936, pp. 142-48 and 1974-83.

36. John Gray, Art.: "Exodus," *ICOB*, p. 58, col. 2.

37. Art.: "Ras Shamra Tablets," *DBH*, pp. 833-834.

38. Gray, *ICOB*, p. 66, col. 1.

39. See Lev. 20:6,27; Isa. 2:6; Ezek. 13:18. Magic, which is the attempt to control the higher powers, was rife in the ancient world, especially in Babylon and Assyria; the Code of Hammurabi and Assyrian law prescribe the death penalty for it. D.M.G. Stalker, *op. cit.*, p. 231, col. 2.

40. K.A. Kitchen, Art.: "Food," *NBD*, p. 431, col. 1.

41. G.W. Anderson, Art.: "The Religion of Israel," *PCB*, p. 163. col. 2.

42. W.F. Boyd–A.R. Johnson, Art.: "King" (in the OT), *DBH*, p. 551, col. 1; cf. B.O. Banwell, Art.: "King," *NBD*, p. 692, col. 1.

43. von Rad, Art.: "Basileus," *Theological Dictionary of the New Testament (TDNT)*, Gerhard Kittel, ed., Geoffrey W. Bromiley, trans. and ed., Grand Rapids, 1964, Vol. I, pp. 565-66.

44. A. Lykyn Williams, Art.: "King," *HDB*, II, 1910, p. 842, col. 1.

45. *Ibid.*, p. 842, col. 2: "A further question arises whether the early Semitic custom of the king being the religious head of the nation and the chief sacrificing priest obtained also in Israel. It has been asserted that this was the primary object of the anointing of the Israelitish kings, but no hint to this effect is given in the OT. . . . Yet there are certainly traces of the old custom, whether it is to be regarded as held legitimate by the Israelites themselves (till quite late times) or not."

46. W.F. Boyd–A.R. Johnson, *op. cit.*, p. 551, col. 1.

47. A. Lykyn Williams, *op. cit.*, p. 841, col. 2; A.J. Maclean-E. Haenchen, Art.: "Sceptre," *DBH*, p. 890, col. 2.

48. von Rad, *op. cit.*, p. 566: "At oriental courts, where a divine human person stood at the centre, the presuppositions were present for fashioning a distinctive courtly language...."

49. *Ibid.*; in other words, Israel adopted many thoughts and formulations from the Canaanite kingship institution and incorporated them into its circle of Yahwistic ideas. The status of the Davidic king as the son of Yahweh seems to have been conferred on him at his accession (Ps. 2:7). It was sonship by adoption; see G.W. Anderson, *op. cit.*, p. 163, col. 2.

50. This was common in all the ancient Orient (cf. in the immediate environs of Israel: "melkart," the Phoenician diety; "Milcom," the god of the Ammonites; "Chemosh," or "Melech," the national god of the Moabites); indeed, this usage is probably pre-Semitic. See von Rad, *op. cit.*, p. 568; also Peter Hunnerman, Art.: "Reign of God," *SM*, Vol. V, p. 233, col. 2.

51. von Rad, *op. cit.*, p. 566.

52. *Ibid.*

53. The deification of the king lay at the heart of the court

style of Babylon and Egypt. The one relic of this view which escaped strict censorship is in Ps. 45:7. The declarations of divine sonship are formulae of adoption; see von Rad, *op. cit.*, p. 566. In Egypt the tendency was for the king or pharaoh to be regarded as identical with the god; in Assyria, rather as representing the god. B.O. Banwell, *op. cit.*, p. 692, col. 1; see also G.W. Anderson, *op. cit.*, p. 163, col. 2.

54. G.W. Anderson, *ibid.*; at the same time, W.F. Boyd and A.R. Johnson (*op. cit.*, p. 552, col. 1) say, "while the monarchy in Israel differed considerably from other Oriental despotisms, it could not be called a limited monarchy in our sense of the term. The king's power was limited by the fact that, to begin with, the royal house differed little from other chief houses of the nation. . . . On the one hand, law and ancient custom exercised considerable restraint on the kings; while, on the other hand, acts of despotic violence were allowed to pass unquestioned."

55. von Rad, *op. cit.*, p. 566.

56. Monogamy would appear to be implicit in Gen. 2:24. J.S. Wright-J.A. Thompson (Art.: "Marriage," *NBD*, p. 787, col. 1), William Smith (Art.: "Marriage," *A Concise Dictionary of the Bible (CDB)*, London, 1874, p. 516, col. 2: "monogamy as the original law of marriage") and Eugene H. Maly (*op. cit.*, p. 12, col. 2: commenting on Gen. 2:24 he says, "The author concludes this first part of his narrative with a general principle--a theological conviction that had prompted and conditioned the story of woman's formation. The unity of marriage and its monogamous nature are God-willed.") support the implications of monogamy. M. Burrows (Art.: "The Social Institutions of Israel," *PCB*, p. 135, col. 2) thinks otherwise. Halley supports the first view: "God had ordained, at the start, that One man and One woman live together in marriage. . . . But man soon managed otherwise" (*HBH*, p. 70). H.E. Ryle also supports it: "Polygamy is not definitely excluded; but the principle of monogamy seems to be implied in the words 'cleave' and 'shall be one flesh'" (*op. cit.*, p. 39; see also p. 79). William Smith, *op. cit.*, p. 516, col. 2: "Monogamy . . . as the original law of marriage. . . . The rule of monogamy was reestablished by the example of Noah and his sons. . . . The principle of monogamy was retained, even in the practice of polygamy, by the distinction made between the chief or original wife and secondary wives."

57. M. Burrows, *op. cit.*, p. 135, col. 2.

58. For instance, sacred prostitution; see A. van Selms, *Marriage and Family Life in Ugaritic Literature*, 1954, pp. 80-1; R.J.A. Sheriffs, Art.: "Prostitution," *NBD*, p. 1048, cols. 1-2; A.R.S. Kennedy-B.J. Roberts, Art.: "Crimes and Punishments,"

DBH, p. 189, col. 2. Another example is human sacrifice, which was prevalent in other religions of the OT period; see A.R.S. Kennedy-J. Barr, Art.: "Sacrifice and Offering," *DBH*, p. 871, cols. 1-2; also see Lev. 18:21; 20:2-5; 2 Kings 3:27; 23:10; Jer. 32:36; Micah 6:7-8.

59. E.G. Romanes-A.G. MacLeod, Art.: "Family," *DBH*, p. 292, col. 1; see also H.E. Ryle, *op. cit.*, pp. 39, 79, 193. While polygamy existed within the framework of marriage, concubinage seemed to have been outside it but within the framework of one's family, in which both male and female slaves were also members. While the legal wife or wives were bound to be faithful to the husband and had no legal right to leave him (see W.H. Bennet, Art.: "Family," *HDB*, Vol. I, p. 847, col. 2), the concubine or concubines could leave the "husband" (cf. Judg. 19:2-4; see also Wright-Thompson, *op. cit.*, p. 787, col. 2). On the other hand, the husband was not required to be "faithful" to his wife or wives, so long as he did not injure the rights of any other man.

60. E.G. Romanes-A.G. MacLeod, *op. cit.*, p. 292, col. 1.

61. Polygamy represents a form of "family planning," motivated by concerns quite opposite to ours in the twentieth century!

62. William Smith, *op. cit.*, p. 516, col. 2.

63. C.W. Emmet-J. Paterson, *op. cit.*, p. 624, col. 1.

64. Barrenness could lead to divorce or move one to commit suicide. See Gen. 18:12; 30:1; 1 Sam. 1:10 ff.; Luke 1:25; Exod. 23:26; Deut. 7:14. Also see J.W. Meiklejohn, Art.: "Barrenness," *NBD*, p. 134, col. 2; E.G. Romanes-C.F. Kraft, Art.: "Child, Children," *DBH*, p. 134, col. 1.

65. K. Fullerton-J.P. Hyath, Art.: "Slave, Slavery," *DBH*, p. 924, col. 2.

66. J.S. Wright-J.A. Thompson, *op. cit.*, p. 787, col. 2; in the Book of the Covenant it is assumed that the maid-servant is at the same time a concubine (Exod. 21:7 ff; cf. Hagar, Zilpah, and Bilhah in the patriarchal narratives). Also see K. Fullerton-J.P. Hyath, *op. cit.*, p. 924, col. 1.

67. At one time Herod the Great had nine wives. Josephus, *Antiquities of the Jews*, XVII, 1.3.

68. The Code of Hammurabi allowed a childless wife to give her husband children by her slave. See S.A. Cook, *The Laws of Moses and the Code of Hammurabi*, p. iii, and Eugene H. Maly, *op. cit.*, p. 20, col. 1. According to this code both Abraham and Sarah

were within the law, but Jacob and Leah were not; in the case of
the latter, the Canaanite law may have permitted it. According
to the Code of Hammurabi Hagar's behavior of despising her mistress after she became a mother was against the law; but perhaps
there was no such law in Arabia or Egypt.

69. See A.R.S. Kennedy, Art.: "Family," *DBH*, p. 292, col. 1.

70. C.W. Emmet-J. Paterson, *op. cit.*, p. 624, col. 1.

71. J.S. Wright-J.A. Thompson, *op. cit.*, p. 786, col. 2.

72. Gen. 16:1-6; 21:1-19; Deut. 21:15-17; Judg. 8:29-9:57;
1 Sam. 1:6; 2 Samuel 11-13; 1 Kings 11:1-8; Deut. 17:17. See
also C.W. Emmet-J. Paterson, *op. cit.*, p. 624, col. 1, and J.S.
Wright-J.A. Thompson, *op. cit.*, p. 787, col. 1. Almost all the
stories of polygamy and bigamy in the OT were written with a
view to show that they cause evil and sorrow in the family. See
Eugene H. Maly's comment on Gen. 16:4-6 (*op. cit.*, p. 20, col. 1).

73. *HBH*, p. 70.

74. William Smith, *op. cit.*, p. 516, col. 2.

75. J.S. Wright-J.A. Thompson, *op. cit.*, p. 787, col. 1.

76. A.R.S. Kennedy, *op. cit.*, p. 292, col. 1: "In the prophetic
writings the note of protest (against polygamy) is more clearly
sounded. Not only Adam but also Noah, the second founder of the
human race, represent monogamy, and on that account recommends
it as God's ordinance. . . . Hosea and others constantly dwell
upon the thought of a monogamous marriage as being a symbol of
the union between God and His people. . . ." C.W. Emmet-
J. Paterson, *op. cit.*, p. 624, col. 1: "Polygamy is, in fact always an unnatural development from the point of view both of religion and of anthropology; monogamy is by far the most common
form of human marriage; it was also amongst the ancient peoples
of whom we have any direct knowledge. . . . Polygamy . . . in Hebrew society . . . fell into disuse; the feeling of the Rabbis
was strongly against it. . . ." William Smith (*op. cit.*, pp. 516-
17) says, "In the post-Babylonian period monogamy appears to have
become more prevalent than at any previous time: indeed we have
no instance of polygamy during this period of record in the
Bible, all marriages noticed being with single wives. . . .
During the same period the theory of monogamy is set forth in
Eccles. 25:1-27. The practice of polygamy nevertheless still
existed. . . ."

77. *The Distinctive Ideas of the Old Testament*, London, 1955,
pp. 11-17.

4

Towards a Theology
of Gospel and Culture

Bruce J. Nicholls

A theology of Gospel and Culture is an exercise in contextualization. The shift from discussions on the indigenization of the life and witness of the church to discussions on contextualization as the interaction of the Gospel with receptor cultures has been accelerated by recent events, especially the Fourth Faith and Order Commission at Montreal in 1963 where E. Käsemann raised the hermeneutical question, and by the Theological Education Fund's report *Ministry in Context 1972*, where contextualization was discussed in the context of the technological revolution and the spread of secularity. At Lausanne evangelicals began to take seriously questions concerning the relationship of the Gospel to culture.

TWO APPROACHES TO A THEOLOGY OF GOSPEL AND CULTURE

As a broad generalization we may speak of two approaches to this subject, one of which we will call "existential contextualization" and the other "dogmatic contextualization." The first approach begins with culture. It seeks to develop a dialectical interaction between questions of man in history and an existential understanding of the word of God. It is the way of dialogical theology which the recent Chiang Mai consultation *Dialogue in Community* began to popularize especially in ecumenical circles.

It begins with two relatives and expects to find tentative theological formulations in a progression to synthesis of understanding.

The second approach begins with a concern for biblical theology as a fixed and authoritative orientating point for contextualization. It seeks to translate and communicate the biblical message with understanding to each particular culture. It transcends the boundaries of particular cultural conceptual forms and practices. It begins with a dogmatic framework rather than a cultural one.

Both approaches recognize that understanding culture involves understanding the integrated worldview, consciously or unconsciously expressed, of any cultural group and that religion and spirituality are normally the dominant factor in any cultural conceptual framework. Further, culture is a total "design for living," a way of behaving, thinking and reacting. It includes the group's value systems and the institutions of family, law and education. Because culture is the sum total of behavioral patterns learned by instruction, observation and imitation, it is constantly changing, and therefore the task of contextualization, however understood, is always a continuing one.

An important study of existential contextualization has been given by Dr. Daniel Von Allmen, formerly of the Protestant Theological Faculty at Yaounde, Cameroons, in an article entitled "The Birth of Theology" (*IRM* January 1975, pp. 135-153). Von Allmen defines Christian theology as a reflection on living preaching of the Gospel of Jesus Christ who died and was raised for us. It is existential theology in Bultmannian terms. He believes that New Testament theology is contextualized in the cultural forms of Hellenistic Judaism and influenced by "a dying and a rising god" of the mystery religions. Paul corrects and adapts this Hellenized Gospel. This is a model for the contextualization of theology in Africa and elsewhere. Further, Von Allmen argues that contextualization cannot be built on any existing theology but must ever begin anew. Thus, a truly African theology must presuppose a *tabula rasa*, stripped of existing, especially western, theologies. African culture has a value of its own and must become the framework for doing theology. He suggests that just as New Testament theology grew out of preaching and worship and not out of dogmatic formulations propositionally conceived, in the same way African theology must develop from the experience of faith, rather than from a defined body of Gospel truth received by revelation. This is a point of view evangelicals will want to question.

SOME QUESTIONS RAISED BY EXISTENTIAL CONTEXTUALIZATION

We may begin with the question "Can existential contextualization avoid the dangers of syncretism and religious universalism?"

Because this method begins with a dialectical process between a changing context and a subjective existential word of God, it has no normative theological framework of belief and practice. I suggest that deviation from an authoritative and infallible Scripture as the word of God is almost inevitable, leading to a syncretistic set of beliefs and practice and a universalistic understanding of salvation, for it is difficult to live within the framework of relative thinking. If the biblical account of the Gospel is not normative, then culture tends to become semi-absolutized. This, I suggest, is what is happening in many emerging Third World theologies and it is being accentuated by the non-theological cultural factor of those who now freed from colonialism are searching for national identity and who are over-reacting to the western paternalistic Christianity to which they were previously subjected. In such discussions rarely do we find any attempt to distinguish between a biblical theology and western theology.

A recent paper "Towards a Theology of Dialogue" by S. Wesley Ariarajah of Sri Lanka (*Ecumenical Review*, January 1977, pp. 3-11) illustrates this point. He reacts against the "teutonic captivity" of Christian theology. In arguing that all theology is "story telling," he says, "All religions seek to tell their religious experience within the framework of 'a story' of the nature of the world, of man, of God and the destiny of life" (p. 5). All stories have no enduring value in themselves except to give this framework. And therefore the Judeo-Christian "Creation-Fall-Redemption" story is no more valid than the Hindu or Buddhist story. He adds, "Anyone who approaches another with an *a priori* assumption that his story is 'the only true story' kills the dialogue before it begins" (p. 5).

Most attempts to contextualize theology in India have tended to follow the same path of relativizing the Gospel and absolutizing one or other of the Hindu conceptual frameworks. For example, Brahmabandhav Upadhyaya (1861-1907) attempted to indigenize Christian theology in terms of Shankara's *advaitic* philosophy of non-dualism. He interpreted the trinity in terms of *Brahma* (the Absolute or Pure Being) as *sat chit ananda* (being, intelligence and bliss). His use of these impersonal categories resulted in his natural theology progressively weakening biblical concepts. He, himself, adopted Hindu cultural practices and on his death was cremated according to Hindu rites. More recently other Roman Catholic scholars, such as Raymond Panikkar, author of *The Unknown Christ of Hinduism*, have given new credence

to Upadhyaya's ideas. In passing it may be noted that Bishop
J. A. T. Robinson's interpretation of Tillich and Bultmann in
Honest to God comes close to the language of Shankara's *advaita*.
A second example is A. J. Appasamy's attempt to indigenize the
Gospel using the concept of *bhakti* (which he translated as love)
as interpreted in the modified non-dualism of Ramanuja. This
also led to a reduction of the Gospel, as for example in his
treatment of the Johannine "I and my Father are one" which he
limited to a moral union of love and obedience. However, his
involvement as a pastor and later as a Bishop progressively led
him back to a more biblically theological framework. A third
example is P. Chenchiah's (1886-1959) use of the philosophy of
Shri Aurobindo and of the emergent evolution of Bergson. In his
Aryan cultural framework he found no place for atonement or conversion or for the church. He left us with an Arian Christ and
a truncated Gospel.

A second key question raised by existential contextualization
follows: "Is revelation in any sense verbal and propositional?"

I have come to see that this is a very crucial question in
the debate on contextualization and in the contemporary discussions on dialogue between living faiths and ideologies. Those
who argue for an existential contextualization generally deny
on philosophical grounds that God's self-revelation could be
verbal and propositional. Instead, many theologians of the
biblical theology school limit revelation as man's reflection on
and interpretation of God's acts in history. In place of an objective word of God, they look to the immediate guidance of the
Holy Spirit. Lesslie Newbigin comments, "Revelation is not the
communication of a body of timeless truths which one has only to
receive in order to know the whole mind of God. Revelation is
rather the disclosure of the direction in which God is leading
the world and his family. The stuff of the Bible is promise and
fulfillment. It is the story of a journey, of a pilgrimage, of
a moment" (*The Good Shepherd*, GLS, Madras, 1974, p. 123). He
adds, "The work of the Spirit then is to lead the church to see
all things, the whole creation, all powers, systems, ideas, cultural achievements, all intellectual structures, all things in
their relation to Christ as head of all men and all things. He
will lead the Church into the fullness of truth as it is in
Jesus, that is to say, to the point where it is made manifest
that all things are subject to him" (p. 129). In existential
contextualization there is generally a fusion between the work
of the Holy Spirit inspiring the biblical writer and the Holy
Spirit illuminating the believing receiver.

All contextualized theologies are culturally conditioned. We
may think of Thomistic theology, Calvinist theology, Liberation
theology, Indian theology, Water Buffalo theology (Kosuke Koyama)

and African theology, etc. Jesus Christ was born a Jew. How
valid is it to speak of a black Christ or an Indian Christ? On
what basis are these attempts to interpret theology to be evaluated? I suggest that there is only one basis, namely, biblical
theology. This raises another set of questions.

SOME QUESTIONS RAISED BY DOGMATIC CONTEXTUALIZATION

We may begin with a fundamental question, "Can there be an objective dogmatic contextualization?" In an absolute sense, no.
All attempts at theologizing are colored by the pre-understandings
of the enculturalized receiver of the message. Luther's commentary on Galatians was influenced by his antagonism to the Pope,
Barth's commentaries on Romans by his existentialism and so
forth. No commentator can bypass his own pre-understanding.
There can be no doubt that Luther and Barth's commentaries have
made the Pauline epistles come alive to their own age. But how
do we test their faithfulness to the biblical norm? Is a "distancing" between the theologian and the biblical writer possible?
The Reformation grammatico-historical exegetical method, which
takes seriously the language, historical background and purpose
of the biblical writers, when used by the "believer" who sin-
cerely seeks to put himself "under" the authority of the Scriptures, reduces cultural pre-understanding to a minimum and makes
possible comprehension of biblical theology. Evangelical scholars such as James Denney, Leon Morris, F. F. Bruce, are good examples of those who have used distancing to good effect. The
Bible's teaching on its own perspicacity assures the faithful
student of this possibility. It is on this basis that we can
speak of the Scriptures as "the only infallible rule of faith
and practice." While we may rightly speak of Pauline or
Johannine theology, these are harmonious and complementary elements of the one unitary biblical theology.

But distancing by itself is no guarantee against distortion.
The Lausanne Convenant states, "He (the Holy Spirit) illumines
the minds of God's people in every culture to perceive its truth
freshly through their own eyes and thus disclose to the whole
Church ever more of the many-colored wisdom of God." Evangelicals standing within the tradition of Anselm's *credo ut intelli-
gam,* "I believe so that I may understand," believe that by the
Holy Spirit enabling the reader to identify with the word of God
he can know the mind of God. Biblical hermeneutics requires
both distancing and fusion of our horizons.

This leads us to ask, "Is there an unchanging Gospel core?"
This issue was raised at Lausanne. The report on the theology
of evangelization paper "The Gospel, Contextualization and Syncretism" suggested criteria for isolating the Gospel core from
other biblical elements. While we may summarize biblical truth

in a number of propositions I have a certain uneasiness about
the concept of a Gospel core for it is open to the same subjective dangers as the neo-Orthodox concern that the Bible "contains" the word of God or a canon within the canon.   Chris
Wright, in "Ethics and the Old Testament; cut-price hermeneutics?" (*Third Way*, 5 May 1977, pp. 7-9), has rightly argued that
the common practice of dividing Old Testament laws into the
categories of moral, civil and ceremonial, of which only the
moral is unchanging, is unsatisfactory.   All the laws of the Old
Testament are the word of God and speak against their social
background to the ethical task of Christians in the modern world.

Any attempt to formulate a biblically dogmatic theology in
order to contextualize it in a particular culture raises the
question, "Can the form of the Gospel be changed without changing the content?"   The distinction between content and form is
relevant to any discussion on the meaning of language.   Can the
linguistic form of the Gospel be changed without changing its
content?   The answer must be both yes and no.   On the pre-
understanding that the Bible is the inspired word of God it must
be affirmed that God the Holy Spirit overshadowed the cultural
forms through which he revealed his word in such a manner that
these cultural forms conveyed what God intended to be revealed.
God was not at the mercy of human culture.   He controlled the
use of it for his particular purpose of revelation.   Therefore,
the way in which the biblical writers use their own culture cannot be made a corresponding model for our contextualizing of
theology.   There is a uniqueness about biblical theology that
does not carry over to our contextualizing of theology.   Our approach to contextualizing must include a process of elimination,
adaption and transformation of pagan cultural forms but biblical
inspiration goes beyond this process.   There is always a supra-
cultural newness about God's self-revelation.   He is not impris-
oned by any culture.   In his sovereignty God chose a Hebraic
cultural form and transformed it over the centuries which cover
the biblical record.   It might be argued that he could have chosen an Indian or Chinese cultural form.   If he had done so, then
I suggest that the nature of these cultures would have been different from what it is today.

In discussing the question of the permanence of the form of
the Gospel I suggest that we distinguish between what we might
call "symbolic" and "conceptual" forms.   By symbolic form I mean
the biblical language that uses analogy of nature, parables and
metaphors.   In the process of contextualization, new symbolic
forms may be found useful without changing the content of the
message.   For example, symbols such as "white as snow" or "small
as a mustard seed" are not essential to the conceptual meaning.
They may be legitimately changed for other cultural forms if the
biblical forms are outside the experience of the receiving culture.

By conceptual form I mean the form that is ontologically essential to the message because these forms are consistently used
throughout Scripture. This will include the use of analogy of
divine relationships. For example, the Bible speaks of God as
"our Heavenly Father." Granted the term father carries different conceptual images in patriarchal, matriarchal and in Marxist
cultures and therefore the biblical form will need to be translated with cultural sensitivity. But we have no authority to
de-mythologize father in favor of some such form as "Ground of
Being." I am unable to accept the plea of Dr. Itofo Bokeleale
of Zaire at PACLA, Nairobi, that because the term father was up-
setting to Africans it should not be used of God in the African
context. In this case to change the form is to change the essential meaning for the term father is the unique way God has
revealed his attributes to us.

This in turn raises another important question, "Is a dynamic
equivalent theology adequate?" A model that is particularly
relevant to this consultation is that of the relationship between "formal correspondence" and "dynamic equivalence." This
consultation is rightly motivated by a desire to communicate the
Gospel to other cultures and several of the papers are emphasizing the dynamic equivalence model over and against the formal
correspondence model. A word of caution is needed here. The
former without the latter falls into the trap of cultural con-
tainment and the latter without the former may fail to communicate. Cultures are not neutral. They are generally orientated
to a particular religious worldview which may be alien to the
biblical worldview and may need to be judged rather than fulfilled. Culture is always the interaction of the supra-cultural
and the human. There is no dynamic equivalence in some cultures
for some biblical concepts. In the several Hindu cultures, there
is no dynamic equivalence to the biblical concepts of creation,
incarnation, resurrection of the body, substitutionary atonement
or grace. There are, no doubt, glimpses of these biblical concepts in the Hindu Scriptures, but I believe they belong more to
the realm of God's general revelation than to his special revelation. I am unable to accept Dr. J. S. Mbiti's statement that
"each culture must count it a privilege to have the Gospel as
its guest." The Gospel is the guest of no culture, including
the Hebrew culture. Jesus was a severe critic of the culture of
his birth. Where there are no dynamic equivalent forms in the
receptor culture, it is essential that "a formal correspondence"
to the biblical form be explained and taught. In the last analysis only the Holy Spirit can make this new concept understandable to the receiver, otherwise it is not possible to communicate Christ as "the lamb of God" to a Buddhist, or the Trinity
to a Muslim.

In many cases it is legitimate for the Christian communicator to use a pagan cultural form and give to it a new meaning which corresponds with the biblical thought. Paul did this when he chose a term such as *metamorphosis*, transformation, which he took out of a Hellenistic structure, and set it in a Christological framework. Numerous parallels may be quoted from Third World situations. On the other hand, Paul sometimes chose a word that had a common usage in Hellenistic and Jewish cultures, and used it in the Hebrew sense when there were differences in its meaning. When Paul used the word *mysterion*, mystery, he used it in the sense in which it was used in the Septuagint. In Hellenistic culture *mysterion* belonged to the cultic practice in which the participants received a secret initiation in order to be identified with the deity and the cosmic forces represented by it. Instead Paul uses it in the Jewish sense of a special revelation made by God about his plan for the future, whereas in Hellenistic thought to disclose a secret was to forfeit the power of mystical identity. In the development of contextualized theologies there is always the danger of attempting to retain an unbiblical conceptual form at the expense of the biblical meaning. To do so is to open the door to syncretism.

SOME BIBLICAL FOUNDATIONS TOWARDS A THEOLOGY OF GOSPEL AND CULTURE

The foundation of a theology of the Gospel and culture is the doctrine of God as the Creator-Savior. We will focus our attention on two implications of God's work as Creator-Savior, our solidarity in Adam and our solidarity in Christ.

1. *Solidarity in Adam*

The high point of divine creation is man made in God's image. Three observations following this divine act may be noted:

  a. *There is a Relational Continuity of Man Created in the Image of God and God Himself*

Man was created in the image of God (Genesis 1:26, 5:1, 9:6; 1 Cor. 11:7). The early church and the Eastern Orthodox churches have stressed the ontic or essential content of this image, usually in terms of reason, freedom and personality. Brunner, in his distinction between the formal and material image, comes close to the Orthodox view. The reformers and evangelical theologians have generally stressed that the image is primarily relational in terms of knowledge, love, righteousness and holiness (Eph. 4:24; Col. 3:10). Universal elements in this relational continuity that provide a positive basis for contextualization as the fulfillment of culture include:

The Obedient Worship of the Creator. The chief end of
man is to worship God and enjoy him forever. This is true of
man as an individual and corporate man in society. All religious
cultures have some concept of the Supreme in either personal or
impersonal forms. The concept of worship is the dominant factor
in most Third World cultures revealing man's insatiable desire
to know God and to worship him. Beauty in most cultures is invariably associated with worship.

The Choice of Moral Values. All cultures have a sense of
justice based on an understanding of moral law and the belief
that man has a degree of freedom to choose right and wrong.
Conscience is either good or bad depending on man's response to
the ever present call of the living God and the dictates of his
moral law. Therefore there is truth and goodness in every man
and every culture. All religious scriptures contain some truths
that are in conformity with the biblical doctrine of law (Romans 2:14,15). The Hindu concept of *karma* parallels the biblical injunction "as a man sows so shall he reap," good is rewarded and evil is punished.

The Power of Rational Communication. Man is able to
formulate rational concepts and to communicate them to others.
He has the capacity to distinguish truth from falsehood. He
understands the law of contradiction as the chief law of logic.
There is a basic logical coherence in every worldview, for example, on the assumption of the Buddhist understanding of suffering, the four truths and the eight-fold path are rational and
logical.

The Gift of Creativity. The Creator has given to mankind
the gift to be able to create out of the existing creation
pleasing aesthetic forms of sculpture, art, music and poetry,
conceptual forms of philosophy and, through scientific knowledge,
to have dominion over creation itself. Man's creative capacity
is derived from the Creator himself enabling him to create and
enjoy beauty and order in form and design.

The Corporate Basis of Society. God created man, male
and female, with the family the basic relational unity of society (Genesis 2:18-24). Marriage and the family belong to the
creation order and may be enjoyed in peoples of all cultures.
God created man for the wider society of community and ordained
the structures of government and property ownership for order
and human well being.

If these component elements of man's relational activity to
God's work in the world were the whole story a theology of the
Gospel and culture would be self-evident. The tragedy is that
man not only seeks God but also rebels against him and selfishly

demands his autonomy, creating tensions in human society that
demand the judgment of God on culture. Theologically we may
speak of our discontinuity as well as our continuity in Adam.

   b.   *There is a Relational Discontinuity between Man and God
        Caused by the Fall*

   The account of the Fall in Genesis 3 and man's oppression of man in Genesis 4 and its theological interpretation in
Romans 1 and 2 is also an up-to-date microcosm of man in society.
There is no part of man's constitution that is not corrupted by
the Fall, and consequently no element of culture that does not
abuse the *imago Dei*. The end is death (Gen. 2:17, 3:4, 14-17).
Culture is never neutral, it is always a strange complex of
truth and error, beauty and ugliness, good and evil, seeking
God and rebelling against him. Elements in this relational discontinuity that evidence God's judgment on culture include:

   The Rebellion Against the Obedient Worship of the Creator.
Idolatry is the practice whereby man closes the gap between the
Creator and the creature, creates deity in his own image or the
image of the created world, and through the mystic of magical
identity with creation placates or controls his man-made gods.
Idolatry is the fundamental sin of man and of society. Romans
1:18-32 is an accurate description of his rejection of obedient
worship.

   The Abuse of the Moral Law. All men abuse their conscience and rebel against the moral law. Justification by the work
of the law is in reality the abuse of the law. The history of
World Wars I and II and of social injustice in this century is
evidence of the out-working of this principle in western society.
In Hindu culture the principle of *karma* is divorced from the
law-giver and becomes an absolute principle to which even the
gods are subject. It becomes a tyrannical master making forgiveness impossible and any idea of substitutionary atonement
absurd. Ultimately man becomes a slave of the gods he creates,
the occult or the spirits of the unseen world.

   The Perversion of Man's Rationality in Communication.
Man rationalizes his desires and experiences and life ends in
meaninglessness and silence. This is true both of the Hindu
advaitic philosophy of non-dualism and of western existentialism
and logical positivists. Francis Schaeffer in *The God Who Is
There* has ably demonstrated this line of despair through philosophy to art to music and to the new theology.

   The Misuse of the Gift of Creativity. Man creates that
which is ugly and cruel, wantonly despoils creation, turns
fields into deserts and through the abuse of scientific knowl-

edge, hastens his own self-destruction and that of the whole
created world.

   The Fragmentation of the Corporate Basis of Society.   Man
abuses the principle of sex and marriage, creates disorder and
lawlessness in the family and in society.   In the assertion of
his autonomy man perpetuates acts of aggression and of cruelty.

   c.   *There is a Divine Mystery between the Sovereignty of God
        and the Freedom of Man in Culture*

        The living God is not a deistic God who stands indiffer-
ent before the arrogance of man in his rebellion.   He is the
sovereign God who loves the whole world and calls all men to
himself in repentance and faith.   He leaves no man without a
knowledge of himself and all are "without excuse" (Rom. 1:20).
Because of God's general revelation to mankind, sin is always
sin against better knowledge.   Man knows he ought to love the
creator and obey the moral law.   It is only the goodness of God
that keeps man from self-destruction and from the total disintegration of society.   Calvin's term "common grace" is not an
entirely satisfactory term but it does point to God's provident
care of the world.

        Revelation is a unity, though a clear distinction in
understanding between general revelation and special revelation
is necessary to develop an adequate theology of the Gospel and
culture.   This double form of revelation was in the heart of
God from the beginning.   Revelation is always supernatural.
Without a general revelation man would have no knowledge of God
as creator.   Without special revelation he is ineffective and
powerless to obey the moral law and find salvation.   The concept
of an atoning sacrifice for sin is common to many non-biblical
cultures.   Perverted forms of propitiation and expiation are
found in the earliest Hindu *Rig Vedas* but the Hindu sacrificial
system offers neither hope nor power of salvation.   If the distinction between God's general revelation and his special revelation given in Scripture is lost, salvation is generally reduced to the level of the mystical identification of the creature with the creator or to agnosticism.   Theology becomes anthropology.   Further, it leads to a confusion between salvation
in Christ and God's sovereign action in history.   Salvation history becomes the salvation of history as in liberation theology.
Chairman Mao is not merely "my servant" alongside Nebuchadnezzar
and Cyrus but becomes "a savior" of his people and of the world.

2.   *Our Solidarity in Christ*

        The transformation of our solidarity in Adam into solidarity
in Christ (Rom. 5:12-19) is the Christian hope for a new society

and for a new culture. Christ is the New Man, the beginning of
a new humanity. In Christ, the image of God in man is restored
and in the lordship of Christ, the Kingdom of God becomes visible.
The Church, as the new community of the people of God, is the
mystical body of Christ and when his lordship is explicitly
acknowledged, becomes the visible expression of Christ's reign.
The institutional church is no guaranteed sign of the Kingdom.
The vertical dimension of personal salvation in Christ is invali-
dated if it does not result in a renewal of horizontal relationship with one's neighbor, for as James argues, "faith without
works is dead" (James 2:17, 20, 26). Therefore, while the Church
is distinct from the world as a new called-out community, it
cannot be separated from involvement in the world. It must always be light and salt to all men.

Where the people of God are truly the realm of God's reign
they must progressively manifest new cultures, transforming existing cultures into conformity to the image of Christ. While
we cannot at present speak of a Christian culture, for the sinner
is never wholly sanctified in this life and society never per-
fected, yet we must be bold to work towards new cultures which
become the dynamic equivalent of God's plan for society under
the lordship of the resurrected Christ. The lifestyle of the
universal Church ought to be a model of Christ-centered cultures
which are both universal in their expression and at the same time
rooted in the historic cultural situations of each particular
people.

The Church's function in the world is to be God's agent to
plant new churches, to expand the boundaries of the Kingdom and
to demonstrate the reality of the new society. It is to be a
model for the world to see. But this is not all. God's sovereign action over the world as the Creator-Savior extends beyond the church to all men, for the creation mandate is for all
men. God is at work in China today as he was in ancient Nineveh
or Babylon. He restrains the evil actions of men, demonic
principalities and powers, institutionalized social and political
evils and prepares communities to receive the Gospel. At the
Cross these powers were dethroned, but their final destruction
awaits the return of Christ. Therefore the church has political,
economic and social responsibilities under the hand of God. It
ought to become the conscience of society, the inspiration for
human justice and a testimony to the love of God for all men.
The church as a covenant community points to the millennial reign
and to the new heaven and the new earth in which dwells righteousness. As Christians we humbly believe that the inner renewal of
the church as the agent of God on earth, is God's chosen agent for
bringing about God-centered cultural change. I believe that the
church in India, small and weak as it is, is the ultimate hope of
a better "design for living" for the whole of Indian society.

THE PROPHETIC PRINCIPLE IN CULTURAL TRANSFORMATION

The ministry of the prophet of the Lord in the cultural over-shadowing of the word of God in biblical times is the key to understanding the conditioning of the Gospel in our contemporary cultures. The prophetic principle is the opposite of the accommodating syncretistic principle which seeks to harmonize man in society with the forces of nature and the spirit world.

The prophetic principle runs through biblical history separating Israel into "my people" and "not my people" (Exod. 3:7, 6:7). Israel was "not my people" in times when they were self-confident, proud of their distinctive kingship and nationhood, victorious over their enemies and in full possession of their land. These were times when their faith was noticeably conditioned by the surrounding pagan cultures of Canaan and Assyria, times when they assimilated pagan religious ideas and customs and entered into mixed marriages.

Israel was "my people" when they were conscious that Yahweh was their King and they lived by their covenant promises in obedience to the Law. At such times they were living communities of faith. These were usually periods of weakness and oppression and times when they were conscious of their calling to suffering servanthood. At such times the cultural conditioning of their faith was minimal and the rebuke of the prophet effective. The "thus saith the Lord" was God's way of restraining the conditioning influence of pagan culture and discipling the people in obedience of the Word of God. True dogmatic contextualization is always reforming. It is the opposite of a pan-en-theism which is man's natural tendency to synthesize creation and redemption. The prophetic voice was a call for reformation of belief, worship and fidelity to the law. It was also an appeal for social and economic justice. The prophetic voice was one of promise and fulfillment, of judgment and hope. In present day attempts at existential contextualization the eschatological note of the return of Christ, the resurrection of all from the dead, the final judgment, the promise of a new earth and a new heaven are often missing. It is only a church that is sure of its calling as a covenanted community of faith and obedient in going into the world as God's servant for mission and world evangelization, that will be able to adapt and transform the symbolic forms of other cultures and give to them new meaning so that they become the bearers of the word of God. Such a Church need not fear syncretism or loss of evangelistic motivation through involvement in society. The free exercise of the prophetic word of the Lord is the only sure basis for faithful dogmatic contextualization. The prophetic principle brings about cultural transformation in four ways:

a. The prophet calls for a de-culturalization of the accretions to biblical faith. In the patriarchal period we see how Abraham and his descendants were progressively de-culturalized from their Mesopotamian culture as nomads in the promised land, during captivity in Egypt and in the Wilderness journeyings. The Exile was another period of de-culturalization.

In western culture the Gospel is distorted by accommodation to Platonic and Aristotelian philosophy, by the humanistic enlightenment and by egalitarian and Marxist ideologies. In Asia and Africa, contextualization must include not only the de-culturalization of western accretions but also of indigenous culture concepts that are contrary to the word of God.

b. The prophet of the Lord judges and condemns those elements of culture that are contrary to the word of God. Idolatry, pagan sexual morals and corrupt political and economic practices come under the judgment of the prophets from Moses to John the Baptist. Much of Israel's history is written from the point of view of the call for the destruction of the Baalization of Yahweh-worship. Jesus Christ was a severe critic of the Judaism of his day. Similarly, in the contextualization of the Gospel in Indian cultures the prophet of the Lord will condemn such evils as idolatry, tantric philosophies of ritualistic sex, caste distinctions, unjust dowries and so forth.

c. The prophet of the Lord is God's agent to re-create and transform cultural elements that are consistent with God's revelation and which may be adapted and utilized in the service of the Kingdom. The Gospel fulfills as well as destroys. For example the adaptation of "meditation" in worship and the transforming of the Hindu "extended family" are Indian cultural forms that find a new level of fulfillment in the Gospel. Similarly there are elements of Islamic culture and worship that are "convertible."

d. The Gospel brings with it new elements in culture. There is no dynamic equivalent to the messianic hope in many Third World cultures. Its prophecy has to be explained and taught. Some Asian cultures interpret sin only in terms of "shame." The biblical concept of guilt, atonement and forgiveness are new elements which the Gospel brings to these cultures. Similarly, the biblical experience of the grace of God is distinctive because it flows from a unique Cross. The hope of the resurrection as distinct from the common Asian view of immortality transforms one's attitude to the body.

We need to recover the place of "Thus saith the Lord" if our task of contextualizing the Gospel is going to be true to the normative word of God and effective in communicating the Good News to those who live in darkness.

5

Hermeneutics and Culture:
A Theological Perspective

C. Rene Padilla

The basic problem of biblical hermeneutics is to transpose the
biblical message from its original context into the context of
the modern readers or hearers so as to produce in them the same
kind of impact that the message was meant to produce in the original readers or hearers. Another way of stating this would be
to say that hermeneutics is essentially the science and art of
explaining in a contemporary situation the Word of God which was
originally explained in a Hebrew or a Graeco-Roman *milieu*, for
the purpose of bringing the lives of readers or hearers into
conformity with the will of God. Understood in these terms,
hermeneutics is strongly linked to the concrete historical context of the modern interpreter. It has to do with the Word of
God which can only be understood and appropriated as it becomes
"flesh" in a specific historical situation with its particular
culture[1] and all the political, social and economic factors
present in it.

The importance of awareness of the particularities of a situation and their bearing on the task of making the biblical message meaningful within a specific historical context can hardly
be exaggerated. Where this kind of awareness is lacking, the
final result is the confusion of culture-Christianity with the
Gospel. This confusion has been frequent in Western-based mis-
missionary work and is (at least in part as a result of it) a

problem affecting the worldwide Church today. The solution can
only come through a recognition of the role that the historical
context plays in both the understanding and communication of the
biblical message. The present paper is an attempt to suggest a
hermeneutic which takes the situation seriously and makes it
possible for the biblical message recorded in ancient texts to
engage with the situation of the modern readers or hearers, yet
at the same time to remain true to its original purpose. In the
first part, I shall describe three different approaches to Scripture according to the importance given to the historical context.
In the second part, I shall propose a hermeneutical circle as an
essential means to relate the biblical message to the situation.
Finally, in the third part, I shall outline the implication of
this hermeneutical approach for the contextualization of the
Gospel.

I.   THREE APPROACHES TO SCRIPTURE

Roughly speaking, there are three approaches to Scripture,
depending upon the attitude to hermeneutics adopted by the interpreter: the intuitive approach, the scientific approach, and
the contextual approach.

A. *The Intuitive Approach*

Over a century ago, Hudson Taylor, the founder of the China
Inland Mission, wrote a letter to a Miss Desgraz in which he
shared what later would be regarded as his "spiritual secret."
After quoting Jesus' words according to John 7:37, "If any man
thirst, let him come unto me and drink," he added:

> Who does not thirst? Who has not mind-thirsts or
> heart-thirsts, soul-thirsts or body-thirsts? Well,
> no matter which, or whether I have them all--"Come
> unto me" and remain thirsty? Ah no! "Come unto me
> and *drink*."

> What, can Jesus meet my need? Yes, and more than
> meet it.... He not only promises me drink to allevi-
> ate my thirst. No, better than that! "He who trusts
> Me in this matter...out of him shall *flow*..."

> Can it be? Can the dry and thirsty one not only be
> refreshed--the parched soil moistened, the arid places
> cooled--but the land be so saturated that springs well
> up and streams flow down from it? Even so! And not
> mere mountain-torrents, full while rain lasts, then
> dry again...but, "from within him shall flow rivers"--
> rivers like the mighty Yangtze, ever deep, ever full.
> In times of drought brooks may fail, often do, canals

may be pumped dry, often are, but the Yangtze never.
Always a mighty stream, always flowing deep and ir-
resistible![2]

Taylor's reading of Jesus' words pronounced at a festival of
shelters in the first century in Jerusalem, illustrates an approach to Scripture commonly taken by Christians everywhere. A
few observations regarding it are here in place:

1. The main concern of the interpreter is with the relevance
and personal appropriation of the message in his own situation.
Hermeneutical considerations are either set aside or minimized.
In more technical terms, the *Sitz im Leben* ("life situation")
fades away and the *Sitz im Glauben* ("faith situation") becomes
prominent. The assumption is made that the modern reader has
access to the meaning of the ancient text as long as he is able
to read it in his own language. There is no awareness of the
role of the historical context either in relation to the text or
in relation to the modern interpreter. The basic assumption is
that the situation of the contemporary reader largely coincides
with the situation represented by the original text. The interpretative process is portrayed in Diagram 1.

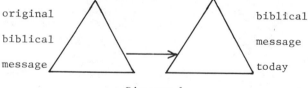

original   biblical

biblical   message

message   today

Diagram 1

2. The value of this approach is that it brings out three
facts essential to biblical hermeneutics. First, that Scripture
was meant for common people, not exclusively for trained theologians. (Was it not the re-discovery of this truth that led the
sixteenth century Reformers to translate and circulate the Bible
in the vernacular?[3]) Second, that there is a mystery about
Scripture, in that the Word of God is given in human words and
understood through the illumination of the Holy Spirit. Third,
that the purpose of Scripture is not merely an intellectual apprehension of truth, but a conscious submission to the Word of
God speaking in Scripture. Properly qualified (as they will be
further on) these three facts are of particular importance at a
time when, in Robert J. Blaikie's words, "Only as mediated
through the scholarly priesthood of 'Biblical Critics' can ordinary people receive the truth of God's Word from the Bible!"[4]

3. On the other hand, the intuitive approach to Scripture
can easily lead to allegorizations in which the literal meaning

of the text is lost. Someone has said that allegory is the son
of piety, and this statement is certainly corroborated by the
history of biblical interpretation from the time of the early
church fathers to modern days. The fantastic interpretations by
such reputable theologians as Origen and Augustine, Luther and
Calvin, are more or less sophisticated illustrations of a piety-
inspired approach to the Bible--the same kind of approach that
many a modern preacher adopts in his effort to make the biblical
message relevant in his own situation. The question to be posed
to this approach is whether the appropriation of the biblical
message is possible without doing violence to the biblical text.

B. *The Scientific Approach*

To anyone with even a superficial understanding of the role
of the historical context in relation to biblical revelation,
the importance of linguistic and historical studies to the interpretation of Scripture is obvious. If the central theme of
the Bible is God's action in history that reached its culmina-
tion in the person and work of Jesus Christ, then it is impossible to understand the biblical message apart from its original
cultural setting. The raw material of theology is not abstract,
timeless concepts which may be merely taken over from Scripture
simpliciter as the Word of God, but rather a message relative to
historical events, a message whose narration and interpretation
are colored by the Semitic and Graeco-Roman cultures of the biblical authors. One of the basic tasks of theology, therefore,
is the construction of a bridge between the modern readers or
hearers and the biblical authors by means of the historical
method, the basic assumption of which is that the Bible cannot
be understood apart from its original historical contexts.

This is the approach adopted by a large majority of biblical
scholars dedicated to the academic study of Scripture. But it
is also the approach preferred by educated Christians interested
in "serious Bible study" (as contrasted with mere Bible reading).
What are we to say with regards to it?

1. The main concern of the interpreter is with the understanding of the biblical message oriented by the conviction that
what is needed for this understanding to be possible is to go
back to the *Sitz im Leben* of the biblical authors. His effort,
therefore, is by means of grammatico-historical exegesis, to extract from Scripture those more universal elements which the ancient text relays. These elements may then be applied to the
modern readers or hearers, but this task is usually conceived as
one which falls outside the field of biblical scholarship and
should be left to preachers and devotional writers. The interpretative process is represented in Diagram 2.

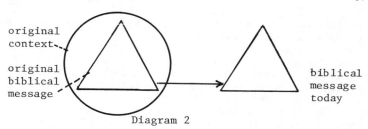

Diagram 2

2.   The value of this approach is that it throws into relief
the historical nature of biblical revelation.   In a way, the
historical interpretation widens the gulf between the Bible and
the modern readers or hearers.   In doing that, however, it witnesses to the fact that the Word of God today has to do with the
Word of God which *was* spoken in ancient times by the prophets
and apostles.   Unless the modern interpreter allows the text to
speak out of its original situation, he has no basis to claim
that his message is continuous with the message recorded in
Scripture.   If the events of revelation and their interpretation,
which are the subject-matter of Scripture, are to be taken seriously, then no interpreter is free to engage in *eisegesis*; his
task is to actualize the past, and actualization is related to
unique historical events inextricably tied to *normative* (though
not exhaustive) meanings and contemporaneous with all succeeding
generations.

3.   The limitation of the scientific approach to Scripture
per se is that it assumes for the interpreter an "objectivity"
which (as the "new hermeneutic" has argued)[5] is both impossible
and undesirable.   Impossible, because the interpreter inevitably
comes to the text with presuppositions that color his exegesis.
Undesirable, because the Bible can only be properly understood
as it is read with a participational involvement and allowed to
speak into one's situation.   The hermeneutical task is not
merely to define the original meaning of the text, nor can the
interpreter assume that the only historical context he has to
deal with is the ancient one related to the text, as if he himself were above history.   Hermeneutics has to do with the transposition of the biblical message out of its original historical
context into the historical context of the modern interpreter,
in such a way that the text written in the past strikes home in
the present.

C.   *The Contextual Approach*

The two previous approaches to Scripture are one-sided; they
fail to do justice either to the original historical **context of**
the biblical text or to the historical context of the **modern**

readers or hearers. As a result, no meaningful dialogue between
the past and the present takes place. In the intuitive approach
the biblical message is prematurely adapted to contemporary
needs for the sake of actualization. In the scientific approach,
on the other hand, the biblical message is considered in its
original context, but its meaning is removed into a world which
is definitely not our world. How can the chasm between the past
and the present be bridged? How can the message recorded in ancient documents speak to the interpreter in the present day,
without losing its original meaning? A number of exegetes have
addressed themselves to this problem. Here I will limit myself
to proposing a way to make our message both biblical and contemporary by means of an approach which combines insights derived
from classical hermeneutics with insights derived from the modern hermeneutical debate--*the contextual approach.*

In this approach the basic assumptions of the two previous
approaches, i.e., that the context of the contemporary reader
has much in common with the original context of the biblical
message and can therefore be appropriated today, and that the
biblical message can only be properly understood in the light of
its original context, are taken up and counterbalanced. Both
the context of the ancient text and the context of the modern
reader are given due weight. The aim is that the horizon of the
contemporary historical situation be merged with the horizon of
the text in such a way that the message proclaimed in the contemporary situation may be a dynamic equivalent of the message
proclaimed in the original context. In its simplest form, the
interpretative process may be portrayed in Diagram 3.

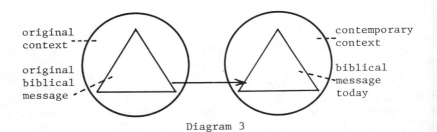

Diagram 3

In a simplified form, Diagram 3 brings out the aim of the
contexutal approach. It illustrates the importance of the historical context to the biblical message, in both its original
and its contemporary forms. There is no such thing as a biblical message detached from a particular historical context. The
representation of the interpretative process involved in transposing the biblical message from its original context into a

contemporary context, however, needs to be refined. I shall attempt to do that by describing the process as a hermeneutical circle.

II. THE HERMENEUTICAL CIRCLE

The simplification of the interpretative process in Diagram 3 lies in the fact that it views the process as a one-way movement, i.e., from the original context to the contemporary context, when in actual fact, no interpretation of the biblical message is possible except one which is necessarily conditioned by the particular contemporary context in which the interpreter finds himself. We need not agree all the way with Bultmann and his followers in order to admit that whenever an interpreter approaches a particular biblical text he can only approach it from his own perspective. If that is admitted, however, it becomes obvious that the interpretative process involves a hermeneutical circle in which the interpreter and the text are mutually engaged and that the interpretation inevitably bears the marks of its historical context.

The process involves, therefore, a two-way movement. The dynamic interplay which takes place in interpretation will be more clearly seen after we have described the various elements of the hermeneutical circle.

A. *The Elements of the Hermeneutical Circle*

The elements that come into play in the hermeneutical circle are four: (1) the interpreter's historical situation; (2) the interpreter's world-and-life view; (3) Scripture, and (4) theology.

1. *The interpreter's historical situation*

No interpreter lives in a vacuum—he lives in a concrete historical situation, from which he derives not only his language but also his patterns of thought and conduct, his methods of learning, his emotional reactions, his values, interests and goals. If God's Word is to reach him, therefore, it must reach him in terms of his own context or it will not reach him at all. The knowledge of God is possible only when the Word, so to say, becomes incarnate in the situation of the interpreter.

Because understanding of the biblical message is always relative to the situation of the interpreter, there is no guarantee that his interpretation (his theology) will completely coincide with the message in its original context. No historical situation as a whole reflects the purpose of God; in all cultures, therefore, there are elements which conspire against the under-

standing of God's Word. In more technical language it may be
said that the interpreter's "pre-understanding" can prevent his
interpretation from being a true reflection of the biblical message. If this is recognized, it follows that every interpretation should be open to correction and refinement. It follows
also that in every situation there is a need for safeguards
against distortion of the Word of God. Whenever in the process
of interpretation any of the values or premises of the interpreter's historical situation which are incongruent with the
biblical message become a part of the interpretation, the result
is syncretism. In every syncretism there is an accommodation of
the biblical message to some value prevalent in the situation,
an accommodation which usually stems from the desire to present
a "relevant" message.

On the other hand, every situation possesses positive elements, favorable to the understanding of the biblical message.
In other words, every situation makes possible a certain approach to Scripture which brings to light aspects of the message
which in other situations remain less visible or even hidden.
Different facets of the message are more meaningful in one situation than in another. Consequently, the same differences that
hinder intercultural communications turn out to be an asset to
the understanding of the many-sided wisdom of God; they serve as
channels to aspects of God's Word which can be best seen from
within a particular historical context.

Eugene Rubingh illustrates this in his article on "The African Shape of the Gospel,"[6] showing that the "primal vision"
characteristic of African culture places the African in a privileged position to understand that "each is part of all, and the
Kingdom embraces every facet, every moment, every act."[7] Another illustration is provided by Don Richardson in *Peace Child*,[8]
which more than a fascinating missionary story is a valuable
case study of contextual hermeneutics. The Sawi people—head-
hunting cannibals of the former Netherlands New Guinea—at first
acclaimed Judas as the hero of the Gospel story because they ide-
alized treachery; but the Gospel struck a responsive note in
them when it was presented in terms of a *tarop tim*, a peace
child given by God for all mankind. Richardson concludes,

Redemptive analogies, God's keys to man's cultures,
are the New Testament-approved approach to cross-cultural
evangelism and only in the New Testament do we find the
pattern for discerning and appropriating them, a pattern
we must learn to use.

Some redemptive analogies stand out in the legends
and records of the past; Olenos the Sinbearer; Balder
the Innocent, hounded to his death, yet destined to

rule the new world; Socrates' *Righteous Man*; the unknown
God of the Athenians, an analogy appropriated by the
apostle Paul; the Logos, appropriated by the apostle
John; the sacrifical lamb of the Hebrews, appropriated
by both John the Baptist and Paul.

Other redemptive analogies have been found hidden away
in the cultures of the present--dormant, residual, waiting....

How many more are yet waiting to be found, waiting to
be appropriated for the deliverance of the people, who
believe them, waiting to be supplanted by Christ, that
they may then fade from sight behind the brilliance of
His glory, having fulfilled their God-ordained purpose?[9]

The interpreter's historical situation does not only supply
"redemptive analogies" which can serve as hermeneutical keys to
God's Word in that particular context; it also poses questions
demanding scriptural answers. It is with *these questions* that
theology has to deal in each situation. If God is to confront
man with his Word within a specific situation, there must take
place an engagement with the horizons of the reader or hearer of
the message in his historical context. God does not meet man in
the abstract; God only meets him as a concrete historical being,
in the context of his bodily existence.

This means that the hermeneutical task requires an understanding of the interpreter's historical situation as much as an
understanding of Scripture. No transposition of the biblical
message is possible unless the interpreter is familiar with the
frame of reference within which the message is to become meaningful. There is, therefore, a place for auxiliary sciences (such as
economics, sociology, social psychology and anthropology) which
can enable the interpreter to define more precisely the horizons
of the contemporary historical context even as linguistics, literature and history can help him in his study of the text and
its original context. The deeper and richer his understanding
of the life situation, the deeper and richer will be the questions he asks from the Bible and the answers he finds in it.

The so-called "theology of liberation" in Latin America has
given a great deal of attention to the whole question of the
historical situation of the interpreter and its decisive role in
the doing of theology. In fact, one of the main representatives
of this "school," Juan Luis Segundo,[10] claims that the basic difference between a liberation theologian and an academic theologian is that the former is "step by step obliged to put together
the disciplines that open up the past and the disciplines that
explain the present in the very act of doing theology, that is,

in his attempt to interpret the Word of God addressed to us,
here and now."11 He then proposes a hermeneutical circle in
which he distinguishes four points. First, our way of experiencing and evaluating concrete reality, which leads us to "ideological suspicion." Second, the application of this suspicion to
all the "ideological superstructure," of which theology is a
part. Third, a new way to experience the theological reality,
which leads us to "exegetical suspicion." Fourth, a new hermeneutic, that is, a new way to interpret Scripture, which includes the new elements gained in the process. By opting for
the Marxist sociological analysis of reality as his starting
point,12 however, *a priori* he blocks the possibility of letting
Scripture speak for itself. If the interpreter comes to the
Bible with questions emerging out of an ideological construction
of reality, how can he prevent his theology from becoming a mere
echo of his ideology? No one can claim absolute objectivity, but
that is no basis for supposing that theology must be made to conform to a pre-packaged ideology in order to be relevant. The
errors of a theology that has been put at the service of the de-
fenders of the *status quo* will not be corrected by tying theo-
ology to a different ideology but by letting Scripture be free
to speak into our situation and to reformulate the very questions that concrete reality is to ask from it. Without that
freedom, the hermeneutical circle turns out to be a vicious
circle.

This is not to deny the need to develop adequate instruments
to analyze concrete reality. All scientific pursuits, however,
are in the final analysis based on a religious commitment and
cannot therefore be regarded as autonomous from the Word of God.
Furthermore, it must not be forgotten that personal experience
and observation of reality by a culturally-sensitive person are
by themselves a valid means to understand the horizons with
which the Word of God will have to engage in the contemporary
situation. Science can certainly add new and valid insights,
but it is by no means the only way to attain knowledge of reality; it must not be absolutized.

In conclusion, a proper understanding of the concrete situation is essential because hermeneutics is not merely concerned
with the meaning of the message for the original readers but
also with its relevance to the life of the modern readers or
hearers in their own historical situation. The incarnation
makes clear God's approach to the revelation of himself and of
his purposes; God does not shout his message from heaven; God
becomes present as man among men. The climax of God's revelation is Emmanuel, and Emmanuel is Jesus--a first-century Jew!
This incarnation unmistakably demonstrates God's intention to
make himself known from within a concrete human situation. Be-

cause of the very nature of God's Word, we can only know this
Word as a message contextualized in a particular culture.

2. *The interpreter's world-and-life view.*

We have already pointed out that the interpreter approaches
Scripture from a particular perspective. He has his own world-
and-life view, his own way of apprehending reality, in a great
measure derived from his situation but also enabling him to see
it as a coherent whole. Whether or not he is conscious of it,
this world-and-life view, which is religiously determined,[13]
is behind all his activities and colors his understanding of
reality in a definite way. As Peter Berger has put it, "Every
'definition of the situation' implies specific theoretical presuppositions, a frame of reference, in the last resort a view of
reality."[14] We can extend this observation to biblical hermeneutics and say that every interpretation of the text implies a
world-and-life view.

Western theology has generally been unaware of the extent to
which it has been affected by the materialistic and mechanistic
world-and-life view which has gained hold on the West.[15] For
the interpreter who without question accepts the modern "scientific" world-and-life view according to which empirical science
is the only source of knowledge and nothing lying outside its
scope can be real, it is natural to assume that whenever Scripture points to a spirit-world or to miracles, for instance, it
can hardly be taken seriously. He may not go all the way with
Bultmann, who claims that the world-and-life view of Scripture
is obsolete and that demythologizing is therefore an essential
hermeneutical method if the New Testament message is not to be
regarded as outmoded; but he will at least have mental reservations as to the validity of what he would regard as a pre-
scientific world-and-life view.

The interpreter whose world-and-life view has been framed in
a historical situation by the assumption of a closed universe
where everything can be explained on the basis of natural causes,
needs the corrective provided by Scripture in its emphasis on a
personal Creator who acts purposefully *in* and *through* history;
on creation as totally dependent upon God; on man as the "image
of God," affected by sin and redemption. Such elements are the
substance of the biblical world-and-life view apart from which
there can be no proper understanding either of reality or of
Scripture. The "scientific" world-and-life view is centered
around man in a closed continuum in which no intentional acts
(and therefore no truly *human* acts) but only occurrences in a
chain of world-and-life natural causality are possible. By contrast, the biblical world-and-life view is centered around the
living God who in his own communication through his Word has

given and continues to give the ultimate proof of his existence. And the Bible must be read on its own terms.

In order to read the Bible on its own terms, however, people who are conditioned by what Donald M. Mackay has called "nothing-buttery"--"ontological reductionism" in philosophical terms--need a real "epistemological conversion." They need to see that the assumption that reason is able to grasp the totality of reality may be an assumption solidly established in the West, but it is not universally accepted or beyond doubt. It may well be that what prevents them from entering into the "strange world of the Bible" is not its obsolete world-and-life view but their secularistic and unwarranted assumption with regards to the powers of reason!

3. Scripture.

Hermeneutics has to do with a dialogue between Scripture and a contemporary situation. Its purpose is to transpose the biblical message from its original context into a particular twentieth-century situation. Its basic assumption is that the God who spoke in the past and whose Word was recorded in the Bible continues to speak today in Scripture; that "the revelation of God and man that was reality in Israel and that in Jesus Christ burst its national limitations to become the faith and life of all mankind has access to each new age only through the narrow channel of Scripture."[17]

From one point of view the Bible must be read "like any other book," which means that the interpreter has to take seriously that he faces an ancient text with its own historical horizons. His task is to let the text speak, whether he agrees with it or not. If the theological is dependent upon the historical, then the effort of the interpreter must be to understand what the text meant in its original situation. In James Smart's words,

> All interpretation must have as its first step the hearing of the text with exactly the shade of meaning that it had when it was first spoken or written. First the words must be allowed to have the distinctive meaning that their author placed upon them, being read within the context of his other words. Then each word has to be studied in the context of the time in order to determine not only what meaning it had for the author but also what meaning it would have for those to whom it was addressed, the two not always being identical and both playing a part in the origin of the text. The religious, cultural and social background is of the greatest importance in penetrating through the words to the mind of the author, but it must not be assumed

that he used words always with the same significance as his contemporaries. The omission of any of these disciplines is a sign of lack of respect not only for the text and its author but also for the subject matter with which it deals.

It has been argued, however, that the grammatico-historical approach described in this quotation is itself typically Western and consequently not binding upon non-Western cultures. After all--claim the advocates of this position--a hermeneutics itself is dependent upon presuppositions which are culturally determined; it must not be regarded as having universal validity.[19] What are we to say to this thesis?

First, no interpreter, regardless of his culture, is free to make the text say whatever he wants it to say. His task is to let the text speak for itself, and to that end he inevitably has to engage with the horizons of the text via literary context, grammar, history and so on. In the West or outside the West, the Bible is an ancient book and must be read "like any other book" in order to be understood. It is also true that it is the Spirit who makes it possible for us to hear the Word of God in and through the Bible, and we shall have more to say about that further on; but in no culture is the Spirit a short cut to the understanding of the biblical message.

Second, Western theology has not been mainly characterized by a consistent use of the grammatico-historical approach in order to let the Bible speak, but by a dogmatic approach, by which competing theological systems have muted Scripture. Abstract conceptualization patterned on Greek philosophy have often gone hand in hand with allegorizations and typologies in which the historical nature of revelation completely subsides and the interpretation of the Bible becomes a capricious literary or homiletical exercise. Western theology provides abundant illustrations of the conscious or unconsicous avoidance of grammatico-historical exegesis as a device to maintain a particular theological position.[20]

Third, in order to minimize the importance of the grammatico-historical approach one must not appeal to the New Testament use of the Old as if it were settled beyond question that the New Testament writers were not particularly interested in the literal meaning of Old Testament Scripture. Of course, the problems in this area of biblical studies cannot easily be dismissed.[21] But there is no basis for the idea that the New Testament specializes in highly imaginative exegesis, quite similar to that of rabbinic Judaism. Even in Paul's case, despite his rabbinic training, there is such a restraint in the use of allegory, for instance, that it can hardly pass unnoticed. As

James Smart has put it, "The removal of all instances of allegory from his (Paul's) writings would not change the structure
of his theology. This surely is the decisive test."[22]

The effort to let Scripture speak without imposing upon it a
ready-made interpretation is a hermeneutical task binding for
every interpreter, whatever his culture. Although attention to
the historical factors may sometimes appear to result in widen-
ing of the gap between the interpreter and the world of the
Bible, still this distancing is essential if the biblical message is to be seen for what it is—a message coming out of a
definite historical context far removed from that of the interpreter. This does not mean, of course, that total objectivity
is possible, but it does mean that unless objectivity is set as
a goal, the whole interpretative process is condemned to failure
right from the start. We must certainly be suspect of our objectivity, but we must also maintain the hope of understanding
the text without having our preconceived ideas obstruct the task
of letting the Bible speak.

Objectivity, however, must not be confused with neutrality.
That the Bible should be read "like any other book" has been
taken as an affirmation of the need to take seriously the literary and historical aspects of Scripture, but it can also be
taken to mean that the Bible must be read from the perspective
of faith. Since any book should be read in the light of the
purpose for which it was written, and since the Bible was written that God may speak in and through it, it follows that reading the Bible "like any other book" implies reading it with an
attitude of openness to God's Word. "The historian who claims
to be an interpreter of the Scriptures, a biblical scientist,
must be a sufficiently open-minded scientist to let his subject
matter determine the character of his approach. If the Scriptures confront him with theological realities, i.e., mysteries
. . . then he will need theological as well as historical and
literary equipment in order to deal scientifically with their
full content."[23] Another way of saying this is to say that because Scripture is not meant simply to give information but to
communicate the Word of God, there must take place an engagement
between the horizons of the text and those of the interpreter.
It is only when the interpreter is willing to ask himself, "What
does this message mean to me now, within my own context?" that
he is prepared to understand the meaning of the message in its
original context. The understanding and the appropriation of
the biblical message are two aspects of an indivisible whole—
the *comprehension* of the Word of God.

If the interpreter is to move beyond a mere intellectual
understanding of Scripture, however, he needs the illumination
of the Holy Spirit. The same Spirit who inspired Scripture in

the past is active today to make it God's personal Word in a concrete situation today. The written Word, whose central content
is Jesus Christ, fulfills its purpose when the Spirit, whose
task is to bear witness to Jesus Christ, enlightens the mind,
thus enabling it to see Jesus Christ in Scripture and its relevance to life in a specific historical context. The testimony
of Scripture is inseparable from the testimony of the Holy
Spirit.

In conclusion, the hermeneutical task is both a scientific
and a pneumatic task at the same time. It has to do with the
understanding of the text in its original context and with the
appropriation of its message in a contemporary situation. It
requires the use of exegetical tools but it also requires the
illumination of the Holy Spirit.

4. *Theology*

Whether in the shape of "biblical theology" or in the shape
of a "Bible exposition," theology is the result of a merging of
the horizons of the contemporary historical situation and the
horizons of the text, without which merging the transposition
of the biblical message from a concrete situation in the past
to a concrete situation in the present cannot take place. Such
theology will be relevant to the particular situation to the
extent to which it is expressed in symbols and thought forms
which are part of that situation, and it addresses itself to
the questions and concerns which are raised in that context. It
will be faithful to the Word of God to the extent to which it
is based on Scripture and it has the Spirit-given power to accomplish God's purpose.

In and through the theology in which there is a genuine
fusion between the ancient text and the contemporary situation,
the Word of God becomes incarnate. The historical context thus
plays a decisive role in the formulation of a theology which is
both biblical and contemporary. There are at least three reasons for this.

First, since the Word became man, the only possible communication of this Word is that in which it becomes incarnate in
history in order to put itself within the reach of man as a
historical being. All authentic communication of the Word of
God is patterned on the incarnation and therefore seeks to find
a point of contact with man within his own situation.

Second, without a translation which goes beyond the words to
break into the raw material of life, the Word of God is an ab-
straction. The Word of God is related to the totality of the
universe and of human experience. If its proclamation is not

directed to specific needs and problems in a particular situation, how can the reality of the Word be concretely experienced?
The Word of God is not an abstract principle or a mere doctrine,
but the determining factor of life in all its dimensions, the basic criterion by which all the values which are the substance of
human life are evaluated. Without contextualization, therefore,
the Word of God will necessarily touch life only on a tangent.[24]

Third, in order for the Word of God to receive an intelligent
response, either positive or negative, there must be effective
communication, communication which takes into account the point
of contact between the message and the historical context. If
such is the case, the communication of the Word of God cannot be
reduced to the repetition of literally translated doctrinal formulas whose success has been demonstrated in other latitudes. If
the proclamation of God's message is to go beyond the conscious
level and its call is to be more than an invitation to mere intellectual assent, it must include the contextualization of the
Word of God as one of its essential elements. Otherwise it will
produce spurious conversions or negative responses which reflect
faulty communication but not a rejection of the Word of God.

If theology represents a real merging of horizons, old and
new, however, it will not be limited to dealing with the questions raised within the concrete situation, but it will also
communicate the questions that the Word of God poses to that
situation. The hermeneutical task is not completed until the
whole of reality is placed under the Word of grace and judgment
and people in it are able to hear that Word from within their
own historical situation.

B. *The Dynamics of the Hermeneutical Circle*

Having considered the elements of the hermeneutical circle,
we are now ready to take a look at the way in which these elements are interrelated in the interpretative process. In order
to represent this adequately, it would be necessary to employ a
motion picture rather than a diagram. It would then be possible
to show more accurately the way in which a change in the situation of the interpreter brings about a change in his comprehension of Scripture, while a change in his comprehension of Scripture in turn reverberates in his situation. It would be seen
that a genuine hermeneutics involves a dialogue between the
historical context and Scripture, a dialogue in which the interpreter approaches Scripture with a particular perspective (his
worldview) and approaches his situation with a particular comprehension of the Word of God (his theology). In spite of the
limitations of a static drawing, we may represent the interpretative process as a circle in which the four elements of the
hermeneutical circle are connected as Diagram 4 shows:

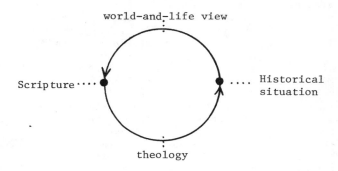

Diagram 4

The aim of the interpretative process is the transformation
of the historical situation. For that purpose the interpreter
listens to the questions being raised in his situation and comes
to Scripture asking, "What does God say through Scripture regarding this particular problem?" The way he formulates the specific questions will of course depend on his world-and-life view.
It may, therefore, be said that the concrete situation can only
approach Scripture through the world-and-life view of the interpreter.

The richer and deeper the questions brought by the interpreter from his historical context, the richer and deeper the
answers provided by Scripture. It follows that without a good
understanding of the real issues involved in living in a particular situation, there cannot be an adequate understanding of
the relevance of the biblical message to that situation. Each
new formulation of the questions based on a more refined understanding of the situation makes possible a new reading of Scripture and consequently the discovery of new implications of its
message. If it is true that Scripture illuminates life, it is
also true that life illuminates Scripture.

Scripture does not answer questions which are not posed to it.
A lack of perception of reality in the historical context may impede the interpreter from properly detecting the questions which
are being raised in his situation, in which case his theology
may specialize in answering questions which no one is asking
while ignoring questions which demand a biblical answer.

We must not forget, however, that Scripture does not directly
answer every question which may be posed to it from within a
particular situation. There is a large number of topics on
which Scripture says nothing or very little. It is therefore

legitimate to ask whether there is a place for the hermeneutical
approach adopted by J. Severino Croatto,[25] an Argentine "liberation theologian" who claims that although the biblical text is
"contextually limited," i.e., it expresses the meaning of the
saving Event in terms of a specific ancient culture, it is capable of conveying an infinite number of meanings depending on
the horizons of the interpreter. According to Croatto, the biblical writer, because of the limitations of his own horizons,
may have very little to say which is relevant to our action in
the modern world, yet he is able to give us a "kerygmatic nu-
cleus" whose horizons we must enlarge if we are to have an answer to our questions. The task of the interpreter is thus to
"de-contextualize" the text in order to go beyond the meaning
originally given by the author to his words, so that the kerygma
may be actualized in terms of a praxis which is relevant within
the present-day situation and God's continuous revelation may
become visible in new events. If the original Event is to be
proclaimed again but in a different context, claims Croatto,
then it must be re-structured in the light of what is happening
here and now, it must be "re-contextualized" on the basis of a
definite praxis.

Croatto's approach brings out three important facts with regard to Scripture. First, that the meaning of the original
events in Scripture may go beyond that which was in the mind of
the original writers--a fact that can hardly be denied by anyone who regards Scripture as the Word of God which transcends a
specific historical situation and is relevant to the whole of
human history. Second, that the wider implications of God's
action in the past are properly comprehended from within the
context of practical obedience (*praxis*, in Croattos' terminology). Third, that Scripture does not often give direct answers
to the questions which are posed to it by the modern interpreter,
particularly in relation to ethical issues. But Croatto fails
to see the unique role that both the prophets and the apostles
have in the history of salvation as authoritative interpreters
of the original events, whose word of interpretation is inseparable from the events themselves.[26] As a result, he leaves the
door open to an *eisegesis* of the most arbitrary kind. It may be
that a *sensus plenior* in Scripture is the logical inference from
a biblical doctrine of inspiration. But no modern interpreter
can claim that his interpretation stands on the same level with
that of prophets and apostles in Scripture without falling into
total subjectivism. The interpretation of salvation events
given in the Bible is not exhaustive, but it certainly is normative.

This, however, does not solve the problem of those questions
for which no explicit answer is given in Scripture. One need
not be facetious to ask, "What is the use of a normative Scrip-

ture if Scripture fails to answer the questions which are raised within one's contemporary situation?" The answer is, in the first place, that even though Scripture does not give an exhaustive answer to a number of contemporary problems, it does provide guidelines which are sufficient for the interpreter to deduce what Scripture *would* say if it specifically dealt with those problems. All the answers will have to be regarded as improvisations, but it will still be possible to judge which of them are more in keeping with the general tenor of authoritative Scripture and which ones are mere reflections of the historical conditioning to which the interpreter is subject. Furthermore, the Spirit of God is active to enable his people to walk in obedience even though they are not able to articulate *a priori* all the answers for every specific situation.

When it is recognized that Scripture does not mean to provide opinions which may or may not be accepted by the modern reader but to serve as the God-given norm for faith and practice throughout all succeeding generations, the basis is laid for a hermeneutical approach in which every effort is made to let Scripture speak. The initial questions, coming out of our concrete situation, may then have to be reformulated. The content of theology will consequently be not only answers to specific questions previously raised within our historical context, but also questions which the text poses to the initial questions. The grammatico-historical approach to Scripture is thus a logical consequence of the view in which Scripture is regarded as authoritative for faith and practice.[27]

The deeper and richer our comprehension of the biblical text, the deeper and richer will be our understanding of our historical situation and of the meaning of Christian obedience in that particular context. The possibility is thus open for changes in the world-and-life view of the interpreter and consequently for a more adequate understanding and appropriation of the biblical message, for in answer to more adequate questioning and a world-and-life view more congenial to Scripture, the text itself will speak more plainly. The more the Bible is allowed to speak for itself, the more the questions which are posed to it from within the concrete situation will be the questions that really matter; the more congenial the world-and-life view from which Scripture is approached, the more relevant will be the theology formulated in response to the burning issues which the interpreter has to face in the concrete situation.

In conclusion, the interpretative process involves a continuous mutual engagement between the horizons of the text and the horizons of our historical context. Neither our understanding of the text nor our understanding of our concrete situation is adequate unless both of them constantly interact and are mutu-

ally corrected. When that is done, the interpreter progressively approaches Scripture with the right questions and from
the right perspective, and his theology is in turn more biblical
and more relevant to his situation. He goes from his concrete
situation through his (increasingly biblical) world-and-life
view to Scripture, and from Scripture through his (increasingly
relevant) theology to his situation, to and fro, always striving
for a merging of his own horizons with those of Scripture. Hermeneutics may thus be conceived as having a spiral structure in
which a richer and deeper understanding of the Bible leads to a
greater understanding of the historical context, and a deeper
and richer understanding of the historical context leads to a
greater comprehension of the biblical message from within the
concrete situation, through the work of the Holy Spirit.

III. THE CONTEXTUALIZATION OF THE GOSPEL

    Daniel von Allmen[28] has argued that contextualization was
"the dynamic element in the formation of New Testament theology.
The Hellenization of the Church which took place in apostolic
times was initiated by Hellenistic missionaries who, in a spontaneous movement and under the pressure of external factors (of
persecution), undertook the work of evangelism and tackled the
Greeks on their own ground. It was they who, on the one hand,
began to adapt into Greek the tradition that gave birth to the
Gospels, and who, on the other hand, preached the good news for
the first time in Greek."[29] Their aim, however, was not a
"Hellenized theology," but simply a faithful transcription of
the Gospel into Greek. After the translators came the poets--
Greek-speaking Christians who gave expression to the faith received, not in a systematically worked theology, but by singing
the work which God had done for them. (According to von Allmen,
here is the origin of a number of hymns quoted by the New Testament writers, particularly the one in Phil. 2:6-11). Finally,
after the poets came the theologians, with the twofold function
of insuring that the new ways of expressing the faith correspond
to apostolic doctrine (a critical function) and showing that all
theological statements must be set in relation to the heart of
the Christian faith, i.e., the universal lordship of Jesus
Christ. Von Allmen maintains that the way in which Christianity
was Hellenized in the first century sets the pattern for contextualization today. What is needed in his view is missionaries
like the Hellenists, who "did not set out with a theological intention"; poets like the authors of the hymns quoted in the New
Testament, who "were not deliberately looking for an original
expression of their faith," and theologians like Paul, who did
not set out to do theology. "The only object of research which
is allowed, and indeed commended," he concludes, "is the kingdom
of God in Jesus Christ (cf. Matt. 6:33). And theology, with all
the other things, will be added unto us."[30]

The value of von Allmen's article lies in that it brings out
the importance of obedience as the driving force in the contextualization of the Gospel in apostolic times. It is certainly
true that the primary concern in the primitive church is not to
"do theology" but to obey God's call to mission. It is, however,
a mistake to suggest that the Gospel could be preached and the
faith sung, without theology. Neither the proclamation of the
Gospel nor the worship of God is possible without theology, however unsystematic and "implicit" it may be. In other words, the
Hellenistic missionaries and poets were also *theologians*--cer-
tainly not dogmaticians, but proclaimers and singers of a living
theology through which they expressed the Word of God in a new
context.

Because, as P.T. Forsyth insisted, "the object of our faith
is a theological God, or He is not Holy Love,"[31] the theological
task, which is in essence a hermeneutical task, is inevitable.
Even at the most elemental level, the communication of the Christian faith poses to the communicator the question of how to express the old message in terms which make sense to his hearers;
and the categories in which he expresses it will necessarily be
those of a specific historical situation. There is therefore no
way to avoid the hermeneutical circle.

The present situation of the Church in many parts of the
world, however, provides plenty of evidence to show that all too
often the attempt has been made to evangelize without seriously
facing the hermeneutical task. Western missionaries have often
assumed that their task is simply to extract the message directly from the biblical text and to transmit it directly to
their hearers in the "mission field" with no consideration of
the role of the historical context in the whole interpretative
process. This attitude follows a simplistic pattern (Diagram 5)
which does not fit reality.

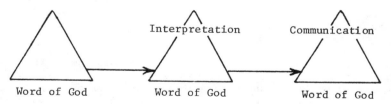

Interpretation   Communication

Word of God   Word of God   Word of God

Diagram 5

This simplistic approach to evangelism has frequently gone
hand in hand with a Western version of Christianity which combines biblical elements with elements of Greek philosophy and of
the European-American heritage[32] and places an unbalanced empha-

sis on the numerical growth of the Church. As a result, in
many parts of the world, Christianity is regarded as an ethnic
religion--the white man's religion. The Gospel has a foreign
sound, or no sound at all, in relation to many of the dreams and
anxieties, problems and questions, values and customs of people.
The Word of God is reduced to a *logos asarkos* (an unincarnate
word), a message that touches life only on a tangent. When this
problem is fully appreciated, one can hardly disagree with
Wibert R. Shenk's affirmation, that "in spite of some surface
signs of success, the modern missionary movement has failed at
a profound level until today. The church which is the product
of this historic movement suffers seriously from spiritual and
intellectual rootlessness."[33]

It would be easy to illustrate the "theological dependence"
of the "younger churches" on the "older churches," which is as
real and as damaging as the economic dependence that character-
izes the "underdeveloped countries." Suffice it to mention that
an amazing quantity of Christian literature published in these
countries consists of translations from English (ranging from
"eschatology-fiction" to "how-to-enjoy-sex" manuals) and that
in a number of theological institutions the curriculum is a
xeroxed copy of the curriculum used at similar institutions in
the United States.[34]

The urgent need everywhere is for a new reading of the Gospel
from within each particular historical situation, under the
guidance of the Holy Spirit and for the sake of a contextualized
Church. It is only as the Word of God becomes flesh in the
people of God, that the Gospel takes shape within a historical
situation. According to God's purpose the Gospel is never to
be merely a message in words, but a message incarnate in his
Church and, through it, in history. The God who has always
spoken to men within a concrete situation has appointed the
Church as his instrument for the manifestation of Christ's presence among the nations of the earth. The contextualization of
the Gospel can never take place apart from the contextualization
of the Church.

If the Gospel is to become visible in the life of the Church,
the whole Church has to be recognized as "the hermeneutical community," the place where the interpretation of Scripture is an
ongoing process. God's purpose in speaking through Scripture is
not to provide a basis for theological systems, but to shape a
new humanity created in the image of Jesus Christ. Biblical
hermeneutics is a concern of the whole Church for it has to do
with God's creation of a community called to manifest his Kingdom in every area of life.

NOTES

1. Throughout this paper "culture" is used in a comprehensive way, as including not only the technical skills, life style, attitudes and values of a people, but also their thought patterns, cognitive process and ways of learning, all of which ultimately express a religious commitment.

2. Howard and Geraldine Taylor, *Hudson's Taylor's Spiritual Secret*, China Inland Mission, Philadelphia, 1932, p. 122.

3. "All the Reformers of the sixteenth century, whether Luther, Zwingli, or Calvin, believed that in the Scriptures God spoke to them in the same way as He had done in earlier days to His prophets and apostles. They believed that if the common people had the Scripture in a language which they could understand, they could hear God speaking to them directly, and could go to Him for comfort, warning or instruction; and their description of what they meant by the Holy Scriptures is simply another way of saying that all believers can have access to the very presence of God. The Scriptures were therefore for them a personal rather than a dogmatic revelation. They record the experience of a fellowship with God enjoyed by His saints in past ages, which may still be shared by the faithful. In Bible history, as the Reformers conceived it, we hear two voices--the voice of God speaking love to man, and the voice of the renewed man answering in faith to God. This communion is no dead thing belonging to a bygone age; it may be shared here and now" (T.M. Lindsay, quoted by Allan M. Stibbs in *Understanding God's Word*, The Intervarsity Fellowship, London, 1950, pp. 58-59).

4. *Secular Christianity and God Who Acts*, Hodder and Stoughton, London, 1970, p. 27.

5. On the positive values and the limitations of the "new hermeneutic," see A.C. Thiselton, "The New Hermeneutic," *New Testament Interpretation*, ed. I. Howard Marshall, the Paternoster Press, Exeter, 1977, pp. 308 ff.

6. *HIS* Magazine, Vol. 33, No. 2, (October 1972), pp. 9 ff.

7. *Ibid.*

8. Don Richardson, *Peace Child*, Regal Books, Glendale (California), 1974.

9. *Ibid.*, p. 287.

10. Juan Luis Segundo, *Liberacion de la Teologia*, Ediciones Carlos Lohle, Buenos Aires, 1975.

11. *Ibid.*, p. 12.

12. Segundo makes it clear that his choice of this starting point is made "certainly not because of theological criteria but because of human criteria" (*ibid.*, p. 13). Yet, if he believes with W.H. van de Pol that "every choice of a starting point in science, philosophy and theology means *a priori* the choice of a definite world-and-life view" (*ibid.*, footnote 9), it is difficult to see how the choice of a starting point can be for him autonomous from theological criteria, as if the *Christian* world-and-life view had nothing to do with regard to the evaluation and devising of theories. For a corrective to this approach, rooted in the Roman Catholic dualism between nature and grace, see Nicholas Wolterstorff, *Reason Within the Bounds of Religion*, William B. Eerdmans Publishing Company, Grand Rapids, 1976.

13. Cf. L. Kalsbeek, *Contours of a Christian Philosophy: An Introduction to Herman Dooyeweerd's Thought*, ed. Bernard and Josina Zylstra, Wedge Publishing Foundation, Toronto, 1975, esp. Chap. 2.

14. Peter Berger, *Pyramids of Sacrifice*, Doubleday, Garden City, N.Y., 1976, p. 30.

15. Cf. Robert J. Blackie, *op. cit.*

16. Donald M. Mackay, *The Clockwork Image: A Christian Perspective on Science*, InterVarsity Press, London, 1974, pp. 42 ff. "Nothing buttery," says the author, "is characterized by the notion that by reducing any phenomenon to its component you not only explain it, but *explain it away*" (p. 43).

17. James D. Smart, *The Strange Silence of the Bible in the Church*, SCM Press Ltd., 1970, p. 144.

18. James D. Smart, *The Interpretation of Scripture*, SCM Press Ltd., 1961, p. 33.

19. Cf. Charles R. Taber, "Hermeneutics and Culture," page 116 of the present volume.

20. Karl Barth provides a clear illustration of this in his "Christological" interpretation of Genesis 2: That man should not be alone means that Christ needed the church as his helpmate. That man was put to sleep to the end that woman come into being means that the church could only come into being through Christ's sleep of death followed by his resurrection. That man had to give his rib for woman to be made means that Christ had to give himself for the sake of the church, receiving in return the church's flesh, i.e., the church in its weak-

ness, even as Adam received Eve. That man was asked to leave his father and his mother and cleave to his wife means that Christ had to leave the glory of his Father and unite the church to him. That Adam and Eve were naked yet not ashamed means that Jesus and his church are face to face yet not ashamed (*Dogmatic* III. 1, pp. 367 ff.).

21. Cf. E. Earle Ellis, "How the New Testament uses the Old," *New Testament Interpretation*, ed. I. Howard Marshall, The Paternoster Press, Exeter, 1977, pp. 199-219. In answer to the question, "Can We Reproduce the Exegesis of the New Testament?" (*Tyndale Bulletin* No. 21, 1970, pp. 3 ff.), Richard N. Longnecker suggests that a distinction should be made in the New Testament between revelatory and circumstantial exegesis, which we must not attempt to reproduce, and historical-grammatical exegesis, which we must seek to reproduce.

22. *The Interpretation of Scripture*, p. 130.

23. *Ibid.*, p. 31.

24. Jacob A. Loewen agrees that in order for the biblical message to be relevant it must speak to specific needs of the culture, but he rightly observes that "the truly relevant message speaks not only to an immediate need, but to a range of basic problems. As a true message from God it will provide a new and renewed reason to be for both individual and society" ("The Church: Indigenous and Ecumenical," *Practical Anthropology*, Vol. II, No. 6, [November-December 1964] p. 244).

25. Cf. J. Severino Croatto, *Liberacion y Libertad: Pautas Hermeneuticas*, Ediciones Mundo Nuevo, Buenos Aires, 1975.

26. The impossibility to separate the Christ-event from its apostolic interpretation was underlined by P.T. Forsyth in *The Principle of Authority*, Independent Press Ltd., London, 1913. According to him God's revelation was to go on, but *in the apostolic Word of revelation*. "The apostolic interpretation is an integral part of the revelatory fact, process, and purpose, a real though posthumous part of Christ's own continued teaching. In the Apostles took place a revelation of revelations-- and a revelation of it once for all" (p. 133).

27. Cf. James Packer, "Hermeneutics and Biblical Authority," *Themelios*, Vol. 1, No. 1 (Autumn 1975), pp. 3-12.

28. Daniel von Allmen, "The Birth of Theology," *International Review of Missions*, Vol. 64, No. 253 (Jan. 1975), pp. 37-55.

29. *Ibid.*, p. 40.

30. *Ibid.*, p. 52.

31. P.T. Forsyth, *op. cit.*, p. 211. Forsyth adds: "It is impossible to separate the questions, 'Whom do you trust' and 'What do you believe about Him?' For the latter only means, 'For what do you trust Him?' We only trust Him in a theological function as our Saviour; not only as our Father--that is not Christianity--but as the Father of the Eternal Son and sole Redeemer" (*ibid.*, pp. 211-12).

32. Elsewhere I have pointed to the problem posed all over the world by a "culture-Christianity" in which the Gospel that is preached bears the marks of "The American Way of Life." Cf. "Evangelism and the World," *Let the Earth Hear His Voice*, ed. J.D. Douglas, World Wide Publication, Minneapolis, 1975, pp. 125-126.

33. "Theology and the Missionary Task," *Missiology: An International Review*, Vol. 1, No. 3 (July 1973), p. 295.

34. In the case of Asia, the situation has been recently described by a respected evangelical leader in the following terms: "Schools that link up with foreign institutions to grant degrees have to follow the foreign curriculum. At many points this curriculum is irrelevant to the situation in Asia. For example, in Western evangelical theological schools, students study defences against liberal theologians. But most Asians have no questions about accepting miracles, supernaturalism, and the authority of the Bible. Asians shouldn't have to spend the time answering questions that aren't being asked in Asia. But they do need to concentrate on questions concerning suffering, poverty, demon-possession, urbanization, Communism, and other living Asian religions. Therefore, we must contextualize our curriculum" (Bong Rin Ro, "Why Accreditation?", *Asia Theological News*, Vol. 3, No. 2 [July 1977], pp. 2-3).

6

Hermeneutics and Culture:
An Anthropological Perspective
Charles R. Taber

The question I am addressing in this paper is easy to state,
but hard to answer. It is simply this: given the Scriptures,
how does one go about discovering what they mean? Notice that
this question will not go away no matter what view one holds
about inspiration. Even if we believed--what few if any Christians today believe--that the Bible was dictated to the writers
word for word by the Holy Spirit, and even if we had the original biblical writings in our hands, we would still be faced with
texts in three very human languages; they would still be texts
composed of sections, paragraphs, sentences, clauses, phrases,
and words, put together according to the rules of those three
languages; they would still be texts written originally to
people whose cultural, social, and historical contexts were very
different from ours. We would still, therefore, be faced with
the question of finding from those texts what God wants *us* to
know and feel and be and do.

Unfortunately, the whole history of Christian interpretation
of the Bible shows that there is no such thing as guaranteed,
infallible passage of information from the Bible to human minds.
If there were, Christians equally competent and honest and committed would come to identical interpretations; but as we can
clearly see, they do not. For reasons which seemed good to God,
and which I am therefore bound to accept, he did not choose,

when he gave us the Holy Spirit to help us understand the Bible, to by-pass normal human approaches to interpreting messages, but to use them. And these approaches are conditioned, colored, and limited by our human finiteness, by our human sinfulness, and our human cultural, social, and historical contexts.

It is my purpose in this paper, then, to explore some of the principal aspects of the processes by which people interpret messages, and to see how these can apply to our own efforts to understand and obey the Scriptures.

I. CHARACTERISTICS OF THE MODEL

This paper is based conceptually on a communication model, enriched by notions from anthropology and linguistics. According to this model, a Source (S) encodes a Message (M) which a Receptor (R) decodes. Note that S and R in the singular stand equally for plural S's and R's. The M may be either an utterance (as were the messages of most of the OT prophets and the earliest Christian witnesses) or a text (which is all we have today of the apostolic testimony). Since we are dealing especially with the biblical texts, we will focus on the interpretation of texts rather than on utterances, though with a minor point or two of difference the basic processes are the same.

A most important fact about any M is that it contains both explicit and implicit information. Explicit information is spelled out in the words and constructions of the text, while implicit information, though it is crucial for the understanding of the text, is not made explicit because the S relies on R to supply it (Taber 1970).

It must not be thought that all explicit information has the same standing with respect to S's intentions and the meaning of M. There is on the one hand information which is explicit because it was so intended by S, and relates directly to what he wants to convey to R. But there is on the other hand information which is explicit merely because the grammatical structure of the language requires that it be explicit, willy-nilly. A moment ago I was obliged to say that a singular form stood in my paper equally for a plural; it would have been very handy if English permitted the mention of noun phrases without the specification of number, but it does not: number is an obligatory category of nouns, as tense is of verbs, and so on. All languages have rules which make certain types of information explicit and which are beyond S's control; think in English of the awkwardness caused, in these days of women's liberation, by the obligatory mention of sex in singular third person pronouns designating human beings. Information which is explicit for these reasons surely does not have the same status in interpretation as information which is explicit because S chose to make it so.

As we have seen, implicit information is information which is not spelled out because S relies on R to supply it. Therefore, whatever information S and R share can potentially be left implicit, provided some explicit pointer to it is given; in fact, leaving information implicit is an important aspect of the feeling of "we-ness" between an S and an R who are close. Making information explicit that should be left implicit can be construed by R as pushing him away from closeness with S, or as an attack on his intelligence (think of how impatiently you say "I know" when someone belabors the obvious). It is chiefly the presence of implicit information that makes communications between intimates so opaque to outsiders. In terms of the biblical texts, many of the difficulties we encounter in interpreting 2 Corinthians derive from the great amount of implicit information in this letter. Note that there is a crucial difference between implicit information, which is necessary for understanding, and omitted information, which is not. Implicit information is an integral part of M, and its loss for any reason mutilates M.

II. DEFINITIONS AND PROCESSES

Hermeneutics is by definition a matter of the interpretation of texts. In order to help you to interpret the present text properly, I will offer a few definitions and characterizations of the processes involved and their background.

1. *Interpretation* is the process by which R assigns *a meaning* to M. Note that I have purposely made this indefinite, to allow for the frequent case in which R assigns a meaning to M which is different from that intended by S.

2. It is also necessary to define the term *meaning*, since it has been known for many years that it is multiply ambiguous and vague (Ogden & Richards 1923). In this paper, I make *meaning* the most inclusive term, comprising R's total perception of the response called for by M. This may, and usually does, involve a number of things.

(a) It involves in the first place the possibility of an addition to or modification of R's worldview, beliefs, and knowledge. In other words, R may see in M a call for him to accept an alteration of his model of reality. This may be simply a matter of adding more data to fill in gaps in a still valid framework, in which case R normally accepts the meaning he assigns to M and assimilates it; we then say that he has learned something new.

Or he may perceive that if he accepts the validity of M, the framework itself will have to be changed; in such a case, R's disposition to accept or reject M will depend on how well the existing framework has worked and continues to work. It would be simplistic and even false to say that R will always reject modification or replacement of the framework, since there are, especially in today's world, cases where traditional worldviews no longer work and are perceived to be unsatisfactory; these are the situations where, in the words of Chinua Achebe, "things fall apart." This is in fact the clear function of revitalization movements, in which dysfunctional old mazeways are replaced by new ones (Wallace 1956). A small, isolated tribal society which has for a long time held a narrow view of the universe known to its members will desperately need a much broader view when it finds itself being fitted, willy-nilly, into a much larger universe.

(b) R may perceive that if he accepts M, he will need to change his behavior. This may involve merely a shift of superficial social custom, in which case calculations of advantage or disadvantage may well determine the response. But it may demand a radical reworking of the whole ethical framework, in which case existential motivations of a profounder nature will be called upon to decide. Considerations of shame and guilt, of incorporation into or alienation from a desirable social group, and so on, will be weighed in the balance. I think here of the fascinating account of conversion among the Sawi of Irian Jaya (Richardson 1976) and of Tippett's detailed account of conversion in Melanesia (1967).

(c) Finally, R may perceive that if he accepts M, it will demand a total shift of existential allegiance and commitment, i.e. a turning to God from idols (1 Thess. 1.9). In fact, as I have argued elsewhere (Taber 1978a), this radical reorientation of the whole life is the core intention of the Christian Gospel, with the informational content as instrumental and the behavioral changes as logical entailment. It is at this point only that the Gospel may be said to have had its true impact. In fact, if we are content with changes of cognitive structures and even changes of behavior without such a transformation of total orientation, we may end up worse than before: we may lose ourselves in dead orthodoxy and/or legalism. The focus on the necessity of being transformed by our study of the Bible is one of the most important contributions of certain new approaches to hermeneutics (e.g. Wink 1973).

But in discussing meaning in the broad sense I give the term, it is not enough to define it in terms of pragmatic correlates; we must also deal with it in the somewhat more technical terms I have given it in another context (Taber 1976). Here the op-

erative distinction is, first of all, between those aspects of
meaning which are internal to language and those which obtain
between language and the non-linguistic world. To the first aspect, the one involving internal linguistic components of meaning, I will assign the term *signification*; to the second,
reference.

Signification, as a part of the linguistic semantic structure,
is further sub-divided into *denotation*, which comprises the conceptual components which are necessary and sufficient to locate
a given sense in the field or domain of all related senses; and
connotation, which comprises less easily specifiable features
which evoke affective responses. For a more detailed description of what is involved, several works of Nida are most useful
(1975a; 1975b; also Nida & Taber 1969:56-98).

Reference, on the other hand, has to do with how linguistic
terms and expressions point to some aspect of reality external
to language. For example, "Jimmy Carter" and "the President of
the United States" have at present identical reference, i.e.
they are both labels pointing to the same human being; but the
one is a proper name with no denotation (other than "male" in
the first name), while the other has a very full set of speci-
fying components (in terms of how its meaning relates to those
of other terms like "dictator," "king," "prime minister," and
so on).

It is crucial for analytical purposes to distinguish these
two kinds of meaning, because they represent very different mental processes in the acts of encoding and decoding. But it is
also crucial to realize that the process of interpreting M involves both. That is, when R assigns a meaning to M, he *both*
assigns denotations and connotations to terms, expressions, and
constructions, *and* determines the referents of each of them. He
will not have the subjective feeling of understanding without
both parts. Thus, when the apostles presented Jesus as the
Christ, it was crucial for their hearers to realize (a) what the
concept "Christ" signified, and (b) that it was properly applicable to a specific human being from Nazareth named Jesus.
Similarly, when the NT uses the term *pneuma* in referring to an
incorporeal being, it is not only important for R to know the
components of meaning of "spirit" (e.g. how it is distinguished
from "ghost"), but also to distinguish those instances where the
term (used without qualification or specification) refers to the
Holy Spirit and when it refers to some other spirit (cf. Matt.
4.1; 12.18; 22.43; 26.41; Mark 2.8; 9.20,26; Luke 1.80; 9.39;
John 1.32ff; 3.5ff; 6.63; 11.33; Acts 2.4). As an aside, in the
process of translation there should be constant evaluation in
choosing terms of the respective roles of signification and reference in the process of communication. The same issue is very

much involved in the question I raise elsewhere (Taber 1978a)
about inadequate conceptions of the true God versus false gods.
To conclude this paragraph: reference answers the question
"What X is being pointed out?"   Signification answers the question "What do the terms tell about X?"

3.   In interpreting M, R makes use of a number of *factors* from
his personal *context* to supply the implicit information.

   (a) He makes use, at the most general level, of his worldview, his knowledge, his beliefs, his values, and his attitudes.
When I was working, a few years ago, with some people in
Khartoum who were translating the OT into several of the Nilotic
languages of the Southern Sudan, I found that they all experienced
great difficulty with the early chapters of Genesis; it turned
out that their views on the composition and construction of the
universe gave them no clues or points of departure for understanding such notions as "firmament" or "windows of heaven" or
"great deep." I had to draw diagrams; and though they at last
made out what was being said in Hebrew, they still found it almost impossible to reproduce in their own languages. At a quite
different level, we are familiar with the grotesque caricatures
of the Jesus of the Gospels created by the culturally biased
minds of Renan, Strauss, and Bruce Barton. I have observed that
gaps in cultural knowledge cause many well educated Americans
either to pass over cultural allusions in the Bible without even
noticing them, or to assign to them quite alien meanings, or
simply to attribute them to the "queerness" of people in the
ancient biblical worlds.

   (b) There are also the social, economic, political, and situational parameters of the communication event. No true communication takes place in a vacuum; S and R either have personal and
systemic relationships along these dimensions, or they are in the
process of establishing them during the communication event itself. Their respective perceptions of these relationships, as
well as the interests they have invested in the communication
process, inevitably color the meanings they assign to M.

   By systemic relations, I mean those that obtain between S and
R by virtue of their respective social statuses: sex, age, kinship, social class, caste, race, nationality, occupation, interest groups, and so on. These tend in all societies to be structured and to be heavily loaded with prescribed and expected attitudes and behaviors which cannot but influence the interpretations they place on each other's messages. It is at this point
that the sociology of knowledge has a good bit to tell us (e.g.
Berger & Luckmann 1967), though it can be exaggerated, as Krass
has shown (see Forman & Baum 1973; Krass 1976). As long ago as

1955, McGavran urged us to make full use of existing systemic relationships as "bridges of God" for the communication of the Gospel (McGavran 1955). Such matters as we are considering have a great deal to do with perceptions of interest and relevance--or the opposite. For instance, the Jesus of Nazareth who fully identified with the poor and oppressed in their plight could urge his disciples to "turn the other cheek" (Matt. 5.38-42); but if a Roman soldier, even one converted to Christ, had offered the same counsel, the perceived message would have been altogether different. I have wondered whether the prevalence of female converts in some countries might not be related to the large number of woman missionaries in those countries.

The personal relationships which affect R's interpretation of M do not substitute for the systemic ones, they are superimposed on them. What I mean is that as persons become acquainted with each other as individuals rather than merely as members of labeled sets, perceptions and appreciations of personal traits begin to modify the stereotypes which normally accompany systemic relations, whether with persons of own group or of out-group, and S can partially overcome handicaps, if any, created by the stereotypes.

The systemic situational context also affects the interpretation of M. There is a time and place for everything, and not all times or circumstances are suitable for all types of M's. Such matters as whether or not R even pays attention or takes M seriously can hinge on just such factors. This is not always understood by enthusiastic would-be communicators of the Gospel, as when some seize the occasion of a funeral to preach a hell-fire-and-brimstone sermon.

R's personal interests and purposes in participating in the communication process must also be taken into account: what does R think he will get out of it? In the western context, an R who sees in affiliation with a church a means of personal economic advancement will interpret M quite differently from an R who sees in M release from guilt or anxiety, even if M is presented in identical words, or even if they both hear the same S on the same occasion.

(c) Different types of texts, different literary genres, are appropriate for and therefore evoke different types of M, and therefore condition interpretation. In every language, there are diverse sorts of texts, including some that can be broadly characterized as prose and others as poetry. Partly cross-cutting this dichotomy, one can distinguish between narrative texts, explanatory-expository texts, argumentative-hortatory texts, and expressive texts. I have in mind empirical properties of texts which serve as signals of text type. What must be added to this sketchy list of some of the parameters of diversity is that (i) not all types of texts are appropriate for all types of communications (consider how we would treat Gospel pericopes if they began in English with "Once upon a time..."); (ii) the inventory of empirically differentiated text-types is not identical from language to language; (iii) the formal distinguishers of types are language-specific, not universal; and (iv) the pairing of type of M with type of text is also language-specific, not universal. For instance, it is today quite inappropriate in English for such a relentlessly didactic text as Psalm 119 to be couched in poetry, though it was apparently quite appropriate in ancient Hebrew.

Since we must assume that the biblical writers made intelligent use of text types in giving form to their M, our interpretation must likewise rest upon a sound understanding of what to expect from these different text types in Hebrew and Greek. A closely related issue is our habit in the West, when theologizing, of transposing narrative and even lyrical texts of the Bible into philosophical-technical discourse, which has quite different properties and therefore cannot help distorting the pristine M. This habit, of course, rests on our prior notion that serious religious discourse *ought to be* couched in technical language, and that we can somehow properly demand of all parts of the Bible that they answer our philosophical-technical questions in a philosophical-technical key. In contrast with this habit, I would as devil's advocate insist that almost none of the Bible is in technical language and therefore that very little of it can answer technical questions (Taber 1975).

(d) Building on what I have just said, it should also be pointed out that the entire presuppositional foundation upon which *any* hermeneutic rests is itself part and parcel of a culture. I have pointed out elsewhere--though it is not a new observation--that the hermeneutic which NT writers used in citing the OT would not be acceptable today, especially in the most conservative circles (Taber 1978b). To put it bluntly, there are times when "X happened so that Y might be fulfilled" seems to mean little more than "X reminds me of Y." Of course, not all OT citations are of this sort; but enough of them are to give us much to think about.

I have already mentioned our habit, when dealing with a very serious topic, of doing it in a technical key. This is clearly related to cultural assumptions about the complex interrelations between truth, truthfulness, facticity, happenedness, precision, objectivity, and the like. Whether we like it or not, these assumptions and equations are not universal; and if we want to claim that our approach to hermeneutics is universally normative, we must make a case for our claim, and not simply take it for granted.

(e) I may add in passing, for the sake of completeness, that when M is an utterance, R will have a variety of perceptible clues which assist him in interpreting M. These include S's body (position, posture, movement, gesture, facial features and expressions), dress, body odor, and of course paralinguistic features of S's speech—pitch, volume, rate and style of delivery, enunciation, pauses, intonations, and so on. All of these are missing when M is a text; they are only partially compensated for by punctuation, penmanship or type face, and various lexical markers. How much easier it would be to understand parts of 2 Corinthians if we could hear Paul saying them!

4. One useful perspective for the examination of these factors is to see them all as parts of R's *culture*. The utility of this point of view is that it highlights certain features of the process which we must bear in mind.

(a) Culture is *learned*. In fact, it is helpful to contrast the patterned responses of animals, which are largely genetic in origin, with patterned human responses, which are almost entirely culturally learned. The human infant is born with very few of the patterns he will need to survive already preprogrammed; what is genetically determined is rather a vast open-ended potential for learning. Animals, on the other hand, have many more patterns programmed in their genes. The animal way makes for much greater security; the human way makes for vastly greater flexibility and adaptability. Whereas it takes many generations for a genetic pattern to be altered significantly by natural selection, it takes only one generation for humans to change—and in fact even less, since humans can unlearn and relearn with varying degrees of success in a single lifetime. I cannot over-emphasize the importance of this fact for our topic.

(b) Culture is *shared*; it is the common heritage of a social group, and is in fact an important part of that group's self-awareness and self-definition. It is what makes communication possible, by investing the environment and its parts and aspects with meaning which is conventionally established and socially transmitted.

(c) Culture is *selective*. This is to permit human experience to have manageable dimensions and to permit the assigning of meaning to traits selected for or against. It also permits specialization in terms of the particular habitat in which each group lives.

(d) Culture is *integrated*. Its various parts, complexes, and institutions tend to fit together in a complementary way, so that life hangs together and all needs are satisfied. Of course, integration is neither perfect nor static; it always tends to be somewhat precarious, and the balance continuously shifts. But the cohesion is good enough so that one cannot readily alter one part without altering other parts via a chain reaction; and the parts also tend to support and validate each other.

(e) Culture is *adaptive* and *adaptable*. That is, it is ideally designed to enable its bearers to make the best possible life out of their environment and its resources, including the other groups with which they are in contact. This fact also highlights the changing nature of culture, since circumstances often change.

In listing all of these properties of culture, it is my intention to underline how much culture develops as well as calls upon the intelligence, imagination, and flexibility of its human bearers. Far from being an unyielding and confining straight jacket, culture is a flexible guidebook and index, often quite open-ended. It is these human qualities that make interpretation of an M from alien cultures possible at all. We must capitalize on the human capacity to wonder, to fantasize, to empathize. I do not want to suggest that the process is easy or inevitable, only that it is possible, so that we need not despair.

Several other remarks should be made in order to round out the picture I am drawing.

First, the knowledge of any individual is only a subset of the total cultural inventory of his society. No single person, even in a small face-to-face society, knows all that can be known in his group. To varying degrees, there is knowledge that is intentionally or accidentally restricted by virtue of age, sex, kinship group, and so forth. In larger, more complex societies, with multiple specializations, each person knows a certain basic common core of his culture, plus knowledge relevant to his specialty, plus a smattering of knowledge of other areas gained through school, the press, and the media, in proportion to his exposure and curiosity. Thus it is true that in complex societies there are multiple worldviews, corresponding to the various classes and sub-groups, each with its own characteristic beliefs, values, and attitudes. This is the area in which the sociology of knowledge is very valuable.

All possible social relations and situations, which we have discussed above, are culturally defined; in fact, each asymmetrical relationship has at least two definitions, one from the

point of view of each participant. This is also true of relations with aliens, whether friendly or hostile. Beliefs and attitudes attending such relations necessarily affect the interpretation any R assigns to any M.

5. In the preceding sections, I developed the notion that R
makes use of all kinds of clues in reconstructing the implicit
information in M. It is equally true, however, that *explicit*
information is subject to the same kinds of slippage between S's
intentions and R's interpretation. This is because S and R assign meanings to the words, expressions, and constructions of
the text independently. R can make use only of meanings known
to him. This is the occasion for untold misunderstandings of
the Bible, even among people who are reputedly very familiar
with it, largely because of the propensity of translators to use
receptor language terms in senses which are quite unusual or
unfamiliar to ordinary readers. I think, for intance, of the
confusion caused by translating *sarks* by "flesh" in passages
where it does not have any of the usual senses of English
"flesh"; or of the difficulty people have with Romans 1.17 when
dikaiosune is translated "righteousness," when in that verse it
does not have any of the normal senses of the English word.
Scholars sometimes seem to labor under the misapprehension that
senses inhere in words, so that using "the right word" becomes
a shibboleth, without regard to how the eventual R will understand it. This, by the way, is one of the reasons I cannot divorce hermeneutics from communication.

   I conclude this section, therefore, by pointing out that R
can respond only to the meaning *he* assigns to M. The intentions
of S can have no weight if R does not discover them in his effort at interpretation.

6. *Understanding* is an instance of interpretation in which R
assigns to M essentially the same meaning as S. Five propositions will elucidate this definition.

   (a) Since R has to supply all implicit information and the
meanings he knows for the explicit terms, understanding is never
automatic. As we have seen, meanings do not inhere in words,
they are socially assigned to them. It follows that misunderstanding, that is the assigning by R of a different meaning than
S intended, is not infrequent. We have already seen illustrations of such misunderstandings. And, beyond sheer error, of
which R may be blissfully unaware, there are many instances of
uncertainty on the part of R; he may find M vague, or ambiguous,
or full of gaps, simply because he is not in a position to supply information which was implicit for S but is missing for him.

(b) Understanding is therefore partly contingent on S and R sharing the same or similar backgrounds and points of view, in terms of the factors discussed above. To the extent that they do not, it becomes necessary for R to do a great deal of research into what can be discovered of S's context, via studies in history, culture, social system, politics, economics, ecology, language, and so on. In other words, he needs to reconstruct as well as possible those aspects of S's world which led S to make certain information explicit and to leave some implicit, and which will permit him in turn to supply the implicit information.

(c) Adequacy of understanding is at its lowest in terms of a word taken in isolation, and at its highest in terms of a whole text. This is a consequence of the dynamic way in which the various senses of the terms mutually select or exclude each other (Nida & Taber 1969:56-63, passim). The more one takes into consideration the entire text, the better one understands each term. This is at the opposite pole from the common technique of attempting to understand each term in isolation and then adding the results. The most heinous popular exemplar of this misunderstanding was the Amplified Bible, which seems fortunately to have gone out of fashion. But the same error can be seen in much more sophisticated form in some of the work of Kittel, as Barr has shown (1961). The way communication really works seems to be as follows: each term, taken in isolation, is *potentially* the vehicle for any one of a number of discrete senses (see e.g., the entry for *head* in an unabridged dictionary), but it is *actually* not the vehicle for any of them (though in some cases there is one sense which pops into people's heads when the word is used without context); as each term is used in an utterance or text, surrounding terms operate selectively to eliminate from active consideration all senses which are not appropriate to that context; from that point on, these other senses are *not present* in the awareness of either S or R (assuming effective communication); and the greater the context being consulted, the less genuine ambiguity or vagueness remains at any point. For this reason, I am convinced that many of the "ambiguities" found in the Bible by lexically minded scholars would vanish if context were seriously and rigorously exploited. In terms of information theory, that sense of each word is selected which adds the least new information to the emerging M. Take the word *stock:* in the dictionary, it will have at least five senses: (i) farm animals, (ii) shares in a corporation, (iii) broth, (iv) type of paper, and (v) inventory of merchandise. If we add the minimal context *He watered the stock,* we have eliminated (iv) and (v), since watering is not an operation normally involving these senses; but the others remain, so that **the sentence is** triply ambiguous. But if we say *He watered the* **stock** *by filling the trough,* we have effectively eliminated all **senses but** (i). By the same token, we have selected for *watered* the sense "supplied water for" rather than "added water to" or "diluted in a metaphorical sense." Precisely the same process is—or should be—involved in understanding biblical texts and their terms. I cite only the case of *sarks* (Nida & Taber 1969: 16-17).

(d) Understanding is never instantaneous, at least if M is at all complex. It is a process which takes place over time, sometimes a great deal of time. It is simplistic to posit a two-place model involving sudden passage from no understanding to full understanding. Rather, what often happens is that R begins by understanding nothing, either objectively or subjectively. If he for any reason is motivated to continue his effort, he will forcibly assign meanings, often erroneous, to M; but as he persists, little by little he eliminates the worst errors and "sneaks up on" the true meaning. Surely that is the normal history of anyone's hermeneutic struggle with the Bible.

(e) A closely related fact is that understanding is never total or perfect. In other words, to talk as I did about R assigning "essentially the same meaning" to M as S is necessarily a relative notion; it does not lend itself to mathematical precision in any but the most sophisticated probabilistic terms, which are well beyond the comprehension of most users of language, including me. Communication is thus a matter of pragmatic degrees of similarity between S's intention and R's interpretation; absolute understanding is not a human possibility, but comprehension adequate for all useful purposes definitely is. I have no patience with persons who bemoan the inherent looseness of communication in ordinary human language and conclude that it is in principle impossible. The very existence of human societies and cultures for so many millenia, and *a fortiori* the existence for almost two millenia of the church, with all its imperfections, is proof to the contrary. The best metaphor I have found for this gradual approach to a true understanding of M is the mathematician's asymptote, a curve which never quite reaches a given coordinate but is forever getting closer, somewhat like Zeno's arrow.

7. I must now make one final comment on the relation between human cultures and the Bible. Because I have been emphasizing the impact of R's culture on his efforts to understand M, it might be thought that the effect is one-way, or that I think it is one-way. Nothing could be further from the truth. For it is also and crucially true that once R has understood the biblical M, it must and will have transforming consequences on his thinking and living and therefore on his culture. For, as I have pointed out elsewhere (Taber 1978a) in relation to indigenization (or contextualization),

> The sharper focus of good indigenization [or hermen-
> eutics] serves to heighten both the positive points
> of contact and the confrontation between gospel and
> culture.... In contrast, bad indigenization [or
> hermeneutics] blunts and emasculates the gospel by
> denying or concealing those parts of the gospel
> which contradict basic cultural values or by focus-
> ing on non-essential or illegitimate issues.

In other words, a truly contextualized hermeneutic best serves
the purpose of the Gospel, which is to transform human lives and
societies.

III. CASES

It may now be helpful for me to illustrate the approach I
have just outlined by examining a number of biblical topics.
The specific topics to be considered were suggested by one of
the anonymous persons who commented on my first outline, when
he said, "bridging the gap between biblical cultures and ours is
crucial. What is to be our attitude to the cultural clothing of
God's revelation (3-decker universe, women, footwashing, logos
doctrine, etc....)? How can we 'de-culturate' without 'demythologizing'?" I accept this suggestion and will now consider seriatim the very topics listed, except for the last which
is too broad. They are sufficiently diverse to represent a wide
range of cultural phenomena: cosmology, social structure,
social/religious ritual, and systematized belief formulations.
Two caveats are in order as I approach these case studies.

First, in discussing these matters I am doing so as an anthropologist, not as a theologian nor as a biblical scholar.
So, though I claim fairly extensive knowledge of the biblical
materials themselves, my knowledge of the voluminous specialized
literature on each of these topics is quite spotty. In a more
definitive treatment, I would of course have to familiarize myself with it.

Second, though I will for the most part confine my comments
to adjustments which might be made in my own western cultural
context, I explicitly disavow any intention of making these
normative for Christians in any other sociocultural context
whatever. It is their right and responsibility to wrestle with
the Bible in their own context *de novo*; they can of course take
note of what we do, but they must not feel bound by it; we are
neither their tutors nor their judges. In fact, a strong case
could be made for the proposition that, taking the biblical cultures as the point of reference, western civilization is the
most remote in many ways, and thus occasions the need for the
greatest dislocations and problems in contextualization. Why

should a Christian, coming to the Bible from a context which
prepares him for immediate grasp of many of its features, make
an extended detour through the swamps of our unbelief and hair-
splitting? Thus, I would see myself as offering a modest example of the kind of thing Christians need to be doing in every
society; but I would be most unhappy if anyone felt that he
needed to make his effort look like mine, or that he could use
my work as a standard for measuring someone else's.

1. *Cosmology*. It is quite clear to anyone reading the opening
chapters of Genesis that the inspired writer(s) conceived of the
universe as being composed of three tiers: the earth *(ha-aretz)*,
which was a roughly flat surface comprising alternating water
and dry land and on which plants grew and beasts and man dwelt;
the "firmament" *(raqiya')*, which was conceived of as a great
dome supporting large masses of water, and to which were fixed
the heavenly bodies; and the "deep" *(tehom)* under the earth,
containing the rest of the water. The space between the earth
and the dome was the sky in which birds flew. The Days of Creation were the successive stages in the establishment of this
differentiation and separation out of original chaos; and at the
Deluge the separation was partially reversed as the "windows of
heaven" were opened and "the fountains of the deep" broke up,
letting the waters re-cover the earth. But normally things
stayed in their places and fulfilled their appointed rounds for
the benefit of God's human creatures.

What can and should we do with this vision of the geometry of
the universe? Are we bound to retain it, in defiance of all
that has been discovered since? Or are we free to reject it,
recognizing its primitivity and its appropriateness to its own
time but not to ours? Or is some compromise necessary or
possible?

Before answering these questions in terms of the 20th century
western world, it must be pointed out that during the period of
the biblical history itself this view underwent progressive modification and elaboration. At some stage between the writing of
Genesis and NT times, the grave became a generalized place of
the dead *(sheol)*, which was then further divided into "Abraham's
bosom" and "the place of torment." Similarly, the heaven above
the dome was elaborated into a structure of several stories
(three? seven?), inhabited by angelic and demonic hosts and culminating in the highest heaven, God's own abode. Though many of
the passages in which these things are mentioned are poetic, and
therefore difficult to interpret in technical terms, it is clear
that by NT times the Hebrews had a much more complex notion of
the universe than Genesis 1-11 reflects, and they did not appear
to feel in any way incommoded by the difference.

Subsequently, when the Gospel moved into a Hellenized gentile world, Christians apparently accepted without question the
various cosmologies of the pagan world; or at least they did
not to my knowledge have any traumatic debates about the differences between Genesis 1-11 and the views they learned as children in their societies. We are familiar with the way in which
Paul simply mentions with no great emphasis or disapproval the
incipiently gnostic notions of heavenly hierarchies. Among
scholarly gentiles, the view that soon prevailed was the
Ptolemaic one, which saw the earth at the center of things and
the heavenly bodies in circular orbits around it. Ironically,
it was this view rather than the Hebrew one which was defended
as biblical in the controversy between the church and Galileo.
But as the weight of evidence accumulated, the view propounded
by Copernicus and developed by Kepler and Galileo prevailed; it
was given its full glory through the work of a devout Christian,
Isaac Newton.

Now, in the 20th century, a new model is gradually emerging
in the popular awareness, coming out of the ivory towers of
Einstein, Planck, and Heisenberg in the early years of the century. It is a view far removed from either ordinary phenomeno-
logical observation or poetry, but it has a compelling inner
logic and elegance of its own. Numerous scientists who are also
Christians have found it necessary, in terms of intellectual
honesty, and possible, in terms of faith in Jesus Christ, to accept this view as the best that can be formulated today.

If the apostles, and other Christians down through the centuries, experienced little difficulty in substituting the various cosmologies of their times for the Hebrew one, and with few
exceptions did not find it necessary to argue the issue, why
should we be more troubled today? Whatever view of the inspiration of the OT these Christians had, it did not bind them to the
simple three-decker universe. Why should we be more squeamish
than they?

Some have expressed the fear that to jettison a vertically
storied universe is to lose the notion of the transcendence of
God. This would be a serious problem, if it were true. But
surely the Scriptures, though they use the metaphor of altitude
to refer to God's transcendence, do so as an accommodation to
our human limitations; *some* metaphor has to be used to give us
at least a glimpse of what is essentially ineffable, the nature
of God. And in other passages, it is said that all spatial
metaphors, as well in fact as all temporal ones, are at bottom
inadequate, and that, far from God being merely "up there," he
is *also* "down there," "beside," "around," "inside"--in fact,
everywhere (Ps. 139.7-12; cf 1 Kings 8.27). The very idea that
we might be able to seize intellectually or emotionally the

wholeness of God's transcendence through any one metaphor is a contradiction in terms; it represents a serious diminution of that very transcendence in our minds. We dare not confuse devices used epistemologically to help our weak understanding with ontological truth about the essential nature of God.

I would add that the same principle applies as well to all the other figures which are used to describe God: figures borrowed from kinship or politics or other socio-economic roles, along with the famous anthropomorphisms and anthropopathisms which so shock people of excessively nice sensibilities. And, I might add, it is also true of Tillich's God "down there" as "Ground of Being." But to say that any one of these metaphors, or even all of them together, cannot give us a grasp of God, is not to deny their usefulness, given an appropriate worldview.

2. *Women.* A totally different issue is represented by biblical teachings concerning the role of women, which have come under increasing scrutiny in these days of women's liberation. The extreme positions are, on the one hand, a total literalism which considers the surface form of the biblical teaching as normative for all time; and on the other hand, a cavalier relativization of everything which people find uncongenial or inconvenient.

Though the direction I will point is not by any means a perfect or final solution, I think the beginning of a sound approach must lie in the recognition that not all biblical statements about this topic, or about any other, have exactly the same status. One must distinguish at least between those statements which are purely descriptive and those which are intended to be prescriptive. In the first category, I place details given in historical passages concerning the relations of husbands and wives at various periods. Unless we are to assume that the people involved were miraculously infallible, it would be absurd to take all descriptions as rules; that would be to confuse what is with what ought to be. I doubt that anyone would commend for our practice Judah's relations with Tamar (Gen. 38), to take an extreme example; but by the same token Abraham's relations with Sarah, in their OT context, are also simply descriptive.

The category of teaching or prescriptive passages is itself not homogeneous. It seems to me *prima facie* evident that some NT teaching—I take it that this is the material most Christians would consider relevant—is explicitly intended to be theological and therefore universal and permanent in import; while some is explicitly or implicitly conditioned by existing circumstances and therefore relative. I include in the former category Jesus' revolutionary insistence that women are just as impor-

tantly involved in spiritual and theological issues as men
(Luke 10.38-42), and that the prevalent notion of "woman's
place" voiced by Martha was invalid; and also Paul's statements
(Gal. 3.28; Col. 3.11) that "in Christ" there are no longer in-
vidious distinctions based on sex. Finally, in the famous Ephesians 5 passage on marriage, the universal statement which serves
as the theme for the entire passage (including master-slave and
parent-child relations as well as husband-wife relations) is
verse 21: "Submit yourselves to one another because of your
reverence for Christ" (TEV). The rest of the passage spells out
the implications of this universal command for both members of
each asymmetrical dyad: not only how a wife should submit to
her own husband, but how a husband should submit to his wife.
This has two revolutionary consequences: first, it removes the
submission involved from any foundation of supposed inherent
superiority of men over women, since it is based on reverence
for Christ; second, it makes the submission mutual, not one-way.

Incidentally, it should be said that neither this passage nor
any other says anything about women in general being subject to
men in general, much less about their being inherently inferior;
OT law, to offer the Hebrew background, specifically and explicitly limits the set of men to which a woman is potentially
subject to her father, her brother, or her husband, depending
on circumstances.

Rather than attempt to deal exhaustively with all of the con-
troverted passages on this topic, that is those which are not
clearly either universal or contextually contingent, I will consider only one of the more difficult passages, 1 Timothy 2.9-15.
The first thing that should be said is that whatever Paul is
teaching here, it surely ought not to contradict his universal
teachings already cited, nor his personal practice in relations
with women, unless we want to accuse him of gross inconsistency.
We find, for instance, that Paul and his companion Luke both accepted without demur and with overt appreciation women in roles
of leadership (cf. Rom. 16.1). It is of great significance that
in Acts 18.26ff, when Priscilla and Aquila taught Christian
doctrine to a man, and one of no mean education and character,
it is the wife who is mentioned first. So whatever Paul meant
by the passage we are considering, it did not prevent women of
talents from exercising them freely in the church. I suggest
that a proper contextual understanding of the passage would
take the following form: given the prevalent sociocultural context, in both Jewish and gentile circles, women were not typically given much education; they were conditioned by the entire
process of feminine enculturation to be dependent, ignorant,
childish, and even frivolous and silly. From verses 9-10, I in-
fer that the stereotypical woman was preoccupied with clothes
and jewelry, to the exclusion of more significant matters. But

it was not universal "feminine nature" that made them so, but
their up-bringing; they were, like women in many other societies, intellectually crippled by the society's ideals of "femi-
ninity" and "woman's place." In such a situation, a woman so
handicapped would not be in a position to offer worthwhile
teaching in a congregation of men who were relatively well educated, or at least literate and accustomed to serious discussion. Women of such limited abilities would cause confusion if
they intervened in church discussions; they would also cause
scandals among outsiders. But in those cases where women, in
defiance of stereotypes, achieved intellectual maturity, Paul,
like Jesus, gave them every encouragement.

Paul's use of a quasi-theological argument in verses 13-14
weighs against my interpretation; but any other interpretation
runs into the problem of making Paul very inconsistent. As for
verse 15, there are so many interpretations that I think it the
better part of valor to admit that no one knows what it meant;
and it is surely unsafe to build a case on so shaky a foundation.

3. *Footwashing.* It is interesting that I should be asked to
discuss footwashing in this context, since I grew up and was
originally ordained in one of the few denominations that practice the rite as an integral part of what is called the three-
fold communion. I am therefore in a good position to appreciate
the weight of arguments that John 13.8b,10 invest Jesus' action
with ritual and theological significance. Here, in other words,
there are two questions: first, was Jesus' action the inauguration of a rite, or merely a moral example? Second, whichever
answer one chooses, what attitudinal and behavioral implications
ought we to see in 20th century North America?

In favor of the ritual interpretation are: the close association of footwashing with the Last Supper, which is clearly ritual in character; the solemn injunction (verses 12-15) that the
disciples ought to follow Jesus' example; and the apparently
theological (soteriological) significance which Jesus attaches
to his action in verses 8b and 10. Against this interpretation
is the fact that nowhere else in the NT is footwashing mentioned
as a rite (adherents so interpret 1 Timothy 5.10, however); and
the fact that it is not mentioned at all in the Synoptics, which
would make it the only sacrament founded on only one Gospel. My
own view is mildly in favor of the latter position, that Jesus
was giving a moral example rather than instituting a rite.

The second question is more relevant to our topic: what are
we supposed to *do* to obey Jesus' clear command in verses 12-15?
Here an understanding of the way footwashing functioned in the
1st century gives us a clear cue: in a day when people wore
open sandals and walked great distances on rough, dusty or muddy

paths, washing the feet upon arrival at destination was an important part of being cleansed and refreshed. But the feet are
not the most exalted part of the body, and to minister to another's feet requires a very humiliating posture.   Thus, the
normal procedure seems to have been that a host provided water
for a guest to wash his own feet (Luke 7.44). However, if the
guest was especially exalted, or the host wished to express extraordinary hospitality, a slave would be assigned to do the
unpleasant chore.   Nothing could be more repugnant to a non-
slave, nothing could more clearly symbolize the non-person status of a slave, than this occasional duty. This can be inferred
from Peter's shocked reaction to Jesus' action (John 13.8).   But
Jesus insisted, and went on to say that he was establishing a
pattern for his disciples. In other words, I interpret the universal significance of this passage to be that it narrates an
enacted form of the same teaching we have already found in Ephesians 5.21:   that each Christian is to voluntarily subject himself to every other, both in attitude and in conduct; and that
it is especially incumbent on those in leadership roles to be
all the more willing to accept humiliation if by so doing they
benefit others (cf. Matt. 20.25-28; Mark 10.42-45; also the example of Paul, 2 Cor. 6.3-10 and similar passages).   It is possible that this teaching more than any other is uncongenial to
the natural human being in any sociocultural context, which is
no doubt why it is so commonly ignored or distorted.

4. *The Logos*. The Johannine concept of the *Logos* is often debated in terms of whether it rests primarily on a Greek philosophical foundation or whether it rests upon a Hebrew OT foundation.   But from my reading of just two treatments of the question (Sanders 1962; Howard 1952), it occurs to me that a question more relevant to this consultation and also more accessible
to me is whether the term is to be taken as a true technical
term in the modern sense, in which case it would be necessary to
pin down its precise conceptual content (either-or); or whether
it is in fact a symbol, in which case it would be perfectly proper and in fact normal for it to resonate on multiple wave-
lengths.   Neither Sanders nor Howard deals with the matter in
these terms, of course. But they both seem in the end to find
it very hard if not impossible to decide between the putative
Greek and Hebrew bases, and they both end up with a more or less
eclectic conclusion.

The Greek component has various strands, including early
writings of Heraclitus, apparently radically reinterpreted by
the Stoics; and the Stoics themselves, with different emphases
at different periods.   In terms of meanings conveyed, the chief
notion was of the divine Reason (sometimes personified, sometimes viewed as an abstract attribute) which is both the creative cause and the explaining principle of the universe.

The Hebrew component, possibly with Greek influence in the later OT period, goes back to the notion of the creative divine Word (Gen. 1), and then later connects up with hypostasized Wisdom (Prov. 8.22-31). Philo synthesized both of the strands in making of the Logos the "intermediary between the transcendent God and his creation" (Sanders 1962:870).

It seems to me that Sanders' position is sound, namely that John arrived at a superficially similar notion independently, but went much farther in identifying the Logos, as creative divine Word (John 1.3), with Jesus Christ; in other words, for John, the Logos is neither an abstract principle nor a personification, but a Person of flesh and blood, a human being of determinate history and location. But this large-scale synthesis is not possible if we are dealing with a true technical term, at least in the contemporary sense (Taber 1975, 1978b). It is possible only for a comprehensive cover symbol, ready to be filled with any congenial content.

I suggest that this gives us considerable freedom, in the various contexts of our day, to assign to Jesus Christ whatever compatible ideas we may have concerning the origins of the universe, its maintaining principles and laws, and so on. For most educated westerners, it is probably the case that the fundamental notion in this area is that of natural law. What the Prologue to John would be telling us, then, is that natural law is not just abstract inference from instances, nor an impersonal determining force, nor a merely immanent property of energy/matter; but rather that under and before and behind all of these is the Creator God, incarnate in Jesus Christ of Nazareth. In other words, the Logos is big enough and flexible enough to serve the purpose whatever the worldview of the people whom it addresses. For after all, *all* worldviews are no more than models, representations of our conception and vision of reality; they are not reality-in-itself. It is the divine Logos who *is* reality-in-itself, and of whom all models are pale, and more or less accurate or inaccurate shadows.

IV. CONCLUSION

I have only a few things to say by way of conclusion. First, this is necessarily an initial stumbling effort by one man, and it is subject to the correction of the entire Body. Second, it is nevertheless a serious and sincere effort, arising out of a profound faith in Jesus Christ as Son of God and Lord of the Universe, and in the Scriptures as the inspired record of the divine self-disclosure. Third, it is based on a glimpse I have had of the enormous disparity between the transcendent God and finite human beings, and therefore between the Person of God and our human minds. Fourth, it also reflects my conviction that

while our cultures and languages do not give us perfect tools
to understand the ways of God, they are none the less all that
we have; and God has sanctified them by using them fully in the
Incarnation of his Son and in the inspiration of the Bible.
Fifth, Christians in all contexts must enjoy the same freedom
we claim in this endeavor. Sixth, while we will never fully
transcend the limits of our contexts, we can by the use of imagination guided by the Spirit of God both grasp and be grasped
by God and so be transformed into the image of his Son. And
after all, isn't that the point of the whole thing?

BIBLIOGRAPHY

Barr, James, 1961. *The Semantics of Biblical Language*. London:
    Oxford.

Berger, Peter L. & Luckmann, Thomas, 1967. *The Social Construc-
    tion of Reality*. Garden City: Doubleday.

Forman, Charles W. & Baum, Gregory, 1973. "Is there a Mission-
    ary Message?" in *The Ecumenist*, March–April 1973. Reprinted
    in *Mission Trends* No. 1, ed. by Anderson, G. H. & Stransky,
    T. Grand Rapids: Eerdmans & New York: Paulist, 1974,
    pp. 75–86.

Howard, Wilbert F., 1952. "The Gospel of St. John," in *Inter-
    preter's Bible*, Vol. 8. Nashville: Abingdon, pp. 437–463.

Krass, Alfred C., 1976. "Accounting for the Faith that Is in
    Me," *Occasional Bulletin from the MRL* 36(2).

McGavran, Donald A., 1955. *The Bridges of God*. New York:
    Friendship Press.

Nida, Eugene A., 1975a. *Componential Analysis of Meaning*.
    The Hague: Mouton.

_____, 1975b. *Exploring Semantic Structures*. München: Wilhelm
    Fink Verlag.

Nida, Eugene A. & Taber, Charles R., 1969. *Theory and Practice
    of Translation*. Leiden: Brill.

Ogden, C. K. & Richards, I. A., 1923. *The Meaning of Meaning*.
    New York: Harcourt, Brace & World (eighth ed., 1946).

Richardson, Don, 1976. *Peace Child*. Glendale: G/L Publica-
    tions.

Sanders, J. N., 1962. "The Word," *Interpreter's Dictionary of the Bible*, Vol. 4. Nashville: Abingdon, pp. 868-872.

Taber, Charles R., 1970. "Explicit and Implicit Information in Translation," *The Bible Translator*, 21.1-9.

_____, 1975. "Problems in the Translation of Biblical Texts," in *Fachsprache-Umgangssprache*, ed. by Petöfi, Podlech & Savigny. Kronberg: Scriptor Verlag, pp. 289-302.

_____, 1976. "Semantics," in *Interpreter's Dictionary of the Bible*, Supplementary Volume, ed. by Crim, Keith. Nashville: Abingdon, pp. 800-807.

_____, 1978a. "The Limits of Indigenization in Theology," *Missiology* 6(1).

_____, 1978b. "Is There More than One Way to Do Theology?" *Gospel in Context* 1(1).

Tippett, Alan R., 1967. *Solomon Islands Christianity.* Pasadena: William Carey Library.

Thiselton, Tony, 1977. "Understanding God's Word Today."

Wallace, Anthony F. C., 1956. "Revitalization Movements," *American Anthropologist* 58(2).

Wink, Walter, 1973. *The Bible in Human Transformation.* Philadelphia: Fortress.

PART II

Culture, Evangelism and Conversion

7

The Gospel—
Its Content and Communication:
A Theological Perspective
James Packer

Let me speak first of three specific benefits which reflection on
our theme--the content and communication of the Gospel, related
together as a single topic--may yield.

First, it will serve to remind us of the obvious but ever-
relevant truth that *the content of the Gospel must always
control the method of its communication,* and that we must judge
the value of the various techniques proposed for use in
evangelism by asking how far they can and do succeed in getting
the message across.

The modern communications industry, and the theoretical
studies which guide it on its way, tend always to detach
questions of method from those of content, and to treat the task
of communicating as if its dimensions were constant, irrespective
of what it is that is being put over. But this is not so, and
an inappropriate technique may limit understanding by inhibiting
challenge at depth even while at surface level it enlarges understanding by bringing conceptual clarity. In the case of the
Gospel, the content includes a diagnosis of the hearer's state
and needs before God, value-judgments on the life he lives as
compared with that which might be his, and a call to judge himself, to acknowledge the gracious approach and invitation of God
in Christ, and to respond by a commitment more radical and far-

reaching than any other he will ever make; and the Gospel is not
fully communicated unless all this comes over.

So the Gospel must be *verbalized* (for none of this *ad hominem*
address can be communicated otherwise, just as the truths on
which it rests cannot otherwise be explained), and in its verbal
form it must be *preached*, that is, set forth by a messenger who,
whether *viva voce* in the flesh or on film or tape or radio, or
in print, interprets and applies it to those whom he addresses
in a way which makes its existential implications for them plain.
Such media of expression as instrumental music, pictures,
sculpture or dance may reinforce the Gospel by the mood or
vision they express, but they cannot, strictly speaking,
communicate it; only preaching can do that. Similarly, teaching
the Christian faith as an academic discipline (as is done in
English state schools and universities) is not strictly
communicating the Gospel, for although the relevant themes are
analyzed the thrust of the application is not present. It cannot be too strongly stressed that since the Gospel is a personal
message from God to each hearer, the only appropriate and
effective way of communicating it is for a messenger to deliver
it on God's behalf, ambassador-style (cf. 2 Cor. 5:20)--that is,
identifying with God's concerns and expressing by the way he
uses words the mind and heart of God, how he hates sin and loves
sinners, and what he has done, is doing and will do for the
salvation of those who turn to him.

God has shown us that preaching is the only natural and
adequate way to communicate the content of the Gospel, by himself actually communicating it this way. "Truth through
personality," which was Philip Brooks' definition of preaching
has been the principle of God's communication throughout, first
through the prophets and then climactically through his own
incarnate Son. It is noteworthy that the writer to the Hebrews
introduces the Son as a God-sent preacher of the Gospel before
saying anything about his role as priest, sacrifice and mediator.
"In many and various ways God spoke of old to our fathers by the
prophets; but in these last days he has spoken to us by a Son...
Therefore we must pay the closer heed to what we have heard...
how shall we escape if we neglect such a great salvation? It
was declared at first by the Lord..." (Heb. 1:1f, 2:1,3). This
chimes in with the evangelists' highlighting of the preaching
of the Gospel of the kingdom as the initial and basic activity
of Jesus' public ministry (cf. Mark 1:14f; Matt. 4:17, 23;
Luke 4:16-21; John 3:3-15). When Thomas Goodwin the Puritan
wrote, "God had but one son, and he made him a preacher," he was
echoing an authentic note in the New Testament witness.

The Gospel can be preached both formally and informally, both to crowds, congregations and to single individuals (cf. Acts 8:29-35), but preached it must be, or its full content as a message from God will not be passed on. This is surely undeniable, and from it two far-reaching conclusions clearly follow. First, whatever experts in contemporary communication may urge to the contrary, preaching must continue as a main activity of the church until the Lord comes. Second, whatever technical skills a Christian communicator may command, what will count ultimately is what he is in himself, whether his manner backs up his matter in making God's mind and heart known or not, and we shall be dealing with Christian communication, intracultural or cross-cultural, in a way that is shallow and inadequate, wrong-headed indeed, if we leave this personal dimension out of account.

Second, our reflections may serve to remind us that *problems in communicating the Gospel raise questions about its content:* questions which it will be ruinous to answer wrongly, but which when answered in the right way can be a source of much help in our communicative task.

It is natural that those who find that they cannot convince others of the truth and relevance of the message which they announce as offering life to all, should ask themselves whether they have yet understood it correctly. The question is a proper one, but wrong turnings are easily taken when answering it. First example: Rudolf Bultmann saw the biblical miracle-stories, and the supernaturalist view of the cosmos which they implied, as an obstacle to acceptance of the Gospel by contemporary Germans, and so in 1941 he proposed his demythologizing program, which removes the stumbling-block of miracles by abolishing the divine and miraculous Christ who performed them. (One thinks of the man who, having bought ointment to cure a wart on his nose, later telephoned the vender to say that his wart had gone, but could he please have his nose back.) Bultmann's program appears to have been doubly mistaken. Hermeneutically, it went wrong in holding that the New Testament witness to Jesus as divine Savior and risen, reigning, returning Lord is myth in a sense which excludes its space-time factuality; theologically, it erred by assuming that the Creator cannot or will not work miracles in the world external to us, but limits his work to the sphere of our self-consciousness and self-understanding, which notion brings an arbitrary and anti-biblical dualism into our thought about God and his world. Second example: in *Honest To God* (1963), J.A.T. Robinson posited "the end of theism" because, as he urged, "supranaturalism," i.e. the idea of transcendent personhood, could no longer communicate any sense of God's presence to modern Western man, and he offered instead a notion of God formed in terms of depth, immanence, love and moral

claims. Here, too, there seemed to be two mistakes: a
hermeneutical error, in not seeing that the biblical writers
offer their account of God not as a human projection but rather
as a revealed description, and a theological error, in shrinking
God by letting go of the Triune aseity which (as I continue to
think though Robinson has explictly denied it) is central to
the biblical disclosure of who and what God is. I cite these
familiar examples as cautionary tales. Both Bultmann and
Robinson aimed at effective communication, but their way of
getting around the stumbling-blocks was to reduce the message in
a way that lost the baby along with the bath-water. It is never
safe for the Christian communicator to conclude that the less
you commit yourself to assert, the easier it will be to assert
it, or to treat objections to a particular tenet as a sign that
it is dispensable.

But for communicators who hold to historic Christianity
problems in making it seem true and relevant can be salutary.
What they may show is that, as a   J.B. Phillips book-title
once told us, *Your God is Too Small,* so we must see our presentation of the Gospel as being too limited, taking too much for
granted and not digging deep enough. What we may be failing to
do, or at least to do clearly and thoroughly enough, is to
highlight those absolutes of God's self-disclosure which show up
the preconceptions and preoccupations that impede communication
as being themselves relative, and therefore arbitrary to a
degree and open to question and revision. The Western
scepticism about the supernatural which sparked off Bultmann's
demythologizing program and Robinson's journeyings beyond theism
would be a case in point; so would the Latin American and
Black American preoccupation with personal freedom and social
betterment which has produced the politically angled "liberation
theology," in which seemingly on a universalist basis, political
action does duty for evangelism; so would any movement which
thinks of our humanness, freedom and dignity as conditional upon
our not being exposed to social, political or economic manipu-
lations by folk for whom we are merely means and not ends. These
perspectives need relating to the true absolutes which our self-
announcing God has made known in Christ--the sovereign
omnipotence of his work in creation, providence and grace; more
specifically, the terms of his plan of salvation; most
specifically of all, the paradigm of humanness, freedom and
dignity in the life of Jesus Christ, not excluding the hours of
his betrayal, show trial, torture and death on the cross. It is
a question whether in cross-cultural communication today Christians are always careful enough to establish these absolutes as
the frame of reference within which all human preconceptions
must be set for checking and correction and any circumstance
which goads us to think and work harder here will be a blessing
in disguise.

For certainly, if this is not rigorously done, the result of not doing it is predictable from the start. Sooner or later, the biblical Gospel, in which God the Creator appears in judgment and mercy reconciling the world to himself, will itself be relativized and thereby distorted through being assimilated to man's prior interests. The world will write the agenda--and it will be man's agenda rather than God's. This seems to be what happened at Bangkok in 1973, where the word "salvation" became the label for many things that men desire, but which are not salvation in the revealed and regulative Bible sense. It happened before in old-style liberalism, which turned the kingdom of God preached as Gospel by Jesus into the kingdom of ends taught as ethics by Kant. It will no doubt happen again, if allowed to. There is no way to stop it happening save to assert the true frame of reference effectively--if we can. So running up against ideas about God or the world or man which challenge the Gospel can be good for us, by prompting us to anchor our message more explicitly and robustly in the divine ultimates and absolutes (as did Paul when on the Areopagus, facing polytheism, he spelled out basic Christian theism at length and with emphasis). Thus, through being stirred to strengthen the foundations, we may end up presenting the Gospel a good deal more adequately than before.

Third, our reflections may alert us to the fact that *our own assumptions about the content of the Gospel can themselves become an obstacle in communicating it;* for we all tend to equate our own culture-bound understanding of Christ with the Gospel itself, and this way trouble lies.

All understandings of the Gospel, whether British, North American, Latin American, African, Indian or what have you, are in the nature of the case culturally conditioned. I cannot jump out of my own cultural skin, nor can you, nor can anyone. Equally, of course, the presentations of the Gospel in the New Testament itself are culturally conditioned; but there we may believe that the Palestinian and Hellenistic cultural settings, so far from being distorting or limiting or obscuring factors, were providentially shaped so as to be wholly appropriate vehicles for expressing and exhibiting God's last word to the world--the word spoken once for all in the Jew who was his incarnate Son, and through his chosen witnesses, the apostolic theologians, in whose minds Rabbinic and Hellenistic culture so remarkably met and blended. That God's revelation of himself in Christ is culture-bound only in the sense of being culturally particularized, as being historical, it had to be, but not at all in the sense of being culturally distorted, seems to me to be a crucial truth for hermeneutics today, and one which urgently needs some fresh exposition and defense; but here I can

only assert it in order then to make the point that there is no
other culture of which this can be said.

We may be sure, therefore, before ever we sit down to look,
that any version of Christianity produced anywhere at any time
will bear marks of one-sidedness or myopia, not only because of
imperfect exegesis and theologizing but also for reasons of
cultural limitation. A culture operates as both binoculars and
blinkers, helping you to see some things and keeping you from
seeing others. So we shall need to be consciously critical of
whatever form of the Christian tradition--in our case, the
evangelical tradition--we have inherited; just as we shall need
to be aware that from the great smorgasbord of international
evangelical tradition no two of us are likely to have ingested
quite the same meal. Being the fallen creatures we are, we
shall always find it easier to see motes in others' traditions
than beams blocking vision in our own, and, being unaware of our
own blind spots, we shall be tempted to ascribe to those
expressions of the Gospel in theology, liturgy and behavior
patterns which we know best a finality, fullness and universality
which may only be claimed for the Gospel itself, and the Christ
of whom it speaks. Then the danger will be that in seeking to
proclaim the Gospel in cross-cultural situations we shall impose
on people our own cultural forms for expressing the Gospel,
forms which to them are alien and unauthentic, and which when
accepted become badges of a dependence that is not wholly
healthy. My knowledge here is limited, but I think as I write
of the zeal of some African clergy for Anglican clerical uniform,
and of a Japanese seminary for instilling the Westminster
Confession.

When a version of Christianity developed in one cultural setting is exported in this way to another, the major trouble is
likely to be not that it includes idiosyncrasies but rather that
it ignores matters of importance. As in our personal discipleship sins of commission are usually less grievous than our leaving undone so much that we ought to have done, so the chief
defects of this or that version of Christianity are likely to be
the things that, unwittingly, we leave out--as, for instance
medieval Christianity left out all sense of history. To give
one example, which comes near home for us all: the Western
evangelical tradition is weak on the doctrine of creation.
Following the almost mortal second-century conflict to establish
against the Gnostics that God the Redeemer is also God the
Creator, the conflict in which Irenaeus achieved so much, belief
in creation, and in the Creator's direct, immediate and particular providential control over all that he had made, became a
Christian theologoumenon which, since the Reformation, evangelicals, concentrating all attention on the doctrines of grace,
have simply taken for granted. The result is a five-fold weak-

ness. First, we still lack any magisterial counter to the deist,
pantheist and materialist versions of the uniformitarian myth of
the universe which grips so many minds these days, and which
modern technology is widely though erroneously thought to confirm.
Second, evangelical discussions of the appropriate way to relate
the witness of Holy Scripture to that of natural science on, for
instance, creation (including evolution), the flood, and the
constitution of the human organism, remain almost discreditably
naive. Third, we regularly ignore the cosmic dimensions of
God's reconciling work in Christ, and of the renewal that is
promised at Christ's return. Fourth, an atomic individualism,
really a product of European rationalism and romanticism two
centuries ago, has crept into our thinking about individuals
before God, making us unable, it seems, to take seriously enough
the family, racial, national and Adamic solidarities which
Scripture affirms as part of the created order, and which the
so-called "primitive" mind grasps so much better than most of us
do. Hence comes theological fumblings when interpreting the
phenomenon of "mass" or "people" movements into the Christian
faith. Fifth, we are short of a theology of nature and the
natural, and so we have constant difficulties in convincing our
critics that the biblical positivism which is our regular
theological method as evangelicals is in fact genuinely attuned
to the nature of things as God made them. Now should anyone
take over any version of the Western evangelical tradition in
theology as a final standard, he would be buying along with many
strengths this chronic and often overlooked weakness on creation.
It is important that such purchases should be outlawed, lest
in retrospect someone should feel himself to have fallen victim
to a confidence trick.

So in cross-cultural Christian communication the right course
will be neither to impose on folk of other cultures forms of
Christian expression belonging to our own, nor to deny them
access to our theological, liturgical, ethical and devotional
heritage, from which they will certainly have much to gain, but
to encourage them once they have appreciated our tradition to
seek by the light of Scripture to distinguish between it and the
Gospel it enshrines, and to detach the Gospel from it, so that
the Gospel may mesh with their own cultures directly. Thus
among younger nations with distinct cultural styles and, perhaps,
some touchiness about cultural imperialism the Gospel may be set
free to do its job, running and being glorified without
hindrance. If it is true (as I for one believe) that every
culture and sub-culture without exception in this fallen world,
whether primitive or tribal or Hindu or Christian, or a form of
the constantly shifting "pop" youth culture which affluent
nations develop these days, is a product not just of human sin
but also of God's common grace (which means, biblically speaking,
of the work of the life-and light-giving Word of John's

prologue), then respect for other cultures as such, and desire
to see them (not abolished, but) reanimated by Gospel grace in
their own terms, must undergird all particular criticisms of
ways in which, missing the good life, they embrace the not-so-
good life instead. This practice of respect will set us all
free for critical dialogue with all forms of human culture,
Christian and non-Christian alike, while safeguarding us
against both the appearance and the reality of cultural
imperialism while we engage in it.

   Putting the point positively, we shall urge Christians of
other cultures to use the resources of our own heritage in the
way that Barth urges us all to use the creeds, namely as a
"preliminary exposition" of the faith, by which they may be
helped to subject their own culture to the corrective and
directive judgment of the Word of God. Long ago that Word
"Christianized" Greco-Roman culture very thoroughly; a century
ago it was Alexander Duff's vision that a similar thing might
happen in India; today, as we face the global cultural
imperialism of Marxists, active attempts to Christianize or
re-Christianize all cultures is much to be desired. And if in
the process Christians of other cultures criticize sub- and
post-Christian elements in our own heritage, we must not mishear
this as cultural imperialism in reverse. The *koinonia* which is
the church's proper life is two-way traffic, taking as well as
giving, and it requires us both to share what resources of
Christian insight we have and to take gratefully any further
insights that others offer us. Only so can we avoid
canonizing the clumsinesses, blind spots and poverties of our
own tradition, and thereby actually misrepresenting the content
of the Gospel which we seek to make known.

THE CONTENT OF THE GOSPEL

   Thus far we have explored in general terms three preliminary
points: first, that the Gospel, being what it is, must be
communicated by preaching; second, that establishing its truth
and relevance involves not diminishing it at the points of
difficulty, but countering directly any preconceptions which
oppose it; third, that the Gospel may not be equated with any
post-apostolic formulation or cultural embodiment of it, but
must be distinguished from them all. Now we move on to look at
its content in more precise terms.

   "Content" could be a misleading word here; not because the
implications of givenness and fixity which follow from its
dictionary meaning, "that which is contained" as in a book or
box or cupboard, are in any way misleading (they are in fact
absolutely correct: remember Paul, in the first paragraph of
Galatians), but because it conveys the idea of something passive

and inert, something that is "there" on a take-it-or-leave-it basis, and thus fails to suggest the dynamism which the New Testament associates with the Gospel, on the basis that whenever it comes before anyone God actually preaches it in the power of the Holy Spirit. But this point, once noted, need not detain us.

A glance at the relevant lexicography shows that the Gospel (*euaggelion*, good news: 60 times in Paul) is the message that God has acted and acts now in and through Christ for the world's salvation. God's saving action was the burden of "the Gospel of the kingdom" which Jesus preached (*euaggelion* appears 7 times in Mark), and Jesus' incarnation, death, resurrection, reign and return was the theme of the Gospel according to Paul. Sometimes "the Gospel" in Paul seems to signify the evangelistic *kerygma* which C.H. Dodd isolated long ago in Acts, sometimes it embraces the whole Christian message as such. To make this Gospel known is God's work through man: God appoints Christians to be his heralds, ambassadors and teachers (*keryx, presbys, didaskalos*) taking the message to the world. This task is regularly described by the use of three verbs: *euaggelizomai* (tell the good news, *euaggelion*), *kerysso* (utter an announcement, *kerygma*), and *martyreo* (bear testimony, *martyria*). The aim is to persuade (*peitho*), to "disciple" (*matheteuo*, Acts 14:21, cf. Matt. 28:19), and so to turn men to God (*epistrepho*).

Laying out the contents of the Gospel in full is a complex task, for the material is abundant, varied and occasional. There is the *kerygma* of the speeches in Acts and such passages as Rom. 1:3f. and 1 Cor. 15:3f., detailing the fulfillment of prophecy in Jesus' life, death for sins, resurrection and kingdom, and the promise of pardon and the Spirit to those who repent and believe. There are the four accounts of Jesus' ministry, each highlighting his death, resurrection and expected return in glory, and each so angled as to present a different facet of his identity and role (in Mark, God's toiling, suffering servant; in Matthew, Davidic king and new Moses; in Luke, God's prophet; in John God's eternal Son, the life-giver, full of grace and truth); each account is called (presumably by its author) "the Gospel." There are also many presentations of Jesus Christ in the epistles, with the thematic changes rung according to what the writers thought their readers needed to hear. All this material has a "between-the-times" perspective, looking back to Christ's first coming, forward to his reappearing, and upward to his present heavenly reign. Perhaps the clearest way to analyze it is in terms of six distinct (though overlapping and complementary) "stories," each of which is the Gospel just as all six together are the Gospel. Two of the stories are about God, two about Jesus Christ, and two about man, thus:

A. Stories about God.

   (i) God's purpose: the kingdom

   The Creator has judicially subjected all mankind to sin and
death, and the rest of this creation to "futility" and
"corruption" (*mataiotes, phthora*), in consequence of the guilty
disobedience of the "first man Adam," in whom all now die.   But
from all eternity it has been his gracious plan, purpose and
pleasure to restore this situation and bring the cosmos to perfection at the end of the day through the mediation of the
"last Adam," the God-man Jesus Christ.   All the decisive events
in God's plan save the last have now been played out on the
stage of world history.   The key to understanding the plan, as
it affects mankind, is to see that by God's appointment each
man's destiny depends on how he stands related to the two
representative men, Adam and Christ.   What God planned was to
exercise his kingship (sovereignty, an ultimate fact) over his
rebel world by bringing in his kingdom, that is, a state of
bliss for sinners who, penitently returning to his obedience,
should find under his sway salvation from sin's guilt, power and
evil effects.   In this kingdom Jesus Christ should be God's
vice-gerent, and trusting and obeying Christ should be the
appointed way of returning from sin to God's service.   God
prepared the way for the kingdom by making himself king of a
national community created out of the family of Abraham: to this
community he gave territory, his law, a national life, prophets
and kings as his spokesmen and deputies, and promises of the
Messiah who would come to reign over them in the new era of
peace (*shalom*) and joy.   When at the appointed time Christ came,
Israel the prepared nation rejected him and compassed his
crucifixion; but God, having achieved world redemption according
to his plan through Christ's death, raised him to life and set
him on the throne of the universe, where now he reigns,
furthering his kingdom by sending the Spirit to draw men to himself and by strengthening them for faithful obedience in face of
mounting opposition till the day dawns for his return to judge
all men and finally to renew all things.

   In this story, the goal of God's action is to glorify himself
by restoring and perfecting his disordered cosmos, and the
Gospel call is to abandon rebellion, acknowledge Christ's lordship, thankfully accept the free gift of forgiveness and new
life in the kingdom, enlist on the victory side, be faithful in
God's strength, and hope to the end for Christ's coming triumph.
New Testament passages of special relevance for this story include Acts 2:14-36, 3:12-26, 10:34-43, 13:16-43, 17:22-31;
John 3:13-15; Rom. 1-3, 5, 8:19 ff; I Cor. 15; Rev. 4-5, 17-21.

(ii) God's people: the church

In this fallen world where men are alienated through sin from
both God and each other, God has acted to create for himself a
new people who should live with him and with each other in a
fellowship of covenant love and loyalty. He acted thus. First,
he made a covenant with Abraham and his descendants, thus binding himself to them to bless them and them to him for worship
and service. When later he brought Abraham's family out of
Egypt he renewed the covenant and gave them, along with the
law which showed what behavior would please and displease him,
a cultus which had sacrifice at its heart, whereby sin might be
put away and communion between him and them maintained. When
subsequently Israel fell into unfaithfulness, a recurring
pattern of divine action emerged--judgment on all, followed by
deliverance and renewal for a faithful remnant. When Christ
came to set up a new and richer form of the covenant relationship by his priestly sacrifice of himself, Israel spurned his
ministry, and he was then the true Israel, the faithful remnant,
in his own person. In him God's Israel was reconstituted out
of believers as such,and in it Jew and Gentile are together as
fellow-citizens, branches of one olive tree and brothers in one
family. Thus reconciliation to both God and each other takes
the place of the alienation that was there before. In glory
the church will remain one city, family and flock together.

Christ's death as sin-bearer under God's judgment, followed
by God's affirmation of him in resurrection, was the definitive
fulfillment of the judgment-and-renewal pattern, and resurrection
out of death in one sense or another, in union with Christ's
dying and rising, is the appointed and abiding shape of life
for God's people, as the symbolism of their baptism shows. It
is a pattern which their physical resurrection at Christ's
return will finally complete.

God's covenant people, the church, lives a public life of
humiliation, dispersion, opposition and distress, but its inner,
hidden life is one of union and communion in the risen Christ
with him and each other, as the Lord's Supper regularly
proclaims. Loving ministry to one another and to needy folk
everywhere is the life-style which properly expresses the hidden
reality: in which connection, Paul pictures the church as
Christ's body, with each limb animated and equipped by his
Spirit for the service which he through it will render.

In this story, the goal of God's action is to have a people
who live with him in love, and whose corporate life, by uniting
the seemingly incompatible in sharing Christ's unsearchable
riches, shows forth to the watching angels the "many-stranded
wisdom of God" (Eph. 3:10). The Gospel call, from this stand-

point, is to accept a share in the life and hope of God's forgiven family by bowing to the Lord whose death redeemed the
church and whose risen life sustains it. This is not (be it
said) to put the church in Christ's place, but to preach Christ
as the answer, through the church, to every man's problem of
isolation and alienation from God and men. The church does not
save, but as the redeemed society it is certainly part of the
Gospel. New Testament passages especially relevant for this
story include John 17; Rom. 6:9-11; I Cor. 11-14; Gal. 3-4, 6;
Ephesians; Colossians; Hebrews; 1 Peter.

  B. Stories about Jesus Christ

  (iii) The grace of Christ

   In Jesus Christ God has given the world a Savior whose great
salvation more than matches man's great need, and whose great
love (which should be gauged from the cross) will not be daunted
or drained away by our great unloveliness. Jesus is set forth
as prophet, priest and king--teacher and guide; mediator and
intercessor; master and protector--and the focal point of his
saving work is identified as his cross, concerning which each
Christian can say "he loved me, and gave himself for me"
(Gal. 2:20). Christ's death was an act of righteousness, for he
endured it in obedience to his Father's will. As such, it
wrought redemption, freeing us from the curse of God's law,
i.e. exposure to divine judgment, at the cost of Christ's own
suffering. His death was redemptive because it achieved an act
of propitiation, quenching God's wrath by dealing with the sin
that evoked it. It propitiated God by being an act of substitutionary sin-bearing, in which the judgment which our sins
deserved was diverted on to Christ's head. From the cross flows
the risen Christ's gift of a permanent new relationship with
God, which Paul analyzes as justification (pardon plus a
righteous man's status) and adoption (a place in the family,
with certainty of inheritance), and the writer to the Hebrews
calls sanctification (acceptance by God, on the basis of consecration to him). With this new status is given new birth, the
indwelling Spirit, progressive transformation into Christ's
image, and glorification--in short, comprehensive subjective
renewal. God's goal in all this is the perfect bliss of
sinners, and the Gospel call is an invitation to faith in Christ,
through which all these gifts come to us, from the Savior's own
hand, "for free." New Testament passages of special relevance
for this story include Romans 3, 5, 8; 2 Cor. 5:14ff; Hebrews.

  (iv) The glory of Christ

   From eternity the Father loves the Son, and delights to give
him glory and see him honored (cf. John 5:20-22). The Son, for

his part, loves the Father and delights to do his will. As the
Father gave honor to the Son in the work of creation and
providence, so he has now resolved to make him pre-eminent in
the economy of redemption (cf. Col. 1:13-20; John 1:1-5, 14).
So he has rewarded the Son's obedient self-humbling to the point
of death by not only restoring to him the glory that was his
before the incarnation (cf. John 17:1-15, 24), but also by
making him head of the church and lord of the worlds, giving
him "the name which is above every name [i.e., *kyrios*, Lord],
that at the name of Jesus every knee should bow...and every
tongue confess that Jesus Christ is Lord, to the glory of God
the Father" (Phil. 2:9ff). Though Christ's mediatorial kingdom
as such will end when the work of grace is done (cf. 1 Cor.
15:24ff), the doxology, "worthy is the Lamb," shall be sung
forever (cf. Rev. 5:12ff). In this story, God's goal is the
praise and glory of Jesus Christ his Son, and the Gospel call is
a summons to join those who, acknowledging that all their hope
is in Christ, are already resolved to spend all eternity
honoring his name.

   C. Stories about man

   (v) God's image restored

   Briefly: man was made to display God's image and likeness
by practicing righteousness in fulfillment of his creaturely
vocation. God's image is more than the rationality which makes
such righteousness possible; it is the actual achievement in
human life of that which corresponds to God's own moral goodness
and creativity. But full God-likeness failed to materialize in
Adam personally, and the same is true of all who are in Adam.
Thus we fall short of our true human destiny, as God planned it,
so now he restores the image in his disciples, by leading us
through his word and Spirit into the life that actualizes it--the
life, that is, of active, habitual, creative response to the
calling of God. This is what Paul refers to when he says that
we are being renewed in knowledge (of God) after the image of
the One who first led us to "put on the new man" (Col. 3:10,KJV).
In this story, God's goal is to see his own character fully
reflected in us, and the Gospel call, quite simply, is to let
ourselves be remade so that we at last become human!

   (vi) Man's joy begun

   Briefly again: man without Christ is in a pitiable state,
whatever may or may not appear on the surface of his life. He
is guilty, lost, without hope as death approaches, short on
self-mastery, pulled to and fro by conflicting allurements and
distractions; there are skeletons of sensuality, callousness,
arrogance and other unlovely things in his cupboard; he regularly

finds frustration and discontent, partly because his reach
exceeds his grasp, partly because he feels thwarted by circumstances, partly because he is so largely unclear what is worth
his endeavor anyway. The various things wrong with the folk to
whom Jesus is seen ministering in the Gospels--hunger, chronic
illness, fever, epilepsy, blindness, deafness, dumbness,
lameness, leprosy, lunacy, organic deformity and in three cases
actual death--vividly picture these spiritual needs (and were
undoubtedly included in the Gospels for that purpose). But
Jesus Christ gives peace--with God, with oneself, with circumstances and with other people--plus his own presence and friendship, plus a call to witness and service as the priority
concerns of life in this world, plus a promise of enabling by
the Holy Spirit, plus an assurance of final glory in the
Savior's own company, and this brings integration, purpose,
contentment and joy such as one has not known before. And the
promise is that as one travels the road of discipleship, so
these things will increase. In this story, God's goal is a
purpose of compassion, namely to impart to us by this means the
joy for which we were made; and the Gospel call is a summons to
enter through faith and obedience into the joy that Christ gives.

   As each strand of a rope is a little rope in itself, so each
of these six stories is itself authentic Gospel, though the
fullness of the message only appears when all six are put together. (The six "stories" cited are not necessarily exhaustive.
One could add, for example, "God's Promise--The Renewing," which
would deal with the new heavens and new earth.) But what precisely are we to suppose that these biblical declarations are
telling us? There is widespread agreement today that such
notions as we have been reviewing--God's purpose; God's people;
the cluster of images expressing different ,aspects of salvation;
the Father exalting the Son; God's image in man; peace, contentment and joy as divine gifts--should be seen as theological
"models," on the analogy of models in physics. This is to say
that they are thought-patterns which function in a particular
way with their own particular "logic," helping us to focus one
area of reality (relationships with God) by conceiving of it in
terms of another, better known area of reality (relationships
with each other). This gives us an idea of *how* they mean, but
does not begin to tell us *what* they mean. And if we press that
question, sharp disagreement appears, for modern theologians
fan out across a broad spectrum between two extremes. The one
extreme is to say that the models are humanly devised for
focusing empirical apprehensions of ourselves and our position
in God's presence (*coram Deo*), and cannot be trusted to yield
any definitive truths about God. The other extreme is to say
that they are divinely revealed anthropomorphisms which God
uses to tell us facts about himself in terms meant to be

normative for our subsequent thinking. Bultmann and exponents
of the "new hermeneutic" like Fuchs and Ebeling stand at the one
extreme, evangelical and Catholic conservatives stand at the
other, and there are many half-way houses.

The choice as to where to stand in this spectrum will be
determined for us by our Christology. If we accept as true anything like the Johannine Christology, we shall treat the things
Jesus tells us about God as normative revelation, and we shall
treat Jesus' own revelatory words as our paradigm for both the
Old Testament (to which, as all scholars today seem to agree,
Jesus listened as to his Father's voice), and also the New
Testament (to whose authors the Johannine Christ promised
authoritative inspiration explicitly, and who often claim to
speak to Christ's Spirit and with his authority). We cannot
here enter into the modern Christological debate, so I simply
put on record that for me, at least, the Johannine Christ is
"for real" (a conviction which can, I think, be compellingly
justified), and that hence I view the models of the six-fold
Gospel story as revealing factual truths about God, not of
course exhaustively (that would be impossible) but truly and
trustworthily so far as they go.

I urge, therefore, that these models should never be
treated, as some treat them, as contingent conceptualizations
in ancient cultural terms of a non-verbal sense of God which
we would today do well to unshell and repack in other terms.
Rather, the conceptualizations themselves should be seen as
divinely given modes of instruction. Hence it should be a
matter of conscience to us, if we attempt "cultural transposition"
of them for some didactic purpose (e.g., to secure "dynamic
equivalence" in a free-flowing Bible translation), to explain
at some point that the transposition merely *illustrates* what the
original means and does not strictly speaking *translate* it at
all. (I am thinking here of concepts with logical substance,
as distinct from conventional verbal forms like the three-decker
universe and diffused-consciousness psychology, which are used
for expressing other truths without being asserted as normative
themselves.) When it comes to the substance of teaching, we may
not cut loose from the biblical categories in which God teaches
us to think.

So if asked the content of the Gospel for today in England,
Chile, Borneo, Bermuda, Tibet or wherever, I shall offer a
formula based on the six-theme analysis above, and urge that
there are five points to be taught.

First, the Gospel tells us of *God* our maker, in whom we live
and move and are, and whom we have been made to worship and
serve, and in whose hands, for good or ill, we always remain,

and whose will and purpose should always determine ours. Like
Paul at Athens, we must introduce folk to the Creator whom they
have forgotten to remember, and go on from there. Not till the
Creator's claim is seen can we ever grasp the sinfulness of sin.

Second, the Gospel tells us of *sin*, defining it as failure to
meet the holy Creator's claim first by aping him and then by
fighting him, and depicting it as rebellion against his
authority, lawlessness in relation to him as our lawgiver,
missing the mark which he gave us to aim at, and becoming guilty
and unclean in his sight in consequence. The Gospel tells us
that we are the helpless slaves of our own rebelliousness and
cannot put ourselves right. Not till we begin to grasp these
things can we ever appreciate the dimensions of the declaration
that Jesus Christ saves us from sin.

Third, the Gospel tells of *Christ*, and we must teach both the
facts and the meaning of his life, death, resurrection and
reign. We must spell out who he is and what he has done, and
we must teach folk to interpret the meaning and purpose of human
life in terms of him. It is sometimes said that it is the
presentation of Christ's person, rather than of doctrines about
him, that draws sinners to his feet, and it is certainly true
that a theory of atonement, however orthodox, is no substitute
for the Savior: it is the living Christ who saves, not any
theory about him. But Jesus of Nazareth cannot be known as the
living Christ unless we are clear that he was eternal God and
his passion was really his redeeming action of bearing away
men's sins; nor shall we know how to approach him till we have
learned that he is now God's king on the throne of the universe.
Not till we are aware of these things can we see what the
response for which Christ calls really means.

Fourth, the Gospel tells of *faith, repentance and discipleship,* and so must we. Faith is credence and conviction regarding the Gospel message, and a consequent casting of oneself on
the promises of Christ and the Christ of those promises as one's
only hope. Repentance is a change of heart and mind, leading
to a new life of denying self and serving the Savior as king in
self's place. Discipleship is a matter of relating oneself to
the living, exalted Christ as both learner and follower, and to
the rest of Christ's disciples as one who longs both to learn
from them and to give to them, and who knows that his master's
will is for him to be in their company. These things must be
clearly taught, or the nature of the Christian life will surely
be misunderstood.

Fifth the Gospel tells of *newness*: new life in the Spirit,
who assures and enables; new relationships in the body of Christ,
where love expressed in fellowship through mutual ministry is

the rule; new goals in the world for all disciples, who find
that, though they are no longer of it, Christ leaves them in it
to render service to it; and new hope for both one's personal
future and that of the world as such, inasmuch as Christ is
publicly coming back. When in 1948 at the first W.C.C. assembly
at Amsterdam Karl Barth led off with a paper entitled "The
Return of Jesus Christ the Hope of the World" he struck a most
proper note; one wishes that over the past 30 years the W.C.C.
had managed to stay with it. When, where, how and with what
measure of discontinuity with what has preceded Christ will
come back we should not claim to know, but the certainty that
he who now reigns invisibly will one day show himself and in
doing so create new heavens and a new earth, wherein dwells
righteousness, and that meantime he stands at the end of the
road of each Christian's earthly life to meet him and take him
home, brings a radiancy of hope to which secular optimism,
however starry-eyed, cannot hold a candle. These points, too,
must be clearly taught, as must the ethical demands of discipleship in terms of love to God and neighbor, the sanctifying
of relationships, and the imitation of God and of Christ.

COMMUNICATION OF THE GOSPEL

Some brief points about the communication of the God-given
Gospel may now be made to round off. They draw together threads
that hung out at various points in our earlier argument.

First, the key to persuasive Christian communication lies
less in technique than in character. Paul was a great
communicator, not because he was eloquent (by the standards of
his day he was not, as he tells us in 2 Cor. 10:10, cf.
1 Cor. 2:1-5, and reading his letters with all their verbal
roughness one has to agree), but because he knew his own mind
and had a great capacity for identifying with the other man. It
is clear that though he has looked to the Holy Spirit to make
his communicating fruitful (cf. 1 Cor. 2:1-5), he knows that
the Spirit works through appropriate means, and so was very
conscious of the human factors in persuasion, namely cogency of
statement and empathetic concern, and was always most conscientious in laboring to achieve them. He set no limit to
what he would do, however unconventionally, to ensure that he
did not by personal insensitiveness or cultural inertia set
barriers and stumbling-blocks in the way of men coming to
Christ. "I have made myself a slave to all, that I might win
the more. And to the Jews I became as a Jew, that I might win
Jews...to those who are without law, as without law...that I
might win those who are without law. To the weak I became weak,
that I might win the weak; I have become all things to all men,
that I might by all means save some" (1 Cor. 9:19-22). It was

to remove possible stumbling-blocks for Jews that Paul had
Timothy circumcised (Acts 16:3) and also, it seems, Titus,
though as he insisted he was under no obligation to do this (see
Gal. 2:3). His loving, imaginative adaptability in the service
of truth and people is a shining example to all who engage in
evangelistic communication, and cannot be pondered too often or
taken too seriously.

Paul was a man who could, and did, share himself without
stint. From his letters we know him well, and we can appreciate
the trauma that lies behind the autobiographical passage of
Philippines 3, where he tells us how Christ stripped him of
cultural pretensions. "Here was a man," F.W. Dillistone
comments, "who possessed all the marks of privilege within a
particular historical tradition. His pedigree, his tribal
status, his religious dedication, his formal education, his
personal commitment, had been such that by every standard of
Jewish orthodoxy and by every sanction of national tradition he
was justified in regarding himself as successful, superior and
secure. He was surely in a position, if ever a man was, to
communicate religious truth to the ignorant and under-privileged.
Yet he had submitted every part of his historical inheritance to
the judgment of the Cross. Nothing could be removed but everything could be re-interpreted. Those things which seemed
positive gain could be judged as of no account in the service of
Christ: those things which had seemed to be hindrances and
handicaps might well prove positive assets in the new order of
living. In any case there was henceforth to be no final
confidence in the heritage from personal and past history..."
Then Dillistone continues: "The missionary today cannot escape
from his own history, national, social or individual. But it
is his duty, as far as possible, to become *aware* of that history
and to bring it under the judgment of the central touchstone of
history. Only so can he dare to approach those who belong to a
different historical tradition and whose personal histories are
very different from his own. He will become aware of their own
pride of history, their own aspirations for a richer historical
destiny. He will judge these not solely in the context of his
own historical framework but in the light of that history held
under the judgment of the Cross and the promise of the
resurrection. It goes without saying that this is no easy
task..." (*Christianity and Communication*, pp. 106f.). For all
who, with Paul, enter the world of cross-cultural communications
these are surely wise and weighty words.

Second, there are procedural guidelines in communicating
Christianity which cannot be ignored without loss. If we do not
stay with the biblical story, and the scriptural text, and most
of all with the person of the Savior; if, while observing the
distinction between milk and meat, foundation and superstructure,

we do not labor to make known the whole revealed counsel of God;
if we do not seek, as part of our communicative strategy, to
show the Gospel shaping relationships in home and family, in
imaginative gestures of neighbor-love, and so on, and to ring
the changes on *both* the "Christianizing" of existing culture and
the forming of an alternative culture as modes of Christian
expression; if, finally, we decline to show any respect for
cultures, however pagan, other than our own; then there is no
reason to expect communication to proceed well in any context,
whether in our local church down the road or on the other side
of the world.

Third, Christian communication cannot be made easy, and there
is not necessarily anything wrong with what we are doing if in
a particular situation at a particular time the task proves
cruelly hard. Our Lord Jesus Christ was a prince and a paragon
among communicators (nobody, I think, can ever dispute that),
yet even he failed constantly to anchor his message in men's
hearts, as his own parable of the Sower declares. His mighty
works were clear proof in themselves of his messianic identity
(cf. Matt. 11:1-6), yet Chorazin and Bethsaida saw them and did
not repent. In a world satiated with communication of one sort
and another, as today's world is, and with human hearts no less
hard than in Jesus' day, the same negative response can be
expected again in very many cases. "A great deal of research,"
writes Dillistone, "waits to be done on the whole subject of
'communications-fatigue.' What produces maximum or minimum
response? When is the limit to effective response reached?
What are the relative values of variations and repetition?
These questions need further investigation, but what is certain
is that in a world in which information of every kind is being
poured through channels of every kind it is becoming increasingly difficult for the distinctively Christian communication
to gain a hearing or to win any response....Today, as in Jesus'
day, there is no *guarantee* that the exhibition of or the
witness to the mighty works of God will not be either ignored
or misunderstood" (*op. cit.*, p. 147). "There is no expeditious
road to pack and label men for God. There is likewise no
guaranteed form of effective communication. Always the struggle
must continue. The end is never in sight" (p. 149).

On which sobering note we close.

8

The Gospel—
Its Content and Communication:
An Anthropological Perspective
Jacob A. Loewen

The approach used in this paper will be a blend of personal testimony, confession, and statement of insights gained during several decades of involvement in cross-cultural communication of the Gospel, especially in South America and Africa. I am very conscious of the fact that all the ideas or "principles" expressed in this paper are of value for this consultation only in as far as they help us improve our communication both within and outside of our own cultures.

PRESUPPOSITIONS

The "sleepers" that often hinder our communication are the differing unspoken presuppositions which the participants bring into a communications context. I therefore want to begin by trying to spell out some of my underlying assumptions so that the receptors of this communication will have at least some points of reference for evaluating the ideas expressed.

1. The Gospel in the person of Jesus Christ is God's Good News for all mankind. For me the simplest statement of the nature and the content of the Gospel we are to share with all the peoples of the world was given by Jesus on that historic sabbath in the synagogue of Nazareth when he unrolled the scroll of the Prophet Isaiah and read:

> "The Spirit of the Lord is upon me,
> because he has chosen me to bring
>   good news to the poor.
> He has sent me to proclaim liberty to
>   the captives
> and recovery of sight to the blind;
> to set free the oppressed
>   and announce that the time has come
> when the Lord will save his people" (Lk. 4:18-19, TEV).

Probably few of those hearing this reading in the synagogue that day realized the import of the words when Jesus cryptically added: "This passage of Scripture has today come true as you have heard it being read" (Lk. 4:21).

2. The life-changing power of the Gospel comes from God. It can never be generated by the efforts of man, no matter how dedicated, how consecrated, or how anthropologically sensitive he may be. On the other hand, no man can stop it no matter how hard he tries or how obstreperous he is. The latter was driven home to me during the height of the drug craze in North America when a well-known anthropologist went to South America to do research on the effects of hallucinating drugs with a tribe of Indians that was known to have wide experience with them. When he arrived there, he informed the shamans that he was going to be with them for six weeks and that he wanted to experience a full range of drugs which the shamans used in order to compare what they and he experienced. The shamans bluntly informed him that his conditioning to the drugs alone would take more than six weeks. At his insistence, however, they finally agreed to try and complete the conditioning in three weeks so that he could then experience a full range of their drugs over the next three weeks. However, already with his first full dose his conditioning turned out to be completely inadequate. Here are his own words.

> "I took my first full dose, and no sooner had I taken
> it, I became aware that I was overdosed. I felt the
> extremities of my body--my feet, then my legs, my hands
> and my arms--grow cold; gradually the coldness
> enveloped the whole of the lower part of my torso. I
> felt 'death' overpowering life in my entire body until
> there seemed to be only a small area around my heart
> that was still alive. I knew I was dying, but I so
> desperately wanted to live. I struggled to hang on to
> my life, but it seemed futile. Just when I thought
> the thread of life was going to snap, the blackness
> of death was shattered by a brilliant light and I saw
> Jesus Christ on the cross saying: 'I will save you.'"

"And the hell of it is," the anthropologist concluded, "that I don't believe in Jesus Christ."

   While the anthropologist was "dying," the shamans, realizing that something had gone wrong, were frantically giving him antidotes to counteract the effect of the drug. The anthropologist's wife and daughter, standing by helplessly, saw how all the frantic efforts of the shamans seemed to be in vain. Then suddenly and unexpectedly the anthropologist opened his eyes. When he told his family of his vision, both wife and daughter responded to the power of God.

3. As in Jesus' day, so today there is more faith among the "Gentiles" than there is in "Israel." When Jesus healed the servant of the Roman centurion, the latter asked the Lord just to say the word--then his servant would be healed. Jesus, hearing the man's words, responded: "I tell you I have never found anyone in Israel with faith like this" (Mt. 8:10, TEV). I have to honestly confess that my experience with so-called animistic peoples in South America and Africa and with western missionaries who are bringing the Gospel to them has convinced me that the capacity to believe among the animists is far greater than among the missionaries who have been conditioned by secularism and materialism, and who today find it almost impossible to believe in a spirit world. In my chapter "Evangelism and Culture" (*New Face of Evangelicalism*, R. Padilla, ed., 1976), I report my own confession concerning the occasion when a fellow missionary and I were pushed out of a circle of Indian believers who were praying for the healing of a sick person. I will never forget their words: "We're sorry, God's power cannot heal when there are unbelievers in the circle." Sad to say, western missionaries do not only suffer from infection by this virus of unbelief themselves, they are carriers of it; in fact, they are conscientiously contaminating the national preachers they are training even today. (For an example of what I mean, see the paragraph on the missionary-trained national pastor.)

4. Anthropology does not have any ultimate answers for the communication of the Gospel. I am firmly convinced that the science of anthropology can provide us with tools to understand culture and cultural problems. It can give us insights into our own behavior and the behavior of people in different cultures, but it can never write *the* foolproof formula for communicating the Gospel. Just as our Lord refuses to be confined to temples built by the hands of men, so his ongoing work will not be confined by any human intellectual structures, be they theological or anthropological. On the other hand, ignorance of the insights of anthropology will be no more valid as an excuse for not having done correctly what God committed us to do, than

not having recognized Christ, as the condemned at the great judgment pleaded: "When Lord, did we see you hungry, thirsty, or a stranger, or naked, or sick, or in prison and did not help you?" (Mt. 25:31-46, TEV).

I hope that the preceding statement of underlying assumptions will provide enough of a basis on which to examine my thoughts on the assigned topic: "The Gospel . . . its Content and its Communication."

THE GOSPEL

I am deeply aware that for many theologians my use of *Gospel* will seem like simplistic ignorance. Like the person who, reading this paper in a preliminary form asked: What do you mean by *Gospel*? Do you mean the *Gospel* (with a capital), i.e. salvation through Jesus Christ? Or do you mean the *gospel* (no capital) i.e., the practical outworking of God's specific word in a specific culture?

Another reader expressed puzzlement about the fact that personal salvation and the solution to cultural problems were treated as equally central to the Gospel. I am aware of all of these distinctions and more, but from the anthropological perspective from which I am writing, there is no value in separating them, because in a religion that embraces all of life and which is concerned with the whole society, the solution to a painful local cultural problem can be as much a part of salvation as the individual's forgiveness of sin, e.g., the Shiriana (Brazil) cultural problem of satisfying sexual needs before personal salvation can have a meaning.

Furthermore, for those African countries who have just undergone their own "exodus" liberation experience, the in-life example of how one *nation of Israel* was formed out of twelve separate and often competing tribes by the religious guidelines God gave, may, in actual fact, be a far more relevant and meaningful message than that the individual sinner can be saved by grace. To be sure, not every individual in these newly liberated countries is equally concerned about nation builing, but the most recent liberation experiences have produced a very widespread felt need for a religion that will help them build a new nation with justice and equality for all.

Here, of course, we also need to be aware of some very fundamental cultural differences, e.g., western individualism stands in bold contrast to African groups that still can find consensus. For the latter highly "individual salvation" is often felt as socially disruptive and negative, rather than truly God-given and beneficial.

On the level of the Scripture, the use of *Gospel* in this
paper embraces not only the New Testament, but the whole Bible
which I accept as the Word of God valid universally and eternally.
But now, having made this broad affirmation, I feel that I must
also point out a number of situational qualifications:

1. The message of the Gospel is a multifaceted one. Not only
did God's people get it over a long period of time, but it was
given to men living within very differing cultural settings and
operating on very different presuppositions. Every student of
the Old Testament is well aware of how the concepts of man and
God underwent extensive and radical changes as Israel moved
from seeing God as the personal God of Abraham to become the God
of Israel when it became a nation, to the God of mankind when
the nation was destroyed and the people of Israel went into
exile. We also need to recognize that as a multifacted Gospel
it does not hesitate to emphasize both sides of an issue, e.g.,
in Romans salvation is by faith alone without works, and in
James works without faith is dead and useless. In fact, multi-
faceted probably suggests that not all facets will be equally in
focus for one person or one people at one point in time.

2. Not only are there radical differences in worldview between
the Old and New Testaments, but within the Old Testament itself
we find that the presuppositions of Abraham, Isaac, and Jacob
were very different from the presuppositions of David and
Solomon, or of Ezekiel and the prophets in exile. Interestingly
enough, Africans say that the New Testament has more or less a
western worldview, while the Old Testament is founded on a worldview similar to their own. In this light it may be significant
to point out that at the present time about 75% of all Bible
translation work in Africa is Old Testament or whole Bible. The
identification of the Africans with God's approach to dealing
with his people in the Old Testament is so strong that up to
World War II (after which so many of the African countries
became independent and the authority of foreign missions
eclipsed) the arrival of the Old Testament again and again
split the existing church. Barrett sets the figure at 81%
(Barrett, 1968). A large segment of the church, rebelling
against what they viewed as the western wrapper in which the
missionaries had given them God's message, started a separatist
movement boldly proclaiming: "The African gospel--the Old
Testament--has finally arrived; the missionaries have kept our
gospel hidden and have preached only **theirs**" (ibid).

3. I as an individual have to confess that at different times in
my life different facts of biblical truth have been more
important to me than others. I grew up in a Mennonite Brethren
community in which revival and conversion were the topics of the

day. The most significant facet of God's truth at that time in
my experience was "escape from hell and to be saved." Later,
when I was at the university and became aware of the fact that
there were brilliant men who, though blaspheming God, were discovering new truths about the world and man, both created by God.
What struck me most deeply was the sharp contrast between these
scientists who were experiencing the excitement of discovering
new truth, and the church which had all its truth canned and
whose leadership was as it were, sitting on the lid busily
trying to smell out heretics, like so many medieval inquisitors.
At this stage in my life the awareness that God's truth was like
a giant piano keyboard was the supreme insight. I saw how
individuals and individual churches played their favorite key
or chord which they accepted as the whole truth. They played
their own note faithfully while fervently condemning all other
notes. I was overwhelmed when I realized that God had to
exercise just as much patience with these people as with the
unbelieving professor who recognized only physics as truth. In
both cases he was beginning where the people were and was trying
to lead them to a greater understanding of himself and of his
truth.

Then as anthropological awareness grew upon me, I became
deeply aware of how my western material-oriented culture with its
total cleavage between the material and the spiritual was
actually stifling my capacity to believe in the spirit world.
By *believe* I don't mean mere mental acceptance of a truth, I
mean to live by it, like the animist who, believing his soul has
been stolen, lies down and dies. During this period I became
aware of God's Spirit as the operative power in this age and
then began to bend my efforts to increase my hearing capacity
for his still small voice.

More recently it has been the incarnation--the truth that God
himself, in order to communicate his good news to men, found it
necessary to limit himself to human nature and to a specific
culture. This is the big truth in my life and thinking today.

4. Different cultures, facing the Gospel for the first time,
will find different facets of it more meaningful than others.
Obviously people cannot continue to live by "one loaf of bread
alone," and as their faith develops they will gradually become
aware of more dimensions. A missionary statesman recently
asked Bakht Singh of India what dimensions of the Gospel he
found most useful in witnessing to his own people.

"Do you preach to them about the *love* of God?"

"No," he said, "the Indian mind is so polluted that
if you talk to them above love they think mainly of sex."

"Well," the missionary said, "do you talk to them about
the wrath of God?"

"No, they are used to that," he replied. "All the gods
are mad anyway. It makes no difference to them if there
is one more who is angry."

"About what do you talk to them? Do you preach on the
crucified Christ?" the missionary guessed.

"No, they would think of him as a poor martyr who
helplessly died."

"Then what is your emphasis? Eternal life?"

"Not so," he said, "if you talk about eternal life the
Indian thinks of transmigration. He wants to get
away from it."

"What then is your message?"

Listen to his answer: "I have never yet failed to get
a hearing if I talk to them about the forgiveness of
sins and peace and rest. That's the product that
sells well. Soon they ask me how they can get it, and
then I can lead them to the Saviour who alone can
meet their deepest longings" (Peters, 1977).

5. Differing cultural backgrounds and their concomitant presuppositions will cause their people to *hear* a differing content
from the same message. This was forcefully driven home to us
when my wife and I tried to serve as resource persons to a
group of missionaries and nationals who were trying to develop a
new meaningful Sunday School curriculum in Africa. They wanted
a curriculum "that would really speak to African people." To
our disappointment we discovered that the Scripture passages
and the truths they were to teach had already been chosen by the
parent church in North America; and what they really wanted was
an artificial African didactic framework. When my wife and I
objected, suggesting that we should let the Africans decide
which truths should be taught and also let them select which
stories taught those truths, the missionaries were incensed.
They were seminary-trained people, they knew the Bible and what
it teaches. In order to make them aware of how different
cultural perspectives cause different people to hear very
differently, we reviewed a number of Bible stories, and asked
both the missionaries and the nationals present to write down on
a piece of paper what they thought the central message of these
stories was. The first example was the story of Joseph. The
missionaries wrote that there was a man who was loyal to God

even to the point of resisting the most fierce of sexual temptations. The Africans wrote here was a man who was totally loyal to his family. In spite of the fact that his brothers had mistreated him, he remained loyal to them even when he occupied the royal throne in Egypt.

6. The believing community in each culture must assume the ultimate responsibility for contextualizing the Gospel in its own setting. If the Gospel is to flourish indigenously, and if it is to help men cope with the problems and contradictions of their own cultural setting, then the believing community in each culture must develop its own patterns of translating the Gospel truth into daily life and worship. However, for a people to be motivated to do this, they usually need a deep consciousness that God is speaking specifically and directly to them. We have recently seen this urgency develop in a number of African language settings. For example, when a consensus-directed believing community within a given language and culture context discovers that their language requires decisions for which no explicit evidence in the original Greek or Hebrew exists (e.g., languages with three rather than one indicative mode: a fact from personal experience, a fact from a reliable source, and "it is said") is moved to pray: "God, how would you have said this if you had spoken in our own language in the first place," and then experience a group consensus in regard to a divine answer, their attitude toward God's Word changes radically. One retired minister in Zambia testified: "For twenty-five years I have told the people that the Bible is the Word of God, but deep down in my heart there was a nagging suspicion that it was white man's God speaking to white man and white man affirming that it was valid also for Africans. But that has completely changed now. God has spoken to us and under his Spirit's guidance we have made decisions which no white man could make."

It is the awareness of the importance of a contemporary en-counter with the inspiration that has led the Bible Society (a) to shift from missionary translators to mother-tongue speakers as translators, and (b) to insist that every generation in major languages should make a new translation so as to experience what J. B. Phillips called the "electric shocks of God's Spirit." (For more detail see Loewen, 1974.)

It is the opinion of this writer that an important factor in the lack of contextualization of the African scene is due to the absence of such a deep consciousness that God has spoken personally and specifically to them.

7. God is always ready to meet man at the point of his greatest
felt need. I have been deeply impressed, while rereading the
life of Jesus, to see how he put Isaiah's definition of the
Gospel into practice by helping men in the area in which they
felt their greatest need. Thus when the four men brought the
paralytic to Jesus to be healed, and were so urgent that they
let him down through the roof, Jesus did not say to the man:
"My son, you are healed," but "My son, your sins are forgiven."
Then for the benefit of the Pharisees who took Jesus' first
statement as blasphemy, he said: "To show you that I, indeed,
can forgive sin, I am going to tell this man to get up and walk."
The healing almost seemed like an afterthought for the benefit
of the Pharisees, and before he did that, he satisfied the
man's deepest yearning for forgiveness. On the other hand, when
Jesus healed the man who had been incapacitated for thirty-eight
years, the latter did not even know who had healed him. Only
later when he met Jesus did he discover who it was that had
healed him. It was then that Jesus said to him: "Go and sin
no more."

8. The aim of the Gospel on a personal level is to set the
individual free from the power of sin, so that he can develop a
character and a life style that will permit him to realize his
unique personal endowments to his own self-fulfillment, to the
enrichment of his fellows, and to the glory of his creator. On
a societal level the Gospel aims to establish a new society of
citizens of the kingdom of God in which justice and brotherhood
shall flourish and bear fruit like trees planted by the "rivers
of water."

THE MESSENGERS OF THE GOSPEL

There are many people who feel called to be messengers of the
Gospel. Here are some prerequisites that should characterize
them all.

1. Each would-be messenger of the Gospel must have personally
experienced the transforming power of the Gospel both in his own
life and in his own culture. Only a person who can testify
from personal experience how the Gospel met his deepest needs
and how "the new spirit" from God provided him with the resources to overcome the personal devils that held him chained,
can be a believable witness on the Gospel's behalf. All preaching beyond one's experience--no matter how well-intentioned--will
at best be hollow human words.

2. Each messenger should recognize that he is a product of his
own culture and become fully aware of the limitations his
culture imposes upon his Christian experience. In my paper
written as a follow-up of the Lausanne Conference on Evangelism,

("Evangelism and Culture") I have tried to show some of the limitations and problems that western culture creates for its believers and missionaries. But western culture is not unique in creating problems for obedient followers of the Gospel, each culture has its own inventory of problems, and the messenger--regardless of his culture--must become fully aware of them.

3. Each messenger must learn to appreciate and to understand the cultural background of the Gospel in the Scriptures. Without an adequate understanding of the biblical cultural settings--and there are many of them, not just two--no one can fully understand its message nor make a dynamic equivalent translation of this Gospel into a new cultural milieu. Working as a translation consultant in East Central Africa my appreciation for the Old Testament has grown immensely, for here I am working with a people whose culture in many ways is more like the Hebrew culture than my own; and these people find great delight in seeing how God operated within that cultural setting. Unless one is aware of the specific cultural framework in which a given biblical message is imbedded, one can readily fall into the trap of defending nonsense, like when my church some decades ago excommunicated women for cutting their hair on the basis of the Pauline prescriptions to the Corinthians.

4. When a messenger of the Gospel has occasion to witness across cultural boundaries he needs to be aware not only of the culture from which he comes, but he must have an equally deep appreciation for, and an understanding of the receptor's culture. (Obviously this presupposes a thorough mastery of the target language.) It is the wholesale condemnation of the cultures of so-called "mission fields" as pagan and evil, and their heavy dependence on interpreters that has led early missionary messengers into all kinds of perversions of biblical truth. As a translations consultant I frequently find myself trying to help national churches to extricate themselves from the meaningless jargon that has been bound upon them by missionaries who had no respect for their culture. Thus in one African language the missionaries rejected the local words for *spirit* as satanic, and on the basis of the Greek and Hebrew used the local word for *breath* to mean "spirit." For this reason we today have the church using *red breath* to stand for "Holy Spirit" (*red* and *holy* are homophonous, but the people tend to hear *red* when the word is uttered in normal conversations), *bad breath* for "evil spirits," and *dirty breath* for "unclean spirits." During a translator training program in this language one of the trainees was asked to put their newly learned techniques of componential analysis of meaning into practice on the various terms for *spirit* in their language. The trainee led the group in an excellent discussion through all the words from the tribal language. However, when she came to these three biblical words,

she turned to the group and said: "There are no components of
meaning here, are there?" And solemnly ministers, teachers, and
laymen alike agreed with her: "There is no meaning here." When
the consultant intervened and said: "But surely *red*, *bad*, and
dirty mean something; "Oh," they said, "yes, those words mean
something, but the whole thing doesn't mean anything." A
hundred years of mission work without an adequate vocabulary for
some very essential truths of the Gospel, all because
missionaries did not respect the culture of the people for whom
they were to serve as a source of the Gospel.

5. Each messenger must approach his cross-cultural witness with
expectancy. Having recognized his own partial understanding of
the Gospel, he must be open and ready for the Spirit of God to
do a "new thing." When Peter had experienced the vision of the
sheet being let down from heaven and being ordered to eat
unclean animals, he, of course, was puzzled by the meaning of
this strange experience; but it had so shaken him that he was
able to break out of his Jewish restraint and racial prejudice
against the gentiles and go to Cornelius' house and witness God
perform a new thing--the gentiles also becoming recipients of
God's Spirit.

The western missionary as a messenger of the Gospel. As
already mentioned, in my "Evangelism and Culture"paper, I have
tried to describe some of the negative aspects of the cultural
wrappings with which western Christianity has clothed the Gospel.
I think I am correct in saying that even today many western
missionaries are still considering this cultural wrapper of
their home Christianity an integral part of the Gospel. I have
found only few western missionaries making a conscious effort to
free the Gospel from its western wrapper, and I have found even
fewer missionaries who are aware of how their culture inhibits
their own faith and obedience. For this reason a missionary
from the West today needs a double dose of humility. It is not
enough for him to be humbly aware of his present inadequacies,
he must also make atonement for the cultural ignorance of his
predecessors.

Local, but missionary-trained pastors. All too often, if the
missionary was blind and unable to separate the Gospel from its
western cultural wrappings, the national pastor who was trained
by him became twice the son of Gehenna. Recently a newly
ordained national pastor came to me and asked: "Do you think it
is true that spirits of the dead appear to the living?" Then
without waiting for my answer he went on:- "I had been in my
congregation for just a few weeks when a man died. There had
been considerable trouble, because this man had lent another
member of the congregation some money and the debtor was
refusing to pay it. On the day after his burial the dead man's

soul appeared to his sister and said: 'You must go to the man
who owes me the money and tell him to pay it at once. I am unhappy to leave this unsettled. If it is not settled I will not
live in the graveyard alone.'" When the family came to the
pastor to ask for his blessing on their new approach to the
defaulting debtor, the pastor had to take refuge behind the
"fifth amendment." He then went and asked a retired lay
preacher. The latter said: "That's exactly what happens."
Unsatisfied he sought out a fellow seminary-trained minister who
reminded him: "We seminary-trained preachers don't believe in
such things." The pastor then told the people that he could not
help them. But then, as if suddenly remembering while talking
to me, he added: "When I was living with my parents in the
village, such a thing would not have troubled me. I would have
believed it. But now I am a seminary graduate and I know I
shouldn't believe such things." In an effort to help him
indirectly I asked him whether there were any examples in the
Bible of dead men appearing to the living. I saw relief flood
his face when he suddenly burst out: "You are right... In the
Bible there too are examples of souls of the dead appearing to
the living."

Third World Christians as missionaries. It is definitely a
healthy sign that many of the Third World countries are launching missionary initiatives in countries other than their own.
On the whole this is most praiseworthy. But sad to say, in many
cases such Third World missionaries are no more sensitive to the
cultures to which they are going than western missionaries were
in the past.

Prophets of Independent Churches. Probably the most
successful witnesses (in terms of the number of members gained)
on the African scene today are the prophets of Independent
churches. Barrett recently observed that six out of ten
conversions in Africa today are to Independent church groups.
To this I would like to add from my own observations that even
the members of mainline (Presbyterian, Methodist, etc.) churches
again and again fall back upon these groups in times of severe
crisis. (My article "Mission Churches, Independent Churches,
and Felt Needs in Africa," which appeared in *Missiology,*
October 1976 gives more detail.)

The prophets usually operate on a very personal encounter
with God who has given them a mandate to preach and teach a
given way of worship. They identify very deeply with Old
Testament prophets. Culturally they usually are single-mindedly
African. This, often coupled with very limited Bible knowledge,
leaves them very vulnerable to syncretism. Recently, however,
I have observed in Zaire, Rhodesia, and Botswana a real openness

on the part of large numbers of such prophets to receive outside
help to up-grade their knowledge of the Bible. This is a very
encouraging sign.

   Culturally aware local leaders. It is gratifying to see a
new kind of leader emerge on the African church scene. These
usually are men who are proud of their African heritage, but who
have had extensive exposure to western culture, and also have
gained some understanding of biblical cultures. It is men of
this culture who will be able to discern both the western
wrappings in which the Gospel came to them, while at the same
time be aware of where the dangers of syncretism in their
own culture lie. They are the great hope of the church to
develop a truly contextualized Christian faith that will meet
the needs of the people and further the growth of God's
kingdom.

THE COMMUNICATION OF THE GOSPEL

A case study of felt needs and church responses. If we accept
Jesus' definition of the Gospel quoted earlier as: "good news
for all--regardless of what their problems," then it behooves us
to find out what the pressing needs of a given people are and
to check whether the message we are giving them is indeed
meeting their felt need, because if our message is not related
to these needs then we may be the modern Pharisees who "bind
grievous burdens upon people but don't themselves lift a finger
to help them carry them" (Lk. 11:46). Jesus condemned
religious teachers who do this in the strongest terms. In
order to provide a ready-made context in which the readers will
be able to make a quick check on felt needs of an area and to
see in how far the Gospel these people are getting is meeting
their felt needs, I would recommend my *Missiology* article. This
article tries to identify the felt needs of a number of tribal
peoples in East Central Africa, and then illustrates the reaction of the missionary and of the western inspired national
church to them. Only if we face the actual facts of the
situation, and become personally convinced of how seriously our
Gospel falls short of Jesus' definition, will we realize how
desperately we need to re-evaluate the content of the Gospel
we are communicating.

   *Recognizing the weaknesses and failures and potential problems
in the process of communication itself.* Every human activity,
even the best, is not without difficulties, and the
communication of the Gospel is no exception. This is not the
time nor the place for full-scale analysis of the problem of the
communications process. However, it does seem essential to
mention at least the ones most crucial to the contextualization
of the Gospel.

1. Willful or accidental misuse of the Gospel. As pointed out in my "Evangelism and Culture" paper (pp. 80-81), the missionaries who accompanied the Catholic conquistadores and the Protestant colonizers did so with the highest motivation and found ample scriptural justification for their "Christian-lord-to-pagan-servant" approach. Today we look back and say their approach was entirely wrong--it made a travesty of the Gospel. But the question that we need to ask is: Has that old attitude really died? Or has it merely taken a new shape?

The misuse of Scripture is, of course, not limited to missionary effort. The Allies and Axis in World War II both misused the Scriptures to show that their side was on God's side.

The so-called Ethiopian type of African Independent churches who try to by-pass the whole missionary effort and the European-inspired spread of Christianity and to link their present church efforts directly to the Ethiopian eunuch spoken of in Acts 8, are also misusing the Scriptures.

2. Skewing the Gospel because of an inherent bias. Most people, even those who are in the business of communicating the Gospel, have a tendency to fall in love with certain specific ideas to the neglect of other parts of the whole counsel of God. Any bias will automatically result in the skewing of the rest of the truth. Racist white people have for generations been using the curse on Canaan quite out of context and completely erroneously to justify the subjugation of black men by white men. This interpretation may be dying out in Southern United States, but it is flourishing in Southern Africa. And what is most tragic about people having such biases is that they often are fervently religious. In fact, looking at my own Christian experience I wonder whether we will ever be entirely without some bias or another. However, it is my deep and earnest prayer that the amount of skewing would decrease as we grow in grace and in the knowledge of our Lord Jesus Christ.

3. Syncretism. By syncretism I mean the mixing of the Christian faith and local traditional (non-Christian) beliefs and practices with the result that the Gospel is perverted, distorted, or largely voided in the process. A case in point is the South American tribal believer who gave the following testimony to me some years ago: "It is wonderful to be a Christian," he said. "You see, now as Christians we have ever so many more 'hard' words than before. You can heal your friends, or you can kill your enemies, whenever you want to. All you have to do is kneel behind them in a prayer meeting and while everyone else is praying out loud (a standard practice in this mission) you just whisper the appropriate 'hard' words, breathe on the person, and it happens just like that. For example, if you should say words

like *tutechan, wikik, kisimasi* (temptation, wicked, Christmas)
or any of the other bad 'hard' words, the person will die like a
fly. If, however, you use words like *kang, epong, klaiki* (God,
heaven, Christ) or any of the other good 'hard' words, the
person will be well before you know it."

This testimony shared in utter candor by a believer
illustrates an indigenous adaptation of Christianity, but it is
hardly an adjustment in which the Gospel is going to flourish.
You ask how in the world this happened. The reason for this
syncretistic adaptation is close to the surface. First, all the
preaching in this setting is done in English with the help of
local Indians interpreting from English into their own language.
Secondly, a look at their culture reveals that this tribe had
a repertoire of "hard" words--magic words--taught to them by
their creator-culture hero so that they could heal the sick.
Since Christianity came into their language through interpretation, unqualified interpreters, faced with the many Christian
technical words which they did not know how to handle in translation, simply made "hard" words out of them. Those words that
seemed to be associated with evil became bad "hard" words;
and those associated with good became good "hard" words.

4. Restructuring. Restructuring is the reorganization of
individual traits or bundles of traits of the Gospel message in
which the component parts of the message are separately fitted
into a local cultural framework usually resulting from severe
distortion, if not in a total loss of the Gospel message. For
example, the Kako people of Cameroun restructured the communion
service on the model of their own *sataka* "peace-making ritual."
Thus if a person were excommunicated from the communion table
by the missionaries because of some failure, he would merely
send his brother to the next communion service, and then he
himself could personally return to the church because his
brother had "eaten with God" and the tort between the two of
them had been settled   (Reyburn, 1958).

The Toba of the Argentine Chaco restructured their tribal
puberty ceremony and made it the model for young people's
conversions   (Loewen, 1969).

Maximizing communication. I am personally firmly convinced
that effective communication is a cooperative effort between the
source and the receptor. No matter how good the source is in
structuring a message, if the receptor is not receiving properly
the communication will be limited. And likewise, no matter how
hard the receptor tries to receive the message, if the source
severely warps the message for one reason or another, the
reception will be hindered or skewed. For this reason a basic

attitude of reciprocity between the source and the receptor is
fundamental. To my mind this involves at least the following
areas:

1. An honest acceptance of the validity of each other's
cultures. While some things may be new, strange, or even
difficult, they will never suspect each other's motives as
persons nor as members of a culture.

2. A spirit of exchange in which two people can learn from each
other. Missionaries in the past have often been overwhelmed
with the greatness of the message that they had to communicate.
They seldom went prepared to learn from their communicants. I
can honestly say that during some thirty years in which I have
tried to share the good news with people in many languages,
tribes and societies, I have usually been taught more than I
was able to teach. I have invariably come away deeply indebted
to individuals in that culture.

3. Their relationship to each other will be characterized by
self-exposure both on a personal and a cultural level. As they
understand each other's personal and cultural reactions more
fully, they will be able to serve as mirror to each other to
help each other become aware of those things that are incongruent with the tenor of the Gospel in their life style or in
their culture.

4. They need to cooperate in identifying what Donald McGavran
has called "the bridges of God." In every society there are
social institutions, communication networks, strategically
situated groups of people who would be most ready to accept the
Gospel and who would best be able to share it with their fellow-
men.

5. They also need to cooperate in finding indigenous "sources
of steam." When a culture encounters the Gospel, obviously some
things in this culture are going to have to change, but culture
change is often difficult to effect unless there is an adequate
amount of push from within. In the past all too often missionaries have tried to provide the push from the outside, but as
soon as they turned their backs or whenever they had to leave
the field things reverted to the old way. For this reason any
genuine change that is to be effected must be linked to an
indigenous source of steam that will help keep up the momentum
in the cycle of change long after the missionary has disappeared
from the scene.

6. They need to search together for the best ways of
contextualizing the Gospel. This statement, at first blush, may
seem to contradict what was said earlier: "each culture must

assume the ultimate responsibility for contextualizing the Gospel
in its own setting," but to my mind it does not. Adequate contextualization is a difficult task and the sympathetic outsider
can often have a very unique role to play as mirror, source of
alternative, catalyst, friend of the court, etc. (Loewen, 1968).

In North-Central Zambia (name of place purposely withheld)
there is a small village with a very active Christian church belonging to one of the mainline denominations by name, but by
function it is an African church. Because of its isolation it
has received only minimal missionary attention, and due to its
small numbers it had not warranted placing a seminary-trained
resident denominational minister there. This relative isolation
from outside interference has permitted the community to develop
a local form of contextualized Christianity, but largely in
terms of traditional models. For example, on the margin of the
church are mediums and "spirit discerners" who are used by the
Christians and tolerated, if not accepted by the church. Thus
when the local rich man and his daughter, who managed a store
for him, were on a collision course in a conflict of personal
interests, the church-accepted medium discovered that the
periodic acute pains of the store manageress-- a leading
deaconness in the church--were resulting from community jealousy
and that her leaving the store was the only real avenue of cure.
Consequently another sister was installed in the store, but
under entirely new and adequate conditions. The father's face
was saved, the first daughter became well, and everyone was
grateful that the church and the community had been spared an
ugly incident.

In the example cited the result of contextualization on the
exclusively local model proved satisfactory, but obviously the
merely tolerated status of the spirit discerners shows that full
contextualization has not been achieved. I personally feel that
if this church had had or could still find an outside mirror,
the contextualization of the Gospel could be furthered.

The outsider-as-mirror function in the contextualization of
the Gospel is as crucial to the established churches of the West
as it is for the younger churches in the Third World. Contextualization is never a once-and-for-all event--it is an ongoing
process. In fact, what was meaningful and right in grandfather's day may be utterly wrong today. I think it is highly
significant that church people working overseas become deeply
aware of serious problems extant in North American Christianity.
For this reason we of the West will do well to consider
seriously such mirror reflections as that of the South American
Indians who are convinced that money, and not God, is the axle
of our way of life. (See "Evangelism and Culture" pp. 184-185,
for a full account.)

7. Last, but not least, there must be an adequate interchange between the older and younger churches. As a church gets established in a "receiving" society there should early be exchanges between it and the "sending" church. This exchange must always be a two-way street. All too often the older churches have been left unmoved by the criticism leaders of the younger churches visiting them have levelled at them. Older churches found the criticisms quaint, interesting, or sometimes even annoying, but they seldom did anything about them. It will be only when older churches take seriously the challenges given to them by younger churches that their own communication with younger churches will be maximized.

Over and above these requirements, which are equally valid for both the source and the receptor, there are certain specific requirements for each individually.

Requirements for the source. In view of his call to be a witness of the Gospel, I feel that the greater responsibility for effective communication rests on the source.

1. He must take the lead in cultural awareness, i.e. in knowing his own, the Bible's, and the receptor's culture. To be sure, his knowledge of both his own and the receptor's culture will grow as the reciprocal sharing between them develops, but at the beginning it is the source who must take the lead.

2. He must assume responsibility for establishing the proper initial channels of communication. This means awareness of communication roles and of communication principles. E. A. Nida says:

> "The basic principles in such an approach are four:
> (1) effective communication must be based upon
> personal friendship, (2) the initial approach should
> be to those who can effectively pass on communication
> within their family grouping, (3) time must be allowed
> for internal diffusion of new ideas, and (4) the
> challenge for any change of belief or action must be
> addressed to the person or group socially capable of
> making such decisions." (Nida, 1960, p. 110.)

3. A willingness to begin at the felt need of the receptor, no matter what the source himself may feel to be the most important. Earlier we said that my *Missiology* paper had been introduced in order to show how the Gospel was meeting felt need in Africa. There is a second and even more compelling reason, namely, to stimulate missionary awareness of felt need. Western missionaries--even the most evangelical--come from a highly secularized church situation in which God and the church

have largely abdicated their concern for crop growth, human
fertility, illness and health, mental health, social welfare,
etc. In the Third World, however, like in the Bible, all of
these are still major religious concerns. Thus the Gospel will
be the good news for the Third World only if it addresses itself
to their basic concerns. Otherwise Christianity will merely be
a fair-weather religion which people practice when sailing is
smooth. However, as soon as a crisis makes its appearance then
these people have to fall back on some other religion to resolve
the problem, because, as the paper shows, mission-founded
churches offer them no help.

Concomitant with the western church's retreat from daily life
concerns is its overriding concern with propositional truth,
and it's preaching is usually the missionary's first concern.

4. A humble acceptance of the fact that the receptor will
establish an independent relationship with God. Western
missionaries have too long held a spiritual-father complex
toward people to whom they have been privileged to bring the
Gospel. (To be sure, this paternal role has often been aided
and abetted by the receptor's readiness to accept the "child"
role, thereby escaping personal responsibility.)

Requirements for the receptor. I would like to underscore at
least three:

1. An ongoing willingness to put himself, his culture and his
unspoken worldview and values under the scrutiny of the Spirit
of God.

2. An implicit obedience to the truth as God's Spirit gives him
new insight regarding the implications of the Gospel.

3. The willingness to submit himself to the whole counsel of
God. (Acts 20:28)

THEOLOGICAL ISSUES GROWING OUT OF THIS PRESENTATION

1. What parameters or limitations does biblical theology place
on the principle of presenting the Gospel in terms of the felt
need of the receptor?

2. What limits does biblical theology place on the principle of
a new church operating on a limited number of facets, or sets of
facets of the Gospel? This question concerns both (a) the
minimum amount of Gospel truth a society must accept before it
can be considered Christian, and (b) for what length of time can
it function with such a minimum?

3. Is it theologically acceptable that an African society with a culture similar to the Hebrew culture of Abraham's time begin with a similar minimal obedience to God and grow toward a more New Testament Christianity over a period of time?

4. In how far is it theologically sound to speak of new inspiration in those languages that have required grammatical or semantic categories for which no explicit evidence is found in the Hebrew or Greek original?

5. If we accept the principle that in Christ all men are equal before God: (a) Is it theologically valid for each society to develop its own expression of Christianity, or are there theological limits to the diversity of contextualization that would be permissible?

(b) Is it biblical that each believing community develop its own theology? Are there biblical limits to the diversity permissible?

(c) Is it biblical that a "new" thing could develop which would change existing Christian patterns as radically as Jesus' teaching and Pauline preaching challenged God-given Jewish religion?

(d) In how far are western churches "obligated" by Scripture to learn from Third World churches? Western missionaries quickly see syncretism in Third World churches. Should they also be open to Third World challenge re syncretism in their own midst?

6. In how far should cross-cultural missions operate the Jonah principle--that the foreign messenger is merely a catalyst who becomes obsolete once his message is received?

7. What are the practical implications of the divine example in the incarnation for cross-cultural witness of the Gospel? Does our current missionary practice contradict that example?

BIBLIOGRAPHY

D.B. Barrett, *Schism and Renewal in Africa--An Analysis of Six Thousand Contemporary Religious Movements*, London: Oxford University Press, 1968, pp. 105, 256, 268, etc. This catalytic effect of the Old Testament in precipitating African Independent church movements has been noted by many:

Recently an important Mozambican leader said to me: "I have studied the New Testament here and abroad, but still find it difficult and strange. In the Old Testament I have felt at home from the first time I read it." It has been noted for Nigeria in Jospeh B. Grimley and Gordon E. Robinson, *Church Growth in Central and Southern Nigeria,* Grand Rapids: Wm. B. Eerdmans Publishing Company, 1966, pp. 283-316, especially p. 314. Sundkler finds South African Independent church movements largely Old Testament. Cf. B.G.M Sundkler, *Bantu Prophets in South Africa,* second edition, London: Oxford University Press, 1961, p. 277. Mbiti cites it as a rather universal phenomenon for all of Africa. Cf. J.S. Mbiti, *African Religions and Philosophy,* London: Heinenmann, 1960, p. 255. He also cites specifically East African examples, pp. 254 f.

Jacob A. Loewen, "Relevant Roles for Overseas Workers," *International Review of Mission,* 57:233-244, 1968.

_____, "Socialization and Conversion in the Ongoing Church," *Practical Anthropology,* 16, 1969, pp. 10 f.

_____, "The Inspiration of Translation: A Growing Personal Conviction," in Robert G. Bratcher, et. al., *Understanding and Translating the Bible,* New York: American Bible Society, 1974, pp. 86-99.

_____, "Evangelism and Culture," in C. Rene Padilla, editor, *The New Face of Evangelicalism,* London: Hodder and Stoughton, 1976a, pp. 177-189.

_____, "Mission Churches, Independent Churches, and Felt Needs in Africa," *Missiology,* October 1976b, pp. 405-425.

Eugene A. Nida, *Message and Mission,* Pasadena: William Carey Library, 1960.

G.W. Peters, "Is Missions Homesteading or Moving?" *Mennonite Brethren Herald,* April 15, 1977, pp. 21 f.

W.A. Reyburn, "Meaning and Restructuring: A Cultural Process," *Practical Anthropology,* 5, 1958, pp. 79-82.

9

Conversion and Culture:
An Anthropological Perspective
with Reference to East Africa
Donald R. Jacobs

I was slightly starry eyed, a young, eager American missionary
appointed by the church to witness for Jesus Christ overseas.
I was indeed humbled by the task but not consciously plagued
with self doubt. The site for my joust with the devil and myself (the two not always clearly distinguished, incidentally)
was Tanzania, among a dominantly Bantu culture. As all well-
meaning missionaries should, I determined to witness to Jesus
Christ without reference to my Germanic Mennonite American background. I determined to preach the "pure" Gospel, uncluttered
by cultural acretions.

I. THE EMERGENCE OF THE QUESTIONS

The utterly futile nature of this task came home to me like
awaking from a dream. I was assigned to teach Theology. I soon
discovered that I had but a hazy concept of the relationship
between my own culture and my Christian faith. This set me on a
pilgrimage of discovery.

In this matter my heart was much more adventuresome than my
head. I realized intuitively, I suppose, that my own theology
had a heavy cultural base, yet I was very hesitant to upset an

apple cart which had served my purposes so admirably through the years. While in this state of unresolve I chanced to hear another North American missionary say with obvious satisfaction, "(so-and-so) is really converted, he is beginning to think like we do." That laid the issue bare for me. I could no longer avoid the problem. I began to phrase the questions as best I could. Can we assume that conversion will result in moving a person toward "our culture," the culture of the missionary? What, indeed, are the cultural expectations as perceived by the convertee and that of convertor? How should an experience of belief in and of walking with Jesus Christ affect a person's relationship with his own culture? Does conversion, for example, de-Teutonicise or de-Kikuyuize? If so, how much, and toward what else? These became my compelling questions. Having allowed myself to form the questions, I was on a journey of discovery. It was as much a journey of discovery into myself as into the culture which hosted me.

This paper is not really a theological essay because it does not employ theological categories as the starting point for the normal analysis of contextualization. But it is a "Christian" paper, written by a Bible-honoring Christian who employs anthropological and sociological images in speaking of the theologizing process. Nevertheless, I make certain theological assumptions, all of which, I hope, are evangelical in nature.

Firstly, when a man in his fallen state responds in repentant faith to Jesus Christ as revealed in the Scriptures and as known and loved by men and women through the ages, he experiences what is commonly known as Christian conversion.

Secondly, this conversion will exhibit itself in changed behavior no matter what the cultural context. Conversion must be demonstrated in order to be recognized by the community and in order to be consolidated by the believer.

Thirdly, all levels of one's life are not changed or altered to the same extent. It is therefore helpful to understand what happens in the various levels of life as a result of conversion and why such changes do occur.

Fourthly, while it is agreed that conversion is an ongoing process, for we all have many "turnings," nevertheless the conversion which is produced by an assent to the known will of God in Jesus Christ upon the awakening of faith is discernible and consequential.

Fifthly, conversion happens to individuals but it always occurs to persons in cultures, not in vacuums. Were a person to profess, "I believe," but then proceed to live as though nothing had happened is to me inconceivable.

Sixthly, I will employ an anthropological construct which makes no distinction between the sacred and the secular, between religion and a-religion, between pre-literate and literate societies. I see little point in trying to split these hairs in discussing the cultural aspects of Christian conversion.

I have treated the subject in two ways, both synchronically and diachronically. In the first section I will deal with what happens within a person's cultural experience upon and following upon conversion and in the second part I will trace what happens as Christian communities shift their relationships *vis a vis* the cultures from which they sprang.

II. THE HUMAN CULTURAL IMPERATIVE

Human beings are unhappy just to receive data; they have a compelling, almost relentless desire to interpret data. They do this in light of some frame of understanding which helps them to categorize and label. Man therefore creates cultures which are, in the last analysis, his group's grids for analyzing, sorting out and tabulating data. Each group thus provides for itself a way to comprehend and to view life. A person would be hard pressed to cope with life at all if it were not for the fact that when but a child, his group molded his world view which in effect gave him a ready-made structure for his comprehension of life.

Cultures enable groups to accumulate and tabulate the learnings of many generations in their own particular philosophical, ecological, and historical context. These cultures and sub-cultures are, to the participants, absolutely self-evident, universally applicable, and eminently "human." (Outsiders may, however, have a different view).

III. THE PHILOSOPHICAL UNDERGIRDING OF A CULTURE

Due to the vast number of variables, the philosophical systems undergirding cultures can differ dramatically from culture to culture. A culture's epistemology, simply one factor in its philosophical orientation, may illustrate this. The simple question, "What is important to know?" is one of the epistemological questions which is answered in accordance with the group's own way of perceiving reality. There is a serious bus accident, and we say "What caused it?" In seeking the cause, my culture leads me to inspect the steering gear, the brakes, maybe the condition of the road. While a Kuria from Tanzania might find such bits of knowledge interesting, for him it does not encompass a wide enough scope of investigation to solve the riddle as to why the bus flipped over. He will probably look for "facts" which are, in his view, more consequential; for

instance, who was angry with whom? The relational "facts"
not only describe for him more adequately the cause of this misfortune, but will then establish a scenario in which the
malevolent powers are exposed and subsequently placed in a
position where the community can deal with them. Witches are
flushed out of hiding and even ancestral spirits appear in their
true light. Both cultures, mine and the Kuria's, seek for
relevant "facts," "the truth" of the situation, and each
identifies a different set of "facts" to explain the situation.
I say, "The truth of the matter is the steering gear broke and
that is that," and the Kuria says, "That is obvious, but that
is not what ultimately caused the accident. The truth of the
matter is, so-and-so willed someone's death on that bus. To
know how the accident happened is only incidental. To know
why it happened is essential."

We could examine with profit other aspects of the two world
views, mine and the Kuria's, and in so doing discover philosophical matrixes quite out of kilter with one another. "Whose
is right?" we may ask. I suppose all we can demand of a
system is that its parts be consistent with one another. Each
culture has an internal consistency in which the world view
clusters around some self-evident philosophical presuppositions.
It is hardly fair to isolate an element in one culture and then
examine that element in light of the philosophical presuppositions of another culture. Yet I suppose this is a pastime
we all indulge in at one time or another. But it really flies
in the face of the notion of internal consistency within cultures which is obviously a fact which must be reckoned with.

Each culture, in summary, has a view of existence, a sort
of guide to the understanding of what life is all about and how
to survive as happily as possible as an individual in a
community. The primary grid of a group's world view is its
philosophical presuppositions which are more often assumed than
propositionalized. Why, a culture asks, argue with the self-
evident? These self-evident philosophical presuppositions have
to do with elemental concepts such as time, space, ontology, and
epistemology. This does not exhaust the presuppositions but
these are used as indicative. A diagram may be helpful.
(Figure 1)

I will pose a question or so about each section of the grid
simply to illustrate the areas of their consequences for understanding life's mysteries.

Time Concepts: Is time conceived of as quantitative, linear,
or relational, what is meaningful history and how much control
does a group have in shaping its future?

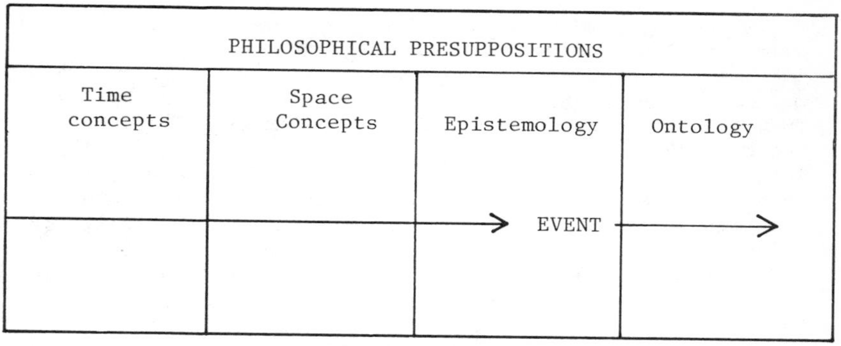

PHILOSOPHICAL PRESUPPOSITIONS			
Time concepts	Space Concepts	Epistemology	Ontology
		$\longrightarrow$ EVENT	$\longrightarrow$

Figure 1

Space Concepts: Is the spatial concept a material one or a "spirited universe"? In other words, what does space enclose?

Ontology: What is a being, do beings influence one another, and what is the nature of freedom and power?

Epistemology: The epistemological questions have to do with what is worth finding out and how to ascertain what is fact and what is subterfuge.

These questions should identify the grids. Events are examined in light of these considerations. Every culture has its understanding of what is logical. It is obvious that cultures differ greatly on the ways they conceptualize their settings. This is at the heart of "tribalness" or ethnicity.

A. *Philosophical Presuppositions and Conversion*

The philosophical presuppositions provide a culture and individuals within that culture with a ready-made key to an understanding of the nature of the universe as they conceive of it. Now we come to the question, what happens to a person's philosophical presuppositions when he is converted to belief in Jesus Christ? Or, we might ask, must these presuppositions be altered *before* authentic conversion can occur? Or do they change at conversion, or do the changes occur after conversion?

After pondering these questions for many years I am slowly coming to the conviction that they are not very relevant questions. Yet they must be addressed. I am convinced that Jesus reveals Himself meaningfully to a person "just as he is." A restructuring of the presuppositional grid is not required as a precondition for conversion.

The New Testament itself tells the story of how the Gospel
which came to one particular people, the Jews, was then
liberated from that culture so that it could be accepted by all
men.   The thrust of the Scriptures is clear; the evangelist must
assume that the receptor's philosophical presuppositions form
the context in which he will comprehend Jesus Christ, at least
initially.   Jesus' own incarnation is the basic model.   Paul,
in his evangelistic methodology, grasped the concept clearly.
His "sermon on Mars Hill" which was preached in the heart of
Hellenism was couched in Hellenistic rationalist presuppositions.
In contrast, his approach to the Ephesian occultists appealed
to the miraculous.   The philosophical presupposition of these
two audiences varied greatly, consequently Paul's philosophical
encouchment of the Gospel was different.

It is quite helpful to remember that the Bible is not a monocultural book.   The Old Testament does have a basic presuppositional undergirding, especially the Pentateuch, but the New
Testament is a different genre of literature.   It is a collection of missionary literature written for more than one culture.   It is not very helpful, in point of fact, to speak about
"the culture" of the Bible.   It is more accurate to talk of the
"cultures" of the Bible, recognizing their plurality.

The story plot of the Acts traces how Christ's presence became
meaningful in both the Hebrew and Hellenistic cultures.   This
happened in such a way that Hebrew Christians were permitted to
retain their Hebrew philosophical presuppositions while at the
same time the Hellenistic Christians experienced Jesus Christ's
presence in their own world.   As I understand it, neither
culture's concepts of time, space, epistemology, or ontology had
to be altered significantly as a precondition to conversion.

In order to grasp the consequences of this problem it may be
helpful to consider briefly each category.   With regard to time
concepts, the least we can conclude is that Jesus Christ can be
meaningfully experienced by cultures which hold to a great
variety of time concepts.   Furthermore it would appear that
cultures need not move toward a linear, quantitative concept of
time in order to believe or grow in faith.   However, in the
process of learning more of the Gospel they may well discover
that by deliberately historicising their minds they can gain new
and important insights in which case they may expand their
understanding of time to include the linear approach as well.
This could be flipped for us Westerners.

Professor John Mbiti recognized the disparity of the time
concepts between Western missionaries and the Kenya Akamba and
the problems of communication which resulted.   In my own studies,
by employing Kuria concepts of time which are basically

relational rather than sequential or temporal I discovered that many previously fogged areas of the Scriptures became refreshingly clear. I then found myself unsatisfied with a purely linear approach. I recognize that Hebrew history and many aspects of New Testament eschatology are stretched across a linear time frame but I also have discovered that God redeems persons who experience time relationally.[1]

We could likewise contrast space concepts. When I as a Westerner think of space I think materialistically. I imagine space as that which contains matter in a variety of shapes and densities. To think otherwise requires effort. I must almost do a "double take" every time I am required to think of that same space as the habitation of spiritual beings. It is not easy to step out of a chemistry class in Philadelphia and go to Sunday School. The Scriptures of the Sunday School admittedly pose a "spirited" universe while Western man tends to conceive of space materialistically. Maybe in this area the Kuria need to shift less than the Westerners in order to understand the Scriptures.

But the truth of the matter is, both cultures can and do experience Jesus Christ within the context of their own understandings. By communicating with one another in love they can enlarge one another's horizons but when it is all said and done the Kuria Christian remains undeniably Kuria in his perception of space and the Germanic American perceives of space as a Germanic American.

In the areas of ontology and epistemology the same can be said. Individuals within these cultures will inevitably respond to the Gospel in terms of their own philosophical presuppositions. Through painstaking effort they may stretch their categories somewhat but the "stretch" will be slight. The findings of cultural anthropologists generally support the premise that at the philosophical presuppositional level shift occurs—very slowly.

B. *The Powers and Conversion*

We now move to a different level within the world view. It is in the area of cosmology in which the "powers" are identified and classified. Each culture conceives of a variety of sources of power which impinge upon it. These are local and exotic, malevolent and benevolent, imminent and distant, demanding and indulging, complicated or simple, tractable or intractable, etc. This, too, is learned quite early in life. Emotions are communicated when reference is made to this power and that. He is to be feared, she to be trusted, never do this or that power will affect you, etc.

Cultures go to great lengths to provide each person with a
glossary of powers and one does himself harm by not taking
proper heed of the wisdom and experience of the group. These
powers are also in conflict with one another at times, at times
they reinforce one another. The constellation keeps changing.
The point is a cosmology of power sources is at the very center
of a culture's existence. This is such a critical area for the
discussion of this paper that I place it right at the center
of the world view.

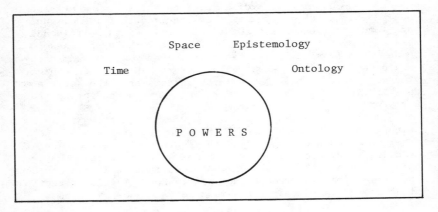

Figure II

When a person is converted to Jesus Christ, what happens at
the level of the "powers"? I am quite convinced that for a
sustained conversion experience a person must elevate Jesus
Christ to a position of Lordship in his power constellation and
keep him there through Christ-honoring living. In fact unless
this happens little else really matters. This will come clear
later.

No matter where in the world a person lives, when he is converted he must make Jesus Christ Lord in order to sustain that
conversion. No culture is amenable to Jesus Christ, even in the
so-called "Christian" west, for even in those cultures anti-
Christly powers are at work and are in fact controlling powers
in large areas of cultures.

Here we are at the crux of the issue. In order for true and
sustained conversion to occur, Jesus Christ must receive His
elevated place in the cosmology of the person as He is elevated

in heaven. Failing this, dualisms persist, syncretism is advanced, and Jesus is reduced to simply an additional helpful source of power.

Is there a rearrangement of the power structures in a person's experience as a result of conversion? I believe that the answer to this question is clearly "yes." In fact one might well scrutinize a so-called conversion experience in which Jesus Christ is not exalted above all powers. He may simply be placed along side of, and somewhat equal in power with, traditional powerful spirits and personalities. Nowhere does belief in Christ eradicate all other powers, rather it places Him above all powers. It is not easy to ascertain the place of Jesus Christ in another person's world, and sometimes not even in one's own. Most of the world's Christians would score high on a doctrinal questionnaire as to the person of Christ. The test comes, however, in times of crisis when we require power or knowledge which we feel Jesus withholds. Such crises bring out one's true cosmology. Conversion which does not include an experiential elevation of Jesus Christ above all other powers may well be short lived unless nurture or spiritual revival can quickly move in and correct the misconception.

C. *Kinetology and Conversion*

Clustered around the central core of "Powers" we can envision another layer for which we will invent the term "kinetology" to denote the science of the ways powers interact or the way power works.

Kinetology is almost philosophical because it is closely allied to a culture's presuppositions. It emerges from the philosophical framework, providing a scheme for understanding cause and effect. Cultures are survival conscious and we know that if we do not constantly analyze events to determine cause and effect connections we are in danger of annihilation. All cultures believe that it is important to discover why things happen in order to better control their destiny. This is the purpose of kinetology, the dynamics of power.

Kinetics defines the nature of power, as perceived by that culture, how power operates, the concept of life-force **and vital** protection, curses, blessings, the dynamics of how events are caused and controlled and how power moves effectively from source to point of motion.

Does conversion alter a person's learned kinetological under-standings? I am quite convinced that this must be answered in the negative. One exception might be an absolute materialist who could never even in his wildest moments imagine the

existence of a disembodied person in any shape or form. This
person now puts his mind to believing in Jesus Christ as a living
Presence.   I would presume that such a person, in order to
believe, must come to terms with the spiritual nature of the
universe, an exercise which would require a significant shift in
his kinetological orientation. Or he might simply believe in a
historical Jesus who once lived but ceased to exist at death.
Normally a person's prebelief kinetology will be the context in
which he experiences the Gospel.

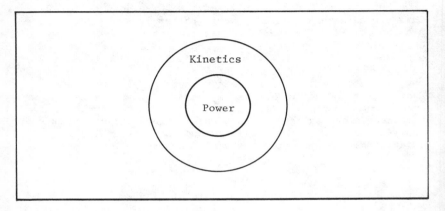

Figure III

Many Western missionaries to Africa have failed to comprehend
the significance of this fact.   That was a mistake because most
of Africa's cultures have elaborate systems which help them to
detect cause and effect relationships which in turn enable them
to incorporate powers into their own life patterns.   Too often
Western missionaries presented the Gospel in such a way that it
had very little to do with the kinetological world of the people.
It was assumed, perhaps, that Jesus should be conceptualized and
not actualized in terms of power. If Jesus is not part of a
person's cause and effect conceptions, He remains an interesting
but irrelevant figure.

I am convinced that Africa's sensitivity to the kinetological
world has beautifully prepared them to comprehend Jesus whose
Name is above every name. I further believe that many Westerners
miss much of God's provision in Christ by failing to grasp Jesus
as "the power of God unto salvation."

D. *Cultural Themes and Conversion*

Philosophical presuppositions and an understanding of powers give rise to cultural themes which are in turn embodied in myth systems which exist in the mind as concepts. To illustrate, an American German theme which arises from our presuppositions is the theme of thrift. This encourages the accumulation of quality products and their protection. It includes a certain disdain for the free-spenders, the non-savers, and people who do not take care of what they accumulate. Many other myths key on this theme which laud work and deplore laziness in culturally conceived terms. Our myths are imbedded in almost every aspect of our lives.

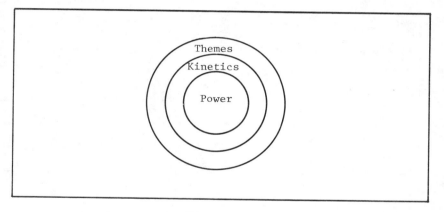

Figure IV

What happens to a person's cultural themes and myths when converted? It is my experience that thematic or mythical shift is a slow process indeed, unless the myth in question is in direct conflict with a theme of the Scriptures which the convert esteems of major importance. Themes such as love and compassion for all men which are also biblical themes will be strengthened and themes such as give rise to avarice and pride will be rejected. For example, among the Wakuria, their strong fertility theme conflicts with the New Testament theme of self-sacrifice, which permits denying spouse, children, and property, if it should be the clear will of God to do so as it was for Jesus and for the Apostle Paul. In such cases the believers must clearly decide to which themes they are going to give priority. Having said this I must hasten to say that prevailing themes, even after conversion, may well reflect some aspects of the pre-conversion ones.

In anthropological theory it is assumed that any one culture will seek to integrate its themes. It is highly unlikely that a culture will be able to sustain at the same level of importance two equal competing themes. One will take dominance.

But thematic shift will not produce sustained Christianity if there has not been a prior adjustment to the "Powers" level. The surest answer to syncretism is to attack the problem at the "Powers" level and not at the thematic level.

E. *Values and Conversion*

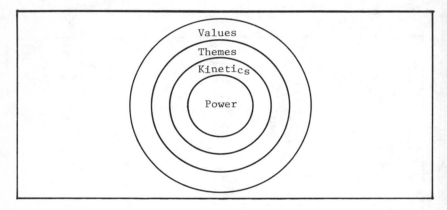

Figure V

As we move to the fourth, the value level, more shift can be expected, in fact is necessary, as a result of Christian conversion. Ordinarily the values grow out of the thematic/mythical matrix and are normally consistent with the dominant cultural themes. Yet within a culture considerable latitude is permitted for differences in value orientation. In fact several quite different value systems may stem from the same commonly held theme. One of them among the Wakuria, for example, is the theme of egalitarianism. Upon conversion, a person of this culture might find this theme reinforced by the Christian doctrine of human equality and the worth of all men. This could conceivably result in the new believer's rejection of one of his culture's myths, that Wakuria should only marry Wakuria.

We might rightly expect some degree of value shift to occur when a person believes. This squares with social change theory which acknowledges that change occurs at the value level before

it does at the inner levels. Cultures, as individuals, can
usually tolerate considerable internal conflict at this level.
At the value level a culture tests the non-traditional ideas
which penetrate its periphery.

We do well to pause at this point and ask a very bothersome
question. When value shift occurs, in which direction will that
shift occur and why? We would normally assume that the shift
would be away from previously held values to the values clearly
expressed in the Scriptures. When a transcultural advocate
(missionary) is involved the shift is probably toward the
"outsider's" value orientation. There are several reasons for
this. A convert is usually well disposed toward the converter
and in symbolizing his new allegiance to Christ may well espouse
some of the outsider's values. Or, it might be that in the mind
of the new believer there lingers the assumption that the
advocate has filtered the anti-Christian factors out of his own
cultural experience and so his culture is a tried and tested
variety of Christian living. So why not imitate at least certain
aspects of it? What often happens is that new believers swap
some of their own cultural values for some of the cultural
values of the advocate. This often serves, incidentally, to
isolate the Christians from their own cultures, a position which
to them seems reasonable because they desire a separate identity
in the early stages of the establishment of a Christian community
in a dominantly non-believing society. Then, too, persons and
communities desire new sources of power, in this case the
advocate's. They therefore develop power linkages with the
advocate, symbolized by a yielding to the advocate's value
orientation. Ideally, the Christian community should, through
meditating on the Scriptures, move their value matrix toward the
values that they see in the Scriptures. However, this is usually
the result of nurture and not of conversion. More of this in
the second section of the paper.

The most obvious metaphysical changes will occur at the value
level and hopefully the change that does occur will be toward
biblical values and not simply toward the values of the
advocate's culture.

F. *Symbols, Ritual, Behavior, and Conversion*

Up to this point we have been dealing with the conceptual
aspects of culture, the world view. But culture does not remain
in the head, it must be formalized in life. Both the metaphysical and the cosmological beliefs will find expression in a
multitude of symbols, rituals, and in everyday behavior. The
process can be diagramed.

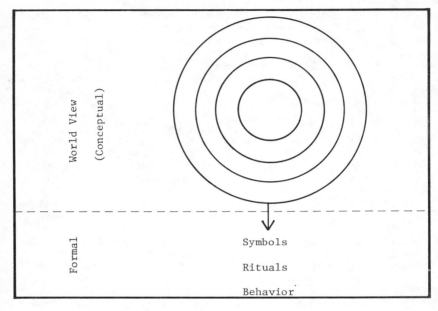

World View
(Conceptual)

Formal

Symbols

Rituals

Behavior

Figure VI

Upon conversion the most obvious changes occur at the formal level. People find ways of symbolizing their newly found relationship with Christ. This is understood by all. The catch is, change at this level may be inconsequential. In the minds of many, a conversion experience can be accomplished by a substitution of one set of rituals and symbols for another. Unless there is a significant shift in the appropriate areas at the conceptual level the formal changes will probably not be sustained.

In summary, as a result of Christian conversion in any culture, we can reasonably expect change to occur at the power level, the value level, the theme level, and the formal level, hopefully in that order. Change at any level has some effect upon all other areas but not equally so. A change at the formal level does not necessarily trigger a change at the world-view level even though this is often the process one is tempted to rely on to effect change. A change at the core of power hierarchy, however, can and does send shock waves through the entire system.

IV. CHANGING CULTURAL EXPECTATIONS AND CONVERSION

When Christianity is introduced into a culture by advocates
of another culture several distinct stages may be defined. As a
small community of Christians emerges, having seen Christianity
modeled by the foreign advocate living among them, they usually
develop an antagonistic stand *vis a vis* their pre-Christian
culture. Rejection might best describe this stage.

A. *The Rejection Phase*

Presumably cultural rejection is seen by the minority as a
way to enhance their chances of survival as a group. For as
they reject their own culture they run the risk of depowering
themselves for which they compensate by laying power conduits to
the foreign advocates.

The new Christian community does not reject its pre-Christian
culture in its entirety, rather it selects very carefully what
it wishes to reject and what it can live with. It is still a
mystery to me how the group decides what they want to reject.
They must in some way detect what will most obviously compromise
their newly discovered understanding of the nature and power of
Jesus Christ and the Christian Gospel and will guard against it.

In East Africa I discovered that the initial confrontation
had to do with the power of Christ contrasted to the power of
the other spirits, especially the spirits of the ancestors. Here
the battle was joined. In order to draw clear lines of demar-
cation between their belief in the supremacy of Jesus Christ as
a Spirit and their previously held beliefs about the power of
other spirits they disassociated themselves from any rituals in
which the ancestral spirits were consulted or even assumed to be
meaningfully present. They had great difficulty in bringing
themselves to even attend traditional funerals or the traditional
puberty rituals which were clearly part of the ancestor cult of
the group. No doubt they were encouraged by the foreign
advocates to move in this direction yet had they refused to do
so there would have been little that the foreign advocate could
have done about it, except, of course, to withhold some power.

I find it interesting that even the paraphernalia employed in
the former rituals connected with the ancestral spirits were
often rejected. The advocates had some difficulty accepting
this cultural stance. I was among those missionaries who thought
it unfortunate that drums were abandoned for so long in regular
Christian worship but I see now that it has taken a long time
to "launder" drums of their association with pre-Christian
ritual. Now in many churches drums are being utilized. The
elders understandably squirm a little because they are closer

to the time when drums were contaminated with pre-Christian associations which were anathema to the Christian faith.

During the Rejection Phase the semi-isolated community, having deliberately cut itself off from many of its traditional sources of power, lay power conduits to the exotic culture represented by the foreign advocate. Having detected some potentially beneficial power sources in the foreign advocate, the new community deliberately built cultural bridges to him. They participated in his ritual and symbolic life to a great extent, hoping thereby not only to demonstrate rejection of much in their traditional culture but also to signify that they were laying new power conduits which would ultimately make the traditional power sources inconsequential.

This process of realigning the power conduits explains why there seems to be an affirmation of the exotic culture and a concurrent denial of the traditional culture.

The new Christian community detects a fountainhead of power in the advocate but does not fully discern the difference between spiritual, sociological, scientific, organizational or other categories of power resident in the advocate. We should hasten to say that the advocate does not either, even though he may suppose he does. The new Christian community may link with the advocate in what the advocate might term secondary sources of power such as education, technology, and management, and miss what is to the advocate the secret of power, a vital living relationship with Jesus Christ as revealed in the Scripture and as experienced by the church for centuries. Some advocates become so incensed by this that they refuse to encourage a coupling in these secondary categories, lest they be accused of making "rice" converts. This concern must be applauded but who in the world has sorted out the "acceptable" motivation for becoming a Christian? I fear that the advocate often withholds from others what to him seems self-evident for he too experiences Christ in a power context which is none too clear to him but which is there nonetheless.

During the rejection phase the local Christian community experiences quite a flood of cultural innovations whose origins are exotic. Many of the new symbols and rituals are borrowed directly from the advocate's culture. This further isolates the Christian community because a gap develops between the code lexicon of that community and the traditional one. This interferes with good communication.

During the rejection phase the new community sees itself in contradistinction to the traditional culture, therefore new believers are expected to exhibit the proper anti-traditional stance. In this case much emphasis is given to the parts of the baptism formula which have to do with the renunciation of the past and the promise to begin a new life in a new community of faith. In this context it is not surprising that so much is made of the ritual of renaming. For many this was and perhaps still is the public demonstration of a shift of sociological base from the traditional society to an exotic one. The renaming consolidated the conversion stance, perhaps even more than the ritual of baptism itself.

Persons who are converted in the context of a rejection phase will have cultural expectations placed upon them which do not apply, at least not as markedly, in later phases. They usually accept Christ and reject their traditional world at one and the same time.

In passing I might venture the assertion that Christians must always see themselves different relative to something. This is especially true for first generation churches which require some cultural self-understanding which enables them to perceive of themselves as different. Usually first generational movements deliberately envision themselves as a counterculture.

The effect of this radical cultural shift can result not only in isolation but the dominant society may encapsulate the new community so that in fact the Christian community is forced to become a sub-culture which then has difficulty communicating with the dominant culture. This process of the establishment of a sub-culture may contribute to a Christian community's stability but it also creates genuine barriers to evangelism.

If a person is converted when the church is in this phase his colleagues will know it because he too will gladly participate in the symbols of rejection.

B. *Accommodation Phase*

Various sources ultimately come to play upon a Christian community both from within and without to effect a shift in their culture stance. When the prevailing national mood, for example, is integrative rather than innovative, as it is in many parts of Africa today, a "stand-offish" group like many Christian communities is made to feel quite uncomfortable. Many African churches have therefore moved into a new phase in which they attempt to accommodate themselves somewhat to the national or ethnic expectations.

This move toward accommodation often accompanies a renewed interest in evangelism on the part of the churches. Since evangelism is basically an exercise in communication it is clear that some of the "petty separation" must go. And so the sharp edges of radicalism are dulled, some cultural innovations which were a bone of contention are modified and the Christian community, in a sense, rejoins society, perhaps two generations after the initial rejection.

The theological perils of this phase include the temptation toward syncretism. For this is the time when the Christian community tries to integrate its own themes, values, and cosmology with that of the traditionalists. Precarious though this period may be it is nevertheless quite a significant one if the Christian community is to evangelize effectively.

During this phase the power conduits are relaid. Many channels which had formerly gone to the exotic culture are now directed toward local power sources. This explains in part why political rapprochement marks this era and why a moratorium is called on the aggressive cultural expansionism of impinging cultures.

Persons who are converted during this era are expected to be respectable citizens as well as keen Christians. If the prevailing mood is accommodation they will, of course, display signs of this attitude by, perhaps, getting involved in social concerns issues, entering politics as Christians or by empowering the Christian community by some other means, usually laying the conduits to local power sources.

C. *Reestablishment of Identity*

A third stage is marked by a renewed desire on the part of the group to come to terms with the dominant culture in a relevant, more dynamic way in which case symbols of separation are again sought. During the first, the rejection, stage the foreign advocate assisted the new community to determine the proper cultural battles, so to speak, which were then symbolized. In the third stage the Christian communities decide for themselves what battles they feel compelled to fight. Usually they choose some social evil which they feel threatens their Christian values. They seek to express their realigned boundary of separation by employing symbols which everyone in the culture is expected to understand. This is generally a period of reexamining the symbols and rituals.

This era is usually noted for its potential of dividing churches because entire Christian communities, due to vested

interests, etc., are unable or unwilling to move at the same
speed. The outcome is usually a new fringe rejection movement
on one hand and the opposite fringe, a more complete accommodation movement, on the other. The accommodation movements tend to
fuzz their boundaries with the dominant society, laying their
power conduits to it without apology. The community of rejection
withdraws many of its power conduits from the dominant culture
and turns these conduits in on itself, hence feeding on its own
internal resources. It may or may not relay conduits to external
sources because by this stage they have become conditioned to
their own style of Christian life and so do not feel compelled
to move very far beyond themselves.

The rejection community is recognizably a participant in the
total culture's ethos yet with a difference. They reject
specific parts of that culture but they do this by employing
meaningful local symbols so that the not-yet-believing people
can see clearly what the Christian community's agenda is. In
this way it differs from the rejection community in stage one.

As the rejection community readjusts its stance *vis a vis*
the dominant culture it becomes a sub-culture. When a person
is converted he is expected to join this group, whether he is a
child of the group or is reared in another home. He is expected
to display signs of conversion by submitting himself to the
discipline of this sub-culture. Where in phase one conversion
was supposed to exhibit itself in a liberation from traditional
culture, phase three determines that conversion should
"domesticate" a person culturally. Denominations, or parts
thereof, which have taken this route relate baptism to puberty
ritual, that is, they assume that the converted one will join
their sub-culture.

Conversion for the group which moves in the direction of even
more accommodation to the dominant culture is not marked with
such radical intent. In fact, other than participating in
certain required rituals from time to time and paying their dues
regularly, nothing much is expected further. Converts in these
groups tend to take a line of accommodation in their own lives.

These three stages are not always generational. They can all
be operating at one and the same time, yet if a particular
Christian community is examined it will be found that such a
sequential development is not unusual.

What are, therefore, the universal signs of conversion? This
question is vexed by cultural evolution and social change. When
an Amish young man in Eastern Pennsylvania in U.S.A. is converted he knows at once how his community will expect him to exhibit

his conversion, in fact his conversion occurs in the context of
cultural expectations. If a Roman Catholic in Eastern Pennsylvania is converted, an entirely different set of cultural expectations come into play.

V. SUMMARY

We have examined the phenomena of Christian conversion from
two angles--the first by asking what occurs in a person's world
view upon conversion and the second by tracing the way cultural
expectations may change as the Christian community readjusts
its stance *vis a vis* the dominant culture in which it exists.

The cultural and psychological variables which go into the
believers' understanding of conversion vary widely. It is
impossible to make very many general statements. Yet a few may
be helpful.

(1) Conversion takes place in the context of cultural expectations and is greatly influenced by the fact.

(2) Unless Jesus Christ enters the convert's cosmology in a
meaningful way as a primary source of power the experience of
conversion will be brought into question as alternative power
sources dominate life.

(3) It is presumptuous for persons of one culture to dictate
the "normal" cultural signs of conversion for another culture.
The culture in question is equipped by the Scriptures and the
Holy Spirit to make these judgments.

(4) Even within one culture the signs of conversion may
differ, depending upon the extent of the formation of Christian
sub-cultures within it.

(5) Conversion must be symbolized. The symbolization is
determined largely by the particular group the person is in.

(6) While conversion may be accompanied by a significant shift
in behavior the pre-conversion culturally defined philosophical
presuppositions will be minimally effected.

In summary, how to get converted and how to witness about
the experience are largely culturally controlled.

---

1. Lesslie Newbigin in *Honest Religion for Secular Man* insists
that any non-linear time framework will ultimately weaken the
Christian faith because historicity is basic to the Judeo-Christian theology. I would, at the same time, like to caution
against the Western tendency to disparage any time concepts
which are not linear and sequential.

10

Conversion and Culture: A Theological Perspective with Reference to Korea

Harvie M. Conn

This chapter seeks to address a complex of questions related to conversion. Is it possible to speak of a conversion to Christ if the person's worldview--which is said to be culturally framed-- has not been modified in the process? What is the proper rela- tion between the Gospel and the person's worldview? Is the Gospel simply accommodated into the person's cultural worldview? When can we speak of repentance being meaningful and adequate in relation to the person's cultural value system and worldview? What are the implications of the answers to these questions for the communicating of the Gospel cross-culturally?

We will seek to deal with these questions by an integration of theological perceptions with anthropological insights. Our goal will be a cross-cultural model heavily indebted to biblical theology understood as the history of special revelation (Vos 1948:23). We do so conscious of the highly selective character of paradigm/models and the humility and patience they demand both from those who analyze existing ones and those who create new ones (Kraft 1977:44-57). Especially is this true of theologically-oriented models where it is all too easy to transfer the inerrancy of the Bible into a mythical inerrancy of our own.

1. *Eschatological dimensions of conversion*

The hazards of this process are amply demonstrated by previous theological formulations of conversion. Calvin used the term as a comprehensive designation for the entire renewal of man. And that same fluidity in understanding the application of redemption seems evident almost a hundred years later in the Westminster Confession, the last of the great Reformation creeds. Though the Confession makes no use of the formal term "conversion," its arrangement of the various topics later identified with what has come to be called *ordo salutis* is not structured around the biblical categories in some strictly chronological or compartmentally logical succession. Rather "it sets forth first the phases which are the actions of God—Calling, Justification, Adoption, Sanctification (X-XIII)—and then those which are concerned with human response—Faith, Repentance, Good Works, Perseverance, Assurance of Grace (XIV-XXIII)" (Murray 1976:320).

In the years that followed, under the growing influence of pietism, mysticism, later Puritan preparationism (Allison 1966; Pettitt 1966), and moralism, the emphasis shifted to individual appropriation of the salvation given in Christ, in preference to questions about the history of salvation (*historia salutis*). Conversion came to be understood as an act of application distinct from such categories as justification and sanctification (Ridderbos 1975:14). Even within the Reformed community, under the growing domination of a Protestant scholasticism that insisted on logical, differentially precise theological categorizations, questions arose over the relation of conversion to the other steps in the plan of salvation. In this process, the meaning of the term was narrowed to fit discussions that distinguished between a *conversio actualis prima,* a *conversio continua,* and a *conversio actualis secunda.* That is, conversion took on a more constrictive shape in order to meet the demands of the emerging *ordo salutis* model. "True conversion" was oriented, whether by Arminian or Calvinist, around individual concerns. Examples of "national conversion" in the Old Testament were dismissed by theologians like Louis Berkhof as "merely of the nature of moral reformations. They may have been accompanied with some real religious conversions of individuals, but fell far short of the true conversion of all those that belonged to the nation" (Berkhof 1949:483).

No doubt, the theological motivation behind these concerns was the preservation of the divine initiative in "turning to God from idols" (1 Thess. 1:9), an initiative reflected in the fact that in the New Testament the verb commonly rendered as "convert" (*epistrephō*), is usually in the middle or passive voice (Matt. 13:15, Mark 4:12, Luke 22:32, John 12:40, Acts 3:19, 28:27). At the same time, we suggest that the formulation of the conversion model was being culturally conditioned by western demands for clearcut, cognitive conceptualizations and an individual-centered view of culture. In the process, the architectonic lines of the redemptive-historical, and in particular the eschatological, character of Paul's preaching, was abused.

The current theological atmosphere seems congenial to an investigation of this cultural conditioning of the exegetical history relative to conversion. Discussions particularly within the Reformed community have become very vigorous over the adequacy of the acculturated *ordo salutis* model. Geerhardus Vos, as early as 1930, in his discussion of "the interaction between eschatology and soteriology," saw the traditional *ordo salutis* categories of justification and regeneration in their broader dimensions, that is, as elements in the present realization of the Age-to-come, inaugurated by Christ's resurrection (Vos 1930: 42-61). Conversion in Paul, as Vos saw it, became "a species of resurrection" (Vos 1930:45).

More recently, the Dutch Calvinist, Herman Ridderbos, has pressed the question even more strongly. Even with respect to the subjective renewal of the individual believer, Paul's approach, he says, "is not of an anthropological, but of a redemptive-historical, eschatological, that is to say, of a christological and pneumatological nature. . . . The result is that in Paul's preaching there is no such thing as a systematic development of the *ordo salutis*, a detailed doctrine of the anthropological application of salvation. The cause for this is not only that the character of Paul's doctrine is not 'systematic' in the scientific sense of the word, but above all that his viewpoint is a different one" (Ridderbos 1975:205-206). Richard B. Gaffin, Jr., of Westminster Theological Seminary, is now asking how this legitimate distinction of Ridderbos' between history of salvation and order of salvation must affect the very method of our doing theology. While properly fearful of Ridderbos' tendency to see these alternatives as mutually exclusive rather than complementary (Gaffin 1968:232), he also credits Ridderbos with an "insight of a magnitude that requires recasting not only eschatology but also the other loci as traditionally conceived, especially Christology, soteriology, both accomplished and applied, and ecclesiology" (Gaffin 1976:50). We anticipate the publication of Gaffin's forthcoming title, *The Centrality of the Resurrection: A Study in Pauline Soteriology*, as taking the discussion even further.

Our own desire at this stage is to stress the importance of this eschatological dimension of the conversion experience in terms of its cross-cultural implications. Western theological discussion in the past, not sensitive to these broader eschato-

logical dimensions and oriented by a cultural overlay of individualism, has divided over whether conversion is a definite crisis in life or may not also be a very gradual one. Even the
helpful defense by Alan Tippett of "conversion as a dynamic process" (Tippett 1977:218-220) does not altogether escape the
fruits of the past. Seeking to modify his own earlier paradigm
of conversion by allowing for a "period of maturity" beyond what
he calls "the period of incorporation," he calls for a "point of
consummation" between these two periods which, he says, "should
be a *precise experience* of the work of the Spirit within man."

Tippett's amplification of his model does not flow from his
theological formulary but from the question raised by his own
field of study: How is it possible for so many village groups
to abandon Christianity after, say, 20 years of post-baptismal
Christian instruction? This is a question every non-Wesleyan
must also ask with equal sensitivity. But we fear Tippett's
formulation may be controlled by a theological controversy of
the past, partially indebted to a western cultural overload of
individualism which demanded that conversion be "a precise experience" of the individual, not simply a personal process. This
overload may also form part of the background for the theological controversy over whether conversion may ever be repeated.

Our effort is not to excuse the Calvinist from blame in this
area. There are many in the Reformed community, like Berkhof,
who insist that "if we take the word 'conversion' in its most
specific sense, it denotes a momentary change and not a process
like sanctification" (Berkhof 1949:485). We suggest that this
emphasis on the "most specific sense" of conversion accompanies
a reduction of other biblical usages of the term to serve the
individualistic orientation demanded by the culturally patterned
ordo salutis model. Thus, Berkhof continues, conversion "is a
change that takes place once and that cannot be repeated, though,
as stated above, the Bible also speaks of the Christian's return
to God, after he has fallen into sin, as conversion."

Our purpose in this discussion is not to escape important
theological questions raised in the past or even to suggest they
are inappropriate. It is rather to draw attention to the fact
that such questions cannot be answered adequately until conversion as "turning to God" is seen in its basic, structural relation as a sign of the age of salvation promised in the days of
the old covenant and now beginning to be fulfilled in Christ.
That sign character is displayed, in the words of Warfield (1952:
362), in "the great change experienced by him who is translated
from the power of darkness into the kingdom of the Son of God's
love" (Col. 1:13). In describing that change from its God-ward
side, a whole group of terms are used in the New Testament
(*gennēthēnai; anōthen; ek tou theou; ek tou pneumatos; palin-*

genesia; etc.). Describing its manward side, says Warfield, are such terms as *metanoein* and *epistrephein*. "We must set over against *metanoia* as the inward word its complement in *epistrophē* as an outward word, denoting the changed course of life" (Warfield n.d.:95). In these passages, Warfield shows a sensitivity to the language as complementary and not simply consequential, that draws them out of the *ordo salutis* usage current today. At the same time, without making them individualistic, he sees their focus on personal, inner change commensurate with gracious initiation and consequent admission to the new day of the Kingdom come in Christ.

Warfield's emphasis in this discussion is on conversion as process, "and a process which has two sides. It is on the one side a change of the mind and heart, issuing in a new life. It is on the other side a renewing from on high issuing in a new creation" (Warfield 1952:369). The entirety of that process, viewed as the work of God in the soul, is what the Scriptures designate as "renewal." In other imagery, it is a change of vesture, the process of laying aside the soiled clothing of the old Adam, and putting on the clean raiment of the new Adam (Eph. 4:24; Col. 3:9-10). It is a metamorphosis, in which the subjects become transformed beings by the renewing of their minds, thus being freed more and more from the fashion of this world (Rom. 12:1-2). Even the fact that repentance can be distinguished from its decisive deeds of expression reflects the fundamental nature of conversion as change-process: "Repentance is known by its fruits, but it is not its fruits. John called on his hearers to show their repentance by their deeds: 'Bring forth, therefore, fruits worthy of repentance' (Luke 3:8, cf. Matt. 3:8)" (Warfield n.d.: 94).

More recently, there have been several efforts to model this process in terms of anthropological and communication insights. The paradigm of James Engel and Wilbert Norton is finding wide usage in the evangelical community as an effort to diagram the process in terms of a communication model. The intent of the model is to affirm that "each person's spiritual journey is a lifelong decision process" (Engel-Norton 1975:46) and to provide some preliminary sequencing of the steps that represent the structure of that process.

While this model of the conversion process is much to be appreciated, there are certain deficiencies. By making "God's role" and "man's response" virtually parallel, the Engel-Norton model can be interpreted as downplaying the divine origin and initiation of man's "turning from and turning to." This would seem to be affirmed by the fact that conversion ("repentance and faith in Christ") is placed in the paradigm before "regeneration," the verbal symbol in the New Testament of God's gracious

GOD'S ROLE	COMMUNICATORS' ROLE		MAN'S RESPONSE
General Revelation		-8	Awareness of Supreme Being but no effective Knowledge of Gospel
Conviction	Proclamation	-7	Initial Awareness of Gospel
		-6	Awareness of Fundamentals of Gospel
		-5	Grasp of Implications of Gospel
		-4	Positive Attitude toward Gospel
		-3	Personal Problem Recognition
		-2	DECISION TO ACT
	Persuasion	-1	Repentance and Faith in Christ
REGENERATION			NEW CREATURE
Sanctification	Follow-Up	+1	Post Decision Evaluation
		+2	Incorporation into Body
	Cultivation	+3	Conceptual and Behavioral Growth
		+4	Communion with God
		+5	Stewardship
		.	Reproduction
		.	Internally (gifts, etc.) Externally (witness, social action, etc.)

ETERNITY

(Engel-Norton 1975:45)

infusing of life. Even more pertinent to our topic, conversion
is apparently restricted to only one step in the process, one act
of the eight-stage progression toward what the authors designate
as "regeneration."

Thus, the model is ultimately self-defeating. It betrays its
western acculturation by isolating several facets of the conversion process and arranging them in individual, sequential, com-
partmentalized units. Not only is conversion restricted to
simply one stage on the chart, it is also placed on the negative
side of the chart. To illustrate the same tendency from the plus
side of the chart, "sanctification" appears to be limited to a
category following regeneration and conversion. Such a narrow
focus makes it impossible for the model to deal adequately with
the wider usage of the term in the New Testament. In Hebrews,
for example, sanctification ordinarily (an exception might be
Heb. 12:14) includes within its orbit much of the forensic element associated by theologians with the Pauline concept of justification (Vos 1956:122-123). The comprehensive, complementary
character of much of the New Testament language relative to
sanctification, supplied by its eschatological character, is
thus lost (Poythress 1976).

Again, this same problem is apparent in the model's +1, +2,
+3, etc., description of our growth in Christ subsequent to the
new birth. These are evidently to be seen as sequential, just
as steps -8 to -1 are sequential. However, it may very well be
that the steps in growth are not sequential but complementary
and parallel.

Further, their manifestation will be radically different in
different cultures, depending on the worldview in which conversion takes place. The model could be taken to imply that conversion begins the process of worldview change. But if so, it
doesn't take account of how the change process will vary from
culture to culture. Thus, in an animistic culture, the earliest,
most prominent shift in worldview, subsequent to the beginning
of our new life in the Kingdom of God, might very well be a
sense of communion with God (+4 on the chart), in response and
contrast to the fears of supernatural powers implicit in animism.
Biernatzki and his colleagues seem to write of early Catholic
conversions in Korea this way: "Without ignoring the role of
supernatural faith, it seems reasonable to suppose that they
initially turned to Catholicism to seek consolation and refuge
from their earthly suffering in much the same way that their
pagan counterparts sought shelter and salvation in animism, popular Buddhism, or in the new religions which bloomed in such pro-
fusion during the troubled final decades of the Yi dynasty"
(Biernatzki, Im, and Min 1975:22-23). Similarly George Paik
describes the experience of early Protestant converts in Korea:

"There was a fellowship among converts that was attractive to an outsider. The Christians were sympathetic toward each other and stood together in sorrow and joy" (Paik 1929:284).

In the same way, among those Koreans whose worldview was deeply motivated by their political and social interests, the most visible first signs of conversion might carry a political flavor not even listed on the Engel-Norton chart. Yi Seung-hoon who was suggested as a signer of the 1919 Declaration of Independence in Korea, was a dissatisfied Confucian who had "wanted, from his youth, to eliminate social differences between *yangban* and *sangnom* (high and low classes), but had no biblical conception of God as the Creator who had made all men equal" (Clark 1971:429). Clark notes, "He was first converted to popular reform, then to Christ" as he came to realize "that the Christian Church had the real power needed for the future."

Charles Kraft's modifications of the Engel-Norton paradigm is much more suitable for reflecting the complementary and culturally flavored character of conversion (Kraft 1977:613).

GENERAL AND SPECIAL REVELATIONAL INFORMATION

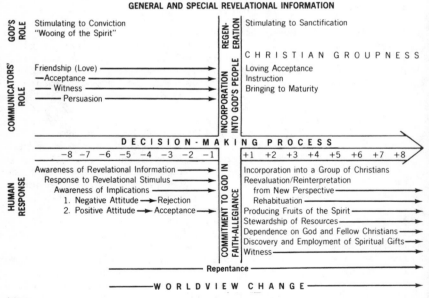

NOTES:

God's Role: Revelational information and Holy Spirit stimulus are constantly operating.

Communicators' Role: (1) Note that there are ordinarily many communicators, not just one. (2) Friendship, acceptance, witness and persuasion are all to operate simultaneously but may start at different times. (3) The communicators' role does not end at the receptor's conversion. It simply changes its function.

Human Response: (1) Note that each aspect involves the making of many decisions. (2) Since the various aspects may occur in different sequences for different people, they are not listed according to a set sequence as in the Engel-Norton scale. Those steps that seem to depend on previous steps are indented. (3) Worldview change and repentance are constants once the positive attitude decisions have begun.

Kraft refrains from a chronological succession in his paradigm
and seeks for a better way to outline what he terms "a dynamic
view of the decision-making process" of conversion (Kraft 1977:
606). He also distances his model from that of his colleague,
Alan Tippett (1973:123), which he calls "similar"; but Kraft's
differs in its focus "on the fact that the process of conversion
is made up of a multitude of (often very small) decisions by human beings in interaction with God" (Kraft 1977:606). He notes
especially that each aspect of his model "involves the making of
many decisions" and that "since the various aspects may occur in
different sequences for different people, they are not listed
according to a set sequence as in the Engel-Norton scale" (Kraft
1977:613). Unlike Engel-Norton, Kraft avoids an identification
of conversion with one point on the scale and draws an arrow
continuum for repentance that moves from the - side through the
+ side of the diagram. "Worldview change" he sees as complementary and parallel with repentance. By dissociating the + and -
scale from specific events in the conversion process, Kraft
would seem to be indicating the intensification and increasingly
meaningful nature of the change which conversion brings about in
worldview.

Perhaps the major drawback of Kraft's model is its lack of
orientation to the eschatological dimensions which demand a more
dynamic view of conversion. Without that "theological" side,
any attempt to offer a paradigm integrating biblical and anthropological insights will tend to suffer from an anthropological
captivity that so filters biblical data as to leave the impression of distortion and prooftexting. We quickly grant an equal
danger in the reverse direction, the possibility of distortion
of anthropological insights through theological filtering.

At that risk, we suggest the relationships may be seen with
the use of two mutually explanatory models, the second very much
like that of Kraft's. The first, however, is essential in providing the general framework by which the second is seen.

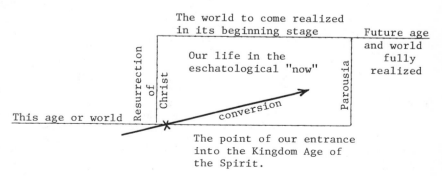

The paradigm is meant to suggest that the Christian's present
life is structured eschatologically in the cultures of this
world by his "being raised in or with Christ" (Col. 3:1). Res-
urrection--one of the most fundamental acts of eschatology--is
regarded by Paul as the Christian's present possession and position through that radical change of life by which he moves from
the kingdom of Satan to the Kingdom of God's dear son, by virtue
of his union to Christ in his death and resurrection. Thus,
while still living in the cultures of "this age or world," he
lives also through the redemptive work of Christ "in the heavenly
places," our citizenship in heaven being a present reality (Phil.
3:20).

In this model, then, "conversion" is the term used to signify
the manward response of faith in acknowledgment of the reality
of the believer's life in the Kingdom of God come in Christ, a
manward designation for the change of life demanded by the realization that the Messiah has come to begin the "new creation"
(2 Cor. 5:17). And, since the Christian lives in two worlds,
the world of "this age and that which is to come" (Eph. 1:21),
his dynamic, continuous task becomes the daily reappraisal of
his lifestyle, his worldview, his culture, to bring all more and
more into conformity to the new truth of the Kingdom come and
coming in Christ. Thus, in our model, conversion is pictured as
an arrow, moving in increasing depth from the point of entrance
into the Kingdom to the "future age" and the final "regeneration."

The Good News of the Kingdom and our place in the Kingdom
through Christ does not simply accommodate itself to our culture
and its worldview. On the contrary, our demanding task is the
accommodation of our culture and worldview to the Good News of
the Kingdom. Within this eschatological perspective, an expression of our understanding of conversion in relation to the cultural reality of "this age" can be modeled, with some modification, after the suggestions of the Kraft paradigm.

The paradigm is obviously more complex than that of Engel-
Norton. But it makes conversion less liable to the charges of
"easy believism" and the dangers that come with it. It encourages the restraint urged by Charles Taber, who asks, "When is a
Christian?" In answer, he draws attention to "the distinction
...between what *makes* a person a Christian and what *shows out-
wardly* that he is a Christian" (Taber 1976:1). Understanding
conversion as a process, and not simply an affirmation in propositional form, Taber restrains our propensity for instant perfection by reminding us that "it is not an absolute degree of
attainment that proves that one is a child of God, but discern-
able progress *in the right direction*" (Taber 1976:3).

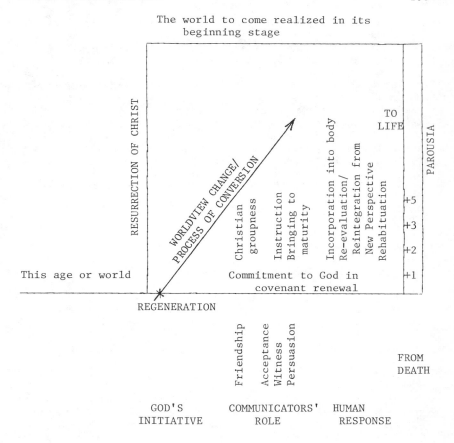

The world to come realized in its
beginning stage

GOD'S   COMMUNICATORS' HUMAN
INITIATIVE   ROLE   RESPONSE

With this paradigm, baptism regains its place as the sign and seal of our entrance into the Kingdom of God and the beginning of life-long training as Kingdom subjects (Shepherd 1976:71). As the mark of our passage from death to life, it can then be coupled directly in the Great Commission with instruction in obedience to the commands of Christ, and properly caution us that "all who have been baptized and are seeking to do the will of God are to be regarded as Christian brothers. There are those who are going to stumble along the way, but the goal is a people of God who do not stumble" (Shepherd 1976:74). Discipline, the God-given tool for discipling, does not then begin with mental excommunication from the ranks of the "converted," but becomes a matter of teaching and encouraging the brother to observe all that Christ has commanded in view of the hope that is laid up for all who love Christ and keep his commandments. So Paul, in ex-

horting the Romans to obedience, does not remind them that they
were regenerated or suggest that they might not be regenerated.
He points to their baptism and calls them to live out of that experience and the conversion it signifies (Rom. 6:1-11).

The flexibility we suggest in not nailing down conversion to
a single stage at the end of a set continuum seeks to ensure its
essence as dynamic process of "turning from and turning to." It
seeks to recognize the diversity of personal context and worldview around which and in which conversion takes place. The converts at Philippi help exemplify this diversity: "There was
Lydia whose heart 'the Lord opened.' Then, there was the slave
girl with a spirit of divination which Paul charged 'in the name
of Jesus Christ to come out of her.' In contrast to both, there
is the jailor 'about to kill himself.'... And finally, ...there
are the 'households' of both Lydia and the jailor" (Shank 1976:
3).

Understanding conversion as eschatological process should also
make us more alert to the ease with which syncretism may occur.
It does not wait for one particular stage in the continuum!

The enthusiastic missionary endorsement of the Korean designation, *Hananim*, as a rendering of *Theos*, illustrates the need
for sensitivity in this area. The term was apparently borrowed
from Shamanism during the period of the Protestants' early efforts. Though the term was apparently selected because of the
missionaries' tracing it too simplistically to a "primitive pure
monotheism" (Underwood 1910:103-111), translating it as "the one
Great One" (Gale 1906:78), it remained a useful point of contact.
Hananim, in the Shamanistic legend, had given life to the people
and their civilization by sending his divine son, Tan'gun, into
the world. His grandson had been the first Korean king. Comments Gale, "Immediately when the Bible is read, 'In the beginning some One created the heavens and the earth,' they answer,
'Hananim.'..."(Gale 1906:78-79). Thus it was that when the
Korean, "standing by his simple altars, where, with neither image
or spirit tablet his fathers have for generations worshipped the
God of Heaven, learns that God is a spirit and truth, he believes
that this is the God of his fathers. When still further he pur-
sues his oldest histories and reads that his most ancient Tan'gun
had built an altar in Kangwha, and there worshipped his 'Father
God,' 'the Creator,' he is more than ready to say, 'This and no
other shall be our God'" (Underwood 1910:261).

There were many benefits in the choice, besides what Underwood
called the "strong possibility" of its monotheistic implications.
If the thesis of Park Pong-bae is correct, the concept was drawn
from a Shamanism syncretized not with Buddhist pantheism but with
Confucian heaven-worship and its ethical implications of kindness

and love, filial piety, purity and chastity (Park 1970:40-46).
Some, like Yun Sung-bum, have even advocated a pseudo-Trinitarian
coloring to the Tan'gun myth from which it was drawn, perhaps
borrowed from Christianity through the impact of Nestorianism
which came to China during the seventh century.[1] In any case,
the myth and the title, *Hananim*, carried with it a social or
ethical dimension of "man for the public interest" (Park 1970:
52-53), and deep moral connotations revolving around the Confucian concept of the "mandate of heaven" (Fung 1952:30-31).

At the same time, in this very Confucian coloration lay the
seeds of syncretism. The transcendental concept implicit in the
term was a negative and escapist one, to affect both Catholic
and Protestant in Korea. Reinforced by the government persecution of Catholicism until the late nineteenth century, it gave
that church an increasingly otherworldly flavor which could make
little contribution to radical social change. This was reflected
in the strong Catholic reluctance to participate in the 1919 Independence Movement. Conversely, the moralistic humanism of the
Declaration could be (naively) endorsed by the Protestants since
the transcendental conception present in the background of the
Hananim terminology blurred any Christian distinctives "into
either the Confucian pattern of identification with socio-
political programs or the Shamanist-Buddhistic pattern of escapism" (Park 1970:189-198).

Finally, an understanding of conversion as eschatological
process should make us more sensitive to the dangers of "lapse"
after the entrance into the Kingdom has been "signed and sealed"
by baptism. Conversion has its consummation not simply in "turning to God from idols to serve a living God" but "in waiting for
His son from heaven...who delivers us from the wrath to come"
(1 Thess. 1:9-10). The line between what might be called "cultural conversion" and "conversion to Christ" is a very real one,
but it can also, through the stress of history and cultural persuasions, be a very thin one.

Again, the early history of Christianity in Korea illustrates
both the advantages of an identification of Christianity with
cultural selfhood and identification as a stumbling block. Unlike China, Korea saw the Protestant movement as "an agent of
continuity" with her national destiny, not "the unwelcomed face
behind the iron mask of Western imperialism" (Palmer 1967:48).
A year before the arrival of the first preaching missionaries to
Korea, the intervention of a Presbyterian missionary, a medical
doctor, Horace Allen, had saved the life of the crown prince
from an attempted assassination by a Japanese-inspired political
group (Harrington 1961:19-23). Out of that intervention came
easy access to the royal chambers (Underwood 1918:221), and, after the turn of the century, a royal request for the establish-

ment of a State Presbyterian Church in Korea. "The Emperor himself and all the court were to be baptized. Fearing the power and influence of Russia, they reportedly dreaded the possibility of being forced to join the Greek Church, which would make them practically the subjects of the Czar" (Underwood 1918:204-205).

In the years that followed, that cultural identification with Christianity was reinforced on several levels. Through the missionaries' decision to translate the Bible into Korean script, a renaissance of the alphabetic script took place. Long out of use since its development by King Sejong (1418-1450), spurned by educated classes as "vulgar," the script was popularized by missionary and church, bringing it into general use even in non-Christian circles (Kay 1950:116-117).

With the revival of the vernacular script came the basis of a new literature closely associated with a reformist-nationalist movement. Korea's first vernacular newspaper appeared in 1896; its editor was Philip Jaisohn, a convert to Christianity, who saw the paper as a call for Korean national independence from Japan and for "the moral and spiritual regeneration of Korea" (Palmer 1967:75-76). Christian secondary schools became seedbeds for the incubation of ideas of nationalism and independence. Many of the early Korean leaders in the struggle against Japanese colonialism in the years from 1905 to 1945 were trained in such schools.

One of the earlier climaxes of this identification of Christianity with Korea came with the March First Independence Movement of 1919, when nation-wide peaceful demonstrations took place upon the public reading of a Declaration of Independence from Japan by 33 Koreans of national prominence. Fifteen of the signers were Christians and of the 19,525 who were arrested in connection with the demonstrations, 3,428 of the 6,312 with "religious affiliations" were Christian. "There is no question that the Japanese blamed the Christians more than all the others" (Palmer 1967:65). And the results were reflected in the growth of the church. Shearer notes that most of the Presbyterian mission station reports for 1920 read like, "Perhaps the work of no year ever began under such adverse circumstances or closed with such bright prospects as the year 1919-1920. Membership rose from 69,025 reported in 1920 to 72,138 in 1921, an upsurge of 4½% and especially notable for a church which registered a slight loss for the previous year" (Shearer 1966:65).

At the same time, this cultural identification opened the way for Christianity's losing its eschatological tension between the Kingdom's "now and not yet" and lapsing simply into a "this world's now." "Christian churches were involved in politics to such a degree that Korean religious institutions became virtual

political institutions" (Park 1970:163), following a Confucian
social ethic of involvement. On the other hand, the Shamanistic,
Buddhistic escapism, unreconstructed by the radical demands of
the Gospel, turned other churches inward, towards a non-
involvement with this world, eyes set only on heaven. When conversion is abstracted from its eschatological integrity as a
process, that liability to blindness regarding cultural pressures grows more real.

2. *Covenant dimensions of conversion*

Repeatedly the conversion process is described in the Bible
in terms of the "turning" of a people to God in covenant. That
language is used preeminently of Israel in the Old Testament.
Her confession of sin at not entering the promised land (Deut.
1:41) comes too late to escape defeat at the hands of the
Amorites (Num. 14:40-45). Moses describes her reaction in terms
of "returning and weeping before the Lord" (Deut. 1:45). Living
under the curse of covenant judgment, Moses predicts, will cause
Israel to "return to the Lord, your God," a returning which will
be mirrored in "obeying him with all your heart and soul according to all that I commanded you this day" (Deut. 30:2,8). Tied
in with this "returning" will be a restoration from captivity,
and a gathering again "from all the peoples where the Lord your
God has scattered you" (Deut. 30:3).

This eschatological dimension to "returning" is enlarged
further by the universalistic emphasis of the prophets. Egypt
will be numbered among the remnant who "return" (Isa. 19:22).
"All the ends of the earth" will turn to the Lord and be saved
(Isa. 45:22). In the last day "many nations" will "go up to
the mountain of the Lord" (Mic. 4:2). Israel, the suffering
servant, will suffer in solidarity for the "many" (Isa. 52:13;
53:6).

A western cultural emphasis on the individual-centered nature
of conversion balks at these examples of "national conversions."
As noted earlier, Berkhof sees them as "merely of the nature of
moral reformations." This, I would suggest, does injustice to
the redemptive-historical *covenant* dimension of conversion.

It is this solidarity-in-community character of covenant
which lifts the instances of Gentile household baptisms recorded in Acts out of the realm of simple prooftexts (whether
for infant baptism or for apostolic sensitivity to winnable kin
structures; Tippett 1970:33, McGavran 1955:29-30). They are
rather signs of the fulfillment of the Lord's word regarding the
conversion of the Gentile remnant. The covenant solidarity of
grace that formerly included only Hebrews and their seed now includes Gentiles. The narrative of Cornelius' conversion parti-

cularly underscores this. It is prefaced by Peter's reluctance
as a Jew to associate with a Gentile (Acts 10:9 ff., 33 ff.).
It is concluded by the church's admission that "God has granted
to the Gentiles also the repentance that leads to life" (11:18).
The point is not a canonical illustration of the sociological
bridge over which the faith passed (McGavran 1955:24), but the
redemptive-historical, eschatological affirmation of the one new
"remnant" that God now builds from Jews and Gentiles, who have
turned from death to life (Eph. 2:1-14).

It is in the light of this covenant solidarity that the
church finds its richest meaning as covenant community, the fellowship of the Spirit formed by the gifts of the Spirit (1 Cor.
12:4-11), the body of Christ expressing its communal nature in
service directed to the world (1 Cor. 12:12-27).   Conversion becomes turning from the community shaped by the sin of the first
Adam to the community shaped by the redemption of the second
Adam, "turning *from* ethnicity and tribalism *to* open covenant
based on Jesus' Lordship (within the church) and *from* geographic
and temporal parochialism (nationalisms) *to* the universal (present and coming) Kingdom" (Shank 1976:6).   Solidarity in covenant finds its fulfillment not in the Promethean spirit of independence and domination but in the servant spirit of Jesus,
reflected in his community.   The community broken in the Garden
is restored in Christ.

The Christian church owes a deep debt to Donald McGavran and
his colleagues for reminding us of the importance of the covenant solidarity concept in the work of converting the ethne of
the world.   Relentlessly, he has warned of the negative impact
our extreme western cultural individualism has had on evangelism,
as mission has sought to cultivate conversions "one by one
against the social tide" (McGavran 1970:299, Kraft 1977:620).
In language that has been refined from the original "mass movements" to "people movements" to "multi-individual decisions,"
we are reminded of the communal way in which conversion repeatedly takes place among the majority of the world's cultures
(Tippett 1973:139-142).[2]

Charles Kraft has refined this into a principle for the "outside advocate" (missionary) seeking cultural transformation.
It is "the recognition that transformational change is accomplished more efficiently and effectively if *advocated by groups*
than if advocated simply by individuals. 'Social change of any
magnitude at all cannot be made by individuals' (Gerlach and
Hine 1970:xxii). This is why movements are of such great importance in cultural transformation" (Kraft 1977:664-665). So,
he concludes, appeals for both conversion and cultural transformation should, for maximum effectiveness, be directed primarily to socially homogeneous groupings of people and to lead-

ers who will influence such groups. That advice, with modifications, seems eminently practical.[3]

My modifications flow from my concern that McGavran's model is more controlled by sociological dimensions than by the biblical-theological dimensions of religious solidarity in covenant. A people's homogeneity is never simply provided by cultural or sociological bonds but by the religious direction of the heart, expressing itself in the solidarity of the ethne (Conn 1977b:15-19), and controlling, in turn, sociological and anthropological dimensions.

That covenant solidarity is most visibly expressed in the family, "the *only* divinely instituted natural social unit" (Boer 1961:176). Vastly modified by historical forces, twisted and devastated by the machinations of sin, reduced by western individualization from "extended" to "nuclear," the family (including its "people" and "clan" forms) remains the patterning relationship for covenant expressions of conversion. Against this background, "biological growth" (a term helpfully provided by McGavran) means more than simply a potential pool for utilization in the expansion of the church. Influenced by his theological background in the Restoration movement, McGavran may not see "biological growth" as a covenant-structured means of conversion; he may be content with a simple admonition that "children born to Christian parents should be brought to an experience of commitment" (Tippett 1973:149). Without in any way disclaiming the need for each generation to live out its commitment to God in Christ, we suggest that circumcision and baptism signify and seal more than potential commitment to covenant. They are *incorporation acts of covenant* par excellence, the real introduction of disciples into the communal jurisdiction of the new covenant (Matt. 28:18-20), the consecration of a people into the solidarity of allegiance to Jehovah, the Great Suzerain (Kline 1968:79-81).

Roy Shearer provides ample documentary evidence from Korea for the authentication of the solidarity-in-covenant model as a workable concept. Analyzing the rapid growth of the Presbyterian Church in the northwest particularly, he sees "the structure of Korean society," specifically, its family orientations, as "one most important factor" in growth (Shearer 1966:146). Citing example after example from early missionary observations, he sees a "people movement" in Korea where "the Gospel flowed along the web of family relationships" (Shearer 1966:150). "This," he argues, "is the means by which the Korean Church multiplied ahead of the missionaries. Because of the close-knit web of family relationships and the interfamily relationship through the clan, no one wished to make a great step in accepting a new religion which would break down these family ties. A person

hearing the Gospel of Christ, or reading it from a Bible sold to
him, would go back to his own village, talk it over with the
members of his family and clan, and if a positive decision was
made, the entire group often quite naturally became Christian,
still holding fast to its family relationships.... If all were
not immediately won, each family member in his own time became
Christian, until soon the whole family and sometimes the entire
clan was won to Christ" (Shearer 1966:148-149).[4]   The identification of Christianity with Korea's own national aspirations
would quite naturally reinforce this decision-making process.

In keeping with our suggestions regarding the solidarity-in-
covenant dimension, we would express our concern for the tendency to see culture as a "neutral" set of separate components
(in contrast to a religiously integrated expression of worldview).   This tendency is strong in McGavran, whose view of culture is far less integrative than that of Kraft.   McGavran
looks upon "cultures as aggregates rather than as organisms,"
containing "components...seldom essential to the culture"
(McGavran 1974:38).   "Christianity," he contends, "is wholly
neutral to the vast majority of cultural components" (McGavran
1974:39-41).

But if one supposes some components of culture to be religiously neutral, if one takes a segmentalist view which sees religion merely as a class of "meaning level" phenomena, how then
may one account for the demonic side of the integrating process
of cultural homogeneity?   Must we not have a solidarity-in-
covenant dimension to our understanding of culture that recognizes the religious resistance of all ethne to a God-centered
direction?   So the church's struggle to transform or "possess"
the cultural unit is always a concrete manifestation of its ongoing struggle with the powers (Eph. 6:12).   "Multi-personal decisions," then, are not easily made for Christ, whatever the insights of sociology and anthropology may imply to the contrary.

Men, to use McGavran's language, do like to become Christians
without crossing racial, linguistic, or class barriers.   But
each of these cultural barriers have religious dimensions, flowing from man's integrity as image of God.   Man, even in his
fallen state as covenant breaker and God-resister, remains man
in solidarity.   While we seek to make use of his covenant desire
for community, we must also be wary of his abuse of that solidarity as covenant breaker.

Again Korea provides us with ample reason for caution in this
area.   At the roots of the family bridge across which Christianity entered into Korea was a Confucian worldview, the religious
depths of which were slighted by mission and church.   Confucian
family patterns called for a solidarity in which the final cri-

terion for ethical decisions became the "sake of family" or "the honor of family." Filial piety was the "supreme virtue and the basis of general morality" in the Confucian worldview, expressing its religious character in the practice of ancestor worship. Within this religious particularism, loyalty as a primary virtue "usually did not go over the line of family, clan, locality, and faction" (Park 1970:114). Solidified during the Yi period which preceded the Protestant entrance to Korea, the particularistic ties of family and kinship reinforced an exclusivism which enslaved individuals to family and clan and worked against the establishment of open community or any attachments outside the family.

These religious roots were unchallenged by the missionary except in their overt manifestation in ancestor worship. And the results have been seen in the church's sad history of regionalism, geographic sensitivity to family or clan origins, and factionalism along clan and regional lines. The church has not been able to develop fully the idea of an open community of grace and service but has oriented its structure and understanding of "authority" along familial lines. A simple appeal to family ties as "bridges of God" will not help in reorienting, transforming and possessing the social units for Christ.

3. *Kingdom dimensions of conversion*

Still another biblical image associated with the eschatological nature of conversion is that of the Kingdom of God. The prophetic promise of the return of the remnant to the promised land is concomitant to the return of the remnant to God (Jer. 12:15-17), "the poor" to whom the Lord will one day manifest his kingly redemption (Pss. 22:27-28; 72:8-12). At the heart of the kingdom dimension to conversion will be the initiative of God's grace (Ps. 80:3,7,19), God's "turning again" to his people (Kittel 1971:724). The eschatological day of the Kingdom will come when chastened Jerusalem, the city of the great king, will seek conversion of heart at the hands of divine grace. "Bring me back that I may be restored, for thou art the Lord my God" (Jer. 31:18). And the Lord will answer at the time of the new kingdom covenant (31:33). "I will give them a heart to know that I am Jehovah; they shall be my people and I will be their God, for they will come back to me with all their hearts" (Jer. 24:7).

The message of the New Testament is the word of the inauguration of the Kingdom (Luke 1:33). It is commensurate with the angelic announcement to Zechariah that the day of repentance has commenced in the ministry of John the Baptist as the forerunner of Jesus. "He will turn back many of the sons of Israel to the Lord their God" (Luke 1:16). John's announcement of the coming

of the Kingdom of God in Christ is thus linked to the call to
conversion: "Repent, for the kingdom of heaven is at hand"
(Matt. 3:2). The disruption of the people will be ended with
the sign of the age of conversion, the turning of the fathers
(Mal. 4:6).

It is this kingdom dimension that colors the ministry of
Jesus as he calls God's people to "turn" and "repent" (Luke 5:
32). The "coming to himself" of the prodigal son (Luke 15:17)
is a mark of the Kingdom, a turning to the Father (15:18).

These emphases are not accidental to the announcement of the
Kingdom come in Christ. "Repentance and faith are simply the
two main aspects of the Kingdom, righteousness and the saving
grace of God, translated into terms of subjective human experience" (Vos 1972:91). So too, in the apostolic preaching, conversion becomes the mark of those who see the Kingdom come in
the redemptive victory work of Jesus. Peter's sermon in the
temple points to the fulfillment of the prophetic word in the
death and resurrection of "the Prince of life" (Acts 3:13-18)
and concludes with a call to "repent and return" (Acts 3:19).
The Pauline commission to preach to the Gentiles is outlined in
terms of a call for "repentance and turning to God" (Acts 26:20).
However these two actions are conceived, they designate the
coming of the new covenant in Christ the king (cf. Acts 15:3,7,
19).

This kingdom dimension to conversion calls for a comprehensive, thoroughly radical (derived from the stem *radix*, meaning
"root") approach to culture which has not been characteristic
of the history of missions. Bavinck notes that the Pietistic
movement of the seventeenth and eighteenth centuries displayed
"a remarkable hostility to the cultural side of the missionary
task.... These...missionaries confined themselves to preaching
to individuals whom they sought to impress with the eternal
judgment of God" (Bavinck 1949:45). Cultural anthropology has
increasingly refuted that bifurcation of religious from cultural
life, of the sacred from the secular in the world's ethne. But
the Pietist mythologization of individualism into a theological
construct has hindered the church from incorporating that insight into missionary methodology.

Conversion as a sign of the Kingdom of God come in Christ
underlines the claim of the kingship of God over the whole of
life. "Jesus Christ is Lord of everything. The whole of life
ought to be subjected to the royal authority of Him who has redeemed us by His precious blood. It is noteworthy that the
missionary command in Matthew 28 follows upon the declaration
of Christ Himself that all power in heaven and on earth has
been given unto Him" (Bavinck 1949:30). The comprehensive de-

mands of the so-called cultural mandate (Gen. 1:28-30) find
their covenant fulfillment in the Kingdom of God initiated by
the redemptive deliverance of Jesus, the second Adam, the ful-
filler of culture. That work of the Kingdom is not narrowly
cultic or religious. Using constant allusions to the Genesis
record of history, and to the cultural call of Adam, Paul in
Ephesians describes "not only Christ's dominion over all but
also his filling of all (Eph. 1:22, 4:10). The cultural mandate
is fulfilled by Christ, in the heart and fulness of its meaning.
In him dwells all the fulness of the Godhead bodily (Col. 2:9,
cf. 1:19)" (Clowney 1976:10).

Here the rich insights of Charles Kraft are most useful. The
impact of the kingdom rule of Christ, as a radical demand, must
always "modify" a person's worldview. And, if true transformational change (as opposed to superficial external alteration) is
to take place, the change must occur not on the merely behavioral
edges of the worldview's manifestation but at its center. Sensitivity to the Kingdom as a radical direction should keep that
insight constantly before us. Kingdom-style conversion begins
with a change "from allegiance to such things as self, tribe or
occupational or material allegiances to faith-allegiance to God
through Christ" (Kraft 1977:631).

The task of kingdom conversion, however, does not end at the
beginning! Conversion as a process structured by the all-
embracing claims of the Kingdom in Christ never allows us to
speak of repentance as "adequate," with respect to culture and
worldview, until the process of possessing or transforming that
culture has been completed. Here begins the process Kraft de-
signates as reinterpretation, reevaluation and rehabituation.
Out of a worldview now Christ-possessed at its root, the convert
starts the lifelong process of worldview reformation, evaluating
and interpreting each aspect of life in terms of the kingdom
claims of his new allegiance. From this reflection will flow
action "rehabituation," "changes in habitual behavior issuing
from the new allegiance and the consequent re-evaluational process" (Kraft 1977:103). Life in the Kingdom bears the stamp of
covenant praxis. It is the process mirrored in Joseph's reflection on life, "You meant to do me harm; but God meant to
bring good out of it by preserving the lives of many people"
(Gen. 50:20). It is the kingdom re-evaluation of handicap by
Paul who sees it now as the medium of expression for Christ's
resurrection power (2 Cor. 12:7-10), death becoming "gain"
(Phil. 1:21), suffering a mark of sonship (Heb. 12:5-7).

In formulating these principles into a methodological rule
for the missionary or "change advocate," Kraft proposes that the
advocate "seek to encourage a minimal number of critical changes
in the worldview, rather than a larger number of more peripheral

changes" (Kraft 1977:659). His concern is over the danger of
the missionary identifying as "central" what really might be a
peripheral cultural theme, and thus either block the appropriate
human response of repentance and faith or encourage "cultural
conversion" rather than "conversion to Christ." Concentration
on the evils of polygamy, a peripheral issue, for example, can
easily provoke this response. A missionary's opposition can
carry a message to the culture which says: "(1) He has turned
against traditional leaders (because they have more than one
wife) and (2) against traditional customs in general. Furthermore (3) he favors familial irresponsibility on the part of
men.... (4) He no longer wants the women to be socially secure
...nor (5) to be able to get assistance with their work around
the home (traditionally provided via polygamy). (6) Nor does God
want men any longer to strive to attain prestige (traditionally
associated with investment of surplus wealth in larger families
involving more than one wife) but, rather, (7) wishes them to be
dominated by their wives..." (Kraft 1977:660). The result of
this kind of message can be "such a high degree of confusion and
disequilibrium in the...core (worldview) of the culture that
there is little chance that the Gospel message concerning salvation through a faith relationship with God will be heard clearly.
Nor, if it is heard, will it be attractive to them (since this
God appears to be so unreasonable)" (Kraft 1977:661).

All this seems eminently true to me and practical. Korea's
mission history illustrates the failure to make this distinction. In 1895, the Methodists passed a resolution arguing that
"in the judgment of this meeting no man or woman living in polygamous relations can enter or retain membership in the Methodist
Episcopal Church" (Paik 1929:210). Thoroughly debated and
studied by the Presbyterians, their eventual judgment was the
same as the Methodists. From it flowed a heated discussion
among the missionaries as to requirements for church membership
and what constitutes a credible profession of faith. The eventual outcome was much more rigorous demands for membership. The
Methodists separated the rite of baptism from reception into
church membership, apparently as a probationary measure. From
it came four classes of church adherents: "the first made up
of full church members; the second consisting of the baptized
probationers, who have all the privileges of church membership
save they cannot vote in church meeting and can be dropped without church trial; third, probationers; fourth, inquirers" (Paik
1929:214). The Presbyterians adopted a pre-baptismal probation,
known as the catechumen class. After six months' probation, the
candidate for baptism was reexamined, and either admitted, continued or dropped. Missionary concentration on the evils of
polygamy in Korea changed the significance of baptism from conversion sign to sanctification sign.

I experience, at the same time, some difficulty in understanding Kraft when he speaks of "a minimal number of critical
changes" in the worldview. (I do not think he means "minimal
changes," for the changes he has in mind are designated as
"critical.") The language might be misleading, especially in
view of our insistence on the necessity of change at the core.
I find it more useful to speak of a "power encounter" in the
worldview. Here we are using the helpful terminology of Alan
Tippett (Tippett 1973:88-91). Tippett's usage is controlled by
his understanding of the conversion process of group movements
(Tippett 1977:202ff) in which there is "a public testimony of
conversion that is the functional equivalent of an altar call
in an evangelical church" (1977:213).

Without space to judge Tippett's model, I prefer to use the
term "power encounter" in what may be the wider dimensions he
gives it in his earlier work. It is that clash in cultural
worldview between the redeeming, liberating power of the Kingdom of God manifest in Christ (including his victory over the
powers; Eph. 6:10-12; 1 John 3:8), and the kingdom of Satan in
which the whole world lies (1 John 5:19). It is the elenctic
call in which the cultural worldview becomes the battleground
(not simply points of contact but *points of attack*) on which
the advocate proclaims the defeat of sin and death through the
resurrection of Christ and his consequent authority ("all power
is given unto me," Matt. 28:18). That kingdom power encounter
will be shaped by the varieties of the world's ethne and worldviews. But it must always retain its God-ward side of conversion, God's saving power affirmed in turning from and turning
to.

Within Korea's Confucian cultural worldview, one can see
traces of that power encounter in the introduction of the Christian concept of sin and its impact on the Korean worldview. In
the Confucian setting there is no concept of radical sin or evil
because of a worldview where opposites constantly blend into
the complementary and mutually necessary harmony of "becoming."
The Confucian worldview speaks of "impropriety or offenses
against traditional authorities, parents, ancestors, and super-
iors in the hierarchy of office" (Park 1970:213). Against this
background, the Christian concept of sin is "rather shocking
and lacking in dignity" (Weber 1968:228), and as such it became
the occasion for a power encounter in Korean culture. "It destroyed the self-asserting and self-righteous attitude of Confucianism. For the first time, Koreans were forced to reflect
upon the religious and ethical meaning of humility. The new
awareness of the radical nature of sin made Korean Christians
deathly afraid of the divine judgment.... The humble recognition of one's weakness and imperfection also opened the door

for compromise and reconciliation in the midst of factionalism
and enmity" (Park 1970:219).

The place in Korean history where that power encounter with
Confucianism took most visible form was the Great Revival of
1907.   Shearer may be partially right in disclaiming the revival
as "the *cause* of the growth of the Church in Korea" (Shearer
1966:56).   But we wonder if that judgment does justice to the
significance of the revival as the first open demonstration of
a previous power encounter of the Kingdom of God with Korea's
Confucian cultural worldview.   In Korea's shame oriented culture, the desperate prayers of confession and petition, which
marked the 1907 revival, signalled a "collapse of the self-
righteous attitude, the deepening of the concept of sin, the in-
ternalization of ethical motivation, and the elimination of
rigid exclusivism" (Park 1970:220).   James Gale observes, "Old
conservative Koreans who had drunk deep of Confucius..., whose
pride of spirit made them un-approachable, were among the
broken-hearted and the contrite" (Gale 1906:213).   "A deep impression of the exceeding sinfulness of sin and of the everlasting obligation of righteousness" flowed from the revival (*Korea
Mission Field* 1908:70).   The patterns of prayer and contrition
formed during the revival continue in the Korean church today.
Prayer is accompanied by weeping and often shrill pleading,
stopped only by the ring of the pastor's bell on the pulpit.
The forms of prayer have been shaped by the cultural worldview's
earlier clash with the reality of sin.

4.   *Worldview dimensions of conversion*

To ask about the relation between conversion and worldview
demands a definition of worldview that is difficult to provide.
Much of that difficulty lies in differences of approach, depending upon whether one relies primarily on insights drawn from
anthropology or theology.   In addition, the task is complicated
by the diversity of definitions provided in either discipline.
An ideological overview seems almost a necessity, and yet that
has seldom been undertaken by Christians working in either discipline.

The dangers flowing from this lack of attention are many.
The risk is increased that one will inadvertently incorporate
into one's synthesis elements hostile to Christian presuppositions.   The possibility of misunderstanding between Christians
struggling with worldview concerns is magnified.   Theologians,
for instance, more often trained in philosophy than the behavioral sciences, see worldview as "a definite theory of the metaphysical character of the universe" (Ramm 1966:138), and ignore
its role as "the central control box of culture" (Kraft 1977:
121).   On the other hand, anthropologists, steeped in an aca-

demic tradition that has long insisted on the religious presuppositionlessness of the social and behavioral sciences, see
worldview as more or less religiously neutral conceptual models
which "attempt to represent symbolically, for restricted purposes, aspects of a world whose structure is not accessible to
us" (Barbour 1974:37-38); this stance ignores or slights the
place of religion as a vertical, integrating dimension of the
worldview.

More recently, contemporary anthropology, in its exposure to
those complex societies whose basic values are less explicitly
supernaturalistic, has complicated this struggle for definition
by restricting "religion" to those beliefs that relate to supernatural beings; accordingly, they use "worldview" in a broad,
neutral sense, to cover the core beliefs and values of a society
whether or not those be "supernaturalistic." Thus worldview is
understood as the core value system that underlies the whole
culture, and religion becomes a sub-system (alongside such dimensions as politics, economics, social structure, etc.), a "non-
relative, basic human function" among others (safety needs, love
and belongingness needs, esteem needs, etc.).

Using the language of Charles Kraft, we prefer to see worldview as "both the repository and the generator of the conceptual
models in terms of which the adherents of that entity, the sub-
scribers to that value system, perceive of and interact with
reality" (Kraft 1977:78). It is that which "defines its own
criteria for evaluating the way the forms and people of that
culture function" (Kraft 1977:187). As such, it performs at
least a five-fold function in a distinctive culture. It explains how and why things got to be as they are and how and why
they continue or change. It validates the basic institutions,
values and goals of a society. It provides psychological re-
inforcement for the group. It integrates the society, systema-
tizing and ordering the culture's perceptions of reality into an
overall design. It provides, within its conservatism, opportunities for perceptual shifts and alterations in conceptual
structuring (Kraft 1977:121-125).

At the same time, these functions are religious in their
direction (an emphasis lacking in Kraft), for culture ultimately is a product of the human "heart," of man as image of
God, as *homo religiosus*. Cultural worldview remains the all-
inclusive, radical response of man-in-covenant to the revelation
of God (Prov. 4:23, Jer. 29:13, Matt. 12:34). It consists of
"powerful, life-controlling entities, . . . completely indivisible structures, because each element coheres with all the
others and receives its meaning from the total structure"
(Bavinck 1960:172-173).

Thus, "culture...is that complex of spiritual, moral, technical and agricultural forces wherein a tribe or a people tries to express its basic feelings towards God, towards nature, and towards itself. The culture of a people is in its common attitude of life, its style of living and thinking, rooted in its apprehension of reality" (Bavinck 1949:55). That apprehension is always religious, either defining reality, on one hand, in terms of the Creator God, or, on the other hand, in terms of some aspect of the creation, which it seeks to make meaningful apart from the Creator. In this sense, "there is not a single element in the cultural structure that can be called absolutely neutral; all elements have their secret ties with the religious faith of the people as a whole. Nothing is to be found anywhere that can be called a 'no-man's land.' Culture is religion made visible; it is religion actualized in the innumerable relations of daily life" (Bavinck 1949:57).

The following model might come close to expressing our viewpoint.

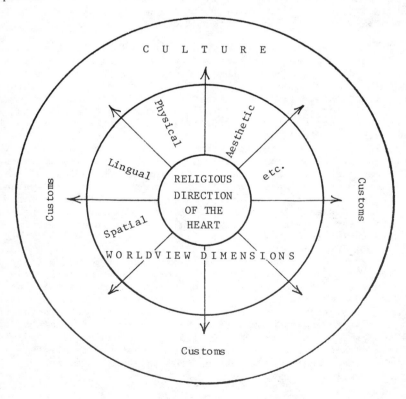

Admittedly, the model makes religion the crucial allegiance dimension of worldview and therefore uses the term in a way not at all congenial to its contemporary usage in anthropology (where it is isolated from worldview as those beliefs that relate to supernatural beings). The model also refuses to see religion as simply one part (albeit vital) among many on the cultural scale of function. Anthropological theory since 1920 has been willing to include religious phenomena within the cultural matrix of society (van Baal 1971:165), culture serving as "a vast instrumental reality" for the satisfaction of religious needs. But even this concession is not enough. Behind it lies the utilitarian monism of functionalism, culture conceived of as "an instrument serving man's biological and psychological needs" (Hatch 1973:320).

Our desire, in our model, is to stress the core place of religion in the formation of worldview and, through worldview, the structuring of cultural forms and functions. We leave as problematic at this stage the number of needs which are basic in culture formation and their order in relation to one another. Herman Dooyeweerd, a Dutch philosopher working within the Reformed tradition, has offered suggestions well worth studying in this connection (Kalsbeek 1975:95-103). We concur in his insistence that even the culture's judgments as to which of these functions will receive proportionate attention in relation to, or in distinction from, the others, is a religious judgment. At the same time, religion is not simply worldview. It is that which forms worldview from its prior commitment either for God or against him.

On this view, religion in culture is response to the "supracultural" God. Fallen Adam does not escape the covenant obligations of culture building (Gen. 1:28-30). But that calling is now burdened by covenant curse, Adam's painful labor subduing the earth, Eve's travail filling it. So too, in that culture building, the apostasy appears. "Cain the murderer builds a city to bear his son's name, the pride of the builders of Babel anticipates Tyre, Nineveh, and Babylon—the exalting of man's name that invites divine judgment. When metals can be smelted, swords can be made, and Lamech can sing his boastful hymn of hate (Gen. 4:23 ff.), the demonic dynamic of the 'abominations' of the heathen begin to appear. The kingdoms whose cultural riches Satan will show to Jesus begin to rise like beasts out of the sea" (Clowney 1976:5). Though they do not necessarily share a commonality of meaning and usage across cultures, culture's forms are universal—poetry (Gen. 4:23-24), music (4:21), forging metals (4:22). But they are never religiously neutral; they remain the symbols of man functioning always as image of God. And whatever use those cultural forms serve is, on the deep structure level, transformed by our self-service as "sons of Cain" or by our "spiritual service" (Rom. 12:2) as "sons of God."

Thus the "spiritual" dimension every Christian wishes to guard in its cultural role is not simply one human universal among others, nor even a synonym for the cultural commonality of religion, a la Kraft (1977:177). It is not an area of life but primarily a direction of life, specifically, a Christian direction of life. The entire scope of man's living in Christ in his culture is "spiritual service."

The task of Christianity vis-a-vis any given culture or subculture becomes, then, primarily the transformation or possession of the worldview of that culture. That transformation is accomplished by bringing Christian understandings of supracultural truth to bear on the worldview. In this process (Charles Kraft calls it a "paradigm shift"[5]), three steps need to be followed to make conversion "meaningful." There must be (1) "a change of allegiance that issues in (2) a concomitant change in the evaluational principles within the person's/group's worldview and (3) a resultant series of new habits of behavior" (Kraft 1977:631-634). Thus, when people are converted, they begin to change their worldview.

Homer Barnett's language in describing what he sees as the three characteristics of people ready to receive a new idea may be helpful here as a summary tool in seeing this interaction between the Gospel and a cultural worldview. He notes (1) they will receive the new idea only if it satisfies a want better than some existing means; (2) the reception of this idea depends in part on the previous life experience of the person; (3) dissatisfaction may be a pervasive attitude in some individuals (Barnett 1953:378 ff.).

This recalls "the psychology of receptivity" (Shearer 1973:160-165), which was characteristic of Korea in the early days of Protestant work. Gabriel Lee has drawn the elements of this receptivity in full scale for us in his use of Emile Durkheim's concept of social anomie to analyze the social conditions of Korea in its initial encounters with Catholic and Protestant Christianity (Lee 1961:35-36, 102-123).[6] The anomic situation of worldview collapse and social disintegration paralleled the early growth of Protestantism from 1884. Political disintegration through nepotism and bribery, cupidity and luxury had long before "sapped the strength and wealth of the land; the whole commonwealth was diseased and rotten to the core" (Hulbert 1905:92). Confucianism, the stabilizing cultural core of the peninsula from the fourteenth century, had become the symbol of social exploitation.

Thrust into the maelstrom of international politics after three centuries of isolation, the society had broken up into traditionalists yearning for the old isolationism, pro-Chinese

and pro-Japanese parties. An 1894 rebellion by the *Tong-hak*
(Eastern learning) movement, a syncretistic amalgam of eastern
religions in conscious reaction to the West, particularly Catholicism (Weems 1964:7-48), was directed against the corruption
of the Yi dynasty government, an expression of mass discontent.
To quell it, the king, at the insistence of the pro-Chinese faction, asked China for aid in putting down the rebellion. Under
the guise of protecting its residents in Korea, Japan dispatched
troops and ships to make war with China on Korean soil. The
victory of the Japanese opened the way for the protectorate and
eventual annexation of Korea by Japan that ended in 1945. In
the years following annexation in 1910, Korea wrestled with the
Japanese effort to obliterate its own cultural worldview and
make it Japanese. Korea, to use Barnett's language, was ready
for new worldview substitutes.

C. E. Sharp, writing in a 1906 issue of the *Korea Mission
Field*, divided the motives which led the Koreans to become Christians into three categories. There were those driven by "the
desire for protection and power.... Owing to the uncertainty of
the time, people have been banding together for mutual help....
These people were simply after the help that comes from union...
[and they believed] that there was only one society that amounted
to anything...the Christian Church.... Another motive that is
moving many at the present time is more refined than the above.
Many are realizing the failure of the ancient civilization of
their fathers, in the stress of the twentieth century. They see
that the nations styled Christian are the ones that today possess the highest civilization and culture, and, turning from the
old, they are seeking the new. But with many of these, Christianity means a kind of civilization only.... But there is also
a third phase of this turning to Christianity at the present
time. There does exist a real soul hunger and there is a real
work of God's Spirit in the heart of many" (Sharp 1906:182).
Sharp's presuppositions concerning culture and theology no doubt
made him differentiate too sharply between the first two motives
and the third, but his remarks certainly underline Barnett's
judgments. A letter from Sharp to his board that same year re-
inforces his sensitivity to the cultural shifts as he recalls
the remarks of a public magistrate who attended an evening service of a Bible training class. "He expressed a sentiment which
shows the present attitude in many minds towards Christianity.
'There is nothing left for us to do now but to put our trust in
the Christians' God'..." (Shearer 1966:54).

Korean sensitivities to their own cultural disintegration and
to Christianity as a "better way" were also reinforced by the
providential ties the missionary sought with Korea's religious
past and by the general appreciation of the missionary for the
traditional culture.[7] Underwood, responding to the hypothetical

question, "What religions are chiefly attacked by the missionaries?" perceptively wrote, "I think no attack upon any religion
is usually made. The missionary who goes to a foreign field has
not the time to spend in attacking its old faiths. His work is
simply to hold up Christ and Him crucified, and in His presence
no other faith can live.... We found that God, by His spirit,
had been at work throughout the length and breadth of this land
before we reached here, however; that all over it men and women
were being led to lose faith in their old religions. The common
remark of the educated gentlemen, that such things are good
enough for women and children, will show plainly the trend of
thought" (Underwood 1908:90-91).

Behind the celebrated Nevius plan and its three-fold formula
promoting self-government, self-propagation, self-support,
adopted almost wholesale among the dominant Presbyterians of
Korea, was a confident assurance not only that Protestant Christianity was relevant to native culture but that Koreans could be
trusted to promote the Gospel without having it suffer serious
distortion. Typical of missionary sentiment may be the words of
Mary F. Scranton, founder of Ewha Girls' School, the first of
its kind in Korea in 1886. "They, the girls, are not being made
over again after our foreign way of living, dress, and surroundings," she wrote. "We take pleasure in making Koreans better
Koreans only. We want Korea to be proud of Korean things, and
more, that it is a perfect Korea through Christ and his teachings" (Paik 1929:119).

In assessing a worldview change such as occurred among new
Christians in Korea, we must ask whether the Gospel has effectively addressed the radical dimensions of sin and man's covenant
rebellion in culture building.

Much Christian construction in this very area can easily
slight the more subtle and profound areas of worldview, especially when there is borrowing from theological or anthropological
frameworks unchallenged by a radical Christian perspective. A
Christian construction of conversion and worldview oriented, for
example, to a Thomistic view of deprivation—in which culture
functions as the religiously pseudo-neutral "configurations" of
natural law, and grace merely perfects it as a *donum superaddi-
tum*—can distort the anthropological "point of contact" between
the themes of Christianity and cultural worldview into a "common
ground" shorn of a "point of attack" (Bavinck 1960:141).
Through this approach, parallelisms can be too easily "emphasized
in order to ease the transitions, through minimizing differences
and maximizing similarities" (Nida 1960:213-214). No accounting
of the noetic effects of sin on worldview can then be radical
enough to prevent an Asian religious predilection for a form of
syncretism.

Recent Catholic scholarship speculates that this happened in Korea's early history as believers carried over from their Confucian and monarchial tradition a highly authoritative view of God and the sacralization of hierarchy and authority in social relationships. "From Buddhist sources Korean Catholics might be expected to have derived a negative attitude towards the world, an attitude easily reinforced by the dualistic and individualistic spirituality they received from Europe. Their persecution experience would have encouraged attitudes of in-group exclusivism and diminishing concern for the out-group, thereby threatening the universalistic, loving concern for one's neighbor which is the identifying mark of the Christian" (Biernatzki, Im, Min 1975:23). Nor would "the beggar mentality which dominated animistic prayer and the prayers of popular Buddhism conflict with the great stress on prayers of petition found in the Catholic prayerbook" of Korea's early Catholicism (Biernatzki, Im, Min 1975:9-11, 25).

On the other hand, an evangelical construction may not fare much better. Although it may recognize that the human use of cultural forms, patterns and processes is always affected by sin, leaving no aspect of culture unaffected, it can minimize that pervasive influence by questioning the nature of culture as a patterned, comprehensive, cohesive system, in terms of which our entire life is organized. (We have already noted McGavran's reduction of cultures to "aggregates rather than...organisms," to collections of components "seldom essential" to the culture, most of which "can be changed or even abandoned without trauma"; 1974:38). Or again, serious loss may occur if, even though the integrating character of culture and its relation to worldview is recognized, religion as the covenant direction of man's "heart" is minimized to a functional expression of worldview (the argument of Malinowski), or if religion is isolated (following more recent anthropological theory, a la Geertz) to describe those complex societies whose basic values are said to be not supernaturalistic. Either way, religion cannot function fully as the basic allegiance dimension of the culture.

We see the former danger exhibited by Nida when he rejects the view of religion as a "cultural capstone--a kind of overarching worldview of the supernatural" and reduces it to an "all-pervading component of 'desire for meaning'" (Nida 1971:12). We see the latter danger appearing in Kraft, who, in modification of Kuhn and Barbour, makes worldview largely a "mental map" of reality and (in his proper desire to escape a definition of "Christian culture" which too often means "western culture"; 1977:209) speaks of culture "as basically a vehicle or milieu, neutral in essence, though manifesting in practice the pervasive influence of human sinfulness" (Kraft 1977:219).

We prefer to retain a wider usage for the term religion, as
that which controls people and ethne to generate worldviews,
and, flowing from their worldview, cultures. "Man is always *man
of God*, even in his disobedience. Entrusting, believing, confessing, integrating is *constitutive* of his human nature" (DeGraaf
1976:5). Worldview is not religion, but it is the confession,
the root expression of man's religious nature. "In one way or
another, obediently or disobediently, all men give expression to
what lives in their hearts. Some people are very conscious of
the vision of life that drives them and can articulate their
deepest convictions in a clear 'world and life view.'... All
people, however, whether they are consciously aware of it or
not, are in the grip of some worldview or confessional vision
that motivates their activities, as becomes evident in their
lives" (DeGraaf 1976:7). That heart commitment is religion, that
religious response to divine revelation is worldview, a more or
less naive construct shaped by culture's historical complexities,
but flowing from man's religious response to divine revelation.[8]

5. *Contextual dimensions of conversion*

Our emphasis on conversion as an eschatological process and
not simply a one-act decision demands that we pay the most serious attention to the context in which conversion takes place in
culture. It is to recognize that we are engaged in "a comprehensive enterprise where the Gospel is shared in depth and out of
the depth of man's need and life situations, so that the knowledge of Christ may one day truly cover the earth as the waters
cover the sea" (Douglas 1975:212). In that "transculturation" of
the Gospel, our sensitivity to context demands that we go well
beyond the traditional evangelical focus on the original situation in the original frame of reference (the Bible). It demands
that, in addition, we recognize both the formative context of
the sharer (in other words, that which has culturally conditioned
the advocate's understanding of the relevance of the Kingdom for
his audience), and the context in which the culturally conditioned hearer re-encodes the Gospel message within his own frame
of reference. This is obviously far more complex than the traditional evangelical model of simply providing information which
people can understand (Conn 1978). The call to conversion in
culture "must present the message in such a way that people can
feel its relevance (the expressive element in communication) and
can then respond to it in action (the imperative function)"
(Nida and Taber 1969:24).

Bavinck, on a naive level, sees this process in terms of con-
stantly asking four questions: (1) To whom am I bringing the
Gospel? Paul, after all, addressed himself differently to
Festus than to the crowd at Lystra. "The different way in which
God spoke at different times is so essential in the history of

revelation that it constitutes a controlling element. The revelation of God does not hang in a vacuum, it is not an abstract
universal truth that descended upon us, but God's revelation entered into our history" (Bavinck 1960:83). (2) What persons
bring the Gospel? Elijah is quite different from Elisha, Matthew presents the Gospel in a completely different form than
does John. "The milieu in which the bearer of the Gospel is
born, his development, his cultural background, his personal
characteristics, his age all play a part and are used in the
hand of God" (Bavinck 1960:84). (3) What is the time of the
power encounter? Paul spoke differently to the crew of a ship
in the middle of a storm than when the ship lay quietly in the
harbor. "Each moment has its own particular opportunities and
difficulties, its *kairos*" (Bavinck 1960:85). (4) What is the
place of encounter? On a much more sophisticated level, more
alert to culture's anthropological dimensions, we see Kraft asking these same questions with his model drawn from dynamic
equivalence translation (Conn 1977a:20-21).

My own personal experience in Korea with two unique segments
of the population may illustrate these points. For a number of
years, I engaged in evangelistic work among the country's large
population of prostitutes, most of them living near American
army bases. A series of four Bible studies were created and
used repeatedly in hundreds of brothels. Focusing on such basic
themes as the nature of God, man as fallen image of God, Christ
as the reclaimer of a broken world, and the demands of Christian
discipleship, the series made use of the traditional Bible passages I had used in a typical evangelical American pastorate.
The responses from the girls ranged from indifference to luke-
warmness to anger.

Then I began searching for ways to communicate these same
truths within their cultural framework. My study of the nature
of God centered around the book of Hosea and God's faithful love
for his faithless Gomers. My exposition of man as fallen image
of God drew from the Old Testament's repudiation of Canaanite
temple prostitution and the comprehensive restrictions on those
who might enter the city of God (Rev. 22:14-15). I pictured
Jesus as the friend of publicans and prostitutes (Luke 15: 2 ff.)
and discipleship as Jesus' call to the woman taken in adultery
to "sin no more" (John 8:11). My attitude turned from righteous
indignation to compassion, and the Gospel became a word of true
love, love purchased not by the receiver but by the Giver, with
the blood of his own Son. The response was overwhelming as
girl after girl left prostitution to follow the "lover of her
soul." Unbeknownst to me, I had "contextualized" the Gospel!

The same experience was repeated on a smaller scale and time
period in a number of classes in "comparative religion" I was

asked to give in several Buddhist temples, explaining, at the
request of the monks, the nature of Christianity. In my pre-
parations for these sessions, I used the services of a former
monk who had renounced the monastery life but was still an ad-
herent. As we studied together, my eyes were opened not only to
Buddhism but to the cultural themes that gave insight into the
Korean worldview. My search into suffering as a key idea of
Buddhism pointed to suffering as a positive value in the Korean
worldview. Suddenly I understood why my sermons were often
praised by Korean Christians with such strange sounding (to me)
expressions as "hard work" or "you suffered much." (My worldview did not allow me to see suffering as a noble trait, to be
praised. It was rather something to be avoided.) I could now
see why Korea had at first embraced Buddhism and its central
theme but later rejected it as its unfolding of suffering as
something to be escaped became clear in cultural history. The
Korean language's absence of personal pronouns in its purer
forms reflected the Buddhist worldview's rejection of the personality of God or man.

Armed with the beginnings of understanding, I presented the
Gospel in the temples around the theme of suffering. Sin became
the introduction by man of evil in the world, suffering the
judgment of God on man's fallen lifestyle. Christ's redemption
and vicarious atonement was presented as the pain of God borne
through the vicarious suffering of the Servant. Christian discipleship was unveiled as the blessing of persecution and suffering through a faithful life of suffering (Matt. 5:10-11), filling up that which was lacking in Christ's affliction (Col. 1:24,
1 Pet. 4:13). The reading of Kazoh Kitamori's *Theology of the
Pain of God* (John Knox Press, 1965) made me wary of repeating
the early heresy of theopaschitism but sensitive also to a cultural link between the Christian faith and Korean existence.
By the time the invitations from the temples began to dry up, I
had over one hundred monks enrolled in Bible correspondence
courses and saw a converted bonze enter a theological seminary
to prepare for the Christian ministry. My invitations for week-
long Bible conferences and evangelistic meetings in rural churches began to focus on these same themes with increasing re-
sponsiveness from the non-Christians attending. I was, as I
have since discovered, engaged in the process of "dynamic equivalence translation."

How may one speak of the radical effects of sin on cultural
worldview, of the religious integration of culture by man the
culture-builder and covenant-breaker, and still use such cultural themes as suffering or the prostitution of love as the
gate through which the call to conversion can enter, of awareness of cultural need as a veritable "point of contact" (but not
"common ground")?

Behind the theological terminology of general revelation lies the answer to that question (Oosthuizein 1977:67-70). In the indivisible unity of cultural structure "there is a hidden crack. The culture of a nation is a product of human work, but there is an untraceable influence in it that cannot be scrutinized because it has its origin in the mercy of God" (Bavinck 1949:77). Culture's roots are formed by man always trying to escape from the strong and merciful grasp of God's hands; even when he seems to seek after God he is still flying from his presence. Yet, even as culture mirrors his flight, it mirrors also God's never-ending witness (Acts 14:17), the certainty that God was concerning himself with the ethne before the missionary met them. God was occupying himself with them before we came to them. "We do not open the discussion, but we need make it only clear that the God who has already revealed his eternal power and Godhead to them now addresses them in a new way, through our words.... He turns his face towards this wretched world and reveals his majesty to all his creatures" (Bavinck 1949:109). Culture's patterns display the chisel marks of those "who suppress the truth in unrighteousness" (Rom. 1:18) and also the dimmed glory of God who has fashioned boundaries of habitation and determined appointed time "that they should seek God, if perhaps they might grope for him and find him" (Acts 17:26-27).

"Has this general revelation a good and salutary effect in the lives of the peoples? We are inclined to confirm this question...be it with some caution. There is some effect on human conscience, something causing Paul to say that gentiles having no law 'do by nature the things of the law' (Rom. 2:14)" (Bavinck 1955:53). A knowledge always suppressed and superseded by ungodliness and unrighteousness, still there remains a trace of truth (Acts 14:16-17).

Does God ever use the stained and mutilated knowledge which the Gentile has at his disposal to do his wonderful work in the heart? What part did the shattered politics of Korea's nineteenth century and the bitterness of the Japanese protectorate play in the conversion of men like Philip Jaisohn and Syngman Rhee? Why did a 1907 newspaper correspondent write, "The whole country is fruit ripe for the picking.... If the Christian church has any conception of strategy and appreciation of an opportunity,...she will act at once" (Paik 1929:353)? Did the Nestorian influence on China play its part in the shaping of the Tan'gun myth of Korea and the creation of a term later to be possessed by the Christian mission? Was Korea's culture in the grip of the powerful revelation of God before it was aware of it?

"What does God do with those fragments of knowledge in a Gentile's life? Does he sometimes overcome that suppressing and superseding force that is always at work in his heart? Does he sometimes stop the hidden machinery of unbelief and rebellion by the unconquerable power of his holy Word, even if that Word reaches the heart in disguised form? Here we suddenly feel ourselves confronted with the deepest of all mysteries, the mystery of the power of God" (Bavinck 1949:106 f.).

Does a simplistic one-act conception of conversion located at the end of a set continuum after the model of Engel-Norton not make it impossible to ask such questions?

Should not this alertness to providential creation of context for conversion also require us to recognize that the varied themes of culture's contexts will order conversion's turning from and turning to, as perceived by the converted persons? And should it not demand that the advocate understand that perceived context in promoting the nature of the change that Jesus Christ brings?

How shall we respond to some of the suggestions by David Shank (1976:5), as to possible culturally determined contexts for conversion?

Context of Experience	*From*	*To*	*Through Jesus*
Acceptance	Rejection	Acceptance	Love
Direction	to err about	to aim at	Call
Festival	Boredom	Joy	Feast-giver
Meaning	the absurd	the reasonable	Word
Liberation	Oppression	Liberation	Liberation
Becoming	Nobody	Somebody	Invitation
Fellowship	Solitude	Community	Presence
etc.			

To be sure, any number of things may short circuit this process. There may be too much focus on conversion as a single act, a rite of passage, through a concomitant neglect of conversion as also a rite of consolidation, "the total dynamic relational process that a living, lifetime relationship with God is intended to be" (Kraft 1977:597). There may be lack of sensitivity to the "constants" of biblical conversion—conscious allegiance to God, the dynamic interaction between God and human beings that issues from man's conscious allegiance to God, growth or maturation in Christ, the community nature of the maturation process, the cultural appropriateness of the conversion process (Kraft 1977:604-613). There may be cultural overlays of individualism held by the communicator. There may be inability to differentiate between the cultural forms of conversion often developed by ecclesiastical tradition and experience and conversion as dynamically equivalent meaning-reality. For one reason or another, we may be left with a "cultural conversion" as much as conversion to Christ, illustrated in these models offered by Kraft (1977:621):

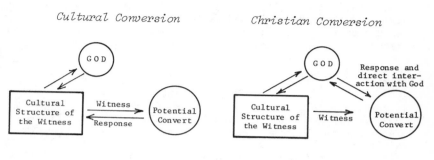

Cultural Conversion   *Christian Conversion*

(Kraft 1977:621)

But is not the ideal reflected in the willingness of a Paul to be "all things to all men, that I may by all means save some" (1 Cor. 9:22)? "Both the context of 1 Cor. 9:19-23 and the content of these verses themselves show that Paul could not modify the Gospel itself according to the particular characteristics of his hearers. The whole of his concern is to make clear that the changeless Gospel, which lies upon him as his *anangkē* (9:16), empowers him to be free to change his stance" (Bornkamm 1966: 196). His methdology is to be understood in the light of 1 Cor. 7:17-24. "In pointed terms this means that in the light of the Gospel Paul does not accept the different *standpoints* (Standpunkte) of Jews and Gentiles, but he does recognize their respective positions as the *historical places* (Standorte) where the 'calling' of each man occurs through the Gospel. From this perspective religious tradition and social position are relativized; at the same time they are highly significant for the realization of Christian experience" (and, we might add, Christian conversion) (Bornkamm 1966:196). They become significant as the lifesituation, the context, in which the Gospel is to accomplish its converting purpose. Paul's principles regarding the cultural context for conversion demanded that (1) the basic content of the Gospel should not be changed and (2) the Gospel should be intelligible and relevant to those felt contextual needs (Shin 1974:75).

In this whole process of understanding culture's contexts, "the Chief Actor in the historic mission of the Church is the Holy Spirit.... He is a destroyer of barriers, a bridge builder, one who enables each to see the other. He opens the eyes to see Christ, but also...to know in order to understand.... He makes

us aware and sensitive" (Oosthuizein 1977:60-61). It is the
Spirit who enables us to listen and learn until one sees the
world of the person in another culture through his eyes. It is
he who opens that culture to the powerful entrance of the Gospel. And it is he who enables the missionary advocate to be
freed from the cultural imperialism that inhibits him from the
freedom of being all things to all men.

FOOTNOTES

1. Yun's thesis was first elaborated in his title, *Kidokkyo wa
Han'guk Sasang* (Seoul: Christian Literature Society, 1964). A
history of the Korean discussion in English can be found in
Palmer 1967:5-18 and Park 1970:48-51. The wider background of
Korea's indigenization discussion of the 1960s is traced rather
sketchily in Shin 1974:133-143.

2. We may be excused a minor alteration if we suggest yet a
further refinement at this stage--a change from the term, multi-
individual (which still bears some cultural stigma) to the term,
multi-personal.

3. Some of the practical dimensions of this judgment are
worked out in more detail by Kenneth G. Smith (1977) and James
Pennington (1974).

4. Out of these observations, Shearer has also suggested a
questionnaire to test religious receptivity to the Gospel. "To
be useful, the questionnaire should be scored to read out and
estimate (a) the amount of dissatisfaction a person has with his
culture, (b) the amount of dissatisfaction he has with his present religion, (c) the strength of bond with his family and clan,
(d) the amount of freedom the respondent has to change, and
(e) the part his family or clan group plays in a decision to
change. Other scales could be discovered during the process of
validation which would indicate aspects of receptivity" (Shearer
1973:163). From that data would then come information for pin-
pointing the segments of a population receptive to change, and
even indicative of the better approaches for eliciting greatest
response, a conversion-readiness scale as it were. The idea
has merit, but perhaps it should also build into the scale the
amount of dissatisfaction a person has with Christianity as an
alternative culture source.

5. I have no problems with Kraft's language per se. However, I
distance myself from what I understand to be Kraft's usage of
it to describe worldview as basically a scientific model, a
theoretical paradigm of a conceptual, analytical, non-naive

sort, a "mental map," "an organization of theories." Kraft's
analysis of paradigm models is deeply indebted at this stage
to Kuhn and Barbour's studies of paradigms (Kraft 1977:45 ff.).
And, though Kuhn's recognition of bias and the abandonment of
the older view of scientific presuppositionlessness is useful,
he never acknowledges the reality of religious bias at the
heart of worldview or modeled worldview. The inadequacies of
modeling drawn attention to by Barbour (1974:37-38) are never
conscious of those inadequacies in the way Kraft suggests, a
form of religious idolatry, worshiping the created model rather
than pointing to the Creator (Kraft 1977:50).

6. I take strong exception to the monopoly Durkheim granted
to the social category in his understanding of the genesis of
religion, and feel this monopoly is a religious one itself, and
one of a radical sort in central conflict with Durkheim's minimal and constructive understanding of religion as a cultic function peripheral to the meaning of culture. But, at the least,
Lee's argument, with his own modifications of Durkheim's thesis,
can be used to authenticate the social dimensions of conversion
as one aspect of a larger picture.

7. This generalization is questioned, among others, by Shin
1974:131, who argues that "generally speaking, early missionaries in Korea were extremely conservative and puritanical, with
the result that they could not appreciate Korean culture."
Shin's supporting reference is a citation from Palmer (1967:26),
which, in turn, is an unacknowledged quotation from A.J. Brown,
one of the General Secretaries of the Board of Foreign Missions
of the Presbyterian Church, U.S.A. (Brown 1919:540). Brown's
comments flow from his own strong lack of sympathy for the evangelical theological convictions of the early Protestants (Conn
1966:26-27). Further, the general thrust of Palmer's argument
is against the overall judgment in support of which Shin uses
it.

8. The relationships of science and worldview are dealt with
philosophically in the work of Herman Dooyeweerd (1953:114-165).
With some questions regarding these formulations (Frame n.d.:
6-14), we still find his discussions fruitful in this area.

BIBLIOGRAPHY

Allison, Christopher F., 1961. *The Rise of Moralism*. London:
    S.P.C.K.

Barbour, Ian G., 1974. *Myths, Models and Paradigms*. New York:
    Harper and Row Publishers.

Barnett, Homer G., 1953. *Innovation: The Basis of Cultural Change*. New York: McGraw-Hill Co.

Bavinck, J.H., 1949. *The Impact of Christianity on the Non-Christian World*. Grand Rapids: William B. Eerdmans Publishing Company.

_____, 1955. "General Revelation and the non-Christian Religions," *Free University Quarterly* 4:43-55.

_____, 1960. *An Introduction to the Science of Missions*. Philadelphia, Pa: Presbyterian and Reformed Publishing Company.

Berkhof, Louis, 1949. *Systematic Theology*. Grand Rapids: William B. Eerdmans Publishing Company.

Biernatzki, William, Im, Luke, & Min, Anselm, 1975. *Korean Catholicism in the 70s*. Maryknoll: Orbis Books.

Boer, Harry, 1961. *Pentecost and Missions*. Grand Rapids: William B. Eerdmans Publishing Company.

Bornkamm, Gunther, 1966. "The Missionary Stance of Paul in 1 Corinthians 9 and Acts," *Studies in Luke-Acts*, Leander Keck and J. Louis Martyn, eds. Nashville: Abingdon Press.

Brown, Arthur J., 1919. *The Mastery of the Far East*. New York: Scribners.

Clark, Allen D., 1971. *A History of the Church in Korea*. Seoul: The Christian Literature Society of Korea.

Clowney, Edmund P., 1976. "Contextualization and the Biblical Theology of Culture," Unpublished paper delivered at the Contextualization Study Group, Fourbrooks, Pa.

Conn, Harvie M., 1966. "Studies in the Theology of the Korean Presbyterian Church: An Historical Outline - 1," *Westminster Theological Journal*, 29:24-57.

_____, 1977. "Contextualization: Where Do We Begin?," *Evangelicals and Liberation*, Carl. E. Armerding, ed. Nutley, N.J.: Presbyterian and Reformed Publishing Company.

_____, 1977a. "Theological Reflections on Contextualizing Christianity: How Far Do We Go?" Mimeographed paper distributed through Westminster Theological Seminary, Philadelphia.

_____, 1977b. "Reactions and Guidelines: The Praxis of a
Covenant Ethnos." Unpublished paper delivered at the Consultation on the Homogeneous Unit Principle, Fuller Theological Seminary, May 31-June 2, 1977.

_____, 1978. "Contextualization: A New Dimension for Cross-
Cultural Hermeneutic," *Evangelical Missions Quarterly*,
14:39-46.

DeGraaf, Arnold, 1976. "An Alternative to Our Traditional Anthropological Models." Mimeographed paper distributed
through the Institute for Christian Studies, Toronto,
Ontario.

Dooyeweerd, Herman, 1953. *A New Critique of Theoretical
Thought, Vol. 1.* Presbyterian and Reformed Publishing Company.

Douglas, J.D., editor, 1975. *Let the Earth Hear His Voice.*
Minneapolis: World Wide Publications.

Engel, James F. & Norton, Wilbert H., 1975. *What's Gone Wrong
with the Harvest?* Grand Rapids: Zondervan Publishing House.

Frame, John M., n.d. *The Amsterdam Philosophy: A Preliminary
Critique.* Phillipsburg, N.J.: Harmony Press.

Fung, Yu-lan, 1952. *A History of Chinese Philosophy, Vol. 1.*
Princeton: Princeton University Press.

Gaffin, Richard B., Jr., 1968. "Paul as Theologian," *Westminster Theological Journal* 30:204-232.

_____, 1974. "Contemporary Hermeneutics and the Study of the
New Testament," *Studying the New Testament Today,* John H.
Skilton, ed. Nutley, N.J.: Presbyterian and Reformed Pub-
lishing Company.

_____, 1976. "Systematic Theology and Biblical Theology,"
The New Testament Student and Theology, John H. Skilton,
ed. Nutley, N.J.: Presbyterian and Reformed Publishing
Company.

Gale, James S., 1906. *Korea in Transition.* New York: Eaten
and Mains.

_____, 1909. *Korea in Transition.* New York: Laymen's Mis-
sionary Movement.

Gerlach, L.P. & Hine, V.H., 1970. *People, Power, Change: Movements of Social Transformation*. New York: Bobbs-Merrill Company.

Harrington, Fred H., 1961. *God, Mammon and the Japanese*. Madison: University of Wisconsin Press.

Harris, Marvin, 1968. *The Rise of Anthropological Theory*. New York: Thomas Y. Crowell Company.

Hatch, Elvin, 1973. *Theories of Man and Culture*. New York: Colombia University Press.

Hulbert, Homer, 1905. *The History of Korea, Vol. 1*. Seoul: The Methodist Publishing House.

Kalsbeek, L., 1975. *Contours of a Christian Philosophy*. Toronto: Wedge Publishing Foundation.

Kay, Il-seung, 1950. "Christianity in Korea." Th.D. dissertation submitted to Union Theological Seminary, Richmond, VA.

Kittel, Gerhard, editor, 1971. *Theological Dictionary of the New Testament, Vol. VII*. Grand Rapids: William B. Eerdmans Publishing Company.

Knapp, Stephen, 1976. "Contextualization and Its Implications for U.S. Evangelical Churches and Missions." Mimeographed paper distributed through Partnership in Mission, Abington, PA.

Kraft, Charles, 1977. "Theologizing in Culture." Pre-publication manuscript distributed through Fuller Theological Seminary, Pasadena, CA.

Kuhn, Thomas S., 1970. *The Structure of Scientific Revolutions*. Chicago: University of Chicago Press.

Lee, Gabriel G., 1961. "Sociology of Conversion: Sociological Implications of Religious Conversion to Christianity in Korea." Ph.D. dissertation submitted to Fordham University, New York.

McGavran, Donald A., 1955. *The Bridges of God*. New York: Friendship Press.

_____, 1970. *Understanding Church Growth*. Grand Rapids: William B. Eerdmans Publishing Company.

_____, 1974. *The Clash Between Christianity and Cultures.* Washington, D.C.: Canon Books.

Malinowski, B., 1948. *Magic, Science and Religion.* Boston: Beacon Press.

Murray, John, 1976. *Collected Writings of John Murray, Vol. 1.* Edinburgh: The Banner of Truth Trust.

Nida, Eugene A., 1960. *Message and Mission.* Pasadena: William Carey Library, 1960.

_____, 1971. "New Religions for Old: A Study of Culture Change in Religion," *Church and Culture Change in Africa,* David J. Bosch, ed. Pretoria: N.G. Kerk-Boekhandel.

Nida, Eugene A. & Taber, Charles, 1969. *The Theory and Practice of Translation.* Leiden: E.J. Brill.

Oosthuizein, G.C., 1977. "The Holy Spirit and Culture," *The Holy Spirit Down to Earth,* Paul G. Schrotenboer, ed. Grand Rapids: Reformed Ecumenical Synod.

Paik, L. George, 1929. *The History of Protestant Missions in Korea 1832-1910.* Pyeng Yang, Korea: Union Christian College Press.

Palmer, Spencer J., 1967. *Korea and Christianity: The Problem of Identification with Tradition.* Seoul: Hollym Corporation.

Park, Pong-bae, 1970. "The Encounter of Christianity with Traditional Culture and Ethics in Korea: An Essay in Christian Self-Understanding." Ph.D. dissertation submitted to Vanderbilt University, Nashville, Tennessee.

Pennington, James, 1974. "Some Principles and Patterns for Family Evangelism in Relation to Church Growth in Japan." Th.M. thesis submitted to Trinity Evangelical Divinity School, Deerfield, Illinois.

Pettit, Norman, 1966. *The Heart Prepared: Grace and Conversion in Puritan Spiritual Life.* New Haven: Yale University Press.

Poythress, Vern S., 1976. "Structural Relations in Pauline Expressions for the Application of Redemption (with Special Reference to Holiness)." Ph.D. dissertation submitted to the University of Cambridge.

Ramm, Bernard, 1966. *A Handbook of Contemporary Theology*.
    Grand Rapids: William B. Eerdmans Publishing Company.

Ridderbos, Herman, 1975. *Paul. An Outline of His Theology*.
    Grand Rapids: William B. Eerdmans Publishing Company.

Shank, David A., 1976. "Towards an Understanding of Christian
    Conversion," *Mission-Focus* 5:1-7.

Sharp, C.E., 1906. "Motives for Seeking Christ," *Korea Mission
    Field* 2:182.

Shearer, Roy E., 1966. *Wildfire: Church Growth in Korea*.
    Grand Rapids: William B. Eerdmans Publishing Company.

_____, 1973. "The Psychology of Receptivity and Church
    Growth," *God, Man and Church Growth*, Alan R. Tippett, ed.
    Grand Rapids: William B. Eerdmans Publishing Company.

Shepherd, Norman, 1976. "The Covenant Context for Evangelism,"
    The New Testament Student and Theology, John H. Skilton, ed.
    Nutley, N.J.: Presbyterian and Reformed Publishing Company.

Shin, Song-jung, 1974. "Paul's Missionary Method and the Indig-
    enization of the Korean Church." Ph.D. dissertation sub-
    mitted to Temple University, Philadelphia.

Smith, Kenneth G., 1977. "The Covenant Family as a Perspective
    in Missions." Unpublished paper delivered at the Third Re-
    formed Consultation on Missions, Beaver Falls, PA., April 4-6,
    1977.

Taber, Charles, 1976. "When Is a Christian?" *Milligan Missio-
    gram* 3(3); 1-4.

Tippett, Alan R., 1970. *Church Growth and the Word of God*.
    Grand Rapids: William B. Eerdmans Publishing Company.

_____, 1973. *Verdict Theology in Missionary Theory*. South
    Pasadena: William Carey Library.

_____, 1977. "Conversion as a Dynamic Process in Christian
    Mission," *Missiology* 5:203-221.

Underwood, Horace G., 1908. *The Call of Korea*. New York:
    Fleming H. Revell Company.

_____, 1910. *The Religions of Eastern Asia*. New York: The
    Macmillan Company.

Underwood, Lillias H., 1918. *Underwood of Korea*. New York: Fleming H. Revell Company.

Van Baal, J., 1971. *Symbols for Communication. An Introduction to the Anthropological Study of Religion*. Assen: Van Gorcum and Company.

Vos, Geerhardus, 1930. *Pauline Eschatology*. Grand Rapids: William B. Eerdmans Publishing Company.

_____, 1948. *Biblical Theology*. Grand Rapids: William B. Eerdmans Publishing Company.

_____, 1956. *The Teaching of the Epistle to the Hebrews*. Grand Rapids: William B. Eerdmans Publishing Company.

_____, 1972. *The Kingdom of God and the Church*. Nutley, N.J.: Presbyterian and Reformed Publishing Company.

Warfield, B.B., n.d. "New Testament Terms Descriptive of the Great Change," Reprint from the *Presbyterian Quarterly*, 91-100.

_____, 1952. "On the Biblical Notion of 'Renewal,'" *Biblical and Theological Studies*. Philadelphia: Presbyterian and Reformed Publishing Company.

Weems, Benjamin B., 1964. *Reform, Rebellion and the Heavenly Way*. Tucson: The University of Arizona Press.

11

Conversion
as a Complex Experience:
A Personal Case Study

Orlando E. Costas

This paper is an exploration of the Christian understanding of conversion as a dynamic, complex experience. Negatively, it is an attempt to call into question the traditional evangelical view of conversion as a static, once-for-all, private, trans-cultural and non-contextual event. Positively, it is a constructive effort toward the development of a more biblical, theological and socio-historically sound formulation of the Christian doctrine of conversion.

Conversion is analyzed in the light of a particular psycho-cultural framework. Culture is conceived as a constituent *part* of the socio-historical reality, and not as an over-arching concept which incorporates all the aspects of this reality. Culture is seen as a social phenomenon. It stands for a people's way of life, including their customs, creations, value system, attitudes and beliefs. For this reason, culture must be viewed historically, as part of long-term, dialectical processes, and analyzed in the context of the macro-institutions (economic, social and political) that make up our respective human societies.

I approach the subject as a Latin American from the Hispanic Caribbean. It is natural, therefore, that I should refer to

Latin American and Puerto Rican cultures. To be sure, there are diversities of cultures in contemporary Latin America, just as there are different types of Puerto Ricans (of San Juan, the rest of the island, the New York diaspora, the outside-New York-North American diaspora and the outside-USA-Puerto Rican diaspora). Even so, there is a common cultural substratum that gives a unique character to the peoples who live or come from South of the Rio Bravo and make up the islands of the Hispanic Caribbean: (1) The two leading languages of Iberia (Castillian and Portuguese) give Latin Americans a linguistic commonality. (2) A dependent, colonial Christendom has given them a common Christian religious heritage. (3) And the convergence of three main ethnic streams (Iberian, African and Amerindian) has given birth to a "new" race, the mestizo, which Jose Vasconcelos characterized in quasi philosophical and/or poetical language as "the cosmic race" with evergrowing common patterns of collective consciousness and world views, expressed in literature, art, music, education, sports, religious beliefs and practices and social formations.

But what gives Latin America its homogeneity is not so much its common cultural heritage as its common historical situation: the fact that it is the offspring of a civilizational process which incorporated into exploitative nuclei the aborigines and their descendants, the slaves brought over from Africa and their children as well as the half-breed and "creole" offspring of the Spanish *conquistadores*. Though the process of historical incorporation was initiated by the Iberian people, it was successfully completed by the Northern European people, notably the British, Dutch, French and more recently the Anglo-North Americans. This latter process, known as the neo-colonial pact, has made of the majorities of the peoples of Central and South America and the Caribbean cultural, economic, social and politically oppressed and marginalized nuclei. It is this reality that gives the peoples of these lands a cultural homogeneity clearly distinguishable from the North Atlantic cultures present in the Americas.

As a Puerto Rican I represent one of the last overt colonies in the hemisphere. As one who lived for many years in the greater New York area, I represent the internal and external migratory process, which has characterized the life of many of the peoples of the region during the present century, largely as a by-product of their socio-economic (and in some cases political) situation. I reflect, therefore, not just the colonial and neo-colonial socio-historical reality of the region, but a migrant sub-culture, concretely that of Hispanic-USA, and stand as a counterpart to the many ethnic groups that have emerged out of the fantastic urban migration that Latin America has experienced since the 1930s.

From this rather complex situation, I wrestle in this paper
with the meaning and distinctiveness of Christian conversion.
Specifically, I try to respond to the following questions: What
is the *locus* of identity of this phenomenon which the Bible and
Christian theology view as an objective of evangelism? Where is
its point of gravitation, what is its aim and how is it
verified?

I try to respond to this question by means of the case-study
method. This, a rather novel approach to theological reflection,
is given an "old touch" by the choice of my own spiritual
pilgrimage as the object of study. In so doing, however, I hold
on to one of the more traditional evangelical approaches to
theology: to reflect on Christian truth in the light of one's
experiences. Yet, so as not to fall into pietistic subjectivism
I try to put this experience against the evaluative control of
biblical revelation and theological analysis. From this I draw
several practical implications which I proceed to outline in
conclusion.

The case study is developed along a twofold model, preceded
by several autobiographical notes. I use, first, a *concentric*
model to explain the facts related to my "complex conversion
experience." I thus speak of a religious conversion to Christ,
a cultural conversion to Puerto Rico and Latin America, and a
socio-political (or missional) conversion to the world, particularly the world of the poor and disenfranchised of society.
I do not see these conversion experiences as divorced from one
another, but as interrelated. Thus the conversion to Christ is
foundational, the cultural a consequence of my new identity in
Christ and the socio-political an outgrowth of my calling as a
follower of the man who wants to be found among the destitute
of the earth. My encounter with an African friend showed me,
however, that even this way of formulating the complexity of
my conversion experience was too static. I suggest, accordingly,
a second model, namely, that of a *spiral*, as a more adequate
way of understanding the meaning of conversion. Christian
conversion is thus defined as "a journey into the mystery of the
kingdom of God, which leads from one experience to another."

A PERSONAL CASE STUDY

Autobiographical Notes

I was born in Puerto Rico, the son of a God-fearing Methodist
family. I was baptized into the Christian faith when I was 40
days old and was consecrated to God's service by my mother even
before birth. I received a high moral example from my parents,
a sound Christian upbringing and fairly good care from the
church, though not without its roughs and tumbles. Yet I lived

a most restless and turbulent childhood. I was (and I suppose
still am to a degree) hot-headed, egocentric, rebellious,
ambitious, proud and boastful.

At the age of 12 my father failed in his grocery business and
(as with many other Puerto Ricans) decided to migrate to
continental USA. I followed my father to live with an aunt in
the Bronx who was married to an Anglo-American. Since I had
been brought up in a middle-class family with many privileges
and freedoms, I was very confident of myself and did not think
as I traveled to New York by myself that the experience would be
as traumatic as it turned out. The encounter with a cross-
cultural marriage, with no children, in a very rough Irish-
Puerto Rican neighborhood and in a school situation which can
only be described, by the title of James Dean's film, as a
"Black Board Jungle," produced such a profound and traumatic
culture shock that I don't think I have ever recovered.

Several months later, my family settled in Bridgeport,
Connecticut. My father had been in Chicago and had not been
able to find a job. (It was in the mid 50's when jobs were hard
to come by, especially if you happened to be a non-skilled
Puerto Rican.) Through the help of relatives on my mother's
side who had settled in Bridgeport, where a small Puerto Rican
community had begun to emerge, a job finally turned up in a
small grocery store. I went to live with my father in
December 1954 and three months later the entire family was re-
united. Our first home was in a run-down, non-heated flat
across from the school my sisters and I attended.

For three years I suffered the impact of a strange environment, full of hostility and prejudice. I developed strong
feelings of shame and self hatred. I tried to overcome the
stigma of being Puerto Rican through an aggressive social
behavior which bordered on what some North American sociologists
would label as juvenile deliquency. When I saw that this was
not getting me very far, I tried new roads to personal status.
First came music. I was discovered as a teenage tenor by the
Police Athletic League Talent Theater Group and was awarded a
scholarship with a teacher from New York. Then came sports.
I became very active in basketball. And thirdly, personal
leadership. I joined a local boys club and within two years I
had been designated "Boy of the Year," the first Puerto Rican
in the USA to receive such an award.

From the moment of our arrival, we became part of the
Hispanic Evangelical Mission, which was sponsored by the local
Protestant Council of Churches. This Mission became a sort of
social refuge for the family. Very soon, however, I began to
branch out into other (English-speaking) congregations. There-

after my religious universe would encompass both the Spanish
mission, where the family interacted with other Spanish-speaking
families, and the English-speaking congregations, where I interacted with Anglo-American peers.

It soon became evident that, though I was attending church
regularly, I was rebelling against the family and my parents'
expression of the Christian faith. I remember, for example, how
whenever I heard my mother praying I would enter into her room,
interrupt, mock and ridicule her to the point that she would
often lose her "cool," stop her prayer and start crying. I
made life miserable for my sisters, bullying them around and
mistreating them. Though I was only 15 years old, I thought
myself big and old enough to come into the house at very late
hours, to hang around with anybody I chose, to go anywhere and
do anything I pleased. My father tried to turn me around in all
sorts of ways. He tried disciplining me, lecturing me, getting
me to read the Bible and even going into my room early in the
morning and praying out loud for me. None of these things
worked. I would not listen, I would not respond, I would not
turn around in my attitudes and behaviour.

In that situation, I attended (at the invitation of a group
of friends) Billy Graham's 1957 New York Crusade. That night
something strange and unusual occurred in my life which I can
only describe as the beginning of a long spiritual pilgrimage.
Looking back and reflecting upon that and the other moments
that followed I can easily recognize lines of continuity with
earlier stages of my life. How much continuity and discontinuity there was between my life before and after that event, I
cannot say. But consciously, at least, there was a new beginning;
something unique did happen on June 8, 1957 in Madison Square
Garden, and has been happening ever since.

A Concentric Model of Conversion

Allow me to describe this pilgrimage in three concentric
circles. The center is Christ, of course, and the first circle
represents my conversion to Him.

Conversion to Christ. An exact reconstruction of this event
is, of course, impossible. Whether it was the exact moment when
I became a true follower of Christ, I cannot assert with
certainty.   It had not been the first time that I had made a
public profession of faith in Christ. Neither can I assert the
exact reason why I "went forward." Certainly it was not due to
the sermon, since I had hardly paid any attention to it. I do
know, however, that the words of the hymn the choir was singing
at the moment of the invitation had a moving impact upon me.

> Just as I am without one plea
> But that thy blood was shed for me
> Now that thou bidst me come to thee
> O Lamb of God, I come, I come.
>
> Just as I am though tossed about
> With many a conflict, many a doubt
> Fightings and fears within, without,
> O Lamb of God, I come, I come.

As I heard the choir sing these words, I could not help but recall many of the things I had read in the Bible, the prayers I had heard my mother and father say, the exhortations I had received from them, the lessons I had been given in Sunday School. I was also conscious of my complex personal spiritual situation: the way I had been trying to push God out of my existence, my rebellious, uncourteous and aggressive relations with my family, my pride and egocentrism. I decided to respond affirmatively to the invitation that was being extended by the Evangelist and *make the words of the hymn my own.*

The quasi sacramental act of going forward and the personal prayer of confession I made later became the outward means through which I expressed my commitment to Christ. The evidence that something positive and unusual had occurred was the change of attitude I began to demonstrate several hours later. When I arrived home that evening, the first thing I did was tell my mother that I had been converted to Jesus Christ and that I had begun a new life. There was a change in my attitude toward prayer and Bible reading. No longer did I get offended by my parents' religious practices. I began to act more considerately with my sisters. I abandoned my irresponsible behaviour outside the house, disciplining myself to act as a member of a family and not as a solitary individual. And I began to think of my future not in terms of personal aggrandizement, but rather of that which would contribute to the enrichment of others.

Yet as I re-oriented my life I began to encounter a number of difficulties, the chief of which was the rather "worldly" environment in which I had begun to move as a result of my musical contacts. My relationship with the PAL Talent Theater Group had set me on the road to a career in show business. This created tremendous demands upon my life which, due to my emotional and religious immaturity, militated against my new Christian life. As I talked the problem over with my parents, we decided to seek the advice of the pastor of the Spanish Mission. He suggested that perhaps I should go to a Christian school to complete my high school, and recommended as one possibility the school from which one of his daughters had graduated: Bob Jones University, which had both a junior and

senior high school. Wanting to give me all the necessary resources that would enable me to follow through on my commitment
to Christ, they opted to send me to this school, at the greatest
financial sacrifice of their entire lives.

Conversion to Culture. It was at Bob Jones that I began to
experience the second great crisis of my life which led
eventually to what I have identified as a cultural conversion.
Bob Jones Academy and University were located in Greenville,
South Carolina. It was (and still is) a center of North
American Southern fundamentalism. I got there in 1958 at the
height of the neo-evangelical-fundamentalist controversy. There
was strong opposition to Billy Graham for his practice of
cooperative evangelism, introduced in the New York Crusade.
Accepting the backing of so-called Protestant liberals was considered by Bob Jones, John R. Rice and others as a "compromise"
of the fundamentals of the faith. They set out to combat Billy
Graham and all those who reflected such "soft" attitudes toward
liberals. This controversy could not but have negative impact
upon my life. As with many of my classmates, I soon began to
take, without understanding all the issues involved, a similar
stand against liberals and neo-evangelicals. I became a
fundamentalist.

Not only did I discover North American fundamentalism at
Bob Jones, but came face to face with Anglo-Saxon culture in its
worst form. The annual Shakespearian productions and the
exaltation of Anglo-Saxon literature; the weekly Vesper Services,
which focused, for the most part, on the great Anglo-American
religious heritage; the daily chapel services, saturated by the
North American revivalistic and crusading spirit; the
puritanical value system, manifested in such things as the
chaperon-controlled dating system and the rigid disciplinary
procedures; the unshameful defense and justification of racism,
so characteristic of Anglo-Saxon culture; and the triumphalistic
belief in the divine destiny of the USA--all of these cultural
configurations led me to ask myself whether I had any part in
such a world. Later on I would come to the conclusion that not
only did I not belong to that world, but that I did not want to,
even if allowed!

Paradoxically, this feeling of not being part of the cultural
milieu portrayed at Bob Jones was intensified by my discovery of
the Latin American world. For there were at Bob Jones many
students from Latin America. As I fellowshipped with them, I
began to discover how close I was to them and how different I
was from the average White-Anglo-Saxon Protestant who made up
the overwhelming majority of the student body. That experience
not only kindled a passionate love for the lands south of the

Rio Bravo, but became the beachhead for the rediscovery of my hidden Latin American identity.

At Bob Jones I also discovered the Christian imperative of evangelism. Through the testimonies of friends who had gone on evangelistic missions to Mexico and Central America and, especially, through the inspiration of a Puerto Rican colleague who had the gift of evangelism, I developed a passionate concern for the communication of the Gospel to those who live outside the frontiers of the faith.

Finally, I discovered the church as something larger than myself, my family or a place where one goes to meet other people or hear someone preach. Partly as a result of my contacts with peers who had a more dynamic understanding and commitment to the church, and partly as a result of the ecclesial consciousness of some of the religious activities on campus (the Sunday School program, for example, was organized along different church traditions), I became convinced of the need to become an official part of a visible church *fellowship*.

One of the results of my studies at Bob Jones Academy was the decision to join a local congregational church in Bridgeport. This act was accompanied by the decision to give public witness to my commitment to Christ through baptism. Though I had been baptized as a child, I felt (at that time) that I should give outward evidence of my new relationship with Christ and that the most Scriptural way to signify it was through what in some free church traditions is known as "believer's baptism."

My studies at Bob Jones had given me not only an evangelistic passion for my people, but a deep concern for preaching. So while fellowshipping at the Black Rock Congregational Church, I became actively involved in ministry among the Spanish-speaking people of Bridgeport and New York. I took my first pastorate at the age of 19. It was a small store-front congregation affiliated with the Christian Church (Disciples of Christ) in the heart of the Latin neighborhood. The work prospered, but after a short period I decided that I needed Bible and theological training. So I enrolled at Nyack Missionary College.

While at Nyack I took a short student pastorate in Brooklyn, at an Evangelical Free Church, where I met my wife and organized a Latin American Evangelistic Team. My wife and team members enrolled at Nyack and from there traveled to New York every weekend for meetings in Spanish-speaking churches. One summer we made an evangelistic tour of Puerto Rico.

During this trip I became aware of the need to study more
closely my cultural heritage and to become part of a larger
fellowship of churches. I came to the conclusion that in order
to minister effectively to Latin Americans I had to understand
their history and culture. I decided to inquire about the
possibility of working with the Puerto Rico Baptist Convention
and of studying at a local university. Both possibilities became a reality when I was invited to become pastor of the First
Baptist Church of Yauco, a town in the southwestern part of the
island and only 30 minutes from the main campus of Inter-
American University (IAU).

Several things occurred during my three-year ministry in that
church. For one thing, I was able to discover the church as an
institution; i.e., as a complex system of distinctive beliefs,
values, rites, symbols and relationships which maintain a line
of continuity with the past and through which the Gospel is
communicated and lived. I became fully integrated to the
Baptist fellowship, and especially into the Puerto Rican and
American Baptist Conventions, when I was ordained to the
ministry (at the age of 21!). For another, I had a chance to
finish my undergraduate studies at IAU, majoring in Latin
American History and Politics. These studies led me to redis-
cover my Puerto Rican identity, to affirm my Latin American
cultural heritage, to begin to question the political hegemony
of the USA in Latin America and to *consciously* break with its
culture.

This did not mean that I had become hostile to North Americans
as persons. It meant rather that I was becoming increasingly
aware of the political oppression and economic exploitation
which their *nation,* as an imperial and neo-colonial power, was
exercising over Latin America as a whole, and in particular
over my own country. It meant, further, that I had finally
come face to face with the fact that I was not an Anglo-American;
that I needed not to be one for I had a rich cultural heritage
of my own which I should accept joyfully; and, therefore, that
I should aim at getting rid of any Anglo-American cultural
influence which stood in the way of the full expression of my
Puerto Rican and Latin American cultural heritage.

I had overcome my cultural crisis. I had experienced an
authentic cultural conversion, an experience which was not
isolated from other moments in my life. For in a sense, it was
the outgrowth of the tensions I had lived from my first contacts
with Anglo-Saxon culture. And in a deeper sense, it had been
stimulated and inspired by my encounter with that Jew who had
transformed my existence once I acknowledged Him as God's
revelation made flesh and trusted Him as my only Savior and Lord.

Conversion to the world. After completion of my university
studies, I returned to continental USA to further my theological
preparation. I enrolled at Trinity Evangelical Divinity School
in Deerfield, Illinois and later transferred to Garrett Theological Seminary in Evanston. I also did parallel studies during the summer at the Winona Lake School of Theology in Indiana.
In order to support my family I accepted the call to pastor an
inner city Mexican-American and Puerto Rican Baptist congregation in the south-side of Milwaukee, Wisconsin.

No sooner had I settled in at the *Iglesia Evangelica Bautista*
when I was called upon by representatives of the Spanish-speaking
community to represent them in the Social Development Commission,
which administered the so-called War on Poverty throughout the
County of Milwaukee. I immediately discovered that I was in a
loaded political situation. The Latin community was a minority
among a minority. Not only the white majority, but also the
blacks were consciously marginating our people from the programs
and social benefits of the War on Poverty. It soon became
obvious that the reason for this was the lack of political
organization which existed in the Latin south-side as against
the sophisticated organization of blacks in the north-side and
the institutional power of the white majority. From the blacks
we learned how important it was to put together a cohesive
organization. So I got involved in community organization,
helping to organize the Latin American Union for Civil Rights.

I should say that in this political praxis I never lost my
Christian and pastoral identity. On the contrary, this process
led me to reflect critically on my ministry and on the nature
and mission of the church. This led me to discover the world of
the poor and the disenfranchised as a fundamental reference of
the Gospel. I came to realize that the Christian mission had
not only personal, spiritual and cultural dimensions, but also
social, economic and political. This meant that the object of
mission was not the community of faith, but the world in its
complexity and concreteness, and that one of my basic responsibilities as a minister of the church was to mobilize it with
all of its resources, and limitations, for a *total* missionary
practice.

My ministry in Milwaukee had led me to experience a missiological (and socio-political) conversion. My conversions to
Christ and to my culture had been complemented by a conversion
to the world, *especially the world of the forgotten and exploited*. Interestingly enough, this enabled both the church and myself to deepen our understanding of our relationship to Christ
and our cultural heritage. The church experienced a well-
rounded, healthy growth. As for me, the fruit of that experience
became evident in the decision of my wife and I to go to con-

tinental Latin America as missionaries and in the publication of
my first book, *La iglesia y su misión evangelizadora*, where I
began to rehearse an integral concept of mission and evangelism
on the basis of my action-reflection experience in Milwaukee.

A Spiral Model of Conversion

I was in Hong Kong lecturing at the Chung Chi Theological
College when I first thought of interpreting my spiritual
pilgrimage in a concentric model involving three interrelated
but distinct conversions. From Hong Kong I continued my journey
through South and West Asia and then crossed over to East and
West Africa. While visiting Cameroon, I had the occasion to
share my three-fold conversion experiences with an African
friend and theologian. His reaction was a straight look and a
"So?"   I asked him what do you mean "so?"   He answered: "So
you think those will be your only conversions? If they are,
then their validity will have been denied. For if you are to
continue to grow as a person and as a Christian, you will have
to experience one turn after another."

These words made me think...and to change my concentric model
into a *spiral* one. For the complexity of conversion does not
lie in a fixed number of experiences, but in the fact that it is
a plunge into an ongoing adventure. Christian conversion is a
journey into the mystery of the kingdom of God, which leads
from one experience to another.

From this definition, it follows that while Christian conversion can be signified by a distinct moment, it is also an ongoing process. Initiation in the journey of the kingdom
implies a plunge into an eschatological adventure where one is
confronted with ever new decisions, ever new turning points,
ever new fulfillments and ever new promises, and this will
continue until the ultimate fulfillment of the kingdom. It also
implies that one is confronted with the need to make ever new
re-routings. The fundamental point of reference, however, is
not a static, fixed point, but a foundational signpost that
accompanies one along throughout the journey, similar to the
traveling tabernacle in the Old Testament or the *anamnesis* that
the children of Israel engaged in year after year in the Passover celebration: a celebration and living again, at whatever
point of their pilgrimage, the Passover experience.

My analysis leads into a theological evaluation. Can my
three conversions be considered legitimate Christian conversions?
What biblical and theological basis do I have in referring to my
cultural and socio-political conversions as part of an ongoing
spiritual process? Does the newness of the kingdom rushed in by
Christ warrant such a dynamic, dialectical understanding of
conversion?

THEOLOGICAL EVALUATION

To evaluate the biblical and theological validity of this way of responding to the question, I shall undertake, first, a brief summary of what biblical scholars have to tell us about the biblical language of conversion, underscoring three main words and their uses: the Hebrew *shub* and the Greek *epistrepho* and *metaneo*, which stand behind the notion of conversion.

The Biblical Language of Conversion

In the Old Testament, the Hebrew word *shub* appears over 1,000 times and means "to return" (Holladay:362-69). It is linked with the prophetic call to Israel to "turn from" its sins, "return to" Yahweh and renew its vows. It also appears in connection with God's acts towards Israel and the nations. In this context, the following words from Christopher Barth are helpful:

> The prophet's call to 'return' derives its special force and urgency from the fact that it confronts its addressees (who include the new people of God from among the pagans) not only with a demand from God, but with the reality of God. Man's return and renewal in the community of God's people is first of all a given event and reality through God's coming, the renewal of His covenant and the coming of His Kingdom. It is only then that conversion becomes an invitation, a call and a demand... (1967:312).

In the New Testament, *epistrepho* stands out. It is the same word which is often used in the LXX to translate the verb *shub* (Bertram:723-724). It means to turn, bring back or return. It is often used in relation to turning of unbelievers (for the first time) to God (Acts 3:19; 26:20) from their sins (Acts 14-15 Barclay:21-22). But sometimes it is linked to erring believers (Jas. 5:19f) who are brought back into a right relation with God (Bertram:727).

Another term which is often used in the New Testament is *metanoeo*, which means "to change one's mind," often feeling regret, and "to adopt another view" (Behm:980-82). It is used both in the context of the call to forgiveness from sin and liberation from future judgment (Acts 2:38; 3:19; 8:22; 17:30; 26:20) and in reference to the problem of apostasy inside the church (Rev. 2:5, 16, 21-22; 3:3, 19).

Metanoeo is closely connected with *epistrepho*, as in Acts 3:19, where Peter calls the multitude to "Repent...and turn again...." It also appears in connection with *pisteuo*, which

means to believe, or "to adhere, to trust or rely on." Thus
Jesus summoned his hearers to "Repent and believe in the gospel"
(Mk. 1:15).

These different words and their various uses in Scripture
underscore several aspects about the various biblical concepts
of conversion. First, conversion means a turning from sin (and
self) to God (and his work). Secondly, this act involves a
change of mind, which implies the abandonment of an old worldview and the adoption of a new one. Thirdly, it entails a new
allegiance, a new trust and a new life-commitment. Fourthly, it
is but the beginning of a new journey and carries implicitly the
seed of new turns. Fifthly, it is surrounded by the redemptive
love of God as revealed in Jesus Christ and witnessed to by the
Holy Spirit.

Let us explore further these biblical perspectives in three
theological propositions. In so doing, I shall attempt to show
the theological complexity of conversion and the validity of
my earlier formulation.

Conversion as a distinct moment
and as a continuous process

In the first place, we should think of conversion both as a
distinct moment and as a continuous process. This seems to
me to be self evident in II Cor. 3:16-18, where Paul states:

> but when a man turns to the Lord the veil is removed.
> Now the Lord is the Spirit, and where the Spirit of
> the Lord is, there is freedom. And we all, with un-
> veiled face, beholding the glory of the Lord, are
> changed into his likeness from one degree of glory to
> another; for this comes from the Lord who is the Spirit.

In this passage, Paul is referring to Israel's incapacity to
understand the old covenant because of its spiritual blindness.
Only "through Christ" can this blindness be removed and Israel
come to see the truth of the covenant (v. 14). This is not only
true of Israel, but of all people. We are all unable to see
God, because we have before us the veil of our sins. But when
we turn (or are converted) to Christ, adds Paul, that veil is
removed. This turning to the Lord puts us in the sphere of the
Spirit of Christ, who enables us not only to see "the glory of
the Lord," but is constantly transforming us "from glory to
glory."

Conversion is then both a distinct moment and the first in a
series of transforming experiences. It appears as a unique
turn and as a continuous transforming movement, made possible by

the enabling power of the Spirit of freedom. The Spirit turns
us towards the Lord, whose unfathomable glory he is always dis-
closing before our eyes.

Elsewhere in the New Testament (e.g., Mk. 1:15), conversion
is described in connection with the kingdom of God. This is the
new order of life which the Father offers in Jesus Christ
through the enabling power of the Spirit. It is a future reality
which is, nevertheless, anticipated in the present. It is a
reality that we experience both personally and in the community
of faith. It is a reflex of what God has done, is doing and
will do, but it is basically discernible in the obedience of
faith. Christian conversion revolves around this future-present,
socio-personal, reflection-action reality. In the words of
Jose Miguez-Bonino, it is "the process through which God
incorporates (women and men), in [their] personal existence,
into an active and conscious participation in Jesus Christ"
(Miguez-Bonino:5).

This process, which has a distinct, though not a consciously
uniform beginning, implies a constant turning from the self to
God. Obsession with the self alienates women and men from their
human vocation, from their calling in creation to be at the
service of one another. The self is the idol which separates
them not only from their vocation, but from their creator. In
turning to God, they are reconciled to the true source of life
and are renewed in their vocation. Conversion is, therefore,
a passage from a de-humanized and de-humanizing existence to a
humanized and humanizing life. Or to put it in other terms: it
is the passage from death and decay to life and freedom. In
conversion, women and men are liberated from the enslavement
of the past and given the freedom of the future, they are turned
from the god of this age, who passes away, to the God who is
always the future of every past (Pannenberg).

Such a passage cannot be limited, therefore, to a single
moment, for this would mean resorting back into the static
existence from which the Gospel liberates. Rather the dynamic
life which is appropriated in conversion implies new challenges,
new turnings and new experiences. It is a life, on the one hand,
which is appropriated in history, in the midst of history's
precarious and evil reality. As historical beings, believers
are always assailed by evil and are always tempted to go back to
the past, and fall into sin. Thus the biblical reminder to be
on the lookout, to resist temptation, to constantly turn away
from evil and commit themselves to God. On the other hand, the
new life is part of the "new creation" which God in Christ is
bringing into being. Believers have been set on the course of
God's coming kingdom. They have been made the pilgrim people
of God, called to set their hopes on "the city which is to come"

(Heb. 13:14) and to participate in the afflictions of Christ in
the world (Heb. 13:13). Accordingly, they are not to escape
from history, but rather to participate in its transformation
through their witness and service. In so doing, they will encounter ever new challenges and should expect ever new turnings.
This, says Paul, "comes from the Lord" who has "put his seal
upon us and given us his Spirit...as a guarantee" (II Cor. 3:18b;
1:22).

Conversion as a Socio-Ecclesial Reality

In the second place, we should think of conversion as a socio-
ecclesial reality. Social, because it is historical. It is not
something which occurs in a vacuum. It takes place in particular social contexts. These contexts bear witness and are
witnessed to by conversion. They are able to see and verify
the change (and the changes) which God by his Spirit operates
in the life of those who trust in his Son. And they cannot help
but name the name by whose power they have experienced wholeness
and freedom (Acts 4:12,20).

Conversion constitutes a break with and a new commitment to
society. It places believers in a dialectical relation with
their environment. Society becomes penultimate in their scale
of values. At the same time, society becomes top priority in
their Christian vocation. Free from its absorbing power,
believers can give themselves completely to the service of their
respective societies. But as with Peter in the case of
Cornelius, so with all believers: perception of this new
relationship requires often "new turnings;" its density is not
easily discernible. In fact, Christians are *always* in need of
more clarifications from God in their relation to society, and
often need, as Peter did, to be transformed in their outlook in
order to adequately fulfill their calling.

Conversion is an ecclesial reality. It is the result of the
witnessing engagement of a visible, concrete community, and
leads to incorporation into that community. This implies a new
set of relationships, participation in a new fellowship,
witnessing with others to a new social reality and sharing in
the hope of a new future. This is what Luke tells us that
occurred at Pentecost:

> And all who believed were together and had all
> things in common;....And day by day, attending
> the temple together and breaking bread in their
> homes, they partook of food with glad and
> generous hearts, praising God and having favor
> with all the people. And the Lord added to their
> number day by day those who were being saved
> (Acts 2:44, 46-47).

This community, however, is affected by the tensions of
history. It is constantly threatened by what the New Testament
calls the principalities and powers of evil. Hence, the
situation described by Luke in Acts 5:1ff, where the fellowship
of Pentecost was broken by the cheating of Ananias and Sapphira.
Situations like this are repeated throughout the New Testament,
the history of the church and can be witnessed everywhere today.
Not only individual believers, but the church as a whole in a
given geographical area can be trapped into sin. The reminder
to resist evil goes, therefore, to every believer and to the
whole church everywhere. By the same token, the call to conversion is not limited to unbelievers and individual believers
who have fallen into sin, but is extended to the church in all
of its density and complexity. Conversion will continue to be
needed until the consummation of the kingdom.

As an ecclesial reality, conversion is the means by which the
church is brought into being and is constantly being brought back
into right living. It is also the way to growth and maturity.
Was this not what happened at the Council of Jerusalem? (Acts 15)
Or was not this the case with the Protestant Reformation or with
so many other *kairoi* in the history of the Church? Indeed, conversion is God's way of renewing and changing the face of his
church, so as to lead it through new paths and enable it to
cross new frontiers.

Conversion as a Missional Commitment

In the third place, we should think of conversion as a
missional commitment. Conversion has a definite, "what for?"
Its goal is not to provide a series of "emotional trips" or the
assimilation of a body of doctrines nor to recruit women and men
for the church, but rather to put them at the service of the
mission of God's kingdom. As Miguez-Bonino has observed:

> The call to conversion is an invitation to disciple-
> ship...whether it takes the direct form of Jesus'
> call to follow him or the apostolic form of partici-
> pation through faith in the Messianic community....
> It revolves around the kingdom. Consequently, it
> involves a community which is engaged in an active
> discipleship in the world (Miguez-Bonino:6).

In the Matthean account of the Great Commission, the call to
discipleship is *mediated* by baptism (which is the outward sign
of incorporation into the body of Christ) and teaching. The
goal of discipleship, however, is the observance of everything
the Lord has commanded to do (Mt. 28:19-20 ff.). And all of
these things can be summed up in the great commandment: "love

the Lord your God..." and "your neighbor as yourself"
(Mk. 12:30,31). Christian conversion aims at putting women and
men at the service of God and neighbor. It is that process by
which they commit themselves to loving God and neighbor in "deed
and in truth." It can only be verified, consequently, in concrete situations, in the efficacy of love. Here the words of
1 John are extremely pertinent:

> This is the message which you have heard from the
> beginning, that we should love one another...We know
> that we have passed out of death into life, because
> we love the brethren. By this we know love, that he
> laid down his life for us; and we ought to lay down
> our lives for the brethren. But if anyone has the
> world's goods and sees his brother in need, yet
> closes his heart against him, how does God's love
> abide in him? Little children, let us not love in
> word or speech but in deed and in truth
> (1 Jn. 3:11,14,16-18).

The foregoing argument, I think, validates the notion of
conversion as a complex experience. While not everyone
experiences conversion in the same way, nevertheless there
is ample evidence in Scripture and in Christian theology to
substantiate the idea of a qualified (by the *parousia*) open-ended
process, grounded on a vital, initial encounter with an
acceptance of Christ as Savior and Lord. This fact becomes
thereafter a key that enables believers to unlock the many turning
points in the course of their spiritual pilgrimage. Thus, for
example, my cultural conversion is not an isolated, secular
experience, but one which finds its roots in Christ. My conversion to Christ is a fundamental reference in my interpretation
and evaluation of other conversions which I may have in my
pilgrimage.

This perspective, to be sure, does overlap somewhat with the
concept of sanctification. But there does not seem to be any
hard biblical or theological evidence for the neat, clear cut
distinction between conversion and sanctification which has been
made in the formulation of the *Ordo salutis* in traditional
Protestant theologies. On the contrary, sanctification seems to
be implicit in conversion and vice versa.[1]

PRACTICAL IMPLICATIONS

It remains for me to underscore several practical implications
which may be drawn from what has been observed heretofore.

First of all, it can be inferred from what has been said that the socio-historical context plays an important role in conversion. There is a correspondence between situation and conversion. The forms which conversion takes vary in accordance with the situation of the person(s) that is(are) converted. Thus, for example, Jesus said to the adulterous woman, "go and do not sin again" (Jn. 8:11), but to the rich young ruler he said, "sell all that you have and distribute it to the poor... and come, follow me" (Lk. 18:22)! It wasn't that Jesus had a double evangelistic standard, but that different contexts demanded different forms of extending the call to conversion and responding to it. This woman had nothing and she knew it! The rich young ruler was also helpless, but his socio-economic situation inhibited him from recognizing his true need. Miguez-Bonino has rightly commented that

> Evangelism must...be related to the forms in which human groups place themselves in the world, their world-vision, their forms of social representation, their class-and-group-consciousness. And, on the other hand, it must be related to the way in which people act, their course of conduct. This means also that 'conversion' may arise within the recognition of a verbally articulated message or through the engagement in a new form of conduct-- consciousness may move through intellectual awareness to the form of life and action implicit in it or an accepted praxis into the self-understanding operation in it (*Ibid.*).

Creative, yet Critical Involvement in Society

Secondly, the understanding of conversion which has been expounded implies both a creative and a critical role for the converted in his or her social milieu. As the Gospel is filtered through a person's socio-historical configurations, so conversion should arise in forms which correspond with that person's reality. Such a person will always be in a dialectical relation with his or her environment. Conversion will both enrich and critically evaluate that person's culture, class-and group-consciousness and social representations. If it is true that the Gospel frees one for creative service in society, it is no less true that it makes one critically aware of the reality of sin and evil. This leads Christians to fully identify with and participate in the joys and hopes, the values and life struggles of their society, and at the same time, to maintain a critical distance so as to be able to detect any form of idolatry or any attempt to absolutize a given practice, person, group, institution or vision.[2]

Imperative of Engagement

A third implication of what has been said is the imperative of engagement for an adequate differentiation between Christian and other types of human **conversions**. Christian conversion can only be verified in the concrete manifestation of a distinctive quality of life. This does not mean that there is a uniform pattern of behavior which corresponds to all believers in all socio-historical circumstances. But it does mean that there is an "ethical minimum" which, though expressed differently in different contexts, maintains, nevertheless, a distinctive quality, easily recognizable everywhere. The "ethical minimum" has been located in the course of our discussion on the command to love God and neighbor. Christian conversion can be said to be taking place whenever people are turning to God and neighbor through faith in Christ and when that turn is being continually translated in outward signs of loving service. Thus, for instance, whenever the rediscovery of one's cultural values or the acceptance of a political challenge enables one to deepen and make more efficacious one's service to God and neighbor, a new conversion can be said to have taken place. Likewise, conversion can be said to take place whenever believers fall away from this missional imperative (or "ethical minimum") and "return" to their vocation.

The Challenge of Conversion
Inside the Church

Finally, what has been said implies that conversion not only confronts the church with an activity that takes place outside its walls, in the world, and for which its witness is vital, but with the challenge of change in its inner life. A centrifugal theology of mission has enabled the church to come to terms with the biblical imperative of the "church for others." But it has also robbed it of the centripetal dimension of mission; i.e., the fact that mission is always a two-way street, a going-coming, outer-inner reality. The church can only be *inside-out*, if it is *outside-in*. In order to minister, it must be ministered to; in order to call others to conversion, it must be converted itself. We have seen how sin and evil are a constant threat to the church. Whenever the church falls into this trap, it enters into a situation of (functional) disbelief, its life and mission become corrupted, it becomes deaf to God's word and loses touch with the Holy Spirit. In such situations, the call to conversion inside the church becomes a missional priority. For, as I have said elsewhere,

> ...a church which loses touch with its source of
> strength (the Word and the Spirit), a community
> which loses sight of the object of its mission

(the world and, particularly, the poor); a people
that are un-responsive to the demands of the gospel,
'cannot be the salt of the earth...[and] the light of
the world...' Indeed, such a church 'is trapped
in its own blindness, its own captivity...[and therefore,] has to be liberated in order to be a liberating
agent in the world.' (Costas:350)

In all of this, we should not forget that though the church
might be unfaithful, God remains faithful, and that though conversion involves our human responsibility, it is made possible
because of the sovereignty of God's grace. "Turning" and
"returning" are thus gifts which God invites us to accept in
Jesus Christ and enables us to appropriate by the liberating
action of his Spirit.

NOTES

1. This is the term which older Protestant theologies coined to
describe the process by which salvation is realized in the life
of women and men. The exact order varies according to the
various traditions. Traditional Reformed dogmatics, for example,
includes seven stages (calling, regeneration, faith [conversion],
justification, adoption, sanctification and glorification);
traditional Lutheran dogmatics has six (illumination, faith,
conversion, justification, mystical union, sanctification and
glorification). Most theologies that prefer to use this kind
of language do insist on separate stages for conversion and
sanctification. They all agree, however, that this is more of
a logical way of describing the process of salvation than an
exact chronology of it, even though it is a fact that they have
often given the impression of a chronological order.

In a cross-cultural theological symposium, Chinese theologian
Jonathan Chao shared how much of a stumbling block the *ordo
salutis* language was for him as a Chinese Christian. He found
it a rigid "package of rationally distilled propositional truths"
which did not permit him to adequately answer the fundamental
theological question of his life: "What can be the meaning of
Jesus Christ, not for the grey past, but for us *today*, and for
the Chinese people in particular?" This led him to a thorough
exegesis of the book of Romans, the results of which liberated
him from the rigidity and culturally bound *ordo* formulation.
He comments:

I came to know that by repentance and faith in
Christ I have been transferred from 'in Adam' to
'in Christ,' and that 'in Christ' is the sphere
where all aspects of my salvation, including

those listed in the *ordo*, are received. 'In
Christ' is also the sphere of the Spirit, where
the Holy Spirit works in me as an individual and
in the corporate body of Christ. Romans 5-8
and the study of the Holy Spirit liberated me
from propositional theology, and I experienced
Christ more personally, pneumatically,
authentically and, in a way, mystically, down
to the deepest level of my being. My personal
quest was satisfied. I leapt for joy...and I
sang Hallelujah from the depth of my heart. It
was the early spring of 1967, just before Easter.
I had experienced a theological resurrection. I
had come to see that Christ is the Gospel. Christ
is all in all. Christ is he to whom I owe my utmost
allegiance, and Christ is the person, the Son of
God, whom I will share with my fellow Chinese
people. What China needs is Christ, not Christ
plus, nor Christ less, but the living and whole
Christ. Of course, I also came to see the
biblical inner pneumatic rationale in God's
salvation. It was a little differently arranged
from the Reformed Theology that I had learned,
and less complicated.

(Jonathan Chao, "The Theological Confession of a Chinese
Believer," a paper delivered at the Study Group on Mission
Issues, Overseas Ministries Study Center, Ventnor, N.J., April
23-24, 1976, pp. 22,23.)

The traditional way of separating different aspects of the
salvific process is more the result of a cultural-intellectual
tradition than the direct teaching of the Holy Scripture. Karl
Barth, however, insisted on the inseparableness, yet distinct-
ness of sanctification and justification (within which he
locates conversion), a point at which he stands in agreement
with G.C. Berkouwer. While he sees them as "two genuinely
different moments," he keeps them within the one event of
salvation, thereby underscoring the fact that they "intersect"
with one another. Cf. Karl Barth, *Church Dogmatics*, IV/2,
Translated by G. W. Bromiley and T.F. Torrance (Edinburgh:
T. & T.Clark, 1958), pp. 500-551. For a similar view see G. C.
Berkouwer, *Faith and Sanctification* (Grand Rapids: Eerdmans,
1922). For expositions of the traditional Lutheran and Reformed
views, see John Theodore Mueller, *Christian Dogmatics* (St. Louis:
Concordia Publishing House, 1955), pp. 319ff.; L. Berkhof,
Systematic Theology (Grand Rapids: Wm. B. Eerdmans, 1939, 1941),
pp. 415ff.

2. It is always difficult to draw the line between the positive and negative impact of conversion upon a person's social milieu, or between the critical and creative functions of the Gospel in a person's life. How far can a person's value-system and world view be integrated into his or her faith in Christ cannot be determined from the outside, since situations vary from place to place. One needs, therefore, to understand in depth each situation and develop a sensitive ear to the Word and the leading of the Spirit.

Jacob A. Loewen says that in the discussion period of a lecture he delivered to a group of missionaries and African believers about conversion, a national leader stood up and said:

> Sir, what you have said about conversion deeply moves
> me because, I must confess: I have not been converted
> that way. My deeper African values have not been
> changed. I have merely become an imitation European
> on the outside. I have not learned to listen to the
> Holy Spirit. I have been trained to listen very care-
> fully to what the missionary who controls the purse
> wants.

(Jacob A. Loewen, "Evangelism and Culture," *The New Face of Evangelicalism*, *suppra* C. Rene Padilla, ed. [London: Hodder & Stoughton, 1976], p. 186.)

If it is true that a critical integration of a person's value system and world view into his or her faith in Christ cannot be effected from the outside, it is also true that in order for that integration to take place the church's representatives must make an extraordinary effort to understand that person's situation, listen carefully to what the Word may have to say about it and be sensitive to the leading of the Spirit in the encounter with the person's milieu. This, in turn, will set the pace for that person to follow through personally with the process. A contextual evangelism is the best guarantee of a contextual self-reflection on the meaning of the Gospel in one's life situations, without which it is not possible to come to terms with the problem of culture and faith.

BIBLIOGRAPHY

Alves, Rubem, 1975. *O Enemiga da Religiao*. Petropolis: Editora Vozes.

Barclay, William. *Turning to God: A Study of Conversion in the Book of Acts and Today*. Grand Rapids: Baker Book House.

Barth, Christopher, 1967. "Notes on 'Return' in the Old Testament," *Ecumenical Review*, XIX:3 (July), 310-311.

Behm, J., 1967. *"Metanoeo, Metanoia,"* *Theological Dictionary of the New Testament*, Vol. IV, edited by Gerhardt Friedrich, translated and edited by Geoffrey W. Bromiley. Grand Rapids: Eerdmans, pp. 975-980.

Bertram. *"Epistrepho,"* *Theological Dictionary of the New Testament*, Vol. VII, edited by Gerhardt Friedrich, translated and edited by Geoffrey W. Bromiley. Grand Rapids: Eerdmans, pp. 722-729.

Costas, Orlando E., 1976. *Theology of the Crossroads in Contemporary Latin America*. Amsterdam: Rodopi.

Fackre, Gabriel, 1975. *Word in Deed: Theological Themes in Evangelism*. Grand Rapids: Eerdmans.

Green, Michael, 1970. *Evangelism in the Early Church*. Grand Rapids: Eerdmans.

Heikkinen, J.W., 1967. "Notes on *'Epistrepho'* and *'Metanoeo,'"* *Ecumenical Review*, XIX:3 (July), pp. 313-316.

Holladay, William L., 1971. *Concise Hebrew and Aramaic Lexicon of the Old Testament*.

Marsh, J., 1962. "Conversion," in *Interpreters Dictionary of the Bible*, Vol. I, George A. Buttrick, ed. Nashville: Abingdon.

Miguez-Bonino, Jose, n.d. "Notes on Conversion--For a Critical Rethinking of the Wesleyan Doctrine," unpublished paper prepared for the Roman Catholic-Methodist Dialogue.

Nissiotis, Nikos, 1967. "Conversion and the Church," *Ecumenical Review*, XIX:3 (July).

Packer, James I., 1976. "What is Evangelism?", in *Theological Perspectives on Church Growth*. Edited by Harvie M. Conn. Nutley, N.J.: Presbyterian and Reformed Publishing Co.

12

Conversion and Convertibility with Special Reference to Muslims
Kenneth Cragg

"The simplicity that is in Christ" (2 Cor. 11:3) is one of those memorable phrases in the A.V. which up-to-date English has to alter but which still fascinate for their older meaning. Of course, "simplicity in Christ" was never the sort to preclude Paul also writing of Christ as "the wisdom of God" where the depth and riches were "unsearchable." "Simple," in archaic usage means "for no other sake but its own," "intrinsically and without reservations," with no "up-to-a-point" about it. A sound modern translation would probably reach for "integrity." It is a term Paul clearly relished (see 2 Cor. 1:12 and Col.3:22 and Romans 12:8) and the LXX translators used it for the whole-heartedness with which David's people offered for the Temple building. The noun means the opposite of duplicity, dividedness, deviousness and inner contradiction. Singleness of mind, whole-ness of heart, are a paraphrase. "Unite my heart to fear Thy Name" the psalmist might have said in context.

There is integrity, then, in Christ and therefore there must be integrity in conversion, a unity of self in which biography past is genuinely integrated into commitment present, so that the crisis of repentance and faith that makes us Christian truly integrates what we have been in what we become.

We are readily familiar with the term conversion and with the

263

issue of its culture context, as it engages us throughout this
Conference. And, traditionally, it is the "newness" we rightly
emphasize, the rupture, as we see it, in vital senses, which
occurs in regeneration, the sinful self transformed into the new
man in Christ.

But that dimension is only one side of the story. For it is
happening within a personal "continuum." Otherwise, *where* is
conversion itself happening? To think of change as total is to
lack any entity in which it occurs. Hence "convertibility" is
an important dimension of study--the identity, that is, in which
conversion happens. Both terms, no doubt, are associated now-
adays with brokers and financiers. But the convertibility of
man is a glorious conviction of Christian hope and mission, and
it focuses our thought about culture realistically by laying
emphasis on that which is going to be there still (like the
fabric of a washed garment) when the meaning of Christ has taken
hold of it.

Nicodemus' question was a sound one. "How can a man be born
when he is old?" He cannot be. The point was that the
questioner had mis-heard Jesus' meaning. Return to the womb,
which Nicodemus rightly knew to be impossible, was not "the new
birth" which Jesus meant, but only a literalist hearing of His
words. "Born of the Spirit" is an event within existing biography, or it is nothing. It does not unmake: it remakes.
Conversion is the transaction of convertibility. Paul never
ceased to be the man who sat at the feet of Gamaliel. The fishing of Peter the Galilean was Jesus' own idiom for his whole
apostolate. We must beware, within our faith and mission, of
what one writer (Gabriel Vahanian) called "the cultural
annexation of God." This means a constantly lively sense of the
convertibility to Christ of every human expression we meet and
its potential for "the integrity which is in Christ." "I will
draw all men unto me, if I be lifted up" is not about a
universally successful salvation but a universally accessible
one.

There is, incidentally, something very heartening about this
realization, this "for-us-men" quality of the Gospel, as the
Creed puts it, confessing the Incarnation as intending and
hallowing a common humanness, male and female, where "Jew and
Gentile," "bond and free," "brown and pale," "Black and white,"
are distinctions so irrelevant that there is no need to make
them. "Us men." Is it not, too often, the contrasts, the
disparities, the varieties, the enmities of species, human and
cultural, which have obsessed us? We have too often been
dominated by those inescapable factors of birth, climate,
territory, speech, nation and religion which so stubbornly
determine the contrasts of culture. But if we believe these

surmountable, convertible to what is "in Christ," then, by the
same token, we must acknowledge how deep-seated they are. "The
integrity that is in Christ" requires that we refuse the notion
that it is culturally monopolized in ourselves. Rather, we must
trust and serve its viability everywhere in the world in the
Holy Spirit.

With this "convertibility" aspect in general view, we take up
here the particularities of Islam as a determinant of culture,
a theology (if you will) of availability for Christ, being also,
as it is, the determinant of the "natural birth" (to return to
Nicodemus) of Muslims. What follows draws on the background
of two persons of Muslim birth and family, now baptized
Christians, one a noted Christian leader, the other an
influential scholar, poet and translator. Both came to be "in
Christ" by faith and conversion, and have remained so. Both
believe that their Muslim origins have found radical fulfillment
and expression in Christ. It has not been necessary for them,
in mature perspective, to see their heritage as requiring
repudiation. Yet their discipleship of newness in Christ is not
in doubt, and, unlike many short-term converts, it has not been
necessary for them to revert to their former allegiance. We
will not confine ourselves rigorously to these two exemplars but
allow them to indicate other aspects of the Muslim-culture/
Christ-faith equation.

Let us divide the Christ-dimension and the culture-ground
into their three elements, as these belong with personality,
shaped by the past, and coming into the faith, to explore how
the one is "convertible" in the other. They are the mind's
understanding, the soul's expression, and the will's discipleship. These, of course, inter-depend. The first has to do
with what Paul calls "the knowledge and love of God." It under-
girds all else.

(1) The Mind's Understanding

There is, truly, a conversion of the mind. But what of the
convertibility of its natal ideas and concepts, if they can be
so described? Those of Islam and of Muslims need careful study
on our part. For it is customary to stress the features of
tension and even hostility that exist historically between the
two theisms. Strenuous, on all counts, these tensions are--the
denial of the Word Incarnate, the disallowing of the Cross of
Jesus, the astigmatism about what is meant by "Gospel," and the
confusion that obtains about the integrity of the New Testament
faith and how the Gospel *of* Jesus develops into the Gospel *about*
Him.

Nevertheless, the positive implications for the faith of the
Christian within Islamic theology are significant and must, at
all costs, be imaginatively and loyally retrieved. But, first,
it is fair to be reminded that conversion is not simply intellectual, a persuasion of the thinking part of man. In fact, one
of our two representatives tells of no particular emphasis here.
His sense of Christ came, as with many, in the setting of a
Christian school and through its influence in his boyhood.
Though questions of articulate theology came later, they did not
belong in the basic experience which was a response to Christian
love and to the witness of unstinted friendship.

With the other representative, however, a realization of what
he came to call the "worshipability" of God in Christ was
paramount, and this was a deeply theological theme pondered in a
keenly philosophical mind. It stemmed from a childhood made
sensitive to the mystery and dignity of suffering. His father,
a very learned Muslim scholar, had become a widower in his
middle years. He strove determinedly to be a double parent in
loving closeness to his family despite its costly toll in
diverting him from his loved books and studies. The son in
question lived in this way with a growing realization of self-
giving affection, and of how exacting it might be, as well as
with the deep awareness of suffering in general countered by
tenderness. Later, in the pursuit of his own scholarship, he
encountered the bigotry of religious obscurantism and the
unfeeling exercise of dogmatic authority, crushing the spirit
and the wistfulness of inquiry into truth.

Both these issues raised for him the relevance of (his
Muslim) belief in God. "God is greater," says the *Shahadah*, or
Creed of Islam. What should divine greatness mean, he asked
himself, in this realm of compassion and suffering, and with
respect to the custodianship dogma claims to exercise over its
meaning? How was the infinitely estimable thing he found in his
father to be related to the divine sovereignty? If God is indeed greater, then clearly the human could not outdo the divine
in this most crucial realm of bearing with need. It was in
this context that the impact of the Gospel came into his ken.

On the other issue in his mind of insensitive authoritarian-
ism in religious custodians, he asked himself whether this could
square with the notion of divine justice which he knew to be a
deep theme in the *Qur'ān*. Was suppression of liberty of inquiry
a right attitude on the part of those who led the community of
faith in God's revelation? Was there something in the very
greatness of God which was betrayed--or at least forgotten--in
an oppressive zeal for His Scripture?

It was these two areas of sensitive personal experience--a feeling of being reared in suffering and of being meant for liberty of mind--that guided his thoughts towards the Christian faith and, surprisingly, with very little intervention, so to speak, from any Christian apologetic. His interest in Jesus as the Christ belonged with his sense of a divine counterpart to the compassion he had parentally received, while he felt constrained to claim, even within his scholarship about Islam, the intellectual integrity he had known in Christian academic friendship. But this interest in the things of Christ belonged clearly with what that scholarship had involved in its own content.

Is it not a fundamental principle of Islamic faith, not only that what is not God (i.e. idols) must be denied worship, but that what is divine must be adored? What then, further, if one finds in the love of the suffering Christ that which is truly worshipable? Will not this be the meaning and, in experience, the discovery, of His divinity? "God in Christ" is then "learned" (to borrow the language of Eph. 4:20) in the context of the great Muslim obligation to "let God be God." The divine Sonship of Jesus is disclosed in the measure His Cross gives us of the power by which God reigns. This is exactly what Paul claims in affirming "Christ crucified" to be "the power of God," but it is reached by the road of Muslim experience. In this personal case, the very idea of God is seen to contain that relation to mankind which is expressed in Jesus as the Christ--a Christology, first, of action, and only then of status. Jesus, in Kosuke Koyama's words, as "the where-are-you? hands of God stretched out towards mankind." If we can rightly say that Islam means "Let God be God" (there is no surer definition), then the mind-conversion we are describing can be summed up in simply letting God be as God is in Christ-compassion, by this measure, addressing our liberty and reaching our hearts as the One who saves.

Of course there are familiar, and entrenched, Islamic disavowals of this view. It is these that make conversion necessary and right. To see Jesus in these terms, to let Him suffer, so to speak, or, rather, to believe that He does, is to run counter to the Islamic Jesus as Prophet-teacher, whose verbal ministry, though threatened by illwishers, ended in rapture to heaven out of danger. His "vindication" was then by intervention of rescue, not by the wounds that save. But, for our story here, that disallowing of the Cross, however well meant, seemed less fitting to divine greatness than the redeeming alternative. The converting conviction was that the greatness and power of God are supremely present in, and known by, the love that suffers. The mind in the conversion is one that sees the grace and, therefore receives the history, of Jesus as being, in truth, one of death for us, not of rescue for Himself.

That persuasion, however, as to Jesus crucified--always a
vital aspect in conversion--belongs deeply with what Islam
already believes about the divine power and divine sovereignty.
The sense of forgiveness is already there. God is *Al-Rahman
al-Rahim*. The question has to do with how such forgiveness
avails. It may come to the heart of a man (as in this case) to
see as utterly fitting to God the *redeeming* forgiveness he finds
in Christ. Then to think that dimension improper to God is to
impugn His being Lord.

Moreover, the very sovereignty to which Islam has loyally
witnessed need not--the Christian would say, should not--be seen
as a transcendence immune from our humanness in the serenity of
heaven, so that it is inhibited from any enterprise for our
redemption. For then we should be implying some kind of divine
imprisonment in aloofness and we should be found forbidding
things to God--hardly an Islamic posture!--least of all when it
is a prohibition of initiatives of grace. For then we should
have what Louis Massignon, the great French Islamicist, once
called "an intransigent transcendence," which does not "come
over"into our tragedy, because it must always be exaltedly beyond us. On Christian grounds such would hardly transcend at
all, since in the face of human evil the whole creation-venture
would be radically at stake. For evils that characterize our
history certainly question that creation, flout God's law and
plague His creature man--on all of which counts God's creative
purpose, in which Islam believes, is vitally involved.

So we may come to see that believing in Christ is believing
in God. So it was for the mind of the one we are reading here.
He saw in that Christ-measure of the nature of God a kinship
with implications of his own Muslim theology. Not least among
these was the realization of how, in a real sense, the rule of
God in human society is constituted to turn upon the human
recognition of it. God, in the *Qur'ān*'s perspective, has
created a world in which man is free even to have idols, to
prefer false gods. To be sure, orthodoxy claims that this does
not harm God. But here orthodoxy may have to think again. For
manifestly, the Prophet's mission against plural worship matters,
and matters intensely. One cannot, then, assume that its
reception is a matter of indifference. Quite the contrary:
"God and His messenger"--the *Qur'ān* always links them together.
Man is seriously summoned to submission and obedience. We can
hardly then conclude that God is not, in that sense, vulnerable
to man. What Islam calls *Shirk*, or plural worships, is "great
wrong," (Surah 31:13) i.e. wrong against God. The Christian
faith finds this "wrong against God" measured in "the sin of the
world" which the Cross constitutes. Contrasted as many things
are at this point between the two faiths, they are together in
the conviction of "men against God." Could there be a greater

evidence of man's obduracy than the way he uses his liberty to prefer false worship to the rule of God? Is it not precisely that obduracy which Muhammad's mission is understood as sent to overcome? Surely we, and Muslims even more, would jeopardize the whole seriousness of that mission, and of the rule of God believed to be staked in it, if we allowed it to be implied that the sins which defy it do not matter. Is there not, then, a way to the conversion of the mind from the reality of man's "wrong against God" identified as *Shirk*, to the Christian belief that our wrongfulness before God is both registered and redeemed at the Cross?

The reality of man's responsibility is also clear in Islam, despite many impressions or assumptions to the contrary. For *islam* (as a common noun), namely the will to let God be God, must be a willed response. If it is inevitable it is unnecessary. If it is automatic there is no need of a mission to teach or a prophet to demand it. It takes freedom to bring an *islam* to God's claim. He is, then, the God we may ignore--as the un-believer does--if He is to be the God we ought to worship and to serve. The point might almost be put as it is in John Oman's deeply Christian study: *Grace and Personality*. "He (God) will not have us accept His purpose save as our own....Nothing is adequate to our whole moral relation to God short of the identi-fication, through our own insight, of our duty with His Will." (pp. 54 and 68). It will not be God's omnipotence if we suppose it so straitened as to withhold from us, as creatures, the responsibility of being free.

What rich convertibility there is here for Muslims into the Christian dimension of a divine love which suffers our obduracy and waits for our autonomy to coincide itself freely with His rule. The theme resolves itself into the issue about the role of Jesus in man's remaking, into which we have not space here to follow it. No doubt many can, and will, find in Islam a sublime indifference of divine sovereignty to the human unbelief. But, if so, it hardly squares with the intensity, not to say, the necessity of Muhammad's mission.

In any event, these are some of the considerations which led our exemplars Christward and allowed them to feel at the same time that a deep strand of their Islam had found legitimacy, so that their movement of allegiance was not wholly one of abandon-ment but of deeper fidelity. There is need for us, in thinking theology and culture, always to identify and enlist every dis-cernible resource in the potential of what we find outside our own tradition. Such is the way of convertibility and such the benediction of integrity in Christ. Let people, so to speak, persuade themselves that Christ is their own logic.

To think this way does not mean forgetting the human lostness, nor the indispensable illumination of the Holy Spirit. It is, rather, to believe in these more profoundly and more expectantly. The great Augustine (of Hippo) mused in his *Confessions* that "if he were called upon to write a book which would be invested with the highest authority, he would prefer to write it in such a way that a reader could find re-echoed in his words whatever truths he was able to apprehend." He went on: "I will not be so rash, my God, as to suppose that so great a man as Moses deserved a lesser gift from You." Muhammad did not think of the *Qur'ān* as "his words." But it is a book "invested" for Muslims "with the highest authority." Perhaps, then when we relate to the cultures it has generated, we may hope to find its own heirs discovering truths (of ours in witness) by *its* implications.

It is for them, truly, to say. It is for us to cherish the conjecture and perhaps kindle the discovery.

Since the *Qur'ān* is the great denominator of Islamic culture we have been right to develop these theological aspects, incomplete as the discussion is. For they undergird all else that must be said about conversion to Christ within the Muslim milieu. Even when, as in countless folk, theology is inarticulate or dormant, it still qualifies the situations where conversion belongs. All other things in cultural derivation arise from these basics.

(2) The Soul's Expression

We must pass from intellectual reflections on the convertible potential towards "God in Christ" of the Islamic world-view, to issues of culture when personal conversion transpires within it. This is what is meant by "the soul's expression." Here the experience of both our chosen examples is significant.

They came to see their discipleship within their past heritage in its arts and poetry which, in maturity, if not at once, they felt free to bring within their new allegiance. Arabic, Urdu and Persian are, of course, languages that delight in calligraphy and calligraphy of the Arabic *Qur'ān* is both the primary form of "religious" art and the mode of veneration of the world. So biblical Arabic, or Persian, or Urdu, deserves no less, if for a different reason. This may serve as a ready illustration of the new in the shape of the old, even as the early church took over some of the features of the synagogue such as lections and psalmody. The cursive flow of letters, the elaborate over-lay of words and all the ingenuities of fastidious penmanship, schooled by reverence for the *Qur'ān* passed over congenially into the service of the Christian meanings. The same they found true of geometrical and floral design and Arabesque. Islam has no monopoly of graces which belong with space *per se*, or in nature as the matrix of the human arts. Angle, curve and line and sequence allow of no exclusive copyright. Cultural usages, as nature constitutes and nurture teaches them, are in this sense common.

That situation is confirmed by the *Qur'anic* theme of "signs" in the natural order, tokens of divine beneficence, which constantly present themselves in the earthly scene and in its social experiences. These are lost upon the casual but they register with the careful and evoke that gratitude which is a prominent feature of the *Qur'ān's* submission call. Behind them all is the understanding of creation and of the law which charters it for man the creature. That delight in external nature and the sense of the human obligation to receive it reverently provide a validation of all that is consistent with its meaning in the diverse arts that culture affords. The disciple does not have to be imitative of others or to opt out of the patterns of his own ethos. So both the converts we have in mind have possessed and repossessed the cultural language and forms of their birthright within the critical newness they found in Christ. They have been able to express themselves in the poetry of their own heritage. Christian architecture of the last half century in Persia has shown a remarkable capacity to "baptize" to its purpose the traditions of a splendid Islamic inheritance.

But arts and poetry are the readiest of cultural forms for this sort of "baptism." There are other cultural expressions of Islam which pose sterner problems. What of the fast of Ramadan, the direction (or *Qiblah)* of prayer, the forms of prostration, the rite of ablution, the saying of *Takbir* ("God is greater"), the use of the human voice in the summons to worship? Are any of these, in any sense, transmissible from old to new, from mosque to church?

Eastern Christians, generally speaking, maintain a studied otherness and repudiate all that might suggest or venture things in common. This extends, unhappily, even to vocabulary which, in religious usage, tends to keep itself distinctive. What of new disciples? With them, too, the consensus is that the Islamic "institutions" we have just listed *are*, essentially, Islamic and had better remain so. Dangerous misunderstanding would be incurred by seeming to be imitative. The resultant ambiguity would not be "integrity in Christ." But the uniqueness of Ramadan in Islam does not mean that fasting has no place in a Christian discipleship. It can be seen as inviting Christians to some identification with Muslim emphases about discipline and self-restraint, or even solidarity in a social concern for a society in control of its appetites. A Christianity, freed from merit-seeking and communal pressures of conformity, may have some duty

to identify with the relevance of the fast to the life of the
community, vigilant as this attitude must be for the demerits of
the fast itself, in pride, formalism or self-righteousness.

The *Qiblah* provides an intense geographical and historical
focus for the Muslim at prayer and on pilgrimage. How does the
Christian from within Islam realize the unity in Christ? His
faith's transcendence of particular territorial locale requires
him to hold together the fellowship, immediate and universal.
His *Qiblah* becomes the Word and the sacrament, at once local and
inclusive. "At Philippi, in Christ," Paul, for example, would
say. But may the convert legitimately retain a sense of the
direction that physically unifies his old community, in order to
care, as Paul might again say, for his "brethren according to
the *Qiblah?*" (What we would give for some Pauline--or Johan-
nine--Epistles about the Muslim setting.)

How do these thoughts square, it may be asked, with Paul's
"counting all things loss" which were once gain to him? Pride
of works, trust in forms--these, truly, were renounced. But the
"familiars" of the heart, subject always to the rule of Christ,
may be duly integrated and fulfilled.

So doing, of course, the convert, other things allowing, may
be the means of mediating into his old community the arts, the
signs, the symbols, of his new discipleship. He is more likely,
so our instances affirm, to do this, if his openness in the other
direction is retained. It is remarkable--if we may note it
parenthetically--how the image of Jesus crucified, and even of
the crown of thorns, has come into contemporary Muslim Arabic
poetry in the context of the Palestinian tragedy. So far has
this been the case that it has evoked the disapproval of Muslim
orthodox authorities. Even apart from all conversion, human
situations may illuminate the relevance of the unacknowledged
Christ. Sunni Islam, broadly speaking, has not adequate
cognizance of the tragic sense of life and when events make the
latter inescapable, poets, if not shaikhs, may reach wistfully
towards the symbols they do not communally possess. How much
more, then, may the committed disciple bring his new "in Christ"
experience to the positive reckoning of his customary world.

What of the postures of Muslim prayer and the prefatory
ablutions? One might quote Psalm 96:6: "O come, let us worship
and prostrate before the Lord..." But, clearly, Christian
patterns of worship have their distinctive source in Christian
faith and Islam anyway would not want to have its forms borrowed.
To us ours and to them theirs. Nevertheless, is there not something latent in the Muslim form which may escape us and which it
would be important to elucidate? The erect-prostrate-erect
sequence in Islamic prayer ritual is a powerful acted parable of

a view of man under God. It is expressive of man's creaturely
submission and his liability with authority. His proudest
member, the brow, is abased to the lowly earth, but only in
order that he may return to the erect stance, resume his sandals
and go about the business of his life in the meaning of that submission. He does not grovel, or stay prostrate. Yet the claim
of his humbling must be with him in the dominion he wields, of
which erectness has always been the symbol. Milton has it so in
Paradise Lost:

>   "...a creature who not prone
> And brute as other creatures, but endued
> With sanctity of reason, might erect
> His stature, and upright foot serene,
> Govern the rest, self-knowing..."   (vii. 506-510)

And erectness must be repeatedly humbled into the true sense of
its obligation. Together they mean man as the tenant-master, or
servant-in-trust, in the good earth the Creator has set under
him. How does the Christian convert relate to this meaning?
Surely he maintains its truth and develops the Christian understanding of such human dignity under God into a steady witness
to the reality of the sin that blights and the grace that saves.
For both sin and redemption find their meaning from that shared
context of the human calling. The Christian will not share the
ritual, but he will recognize the significance of its reading
of man, alike "humbled and exalted."

Something of the same double relevance applies also to that
God-consciousness which is so central a feature of Muslim
religion. *Allahu akbar* "God is greater," (called the *Takbir*):
"Praise be to God, Lord of all being:" "Exalted be He:"--these
and like phrases express the Muslim's awareness of omniscience
all around the self of man. This penetrates far into culture,
into conversation and greetings, even into the trivia of daily
life, like spurring a donkey or mopping one's brow. Perhaps the
surest clue here for the Christian, whether he be convert or
neighbor, is to acknowledge the mutual theme of divine greatness
and witness to the Christian criteria of what divine greatness
is and does. *Takbir* corresponds, verbally, to *Magnificat*. Our
souls magnify the Lord, tell out His greatness. The issue is
not whether about that greatness, but whereby, wherein and why.
So our task is to magnify the Lord with Muslims, in loyalty to
the Christian predicates of greatness as the Gospel learns them.
The convert was here both a liability and an asset in his
culture's habituation (we might almost say) with the thought and
the immediacy of God, as will and power and mercy.

There are other aspects of culture and soul-expression. But
they are probably best considered under our third dimension in
the study of conversion.

(3)   The Will's Discipleship

"Knowledge of God" and "expression" in the conversion
experience into Christ from within Islam have been our concern
thus far.   These, of course, belong with and proceed through,
that sense of personal identity which is at the heart of all
response.   "My spirit rejoices in God my Saviour," "Lord, here
am I..." "To me to live is Christ." Things conceptual and things
artistic and imaginative are bound up with the personal (if you
like, the psychic) equation.   What of the self in action, and
its convertibility so that it is not lost in some mistaken
question about being "unborn when it is old,"--old meaning here,
formed, as mother's milk, a native landscape, a natal tongue
and a local culture *do* form people, not to be, in that sense,
unformed, nor, we pray, deformed.

Here we need to remember that Islam is far other than a
religious option of opinions, freely chosen or freely abandoned.
It is a totality which includes a dimension very like nationality, as well as belief.   There is no more tenacious community
than Islam.   The traditional concept of apostasy is the negative
side of this.   Islam, at least in Arab and most Asian lands, is
hardly yet a faith one is free to leave.   Its tolerance,
historically, has meant a freedom of continuing what one may have
been, if born outside it, e.g. Jewish or Christian.   Or it meant
a freedom to migrate into Islam.   There was no liberty for the
born Muslim to migrate out of it.   It was never supposed that a
Muslim would desire to become anything else, and were he to do
so it would be indicative of the utmost perversity.   This spells
the tenacity of the *Ummah* concept, both in theory and in practice.
To this day, for example, a Christian Turk or a Christian Malay
is almost a contradiction in terms.   Christians are Armenians or
Greeks, or whatever--the other "faith-nations."   There are it is
true, Christian Arabs, surviving as *dhimmis*, or tolerated
minorities from before the rise of Islam.   So Arabism is not
wholly dominated by Islamicity, though there are those who think
it should be.   The role of minorities is notoriously difficult in
many cultures.   Islam has a better record than some, in letting
"others" be.   But they have to be "others."   Its own denizens do
not, for the most part, enjoy such freedom as might allow them
to become non-Muslims.   It does not envisage that minorities can,
should, or may, expect to recruit from its own ranks.   They may
persist by dint of their own natal fertility and their spiritual
survival power.

Over the centuries, it may be said that the Christian
communities within Islam have accepted this static account of
themselves, as once-born identities.   This has, indeed, been the
psychic price of their durability. They have not lived, or been
allowed to live, in any realistic expectation of conversion,

from Islam, into their fellowship or faith. Emigration,
and naturalization elsewhere (as in one of the two disciples here
concerned) may facilitate a legal change of faith. But, by the
same token, a local ex-Muslim church is not thereby generated.
Persia is one country where a small church, with ex-Muslim
clergy and lay people, does exist. In Africa, because of the
third denominator of animism, and for other reasons, the
situation is more fluid and there is much more inter-communal
liberty of movement and of inter-penetration of ideas and usages.

In central Islamic countries, however, the rigor of the situation is a primary problem besetting feasible conversion--to
speak humanly. As long as Islamic solidarity is politically
determined and sanctioned, viable personal initiatives will face
stern and often impossible strains. In this sense it is
probably wrong to talk of conversion and culture, since the
equation goes far beyond what normally culture would connote.
It might almost be phrased: "Conversion and treachery," or
"conversion and dis-identity." For as such it has so often been
seen by the human context in the *Ummah* of once-born, always,
Islam.

Nor is a plea for heroism the answer if it leaves intact, or
does nothing to bring into question, the pattern which calls for
it. In the existing structure the ultimate hope must be the
realization within Islam that a faith one is not free to leave,
or question, is a virtual prison if one is minded to do so, and
that no self-respecting religion can afford to maintain adherence
by sheer immobility of will. It is in fact odd that a Muslim
may indulge inward, or outward, compromises of Islam and do so
(*pace* the Wahhabis and the Muslim Brethren) with impunity, provided he does not contravene his formal identity.

There are, to be sure, aspects of Islam within the *Qur'ān*
which arguably imply a genuine freedom of movement of faith,
notably the statement that "there is no compulsion in religion"
(Surah 2:256), meaning that there ought not to be. For, manifestly, there is, in the effective denial of what English school-
boys call an *exeat*.

In this situation, what of the will's discipleship? Surely
part of the answer is that convertibility means a studied effort
after continuity. Hence the careful search, in our first
section, for the Islamic dimensions, as they really are, of a
Christian sense of a divine solicitude for man and a divine
stake in human freedom to acknowledge that He *is*, and must truly
let be, God. All our theology and conversion rationale is here--
in God duly known and loved and served for the God He is, and,
for us, the crucified Christ as the ultimate climax of that
theism: "God in Christ reconciling the world to Himself."

In this way the new disciple can affirm a genuine continuity with hope and without compromise. Only so will he really sur-mount the hurdle of a feared treachery (or the accusation of it). Here we do not finally mean the treachery an intimidating, possessive community alleges, but a deep inner feeling of having forsaken one's past and somehow disowned one's community. Both our two examples felt and suffered this acutely. One has given us a moving account of it.

> "The old restlessness of spirit cropped up again and
> this time in a more intensified way. There was a war
> inside me, the old war which must have troubled St.
> Paul when he wrote: 'I do not understand my own actions.
> For I do not do what I want, but I do the very thing
> I hate.' It was as if these words were written for
> me. How long, O Lord?....I was becoming lonelier and
> lonelier within myself. I used to sink down into the
> lowest state of unbelief and despair, and blamed God
> for having taken my mother from me so early in life....I
> used to blame those who were the cause of my separation
> from my own people. What right had they, I used to
> think, to uproot a child from his own environment,
> his cultural and ethnic background, and let him grow
> aloof from everything which he could rightly claim
> to be his own?....
>
> "New life involves new sufferings. God in His inestimable
> love and wisdom regarded me as one of those worthy to go
> through those mental and spiritual torments in order that
> the new life in Christ might be let loose through me...I
> humbly regard myself as honoured to have gone through all
> this; only I would say: 'If those days had not been
> shortened, no human being would be saved.'...
> I used to lie awake for long hours letting my imagination
> be fed by my imaginary misery to such a degree that the
> thought of suicide started to creep in. The rush of the
> waves of self pity and despair was sometimes so tremendous
> that they used to press streams of tears out of my eyes,
> and like Job I used to curse the day I was born."

Through that crisis he was blessedly brought into a mature set of the will in Christ. In that quality of soul he has been able to see his entire Christian commitment within a true possession by, and of, the culture whence he came to it. This has resolved the tensions which otherwise--as in so many cases--would have been the end of his discipleship. It has enabled him to turn to live in that culture, in its poetry and its arts, as one who has found the reality of God in the grace of Christ. Thus, for example:

"It was the fact of the Incarnation which made me fall in love with Christianity. To a Muslim the very idea of God becoming man is blasphemous, but it was this 'blasphemy' that saved me from unbelief. To me it came to be the most natural thing. Stories are told of Shah Abbas (18th Century ruler in Persia) and how, in order to get to know his poorer subjects, he used to dress up as a poor man—a dervish—and thus go among them. This gracious act he was able to do precisely because he was king and by such an action nothing was taken away from the glory of his kingship. If we admire such action in human beings, why should we not admire it in God?

"One of the famous poets of Isfahan, Hatef by name, tried his best to understand the Holy Trinity. In a long and lovely Persian poem about the unity of God, he refers to a visit to a Christian church and a discussion there with a Christian friend about the Trinity. At the end of that part, in exceptionally beautiful language, he says:

'While in these matters occupied were we,
The church bells seemed to peal this solemn chant
God is One: there can no other be:
One is the Lord, and there is none but He!'

Hatef's poem does not fully explain the Christian doctrine of the Trinity, but it lifts it high above the common understanding of Muslims of that doctrine. It was a great help to me, and I am sure it can be to many others."

These sentiments are surely in line with Paul's appreciation of the pagan altar in Athens and his temper of mind on the Areopagus. There, of course, he was not handling the culture of his birth, but only his acquisition, and some would argue that his point was only "tactical." But in this issue, sincerity in Christ has deeper sources than the tactics and, for the convert within his birth-culture it must always be so. The matter here is not how best to plead for a doctrine to be heard: it is how to love the Lord with all one's strength—a strength constituted in all one's origins and depths of spirit.

No Christian approach to questions of conversion and culture within Muslim societies can rightly neglect the necessary battle for liberty of mind to follow persuasions of truth. To believe in conversion without caring—as far as in us lies—for the circumstances preceding and attending it would be disloyal. The issues of freedom of belief are, of course, the responsibility of those inside Islamic communities, not of outsiders. But the latter may help to clarify and foster the thoughts and factors that make for liberty of belief. In some academic areas the

battle has already been largely won. But legal rights, and the
readiness of public opinion to make them effective, are yet to
be made secure. One of the surest ways of influencing cultural
patterns in this respect is simply the quality of Christian relationships as patient, reverent and expectant.

However, it is not only the dominant culture in its attitudes
to movement of religious faith that is involved. How is the will
to receive Christ taken in the churches? One might assume--with
eager warmth and ready welcome. But the fact is often otherwise--
with scepticism or reluctance. Reasons we have already noted in
the long habituation of the old churches under Islam to non-
evangelism, at least in the active sense. Churches, too, of
more recent missionary planting or association tend to stay wary
of the baptizand. Motives may be suspected or professions dis-
trusted, so that the inquirer is liable to find a doubtful
reception. In Africa the situation is easier, in that Islam itself is less rigorous, more relaxed, and there are mixed
Muslim/Christian families, such as rarely, if ever, occur in the
Arab world. Africa, sub-Saharan, puts its own stamp on every
situation.

But what are we to say of convertibility in this external and
"confessional" sense of discipleship *via* baptism and participation in the Christian community? "Baptised into Christ" is
certainly the New Testament principle and the commands to preach
the Gospel and to make disciples of the nations are linked in
one. The faith does not present itself for admiration, or for
ventilation and review, for conversation, but for "obedience."
The waters of baptism are, institutionally, as symbolic and
decisive as the Red Sea and the Jordan, those waters of history
whence the imagery came. Baptism, one might say, is the Rubicon
of discipleship, meant to be crossed, with the boats burned behind us, "risen with Christ in newness of life."

Yet such baptism pre-supposes the welcoming community and it
pre-supposes that it is the person who is meant, not the passport,
the legal identity or the citizenship card. What then, when the
spiritual meaning of baptism is obscured by assumptions that a
treachery has been committed? How can it be known only and truly
as a transaction in discipleship? Should there be other ways of
pastoral acceptance and true incorporation into fellowship which
obviate the distortions of meaning that beset the public mind
and saddle the personal response? These are questions urgently
on the conscience of the Gospel in each local setting. Baptism
cannot be culturally immunized. How, then, should it be
culturally expressed?

Around the answer to that question lurks a surmise some of us
cannot ignore. Is it possible that baptism could even become a

kind of Christian circumcision and so merit the strictures of
the New Testament apostles? May it be seen as a necessary badge
of belonging, a mark of the true folk, when we should rather be
ready to risk community in the Holy Spirit without it? "Christ
sent me, not to baptise, but to preach.." (1 Cor. 1:17) wrote
Paul. It was, clearly, not an absolute negative for, on his own
admission, he did baptize. But a statement of priority is
plainly implied. The apostle would seem to be saying that
mediation of the Word has priority over the initiation of
hearers, the more so if the latter became thereby partisans of a
mission(ary) or a sect, or develop a sense of whose they are as
members which means more to them than the wonder of what they are
in Christ. For what avails finally is "neither circumcision,
nor uncircumcision, but a new creation." There are no easy
answers to this problem. But the worst answer of all would be
to behave as if it did not exist.

Are there, perhaps, further senses, with or without the rite
of baptism, by which Christian discipleship can be known for
what it is in action and in fellowship? Surely Yes! There is
a way to be in the midst of culture as would-be guardians of
truth, servants of faith and people of hope. Culture, in all
its manifestations, is, after all, the quality of society, the
"style" of life. It is always in flux and change, needing to be
leavened, seasoned, lifted, resisted, renewed. This dimension
of vocation lies deeper than discerning ways in which Christian
worship can recruit cultural forms and reject the habit of alien
imitation. It means more caring for vocabulary, artifacts,
music, design and idiom in the local guise, significant as all
these must be seen to be. Conversion to Christ means reaching
out *via* the newness of mind, *with* the authentic idiom, but *into*
the whole context, to "prove what is the good, acceptable and
perfect will of God." That "proving" surely, is not a learning
to accept the circumstances that befall and to find them "working
for good," simply in personal safety and well-being. It is
rather, giving people around us to know for sure what God would
have them be and their world because of them. It means not being conformed but transformed so that "culture"--in its fullest
sense as what life is in the living of it--has present within
it that witness to judgment and to grace by which its norms are
judged and called. This is not some social Gospel. For the
reality of personal conversion is the crux of all other convertibility towards truth and compassion and joy. But the truly
personal conversion never stays with an individual dimension.
For, in our Lord's words, it has its incidence only in that
"wind of the Spirit" everywhere moving "as He lists."

The themes and crises of culture are legion. Much of the
Muslim world is caught in a vast sudden influx of wealth, of
petro-dollars. Of that situation one writer had recently written
as follows:

"The Gulf is an area which has emerged from rags to riches
in the space of thirty years....The changes have been
intense and comprehensive, affecting every area of human
activity and experience....The contrast between a struggling,
labor-based survival economy and a wildly wasteful consumer
economy fuelled by a massive welfare system has been a
shattering experience."

After exploring the "boom-town" analogy, he goes on to note how
in the Gulf situation the incomers are almost all foreigners,
until the local population is wellnigh outnumbered by the influx
from abroad. The resulting tensions, many of them compounded
by religious and racial factors, "conspire to create dividing
walls of suspicion."

"The dominant experience of sensitive souls is one of
despair, restlessness, transience and futility in work....
One gets the feeling that everything is prefabricated,
jerry-rigged, and easily disassembled, from physical
structures to the social matrix itself. In the face of
this overpowering attack upon the quality of human
existence, to what spiritual resources may the people
turn?"

Other areas face the opposite urgency of drastic poverty, of
local population growth far in excess of the capacity to sustain
even a deplorable "standard" of living. What of the struggle
for dignity, not to say survival, in a world of such utter
crowdedness and fragility? What, as Ezra Pound put it, of
"the enormous pathos of the dream in the peasant's bent
shoulders " ?

When mission fields are closed through revolutions or radical
regimes, as of late in Ethiopia and Eritrea, is it enough to
speak simply of a closed door for our evangelism and find the
goodness of God in new opportunities for a visa in another place?
Our wrestling *is* with "principalities and powers" and the current
meaning of that New Testament phrase is, precisely, these
structures of power, of anger, of retribution, of ideology, of
competition, now on stage in the world.

What, again, of all the emotive and explosive issues in the
Arab/Israeli confrontation, where the irreducible claim of
Israeli Statehood (as distinct from presence) within the Arab
world, counters the hardly reducible insistence on Palestinian
rights and liberty to love the same natal territory? There has
surely been no sterner crisis of the Arab soul in all its
history than this of how to resolve relationships with Israel.
The Zionist State may be seen as history's justified reparation
for the holocaust. But the holocaust was Europe's guilt not the

Arab East's. Such invitation to vicarious suffering on behalf
of others' peace is a deep vocation. But the outsider, recom-
mending its acceptance, has no right to be generous with other
people's sorrows. The impulse must come from where the suffering is and that means, if at all, from within Islam. Our
Christian concern for conversion cannot stay aloof from the
"convertibility" of this tragic situation towards healing and
compassion.

There are only random examples of "principalities and powers,"
forces, claims, passions, at issue in the world of our time.
There is, clearly, no theme of culture, of life in its quality
and personal existence in its "style," that can be immune from
the stress of these, and other, factors in the human scene where
we are looking for conversion. With these, says the apostle, is
"our wrestling." What can he mean? Intercession? Truly. But
then the God with whom we intercede is liable, as with evangelism,
to entrust the issues back again to us, that a man may work for
what he prays, but do so in the dimensions his intercession
learns. Prayer is certainly not exoneration, but involvement.

It is, perhaps, possible for some to *identify* the transcendent
will, in some sense with their own structure and their cause.
"The rock of Israel" in the Constitution of the State of Israel,
is an intriguingly ambiguous solution to a deep controversy,
focusing this very question of the nature of culture. The
secular activists, like David Ben Gurion, would have nothing of
"the Lord God of Israel," at least in the Constitution. They
did not envisage a religious "Israel"--a national "ghetto" of
piety, but a self-reliance and resilient new Jewishness, rejoicing in its own vitality. The orthodox Rabbis would have
nothing less than "the Lord God of Israel." For, Him apart, Zion
itself would be presumption. So it was that "the rock of
Israel" proved a reconciling term, that either could interpret
in his own sense. What large areas of culture are implicit
in this equation, which could be paralleled at large?

The Christian cannot rightly allow that structures, our
structures, are the only transcendent there is. This is the
Marxist way. But nor would he be right to leave structures and
powers to themselves, as if faith were a retreat from their
relevance. It is easy to become despairing at this point, and
Muslims are not immune from this temptation. In a recently
translated book, first published in Cairo in 1967, the well-known
Muslim thinker, Muhammad Kamil Husain, has interpreted Islamic
faith as primarily the maturing in the soul of an inner peace.
Writing with the Mosaic title of *The Hallowed Valley* (cf. the
"holy ground" of Exodus 3:5), he records a doubt he has expressed
in other words that social and political institutions can ever
escape the effects of human perversity and self-interest, as

"collectives" arouse and sharpen these, by over-riding both
conscience and compassion.

> "The effect of individual purity on the refining of relation-
> ships between man and his community is less than its
> influence within the person himself. As for its impact
> on the inter-relationship of communities,--that is a frail
> thing and hardly to be depended on."

Many outside Islam, in the light of history, would be disposed
to agree with him. But, in that case, are we not in danger of
leaving the whole sphere of culture, that is, the patterns of
human assumption and intercourse, to the cynic or the casual?

Ours, surely, is the vocation to care for such personal
"peace" and "purity," according to Christ, in conversion, but
then to set such "convertedness" outwards towards the world, in
a spiritual militancy for its institutions and its ways. Ours
it is, if we are in Christ, within all cultures, to affirm the
sacramental earth, the work of the God who created and meant
it unto good, and to witness concretely for that meaning, however paralyzed it may be by man's waywardness. In so doing,
we must recruit all the arguable assets that other faiths afford,
subduing all these to the criteria that we obey in Christ and
Him crucified. That means the local churches as caring communities, reaching into the personal needs, and hopes and fears,
of their neighbors, in an active compassion and a living commun-
cation. Such is the will's discipleship in Christ.

Perhaps we can come round full circle and conclude with
repentance, where conversion begins. Islam, in its emphasis on
Taubah, or penitence, and on God as *Al-Tawwab* or "cognizant of
penitence," has some kinship here, though its accent is on sin
as what we *do* in deeds, rather than on sin as who and how we
are in character and nature. "The valley of Achor" has to be
"a door of hope." (Hosea 2:15) So much of the world is there,
without seeing the door. We need to think of penitence in a
more vicarious way, as the will to make our own the evils of
society, to feel ourselves responsible. This runs against the
grain of all societies and cultures. For we all like to think
ourselves innocent, to be "justified" even though the
"justification" be a false one. Thus even religion, as Albert
Camus had it, may be seen as "a great laundering exercise."
When it is so, then culture becomes impervious, in its smugness,
to a truer quality. Without such accusation, societies decay.

But the only right to press such accusation is in the love
that itself suffers, before it can transform. Here is the whole
secret of the Cross of Jesus as the Christ and, with it, the
whole duty of the Christian in culture.

PART III

Culture,
Churches and Ethics

13

The Church in Culture:
A Dynamic Equivalence Model
Charles H. Kraft

The question to which I seek to address myself here concerns the nature of the relationship between the people of God (commonly known within Christian circles as "the church") and the culture in which groupings of the people of God find themselves. The overall question to be asked is, What should a genuinely Christian expression of people of God-ness look like in relationship to the surrounding culture? Such a question involves the development of an understanding of the kind of help that we can get from the Bible to assist us in answering this question and the way in which we will get that help. It is to these latter concerns that I wish to address myself in this paper.

As one who has been involved in church planting in northeastern Nigeria and who now teaches missiology to those working largely in nonwestern parts of the world, I have a primary concern for developing an understanding of the church in nonwestern contexts. I seek, however, to develop a perspective that is just as applicable within western culture as within nonwestern cultures.

In the development of the topic I will first attempt to outline the two prevailing perspectives or "models." I will then proceed to a critique of these models, followed by a discussion of new understandings concerning culture and language that, if

applied to the subject at hand, can, I believe, lead us to the
kind of breakthrough in conceptualizing the church that has
recently occurred in the conceptualization of Bible translation.
On that basis, then, I will develop the concept of dynamic
equivalence churchness.

PREVIOUS MODELS

There are two previous models of churchness that need to be
treated.   The first of these we will label the *traditional model*.
Missionaries employing this model have ordinarily assumed that
the church in a new area is to be as similar as possible to the
churches that they have experienced in their home countries.   As
one missionary committed to this model once said to me, "We
(i.e., Euroamerican Christianity) have had 2000 years of
experience with Christianity. We know how the church is to be
organized and operated."   According to this position, we who
"know what the church is to be" are simply to instruct the new
believers in our ways.

Such a position or model characteristically assumes that,
though there may be many types of church organization and policy
in existence, the positions advocated by the missionary's group
are more correct (more biblical) than those of any other group.
There is, therefore, only one right way for all peoples--that
developed by the leaders of the movement of which the given
missionary is a part.   These positions are typically justified
in the theological formulations of the movement and labeled by
the movement as "the New Testament pattern," even if some attempt
is made to adapt them to the surrounding culture.   The advocates
of this position tend to hold that

> the question of church government is not an anthro-
> pological but a theological one. Before beginning
> to apply his knowledge of a culture to the establish-
> ment of an indigenous church, the missionary must be
> convinced that either the congregational or the
> episcopal or some other form of church government is
> the kind Jesus Christ meant for every society, all
> over the world and at all times (Samarin 1954:120).

Advocates of the traditional approach tend to try to reproduce
in the receptor culture forms of churchness that are the same as
or, at least, highly similar to the forms employed in the sending culture.   These are imposed from outside of the receptor
culture, on the assumption that study of the Scriptures has enabled the missionaries to see clearly what these forms should be.
Often this approach is employed with a feeling of guilt on the
part of the missionaries that their home churches are not living
closer to the ideal that their denomination advocates.   There is,

therefore, often an attempt on the part of the missionaries to produce a purer form of churchness in the receptor culture than is actually found in the sending churches.

Missiologists have long since found the traditional approach to be inadequate at several points. They see theological naiveness in the assumption that any given denomination can see clearly a single scriptural model that is applicable to all peoples in all times and places. They would see, further, a cultural naiveness in the assumption that models that may serve well in the home country can simply be exported to other cultures without modification. Some time ago, therefore, mission theorists such as Henry Venn, Rufus Anderson and Roland Allen became critical of such a paternalistic approach and committed themselves to the concept that churches are to be indigenous in the receiving cultures rather than simply exported from the sending cultures.

An indigenous church, then, came to be understood as one that is self-supporting, self-governing and self-propagating. In the latter part of the nineteenth century it was quite revolutionary for Venn to contend that the aim of his mission (Church Missionary Society) should be "the development of Native Churches, with a view to their ultimate settlement upon a self-supporting, self-governing and self-extending system" (Stock 1899:2:83). Eventually, though, nearly all mission theorists and a large number of field missionaries came to give at least lip service to these principles.

Many missions gave themselves rather totally to such principles of indigeneity and poured a considerable amount of their energy into training leaders who would take over the church and mission structures. Such activity became more and more common from mission to mission as the day of national independence for the countries in which they worked approached.

CRITIQUE OF PREVIOUS MODELS

No one can doubt the sincerity of missionaries who simply did the best they could, given the training and insights available to them. Committed missionaries have always sought to be biblical. And yet "being biblical" is a matter of interpreting the Bible according to the best insights available to one. We do not see even biblical meanings absolutely, but always as affected by our culturally inculcated understandings of life in general. Interpretation is always a matter of application of one's perspectives to the understanding of the Word. The primary factor, then, in critiquing previous approaches to understanding what the church ought to be in mission lands is not the substitution of something other than the Bible as the basis. It is, rather, a change in the perspective in terms of which the Bible is interpreted.

The perspective underlying the traditional approach to churchness may be labeled monocultural and ethnocentric. It fails to appreciate cultural differences. The way advocated by the denominational perspectives of the missionary is looked on as superior and all other Christian approaches as based on inferior understandings of the Scriptures. Different cultures, likewise, are looked on as inferior to that of the missionary. Implicit in the approaches to mission based upon this perspective is the aim to get converts to think and act like the missionary and his people, since that way is regarded as superior and Christian. From this perspective even the Scriptures seemed to support what was, perhaps, the prevailing missionary philosophy of the day—"civilize in order to evangelize." Schools and other types of training programs common in the sending countries came to be the major vehicles in terms of which people were trained out of their "inferior" ways into "Christian" ways which included both the faith and the cultural trappings of the missionaries' approach to Christianity.

The "three selfs" approach was in theory a considerable advance over the traditional approach. In practice, however, it often devolved into a mere intensification of the training program set up to produce western leaders for a western church. Though the term "indigenous" pointed missionaries in the direction of the receptor culture, the reduction of the definition of indigenous to the three selfs formula enabled missionaries to focus on formal, surface-level changes in strategy. The results aimed at tended to still be in terms of cultural forms more appropriate to the sending culture than to the receptor culture.

In a landmark article published in 1958 William A. Smalley provides what I feel to be the most telling critique of the three selfs formula for indigeneity. Smalley served in a mission that prides itself both in its commitment to biblical Christianity and in its commitment to three selfs indigeneity. Smalley's approach is, therefore, biblical. But his perspective on the Bible is, unlike that of the majority of his colleagues, an anthropological perspective. His commitment is to indigeneity, but to deeply *functional indigeneity* rather than simply surface-level indigeneity of the forms of churchness. He suggests, therefore, that

> It may be very easy to have a self-governing church which is not indigenous. Many presently self-governing churches are not. All that is necessary to do is to indoctrinate a few leaders in Western patterns of church government, and let them take over. The result will be

a church governed in a slavishly foreign manner (although
probably modified at points in the direction of local
government patterns), but by no stretch of imagination
can it be called an indigenous government. This is going
on in scores of mission fields today under the misguided
assumption that an "indigenous" church is being founded
(1958:52).

What Smalley points out is that, though an indigenous church
will ordinarily be characterized by the kind of self functioning
embodied in the three selfs formula, not every church that
governs, supports and propagates itself can be properly labeled
indigenous, except in a very superficial, formal sense. For
"although these three 'self' elements may be present in such a
movement, they are essentially independent variables" (Smalley
1958:51-2), rather than diagnostic criteria of indigeneity. For
it is not the mere fact of self-government or of self-support or
of self-propagation that assures that the church in question
is "indigenous." The indigeneity (if present at all) lies in
the *manner* in which selfhood is expressed. Simple evaluation of
the forms of government, propagation and support is not sufficient.
One has to look also at the ways in which these cultural forms
are operated and the meanings attached to them both by the
church itself and by the surrounding community.

There is, for example, a church which is advertised by
its founding mission as a great indigenous church, where
its pastors are completely supported by the local church
members, yet the mission behind the scenes pulls the strings
and the church does its bidding like the puppets of the
"independent" iron curtain countries (Smalley 1958:54).

There are, in addition, many churches where the real power is
no longer either directly or indirectly in the hands of
foreigners. It is, rather, in the hands of nationals so indoctrinated in foreign ways that they bend every effort to
perpetuate the foreign system in the name of Christ, as if that
were the only possible "Christian" way. In both situations the
"indigeneity" is in outward form only. The essence, the content,
the meanings conveyed, the impressions given are all foreign.

Nor is "indigeneity" necessarily the most appropriate label
for the ideal toward which we strive. For something totally
indigenous would in appearance, functioning and meaning be no
different from the rest of the culture. Christianity, however,
comes from outside of a culture--both in its inception (Christ
entered Hebrew culture from outside) and in its transmission by
cross-cultural missionaries (who by definition are outsiders).
Christianity is, therefore, "always intrusive to a certain
degree." There is "no such thing as an absolutely indigenous

church in any culture" (Smalley 1959:137). Something totally
indigenous would so conform to the culture that it would not be
Christian. There is, thus, a certain basic incompatibility between the terms "indigenous" and "Christian" unless we agree
(as, I think, has generally been the case) that by "indigenous
Christian Church" we mean to imply something less than total
indigeneity.

What, then, is the ideal toward which we strive? Smalley
defines an indigenous church as

> a group of believers who live out their life, including
> their socialized Christian activity, in the patterns of
> the local society, and for whom any transformation of
> the society comes out of their felt needs under the
> guidance of the Holy Spirit and the Scriptures (1958:55).

Such a church will be characterized by an autonomy strongly
reminiscent of the churches described in the pages of the New
Testament. It will, therefore, exhibit "selfhood" at a far
deeper level than can be merely imposed by any outside organization committed to three selfs indigeneity. Alan Tippett
describes this selfhood in terms of six integrally interdependent
characteristics (1973:154-59). 1) Such a church will possess the
kind of self-image that enables it to "see itself as *the* Church
of Jesus Christ in its own local situation, mediating the work,
the mind, the word and the ministry of Christ in its own environment" (p. 155). It will, further, 2) be a self-functioning
Church that, like a body, is made up of interdependent, interacting, yet discrete parts each functioning in commitment to and
for the good of the whole, not at the behest of outsiders.   3) A
third mark of such a Church is that it will be self-determining.
Decisions will be made autonomously according to culturally
appropriate decision-making patterns.

A truly indigenous Church will 4) by nature support its own
operation and outreach in culturally appropriate ways. It will,
further, 5) hear the Great Commission as directly addressed to
itself and, therefore, commit itself to indigenous forms of
self-propagation. Such a Church will 6) be self-giving. It
will serve actively and appropriately as an expression of its
Christian self-image. When, therefore,

> the indigenous people of a community think of the Lord as
> their own, not a foreign Christ; when they do things as
> unto the Lord meeting the cultural needs around them,
> worshipping in patterns they understand; when their
> congregations function in participation in a body, which
> is structurally indigenous; then you have an *indigenous*
> Church (1973:158).

In a similar vein Smalley points to several basic considerations with respect to indigenous churches. He notes that a
church is a sociocultural entity. As such it involves patterns
of interaction between people that will be based on the patterns
of interaction that characterize people outside of the church.
If the patterns of interaction characteristic of a given church
are those of the missionaries from overseas, the church may not
be called indigenous. If the church is to be indigenous, the
patterns of interaction among the members will be based upon
those of the indigenous culture in which the members were
brought up.

A second characteristic of an indigenous church will be the
presence of the Holy Spirit. His presence in a society implies
that there will be transformation both of individuals and of the
group as a whole. Available evidence concerning the working of
the Holy Spirit in various societies leads us to believe that

> such transformation occurs differently in different
> societies, depending on the meaning which people attach
> to their behavior and the needs which they feel in their
> lives....An indigenous church is precisely one in which
> the changes which take place under the guidance of the
> Holy Spirit meet the needs and fulfill the meanings of
> that society and not of any outside group (Smalley 1958:56).

A third point that Smalley makes is that when the Holy Spirit
begins working indigenously within a receptor society, it is
very common for missionaries to dislike the results. Missionaries, even those committed to indigeneity, tend to encourage
culture change that makes people more like themselves in outward
form. But the nature of nonwestern societies and of the working
of the Holy Spirit within such societies are often such that
western missionaries are put off by them. For the deeply in-
grained reflexes of the missionaries have been conditioned by
other social patterns and they have become accustomed to the
way the Holy Spirit works in those contexts. The patterns
familiar to the missionary are, therefore, regarded as natural,
anything else is regarded as unnatural.

Such a perspective on the part of cross-cultural missionaries
needs to be replaced by a more culturally aware perspective on
God and the way he works. We aim to be biblical but, with a
culturally aware perspective, not as naively monocultural in
our understanding and application of the Bible as were many of
our predecessors. As cross-cultural witnesses

> It is our work first of all to see the Bible in its
> cultural perspective, to see God dealing with men
> through different cultural situations. It is our

responsibility to see Him change in His dealings with
men as the cultural history of the Jews changes, to
recognize that God has always, everywhere, dealt with
men in terms of their culture. It is next our
responsibility to take new Christians to the Bible and
to help them see in the Bible God interacting with other
people, people whose emotions and problems were very
similar to their own so far as their fundamental nature
is concerned, but also at times very different from their
own in the specific objective or working of their forms
of life. It is our responsibility to lead them in
prayer to find what God would have them do as they study
His Word and seek the interpretation and leadership of
the Holy Spirit (Smalley 1958:58).

Missionaries, with their own cultural conditioning a primary
factor in their experience, often have a difficult time learning to operate this way, especially when the results may be
expressions of Christianity that are radically different from
what they know at home.

A fourth implication of this critique is that an indigenous
church cannot be founded. As Smalley says

The biblical figure of planting and harvest is far more
realistic than our American figure based on our American
values and expressed in the idea of the "establishment"
or "founding" of a church (1958:60).

It is biblical to plant churches, western to found them.
Founding churches, as Smalley points out, typically involves
the use of organizational procedures familiar to the missionaries from their experience in the home country. This results
in the production of such trappings of western churchness as
constitution, doctrinal statement, procedures for the operation
of business meetings and elections, disciplinary procedures and
the like. In one case, cited by Smalley, the problem at hand
was the production of the constitution by means of which the
church was to be governed. The missionaries generously put
more nationals on the constitution committee than missionaries.

When the committee met, the missionaries asked the tribesmen what they wanted in their constitution. The tribesmen,
of course, did not know what they wanted in their constitution. They had not even known that they wanted a
constitution until they had been told so. The missionaries
suggested some of the possibilities for a constitution
and the tribesmen readily agreed to most or all of them.
The result, worked out in good faith by both the missionaries and the tribesmen, was a replica of the denominational

constitution of the mission body. To this day no one
seems to have sensed the fact that a tribal church with
a constitution is no more an indigenous church than a
tribal church without one, as the existence of a
constitution is entirely irrelevant to the relation of
the church to God and to surrounding human life.

In any honestly indigenous work a true constitution (if
there were any at all) would be one which would describe
the structure of the church society in its workings
(Smalley 1958:61).

A planted church, as opposed to a founded one, may not need a
formal constitution. It certainly will not need one until it
is the desire of the members of the church to produce one,
rather than the desire of outside founders. A planted church
will adopt indigenous governmental and organizational procedures
intact, making whatever modifications need to be made for these
procedures to be appropriate to the Christian community.
Decisions concerning these procedures, their use and their
modification, can only be made by those whose cultural reflexes
have been formed by them. The outside missionary is in no
position to make such decisions. A culturally sensitive outsider can function effectively as a consultant in such matters,
but he must be aware and constantly make his people aware of
his limitations as well.

The fifth point that Smalley makes is that indigenous churches
often start apart from missions. The most indigenous churches
of Africa, for example, are certain of the independent African
churches. An exciting indigenous church among the Meo of
Southeast Asia was planted by a converted Meo shaman who got
excited about the Gospel message and, with another tribesman,
began proclaiming that message from village to village among
his own people (see Barney 1957).

The problem pointed up by this factor and the last is a very
serious one. It stems from the fact that the western cultural
matrix from which most missionaries have come has in several
ways crippled us both in our understanding of the Scriptures
and in our ability to communicate them to people of other
cultures. As Smalley says:

Our distance from most other cultures is so great, the
cultural specialization of the West is so extreme, that
there are almost no avenues of approach whereby the
work which we do can normally result in anything of an
indigenous nature. It is an ironical thing that the
West, which is most concerned with the spread of
Christianity in the world today, and which is financially

best able to undertake the task of world-wide evangelism,
is culturally the least suited for its task because of the
way in which it has specialized itself to a point where
it is very difficult for it to have an adequate understanding of other peoples (Smalley 1958:63).

Given this fact, it is of great importance that we from the
West begin to examine from new perspectives our understandings
of what we do in missionizing. It is the intent of what follows
in this paper, as of this conference as a whole, to develop such
new perspectives. Perhaps it is not too late for some to be
protected from the advocates of the Gospel even while responding to the message that they seek to convey.

TOWARDS NEW UNDERSTANDINGS

The key to the development of a new approach to churchness is,
as Smalley points out, to get beneath the surface formal level
to a deeper level of understanding. Anthropologically we refer
to the surface level of cultural phenomena as the level of
cultural forms. Beneath this level are what may be labeled the
level of function and the level of meaning. As pointed out
above, the Church, in addition to its spiritual nature, is also
a cultural phenomenon. And as a cultural phenomenon it functions
within human society as a conveyer of meaning to human beings.
The Church will, therefore, convey some set of meanings to the
human beings who have contact with it. Just what those meanings
are and how closely they correspond to the meanings that God
intends for it to convey are, however, dependent upon the way
the Church as a cultural form functions in the society of which
it is a part.

The *forms* of a culture are the observable, surface features
of that culture. Cultural forms may be material items such as
houses, clothing, pottery, tools, machines, etc. More
frequently, though, they are non-material elements of culture
such as ceremonies, rituals, organizations, words, grammatical
constructions, ideas, and the like. A word is a fairly simple
non-material cultural form. A wedding ceremony or a church are
much more complex cultural forms made up of many subsidiary
cultural forms. Cultural institutions such as the family or
democratic government, practices such as visiting neighbors or
telling stories, customary ways of eating or farming, rituals
such as baptism and other initiation rites and organizations
such as clubs and churches are all cultural forms.

Cultural forms serve a variety of *functions* in a society.
One of the most important types of function that they serve is
to meet the basic needs of people. Cultural forms such as the
customs employed in eating, sleeping and defecating serve to

meet basic physical needs. Cultural forms such as marriage, family, educational practices, political and economic customs serve to meet basic sociocultural needs. Religious organizations and rituals serve to meet basic psychological and spiritual needs. Quite often cultural forms that were intended to serve certain needs actually perform other functions in place of or in addition to the serving of those needs. Eating together, for example, frequently has ritual or ceremonial significance in addition to meeting people's biological need for food. Jesus criticized the Pharisees for changing the function of Hebrew religious practices from service to God to oppression of the people of God.

The functions that cultural forms are used to serve, then, result in the communication of *meanings* through these forms to the people who use them. When a family is functioning well it communicates love and security to the children within it. If it is not functioning well, however, it may signify tension, enmity, bitterness and insecurity. When a government is functioning well it provides for the greatest good for the greatest number of people. When it is not functioning well, it may become an instrument of exploitation, oppression and self-interest on the part of those in power. When a church is functioning well it successfully communicates the meanings that God intends that it communicate to those to whom it ministers. When it is not functioning well, a church communicates other meanings such as foreignness, oppression, God's insensitivity of people's real needs and superstitious reverence for meaning-less rituals.

Those who study intercultural communication (including Bible translation) have discovered that certain very interesting, and often disturbing, things happen when the cultural forms of one culture are employed in another culture. What the forms signify to the receptors is determined by them, not by the communicator. And there are, apparently few, if any, cultural forms that signify exactly the same thing to people of different cultures (Nida 1960:89-90). Even when the people of two cultures appear to practice the same custom, we can expect the understood meaning of that custom to differ from group to group (and even from individual to individual within each group, though to a lesser degree). The first of two major principles of intercultural interaction thus becomes evident. 1) When a cultural form (like an axe, a word or the church) is borrowed from one culture to another, there will always be some change in its meaning.

In spite of such lack of exactness, however, it does seem to be possible for a member of one culture to communicate *equivalent* meanings to people of another culture. People are

enough alike, in spite of cultural differences, to understand
each other, even from one language and culture to another, if
sufficient adjustment is made. Though the receiver of the
communication will always have to make some adjustment, the
major responsibility for adjustment belongs to the one who seeks
to communicate a message across a cultural barrier. *The major
principle* that such a cross-cultural communicator needs to
learn, though, is that 2) equivalent meanings can only be
communicated in another culture if the forms employed are as
appropriate for expressing those meanings in the receptor
culture as the source forms are in the source culture. This
will ordinarily involve a heavy dependence on terms already at
use in the receptor language and culture and an extremely
limited use of new borrowings from other sources.

The recognition and employment of these two principles is
crucial to an understanding of indigeneity. For if the
cultural form of the church in one culture is simply transplanted to another culture we can be certain that the meaning
will be changed. The people in the receiving culture will not
understand the Church in the same way that those in the sending
culture did. Thus, if those in the receiving culture are to
understand the Church the way that those in the sending culture
understand it, the cultural form of the church *must* ordinarily
be changed. The basic structure and subsidiary forms of the
cultural organization known as the church must be as appropriate
to the receiving culture as they were to the sending culture
if their meanings are to be equivalent.

The great inadequacy of the three selfs definition of
indigeneity is seen when it is understood that each of the
three selfs has ordinarily been interpreted as a cultural form.
According to that model, indigenous churches are expected to
simply take over biblical (usually interpreted as western)
patterns (forms) of government, support and propagation. They
thus perpetuate patterns that meant one thing in the sending
culture but mean something quite different in the receiving
culture--unless, of course, the Christians in the receiving
culture go against what is expected and develop and employ their
own indigenous methods of government, support and propagation.
What is needed is *a kind of translation* of the meanings of the
Church *from* the cultural forms of the source cultures, the
biblical cultures, *into* those forms of the receiving culture
that function in such a way in the receiving culture that they
convey equivalent meanings. Only by changing the forms in this
way can the meanings be preserved.

To further clarify this concept, I will illustrate from the
area of Bible translation. For I am suggesting that a truly
indigenous church should look in its culture like a good Bible

translation looks in its language. In a good Bible translation 1) the original meanings come through clearly, 2) the hearers assume that it is an original work in their language (rather than a transplant) since they are not forced to learn foreign patterns in order to understand it, and 3) the impact of the message in the receiving language is roughly equivalent to its impact on its original hearers. Each of these things should characterize Christian churches as well.

DYNAMIC (OR FUNCTIONAL) EQUIVALENCE VERSUS CORRESPONDENCE IN FORM

Informed Bible translators do not aim for mere "formal correspondence" (i.e., correspondence between the forms of the source language and those of the receptor language) as do literal translations such as the RSV, ASV, and KJV. Such translations have a non-English (i.e., non-indigenous) flavor because the translators have not carried their task far enough. They have not made sure that the English renderings are the functional equivalents (not merely the formal correspondents) of their Hebrew, Aramaic and Greek referents. And the impression is of stiltedness and foreignness, since it does not represent the way people talk and write in English.

Such "formal correspondence translations" force their readers to learn foreign language patterns, since they simply transfer many of the word and grammar forms of the source language into the corresponding word and grammar forms of the receptor language. When Paul employs a word which in Greek is used as the name for "bowels," the KJV renders it "bowels" (e.g., Phil. 1:8, 2:1), in spite of the fact that the term is clearly being employed figuratively in these passages (signifying "affection" or "kindness"). Since the translators understood the basic meaning of the word to be "bowels," they attempted to consistently translate it that way. A formal correspondence translation attempts insofar as possible to regularly render each given word in the source language more or less mechanically by the same term in the receptor language. Thus the RSV translates the Greek word *soma* as "body" in each of the following verses: Mt. 6:25, Mk. 5:29, Lk. 17:37, Rom. 12:1 and Col. 2:11, since in English the word "body" may be taken to be the main meaning of the word and translators wanted to be "consistent." What they did not seem to understand is that the Greek word and the English word are far from exactly equivalent to each other. That is, the Greek word *soma* covers a different area of meaning than the English word "body" and, if the English translation is to be true to the Greek *meaning*, should be differently rendered whenever the context so indicates. In Mk. 5:29, for example, the English rendering that most naturally conveys the Greek meaning of *soma* would be "(her)self," rather than "her body" (RSV, KJV, ASV, NIV). In Lk. 17:37 a more meaningful rendering would be "corpse," in Rom. 12:1 it would be "selves," and in Col. 2:11 it would be something like "lower nature" (rather than the RSV's puzzling literal rendering "body of flesh").

Literally thousands of such illustrations can be produced from the KJV, ASV, and RSV of formal correspondence translations from Greek and Hebrew that obscure and sometimes obliterate the intended meanings. For these translations were produced in adherence to nineteenth-century concepts of the nature of language. These concepts saw languages basically as alternative codes each consisting of a different set of labels for the same reality. Early in this century, however, anthropologists and linguists began to recognize that understandings of reality are structured differently by different cultures and that these differences are strongly reflected in their languages. There is, therefore, no such thing as an exact correspondence between a given word (or other cultural form) in one language and culture and the most nearly corresponding word (or other form) in another.

Since cultures and their languages do not correspond exactly with each other, formal correspondence translations frequently create the misimpression that God requires us to learn a foreign (i.e., Hellenized or Hebraized) version of our own language before we can really understand him. They do this by employing English labels (words) to designate the segments into which the Greek or Hebrew languages are divided, not those into which English is divided. Preachers using literal translations have, then, to devote much of their time to explaining that the apparently English words don't, in the Bible, have their ordinary English meanings but, rather, have Greek and Hebrew meanings that only students of the original languages can properly understand and explain.

Such translations as Phillips, Today's English Version, New English Bible, and Living Bible are, however, much more in line with contemporary understandings of language and culture. Such translations carry their task beyond mere formal correspondence to the point where they endeavor to be faithful both to the original message and to the intended impact of that message on the original readers. For these translations seek to elicit from contemporary readers a response equivalent to that elicited from the original readers of the slangy, communicative Koine (=common people's) Greek. Thus, in recognition of the non-equatability of languages, they employ renderings that go beyond mere correspondence in form. They use English constructions that function in today's English-speaking world to convey meanings that are as equivalent as possible to the original meanings in the New Testament Greek-speaking world.

This type of translation is labeled by E. A. Nida a "dynamic equivalence translation." Such a translation is described as "the closest natural equivalent to the source-language message" and is "directed primarily toward equivalence of *response* rather than equivalence of form" (Nida 1964:166, emphasis mine). Good translation is therefore to be defined in terms

> of the degree to which the receptors of the message in the receptor language respond to it in substantially the same manner as the receptors in the source language. This response can never be identical, for the cultural and historical settings are too different, but there should be a high degree of equivalence of response, or the translation will have failed to accomplish its purpose (Nida and Taber, 1969:24).

An important concomitant of this dynamic view of Bible trans-. lation is the fact that good translation involves more than simply the conveying of information. This fact is of particular relevance to the present discussion. According to Nida and Taber

> It would be wrong to think. . .that the response of the receptors in the second language is merely in terms of comprehension of the information, for communication is not merely informative. It must also be expressive and imperative if it is to serve the principle purposes of communications such as those found in the Bible. That is to say, a translation of the Bible must not only provide information which people can understand but must present the message in such a way that people can feel its relevance (the expressive element in communication) and can then respond to it in action (the imperative function) (1969:24).

This understanding of what is involved in translating the Bible is considerably more aware than previous understandings of the complexity both of language (and culture) itself and of the process of moving concepts from one language to another. This approach recognizes that the central aim is *communication*, not mere transference of the forms for their own sake (out of reverence for supposedly sacred words). The biblical writers (and God) intended to be *understood*, not to be admired or simply to have their writings so highly thought of that they are transmitted in unintelligible or misleading forms. Faithful translation, therefore, involves doing whatever must be done (even including a certain amount of paraphrase) in order to make sure that the message originally phrased in Hebrew and Greek is transmitted in words and idioms in the receptor language that function to produce meanings in the **hearers' minds**

equivalent to those intended by the original authors. For the
real issue in translation lies outside of the mere words of the
source and receptor languages in and of themselves. It lies in
the impact of the concepts (the meanings) embodied in the
linguistic forms on the reader/hearer. If the impact is such
that it results in wrong understanding, misunderstanding or lack
of understanding on the part of the average (that is, unindoc-
trinated) reader/hearer, the translation has failed. Thus it is
that a *primary question asked by the new approach is, "How does
the receptor language require that this concept be expressed in
order both to be intelligible and to convey an impact equivalent
to that experienced by the original readers/hearers?"*

DYNAMIC EQUIVALENCE CHURCHES

All of this is highly suggestive of a new understanding of
what churches should look like from culture to culture. For a
church is a kind of culture-to-culture translation. Churchmen
ought to regard the receptor culture and the biblical cultural
expressions of "churchness" as the contemporary Bible translator
regards the languages he works with. Nida and Taber (1969:3-8)
develop seven basic understandings of language required of
effective Bible translators. Six of these are equally applicable
at the cultural level as requisites for the effective planting
of indigenous churches that have today the kind of impact that
God intends.

1) Each language and culture has its own genius, its own
distinctiveness, its own special character, its own patterning,
its own strengths, weaknesses and limitations. The effective
church planter, like the effective Bible translator must
recognize this distinctiveness.

2) To communicate effectively in another language and culture
one must respect and work in terms of this uniqueness. It is
the receptor language and culture (with both its strengths and
weaknesses) that must provide the matrix for the translation
and/or the church. Whatever changes in linguistic and cultural
forms are demanded by that receiving matrix to assure maximum
accurate intelligiblity must be acceded to.

3) In general, meanings that are communicable in one language
and culture are communicable in another, though in different
forms and always with some loss and gain of meaning. Though the
correspondence between the original meanings and those received
can never be exact, it can be adequate if the focus is on the
content being transmitted rather than on the mere preservation
of the literal forms of the source language and culture. The
essential concept of churchness is, therefore, transferable.

4) "To preserve the content of the message the form must be changed" when that message is translated into another language with its own unique genius. The concept and communicational impact of the church is, therefore, accurately transferred only if the forms that it takes in the new receptor culture are as specifically appropriate for the communication of those meanings in the new culture as the forms employed in the source culture are to that communication in the source culture. The cultural forms of churchness will, therefore, have to differ from culture to culture as much as necessary to assure equivalent meanings.

This principle may be illustrated by contrasting numerous inept renderings in the literal translations of the Bible with the more acceptably English renderings of TEV. Note, for example, the KJV, ASV, and RSV treatments of Mk. 1:4 ("baptism of repentance," which should be rendered by a more natural English verbal expression such as "turn away from your sins and be baptized," TEV); Mt. 3:8 ("bring forth. . .fruits meet for repentance," which was intended to signal something like "do the things that will show that you have turned from your sins," TEV); and Lk. 20:47 ("which devour widows' houses," which means in English "who take advantage of widows and rob them of their homes," TEV). There are, unfortunately, a large number of similarly inept correspondences of churches in many parts of the world to the forms of the source churches produced in disregard of this principle.

If the source and receptor languages and cultures are fairly similar (as with Euroamerican languages and cultures) the appropriate differences in form will not ordinarily be great (though even small differences may carry great significance). In general, however, the greater the distance between languages/ cultures, the greater the number and extent of the differences in the forms employed to convey equivalent meanings. This is the major reason for the greater difference between contemporary western churches and Old Testament and New Testament Hebrew churches than between contemporary western churches and the Gentile churches of the New Testament--the cultural distance is much greater.

5) Available evidence and perspectives strongly suggest that we should not regard the languages and cultures of the Bible as too sacred to analyze and relate to as we do to other languages and cultures. They appear to be subject to the same limitations as other languages and cultures.

With respect specifically to the biblical languages, they appear to be no more perfect or precise than other languages (e.g., over 700 grammatical and lexical ambiguities have been counted in the Greek Gospels alone!) but, in fact, just like all

other languages, the biblical Greek and Hebrew vocabulary, idiom
and grammar participate fully in and have meaning only in terms
of the culture in which these languages were used. The authors
did not invent unknown words or use them in unknown ways except
as anyone is allowed by his culture to innovate on occasion to
convey new insight or for cultural borrowing. "All the vocabulary was itself rooted in the finite experience of men and
women, and all of the expressions must be understood in terms of
this type of background." That is, it is the *message* of the
Bible that is sacred, not the languages themselves, even though
the sacred message was conveyed in terms of these finite,
imperfect, culture-bound languages.

As with the relation between the biblical languages and the
message of God, so with the biblical cultures and the Church of
God. The cultures and the forms employed within them to express
sacred meanings are not sacred in and of themselves. God's use
of them demonstrates God's willingness to work in terms of the
forms of any culture, not a desire on his part to perfect and
impose any single set of cultural forms. It is the message, the
communication conveyed via those forms that is sacred. And that
can be conveyed as well via any other culture and language.

6) "The writers of the biblical books expected to be understood." To many Americans, accustomed to hearing and reading
God's Word from literal translations and hearing preachers trying to explain them, the idea that the authors expected to be
understood may come as a shock. Yet "the writers of the Bible
were addressing themselves to concrete historical situations and
were speaking to living people confronted with pressing issues."
The translator is obligated to produce a translation that makes
that same kind of sense in the receptor language, if he is to
keep faith with the original authors and the God for whom they
spoke.

God expects to be understood through his Church as well as
through his Word. The Church (like the Bible) is meant to be
maximally intelligible to the world around it, conveying to it
meanings equivalent to those conveyed to their cultures by
scripturally recommended examples of churchness (both Old
Testament and New Testament). The faithful churchman is to work
toward this end in consciously attempting to transculturate the
concept of churchness into the appropriate cultural forms of the
receptor culture in which he works.

Applying this model to church planting would mean the eschew-
ing of attempts to produce mere formal correspondence between
churches in one culture and those in another. A church that is
merely a "literal" rendering of the forms of one church--be it
an American church or the first century Greco-Roman Church--then,

is not according to the dynamic equivalence model. Such a church is not structured in such a way that it can perform the functions and convey the meanings that God intended through his Church in a culturally appropriate way. It will always smack of foreignness, of insensitivity to the surrounding culture, of inappropriateness to the real needs of the people and the real message of God to them, since its forms have not been translated or "transculturated" from those appropriate somewhere else into those appropriate in the new setting.

A "formal correspondence church" models itself slavishly after the foreign church that founded it. If that church has bishops or presbyters or elders, the younger church will have them too. If that church operates according to a written constitution, the younger church will as well. If the founding church conducts business meetings according to Robert's Rules of Order, the younger church will likewise. And so it will be with regard to educational requirements for leadership, times of worship, style of worship, type of music, structures of church buildings, behavioral requirements for good standing (e.g., refraining from smoking and/or alcoholic beverages), the types of educational, medical and benevolent activity entered into, and even the expression of missionary concern (if any) on the part of the younger church. And all of this will utterly disregard the culturally appropriate functional equivalents and the indigenously understood meanings of all of these things in the culture in which the young church is supposedly functioning and to which it is supposedly witnessing. The impression such churches give to the people of their cultural world is one of foreignness and outside domination, even though the leadership of these churches may well be "their own people"--though again only in a formal sense, since these leaders have been carefully indoctrinated into the foreign system in order to attain the positions that they have within the system.

The *true aim* in this as well as in every other aspect of the propagation of Christianity is, however, not such formal correspondence, but the same kind of dynamic or functional equivalence discussed above for Bible translation. For, as Nida points out, Christianity is not like Islam which, through the Koran, "attempts to fix for all time the behavior of Muslims" by setting up an absolutely unbending set of forms that are simply to be adopted, never adapted. The Bible, rather, "clearly establishes the principle of relative relativism, which permits growth, adaptation, and freedom, under the Lordship of Christ . . .The Christian position is not one of static conformance to dead rules, but of dynamic obedience to a living God" (Nida 1954:52).

A "dynamic equivalence church," then, is the kind of church
that produces an impact on the people of the society of which it
is a part equivalent to the impact that the original church
produced upon the original hearers. In that equivalence the
younger church will have need of leadership, of organization,
of education, of worship, of buildings, of behavioral standards,
and of means of expressing Christian love and concern to the
people of its own culture who have not yet responded to Christ.
But a dynamically equivalent church will employ forms appropriate
and understandable to the receptors in the meeting of these
needs--familiar, meaningful forms that it, like the early
churches, will possess, adapt and infill with Christian meanings.
Such forms at the beginning of their employment by the church
may be only minimally adequate to the tasks at hand. But they
will thereby begin the process of transformation that will make
them more adequate to fulfill their Christian functions.

What is desired, then, is the kind of church that will take
indigenous forms, possess them for Christ, adapt and employ them
to serve Christian ends and to convey Christian meanings, to the
surrounding society. If this is what is intended by the term
"indigenous Christian church" well and good. But, I fear, that
designation has too readily been assigned on the basis of mere
formal correspondence to the sending church rather than on the
basis of true dynamic equivalence to biblical models for the
church. And such formal correspondence, carrying with it as it
does the pervasive impression of foreignness and irrelevance to
real life, is disturbingly counterproductive in terms of the
kind of powerful, relevant impact on human beings that Christianity is intended to have.

DYNAMIC EQUIVALENCE TO BIBLICAL MODELS

According to the above conception a dynamic equivalence church
would be one that 1) conveys to its members truly Christian
meanings, 2) functions within its society in such a way that in
the name of Christ it plugs into the felt needs of that society
and produces within it an impact for Christ equivalent to that
which the first century Church produced in its society, and 3) is
couched in cultural forms that are as nearly indigenous as
possible.

It is necessary, though, to attempt to ascertain just what
were the biblical forms, functions and meanings to which the
church in the receptor culture is expected to develop dynamic
equivalence. For this information we look primarily to the New
Testament (though for many situations culturally closer to Old
Testament cultures, the Old Testament offers more easily transculturated models). The Book of Acts and the Pastoral Epistles
provide many insights into matters of organization, leadership,

fellowship, witness and worship. Insights into behavioral
matters are likewise found in these books and also in the
Corinthian epistles. Certain other epistles focus more on
doctrinal matters. To these models contemporary churches whether
in Euroamerica or overseas are to develop dynamically equivalent
forms within and relevant to their contemporary cultural matrix.

The techniques of exegesis have, of course, been developed to
enable us to discover these New Testament models for application
in our own life. It is, however, all too easy to exegete well
enough to arrive at culturally appropriate functional equivalents
for our own culture and sub-culture. But we often then insist
on imposing these *forms* on the members of another culture or
another sub-culture within our culture (e.g., youth, those of
another denomination). This has frequently been the result when
missionaries of a particular Euroamerican denominational (or non-
denominational) heritage have simply attempted to organize the
church in the receptor culture according to their own denominational pattern with the particular organizational, doctrinal,
and behavioral emphases. Whereas its functional equivalence
between the New Testament models and their expression in the
Euroamerican denomination may be fairly appropriate in the Euro-
american context, not infrequently much of the functional appropriateness is lost when the representatives of that denomination
export their emphases to another culture. This is certainly true
when it comes to modes of baptism (and especially the apologetics
that accompany them), of the Lord's Supper and of church organization. But it is also, and perhaps more damagingly true of
the forms of worship, doctrine, witness and behavior that are
recommended. Why, for example, should more time be given in
Asian and African Bible schools to discussions of the proofs of
biblical inspiration and of theories of the atonement (problems
which we in our culture may find very important to us) than to
dealing with a Christian perspective on evil spirits and ancestor
reverence (problems of vital importance within their cultures)?
Perhaps we have not learned that just as Euroamerican churches
need to be dynamically equivalent to New Testament models in
their relevance to the surrounding culture, so must the churches
of mission lands with respect to their cultures.

In attempting to discover a dynamically equivalent form of
preaching I once asked a group of Nigerian church leaders how
they felt it would be appropriate to present a message such as
the Christian message to the village council. They replied,

We would choose the oldest, most respected man in the
group and ask him a question. He would discourse,
perhaps at length, on the topic and then become silent,
whereupon we would ask another question. As the old
man talked other old men would comment as well. But

eventually he and the others would do less and less
of the talking and the leader would do more and more.
In this way we would develop our message and it would
become the topic for discussion of the whole village.

I asked them why they didn't employ this approach in church.
"Why, we've been taught that monologue is the Christian way,"
they replied. "Can this be why no old men come to church?" I
asked. "Of course!" they said, "We have alienated them all by
not showing them due respect in public meetings."

Thus it is that a preaching form that may (or may not) be
appropriate enough in Euroamerican culture--dynamically equivalent
in that culture to the New Testament model--loses its equivalence
when exported to another culture. It is found there to be
counterproductive rather than facilitative with respect to the
functions such a form is intended to fulfill.

The models are presented in the Scriptures. It is, however,
equivalence to the functions performed by these groupings of the
People of God and to the ideals that lie behind them that we
seek, not, as has been stressed above, a mere imitation of their
forms. With regard to leadership, for example, simply because
the N. T. churches appointed bishops, elders, and deacons does
not mean (as some contend) that churches today must label their
leaders by these terms or expect them to lead in the same (rather
dictatorial) ways that were appropriate for those leaders in
their society. These were simply some of the types of leadership appropriate to the various cultures and sub-cultures of the
areas spoken of in the New Testament.

We see, in fact, not a single, once for all leadership pattern
(of forms) set down for all time in the pages of the New Testament. We see, rather, a series of experiments with cultural
appropriateness ranging from a communal approach (Acts 2:42-47)
to, apparently, a leadership by a council of "apostles and elders"
(Acts 15:4,6,22), to the more highly structured patterns in the
Pastoral Epistles.   But in each case the pattern alluded to was
developed in response to the felt needs conditioned by the
culturally inculcated expectations of the members of the culture
and sub-culture in which the particular local church operated.
Thus we observe certain organizational differences between the
Jewish Jerusalem Church and the Greek Churches with which Timothy
and Titus were concerned. Likewise we observe, in the Acts
account of the appointment of deacons (Acts 6:1-6), the development in a culturally appropriate way of a new form to meet a need
not anticipated at an earlier stage in the life of the Jerusalem
Church.

DYNAMICALLY EQUIVALENT CHURCH LEADERSHIP: A CASE STUDY

There are, then, in the Pastoral Epistles, rather detailed lists[1] of the kinds of attributes felt to be culturally appropriate to church leaders in the Greco-Roman part of the first century church. But, as is the case with the various types of leaders referred to above, the focus is constantly on appropriateness of function rather than on the standardization of form. The lists of characteristics catalogued for the original hearers (and for us) provide illustrations of some of the things implicit in a person's being regarded as well qualified for church leadership in that society at that time. Such a leader should, according to the author of 1 Timothy, be of unimpeachable or irreproachable character. This implied in that culture being "faithful to one wife, sober, temperate, courteous, hospitable," etc. (1 Tim. 3:2 NEB). If he possessed these attributes he would attain and maintain the proper reputation within and outside of the Christian community.

But, as with the specific forms of leadership and organization in the New Testament, so with the specific forms there listed as characteristics of the leaders. It is not the specific forms that provide us with the model to which contemporary churches are to be equivalent, but the *functions* that lie behind these forms. Contemporary churches need leadership that functions in ways that are as appropriate to the cultural context in which these churches operate as the New Testament examples were to the culture in which they operated. And these leaders are to be of just as unimpeachable character, *in terms of their societies' lists of qualifications,* as the leaders of the N. T. churches were in terms of the culturally appropriate lists of 1 Timothy 3 and Titus 1.

But note that, as in the case of the Incarnation and also in the case of dynamic equivalence translation, the forms in terms of which the content is presented are determined by the receptor culture and language. So must a dynamic equivalence church fulfill its functions in and through the forms of its own culture and language. That is, Jesus Christ, in crossing the cultural barrier between the supracultural and the Hebrew cultural realms adopted the forms of the receptor culture, rather than maintaining allegiance to those (if indeed there be any) of the supracultural realm from which he came. And he so "indigenized" himself that at the formal level he was 100% Hebrew. He looked like a normal product of Hebrew parents at the formal level-- not like a foreigner or a formal correspondence translation. At the formal level he looked (as does a good translation) like an original work in the receptor language.

Thus, if the church in the receptor culture is to be dynamically equivalent to the New Testament models, its patterns of
church government, leadership, etc. and even its definitions of
what constitute proper qualifications (especially irreproachability) for its leaders must be those of the receptor culture.
They will not simply correspond to the forms of the New Testament
cultures, or any other outside culture (such as Euro-American).
Not until there is such equivalence can that church be labeled
dynamically equivalent to the New Testament model.

If, for example, the political structure of the receptor culture is one or another form of democracy, a dynamically equivalent church will manifest the appropriate kind of democratic
government. Such a church, further, in imitation of the scriptural model and claiming the leading of the same Holy Spirit who
led Paul, will be able to state its own culturally appropriate
criteria of idealness on the part of its leaders. There will be
criteria that are functionally equivalent to those in 1 Timothy 3
and Titus 1, but that are not necessarily the same forms. For
different cultures, while showing a considerable degree of similarity in such matters, focus in on slightly differing aspects
according to their differing value systems.

In contemporary American culture the criteria would include
such listed items as: serious, self-controlled, courteous, a
good teacher(or preacher), not a drunkard, not quarrelsome, up-
right, doctrinally sound. Such items as hospitable, dignified,
no lover of money might or might not be specified in such a list
but would probably also be expected. We would not, however,
necessarily be so insistent that our leaders will have already
demonstrated their ability to manage a home and family well,
since we tend to choose younger leaders than seem to be in focus
here.   Such a factor would, however, probably be a consideration with an older man. Nor would we say, as it was necessary
to say in Greco-Roman culture, that irreproachability demands
that a person never have more than one marriage,[2] since we allow
and even encourage a man to remarry after the death of his first
wife. Many churches, though, would disallow(that is, not regard
as beyond reproach) a pastor, at least, who had remarried after
a divorce.

Our list, then, would include most of the items on the Greek
list, though some of those specifically mentioned by Paul would
probably be left implicit rather than made explicit by us. We
would probably want to add a few things such as administrative
ability and perhaps even youth. Due to similarities between
Greco-Roman culture and our own the lists will be fairly similar.

If, though, we develop an equivalent list for a radically different culture such as many in Africa (e.g., Higi of northeastern

Nigeria) we will find some additions to and subtractions from
the lists.   And there will be at least one major reinterpretation of a criterion, though the criterion is basically the same.
Greed, being the cardinal sin of Higiland, would be one of the
major proscribed items, and conformance to culturally expected
patterns of politeness one of the more important prescribed
items.   Hospitality and its concomitant, generosity, would be
highlighted to a much greater degree than would be true for
either Greco-Roman or American culture.   Soberness, temperance,
patience and the like would appear on the Higi list, and more
highly valued than on the American list.   Higis would, in addition, focus on age and membership in the royalty social class.
They would, furthermore, strongly emphasize the family management aspect of the matter—certainly much more strongly than
would Americans and probably even more strongly than Greco-
Romans did.

And herein would lie the most significant formal difference
between the Higi ideal and either of the others.   For, in order
for such a leader to effectively function in a way equivalent to
that intended for the first century leaders, he would not only
have to manage his household well but would (as with many Old
Testament leaders) have to have at least two wives in that household!   "How," the Higi person would ask, "can one properly lead
if he has not demonstrated his ability by managing well a household with more than one wife in it?"   The Kru of Liberia with a
similar ideal state, "You cannot trust a man with only one wife."

If, then, we line the lists up side by side and arrange each
in approximate order of priority, we can compare the similarities and differences between the culturally prescribed formal
characteristics deemed requisite for Christian leadership in the
three cultures:

Greco-Roman	American	Higi

1. Irreproachable:
   One wife (forever)
   Serious
   Self-Controlled
   Courteous
   Not quarrelsome
	1. Irreproachable:
	   Faithful to wife
	   Self-Controlled
	   Serious
	   Courteous
		1. Royal Social
		      Class

2. Hospitable	2. Doctrinally sound	2. Hospitable
3. A Good Teacher	3. Vigorous	3. Mature

4. Not a Money Lover	4. A Good Preacher	4. Irreproachable:
		   Generous
		   Patient
		   Self-Controlled
		   Serious
		   Courteous

Greco-Roman	American	Higi
5. Manage Household Well	5. Personable	5. Managing well a Polygamous Household
6. Mature in Faith	6. Mature in Faith	6. A Good Teacher
7. Good Reputation Outside	7. Manage Household Well	

Chart of leadership lists for Greco-Roman,
American and Higi cultures.

If we added columns listing the formal characteristics of
ideal leaders in the various cultural varieties portrayed in the
Old Testament it would become even more clear that God chooses
to work in terms of the forms of each culture in order to attain
his purposes. We would also note fewer differences between the
Higi list and lists generated from the Old Testament. We deduce,
therefore, that the principle of cultural dynamic equivalence is
the ideal toward which church planters should strive.

It must be made clear, however, that *we are here speaking only
of God's starting point*. Once God begins to work within the
people of a culture his interaction with these people inevitably
results in the transformation of at least certain of their customs. To maintain, therefore, as I have above, that a dynamically equivalent Higi church would have polygamous leadership is
not to say either 1) that God's ultimate standard is polygamy or
2) that this particular criterion for dynamically equivalent
leadership will never be changed. It is, in fact, likely that
it will be changed, just as, through God's interaction with the
Hebrews, polygamy died out in Hebrew culture—over the course of
a few thousand years. If, however, the missionary or other
leader steps in and (as has been done) attempts to impose foreign
criteria on the Higi church, what is produced is some kind of
formal correspondence to that foreign model rather than dynamic
equivalence to the New Testament models. In this way the development of the equivalent of the dynamism so apparent in the early
churches is squelched.

And so it is with each of the elements in the life, doctrine
and worship of churches. The New Testament needs to be interpreted in its cultural context with respect to the functions
served by the forms employed (as illustrated above). Then the
various characteristics of the receptor church should be evaluated to ascertain the appropriateness of the forms employed in
the conveying of meanings and the meeting of needs in ways equivalent to the New Testament models. The priority must be for
the conveying in the receptor culture of a content that is equivalent to that conveyed in the original culture. And this may

require that the cultural forms in terms of which that content is
expressed differ widely in the receptor culture from those of
either the New Testament or the source culture. As with translation, so with the transculturating of the church--the extent
of the divergence of forms should depend upon the distance between the cultures in question.

Evaluating the appropriateness of present and future approaches to churchness may be done by following an analytic procedure parallel to that employed by those involved in dynamic
equivalence translation (note the numbering of the steps).

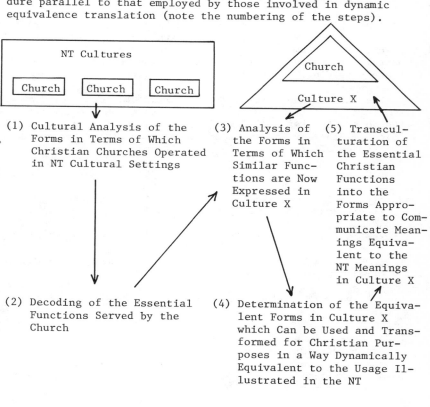

(1) Cultural Analysis of the
    Forms in Terms of Which
    Christian Churches Operated
    in NT Cultural Settings

(2) Decoding of the Essential
    Functions Served by the
    Church

(3) Analysis of
    the Forms in
    Terms of Which
    Similar Func-
    tions are Now
    Expressed in
    Culture X

(4) Determination of the Equiva-
    lent Forms in Culture X
    which Can be Used and Trans-
    formed for Christian Pur-
    poses in a Way Dynamically
    Equivalent to the Usage Il-
    lustrated in the NT

(5) Transcul-
    turation of
    the Essential
    Christian
    Functions
    into the
    Forms Appro-
    priate to Com-
    municate Mean-
    ings Equiva-
    lent to the
    NT Meanings
    in Culture X

Analytic procedure for arriving at the forms
to be employed by a dynamically equivalent church.

CONCLUSION

I have argued that, just as in Bible translation contemporary
theory sees the aim as equivalence of impact on today's hearers
to that experienced by the original hearers, so we should see

the aim of the church in its society. I have contended that the
dynamic equivalence model is more in keeping with the thrust of
Scripture than formal correspondence. Formal correspondence
models of the church result in the same kind of foreign, stilted
product as the Bible translations produced according to that
model. I have illustrated certain facets of the dynamic equivalence church concept, given a case study and suggested an
analytic procedure (patterned after translation analysis) for
arriving at culturally appropriate forms for scripturally im-
pactful churches.

---

1. The making of such "ethical lists" to state the required qualifications of various types of leaders was, apparently, a common
practice in Greek culture. See Easton (1948: 197-202) for a
useful discussion of this custom and examples of lists for such
leaders as King, General, Ruler and Midwife.

2. See such commentaries as *The International Critical Commentary*, *The Moffett Commentary* and others in the interpretation of
the "one wife" verse (1 Tim. 3:2, 12; Titus 1:6) as referring to
"digamy"--the marriage of a man to another wife after the death
or divorce of his first wife.

BIBLIOGRAPHY

Barney, G. Linwood, 1957. "The Meo--an Incipient Church," *Prac-
    tical Anthropology*, 4:31-50.

Easton, B.S., 1948. *The Pastoral Epistles*. London, SCM Press.

Nida, Eugene A., 1960. *Message and Mission*. Pasadena: William
    Carey Library.

_____, 1964. *Toward a Science of Translating*. Leiden: E.J.
    Brill.

Nida, Eugene A. and Taber, C.R., 1969. *The Theory and Practice
    of Translation*. Leiden: E.J. Brill.

Samarin, William, 1954. "Theology and/or Anthropology," *Prac-
    tical Anthropology*, 1:120-21.

Smalley, William A., 1958. "Cultural Implications of an Indige-
    nous Church," *Practical Anthropology*, 5:51-65.

Stock, Eugene, 1899. *History of the Church Missionary Society*.
    London: Church Missionary Society.

Tippett, Alan E., 1973. *Verdict Theology in Missionary Theory*
    (2nd Edition), Pasadena, California: William Carey Library.
    (1969 edition, Lincoln, Illinois: Lincoln Christian College.)

14

Mission
as Inter-cultural Encounter:
A Sociological Perspective
Alfred C. Krass

The present paper will be seen, by those who know my book, *Go...
and Make Disciples* (London, S.P.C.K., 1974), to represent some
movement in my own thinking over the past four years.

As one who entered the field of missionary social science
largely under the tutelage of the Church Growth school of missi-
ology--to the leaders of which I continue to feel grateful--I
recognize that I am offering here a paper which departs significantly from their methodology and approach. This is as a result of a growing perception, during my years as Consultant on
Evangelism for the United Church Board for World Ministries,
that, though church growth theory, and the functionalist anthropology which is its basis, had a direct relevance to the situation I was involved in in mission to the Chokosi people of
Northern Ghana, it had less applicability to the kind of
missionary situation which I was asked to analyze as Consultant
on Evangelism on a worldwide basis.

Functionalism developed largely in small, esoteric, bounded
societies. Though we now know that such societies were not
"stationary"--to use Sir Henry Maine's term--it is nevertheless
true that change such as took place in them was exponentially
smaller than change in societies which were in regular inter-

course with other peoples, other civilizations.   Functionalism
has a bias toward seeing change as endogenous.   Much of the
change that has occurred in societies in inter-civilizational
encounter has been exogenous, being a direct result of forces
not inherent in those social bodies themselves but in the outside world which they encounter, and which most often subjugate
them.

While studying anthropology in prepration for writing *Go...
and Make Disciples*, I became aware that anthropologists had been
having second thoughts about the adequacy of functionalist
models and that, in their study of complex societies, ethnic
groups and boundaries, the cultures of less than total societies,
and the study of different levels of "integration," they had
been constructing different models.   They had, secondly, become
more interested in history.   As a former president of the
American Anthropological Association had declared, "Anthropology
will either become history, or it will become nothing."   History
is, however, the study of change, and for anthropology to become
more historically oriented would mean that it would become a
very different kind of anthropology.

In my own pilgrimage I found a growing partnership with a
kind of social science which had its primary basis in the
discipline of sociology (although anthropologists like Clifford
Geertz were also into it).   Its leading exponent, Benjamin
Nelson--who died as this paper was being written, and to whom I
am heavily indebted for this analysis--called it a comparative,
differential sociology of socio-cultural process.   It is a
sociology which takes its fundamental stand in the fact of encounter, encounter between civilizations, encounter between
peoples, peoples having different "structures of consciousness,"
different mind-sets by which they understand the history in which
they are involved.   In the process of their encounter with
people from different civilizations, changes take place in their
understanding of the world and in the people themselves.

It is not a one-way process, with the exponents of "modern-
ization" being the "change-agents" and the people amongst whom
they work being the "changed."   Both parties are changed, first,
by their encounter with one another, and, secondly, by that fact
that, as a result of their encounter, they are often knit into
a new, larger social body.

The complications of this for missionary social science seem
to me immense.   It will mean that we will need to focus not only
on the "receptor culture," but on the culture of the missionaries
as well.   We will need to analyze who the missionaries are, what
are the mind-sets of the civilizations they represent, and what
kind of encounter was taking place between their civilization

and that of the people to whom they were going in mission, as well as attempting to understand what took place at the micro-level, in the missionary work itself.

The best extant monograph which might be said to represent something of this type of approach is Sidney Williamson's *Akan Religion and the Christian Faith* (Accra, 1965). Williamson had a rare ability, as a historian of the missionary encounter, to see the larger questions and to be critical of the civilization from which he, as a missionary, came. Yet he did not operate out of a sociological basis.

In my attempt to show what the sociology of inter-civilizational process might look like as applied to missionary social science, I have chosen to look at an encounter similar to the one Williamson studies. Mine will be a study of the encounter of missionaries of the American Board of Commissioners for Foreign Missions with the people of Central Angola in the 19th Century. I think this study will point to some of the difficulties of the proposed attempt to establish "dynamic equivalence churches." It will not do this directly. Rather it will do it by demonstrating the extreme complexity of any missionary encounter--even one which takes place in the kind of esoteric, bounded society Church Growth missiology specializes in. It will force us to raise questions about the extent to which it is possible for missionaries to achieve the objectivity which dynamic equivalence principles presuppose. And it will argue--perhaps paradoxically--that missionaries need to operate on a much larger scale than the planting of churches if they are to be faithful to the God of the Bible.

Enough of an introduction. On with the analysis!

THE CASE STUDY

In 1880 four missionaries were sent to "West Central Africa" (present-day Angola) by the American Board of Commissioners for Foreign Missions. The party was charged with the following task:

> The purpose of your mission in general is to make known the gospel and plant Christian institutions in that part of Western Central Africa which lies inland from the Portuguese colony of Angola.[1]

The missionaries, and those who commissioned them, considered themselves to be a part of a history which must be traced back as far as the command of Jesus, to "go to all peoples everywhere and make them my disciples: baptize them in the name of the Father, the Son, and the Holy Spirit, and teach them to obey everything I have commanded you."[2] In many ways they considered

themselves to be quite immediately related to Christ's original
commission to the disciples, to be directly responsive to the
Lord who, in giving his commission to the first disciples,
promised that "I will be with you always, to the end of the age."
And yet they were part of a more specific history as well, part
of a long tradition with many sub-histories and alternative
paths and by-ways.

This can be seen even in the single bare sentence quoted
above. At no point in his original commission did Christ assign
to his disciples the task of "planting Christian institutions,"
and yet, in 1880, it could be assumed *ab initio* that the task of
Christian missionaries was not simply to make disciples but also
to plant institutions. That the making known of the Gospel had
not only logical but also chronological preeminence was not to
be denied, but that the Gospel could truly be made known, that
disciples could in the fullest sense be made, without planting
institutions, was by this time questionable. Still one had to
remember the proper order:

> Do not be in a hurry to teach the natives many things
> until the one thing needful has been learned and re-
> ceived into the heart. Make it your endeavor that
> the civilization you hope to introduce may not be as
> varnish laid on the heathen character, rendering it
> in all likelihood less amenable to the gospel than
> before, but the growth and outcome of regenerated
> hearts. Act upon the principle that Christianity
> must precede civilization if the latter is to be
> of any real value.[3]

It could be assumed that the missionaries would "hope to introduce civilization"; it could be assumed that they were missionaries not just of Christ but of "civilization"; it was accepted
that the people to whom they were sent could fit under the
rubric "heathen"; it was assumed that the process in which they
were to be involved was "the regeneration of hearts"; yet for
us who survey their work from a comparative, differential
sociological, historical point of view, almost a century later,
all of these assumptions must be questioned. How did it come
about that, in the year 1880, four men were commissioned by this
particular mission board with these particular words with the
expectation that they would carry out the task in this specific
way? Why this way and not some other? Why these men and not
some others?

The board was the first North American Protestant mission
board, founded in 1810. By 1880 it was in effect the Congregational churches' mission board, the mission board through
which the biological and spiritual descendants of the Puritans

exercised their missionary vocation. Its headquarters were in Boston. But once it had been in more than just name *the* American Protestant board, dispatching missionaries of other denominations as well. It was not an official agency of the Congregational churches, but operated under an independent charter granted by the Commonwealth of Massachusetts, an expression of the principle De Tocqueville and others found pervasive in American life: "voluntaryism." Its welfare was entirely dependent upon the good offices of its supporters, upon the fervor which it could stir up through local, regional, and national meetings, and through its publications. Its missionaries were not ministers assigned to foreign service but laymen and clergy "called to missionary service" and specially "commissioned."

What happened in 1810 when the Board was founded--and what happened in 1806 when the "Haystack meeting" took place in Williamstown, Mass., when four young college students felt themselves "impressed with the duty and importance of personally attempting a mission to the heathen" and were moved to direct an "inquiry" to their fathers in the faith[4]--had not happened in 1640 or in 1710 or even in 1795. Although some of the early colonists had directed themselves to the conversion of the American Indian, and although Indian missions had continued, with varying degrees of fervor, right up to the time of the Haystack Meeting, there had been no American foreign missions until this time. Why, then, did foreign missions begin at this time, and why not earlier?

A full comparative differential historical sociology of missions would have to seek answers to these questions, and compare them with what it found in 1830 and 1850 and 1880, and with what it found in the Episcopal community and among the Quakers and Roman Catholics, and with what it found in England and France and Germany. Our focus, however, is on a later period, starting with the year 1876, when the Board first seriously proposed a mission to Central Africa, and continuing through the early 1890s, affording us a view of how the task was actually carried out and how it was interpreted. We fish in the same stream, but downstream, past a few bends. Some of the currents are the same--continuing Puritan heritage, American voluntaryism, revivalist theology, an expanding continental nation, the ethos of constitutionalism and democracy, a growing commercial and industrial economy, a largely middle- to upper-middle-class denomination, with a largely (but declining) New England base. But for the differences--and the differences even in what seems the same--we shall have to wait till other chapters are written.

We shall look at the party which went out in 1880 and at those who joined them in the remainder of that decade, at what they

did and what they felt, at what they reported and how they
interpreted it, and--perhaps most important--at the questions
they did *not* ask.

As a history, what follows will be sketchy, for this is not a
history, but an attempt at socio-cultural understanding. What
we are constructing is what Weber called an ideal type. Its
function is heuristic. Its usefulness--or lack thereof--will
lie in what comparative observations it will enable us to make.

The missionaries immediately set out to learn the Umbundu
language, and, with equal dispatch, once they had learned it, to
start to translate the Bible into it (as well as Buynan's
Pilgrim's Progress).

The missionaries were very solicitous from the start to
establish good relations not only with the Portuguese (who were
then in the process of extending their sway inland from the
Angola colony to the Bailundu-Bihé area, where the missionaries
settled) but also with the Ovimbundu kings and chiefs, and yet
to remain somewhat distant from both.

At a very early stage--in most cases after only a few visits
--the missionaries sought to obtain, from the kings, land on
which to build a house, and then proceeded to build what were
intended to be comfortable and permanent dwellings.

In each place they occupied, the missionaries took African
lads into their homes as paid employees and immediately began to
train them. It was from these lads that the first congregations
usually started.

It is impossible to date with any high degree of accuracy the
beginning of a school in each location--there seems to have been
no conscious preparatory period or time of "settling in" before
a school would be started.

The first congregations consisted exclusively of young men
and of boys and girls. No attempt seems to have been made to
make disciples of mature men and women, or of the chiefs.
Preaching services were held for whole villages, or for the
kings' or chiefs' households, but there never seems to have been
any expectation that such preaching would lead more than a
responsive few to baptism and church membership.

The missionaries were in no hurry to baptize anyone--indeed,
the contrary may be affirmed: only those who proved themselves
over a long period of catechesis to be "of serious endeavor"
and ready to "forsake all manner of heathen observance" and
polygamy and alcohol, etc., and who had mastered the requisite

Christian knowledge, were considered fit for baptism. The first congregations were very small, 14 or 9 or 12 "regenerate souls," no more, baptized on individual confession of faith.

The missionaries never became the pastors of the new congregations, but insisted that only natives could be pastors: they chose the one they deemed most fit, gave him special training, and expected the new congregation to support him without any outside subvention.

It was expected that, wherever a congregation was formed, a church building would be erected, but the missionaries expected the members themselves to erect it and offered their good services only as consultants on architecture and engineering, and perhaps to solicit a bell from America.

Only financial difficulties kept the missionaries from establishing boarding schools and institutes in the early years. It was their firm conviction that the work would progress best if the pupils could be kept more completely separate "from the corrupting influences of their heathen homes."[5]

It was assumed that the proper hymns for the new churches would be American or European hymns, that the proper catechism would be a translated American catechism (or preferably two or three, one of which would be "an historical catechism of Biblical history"[6]), that those joining the church would recite a "covenant," and that this could be a covenant from a church in Ohio.[7]

The missionaries were from the start active in introducing, either in their homes or in communal projects, physical amenities like bridges, better roads, superior methods of construction, new crops, new tools.

The missionaries were very solicitous of their health (several died and several had to return to America because of ill health) and of their physical safety. On the latter score they were somewhat welcoming of the extension of Portuguese authority to the interior, and availed themselves of official protection. On the former score, they were also solicitous of the Africans' health and very early on began regular medical treatment, and constantly petitioned the Board for missionary doctors to be sent, until medical work became a regular part of the mission at every station.

The missionaries were ethnocentric in many of their perceptions and value-judgments, though with a difference--the Portuguese, being Catholic, and not being noted for their piety ("they seem wholly given up to business and sin"[8]), were not

quite welcomed as fellow Europeans, and the people of Bailundu
and Bihé, though "heathen Africans," were "vigorous, sturdy, and
even noble."[9]

Two final observations:

--There is no record that any of the early missionaries ever
questioned his mission, or questioned that it was God's will
that the mission should be carried out.

--Although the missionaries anticipated that great effort
would be needed to assure the permanence of the work, in their
writings none betrayed the slightest doubt but that West Central
Africa would be "won for Christ." All that was needed was time
and persistence.

                    *   *   *   *

The ideal type we have constructed raises questions--merely
by isolating certain common features of the missionary work in
West Central Africa in the 1880s, we have seen that things
might have been otherwise. For example:--

--the missionaries might have decided to function not in Umbundu
  but in Portuguese, or perhaps even in English

--they might have cast their lot wholly with either the
  Portuguese or the Ovimbundu, forsaken their neutrality, and
  become partisan

--they might never have obtained land or built any dwellings,
  but merely accepted the hospitality offered them, or perhaps
  they might have led an ambulatory existence

--they might have chosen, instead of working with young men and
  boys and girls, to work with adults of the villages, or to
  concentrate on the royal families

--they might have decided not to accept individuals on confession
  of faith, but to look for the baptism of whole social units

--there was nothing that forced them to start schools: they
  might have restricted their educational endeavors to the
  training of the pastor-elect, or, going beyond that, not even
  anticipated having any trained native leadership, but
  maintained all leadership themselves

--they might have built huge churches, in American style, for
  the converts with funds from America

--they might not have translated the Bible, or at least not
   until a felt need for it arose on the part of the converts

--they might have translated Dante's *Divine Comedy* instead of
   Bunyan

--they might have encouraged the people to make their own church
   music and listened to the questions people were asking them
   about the faith in order to make a catechism, rather than
   importing hymns and catechisms from abroad

--they might either have introduced no physical improvements and
   no medical work or majored in industrial and medical arts

--they might have regarded the Ovimbundu as "noble savages" and
   their own Euro-American cultures as "degenerate"; or, on the
   other hand, they might have regarded the Ovimbundu as of
   racially inferior stock and incapable of civilization

--they might have gone out to find out what the religion of the
   Ovimbundu was, and to consider whether they needed to hear the
   Gospel, without prejudging that, or at least they might have
   waited to learn about the people's religion, before deciding
   what would be an appropriate sharing of the faith with them

and, finally,

--they might have been very pessimistic about the chances of
   success for their work.

   All of these alternative possibilities (with the exception of
the suggestion that they might have translated Dante instead of
Bunyan) *can be documented*--not once, but many times--*from the
history of Christian missions*. They are not posed fancifully,
but seriously. Other missionaries at other times have insisted
on working only in their own language, baptized only whole
villages, built huge churches for the people, etc. But the
American Board missionaries in the 1880s did not, and our
purpose is to ask why.

   The first thing to be remembered is that these missionaries
were not free agents--they were commissioned, given special
orders, and were maintained by the Board on condition that they
carried out their orders. They were individuals--this definitely
comes out in the reports--but they were individuals under
assignment, and just as those who applied for missionary service
had to pass through recruitment procedures which weeded out many,
so missionaries who did not while in service exemplify what the
Board desired could be released, recalled from overseas, or not
be sent back from furlough.

So, if we want to know why the missionaries did what they did
in Africa--and did not do what they did not--we have to turn
first to America, to Boston, to the *Missionary Herald* magazine,
to the Annual Reports of the ABCFM, and try to understand how
the Board secretaries and the Prudential Committee and the
Corporation of the ABCFM understood the world and the missionary
task. We shall do this under three heads: (1) how the Board
understood the missionary task, (2) how the Board understood
Africa and non-Christian and non-"Evangelical" religions, as
well as how it understood the conditions it described as
"savagery," "barbarism," and "heathenism" and, finally, (3) how
the Board understood America and "Evangelical (Protestant)
Christianity" and what relation it saw between them.

(1) The missionary task

In the Annual Report of 1883,[10] we find the work of mission
described succinctly:

> Missionary work involves (1) conversion of lost men,
> (2) organizing them into churches, (3) giving them a
> competent native ministry, and (4) leading them up to
> independence and in most cases self-propagation.

A close examination of the Board's "Outline of Missionary Policy"
in 1856[11] reveals that the 1883 formulation is a faithful
replication of the policies of the Board, framed by the
Prudential Committee under the pioneering leadership of Rufus
Anderson, who dominated the Board--and indeed much of American
and even European Protestant mission work during the middle
decades of the century. Anderson, in America, and Henry Venn,
of the Anglican Church Missionary Society, in England, pioneered
what later became well known as the "three-self" understanding
of Christian missions--missions should lead to self-supporting,
self-governing, and self-propagating churches; the work of
missions was temporary--it continued only until churches were
planted in a given location--and then the task of the missionary
was to move on to areas where the Gospel had never been heard.
(Venn spoke of "the euthanasia of missions.")

Yet the 1883 statement, for all its theoretical orthodoxy, is
found in the midst of a different ethos. The differences were,
to some extent, subtle, and yet, upon a close reading of the
documents from the '80s, we might conclude that, the more things
remained the same, the more they had changed.

Certain things had remained the same. The basic distinction
between people was between the "lost" and the "saved." This was
a distinction fundamental to revivalistic theology. Though the
words were in the biblical canon, they did not have uniform

emphasis, but were found in certain strata and not in others, and with various possible interpretations. They became key concepts during the 18th Century revivalistic movement known as The Great Awakening. During Puritan times theologians looked at societies more holistically: the talk was more of a "holy commonwealth," or a "righteous empire." The Great Awakening was the first movement within New England religious history in which distinctions were drawn primarily between individuals, members of the same society, rather than between societies. The holy commonwealth, the great theologian Jonathan Edwards was the first to admit, no longer existed: its charisma had been routinized and had become less than charisma; not all members of the commonwealth were in fact saved; unless men had an "awakening," a decisive religious experience, their faith and salvation could not be unquestioned. They might in fact be "lost."

And so, in the Second Great Awakening, which began under Timothy Dwight, President of Yale College and member of the Board's first Prudential Committee, in 1810, the attempt to "revive" men continued. The "New Divinity" of Samuel Hopkins (whose grand-nephew, Mark Hopkins, was the President of the Board during our period) and Nathaniel Taylor did for the 19th Century revival what Edwards had done for the 18th: provided a theological basis for the work of home missions. Distancing themselves from the old-line Calvinists, the New Divinity men at Yale added to the old, once supreme theologoumenon of the sovereignty of God a qualified respect for what man, responding to God, could do (this came to be called "Arminianism," after a supposed connection with the Dutch theologian Arminius), and offered a theological justification for the "enthusiasm" of the revival spirit, its tears and outpourings, its uncalvinistic emotion--the "outward signs," the New Divinity men said, of the process of "regeneration"--lost men becoming saved.

What had remained the same was the interpretation of the mission task--home and foreign--as leading the unconverted to a dramatic conversion experience. "Except ye be born again," the revivalists echoed the Jesus they heard in John's Gospel, "ye cannot be saved." Mission aimed at the regeneration of the "unregenerate"--those who had not had a conversion experience. The universality here was remarkable--the unregenerate were to be found both in "Christendom" and in "heathendom." Preacher after preacher in the Board's annual meetings in the '80s repeated the proposition that foreign missions were just the extension abroad of home missions.

Similarly the assumption that the outgrowth of conversions should be the gathering of the new-born into churches remained unchanged. Missions meant church-planting. Churches once

planted, if they were to be permanent and grow, needed to have a
competent, educated ministry as well: the minister was not just
an administrator of sacraments but a preacher and teacher. His
primary ministry indeed was the ministry of the word. This also
remained unchanged.

But in the addition of the words "in most cases" to the fourth
point, "leading the churches up to independence and self-
propagation," a change was beginning to be felt. The Andersonian
principle was experiencing some difficulty. The "euthanasia" of
missions might, it seemed, need to be put off:

> In the early days of mission, it was enough to bring
> men to the acceptance of the great facts of the
> gospel, who should make it known to others, and so
> the divine leaven spread from one to another. Life
> was simpler in its elements....But in the orderly
> growth of the work a change comes. Other wants are
> to be met. A Christian civilization as a proper
> expression of the new life makes it demands....New
> institutions [literature, schools and colleges are
> mentioned] are to be established....In the foreign
> field, to the missionary is given the creation of
> this social order, and the shaping of institutions
> to be for the welfare of the millions of his
> fellow-men.[12]

The mandate is coming to be understood more broadly--not without
difficulty, for the Scriptures do not seem, at first sight, to
warrant a "civilizing mission":

> Our aim is to Christianize and not to civilize.
> Deliberately we choose to render the supreme service,
> and leave others to follow in its train. We do not
> go to the heathen nations with steam-reapers and
> railroads and telegraphs and universities and art-
> collections, to initiate them at once into our better
> forms of life. We undertake a greater and more help-
> ful service; instead of new conditions and surroundings,
> we strive to develop a *new manhood* and thus to provide
> the soil in which all those other things at length will
> take root and flourish and yield their noblest fruits.[13]

The problem is recognized--that which the missionaries find themselves yearning to do, to "elevate" as well as to convert, that
which the world around the mission board encourages the mission
to undertake, seems to have no biblical warrant. A casuistry
is necessary, the *novum* will have to be insinuated into the conception of what is legitimate. Watch it happen, as the speaker
goes on:

... all such results, invaluable as they are, do not
constitute the principal end to which this movement
is directed; they are, at the most, but secondary
and incidental. The inspiring of human hearts with
the thought of the living God, the renovation of
personal character in the image and spirit of Jesus
Christ, the regeneration of the family *and society*
(my italics) according to the power of the Christian
faith: this is our great aim, to this end all
missionary labor is primarily directed.

What has happened? The converts are no longer seen as so
many discrete individuals. Human life, it is recognized, goes
on in society. A Gospel just for the individual is not--to use
a favorite term--a "Gospel for the whole man." A Gospel for the
whole man is a Gospel for society as well as for the individual.
Missions are directed not just to the regeneration of individuals,
but to the rebirth of societies as well. There is a synonym
we can use. It is the word which troubled the speaker above,
but which is found throughout the annual reports. It is the
word *civilization*. To heathen societies is to be imparted the
blessings of civilization. The mission is not just to convert
the individual soul, but to *civilize*. In the slip of a tongue,
one speaker lets the secret out:

The gospel of Jesus Christ, let us remember, is the
power of God. It is the power of God unto civilization
[he was quoting St. Paul, but he has gotten his
quotation wrong; Paul wrote that the gospel is the
power of God unto *salvation*; he explains that it is
not really an error:], for civilization is included
under salvation. This gospel has proved itself mighty
enough to lift the most degraded. It can and will lift
Africa, only let its forces be applied. Instead of
the hopeful indications in the land and in the people,
let it be that there is all the inferiority and help-
lessness which the most perverse pessimist asserts: the
gospel of the Son of God can make a new world out of it.

We ourselves have come out of as savage barbarism as
now exists in Bihé and Bailunda. The roll of the
centuries has seen barbarous Britain and Scandinavia
transformed into England and America. The power which
has wrought the transformation has been Christian
civilization....If it were not so, if no reasonable
hope could be cherished of bringing Africa into the
number of civilized continents, something can be done
to better her condition. The more hopeless, the more
to be pitied she is, and the louder is the call upon
Christian compassion to mitigate her wretchedness.

> In our days philanthropy is heroic, and draws
> back from no magnitude of degradation.[14]

The task is "heroic," but at the same time it has become more
complicated. The same words can be used to describe it, through
various casuistries--"salvation," "regneration," and--above all,
"the kingdom of God" can be redefined to give warrant to the
task more broadly conceived. See how Secretary Clark defines
"Thy kingdom come, thy will be done":

> When art and science, literature and philosophy,
> shall lay their tribute at the feet of our risen
> Lord, and when the social and political, as well
> as the religious, life of manhood shall bear witness
> to the transforming power of the gospel of Christ,
> and the Kingdom of God be set up on the earth.[15]

Thereon hangs a tale. The concept of the Kingdom of God,
Richard Niebuhr has demonstrated,[16] has been a powerful
leitmotif of American church history, but it has meant, at
different stages, at least three different things. By it the
Puritans meant the sovereignty of God, as opposed to the
sovereignty of human initiative--a continuation of the Reformation emphasis on *sola gratia*, in contrast to the Roman Catholic
emphasis on grace plus works.

> These early American Protestants believed in the
> kingdom of God, but it was not a society of peace
> and concord to be established by men of good will;
> it was rather the living reality of God's present
> rule...(which was) not an ideal dependent for its
> realization on human effort; men and their efforts
> were dependent upon it; loyalty to it and obedience
> to its laws were the conditions of their temporal
> and eternal welfare.[17]

By the kingdom of God the Puritans thought of "the cleansing of
the inward parts, the restoration to man of inner harmony, and
the elimination of the war in the members, whence all other wars
and fightings come."[18]

In the Great Awakening the same term was defined in a second
way. The idea of the kingdom of Christ became dominant--it had
been at most secondary before. God was now seen to be acting in
history: "In Jesus Christ he has brought in the great change
which has opened to men the kingdom of liberty and love....The
kingdom of Christ as the liberty of those who had received some
knowledge of the goodness of God and who reflected in their lives
the measure of their knowledge and devotion....The reign of
Christ was above all a rule of knowledge in the minds of men."[19]

It was the concept of the kingdom of Christ which was integrally related to the founding of the missionary movement: people everywhere had to *know* the truth of the Gospel. Under this impetus the ABCFM was founded.

But the idea of *the kingdom on earth* was the new idea which developed in our period, the idea Secretary Clark had been dealing with in the passage quoted above. This belonged neither to the Puritan conception of the kingdom nor to that of the Great Awakening. When we deal with the concept of the kingdom on earth, we are in the realm of millenarianism. Edwards allowed himself to suspect that it might be coming--"The New Jerusalem... has begun to come down from heaven, and perhaps never were more of the prelibations of heaven's glory given upon earth"[20]--but it surprised him. It was "a great and wonderful event," "a strange revolution, an unexpected surprising overturning of things, suddenly brought to pass," the concept that God's great millennial work might be beginning in America.[21] He was unprepared for it and he never fully developed the idea. The specific events which made him expect that it was in fact happening were the unexpected evidences of spiritual revival which appeared in connection with his preaching, preaching which was aimed at the mind and not the heart, but which had strange effects on the hearts of his hearers.

Hopkins developed the idea further--he foresaw a time of universal peace, love, and general and cordial friendship, a time of religious unity and political peace, a time of universal joy, not only for spiritual but also for material reasons:

> the art of husbandry will be greatly advanced, and
> men will have skills to cultivate and mature the
> earth in a much better and easier way than ever
> before...[a time of] great improvement in the
> mechanic arts by which the earth will be subdued and
> cultivated, and all the necessary and convenient
> articles of life, such as utensils, clothing, build-
> ing, etc. will be formed and made in a better manner,
> and with much less labor than they now are....There
> will then be such benevolence and fervent charity...
> that all worldly things will be in a great degree and
> in the best manner common, so as not to be withheld
> from any who may want them.[22]

But it was not until after the Civil War that the idea came to full fruition. Edwards and Hopkins were going somewhat against the grain to affirm what they did--they scarcely believed what they found themselves predicting--this was not part of the "bag" of mainline revival preaching. Millennialism and Calvinism were not wont to consort with one another.

This is not to say that millennialism was a new thing in
Christian history--far from it. It was, however, a product of
the kind of chiliastic "enthusiasm" from which orthodox Roman
Catholics and Calvinists, Lutherans, and Episcopalians distanced
themselves. The medieval Catholic sects might indulge mille-
narian enthusiasm. Millenarianism might be appropriate for
Anabaptists or Quakers or Methodists, but more orthodox
Protestant types stayed far from it.

What took place in the nineteenth century in America was that
those Protestants who had throughout history eschewed mille-
narian expectations were converted to them. "Respectable folk"
at long last fell prey to what had been the indulgence of
Christian outsiders.

The theologian who is credited with having finally stated,
and justified, what the others suspected yet feared was Samuel
Harris of Yale who, in 1870, delivered a course of lectures at
Andover Seminary, the bulwark of the New Divinity, from which
many of the main elements of the Congregational ministry in New
England were drawn. The lectures were entitled *The Kingdom of
Christ on Earth*. Most of them were published in *Bibliotheca
Sacra*, a widely circulated theological journal of impeccable
credentials,[23] before being published in a separate volume.[24]

Harris pulled out all the stops. Taking his stand firmly on
solid, mainline Protestant doctrine, he proceeded from the known
and accepted to the suspected yet suspect. "Christianity," he
said,

> is not only a power of spiritual regeneration to
> the individual, but, because it is so, is also
> the power which restores human nature to its com-
> pleteness and society to its best condition. *The
> transformation of human society into the kingdom
> of God* [my italics] creates the highest and best
> civilization.[25]

The process was not apocalyptic but cumulative:

> By this cumulative progress Christianity is working
> out in human history a demonstration of its divine
> origin and power. And when it shall have prevailed
> through the world, the demonstration will be complete.
> Humanity itself will have become a living epistle,
> known and read of all men--a word of God, declaring
> Christ the living Word--a second incarnation of the
> divine in humanity....[26]

He outlined how, by the preaching of the word, men become converted and work for the world's conversion, each working for the
triumph of good and the defeat of evil and bringing others to
Christ, and the ideas which they espouse becoming incorporated
into society, so that they "form public sentiment, determine
customs, laws, and institutions, and thus create for themselves
an organic force." Then the customs of civilization in turn
help the progress of Christ's kingdom.[27]

Wherever Harris looked around him, he saw the kingdom growing
like a mustard seed, until all the birds of the air would find
their nests in its branches. The vehicle for the growth of the
kingdom was the profound activity of "the Christian nations,"
which he saw as being "characterized by energy, progressiveness,
and expansiveness." In their face, idolatry was doomed.
"Idolatry," he confidently predicted, "cannot live by the side
of steam-engines and telegraphs."[28]

It was because they were Christian--and Protestant Christian--
that the nations of Northwest Europe and America had achieved
the heights that they had. They were obviously God's chosen
peoples:

> God has always acted by chosen people. To the
> English-speaking people more than to any other the
> world is now indebted for the propagation of
> Christian ideas and Christian civilization. It is
> a remarkable fact in this day that the thinking of
> the world is done by the Christian nations; that the
> enterprise and energy of the world are mainly theirs.
> They alone are colonizing, and by their commerce and
> enterprise pushing their influence throughout the
> world. So also the political condition of the
> Protestant nations is that of constitutional govern-
> ment, popular education, and a growing regard for the
> rights and welfare of the people.

And he concluded:

> These are conditions more favorable to the advancement
> of Christ's kingdom than have ever before existed.
> And in view of both the thinking and the practical life
> and character of the age, I believe that no preceding
> age has presented conditions so favorable to the
> advancement of Christ's kingdom and so encouraging
> to faithful Christian effort.[29]

Richard Niebuhr goes on to document how the idea of the
kingdom on earth was secularized, nationalized, and **confused**:

Christianity, democracy, Americanism, the English
language and culture, the growth of industry and
science, American institutions--these are all con-
founded and confused. The contemplation of their
own righteousness filled Americans with such lofty
and enthusiastic sentiments that they readily
identified it with the righteousness of God....Hence-
forth the kingdom of the Lord was a human possession,
not a permanent revolution. It is in particular the
destiny of the Anglo-Saxon race, which is destined
to bring light to the gentiles by means of lamps
manufactured in America. Thus institutionalism and
imperialism, ecclesiastical and political, go hand
in hand.[30]

But that carries us farther than we need to go. Our goal--to
understand the ethos under which the missionary task in Angola
was understood in the 1880s--has been achieved. We have gained
a vision of why the casuistries in which the mission leaders
engaged were necessary: they had a larger vision of what was
possible, and therefore of what must be attempted, than the
scriptures, understood in their proper context, could account
for. They had to bend the scriptures to the cultural mandate
which they so strongly felt. Agents of the millennium, they
could not limit themselves to the planting of churches. That
they did more, that they did not readily accede to the
euthanasia of missions, is easily understood. That they did not
go even farther than they did and espouse the nationalism, the
colonial fervor, the extreme ethnocentrism and even racism of
many of their compatriots is perhaps more to be wondered at.
With all their millennial enthusiasm they still maintained a
certain sense of perspective on their task, a certain openness
to worlds different from their own, a certain sense of judgment
on the civilization of which they were a part.

(2) How the Board and its missionaries understood the world in
which they worked.

We are likely to be rather hard on the late 19th Century
missionaries when we are asked how they saw the world. Their
categories--"savagery," "barbarism," and "civilization";
"Christendom" and "heathendom"--are not ones modern Americans
or modern missionaries are likely to use. Whether, in rejecting
such terms, modern missionaries have followed the fashion of the
times or whether they have in fact helped to bring about the
change is a question beyond our present scope. What we should
now note is that missionaries, both then and now, tend to use
the same terms their contemporaries do.

The triad "savagery, barbarism, and civilization" was not coined by the missionaries. It was part of the general currency of the times. What is typical of the missionary usage is its unsystematic character. The contemporary 19th Century American anthropologist Lewis Henry Morgan used the terms in a systematic way: savagery was the lowest rung of the ladder of civilization, barbarism a step higher, and civilization the highest rung. In missionary usage, however, savagery and barbarism are used interchangeably, and civilization is thought of as higher than the other two but not *ipso facto* as implying in the fullest sense the highest stage of human development. I shall explain this in the next section.

The fact that the missionary statesmen used the terms in an unsystematic way is an indication that they had not yet "progressed" from the rather rough, polycentric world of the 18th Century anthropologists to the brave new world of Tylor in England and Morgan in America, who first systematized anthropological classification on a single, unilinear ladder of the development of "culture." As George Stocking points out,[31] it was only when anthropology began to see "culture" as one "thing"--different societies have more or less of "it"--that the inference became common that those who had more (i.e., of European culture) were more highly developed and those who had less were "still" undeveloped. This begged the question: why should some peoples of the world have more and others less?-- and the answer was commonly given, with less and less trepidation (until Boas shattered the myths in the 1920s), "because they have less innate abilities," "their brains are smaller," "they are of inferior racial stock," etc.

The missionaries, on the other hand, were less scientific for one thing and forced to be more charitable by their doctrine for another. No text seems quoted more often in the meetings of the '80s than "He hath made of one every nation of men to live on all the face of the earth,"[32] and the inference was drawn from this that "human nature is one":

> It may be dwarfed, perverted, corrupted, lost sight
> of in its moral debasement and bondage to evil, but
> its existence under all its coverings and wrappings
> is the sole possibility of an awakening from death
> until life.[33]

Not altogether different from Edwards' and Hopkins' understanding of the effect of the Fall on human nature in New England! Race and physical surroundings could be described as "accidents," not belonging to human nature. Human nature was one the world over, well suited to the Gospel the missionaries proclaimed:

> The gospel is cosmopolitan and universal. It knows
> nothing of a favored land, a peculiar people, or
> limits to Christian love and service and duty. An
> American is just as dear to Christ as an African, and
> no more. Christ seeks the salvation of the German,
> but that of the Chinaman as truly, and with as strong
> an impulse of love. In the kingdom of our Lord there
> is neither Greek nor Jew.[34]

As far as their *mission* was concerned, there was no problem:
the theology on which the mission was based was clear--there was
no place for the compartmentalization of peoples into classes or
higher and lower races. Moral judgments there could be ("the
cruelties and debasing, bloody superstitions which everywhere
prevail among them"[35]; the "Dark Continent--dark in our
knowledge of it and in its moral coloring"[36]; and many other
examples), but the categories were in general those applied to
moral reprobates at home as well. But where the difference
came in was when the missionaries started making judgments about
the development or non-development of civilization.

In 1880 *The Missionary Herald* reported, in its youth section,
the visit of three young men from King Mtesa of Buganda to the
Queen of England. The author was ecstatic about what might
happen as a result. "They will go back with a story that will
convince the Emperor and people of Uganda that the missionaries
who are laboring among them came from a wonderful land, and on
an errand of love," he hoped. For how could he hope otherwise?

> What a contrast there is between Africa and a
> Christian country like England or the United States!
> ....If these envoys from Uganda should go back and
> tell of what they had seen in the Christian homes
> of England, of gentle fathers and mothers and happy
> children, it would seem as if the men and women of
> the "Dark Continent" would listen to the gospel....
> The African savages who have seen the wonders of a
> civilized land cannot say or do anything to help
> those to whom they return to be better than they
> now are, only as they convince them that Christ is
> a mighty Savior and the Bible a sure guide.[37]

And that in Dickensian England!

And so the pejorative comparisons could go on, and did,
comparisons based upon "civilization," defined ethnocentrically:

> Mohammedan and heathen Africa alike know nothing
> of domestic purity and peace, and contain within
> their vast domains scarcely a family ordered after
> *the natural, which is the Christian pattern* [my
> italics]. The African family is simply a cattle
> kraal on a slightly elevated scale.[38]

Many of the descriptions make embarrassing reading today. The
moral righteousness, the lack of self-critical ability, the
fawning paternalism, the confusion of the mission of the Gospel
with *la mission civilisatrice*--all of these are things missionaries and secular change-agents from the West would like to
forget.

And yet, with all of the prejudices, there was a certain
openness, which fought, as it were, against the grain but
occasionally broke through, to new perceptions and new questioning of the accepted wisdom. In 1883, less than three years
after the work in Angola began, reports went back to the Board
that "the superior character of the people in kindness,
intelligence, and attractiveness is becoming more and more
apparent."[39] In the same year Missionary Stover reported, "The
people disappointed me agreeably. They are really a fine race,
and, I would say, worth all the expense necessary to save them,
were the country as barren as Sahara itself."[40] Mr. Fay added,
"To me now the tone given to the word *heathen* in many of our
home prayer-meetings would be utterly offensive, and I think
the tone would be changed and a new meaning be put into the
word, or a new word be used in their prayers, if our Christian
people could see the bright, intelligent faces of many of these
people."[41]

In the schools of the mission as well as at worship the
Africans "disappointed the missionaries agreeably." Mr.
Woodside reported in 1890 that it was his belief that, if given
the same opportunities as American boys and girls, his African
pupils "would not be left far behind."[42]

Although the missionaries have been accused of not even considering to study religions they deemed "heathen," Mr. Currie
had this to report in 1890:

> These people have a somewhat elaborate system of
> religion, and a much more methodical form of
> worship than most people imagine; while both form
> and system are protected by superstitious beliefs
> so that neither is like to change quickly.[43]

One cannot do a revisionist history of nineteenth century
missions which would make the missionaries out to be far better

than their contemporaries, or erase their undoubted ethnocentrism. They were, beyond a doubt, men of their times, and
their times were increasingly arrogant and ethnocentric. But
one can, by studying their writings carefully, come to understand both why they failed in the common failings of their age
and why they offered at the same time something unique. Such an
understanding leads us a long way toward a comprehension of why
they carried out their mission in the way in which they did. In
the light of a total taxonomy of available missionary methods,
it can be maintained that there were alternative possibilities
open to them in every aspect of their work, but an analysis of
missionary methods in civilizational perspective leads us to
recognize that the alternatives open to any given set of
missionaries at any given time are far fewer than a broad
taxonomy might indicate. The task of a comparative differential
sociology of missions is to indicate the differential in
different times and societies.

(3) How the Board understood America and Evangelical Christianity, the West and "Christian Civilization."

There was no crisis of confidence in the America of the 1880s.
No matter what the injustices of the times may have been, no
matter how many treaties with the Indians might have been broken,
no matter what critical appraisals budding socialists might have
offered of the social fabric of the United States, those proud
to be at the center of American life--and that certainly included the Congregational establishment--had no doubts that the path
of the nation was the correct one and that its course was upward.

In 1881 Secretary N.G. Clark gave a major address at the
Board's annual meeting on the "special trust" which the U.S. had
to fulfill in the "economy of Divine Providence."[44] He contrasted America's place with the high place Providence had
evidently assigned the British. Say what one might about the
role of Britain, "no island could give scope to the divine conceptions of man and his destiny. A virgin soil was required for
the grandest development of a higher civilization. A continent
was needed."

America, Clark went on, contained "the choicest elements of
Protestantism." Its "controlling sentiment was English--and yet
not so much English as Christian--Christian thought, only more
fully realized in English life and character."

America had "forgotten race in the larger love of man," and
so, as a result, it could offer a vital force made up of "what
was best in each nationality, and to blend the varied elements
into one grander whole, capable of worldwide aspirations and
endeavors, to be, not English or Anglo-Saxon, but henceforth and
forever AMERICAN."

Key to America's success, Clark felt, was its freedom from "the traditions and conventional usages of the Old World." In America Christianity was to be organized into a new social life, offering the highest opportunity to all.

> There was to be developed in this land, thus prepared of God, a chosen people, a peculiar nation, with a growth in numbers and power unrivaled in the annals of time. Through a baptism of fire and blood it was to purge itself of the last remnant of the old-time civilization, and then press on to a career of national prosperity that should be at once the despair and the wonder of the civilized world, which all men, of whatever land or race, should see and feel to be due to the freedom of a life begotten and energized by the gospel of Christ.

Thus God intended that America should hold "a great trust for mankind."

It was obvious, Clark felt, as he surveyed the American scene, that America was worthy of the trust. Anyone could see

> an advance in public morals, in Christian activities of all kinds, in keeping with the growth of the church and of our educational institutions. The very atmosphere is charged with moral and religious ideas; the common sense of the average American represents an amount of knowledge and moral perception quite unknown to the average man of any other age or country; it is so far Christianized that thousands of men and women outside the pale of any existing church are an honor to the institutions amid which they live.

Such a nation could not have any lesser mission than to participate in "the spiritual and social regeneration of mankind." To America "preeminently is given the establishment of Christian states and empires around the globe."

The difference between America and the other Christian nations was that whereas they were Christianized from heathendom

> This nation alone was born Christian, and born again of blood in the Revolution, securing nationality; and born still again of the Holy Spirit through the word of God, in home and Bible, in school and church, and in continuous revivals throughout our history.

God could therefore be forgiven if he had kept Japan, China, and Africa virtually closed to mission work till such time as America would be ready to bring the Gospel to them, and therefore he deliberately forestalled the development of the steam-engine and the telegraph until his chosen people would be ready.

Clark was not the only one to speak thus of America in the meetings and annual reports of the Board in the '80s. Such visions of America's divine destiny dot the pages of the documents the Board produced in those years. The aphorism Secretary Alden quoted in 1886 (which he thought was "a most inspiriting idea") expressed the sense of the Board through those years: "As goes America, so goes the world."[45] The committee reviewing Alden's paper that year felt it only fair to conclude that

> Our Christian institutions are to be reproduced in
> other lands. The eyes of the world are upon us.
> What an impressive thought that America is expected
> to set the fashion for the world in the transcendent
> business of building a Christian civilization![46]

At times, though, the Board was less narrowly chauvinistic. It accorded the same accolades to the other "Christian nations" as well. Secretary Means was fond of quoting a French statement which expressed the mission of all Europe in the world of heathendom: In the 19th Century the white has made a man out of the black; in the 20th Century Europe will make a world out of Africa.[47]

The Board was therefore quite impressed with King Leopold of Belgium's "International Association for the Suppression of the Slave Trade and Opening of Central Africa." Leopold in turn expressed the hope that the Board in its proposed mission, would find his relief stations helpful.[48] The Board rejoiced over the Christian cooperation which made the Berlin Conference of 1884 possible, and over the establishment by that conference of the notorious Congo Free State. Secretary Smith was sure that these events "mark the dawn of a new era in human history, a new age in the political and moral order of the world."

> An imperial domain of vast population, of superb
> resources, the natural seat of a power that should
> influence every part of the Dark Continent and shape
> its future for ages, was solemnly dedicated to the
> best arts and culture and faith of the Western world.[49]

It was, thus, not only the endeavor to end the slave trade and establish civilization which won the Board's approval, but the colonial enterprise and the establishment of commerce as well. "Let Christian civilization pervade Africa," Secretary Means

said, "and she will take her share in the world's business....It
is a reasonable and moderate expectation that Africa, pervaded
by Christian civilization, with such marvelous resources, will
come up to the average per capita of the business of the world.
This average...will swell the volume of business and augment
the profits of labor and of capital the world over, as the high
tide swells the Bay of Fundy."[50]

With such an attitude toward what the Western nations were
doing, it was no wonder the missionaries in Angola accepted the
protection of the Portuguese when once they were expelled by the
Ovimbundu king. They rejoiced that the Portuguese had pledged
themselves "to the protection of the missionaries and to the
peaceful prosecution of their work."[51]

Yet the Board's enthusiasm for the Western powers was not
boundless, nor was their admiration of America without qualification. At times the word of judgment was spoken. In 1890
the Committee to Review Secretary Smith's paper pronounced a
gentle but highly significant rebuke to the Secretary's boundless enthusiasm for what the West was doing:

> ...let us caution ourselves as to expecting overmuch
> from the leadership of Christian nations in the world's
> affairs. Undoubtedly they are becoming more and more
> the dominant forces in its civilization. But it is not
> to be forgotten that while they are thus opening the
> way for the incoming of Christianity among the nations,
> they are at the same time furnishing the most potent
> hindrances to its success. Behind the opium traffic,
> that awful curse whose withering touch is like a
> plague of death upon not less than 150,000,000 of Chinese,
> is Christian England; and with no excuse whatever save
> the profits she wrings out of the bodies and souls she
> helps to destroy. Behind the infernal liquor traffic,
> with which the Dark Continent is being scourged worse,
> even, than by the infamous slave-trade, are Christian
> Germany and Christian America, and with the profits
> of their rum and gin as their only excuse. Behind the
> flood of infidelity and rationalism pouring steadily
> into India and Japan and counter-working powerfully
> the efforts of our missionaries, are all three of
> these Christian nations, and with avowed hostility
> to Christ and his gospel as their inspiring cause.
>
> While therefore we rejoice in seeing these great
> Christian powers enlarging their sphere of influence
> over the nations, let us not fail to pray, and to
> pray earnestly, and, as respects our own country,

> *to vote as we pray*--that these mighty dominators of
> national destiny may be led to wield their powers in
> the fear of God and for the furtherance and not the
> hindrance of his gospel.[52]

The memory of slavery was also a potent reminder not to equate
Christianity and America too closely:

> The evangelization of Africa has peculiar claims upon
> American Christians. Whatever the horrors of the
> slave trade, as it exists today among these African
> tribes, some part of the responsibility lies un-
> questionably at our doors....For as many years as
> American ships tracked the seas with curses and
> blood, in the interest of American slavery, we can
> keep them re-tracking it with Bibles, and missionaries,
> and prayers, and songs of jubilee, in the interest
> of our Lord Jesus Christ, and the evangelization of
> Africa.[53]

A distinction had to be drawn between what men proposed and what
God was disposing:

> What Belgium means, what Germany desires, what England
> intends, what the nations expect, perhaps we cannot
> tell. But what the King of nations means we know
> full well. And what he intends--*that* is the true
> meaning of it all. Bismarck holds his own policy
> in his hands and spins it well. Leopold draws well
> the thread which passes to his control. Stanley
> guides shrewdly the lines of power that fall to him.
> But not one of these alone, and not all of these
> combined, hold the destiny of Africa within their
> grasp. The thread of fate for this new world
> proceeds from the mighty throne of God. And his
> will for Africa is the conversion of her sons and
> the Christianization of her social and political
> life.

God, the secretary was implying, was using the empires for his
ends. So long as that distinction was maintained, the possibility of prophetic judgment remained. Could the same Lord who
once used a tool not discard that tool or even smash it? But
for the moment the judgments were few, the praises many. So far
as the Secretary could see, the powers were serving the Power,
not just in a secular way, but, through their secular deeds,
they were serving the purposes of the Kingdom:

> One and all, they serve his purposes; one and all,
> dumbly or with articulate speech, they cry, "Repent!
> for the kingdom of heaven is at hand."[54]

Perhaps that was the ultimate casuistry of the era, to say that
the forces of imperialism and commerce and colonialism were
crying "Repent!"

SOME TENTATIVE CONCLUSIONS

The question with which we began, you will remember, was the
question why this particular group of men carried out their
mission in Angola in the way in which they did. The question a
comparative, differential sociology will ask of mission history
is, why this approach here and that approach there? Why this
approach now and that approach then? Why any given approach and
not another?

We began by creating an ideal type. It had many features. I
think by now most of those features are easily explained:

--the missionaries built permanent homes because, though they
  continued to mouth Anderson's formulas, they no longer had a
  conception of mission which would enable them to move quickly
  on; they were to civilize as well as Christianize, and that
  work would require generations of missionaries

--the missionaries chose to work with young lads rather than
  adults because their concept of what true Christianity meant
  was such a total change of life--of socialization as well as
  of creed--that they doubted whether they could Christianize
  unless they started with the trees when they were green; full
  Christian life would, in addition, involve, the missionaries
  felt, the ability to read the word, and so the logical place
  to begin, in an era which preceded adult literacy work, was
  with the young

--the missionaries were in no hurry to baptize anyone, but insisted on tried and proven candidates (a) because they were
  sure of the ultimate triumph of Christ's cause and (b) because
  their model of conversion was a total one and not a partial
  one (*fides implicita* was not enough; *fides explicita* was required for salvation) and an individual one and not a social
  one (the social was in their understanding the product of the
  actions of individuals)

--the missionaries used American hymns and catechisms and
  covenants and helped design American-style churches because
  what was American was not just "American" to them, but the
  new experimental forms for the new humanity, merely developed
  and tested in America, but of universal import

--the missionaries got involved in physical amenities (a) because
their religion was not a rejection of the world but a religion
which enabled them to practice a kind of inner-worldly
mysticism on the one hand, and a kind of inner-worldly
asceticism on the other: the "new world" of the "new Adam"
was the arena of divine grace and human vocation, and (b) because they were late-19th Century Americans and took pride
in being "the wonder of the world"

--the missionaries were ethnocentric because, with the rise of
self-confidence in the West in the 19th Century, the myth of
the "noble savage" was swept away for a century (Cf. the fine
book by Henri Baudet, *Paradise on Earth*, New Haven, 1965 for
an analysis of the vicissitudes of the idea of the noble
savage in European history); the noble man was the civilized
man, and civilized men felt they were not merely cultural
types but expressions of the new manhood, universal men

--the missionaries had no doubt of the ultimate success of the
work because they felt they saw history as pointing clearly
in the direction of American development, that America--an
Evangelical nation--had set the path in which the world
would walk, and that path was Christian and evangelical

--the missionaries did not major in physical and "civilizing"
ministries because they felt social and physical changes would
naturally come as the outgrowth of spiritual changes; by the
regeneration of the hearts they would let loose the leaven
which would change all else.

All this seems clear, and not hard to envision. Several
questions remain, nevertheless:

--why did the missionaries become such good linguists and translate the Scriptures into Umbundu if they thought that the
Anglo-Saxon nations were leading the way to the future? Would
it not have been more logical to "elevate" the natives to the
English tongue?

--why did the missionaries insist on self-support for the
churches, and upon an independent native ministry? their
ethnocentrism might have logically led to paternalism.

--why did the missionaries not fall prey to the racism of many
of their contemporaries, when they obviously conceived of
America as so far ahead and of Africa as in such darkness?

--why did the missionaries accord the respect they did to the
native kings and chiefs? did they not see that the future lay
in the hands of the Portuguese?

--why did the missionaries so early translate the Bible? would it not have been sufficient to give the latest, best inter- pretation of the faith? why did every person need to read the Bible for himself? did not American Evangelicals have the authentic interpretation?

On these questions the logic seems to break down. Our ideal type is not all of a piece. It is a type of process in history. The missionary movement of the 1880s did not spring full-grown from the head of 1880--it was a continuing movement with roots in a remembered and celebrated past. That the many casuistries we have noted had to be made is a sign of the power of the past over the present. That in some cases "legal fictions" prevailed (as in the claim that the Board was following in the "three-self" formula of Anderson) shows that the present can trick the past, but in many ways the past maintained its power over the present. "Every man a Bible reader," "every man a priest" were two of the dicta of the past which were too powerful to be changed by the present. The Bible *had* to be translated. The Bible was pre- eminent in Protestant faith--it could not be a secondary intro- duction.

Similarly, the concept that God had made of one all the races of the earth acted as a check on racism. Human nature was one, and one would have to work extremely powerful casuistries on the Scripture (as the German Christians did in the 1930s) to deny it. The Ovimbundu was as fully human as an American. He had a claim upon the American, and a right to his respect. His language was an expression of who he was, and it was important. His system of government, barbaric though it seemed, was part of what made him who he was, and it ought to be (somewhat) respected.

That leaves the stress on self-support and an independent, trained native ministry unexplained. Perhaps all that we can say is that Rufus Anderson's missionary policies had come to have an almost scriptural authority for the ABCFM, and they accorded well with the imagery of the American frontier. Even if they did not "fit the type," they could not be done away with, but they could be--and they were increasingly--disregarded and postponed. (Note: missionaries exercised pastoral authority in Angola until very recently.)

APPLICATION TO CONTEMPORARY MISSION METHODS

This has been a study of missionaries and their methods, not of the Angolan church--The Protestant Church Council of Central Angola--and its history. I deliberately focus on the mission- aries in order to illustrate the difficulty of speaking about dynamic equivalence churches. The initial literature on dynamic

equivalence churches[55] removes the missionaries too much from
its center of focus: it assumes that, at the ideal, the
missionaries are catalysts--they help to create the conditions
in which dynamic equivalence churches can emerge; they are not
themselves part of the equation. Intelligent missionaries,
writers like Kraft assume, can stand back and look at the
situation objectively and decide how they can create a condition
in which dynamic equivalence churches will emerge.

My case study, on the other hand, questions Kraft's optimism.
It argues that missionaries cannot attain such objectivity. It
contends that the missionaries, and the culture they represent,
are important parts of the process of church growth. It further
argues that--despite the best intentions of the missionaries--
they do not operate in a vacuum. That the missionaries are even
present in a given situation is a sign that an inter-civilizational encounter is taking place, that the civilization and
society from which the missionaries come are in encounter with
the civilization and society of the "receptor culture." More
is happening in the place where the missionaries do their work
than a process of church planting. The story of the church's
growth is just one chapter of a larger story of inter-civilizational encounter.

The missionaries cannot, for example, tell the people to turn
off their transistor radios. They cannot blockade the
"receptive culture" against the weekly visits of the van from
the Anglo-American Tobacco Company. They cannot keep Bristol-
Myers from selling infant formula. They cannot keep Harry
Oppenheimer's consortia from recruiting migrant workers. They
cannot keep the nation's political parties from calling local
people to conventions and seminars. They cannot impede the
progress of literacy and planned parenthood campaigns. They
cannot forestall fluctuations in world market prices for primary
products. They cannot block off the people's vision from jumbo
jets flying overhead, nor keep people from knowing about the
latest heavyweight championship fight.

Nor will the missionaries stop receiving their weekly copies
of *Time* and *Christianity Today*, or cease listening to Voice of
America broadcasts. They will notice that their salary payments
buy less or more goods at the local market as a result of
fluctuations in the value of the dollar and local currency.
They will know that relations between their country and the host
country are different under Carter and Andrew Young than they
were under Ford and Kissinger. As intelligent beings, they will
seek to modify their missionary practice in accordance with the
best modern insights into methods of communication and leadership training, of community development and health education.

If the missionaries know how to "read the signs of the times,"
they will revamp their ideas on the role of women and the
function of government, on the nature of racism and the social
function of ideology. They will become, perhaps painfully,
aware of the ways in which the people with whom they work belong
to a directed society and of how they as missionaries come from
the director society. They will understand that colonialism has
been replaced by neo-colonialism, and that vital decisions about
the life of the people to whom they minister are made, not by
the people themselves, but by the Western world and the country's
internal ruling elite--or else the country's dominant socialist
party and its allies in Moscow or Peking. They will see that
they are parties to the major drama of our time: the question
of power and who will have it, the struggle for domination and
liberation.

As they read their Bible with the people, they will discover
that the Bible is not biased toward equilibrium and stasis, but
toward change, that the God to whom the Scriptures bear witness
is a God of change, who liberates people from their shackles,
who overthrows the mighty and exalts the humble and meek, and
whose will it is that a new Kingdom should be established, a
Kingdom of justice and love, of brotherhood and sisterhood.
They will recognize the high role which the Scriptures give to
the church, as a sacrament of the salvation God is bringing,
the first-fruits of a new creation. They will hope and pray
for the new church which is emerging, that it will be dynamically
equivalent to the church in the Book of Acts, a church in which
the dynamism was that of the Spirit who was creating then--and
still seeks to create--a new Kingdom order. Just as it was
once said, "These Christians are turning the whole world upside
down," they will hope that the new Christians in the place in
which they are working will "turn the world upside down."

There is a danger here, of course. The danger is that, in
the place of the old Christendom mentality, which was beginning
to dominate the world of the early Angola missionaries and which
came to full bloom in the early 20th Century under such
ideologues as Josiah Strong, will come what John Howard Yoder[56]
has called a "new Christendom mentality," in which a "crusade"
is carried out--of "courageous attack on unjust authority in the
name of greater democracy "--which does not challenge the
world's agenda but merely, in the old Constantinian pattern,
adopts it. Is this God's way? Yoder asks. Must we always be
changing things? He calls rather for "acquiescence in the
presence of a given power structure," the position which he has
elsewhere called "revolutionary subordination." He describes
this as "neither approval nor rebellion," but "a willingness
to live in a world one cannot control," a "diaspora approach."

Yoder is concerned to save the church in mission from becoming victim to yet another unholy accommodation. Certainly
there is a reductionism in some "liberation theology" which
merits his warning; God's sovereign independence is compromised,
his majesty is reduced. No longer "the opiate of the masses,"
he becomes their "speed." Utopia is confused with the Kingdom,
and ideology with theology.

Against such criticism those who speak of dynamic equivalence
churches are secure. Their stage is far more narrow than that
of the liberation theologians, their desire more modest. The
world they see themselves as working in is much smaller; the
task to which they feel called much simpler: to midwife the
birth of a church which the local Christians will "feel is an
original institution within their own culture,"[57] a "church
which will possess indigenous forms for Christ, adapting them to
Christian ends by fulfilling indigenous functions and conveying
Christian meanings through them to the surrounding society."[58]

We must, in one real way, welcome their modesty. They have
discovered, through functionalist anthropology, a way of overcoming the ethnocentrism which has characterized most Christian
missions from the West. They have discovered a biblical way of
adopting a certain modicum of legitimate cultural relativism.
Their methods are undoubtedly freeing up many African and Asian
peoples from cultural imperialism. They can speak with much
greater confidence to an American church public which is increasingly out of sympathy with the old missionary arrogance.
Missionaries trained by their methods are a new breed, sensitive
to cultures, less given to evolutionary racism, full of respect
for Third World people's desire for "selfhood."

It is a fact not to be denied, however, that "liberated"
missionaries—and I was one—often run into conflict with the
church and people to whom they are ministering. Second-and
third-generation Christians accuse them of "syncretism."
Educated people accuse them of "romanticism." Politically con-
scientized people fault them for "irrelevance" and "other-world-
liness." In their own perception, this is highly ironic: they
are the local tribal people's best friends—no one else (not
outsiders, not the older generation, not the upcoming youth)
understands the people as well. If the others only knew the
people as they really are, and shared the missionaries' concern
for authentic cultural patterns and "dynamic equivalence," they
would recognize that what they are trying to do is worthy of
their fullest support. Only through some such means will a
strong church come into being, will true economic and social
development take place.

But the young people call for technical schools and modern church music; the old people ask for Moody and Sankey and more missionary doctors; and the politically inclined ask the church to support the national revolution. And the missionary doesn't know what to do about it.

If he is a typical Westerner, he believes in change--change is "good," what is "modern" is to be recommended. But, in his semi-romanticism about the people to whom he has been sent, he probably imagines the same people living in (aluminum-roofed) round houses, taking chloroquine and boiling their drinking water, while singing traditional songs and carrying on decision-making as it has always been done. He is not as fearful of Western technology as he is of Western "culture " (and he separates the two).

If he is like me, he probably welcomes the entry of Western business firms into the nation's economy, and never questions whether they bring bane as well as blessing, dominance and oppression and alienation as well as the opportunity for people to find new jobs and earn money with which to improve their lives materially.

His missiology is most likely not suited to discussing questions like migration within the country, except in so far as migration leads to new possibilities for planting churches--the ethics of a migrant economy, the values of a wage-based society, the questions of industrialization and urbanization don't figure into such a missiology. They are part of "secular history," and the missionary deals with "sacred history."

I say this by way of confession, not accusation. It has taken me all these years to recognize how unliberated a "liberated" missionary I was, how small the stage was to which I had consigned God's action in history. Now I recognize that the missiology which I studied and practiced was only a partial missiology. And I do not find in dynamic equivalence theory the advance church growth thinking must make if it is to become faithful to God in today's world. A missiology which will speak to South Korea in the throes of industrialization, to teeming Lagos and impoverished Northeast Brazil, needs to introduce far more parameters than dynamic equivalence missiology uses. And there--rather than in exotic, isolated places--is where the predominant missional challenge of our days is to be found.

Where, then, can we find a missiology which is adequate to cope with today's world and which does not succumb to the temptation of which Yoder speaks, of mounting a new "crusade" akin to the old Christendom mentality?

Our starting-point should be with the God of the Bible, a God
who rules people and nations in accordance with his sovereign
will, who can use a leader or a nation as his instrument or
dispense with them in sovereign freedom, who is concerned for
every sparrow that falls as well as for the whole cosmos, who is
actively working to bring in his Kingdom, who forgives sins and
raises the dead. He is a God whose concern spans the gamut from
the particular to the universal. It is no mythical use of
language to say that he is present to every one of his creatures,
and no exaggeration to claim that he is Lord of all.

The sovereign God has chosen to be a God of freedom. His
creation is plural and he wills that individuals and individual
societies and their cultures should be as jewels in his crown.
Everything that we have learned about societies and cultures
from functionalist (and other types of) anthropology will be of
use to us in learning how we can relate to his people--he does
not choose to use only methods of mass communication. The
primary quality of his communication is its specificity.

At the same time, this God's purpose is to "unite all things"
in Christ (Eph. 1:10). As the hymn puts it, he is "working his
purpose out, as year succeeds to year." In the midst of this
complex and confusing world--more characterized by struggle and
competition than by solidarity--he is working to bring new
unities into being. It is not his will that, at the end of time,
each tribe and clan and nation will be isolated in its own
cubicle waiting for the judgment (certainly that is not the
meaning of "In my Father's house are many mansions"!). Rather, he
is the force behind every movement which transcends barriers.
The God in whose Son there is "neither slave nor free, Jew nor
Greek, male nor female" (Gal. 3:28) is a God who wills that
people should now experience new unities across linguistic,
racial, sexual, national, and religious boundaries. Under his
sovereignty, clans have united into tribes, tribes into nations,
and nations have coalesced in civilizations. Today, under that
same sovereignty, civilizations and nations are forced to confront the need to construct the world's first planetary society.
Just as neo-colonial nations and multi-national corporations
have discovered the opportunity they have to gain power and profit through transcending national borders (creating an international ruling elite and an international class of oppressed
people in the process), so responsible citizens and visionary
leaders of nations are working for the creation of a new international order of justice and equity ("As sin increased, grace
abounded all the more." Rom. 5:20).

The early missionaries to Angola and the Board that sent them
knew that, with the coming of the telegraph and the steamboat, a
new oneness was in store for the world. They interpreted that

oneness in an ethno-centric way, feeling that they were called
to make all peoples over in the image of the Anglo-Saxon, and
particularly the American, people. They confused the Kingdom
of God with "manifest destiny," and missionary responsibility
with the "white man's burden." They were far too uncritical
of the structures of American and Western European capitalism,
and far too judgmental of non-Western peoples. They assisted in
destroying many cultures and established too many "formal
correspondence" churches, and they provided a gratuitous apologia
for Western imperialism and commercial expansion. They contributed to a world in which a "Third World" would produce the
primary products that fed a growing "First World" industrial
revolution. They contributed to the alienation of land, material
resources, and culture from the dark-skinned people of the world.
Profiting from the largesse of the commercial entrepreneurs and
the colonial governments, they raised their voices all too infrequently at attendant injustice.

But most of them lived according to their own best lights,
and it is far too easy for us, with our hindsight, to condemn
them for lacks of which they were, largely, unaware. We must at
least accord to them the recognition that they differed in a great
many ways from the colonizers and exploiters. Their efforts
led to the birth of churches around the globe, and members of
those churches remember them with deep gratitude, for they made
Christ known in places where otherwise his name might not have
been heard or his salvation appropriated.

I would like to suggest that, in another important respect,
they were closer to the truth than we may have been liable to
admit. That is in terms of their world-historical vision. In
a day of minimalism in evangelical mission theory--when we have
set our sights on nothing more than planting churches and
multiplying cells of believers--we would do well to be skeptical
about our skepticism concerning a "cultural mandate." Chastened
as we are by the taunt of "Missionary, go home," and "Don't
export your culture to us," we are all too likely to retreat to
the "safe" fortress of "doing only what the Bible tells us"--
converting individuals, starting dynamic equivalence churches,
and seeking to assume an "objective" position with regard to the
affairs of the world.

The study of the Angola missionaries should convince us of
how difficult this indeed is--and even make us question whether
it is possible. *Can* we be objective? To claim to be may be a
more arrogant claim than the recognition by the early missionaries that they were seeking to civilize as well as evangelize.
Such a claim presumes a dichotomy between subject and object
which has come under question in discipline after discipline
in the post-Vietnam era. Perhaps the time has come to put it
under question in missiology as well.

Missiology is not a "value-free" science. Missionaries are
not of the order of Melchizedek, "having neither father nor
mother." The Gospel we proclaim does not spring full-blown from
the forehead of the apostolic age. It has had a long history.
We have all learned certain ways of understanding the Gospel.
We all have a definite hermeneutic or principle of interpretation
and modes of application. There can be no such thing as a
missionary who enters the mission process only as a catalyst.

The important thing is not to be "value free" or to pretend
to "Gospel objectivity," but--in fear and trembling, and with
a full faith in the justification of sinners--to be conscious of
what our values are, to make them explicit, and to discover what
the values of Scripture are, and to ask how far our values
accord with what we perceive those of the Scriptures to be.

The God of the Bible is not a "value-free" God. He has a bias
on behalf of the poor and oppressed. He is engaged in the work
of their liberation. He is a God of judgment--he looks with
scorn on the proud and stiff-necked. History is strewn with the
wrecks of misplaced zeal, much of it carried out in the name of
God, most of it not. Just as we criticize our forebears, in
the socialist world voices are being raised criticizing the
failure of the revolution to lead to the overcoming of alienation.
Roger Garaudy, a leading Marxist philosopher, fears that the
trouble was that the renovation of life on earth was not ordained
to a finality which was higher. Now a confessing Christian, he
says that history must be kept open to a fulfillment partially
outside history.[59]

Denis Goulet, a perceptive observer of recent developments in
both East and West, writes that

Perhaps the human race, like Adam is summoned by destiny
to display a modicum of ontological humility, to recognize
its finiteness by admitting that perhaps it may be radically
unable to achieve total redemption in time.[60]

The "openness toward transcendence," as Goulet calls it, frees
us for the attempt to shape a new future today. No longer
obsessed to do it, *and do it now*, we can--as the contemporary
adage puts it--"hang loose" with regard to ultimate results,
and invest ourselves joyously in the effort to let the winds of
the Spirit blow, that communities may be renewed, that relationships may be transformed, that people everywhere might find
abundant life, the life we believe Christ came to bring
(Jn. 10:10). No ideology can demand our ultimate allegiance,
no party platform our unquestioning support. As a "loyal
opposition" we may work with others for the achievement of
terrestrial goals, but we march to a different drummer. We will

be better allies--more trustworthy co-workers--with those in the
struggle for liberation because we will not be "yes-men." As
Che Guevara recognized, Christians have a contribution to make
to the revolution, but only if they are courageous enough to
show their faith.[61]

"A dynamic equivalence church," Kraft writes, "is the kind of
church that produces the same kind of impact on its own society
as the early church produced upon the original hearers."[62] That
is a wide-ranging reflection. Look at what historical forces
were set in motion by the first announcement of the Gospel in
the Roman Empire! To be faithful to what Kraft proposes means
that we must go beyond the methodology Kraft introduces, and
seek to find the ultimate meaning of dynamic equivalence in a
theology and mission practice which is related to the Kingdom.
The Kingdom of God--and that includes much more than the planting of what Kraft describes as dynamic equivalence churches--
ought to be our guiding star in mission. If it is true, as
Lausanne put it, that God "has been calling out from the world
a people for himself" in order that he might "send his people
back into the world to be his servants and his witnesses, *for
the extension of his kingdom*," (Art. 1, my italics), then we
will need a missiology which enables us to see that Kingdom in
larger than ecclesiastical terms. The "unfinished task of
evangelization" will only be finished when the church has
brought the good news of God to bear on the totality of God's
fallen creation. As the Covenant puts it, "When people receive
Christ they are born again into his kingdom and must seek not
only to exhibit but also to spread its righteousness in the
midst of an unrighteous world" (Art. 5). This, the Covenant
elsewhere explains, is a matter of seeking "to transform and
enrich culture for the glory of God" (Art. 10).

NOTES

1. American Board of Commissioners for Foreign Missions, Annual
Report, 1880, p. 24.

2. Matt. 28:19 f.

3. ABCFM, *op. cit.*, p. 30.

4. Strong, William E., 1910. *The Story of the American Board*,
Boston, pp. 4 f.

5. ABCFM, Annual Report, 1891 (the reference is to the work in
East Central Africa).

6. *The Missionary Herald*, 1890, p. 291.

7. Annual Report, 1887, p. 63.

8. *Missionary Herald*, 1890, p. 239.

9. *Ibid.*, pp. 238, 67; Annual Report, 1879, p. lix et passim.

10. *Ibid.*, p. xliv.

11. Annual Report, 1856, pp. 51-67.

12. Annual Report, 1880, pp. xxxvi f.

13. Annual Report, 1886, p. xxvii.

14. Annual Report, 1880, p. 383.

15. Annual Report, 1886, p. xxix.

16. Neibuhr, H. Richard, 1937. *The Kingdom of God in America*, New York, 1937.

17. *Ibid.*, p. 51.

18. *Ibid.*, p. 91.

19. *Ibid.*, pp. 103,105.

20. *Ibid.*, p. 142.

21. *Ibid.*, p. 141.

22. *Ibid.*, pp. 145 f.

23. Handy, Robert. *A Christian America*, p. 98.

24. Harris, Samuel, 1874. *The Kingdom of Christ on Earth*, Andover.

25. *Ibid.*, p. 203.

26. *Ibid.*, p. 197.

27. *Ibid.*, p. 196.

28. *Ibid.*, p. 254.

29. *Ibid.*, p. 255.

30. Niebuhr, *op. cit.*, p. 179.

31. Stocking, George, 1969. *Race, Culture and Evolution*, New York.

32. Acts 17:26.

33. Annual Report, 1887, p. xxiii.

34. Annual Report, 1885, p. xxxi.

35. Annual Report, 1879, p. lix.

36. *Ibid.*, p. xxxviii.

37. *Missionary Herald*, 1880, p. 368.

38. Annual Report, 1880, p. 212.

39. Annual Report, 1883, p. xviii.

40. *Ibid.*, p. 28.

41. *Ibid.*, p. 29.

42. *Missionary Herald*, 1890, p. 238.

43. *Ibid.*, p. 67.

44. Annual Report, 1881, pp. xii ff.

45. Annual Report, 1886, p. xv.

46. *Ibid.*, p. xxxvi.

47. Annual Report, 1879, p. xxxvi.

48. *Ibid.*, p. xliv.

49. Annual Report, 1887, p. xlvi.

50. *Missionary Herald*, 1880, Means.

51. Annual Report, 1885, p. 24.

52. Annual Report, 1890, p. xxi.

53. Annual Report, 1879, p. lx.

54. Annual Report, 1885, pp. xxvi f.

55. See particularly Kraft, Charles, 1973, "Dynamic Equivalence Churches," *Missiology*, Vol. 1, No. 1, Jan. 1973, pp. 39-57.

56. Yoder, John Howard, "Between Christ and Caesar," unpublished address given at the Ventnor Consultation on Christian Mission Under Authoritarian Regimes, May 1977.

57. Kraft, *op. cit.*, p. 41.

58. *Ibid.*, p. 49.

59. In Goulet, Denis, 1974, *A New Moral Order*, Maryknoll, New York, p. 119 f.

60. *Ibid.*, p. 119.

61. *Ibid.*, p. 133.

62. Kraft, *op. cit.*, p. 43.

15

Contextualization
of the Church in Bali:
A Case Study from Indonesia

I. Wayan Mastra

God's purpose in Christ was to offer salvation not only to the Jews, but also to the entire world. Christ is the Light of the World, which means all the people in the world. Following their Master's Great Commission, and driven by the persecution at Jerusalem, the disciples journeyed to distant lands to bear witness to Christ. To the amazement of the Jewish Christians, Gentiles responded to the Gospel in faith and the Christian community grew significantly. The disciples soon felt the need to resolve the problem of how to integrate people of different religious traditions into a unified Christianity. The decision of the Jerusalem council was to not trouble those of the Gentiles who turn to God with the trappings of Jewish culture and religion (Acts 15:19).

In the second and third centuries, Christian apologists felt the need to defend the faith against the charges and suspicions of the so-called pagan peoples. The most outstanding of these was Justin Martyr. He believed that traces of truth were to be found among the Gentile philosophers since all men shared in the "generative" or "germinative" Logos, *logos spermatikos* (Walker 1959:47). "Thus the Church Fathers," says Paul Tillich, "emphasized the universal presence of the Logos, the Word, the principles of divine self-manifestation, in all religions and cultures" (1963:34). In this way the Logos is to be found in

every land as the forerunner of the historical appearance of the
Logos in the person of Jesus of Nazareth (ibid.).

Later, Christianity became for a time a self-contained religion in Europe, unchallenged by other religions and cultures;
but the advent of Islam with its victorious wars of conquest in
North Africa and Spain forced Christianity to conceive of itself
as one religion and culture. The result of this new self-
awareness and of the encounter with another religion and culture
was the Crusades (ibid.:38). The Crusades did not bring political success to Europe, nor did they bring a solution to the problem of the confrontation with non-Christian religions; when they
were ended, Palestine was still occupied by the Muslims and
Christianity was still challenged by Islam.

But as a result of the cross-fertilization of eastern and
western ideas, the Crusades enriched the Christian nations of
Europe with culture and science, which became very important
factors for the later expansion of the church. The acquisition
of new techniques enabled the adventure-loving Christian nations
in Europe to engage in new explorations and discoveries, which
in turn led to colonial and church expansion.

After the arrival of the Portuguese and Spanish in the East
and discovery of America by Columbus in 1492, the church prepared itself for new expansion and confrontation with other
world religions and cultures. The Christian message was carried
around the world so that Christianity was ultimately found in almost every land. Hence Christianity is today confronted not by
one religion as was the case with Islam of old, but by many religions and cultures; and ultimately by all conceivable religions
and cultures.

Because of this expansion, Christian theologians began to take
great interest in the study of non-Christian religions and cultures; they developed the phenomenology, history, and philosophy
of religions, which are known collectively as the science of
comparative religion. The motive underlying this newly found interest in comparative religion was an apologetic one: to show
the superiority of the Christian faith over non-Christian religions (Braden 1964:190). However, comparative religion cast some
doubts upon the veracity and authenticity of Christianity. Some
theologians raised the question as to whether the Christian message was still needed by non-Christian people, since there was a
great deal of similarity between all the religions of the world.
Thus, baptism, circumcision, the eucharist, prayer, and many
other religious practices did not belong exclusively to Christianity, but were also to be found in many other religions.
Some of these doubts concerning Christianity are best expressed
in the famous play, *Nathan der Weise*, written by Lessing in 1779

(Verkuyl 1961:14,15). Later, when the Christian nations of Europe had become world powers and had occupied and were ruling almost all the non-Christian nations of the world, Christian theologians formulated a theological position that reflected the feelings of superiority experienced by the Christian nations. Hence Christianity was formulated as a religion and culture superior to the non-Christian religions.

After World War II, when the non-Christian countries became independent and respected nations, Christian theologians began to see the world as one plane, filled with a multiplicity of societies, and characterized by religious, cultural, and racial pluralism. They encouraged new approaches based upon mutual respect in the relationship between races, religions, and cultures. They produced the catchword *contextualization*. These new approaches showed a tendency to return to the approach of the early Church Fathers.

Moreover they recognized that religion is heavily loaded with local features. It is embedded in historical things such as custom, language, and art, which are not universal. Thus, understanding the non-Christians in both their religious thought and their cultural background is a very important factor in mission work, since it will enable us to communicate the Gospel in the thought, language, culture, and feeling of the people.

BALI: ITS LIFE, RELIGION, AND CULTURE

Bali, an island of 2,000 square miles east of Java, is very small compared with many other Indonesian islands; it is only one hundred miles long and fifty miles wide. But it is perhaps the most famous and unique of all, with epithets such as the "lost paradise," "morning of the world," and "island of many temples."

The mountains that run across Bali from its western to its eastern tip divide it into two parts, South and North, and play a very important role in the life, religion, and culture of the Balinese. The craters that have turned into lakes have served Bali as reservoirs for water. The heavy forests on the slopes of the mountains cause a lot of rain, and hold water and distribute it during the dry season. Rivers flow from the mountains south and north, eroding the soft soil of the slopes and creating deep valleys and ridges. All the roads and paths in the north-south direction are relatively straight and unobstructed, while the east-west roads and paths are very crooked and twisting and need many bridges. Before bridges were built, it was very difficult to have communication between people from one village to the other and to have a strong central authority in all aspects of the life of the island (Swellengrebel 1960:4). That was why prior to World War II Bali was divided into eight kingdoms that

had great rivalry between them. Originally there was only one
Hindu kingdom, but when the central government became weak, the
eight countries became stronger and broke away and established
their own kingdoms.

Water plays a very important role in the life of Bali. As the
rivers flow to the ocean, they give life to the rice in the *sawah*
(wet rice paddies) as well as to the people who live on the
plains and lowlands. The rivers then continue their journey to
the sea, taking with them all the dirt and filth. That is why,
according to the Balinese, the gods and goddesses live in the
mountains, people live on the plains or lowlands, and the dead
are in the sea. Temples and monasteries are built on the slopes
of the mountains and in each *desa* (village) the main temple faces
the mountain. The people turn their backs to the sea and face
the mountain. The mountains are symbols of stillness, calm, and
peace, the origin of life; the sea is a symbol of roughness and
anger, the destination of the dead. The character of the Balinese people can be likened to the mountains and volcanoes. Generally they are mild, friendly and generous, but when they are
being insulted they can be quite angry like a volcano. That is
probably why they could purge and kill more than 100,000 communists during the *coup d'etat* in 1965.

Like other Indonesians, the Balinese belong to the Malay
stock. But because of Bali's splendid isolation and the rough
sea surrounding it, the people have developed unique traits. The
population of 2,500,000 is divided into three major religious
groups: Bali Hindu, 98 percent; Bali Islam, 1 percent; and Bali
Christian, 1 percent (1976 census). The language, a dialect of
Malay, has three levels as a result of the caste system of
Hinduism. A court action can result if someone uses the wrong
level of language, because it indicates contempt. During the
period of the Hindu kingdom, people from the superior caste could
kill a person of inferior caste if he made a mistake in level of
language.

In talking about Bali one cannot escape discussing the Hindu
Dharma religion which is the source of Balinese culture. Originally the religion was called Bali Hindu, and it was exclusively
related with the Balinese people. Now they call themselves Hindu
Dharma in order to give room for non-Balinese to join. But in
fact no non-Balinese can join, because the main sanctuary or
temple or shrine in Bali is related to the ancestral spirits;
each Balinese family is related to its forefathers in a mystical
union between the living and the spirits of the dead. It is only
non-Balinese women who can become Balinese by marrying a Balinese,
because the woman does not bring her family gods or ancestral
spirits to the home of her husband. In that way her husband's
gods or ancestral spirits become hers.

From the term "Bali Hindu" it is obvious that this religion is a mixture of Hinduism and the native Bali religion. The oldest account of religion in Indonesia shows that Brahmanism and Buddhism came to Yavadvipa (Java) around A.D. 413 (Fa-hsien 1965: 29). There is no such early account of religion in Bali, but archeologists believe that Buddhism has been known for a long time there. Clay seals which had been kept in a small *stupa*[1] had engraved upon them a Sanskrit rendering of a Buddhist magic formula of the Mahayana sect. The same magic formula was also found in Candi Kalasan in Java, dated A.D. 778. A round stone monument with Sanskrit and ancient "pre-negari" Balinese writing on it can be found at Sanur (South Bali).[2]

Buddhism, therefore, has been known in Bali for eight to ten centuries. During this period a Balinese king, Dharma Udayana, married a princess from East Java named Sri Gunapriya Dharmapatni, a descendant of Empu Sendok. Of this marriage a child, Airlangga, was born in A.D. 991. Upon his grandfather's death, Airlangga went to Java and became king. Then, when his father in Bali died, he annexed Bali and let his younger brother rule in Bali in his name. He sent a Hindu priest from Java to Bali who translated the *pracasti*, or law, from ancient Balinese into Javanese. During his reign the king managed to save his people from a plague. Out of this mythical struggle against the plague there arose a legend called "Calon A-rang" which keeps the memory of Airlangga alive in Balinese tradition. He eventually abdicated, became a hermit, and built a Siva Hindu monastery which can still be seen.

After Airlangga's death, Bali became independent again and remained so until A.D. 1343, when it was conquered by Gajah Mada of the kingdom of Majapahit in East Java. He managed to unite under his rule Malaya and all the islands that presently belong to Indonesia. This was the last and the greatest of the Hindu kingdoms in Indonesia. When Majapahit fell in 1478 to Islam, the son of the king of Majapahit fled to Bali, the remaining part of his kingdom. He was followed by his entire court, priests, artists, and intellectuals. They were the most "civilized" in the whole region, the cream of Javanese culture. They transplanted to Bali their art, religion, and philosophy which have flourished ever since.

During Majapahit's rule a Sivaist Hindu priest, Dang Hyang Nirarta, an expert in ancient Javanese and Sanskrit, came to Bali and diligently went from one village to another teaching Hinduism. It was he who introduced the caste system in Bali. His sons were honored as members of the highest caste, the *Brahmana*. The families of the king who ruled Bali at that time were called *Ksatria*; their helpers were called *Vaisya*. These three honored groups, the *Trivangsa*, all came from Java. The native Balinese were called *Wong Jaba,* meaning "people who live outside," because they lived outside the city walls. The Javanese built walls around their houses because they feared an uprising of the native Balinese. Later on, foreigners who knew the caste system in India came to Bali and called these native Balinese the *Sudra* (Pandit 1960:41). Among the Balinese, those who rejected Javanese Hindu influence went to the jungle or remote areas and built their villages there (the Bali Age); and those who accepted it were the Wong Majapahit (the people of Majapahit) (Kempers 1955:15). They later considered themselves higher in position than the Bali Age. In this way Hinduism penetrated Balinese life.

As for the native beliefs in Bali, they are basically animist in nature. The Balinese believed that everything had a soul and that souls were the natural forces that gave life and movement to all things. They worshiped such natural forces as the wind, the sea, volcanoes, springs of water, valleys, jungles, rivers, big trees, etc., which they considered to be spirits. They brought offerings for these spirits, in order to prevent them from becoming angry at the people. When someone was hurt in an accident or was killed, the Balinese believed that the spirit of the thing which caused the accident was angry.[3] In such a case, the injured person needed someone who knew how to deal with the angry spirit. Usually they would go to the *pemangku* or priest-magician, whom they believed to have extra-sensory perception and to be able to make an advantageous exchange with the spirit for the recovery of good health. Thus, the *pemangku* would tell the family what to do in order to charm the angry spirit.

The belief that everything had a soul entailed that man also had a soul, a belief which led the people into ancestor worship. The people considered that the souls of their ancestors were still alive after the death of their bodies and dwelt at the temple of the dead or in the mountains and volcanoes. Hence in Bali there are still many people who claim to be mediums and clairvoyants, capable of talking with the souls of the dead.[4]

When the Buddhists and the Hindus came to Bali, they did not change the beliefs of the people, but merely gave new names to the spirits or divine beings in which the people already believed. Since animism, pantheism, and polytheism are very close to nature, there was an easy transition from animism to Buddhism and Hinduism.

For example, when the Hindus came to Bali, they gave the name *Brahma* to the spirit of fire, *Vishnu* to the spirit of water, and *Siva* to the spirit of the air or ether. These three main spirits manifest themselves in the sea, in volcanoes, in the jungle, and so forth, and receive a special name in each manifestation. The present generation of Balinese Hindu priests and leaders have formed a doctrine of trinity out of these three main spirits or deities. When the spirit manifests himself as creator, he is Brahma; as maintainer, he is Vishnu; and as destroyer, he is Siva. They claim, however, that this trinity is monotheistic because the Brahma, Vishnu, and Siva are the manifestations of the one true God, i.e. the *Sang Hyang Widhi Wasa* in Balinese.

Although the process of Hinduization went on for many centuries, the original character of the Balinese remained, as may be seen in the way people deal with their dead, even today. Some do not bury the corpse, but leave it on a stone in the cemetery where birds eat the flesh, thus carrying the body to heaven. Others bury the dead. Still others cremate the body following the Hindu custom, because they believe a body consists of three things: air (Siva), fire (Brahma), and water (Vishnu). Through cremation the body is returned to the essences that make it up. The body having gone back to its origin, the soul is then free to go to heaven or *atman* where it can join the *Brahman;* the soul of the microcosm unites with the soul of the macrocosm.

There is other evidence that the Balinese tradition remains in spite of the long process of Hinduization. The Hindus introduced a new priesthood, descendants of Empu Dang Hyang Nirarta, the first Hindu priest who spread Hinduism in Bali. But the native priest, the *pemangku,* who functions like the *shaman* or priest-magician among the people of Central Asia and Polynesia, still plays a very important role in village temples and lives. The Hindu priests are from the Brahman caste, the scholars of sacred *vedas* and *mantras,* while the *pemangkus* are native Balinese. They are chosen by appointment or by trance from within the clan, so the people believe they are chosen by the deities.

The original Balinese tradition and culture can also be seen in the way temples are built; these differ considerably from Hindu temples in India. Bernet Kempers, a Dutch archeologist, believes the temples in Bali to be in direct line from the old sanctuaries where the spirits of the ancestors as well as the great nature gods were worshiped by the native Indonesians and Polynesians. The sanctuaries were always an open space surrounded by walls. Inside the wall there was usually the *tachta batu* or throne made of stone where the deities were worshiped. Through Hindu influences the *tachta batu* has developed into *padmasana,* a shrine which is beautifully decorated and carved, made of black rock, that can still be found in Sanur, a village in South Bali. This sanctuary can be compared with the *marae* of Polynesia (Kempers 1955:20).

The old Indonesian and Polynesian sacred places were often stepped pyramids made of stones, which represented the celestial

mountain; they are similar to the multiple roofs of the Balinese
pagodas, such as are to be found at the mother temple of Bali at
Besakih and Pura Kehen at Bangli (Wertheim 1960:28).

Thus, the Hindu religion and the ancestor worship and animism
of Bali have molded Balinese religion and culture. Because of
Bali's isolation, it is very hard for outsiders to come to Bali;
thus, the religion and culture of Bali became unique. The religion became the source of its culture, as is evidenced in the
life and activities of the people: dances, paintings, wood
carvings, temples, and numerous ceremonies, as well as the music
of the *gamelan* orchestra and several other features of Balinese
culture and life. The Balinese are very proud of these and
strive to retain them.

Moreover, because of the mixture of religions, the people accept the idea that all religions are the same; all are seeking
an experience with God, like so many rivers flowing to the sea.
The differences between them are those of stages on the way, one
religion being higher, another lower than the other. This attitude towards religion can produce religious tolerance, and religious tolerance can develop into syncretism and make it very difficult to proclaim the Gospel which claims that Christ is the way.
the truth and the life.

The Dutch did not conquer Bali until the beginning of the
20th century, because Bali was not tempting economically. But
after a series of bloody battles with the Balinese in this century's early years, the Dutch managed in 1914 to conquer the
whole island, and to deploy a police force throughout. The
Dutch maintained the indigenous political structure, restoring
to power the aristocracy in the eight kingdoms of Bali. They
introduced western style administration and education and built
many roads, so that Bali today has one of the finest road networks in Indonesia.

The very first Christian missionary to Bali was J. de Vroom
of the Netherlands, who came to Bali in 1866. After much hard
work, he succeeded in winning his first and only convert in
1873. But when this newly converted man returned to his village,
he had great difficulty with the other villagers. De Vroom apparently did nothing to console him when they met again, and so
the convert killed him in 1881. The convert was captured and
hanged by the Dutch in Jakarta. As a result, Bali became a
closed area to missions from 1881 to 1931, especially under the
Dutch East Indies Company, for the sake of law and order.

In the 1920s, scholars and writers from Holland, Germany, and
America "discovered" Bali and were deeply captivated by the
people and culture. Many books were published, and in a short

time Bali became the 20th century paradise for tourists. Because of the beauty and uniqueness of Bali, the government wanted
to preserve it as a remnant of Hinduism. This reinforced the
ban on missionaries. In 1923, applications from Roman Catholic
and Lutheran churches to be allowed to send missionaries to Bali
were rejected by the Dutch governor-general with the whole-
hearted support of those western residents and tourists who
feared a Christian "invasion" of Balinese culture.

But Bali could not be kept closed to Christ. In 1929, when
the ban on missionaries was still on, Tsang To Han, a Chinese
evangelist of the Christian and Missionary Alliance, received
permission from the governor-general to come to Bali to take
care of two Chinese Christians who had arrived from China. He
was allowed to work only among the Chinese. His work among them
was not successful, but through a Balinese woman who married a
Chinese in Denpasar, he became acquainted with some Balinese who
were looking for a new religion. Although he could not speak
Balinese and his knowledge of the Indonesian language was inadequate, he could not reject the invitation of these people to
come to their villages.

It happened that in 1908 Radem Atmajakusuma, a Javanese *guru*
belonging to a mystical spiritualist group, had come to Bali.
In 1927, linked with the Communist movement in Java, he was captured and removed by the Dutch, but his followers remained and
spread his teaching. When Tsang came to Bali to teach the new
religion, the villagers thought he was the successor to Radem
Atmajakusuma, which is why they asked him to visit their village.
The Spirit of God worked through him so that on 11 November 1931,
the first baptism was administered to a group of 11 believers.
The flame of Christianity spread very rapidly from one village
to the other along family lines, which served as "the bridges of
God" (McGavran 1955).

A second baptism took place in November 1932, which created a
great sensation in the whole island and even in the central government in Jakarta. First, it was illegal; second, the manner
in which Tsang administered baptism aroused feelings, as did his
way of speaking about the Bali Hindu religion. As an evangelist
of the Christian and Missionary Alliance, he was motivated by
great courage and zeal to win people for Christ, but he had no
respect for anyone else's feelings. With R. A. Jaffray, who,
according to Kraemer, displayed a typically American lack of
hesitation (Kraemer 1958:159), Tsang exhibited the new converts
on the bank of a river close to a market, baptizing them by im-
mersion, so that many people could see the event. He told the
converts to burn their idols and destroy their temples, because
he considered these things to belong to the demons. He had no
consideration for the fact that those idols were still worshiped

by the Balinese Hindus, and those temples still played a very important role in their religious life.

The Balinese Hindus felt attacked and insulted by these actions. Moreover, in accordance with the Balinese Hindu conception of the world as macrocosm and man as microcosm, the land could not be separated from man. If a man was not a Hindu, he had no right to be on Hindu land. People of the village who became Christians were considered traitors and destroyers of their culture. Therefore they had no right to stay in their village. There was, therefore, unrest in Bali, and the government expelled Tsang in 1933. But Christianity was born! Two hundred sixty-six Balinese had been baptized. It was a spontaneous expansion of the church from one family to another, from village to village. But when Tsang left Bali, the new converts were left alone without leadership and guidance, a flock without a shepherd. The missionary had to go, but God continued to build his church.

During this period of unrest, Hendrik Kraemer visited Bali to study the situation; he later made an appeal to the governor-general for permission to take care of the newly converted people. After a long period of struggle and persuasion he got the government's permission. Thus the converts moved from the Christian and Missionary Alliance tradition to the Dutch Reformed tradition. Then they called themselves the *Gereja Kristen Protestan di Bali* (the Protestant Christian Church of Bali), commonly known as the Bali Church. The church grew steadily in spite of many difficulties and ostracism, so that at this time it has 6,000 members who are living in Bali and some 12,000 people who have migrated to Sulawesi.

INDIGENIZATION IN HISTORICAL PERSPECTIVE

The success of the Hindus in winning Balinese for Hinduism was the result of their efforts in introducing Hinduism not in the form of a foreign religious and cultural invasion, but as a seed planted in Balinese soil and growing up in its own way. Thus Hinduism in Bali becomes indigenous, unique in culture and appearance. The people could worship God in their own atmosphere and glorify him with their own talents.

This effort can be compared with the effort of the church fathers to win Europe for Christ. One cannot really plant the Gospel as a seed which grows in indigenous soil without having a thorough knowledge of the thought trends of the people.

In this connection, Martin Dibelius credits Paul's success in his missionary work to his thorough understanding of the non-Christians with whom he dealt (Dibelius and Kümmel 1966:21). He was born in the city of Tarsus in the province of Cilicia (ibid.: 16), which was the center of the heavy traffic passing through the Cilician plain. Tarsus was a famous university town, and a meeting place for Hellenism and Orientalism where they developed and blended into

> the idea of cosmopolitanism and the doctrine of the
> *logos*...the supreme wisdom governing the universe....
> The stoic philosophy, whose great teachers nearly all
> came from the East, had prepared the ground on which
> naturalization and philosophic interpretation of
> foreign deities...Isis, Osiris, the Egyptian Hermes
> Trismesgistus (i.e., the Egyptian god Thoth), and
> Attis...could be carried through (ibid.:17).

Because Paul knew Greek, he could appreciate Hellenism and Orientalism and knew their thought and culture. His approach is well exemplified in his mission to the people of Athens when he said on the Areopagus:

> Men of Athens, I perceive that in every way you are very
> religious. For as I passed along, and observed the ob-
> jects of your worship, I found also an altar with this
> inscription, "To an unknown god." What therefore you
> worship as unknown, this I proclaim to you (Acts 17:
> 22,23).

Paul did not want to be accused of bringing foreign gods to the people of Athens, but to plant the Gospel inside the minds and hearts of the people by using their own expressions. He as- serted the existence of an unknown God for whom the people of Athens had erected an altar (Barnes 1949:26). He respected the people of Athens' belief and used it to explain his message:

1. It was not his custom needlessly to blame or offend
   his auditors.

2. It was not probable that he would commence his discourse in a manner that would only excite prejudice
   and opposition.

3. In the thing which he specified (verse 23) as proof
   on the subject, he does not introduce it as a matter of blame, but rather as proof of their devoted-
   ness to the cause of religion and their regard for
   God.

4. The whole speech (Acts 17:22-34) is calm, dignified,
   and argumentative--such as became such a place, such
   a speaker, and such an audience (ibid.:259f).

On another occasion, in Corinth, Paul found a problem of division within the church among the parties of Peter, Apollos,
Paul, and Christ that was tending to rupture the unity of the
church. To counteract the new division Paul developed the idea
of the church as the body of Christ (Cerfaux 1959:228-231).

He used the word "body" (*sōma* in Greek) in order to describe
the unity of the church. This concept came from the Hellenistic
fable of the body and its members, taken from the tales of
Aesop and adapted by Menenius Agrippa to the social order. This
tale was obviously very familiar to everyone at that time since
it was much used for illustrating the various aspects of the
corporate life of the community (ibid.:266). Here again it is
clear that Paul was able to understand the Hellenist thought of
his time and then to apply it to his teaching so that it would
be relevant to its hearers (1 Cor. 10:11; 12:12-27; Rom. 12:
4,5).

Paul dealt with the same subject of the church as the body of
Christ, but from a different point of view, in his letters to
the Ephesians and Colossians.[5] This new usage is clearly stated
by the expression "body-head" (Eph. 1:22f; 4:15f; 5:23; Col.
1:18; 2:10; 2:19), in which the relationship between the church
and Christ is represented (Schlier 1963:15). The central organ
in a human body, according to Paul, is the head, which is considered as the seat of life. This life can be compared with the
life of the "members" of the body of Christ--the church, which
depends on its head for its life, that is, Christ (Col. 2:18,19)
(Kee, Young, and Froehlich 1965:207).

This analogy was taken by Paul from the Hellenistic understanding of the world as a *cosmos* (universe). The Greeks conceived of the world as a totality bound together into a unified
structure containing heaven and earth and all living creatures,
including God and men. This concept was foreign to the Old
Testament Hebrews, who always excluded God from their concept of
the world in order to distinguish the creation from Creator. In
this sense, Hellenistic Judaism appropriated for itself and used
the term cosmos as it was used later by Paul in explaining the
church as a cosmic man (Bultmann 1951:254). Paul tried to make
his teaching concerning Christ and the church relevant to the
people by Christianizing the Hellenistic and gnostic understandings of the body, thus giving them a meaning consonant with his
teaching (Cerfaux 1959:325).

The church leaders in Europe later followed Paul's method in
adopting and adapting the people's beliefs and worship into the
Christian tradition. Thus the cradle of Christ which is used in
the Roman Catholic tradition is borrowed from the cult of Adonis.
The cave where the child Adonis was born was adopted into Chris-

tian worship by the Empress Helena, and later, in A.D. 355, it was richly endowed as a shrine by the Emperor Constantine (Hastings 1928:608f). Similarly, when Boniface, the apostle of Germany (680-754), brought the Gospel from England to Germany, he baptized German cultic practices into a new variety of Christian liturgical tradition. "He replaced the sacrifices to Odin's sacred oak by a fir tree adorned in tribute to the Christ Child" (*Encyclopaedia Britannica* 1962:643).

Following such an unbroken sequence of repeated usages of the same mission technique, one can see a spiritual and cultural continuity between pre-Christian and Christianized Europe. In this connection Father Thomas Ohm has said:

> When the Germanic tribes received and accepted the Gospel, they took it up in their own way and formed their own pattern. The nations of Asia may do the same. Just as the Reformation served as an occasion for genuine reforms in the church, Asia may in a similar way serve the church (Ohm 1959:227).

CONTEXTUALIZATION BALI STYLE

The *Gereja Kristen Protestan di Bali* has started to take some steps in communicating the Gospel to the people of Bali in the language, culture, and feeling that can be easily understood by them. At the same time, it endeavors to retain its identity as a church which is called from the Balinese, placed among the Balinese, and sent to the Balinese.

The fact is that the Word has become flesh, and so the Word and the world are in polarity and closely related to each other; the *logos* is rooted in the world of culture (Marty 1964: 132). In the same way, the Christian message and the community must be related to each other. But too often our message and action may hurt the feelings of the community, because they may feel that they have been insulted. That is why in many cases people respect and love Christ, but they resent the Christians and the missionaries.

1. *The message must be concrete, visible, and tangible.*

Balinese like many other Asians are extraordinarily visual. They can understand things after they have seen them. They want everything to become concrete, visible, and tangible. That is why they look for signs of their faith in significant happenings in nature and human life. It is important for them to symbolize their faith in action—drama, dance, painting, carving, and architecture, which are seen in temple ceremonies as well as in the temples themselves.

In the West where most missionaries come from, the thought
trend is basically abstract. They tend to speak about their
faith intellectually. That is why church services look so dry,
because they are reduced to an abstract verbal proclamation of
the Gospel. It appears that the western nations like theology
which gives intellectual satisfaction; but in the East such as
Bali, the people like religious experience in order to make
their faith become a real and not merely a theoretical conviction.

The verbal proclamation of the Gospel can also give a feeling
of superiority of the Christian religion and culture over non-
Christian religion and culture. In the past, missionaries and
early Balinese Christians used to say their new religion was
superior to their traditional religion, which they said was related to demons and evil spirits and filled with superstitions
and idols, which kept the people in darkness. They also considered their traditional culture to be inferior to the western
culture. They did not distinguish between Christian faith and
western culture.

That is also why in the past the non-Christians considered
Balinese Christians as the accomplices of the colonialists,
traitors to their country, betrayers of their national identity,
and deniers of their own culture and ancestral religions.
Christianity was generally labeled as a foreign religion with a
foreign God and Savior. This accusation was partly true, because the missionaries not only taught the new converts Christianity but also taught them foreign customs and languages,
which in Indonesia meant the Dutch language and customs. Hence
Balinese as well as other Indonesian Christians were often given
the epithet "Black Dutch"!

During the struggle for national independence in 1945-1949,
many Christians suffered persecution at the hands of the revo-
lutionaries because they were considered as collaborators of the
Dutch. After the revolution in which the country obtained its
independence, the Balinese Christians suddenly found themselves
in a totally new situation to which they were forced to adjust.
Since foreign missionaries were identified with the Dutch colonialists, there was great pressure from the people in general
upon the church to expel its missionaries. In these circumstances the Balinese Christians were not only forced to stand on
their own two feet, but most serious of all they found themselves as alienated groups among hostile neighbors, as foreigners in their own land, and as a little flock in the midst of
masses of people who challenged their faith and attitude to
their people and culture. Balinese Christians were confronted
with two major problems:

a. They had to struggle hard to be accepted as part of the Balinese community, and

b. they had to prove the validity of their faith, i.e. that Jesus was really Lord of the world, of all nations, and above all, of the Balinese as well.

That is why the Balinese Christians take the attitude that because they love their own people and cultures, they try to adapt as much as may be permissible for the church. For them, the Gospel in the Bible is a simple message about God's redeeming act in Jesus Christ, the incarnate God. The Gospel comes to a culture, it is not part of that culture. It is an offer of a new bread of life and living water. How do the people want to accept this offer? The Europeans will receive and eat the gift by using their tools such as spoons, knives, and glasses. The Chinese, perhaps, will receive and eat the gift by using their chopsticks and porcelain, while the Balinese will surely receive and eat the gift by using their fingers and clay cups.

The Gospel will transform the culture into a new creation. In this way the New Testament very often describes it in terms of both birth and death. To have faith means to be born again into a new religion and also to die to one's old religion. This view is represented in the New Testament by John and Paul, as for example in John 3:3, 1 John 2:29, and Rom. 6:1. In baptism, as in the decision of faith, the "old" man is dead and the "new" man is born. In this sense there is no continuity between traditional religions and Christianity, for although there is a continuity at the beginning of the conversion process in externals, yet after one becomes a Christian the old is transformed into a new being (2 Cor. 5:17).

Once when I was preaching the Gospel to the Balinese, I found a lady who was not happy because her husband and children had become Christians. When I talked to her, she expressed her anxieties. I discovered that she was unhappy because she was afraid that her ancestors and deities would punish her husband and children because they no longer brought offerings to the family temples. She had been brought up and nurtured in a tradition in which offerings were the most important factor for achieving salvation. She could not understand how Christianity could bring salvation, because the Christians did not bring offerings to the church. (She understood offerings as consisting of burnt offerings, i.e., food offerings which are very close to the offerings mentioned in the Old Testament.)

I told her that there were some similarities between Christianity and the Balinese Hindu religion. The Balinese Hindus bring offerings and sacrifices to the temples of their gods. One of the most important of the temples is *Pura Besakih*, which is located on the slope of Gunung Agung (Great Mountain), Bali's highest and holiest mountain, "...where the god of the mountain and the deified spirits of mythical founders and ancestors of various families and castes are believed to dwell" (Hooykaas 1964:177). The offerings and sacrifices made there consist of flowers, foods, and animals (chickens, ducks, goats, and black bulls). The animals are killed and their blood shed in order to charm the angry spirits and deities.[6]

I then told her that the Christians had already made their offering at mount Golgotha in Palestine once and for all in the person of Jesus Christ, God himself who became man for our sakes. Hence Christians do not have to bring offerings and shed blood anymore because the offering of Jesus Christ was enough. Christians, however, do bring offerings to church in the form of money out of a spirit of dedication and love, for the continuation of God's saving act in the world.

The woman accepted my explanation and wanted to become a Christian, so that now she is one of the most active Christians in Bali.

Following the above example, we should not try to condemn or attack the non-Christian religions and cultures because condemnation and attack only excite a hostile reaction and hate from the non-Christians, emotions that may eventually endanger Christians themselves as well as the mission of the church.

Even the Communists, who consider religion as their most ardent foe, following Karl Marx's denunciation of religion as the opiate of the people, do not condemn or attack religion for tactical reasons, in an effort to win the people in Indonesia. In fact, the people's strong faith in spirits and deities protected Indonesia from becoming communistic during the Communist *coup d'etat* in 1965.

This kind of approach raises the problem of the continuity and discontinuity between religions. As a convert from Hinduism to Christianity, I myself find that there is both continuity and discontinuity between religions. Since I was raised in the Hindu Balinese religion, I understood Christianity from the point of view of the Hindu Balinese religion from the very beginning of my conversion. I was just like the woman whom I discussed above. She understood Christianity as the continuation of her perception concerning the offerings and sacrifices that she used to offer to the spirits of the ancestors and the deities. Similarly, Empress Helena adapted the cult of Adonis to Christianity and the Germanic tribes adapted the sacrifices of Odin's sacred oak to Christianity. Thus a continuity exists between the traditional religions and Christianity.

In this manner the conversion of an entire people occurs gradually today just as it did in the early church. The people of the early church as a community of Christ first accepted Christ as their Savior and hope through their traditional faith. Then they formulated their faith in the form of theology step by step, and this process has continued up to the present day. Though we cannot avoid the continuation of the traditional religions and cultures on the mission field for some time to come, yet the faith of the new converts to Christianity will grow gradually from their traditional faiths to Christian faith. In other words, they will formulate their faith and understanding of the Gospel of salvation in Christ from the religious perceptions that they already have. Through the guidance of the Holy Spirit they will grow and become more mature in their faith and knowledge concerning the essence of the Gospel of salvation in Christ, for as Paul says: "When I was a child, I spoke like a child, I thought like a child, I reasoned like a child; when I became a man, I gave up childish ways" (1 Cor. 13:11).

When we respect non-Christian religions and cultures, it does not mean that we abandon the mission of the church. Nor does this approach lead to syncretism or defeatism in our missionary endeavors. The main point in this approach is none other than "that the Christian attitude is not one of judgment or condemnation [of non-Christian religions and culture]; it is an attitude of witnessing and prayer for and with the world" (Neuner 1967:24).

We must approach the non-Christian with the same tolerance and humility that Paul had when he said in the Areopagus, "What therefore you worship as unknown, I proclaim to you" (Acts 17:30).

Thus in our task to witness to God's salvific work in Jesus Christ, we merely come to the non-Christians to present our Christian faith whereby God shows his involvement with mankind through Jesus Christ. We can only hope that the non-Christians may encounter Jesus Christ and become his followers in order to continue his work (Niles 1962:237f). We do not approach their religious systems, but we approach them as men of other faiths. Hence we do not need to compare one religious statement of truth with another statement of religious truth, nor do we need to challenge one claim with another. Religious truths are different from those scientific truths which have complete certainty and can be tested by their own inherent logical truth, a truth which cannot be denied. Rather, religious truth is based upon faith which one can only accept or reject, believe or disbelieve (Ferris 1969:4,5).

In confronting the world of religions and cultures, perhaps the best method of approach is to follow Jesus' advice to his apostles when he sent them out to preach the Gospel: that they should be wise as serpents and innocent as doves (Matt. 10:16). From experience in Bali it is very clear that one should avoid arguments over religion, because in such disputes each man inevitably claims out of self-defense, rivalry, and even anger that his religion is the best. It is difficult to discuss religion in a meaningful way unless each side is willing to sacrifice some of its claims.

Religion is a very personal thing and is related to personal religious experience in faith. That is why in Bali, where people are still strongly believers in the role of the spirits of the ancestors, when a person dies, and relatives try to consult the spirits through mediums, we stress the need and the important role of prayer. People have religious experiences when they encounter Christ directly in their prayers and find him answering their prayers. Prayers are very important in order to dramatize our faith in Christ that he is the same yesterday, today, and forever (Heb. 13:8). If he could cure a person who was sick in the past, surely he will be able to at this time, because he is the same. In Bali we have at least two congregations which were started because people felt they met Christ personally in the answers to their prayers. Thus their faith became real, and they became strong in their faith and they were able to overcome many temptations and persecutions. Because their faith became real, they will also follow Christ's commandment, so that they will have a high ethical life and deep social concerns. Thus the religious experience dramatizes Christ's presence, and it helps to meet the needs of the people who want everything to become concrete, visible, and tangible.

Moreover we need to demonstrate lives which are ruled by Christ, by bringing forth the fruits of the Spirit as they can be seen in our high ethical conduct in following Jesus' steps. The people know the trees through their fruits.

The people also want to see the sign of Jesus' sincere concern for people who are in need and trouble. That is why we have to be involved in social action in order to dramatize Christ's love and concern through our actions in helping people. As we can see in Holy Communion, Christ invites us to come to his table; in the same way he will invite us to come to his providence in the life hereafter.

It is in this light that the Balinese Christians see their efforts to bring the Gospel to the Balinese. We avoid communication in verbal abstractions that the people find too difficult to understand. We also avoid preaching too much on sin and punishment but rather demonstrate Christ's love and concern. People do not know the Christian concept of sin unless they read and know the Bible and want to accept the proclamation on sin. In any case, they usually already lead a high ethical life, so that our message on sin does not meet their need. But it is quite different with love, because they live in constant anxiety. They are frightened by the evil spirits and they are oppressed by the ruling class, so that Christ's invitation--"Come to me, all who labor and are heavy laden, and I will give you rest" (Matt. 11:28)--really becomes attractive to them. Many peoples are converted because of this invitation; the stress is not on sin but rather on difficulties in life.

2. *Some focal points in indigenization*

As we have seen, church leaders in Europe through time have baptized or Christianized pagan, religious, and national practices together with art and legend, and as a result these elements have become identified with western Christian culture. Thus the Gospel has been planted and grows in each section of Europe; it has become indigenous and unique in its own area.

But when Christianity was introduced in Bali the missionaries identified the European Christian culture with the Gospel and tried to impose it on the new converts. Missionaries told the newly converted people that their culture and religion belonged to the demons and urged their destruction. They did not distinguish between western culture and Christian culture, between European Christian culture and the Gospel. Alarmed by this kind of attitude, a strong reaction arose among non-Christian Balinese and foreigners in Bali, mostly archeologists, artists, linguists, and novelists who had come to Bali to find inspiration for their work and who had a genuine sympathy for Balinese culture. They worried that the beauty of the unique Balinese culture would collapse because of Christianity.

The church becomes conscious of the fact that if it wants to win the people for Christ, it should take some steps in bringing the culture as much as possible to the church. This thought is especially strong among the younger generation Christians. But these efforts have not always been welcomed by all Christians, particularly the older generation--those baptized in the 1930s. They well believed these things belonged to the demons. They said: "Why should we try to use these cultural practices that we have tried to avoid and to leave behind?" Once I met a minister who was converted during the 1930s. He wanted to build a new church building for the congregation. I suggested building the church in Balinese style by using Balinese artistic expression and philosophy. But the minister said: "Why do I have to build a church which does not look like a church?" Consequently

he built the church as a garage with a small window, because
that was the kind of church building first built in Bali. The
minister gave a magical meaning to the small window, so that the
Word of God would not "run away" from the people. But in Bali
there is no winter, it is summer all year round. Such a church,
therefore, is very hot inside, much like hell! This western
style construction is also too expensive, because many things
have to be imported, and the local village carpenter cannot make
them.

But if we look at the village temple, it is beautiful from
the artistic point of view; it fits the tropical climate; it is
cheap because local materials can be used; and the village artists have a chance to glorify their deities through their artistic talents. Why does not the church give a chance to the
newly converted people to glorify their God through their artistic talents which have been inherited from their ancestors?

In this context there was a reappraisal within the younger
generation toward the Balinese culture. The Synod meeting of
the church held 21-24 March 1972 developed a program for building a cultural and training center with specific goals:

1. Seek to proclaim and live the Gospel of Jesus Christ
    in ways relevant to the Balinese people.

2. Help Balinese Christians to gain a greater apprecia-
    tion of their cultural heritage within the context
    of their faith and to find new ways of expressing
    that faith within the culture.

3. Stimulate greater use of Balinese architecture and
    cultural symbols in expressing the Christian faith
    within the Balinese culture.

4. Develop vocational training programs for youth which
    will lead to specific jobs and will help perpetuate
    their cultural heritage.

5. Help modern youth to learn ancient skills of danc-
    ing, wood carving, art, etc.

6. Establish a craft cooperative, a tour service co-
    operative, and other organizations and programs
    which would be helpful in achieving the other spe-
    cific goals of the church.

7. Build and improve the lay training center so that
    it can be used as a guest house during the tourist
    season.

8. Stimulate greater inter-religious dialogue and co-operation among Balinese residents.

9. Seek to find ways to gain greater social and financial benefits from the expanding tourist industry for Balinese people.

10. Attempt to provide a relevant ministry and mutual self-help program among young travelers from all over the world, especially those who establish semi-transient residence in Bali.

11. Help villagers to learn new skills of modern farming, nutrition, health care, and family planning.

12. Improve youth counseling service in the cities and in the villages.

13. Improve and expand the migration programs.

The Bali Cultural and Training Center that was planned above was completed and dedicated with the name *Dhyana Pura* ("meditation center") 21 May 1977.

The theme for Dhyana Pura is taken from Isaiah 6:1-8. When Isaiah was in trouble, he went to the temple to meditate. He was purified and then heard the Word of God. As a result he became sensitive to the needs of his people and offered himself by saying: "Here am I, Lord! Send me!"

Thus the center is expected to serve the church so that it can find spiritual renewal that strengthens its dedication and loyalty to Jesus Christ, its Lord and Savior. The center will help the church to talk in concrete ways in communicating the Gospel to the people, in the flux of their thought. They need pictures, symbols, drama, and action. The church wanted to use its Balinese cultural heritage to concretize its message, by bringing out the culture as much as is suitable for the church. In this way the church just finished its work in translating the New Testament into Balinese and now proceeds to translate the Old Testament. It is busy rebuilding and remodeling the church building by bringing in the traditional Balinese art and architecture as well as inserting Balinese symbols and philosophy in the light of Christ. Balinese traditional decorations have been used in the church for church festivals. When there is a wedding people prefer to use Balinese ceremonial dress, while in the earlier days they used the western dress. This ceremonial dress is also considered proper when they celebrate Christian festivals such as Christmas, Easter, and Holy Communion. They also use the *gamelan* orchestra during the church festival services.

In order to meet the need of the people's lively imagination, the church encourages the people to paint the biblical stories in the Balinese traditional way of painting. The church building is also decorated with reliefs telling biblical stories in traditional Balinese carving. The new church building at Denpasar is being built according to the Balinese tripartite division which is very close to the Christian conception of the Trinity. In Bali the people have three basic needs of their bodies-- stomach, heart, and mind. God gave three important elements for our life: air, water, and fire. That is why the church floor was built on three levels. The roof is also on three levels. The three steps of coming to Christ: hearing the Word, being baptized, and participating in Holy Communion, are also clearly pictured in the church. Behind the altar or communion table is built the traditional temple gate with a cross in the opening, which represents Jesus as "the way, the truth and life" (John 14:6). A roof is being built which looks like the wings of a bird that protects its young in order to give warmth, comfort, and security, which is the same way God has protected us. Thus the church building preaches a sermon to people in symbols.

The Balinese love dramatic symbols; this can be seen in their dances, where all the beautiful movements represent symbolic presentations of the faith. The eyes, hands, and feet movements represent the fact that they live by air, work, and soil. Traditional Balinese dancing has also been used for telling biblical stories in the form of pantomime and drama. The Bible itself is full of redemptive drama such as the Exodus, the Exile, the Incarnation, and the Cross, in order to show God's plan and purpose for mankind. In this connection the Balinese *tembang* (opera) has also been used for preaching the Gospel to the people.

Hence the people feel closer to the Gospel. They do not think of Christianity as a foreign religion any more when they can see and hear that the Gospel has been given Balinese clothes. Since the people love their culture and art, performances in Balinese dance and drama are always crowded. If we were to bring moving pictures or slides about the life of Christ, we would have to get special permission from the government; and we would not have many hearers, because these media are strange to them. But the Balinese dance and drama do not need a permit, because they are folk dances and drama.

Color also plays an important role in the life of the people and has symbolic meaning. That is why the traditional black robe of the ministers has been replaced by a white robe. White is related to good spirits and black is related to evil spirits or demons. This is related to white and black magic. Hence white will create a feeling of reverence in the Balinese when it is related with the church.

Lastly, the people will not be able to conceive the love of Christ for them if we preach to them in verbal abstractions. People need to see this love being demonstrated or dramatized through our action. That is why the Bali Church is active in social action, in improving the people's condition by building schools, dormitories, a hospital, an experimental farm, a chicken farm, and a fish pond as a demonstration of our love as well as a model for improving the people's condition. This is also the goal of Dhyana Pura.

We try to make the people aware of our presence among them in witnessing and serving Christ's love to them. We hope that they will come longing to drink the living water and make a decision to follow him.

EPILOGUE

These are the efforts that have been made by the Bali Church in planting the Gospel among the Balinese in the Balinese atmosphere. Although the process of taking the indigenous ways of worshiping deities has brought success to the spreading of Hinduism in Bali, and a similar process caused the success of the Gospel penetration in Europe, there are several things that must be considered seriously.

First of all, one must remember that fine art is always expensive. Hence, even though the church wants to use the cultural art forms as much as possible, in many cases it is not able to afford it. That is why the construction of the church building must be extended over a period of several years. But this can become a blessing in disguise. In the past the churches in the mission field had "mothers" in the form of missionary agencies and "uncles" in the form of donor agencies that become their sponsors. Now they have to stand on their own. Mostly the people of Bali liked to sacrifice very much to build their temples before they became Christians. But many times Christians lost their generosity in bringing offerings to God, because they relied on the mother church and donor agencies. We have to revive this generosity. When people learn to give money for building churches over a period of about ten years, they will learn to give money also for church business in carrying on its mission.

Secondly, the contextualization of the church must not be related to the nationalistic movement of the people, because the Gospel is not related to a particular nation. Religion is not identified with particular nations, so that one cannot say

Japanese are Shintoists, Burmese are Buddhists, Balinese are Hindus, Arabs are Muslims, and Europeans are Christians. Religion is rather a feeling of the touch of the soul by the divine as a result of one's inner struggle. One's religious experience is different from that of another person.

On the other hand, the Gospel is universal and does not belong to a certain nation. Jesus is the light of the world, and God is God of all nations including their cultures. This will answer the problem of converting people. Many Christians including many theologians feel that converting people to Christianity is wrong, because we proselytize or bring people away from their environment. They think that Japanese are Buddhists, so it is wrong to proselytize or bring them to Christianity. In that way they ignore the people's religious freedom, freedom to embrace a religion as well as to leave it.

Thirdly, it must not become the goal of the church to preserve a particular culture or civilization. It will be impossible to keep the culture and civilization of one nation as they were before the coming of the Gospel, especially in this shrinking world when people from various cultural backgrounds are brought closer together by modern technology. There is no culture and civilization that can stay unchanged. The culture and civilization of a nation are not dead and static. They are alive and will be changed and developed because of the situation in the society and the influence from outside. In this light the Gospel has an outstanding character of transforming someone or something to a new being (1 Cor. 5:17). Thus the coming of Christ to a nation will transform the language, culture, and feeling of the people into a new being. But the new development will be the continuation of the past.

In this way we approach indigenization or contextualization as a tool. It is merely a tool for communicating the Gospel to the people so that our message becomes relevant to them. Hence it will give some flexibility, it will serve the church as a strategy of mission with the purpose that Christianity can get a home base and be rooted in the soul of the society. In this way Christians will not become foreigners in their own country, and then Christ can be truly felt by the people as the Savior of all nations.

Let the Holy Spirit rule the hearts of the new believers. In this way they can transform their old culture and their ancient view of life into a new being, truly Christian in nature, yet still indigenous in its expression. Thus strong faith in the living Christ, who is the same yesterday, today, and forever, will be able to counter the strong faith in the role of the spirits of their ancestors. We will not be afraid to counter this belief, because if we believe in Christ as the incarnation of the true God, so it must be the strongest possible religion. If we want to be called a religion ten feet tall, we must not ask the other people to kneel. In other words, if we want our church to be strong, then we should not degrade the other religions. Moreover, if our church consists of many people of many racial backgrounds, then it can also include many cultural backgrounds.

Finally, the efforts of making an indigenous church will mean nothing for the strategy of mission if the Christians do not have a real concern or a deep love of the people to whom God wants them to preach the Gospel; as Paul said:

If I speak in the tongues of men and of angels but have not love, I am a noisy gong or a clanging cymbal. And if I have prophetic powers, and understand all mysteries and all knowledge, and if I have all faith, so as to remove mountains, but have not love, I am nothing. If I deliver my body to be burned, but have not love, I gain nothing (1 Cor. 13:1-3).

NOTES

1. This *stupa* (a hemispherical tower in a Buddhist shrine) can be seen in the Bali museum.

2. *Pre-negari* is a language used only by Buddhists up to AD 914.

3. This custom remains to the present, so that people bring offerings to the site of accidents to charm the spirits that cause the accidents.

4. I was raised in this animistic environment until I was baptized into Christianity in 1952 at the age of 21. Last year when I lost a daughter, a friend offered to get a medium to talk to the dead child.

5. Dibelius and Kümmel point out that many biblical scholars had serious questions about the letters to the Ephesians and the Colossians, but that they are now accepted as genuine works of Paul (1966:6,7).

6. The people who lived on the slopes of Mount Bromo, an active volcano in East Java, used to sacrifice a girl at the crater of the volcano every year until the Dutch stopped the practice at the beginning of this century. The Balinese and the Bromo are connected in faith and race.

16

The Christian Life-Style
Gottfried Osei-Mensah

This paper intentionally lacks a clearly defined "cultural frame-work." It is written against the background of the growing multi-racial, multi-cultural, international "tribe" found in the cities and urban centers of our rapidly shrinking world (the global village). From time to time this process of growing to-gether produces its backlash in the crisis of identity and the quest for "roots." However, the process can be expected to go on with the increasing mobility and intermingling among the na-tions. (Five of the 33 participants in the Consultation happened to be married across both racial and cultural barriers!) The urban congregation to which I ministered for five years included 700 young people from some 15 different nations--including North Americans, Europeans, British, Asians, as well as African peoples. What normative biblical principles apply when we con-sider the Christian life-style in the context of such cultural diversity? This is the basic question with which I have sought to grapple in this paper.

CHRIST-CENTERED LIVING

The goal of the apostolic teaching, exhortation, discipline and prayer was that Christians should live "a life worthy of the Lord and pleasing to him in everything . . . " (Col. 1:9,10 GNB;

see also Eph. 4:1, 4:8; 1 Thes. 2:12; 2 Thes. 1:11; 1 Peter 1:14-16; 1 John 2:6, etc.)

The principles of discipleship which underlie this distinctly Christian life-style were variously stated by the Lord Jesus Christ himself. As the Lord, he claimed the first place in the disciple's life, loyalty, love, affection, and obedience (see Luke 14:26). His disciples must renounce all their personal rights, and hand over the control of everything they have to him (see Luke 14:33; c.f. Mark 10:28). Furthermore, they must submit to him and to his authoritative teaching in a life of daily, costly obedience and service (see Luke 9:23; John 12:26).

If the terms of discipleship are demanding, what the Lord promised in compensation for the disciple's total commitment and costly obedience are even more astounding: "Anyone who leaves home or brothers or sisters or mother or father or children or fields for me and for the gospel, will receive much more in this present age ... and in the age to come he will receive eternal life" (Mark 10:29,30 GNB).

The Lord Jesus taught his disciples that "a man's life does not consist in the abundance of his possessions." Rather, the true self-realization and fulfillment which men and women vainly search for in possessions, pleasures, and personal relationships is to be found in a whole-hearted commitment to him as the Lord. "For whoever would save his life will lose it; and whoever loses his life for my sake, he will save it" (Luke 9:24, 25 RSV).

If these principles are to work out effectively in the daily lives of Christians it is essential that they see themselves in the two-fold role of servants and stewards.

SERVANTS AND STEWARDS

Discipleship is inseparably linked with servanthood (see Luke 17:7-10). The disciple is committed to follow, obey and serve his master, as well as learn from him. By his teaching and especially by his example the Lord oriented the disciples' minds from a master-mentality to servanthood: "You know that the rulers of the Gentiles lord it over them, and their great men exercise authority over them. It shall not be so among you; but whoever would be great among you must be your servant, and whoever would be first among you must be your slave; even as the Son of man came not to be served but to serve, and to give his life a ransom for many" (Matt. 29:25-28 RSV; see also John 13:13-16).

To call Jesus Christ Lord, then, involves a submission not only to obey and serve him, but also to serve other people for his sake (see 2 Cor. 4:5).

When a disciple renounces his rights and hands over the control of everything he has to the Lord Jesus, he becomes a steward of a far greater trust than the privileges and possessions he surrendered. Usually of course he receives back from the Lord his possessions, only now no longer as his own, but on trust, to be used as the Lord directs. He becomes also a steward of the gifts, special abilities and skills (both natural and spiritual) with which he is endowed. The new motivation of his life is to develop all these resources and potentials to the full for the service of the Lord and his people. It is the controlling love of Christ and the solemn sense of accountability to him which leads the Christian to resolve no longer to live for himself but only for the Lord who died and was raised to life for his sake (see 2 Cor. 5:10,14,15). It follows then that a deficient sense of stewardship in a Christian community signifies an inadequate grasp of what Christ in love has done for them, and the reality of the day of reckoning.

In his teachings the Lord Jesus described the qualities he expected of his stewards (see Luke 12:42-48). First and foremost a steward must be faithful to his Master. He must share his Master's concern, purpose and goal. He must be trustworthy and honest with his Master's goods (see Luke 16:10-12); and he must use these resources in the most effective way to achieve his Master's objectives. Christ's stewards must be caring and outgoing to people. People matter (at least to Christ) more than things! His entire mission was people-oriented, and so must ours be if we share his objectives. Our perennial temptation is to squander our Master's resources in creating unprofitable structures which glorify man rather than God. But a far worse abuse of our stewardship is to appropriate our trust for our own selfish pleasure. This is tantamount to robbery and oppression of the needy who are our responsibility, and courts our Master's hot displeasure (see Luke 12:45,46). Christ's stewards must also be wise and industrious in cultivating and developing their gifts and potentials (see Matt. 25:14-30; Luke 19:11-27). The Lord commends diligence in this respect as a measure of his servants' love and loyalty, but condemns slothfulness and shirking as a wicked sabotage of his interests.

Under normal circumstances, hard work combined with modesty in providing for our own needs (and those of our household) will result in increased resources. Our natural temptation is to upgrade our standard of living accordingly; or worse, to become dependent on (or preoccupied with) our growing bank balance. But a wiser course of action is to seek the Lord's help in continued faithfulness to our enlarged responsibility.

"If your riches increase, don't depend on them." "Much is
required from the person to whom much is given; much more is
required from the person to whom much more is given."
(Psalm 62:10; Luke 12:48 GNB; see also 1 Tim 6:17,18).

Two major considerations determine the style of life in every
culture: Survival and Dignity.

SURVIVAL

Every society of people must come to terms with the forces
(benevolent or malevolent) that bear on its survival. The
necessity to develop adequate supplies of the vital resources of
water, food, energy, etc., and to provide security for life and
property is a factor which unites people together in communities.
The Ashanti nation (in Ghana) had a highly organized system of
clans for the purpose of defense against external aggression
and for community development. Social welfare was organized
at the level of the extended families within the clans. The
still smaller units of a compound each consisting of a husband
(the headman) with his several wives, children and dependents
provided the immediate sense of security and belonging. All
made good sense in a tropical, rural, agricultural society with
a rather high mortality rate.

The advantage of such gregarious (closely knit) societies is
that people matter, and on the whole they receive the care and
attention they need as human beings. They used to say there
were no "lonely individuals" (ankonam) in Ashanti, only members
of the families of the nation (omanfo). The security people find
in proper interpersonal and community relationships is an
effective check on the self-seeking instinct. Consequently
material possessions (such as there are) are shared more freely
and evenly. It is an observable fact that people who live in
such societies are usually very generous.

Industrialization on the other hand, tends to orient values
from people to things. Gradually people become merely cogs in
the wheels of good production. A man's value in an industrialized society is inevitably reckoned in economic terms. The
organization of industrial production disrupts normal community
and social life; and even the so-called nuclear family comes under considerable strain.

The resulting loneliness of individualism compels people to
seek security (protection against want, illness or redundancy,
etc.) in the acquisition of material goods. Anxiety, worry,
selfishness and indifference to the needs and interests of other
people are the symptoms of individualism in industrialized
nations. The insatiable urge to acquire more and better

possessions is at the bottom of the rat-race in such societies.
Paul calls it a trap: "Those who want to get rich fall into
temptation and are caught in the trap of many foolish and harmful desires, which pull them down to ruin and destruction"
(1 Tim. 6:19 GNB).   Preoccupation with mammon misses out on the
real values (i.e. wholesome human relationships and a vital
faith in God), and must inevitably lead to frustration and
disappointment.   Paul went on to say, "some have been so eager
to have it that they have wandered away from the faith and have
broken their hearts with many sorrows" (verse 10).

Before we consider Christ's response to the question of
survival, we must note the other factor, namely, the quest for
dignity.

DIGNITY

No people are content merely to exist.   The human urge is to
live in dignity.   Every human society has its ideals, values,
customs and procedures which are considered to be proper.   The
measure of dignity in that society is the degree to which its
members approximate those accepted ideals.   The outward
expressions of dignity and self respect usually include the
quality of clothes and ornaments worn, foods served, and
dwellings lived in.   It may also include a man's estate,
material possessions and the size of his family and dependents.

Egalitarian tribal societies are not necessarily classless.
However many organized tribes have in-built safeguards against
excesses and ostentation on the part of the individual members
of the community.   Among the Ashantis, certain items of clothing,
ornaments and furniture could only be used by chiefs and heads
of clans.   Even if an ordinary member of the clan could afford
those things, he was not permitted to use them.   This policy
contributed to sharing and an even distribution of material
possessions within the extended families and clans.

In our modern industrialized and consumer societies there is
no limit to what an individual may legitimately acquire,
provided he can afford it.   The media and advertising business
exploit to the full the acquisitive instinct which is part of
our human weakness.   Those who can afford surround themselves
with all the status symbols of our age, while those who cannot
admire or envy them!

Christ's answer to the disciples' perfectly human quest for
survival and dignity may be expounded from Matthew 6:24-34.   Man
everywhere looks for his survival and dignity in terms of
material possessions.   The GNP is virtually worshipped by man
and nations as the economic deity of modern society to which all

other values must be sacrificed! It is against the background
of a similar travesty that the Lord Jesus warned the disciples:
"You cannot serve both God and money" (verse 24). He proceeded
to show them the way to adequacy in God who claims their
exclusive devotion and loyalty. The Lord's teaching can be
summarized in three sentences: We have a Father God who cares.
Having such a Father should make all the difference between our
attitude to questions of survival and dignity and that of the
pagans in our society. The primary concern and commitment of
God's people should be the extension of his kingly reign and
the spreading of his righteous requirements.

The Lord's argument is unanswerable. God has done the greater
in creating our bodies and giving us life. We can at least
trust him to do the lesser--to care for our survival and fulfillment (see verse 25). Here are two telling illustrations.
The birds don't have to worry about survival. If any creature
should worry, it is surely they! Why, they have not the
capacity to sow, harvest, and store away; but we have! And the
God who takes care of these lesser creatures of his is our
Father in heaven (whose resources are limitless). The Lord has
a sense of humor: "Can any of you live a bit longer by worrying
about it?" (verse 27). Anxiety and worry, we know, are always
counterproductive. To worry about living longer is the surest
way to die younger!

Again, the wild flowers don't have to worry about beautiful
and dignified clothes. Could any other creature be more helpless in
this respect? They can't even move about, let alone work and
make clothes for themselves; but we can! And the God who takes
such astonishing care of ephemeral things like grass and wild
flowers is our Father! Moreover, he knows that we need food and
clothes. So then we must trust him for our needs and not worry
about them. Rather, our preoccupation should be our personal
submission to his kingly reign, and our commitment to live out
and spread its righteous requirements in society everywhere.

Christ commands and exhorts his followers not to worry about
the necessities of life. Over-anxiety is therefore sinful. It
is a disobedience as well as unbelief. When we worry, we dis-
trust our Father's wisdom, love and ability to keep his promise
to provide for his people. But suppose we argue: We have seen
many go without; and wisdom dictates we must lay up for the
future against such eventualities. Could it be, perhaps, that
many are having to go without the necessities of life because
those entrusted with more than they need are hoarding? What
about the greed of God's stewards who live wastefully on his
resources? God's stewards must function as pipes (channels)
through which his adequate supplies can reach all; not as buckets
to hold all our anticipated needs for the unforeseeable future!

Attempt must now be made to answer a number of specific
questions relevant to our discussion of the Christian life-style:
Can godliness and holiness of life in Christ demand in a given
culture attitudes and behavior that in another culture are not
required? Is true discipleship compatible with acquiescence in
values that weaken and even hinder full obedience to Christ?
Are there aspects of a Christian life-style that may be regarded as normative for the world-wide Church?

ATTITUDE AND BEHAVIOR

The Lausanne Covenant rightly states that "the gospel does not
presuppose the superiority of any culture to another, but
evaluates all cultures according to its own criteria of truth
and righteousness, and insists on moral absolutes in every
culture." (see clause 10: Evangelism and Culture)

Therefore there cannot be attitudes and behavior that
discipleship to Christ demands in a given culture which are not
required in other cultures. However the issues may be different
from culture to culture. For example, to take a personal stand
for Christ costs far more to a Christian (or a Church) in a
Moslem or a Communist society than to others in free western
society. But a personal stand for Christ is required of every
disciple. The issue of stewardship of possessions may be quite
simple to Christians living in more or less individualistic
societies. It is not so simple for those living in closely knit
communities and extended family systems. Their possessions are
really not theirs personally to dispose of as they wish. They
are held in trust for the whole extended family. Bishop Donald
Jacobs cites in his paper (see "Conversion and Culture," p. 175,
this volume) the Wakuria whose culture contains a strong
fertility theme which conflicts with the New Testament theme of
self-sacrifice. However the Wakuria Christians will have to
come to terms with the demands of discipleship which include the
prospect of leaving wife, children and property for the sake of
sacrificial service to Christ and the Gospel. I concur with a
statement by Dr. John Mbiti (at PACLA): "It is within our
culture that we have to wrestle with the demands of the Gospel.
....The gospel does not throw out culture: to the contrary, it
comes into our culture, it settles there, it brings its impact
on our total life within that culture. God does not want us to
be aliens to our culture--but only aliens to sin."

It would seem then that the Church in every culture has the
responsibility to pray, reflect, and work out the implications
of obedience to the Lord in the light of biblical teaching, and
in the context of her cultural situation. In this ongoing
exercise, the shared experience of churches in other cultures
will be helpful; but it should never become a substitute.

But the question may be asked: If the church in every culture sufficiently succeeded in reflecting her distinctive cultural situation, how would the universal, supra-cultural nature of Christianity appear? Could a Christian brother from the United States feel a sense of belonging and welcome in the congregation of a typical African Church in the Ivory Coast? Undoubtedly there will be some feeling of strangeness at first, in addition to the obvious problem of language and communication. But the universal mark of the Church of Christ is his discernible presence among his people everywhere through the Holy Spirit, and the sense of reverence, love, purity, peace and joy experienced in the fellowship of real believers (see Romans 14:17; Gal. 5:22, 23). Moreover, the Spirit-generated desire among Christians to share Christ beyond their own cultural boundaries inevitably exposes many to other cultures. Through the ministry of such international Christians, the universal nature of the Christian Church is manifested and affirmed.

THE PRESSURE TO CONFORM

Christians live in a world in revolt against God and his Christ (see Psalm 2). The Bible teaches that behind man's rebellion against God, and consequent slavery to sin, stands a sinister spiritual personality--Satan. He has hosts of other wicked spirits at his command, by the aid of which he exercises a usurped dominion of darkness over man and his world (see Eph. 6:11-12). He labors unceasingly to insure that the very structures, values, attitudes and life-style of man's world are all organized in opposition to God (Eph. 2:2-3, 1 John 2:15-17). This fact sheds light on the nature of the opposition Christians must expect to face as they seek to live out their obedience and loyalty to the Lord Jesus Christ in human society.

In every society there is usually a small group of the elite who wield ideological power over the rest. Their main interest may be social, political, economic, or religious. Someone has defined an ideology as a system of ideas and attitudes, with pretensions of objectivity and universality, which conceal the interests of a group, a class or a nation. Since the interest of the elite group or class is best protected by the acceptance of (or at least acquiescence in) the particular system by the entire society, every dissent or proposal of a live option becomes a threat. If the Christians' witness and way of life becomes identified with the protest against the particular ideology, they can expect to experience a variety of pressures to conform. National leaders with ideological interests have been known to try to silence the Church's prophetic voice, first of all, through flattery and bribery of her leadership. When this has failed, they have used ridicule and blackmail, followed

by threats and active persecution. The worst the active
persecution can do to a committed people of God is to drive them
to operate underground. But there is no future for a church
which trims its message and compromises its obedience to Christ
in order to become acceptable and respectable in society. But
there is a far worse state into which the spirit of compromise
may lead the Church. This is when the people of God become the
religious advocates of the popular ideology, and thereby
sanction sectional interests in the name of Christ. The Basel
Letter, issued by a WEF Consultation on Church and Nationhood
(1976) had some relevant words to say on this matter. It
recognized the desperate situation developing in many countries
today: "Some churches are growing rapidly but are finding the
civil authorities eager to use them to further political
objectives. Other churches are tiny minorities in vast pagan
populations. Frequently they are oppressed by secular powers
and, on occasion, dismissed with savage contempt. Still others
are being enticed to abandon their distinct Christian identity
and reduce their mission to mere political activity." The
Letter counselled a clear-cut stand on a number of issues including the following:

   Christians should resist pressure on churches to make them
mere religious tools of the State. At the same time, our
churches should not be permitted to enlist the State as their
political tool. We should not tolerate an intermingling of the
Gospel with any political, economic, cultural or nationalistic
ideology in such a way as to compromise the Gospel; nor should
we yield to the temptation of making our people or nation or
our nation's institutions the object of near-religious loyalty.
The loyalty of Christians to the one worldwide Body of Christ
should transcend loyalty to tribe, class, race or nation. Our
Christian concern for the community of mankind, created by God
in his likeness, should enable us to stand firmly against all
forms of legislated discrimination based on race or color.
Churches were called upon to exercise their prophetic role in
society. They should summon civil authorities to their God-
appointed task of promoting justice in society. The cost of
such a prophetic ministry in terms of the Christians' call to
participatory suffering was fully recognized. The prevailing
moral decay, economic injustice and political oppression makes
urgent the church's role as salt of the earth and light of the
world. Crucial to this role is its corporate life, as the
sign of Christ's kingdom, in a visible community that exhibits
the righteousness, peace, and love of his reign.

NORMATIVE LIFE-STYLE?

Can we really speak of a normative Christian life-style in spite of the obvious diversity of our social, political, racial and cultural backgrounds? I believe we can, provided we mean something much deeper than what these superficial differences imply. The rationale behind the distinctively Christian style of life urged on us everywhere in Scripture is the new (divine) nature we now share in common with our risen Lord and Savior Jesus Christ (Rom. 7:4-6). This is the glorious result of our new birth into God's family by God's Spirit with God's Word (John 1:12,13; 3:5; James 1:18; 1 Peter 1:23; Gal. 3:26). The Spirit of Christ has written God's law deep on our hearts and minds as the new principle of life (2 Cor. 3:2,3). He has taken his residence in us as our indwelling source of moral and spiritual strength to live the life worthy of our Lord and pleasing to him in everything (Romans 8:2,9). Submission to the sanctifying and renewing work of the Holy Spirit with God's Word produces in every Christian (from whatever cultural background) the same fruit of the Spirit. Essentially, then, a normative Christian life-style may be described as a life habitually fed and led by God's truth (the Scriptures), which results in a progressive reflection of God's holiness (Christlikeness) in personal character, and God's love and righteousness in personal relationships.

The Bible contains numerous descriptions of this life and its essential qualities. For example:

The fruit of the Spirit:	love, joy, peace, patience, kindness, goodness, faithfulness, gentleness, self-control. (Gal. 5:22,23; see also 1 Cor 13:4-7)
The Wisdom from above:	pure, peaceable, gentle, open to reason, full of mercy and good fruits, certain, sincere, righteous. (James 3:17,18)
The Blossom of Shared Divine Nature:	faith, virtue, knowledge, self-control, steadfastness, godliness, brotherly affection, love (2 Peter 1:5-7)
The New Being in God's Image:	compassionate, kind, lowly, meek, patient, forebearing, forgiving, loving, peaceful, thankful, etc. (Col 3:10-15; see also Eph. 4:1-3)
The Praise-worthy Conduct:	whatever is true, honorable, just, pure, lovely, gracious, virtuous, etc. (Phil 4:8)

The inner force of the distinctive Christian life manifests
itself in terms of truth, holiness and love. The particular
cultural dress which these qualities may wear from place to
place is of secondary importance. "Here there cannot be Greek
and Jew, circumcised and uncircumcised, barbarian, Scythian,
slave, free man, but Christ is all, and in all" (Col. 3:11).
The most outstanding thing about any Christian therefore should
not be his culture--his hairstyle, his jewelry, his clothes,
etc.--but his "true inner self, the ageless beauty of a gentle
and quiet spirit, which is of the greatest value in God's sight"
(see 1 Peter 3:4). It must be so for it reflects the beauty of
his Son, who invites us to learn from him because he is gentle
and humble in spirit (see Matt. 11:29). By the same token the
Christian's true inner beauty will inevitably manifest itself
in the modesty of his tastes and choices, whether in clothes,
foods, dwellings, furniture, etc., always having an eye to the
needs of others as well as of his own (see 1 Tim. 2:9,10).

LIFE-STYLE AND MISSION

The Lausanne Covenant called for sacrificial living and sacrificial giving with a purpose--namely, in order to contribute
more generously to both relief and evangelism. The basis of the
call is the urgency of the evangelistic task: the spiritual
needs of the more than two-thirds of mankind who have yet to be
evangelized. Then there are the poor, starving millions of
humanity--victims of socio-economic injustice or natural
disaster or both--for whom God's people have inescapable
Christian responsibility (see Lausanne Covenant clause 9: The
Urgency of the Evangelistic Task). That is the task from a
global perspective.

From the point of view of Christians' immediate contact and
involvement with their fellow men, their life-style affects
(for better or for worse) both the credibility and the
communication of their message. Speaking on Christian service
and witness at the Pan-African Christian Leadership Assembly,
John Mbiti gave the following challenge to the Church in Africa:

"The Christian Faith is not just a private bank account which
the depositor uses secretly or privately. It is public property
which has to be shared through service and proclaimed through
evangelism. It is at the very heart of what our Lord himself
did: He went about preaching the Gospel, healing the sick,
raising the dead, feeding the hungry....

"African Church life must reflect and incarnate this work of
our Lord, within the context of the peoples of Africa. There
are many who are ready to listen to the Gospel--but they must
hear it in their own languages and life situations. There are

many who are sick; the Gospel must bring them hope, healing and
newness of life. There are many who are spiritually and morally
dead, politically oppressed, economically exploited, socially
ostracized. The Gospel and the Church must bring healing to
them all. There are many who are hungry--physically starving,
eating only the crumbs that fall from their master's table,
babies suffering from malnutrition, thousands crying out for the
food of love, the food of justice, the food of care....the
Gospel and the Church must feed them first. Unless they have
enough to eat and drink, unless they are touched by the grain
of love, they will be too concerned about their stomachs to hear
the Gospel, unless they are socially and economically given to
eat (set free), they will not understand what the Gospel is all
about. The centre of the hungry man is his stomach, and not his
heart. The centre of the oppressed man is the chains that bind
his legs and hands, and not his head. The centre of the
destitute is not his soul but his basic rights and his craving
for love. African Church life should address itself to these
centres of human life."

This is the language of self-sacrificing, caring love which
is understood in every culture of man.

17

Contextualization of the Gospel in Fiji: A Case Study from Oceania

Alan R. Tippett

In this essay an attempt is made to show that the context of Christian evangelization and application has both cultural and historical dimensions. Contextualization is taken to mean the process of making evangelism and the new lifestyle relevant in the specifics of time and space. This leads us into a study of encounters between the Gospel and culture.

This is a case study from Oceania in which we consider Christian contextualization in the history and culture of a single people--the Fiji Islanders.

The testing tool used is borrowed from applied anthropology (F. E. Williams). It comprises three critical questions to ask and answer about cultural institutions before engaging in "directed change" (i.e. evangelization) if the change is to be relevant and permanent:

> Should it be maintained?
> Should it be expurgated?
> Should it be expanded?

The data is arranged according to the ethnohistorical method
known as the cultural continuum and reveals that cultural context varies at different levels of time depth even within a
single culture.

THEORETICAL PREAMBLE

I write this paper as an anthropologist, but as one with a
strong leaning towards ethnohistory. The Christian lifestyle
of any church, like its planting and growing, always (1) bears
on its cultural context, and (2) has to be considered in time
perspective. There are two ways in which a planted church community can be "foreign." On the one hand the structures, opera-
tions and values may be culturally alien, or on the other hand a
church may have been planted with patterns that are now archaic,
having failed to change relevantly with the times within a given
culture. Thus we need to realize that a comprehensive treatment
of Christian lifestyle, as it relates to context, can be studied
either synchronically or diachronically.

A synchronic discussion of the context of the conversion of,
say, some Pacific Island to Christ permits examination of the
cross-cultural relations of evangelists and converts at a given
point in time (*across* time). A diachronic discussion permits
examination of the changing contexts in which the Christian
lifestyle is manifested through a century or more of culture
history (*through* time). The former relates more particularly to
pioneering thrusts of mission, the latter to second and third
generation communities of Christians. In Oceania (the region
assigned to this paper) we meet both these situations, so the
differentiation has to be made.

The contextualization of the English evangel of, say, 1835 to
1874 in Fiji (the pioneering period of mission) requires the
same form of analysis as that of the Fijian evangel from 1874
onwards in New Britain and New Ireland (also the pioneering.
period). This is not something which applies only to western
evangelism, but to all cross-cultural evangelistic pioneering
thrusts. The problem is always the same--getting the Gospel
from one's own culture into another with which he is less
familiar.

The diachronic approach in the Pacific requires a particular
time-line for each ethnic group because of the differences in
their historic experiences. Thus, for example, many Micronesian
communities have passed through periods of Spanish, German,
Japanese and American influence, with terrific value changes and
discontinuities in each period. This factor has not been considered adequately in Micronesian historical and missionary an-
alyses. Vastly different, however, is the case of Fiji, say,

whose history falls comfortably into three levels of time depth
--pre-colonial, colonial and post-colonial--which reflect not
only the political contexts but many of the social changes and,
to a large extent, the missionary strategy. This group also
provides data for the study of the cultural continuities which
run through the time span of the diachrony, and help us to see
how indigenous the young church was at each level of time depth.

This paper will take the case of Fiji as a basic model for
investigation. It might well have been Samoa, or Tonga, or some
region of Papua New Guinea, but a paper of this kind must be limited in length so a choice had to be made. However we should
be careful before taking one Pacific group as typical because
each has its own unique set of data. The method of analysis used
in the following pages is that known in ethnohistory as the *cultural continuum* approach, and I shall use the diachrony suggested in the above paragraph, after indicating some of the basic continuities that run through all levels of time depth.

BASIC CONTINUITIES

Three notions in the Fijian way of thinking and operating
were accepted from the beginning of the Fijian Mission. They
become basic continuities which ramify through the history of
the Fijian Church to this day. I mention these before turning
to the main body of our discussion, because they are so essentially basic to the Fijian context that the church could not
have been indigenous without recognizing them. They are (1) the
notion of multi-individual people movements as the form of conversion, (2) the notion of the role of herald, or go-between, in
community ceremonial, and (3) the notion of culture change being
possible, provided the approved persons and mechanisms were employed to bring it about.

1. *The Notion of Multi-Individual People Movements*

The mission to Fiji came from the British Wesleyans (W.M.S.).
The pioneering missionaries, Cross and Cargill, landed in Lakeba
in 1835. Both had served a short term in Tonga, where they had
witnessed the Great Awakening--a people movement that spread
throughout Tonga in a couple of years. They had witnessed the
character of these conversions, the confessions of the converts,
their destruction of religious paraphernalia and all the other
aspects of the dynamics of this kind of religious change as it
manifested itself in Polynesia. (For a documented study of this
see my *People Movements of Southern Polynesia*.)

The importance of this to Fiji was that the Fiji Mission began with the acceptance of the notion of large people movements
from paganism to Christ. What came through the 1840s and 1850s

was exactly what they expected and they had an army of Tongan preachers to handle it. They understood the multi-individual character of decision-making and group action. In some places this was a problem to the missionaries, but not so in Fiji. In any case the movements had much in common with the English Evangelical Revival, of which many Wesleyan missionaries at the time were the products only one generation removed.

The missionary documents of the period show that immediate perfection was not expected of the converts, but rather that two spiritual experiences were expected—first conversion from paganism to Christ and later as the Christian *koinonia* began to function there followed a second conversion, an experience of salvation from sin which required a knowledge of the word and a sharing of the *koinonoi*. The first took place in the pagan context itself, the second within the *koinonia*. The important thing to point out in reporting this is that all this was not an imposition of missionary theology on the situation, but rather missionary reaction to what actually happened. They described each experience as "fresh manifestations of grace." The theology came out of what they believed to be "the working of the Holy Spirit" within the Fijian context. They believed that they themselves were in the stream of God's will in going to Fiji, and that he was working in their midst. The conversions were culturally patterned but it never occurred to them to see the group movements as of any other but God. God was working this way and they continually gave him praise for it. As the converts matured in the faith the missionaries found themselves praying for divine manifestations within the contextual pattern.

2. *The Notion of the Go-Between in Community Ceremonial*

Also within their Tongan experiences the pioneering missionaries were introduced to several aspects of the Fijian context. Fiji was not unknown in Tonga. There was considerable trade and social intercourse between the two. Colonies of Tongan carpenters and canoe-builders were scattered about Fiji and many Tongans understood the Fijian languages. Many Fijian chiefs married the lighter-skinned Tongan women. The language of Lau had Tongan constructions and vocabulary, and most of these Fijians to the windward were fluent in Tongan. Likewise there were Fijians in Tonga. One of these, a chief of Fulaga, had been taken there to teach the Fijian war dances to the Tongans. He had been converted in the Great Awakening and became an aggressive evangelical Christian.

This man (Christian name Josua Mateinaniu) taught the early missionaries the rudiments of Fijian and returned with them to his own country in 1835. He guided the first missionaries through the maze of Fijian ceremonials of introduction and re-

quest, which secured the formal acceptance of missionary residence in Lakeba.

Through the efforts of this herald, or go-between, the missionaries went everywhere in the correct manner, they approached
the right people, and performed the right courtesies. Many missions in the Pacific failed at this point. Without a knowledge
of correct procedure they ran into all kinds of obstructions.
But in Fiji, where customary procedure is as complicated as anywhere in the Pacific probably, because they had a good herald
they ran into no trouble. The missionaries were well aware of
this and leaned heavily on Mateinaniu for all kinds of decision-
making, and especially for pioneering missionary thrusts into
new regions of Fiji. He had enough chiefly status to command a
hearing, but not too much so as to be politically suspect.

Again the missionaries interpreted this theologically. It
fitted their doctrine of prevenient grace. Was it not the Lord
himself who had sent them on this mission to Fiji, and the same
Lord who had sent this man to open up the way for them? And
God said to Mateinaniu, as he did to Cyrus of Persia, "I have
girded thee though thou hast not known me."

Thus, from the very beginning, the missionaries to Fiji
learned to use the herald, or go-between. The herald is the
cog in the whole Fijian system. This man holds everything together in equilibrium. He holds a sacred and protected position. He stands protected between two enemies, between two
chiefs, between two communities, between two trading parties,
between two occupational groups, between chiefs and commoners,
between families contracting marriage. He interprets the one
to the other. He smooths over the difficult negotiation. He
restores peace in times of disagreement and war, and in times
of peace he sees it is maintained. He says and does things in
the right way so there need be no suspicion or ill-will. This
is the *mata*. He argues. He pleads. He welcomes. He fare-
wells. He negotiates. He interprets. You cannot have a national or civil assembly in Fiji without a *mata*—or a church
one either. This is a major element of Fijian social or religious organization. The missionaries did not impose it on
the Fijian society. They found it already there.

3.   *The Notion of Social Change and How It Is Brought About*

This becomes important if we take social change to include
religious change, as it certainly does. The principle has been
established by anthropologists (e.g., Barnett, Kroeber) that
people change when and if they want to do so. The advocate of
an innovation has to "sell" his idea. The real innovator is
the acceptor of the idea. He alone brings about the change.

Thus the evangelist may advocate the person's conversion, but he does not convert him. The point must be made that historically, in spite of the persecution in some places, Fiji was ripe for the Gospel. In hundreds of ways the place was intensely innovative.

A frequent myth among some popular journalists is to dichotomize human societies as either tribal or static on the one hand, or innovative or progressive on the other. Nothing could be more unfair to tribal societies. The possibility of social and/or religious change is built into every tribal society, its structures and social mechanisms. Every village assembly, every meeting of the gerontocracy, every family council implies some topic for discussion, some potential change to be made, some decision to be debated before action.

As with the legal system in our own society, tradition lays down guidelines with expectation of reasonable stability, and custom conditions lifestyle not laid down legally; but there is no human society so rigid that it will not consider innovation. And a study of pre-Christian Fijian aesthetics--poetry, chanting, art, pottery and the creativity manifest in riddle-making for competitive entertainment, say--all show the pre-Christian society as far from static.

A whole paper, longer than this one, could be given to a study of innovation in the pioneering decade of missionary contact. Pagan values were being discarded and Christian values accepted (even prior to conversion). Sexy songs were being cast aside and a new type was emerging (or new involution of old types). New Christian uses were found for Fijian bark-cloth and given Christian symbolism. The technology of carving warclubs and spears was being channeled into the manufacture of more peaceful artifacts. Some missionaries who were craftsmen in their own peculiar ways (notably Thomas Williams and John Hunt) introduced the Fijians to arts like burning lime and crushing the juice from sugar-cane. Gardens began to appear round the dwelling houses. Missionary wives taught the Fijian women to knit and crochet--the latter being one of their most highly developed skills today, and an interesting case of a western skill which became utterly indigenized immediately.

All these aesthetic and technological innovations date back to the pioneering period and often preceded the acceptance of the Gospel. They show how intensely innovative the people were, even to the cultural borrowing from outsiders, because they saw some advantage in accepting the new ideas for incorporation into their own cultural context.

Customs like cannibalism and widow-strangling, which had a
social and religious underpinning, were very much on the decline
before the Fijians became Christian. Fijian warriors and cannibals were using Tongan-made weapons of war, and Fijian craftsmen
were copying them. They also reflect changes in the techniques
of war. Most craft groups had their Fijian origin myths, but in
the period before the coming of the Gospel we find a spread of
rival myths--all with strong Tongan characteristics. Undoubtedly
Tongan acculturation was widespread in Fiji when the Gospel came.
It also came from Tonga.

Without doubt the Gospel came to Fiji in a day of dramatic
social change, and to a people who were ready to consider the
claims of new forms of prayer and worship, and new kinds of chanting and singing--or at least to change the content of their traditional styles of devotion and music. The whole religious system was open for change. Fiji, at the time, was divided between
seven kingdoms, none with a king powerful enough to reduce the
rest or unify the whole. Western arms and ammunition, alcohol,
venereal disease and cannibal war were reducing the population
at a tremendous rate. Although Fiji was looking for a military
unifier she was open even to a non-military message.

The greatest change advocated by the first missionaries was
the offer of literacy. Within twelve years the New Testament
had been reduced to Fijian writing and printed and every Fijian
convert learned to read and write. It was the Fijian New Testament which gave Fiji a *lingua franca* and unified Fiji except for
two mountain tribes.

Not only were the Fijian people innovative, but they were
more or less free to innovate. They innovated because they
wanted to do so. They were, in most of the commonplace things
of life, their own decision-makers. What was more important to
the Fijian was frequently not "May I innovate?", but "What is
the correct procedure for innovation? How? When?" And this depended on the level of innovation. The craftsman was free
within the confines of his craft. Hunters, fishermen, agricul-
turalists, potters and so on, except for communal social responsibilities, were free to go and come in their own pursuits.
Priests were remarkably free to innovate. They innovated at
will and none dared say them nay. Often they took the initiative
of rejecting the old religion and turning first to the Gospel.
Normally they were either the first or the last to be converted--
i.e. the prime acceptors or the prime objectors.

Any individual could reject his personal religion, domestic
"gods," or cast out his sacred paraphernalia. However, the family gods were a family matter, and the tribal gods were a tribal
matter. These called for group action after discussion. Some-

times several meetings were held before a consensus was reached.
There are even cases on record of the group giving permission to
a sub-group to convert. In such cases usually the remainder followed a month or so later.

On the level of the kingdom which was the highest political
unit and enemy of all the other kingdoms the question of loyalty
to the king was involved and people hesitated to convert without
his approval. However, there are cases on record of Cakobau
finding that the Christians (or those who wanted to become
Christian) were his most loyal supporters, and therefore grant-
ing them freedom of choice in the matter of religion. Several
whole islands immediately became Christian. Apparently the missionaries were nervous at this point and urged their believers
to safeguard their loyalty to the king at all times. They could
have lost their cause here especially during the war period when
these island communities provided the non-military resources of
the king. Loyalty to the king was always a complicating factor
in the Fijian context.

In the case of Cakobau's own conversion, which I have re-
searched at length, he took counsel on three levels before taking the step. The first was on his personal domestic level with
his wife and the evangelist. He made his personal decision here.
Then he called his kinship group and secured their approval.
The next day he called the assembly of his political unit-king-
dom, where the discussion fell very largely on the matter of
loyalty. On the following Sunday he attended worship and symbolically "bowed the knee to the Lord," some 300 of his supporters joining him. Other kin sub-units followed over the next
few months. This was a typical movement. "Bowing the knee" also
is typical of Fiji--a symbolic gesture in the presence of the
Christian group. It brought the convert within the prayer-
support of the fellowship of believers. I believe this had a
Fijian rather than a missionary origin, but I cannot prove the
point.

In passing let me reiterate: there is no doubt whatever about
the freedom to innovate in such a tribal society, a society ready
for religious change will certainly change; but the matter of
deeper concern is how one goes about it, what are the in-built
social mechanisms for such change. The missionary advocate can
win or lose all in this matter of how he goes about allowing his
converts to separate themselves from their old ways and incorporates them in the *koinonia*. The most tragic mistakes of cross-
cultural evangelism have frequently been at this point.

These, then, were the three basics from the very beginning of
the Fiji Mission, the notion of multi-individual group conversions, the notion of the herald, or go-between in all community

ceremonials (which included the young church being planted), and
the notion of the acceptability of religious change provided it
is carried out in line with cultural procedure. These three
factors gave the Fiji Mission a certain momentum from the very
start, and later missionaries would have had no hope of changing
them even if they had desired to do so. Theologically the missionaries accepted the idea that God had sent them there and had
demonstrated his presence even in a cultural situation which was
far removed from their own.

I now turn from these continuities to the changing cultural
context at each of the three levels of time depth I have suggested above; and I hope that by doing so something relevant
will be said for other missions at each of these respective levels somewhere today.

THREE LEVELS OF TIME DEPTH

I. The Pre-Colonial Level

As we turn to examine in more detail the pagan/Christian encounter in the pagan Fijian context in the contact period, I
want to differentiate between two types of encounter which, for
the want of better terms I shall call *direct* and *indirect* encounter. The former were encounters with cultural institutions
founded on false values or beliefs. Here there could be no compromise for Christianity. They were manifestly incompatible and
had to be replaced by Christian values or beliefs. Both the
pioneering evangelists and the pagan Fijians knew this and the
conflict was direct--face-to-face. There could be no dynamic
equivalence here, and probably no Christian functional substitutes because the basic values were anti-Christian.

However there were other types of encounter which came out of
customary procedures, and related to the meeting of felt-needs,
and called for a deeper appreciation of function. Sometimes
they created moral problems for Fijian converts and these often
came after conversion rather than as obstructions to conversion.
The issues were not so clear-cut. These indirect encounters
raised a different set of questions. What should be preserved?
What should be discarded? What should be modified? These are
still the basic questions for the applied anthropologist.

The best examples of direct encounter--i.e., encounters which
became obstructions to conversion--were pagan warfare, cannibalism, widow-strangling and patricide. I shall look at these
very briefly (having dealt with them at greater length elsewhere). Then I shall turn to the more subtle indirect encounters which created problems for the moral life of converts. They
concern social structure, kinship loyalties, rites of passage,

aesthetics, agriculture, economics and technology. Finally, I
shall end this summary of the Fijian context of the pre-colonial
period by raising the question of Fijian thought itself--did it
supply the intellectual conceptualization necessary for the
emergence of a Christian theology which was at the same time
indigenous?

1. *Direct Encounters:*

(a) *Fijian Pagan Warfare:* When the Gospel first came to
the group the Fijian societies were completely involved in war.
In spite of the fact that they were psychologically ready for
religious change, the missionaries' first contextual confrontation was with war itself. They found that war hindered both the
acceptance and the spread of the Gospel. The Fijian wars of the
contact period are well-documented in both secular and missionary
sources and several anthropologists have worked over the material. The greatest ethnolinguistic florescence of the Fijian
language of the contact period was the diversification of war
terminology.

There were two kinds of warfare in old Fiji--(1) petty
skirmishing on the local level, which related to social functions like training youth for war, cannibalism and low-level ri-
valries; and (2) the large scale "war of the chiefs" between two
tribes, a bitter struggle of total communal effort until one of
the paramount chiefs was killed. These I have described in detail in the *Proceedings* of the Fijian Society and in *Fijian Material Culture*. Here I merely point out the existence of the
two types of war and their completely different social functions. The best reporter of these differentiations was John
Hunt (*Journal*) between 1838 and 1848.

The social value which undergirded the war orientation was
the notion of the *perpetuity of the tribe*. The inter-tribal
war--i.e., between the larger social groups, "kingdoms" (*mata-
nitu*), not feuds between villages or families--reached to every
corner of Fiji. At one time in the contact period seven major
wars were being fought at the same time. The loyalty of a
smaller group, family or village, was always suspect, however,
when one became Christian--i.e., pacifist. A Christian convert
(individual) could hardly survive within a pagan village. He
might detach himself from the village and remove to a Christian
village, or join a mixed group of Christian refugees (a Christian sodality) who had settled near some mission station, but
he was branded as pacifist (which meant a defector or disloyal-
ist) and was extremely vulnerable.

When a village turned Christian its very existence was precarious for a period of time. Scores of such villages (I can

supply names and locations of many) were completely wiped out by
pagan war parties, their men eaten, and the women and children
enslaved. Such massacres were either initiated by the pagan war
parties for the sake of plunder, or inspired by the prophetic
oracles of the local heathen priest who felt threatened by the
spread of Christianity. But the rationalization or justification
for all such massacres was that it was appropriate to their tribal disloyalty.

Yet in spite of this, Christianity spread because of the
fearless faith of her converts. It was on this account that the
chief Ra Esekaia surrendered his chiefly inheritance and turned
his office over to his younger brother, because he knew that as
a Christian he could never rule his pagan subjects. He relied
on his high birth to protect him and devoted his energies to protecting the Christian group. This was an interesting political
compromise, a social mechanism which permitted the church to get
established in a bitterly pagan context in the decade before the
people movement phase.

The greatest Fijian peacemaker was Ilaija Varani, whose life
story is well-documented. He was the Viwa war lord and right-
hand man of the famous cannibal king, Cakobau. The heathens
were astonished at his conversion and a plot was organized to
humiliate him and force him into an act of military retaliation.
His Christian reaction convinced everyone of the genuineness of
his conversion, and thereafter he traveled fearlessly from one
warring state to another as a Christian peacemaker, a ministry
which eventually cost him his life.

One of the greatest documents of this period is the autobiographical journal of Joeli Bulu, the Tongan Christian evangelist
in Fiji. It describes numerous war situations in which he was
involved in restraining the new Fijian converts from military
retaliation. What stood out about the character of these Christian converts was the fearlessness of their pacifism. History
showed that no man was more adept than Bulu for turning a hopeless war situation into a faith situation (miracle). One does
not wonder that many of these men, upon Christian baptism, chose
for themselves names of Old Testament heroes of the faith, like
Joshua and Elijah. It was indeed a world of Old Testament power
encounter.

However, the social value of the Fijian context which the
pagan Fijian felt to be threatened by Christianity was the notion
that war (skill in war and victory) was the only way of safeguarding the perpetuity of the tribe. The Christian converts
demonstrated this to be a false assumption, but many lost their
lives doing so. The charge against the Christian convert was

tribal disloyalty. They went out of their way to demonstrate tribal loyalty in non-military ways.

(b) Cannibalism: The first missionaries to Fiji found themselves in a world of institutionalized cannibalism, although this was passing through a rapid transition at the time, and had been doing so for some 25 or 30 years. Prior to that, cannibalism was a ritualized mechanism for correcting social wrongs, prosecuting feuds and relieving feelings of hate. As with many other inhumane customs, it was religiously ritualistic and hedged with taboos. It was confined to certain persons and to specific situations, and completely barred from women and children.

Its secularization began in the first decade of the 19th Century, when sandalwood traders and escaped convicts began bringing western arms and ammunition to Fiji and participating in Fijian wars. They upset the balance of power and by increasing the range of the weapons they provided a surplus of cannibal flesh for the ovens. The taboos broke down. Women began to partake of the feasting, and they rubbed the flesh on the lips of their infants to cultivate their taste for it. By the time the missionaries arrived the system had been completely secularized. The older informants told the missionaries that they remembered the days of the taboos when things had been well under control. Many chiefs were displeased with the changes, and some from quite pagan areas felt that cannibalism had run its course and was no longer socially functional, and therefore should be disposed of.

In areas of Christian influence cannibalism declined even before the people were converted--almost as if the "field was ripening unto harvest." Before long cannibalism survived only in hard-core pagan areas where it was perceived as a kind of anti-Christian resistance symbol. A flow chart of the spread of Christianity in Fiji is also a flow chart of the decline of cannibalism. However, it should be pointed out that while becoming Christian meant rejecting cannibalism, there were also many pagan leaders who had rejected it of their own volition by the end of the 1850s. With or without Christianity, cannibalism, after having been out of control for some 50 years, had now begun to wane. Meantime, for the purpose of this present paper, Christianity stood in direct encounter with cannibalism. There was no middle course, and both Christian and pagan knew it.

(c) Widow-strangling: Widows were strangled for burial with their deceased husbands. This was especially so in the case of great chiefs and warriors. In the case of a regional paramount chief, a bodyguard of warriors and a few slaves might also be strangled. Strangulation was considered an honorable death, and it was shameful or dishonorable for a widow to attempt any

escape from the ritual death. In Christian times when the custom declined, partly because of missionary appeals against it,
many widows who could have been saved from death cried out bitterly for it, and some even committed suicide.

In the case of a powerful polygamous chief *all* the wives were
strangled. The ceremonial was ritually performed and only persons of a specified social status in relation to the victim
could pull the strangling cord. The manner of a widow's death
was a matter of pride and prestige, and they died in a flourish
of glory.

The custom has a theological (eschatological) motivation. A
big chief or warrior, upon his death, would be deified (even a
smaller chief could become an annoying spirit), normally as a
war divinity with a particular interest in his own clan or tribe.
Those who had fought and lived under his authority would begin
to worship him. Their success in war, and therefore the perpetuity of the group, depended on the effectiveness of this worship. To dishonor the dead in any way would bring disaster on
the whole group that remained. The easiest road to dishonor was
to downgrade the funerary rites by dispatching him into the
afterlife without wives and servants, so that he arrived there
as an insignificant person. The living had to retain good relations with the dead for both positive and negative reasons.

The only counter for this complex of belief and custom was a
Christian eschatology--and this was a matter of instruction after conversion.

The missionaries (supported by their converts) battled against
this custom in the pagan context and used all the ceremonial procedures of courtesy and respectful request in their attempt to
persuade the leaders of the funerary rites to spare the lives of
the widows. In the absence of male missionaries, their wives
sometimes undertook the formal ceremonial requesting. These performances throughout were correctly done according to Fijian
respect and custom and the pleaders were given a respectful hearing. Because of this mutual respect they were partly successful.
Some, but not all the widows were spared. Not until the people
became Christian and learned a new Christian eschatology was
widow-strangling brought under control. This new theology alone
revealed the fallacy on which widow-strangling was founded.

The pagan-Christian dialogue on widow-strangling ran like
this:

Christian: We plead for the life of this widow. We love her.
            Spare her life.

Pagan: But we love her also. And we love the dead. We will not shame or dishonor her by denying her the prestige of her ritual duty. Nor will we shame the dead by denying him his place of respect in the world of the dead.

Christian: We talk of love, not of shame.

Pagan: How else can one demonstrate one's love, but by saving a person from shame?

And neither party was able to understand the other, for the pagan and Christian eschatologies offered no common ground for dialogue.

One ought also to add that the woman who escaped the strangling-cord had a miserable life thereafter. Society provided no social mechanisms for her comfort.

We have here an important anthropological point: when the locus of encounter between Christian and pagan values has theological rather than social underpinnings nothing but a theological change can dispose of it. In this case, the compromise of sparing some widows but not all shows that the pagans had not conceded anything at the level of the belief system. They compromised out of respect for requests made correctly, ceremonially and respectfully--and no more. Furthermore they left the "saved" widows without any cultural protections to survive without respect. Such widows had no alternative but to become Christian with or without spiritual conviction. Some such preferred to commit suicide.

    (d) Patricide: Another custom in the Fijian context of the contact period was the killing of the aged. This was either by strangling or by live burial--both were honorable deaths, as distinct from clubbing, say, as one would use against an enemy.

The aged might be strangled or buried for any one of several reasons. Care of the aged was always a social burden in a society subject to sudden enemy attack. When age or sickness rendered a person incapable of caring for himself, he might be ceremonially strangled with all due pomp and ceremony by his eldest son and heir. This was to give him honor and avoid the possibility of his being left behind to be clubbed by the enemy and possibly eaten--a shameful death that demanded retaliation. In some places the aged were placed in a small temporary house, a "waiting house" or a "house for death," outside the village, and visited daily by a servant with food. It was a miserable end to life and normally the "victim" would request his eldest son for strangulation or burial--lest an enemy come and he be

unable to defend himself. At least this would give him the
honor of a noble death and the funerary rites of respect.

A great chief or warrior might become aware that "his hand
had lost its cunning" and know that in the interest of tribal
security his son should take over his office. He might find his
son preparing his funerary rites even while he was yet alive.
Then, with all due decorum he would find himself in the grave,
with his son stamping down the earth on the mat above him with
the ceremonial words--"Sir, your sun has set!"

In all these pagan situations the Fijian argued that this was
the kindest way of doing things, and this he would justify with
theological arguments. They believed that the body passed on
into the afterlife in the state it was at death. It was therefore a bad thing for a man to become aged or decrepit. No
Fijian wanted to be senile forever. A man wanted to die while
he could still hunt and fish and defend himself from his enemies,
using his tools and weapons with dexterity and engage in fluent
repartee. Thus, if he felt his physical decline in any way he
expected his son and heir to take the matter into his own hands
and dispatch him hence. He regarded this as a merciful act.
And here is another example of a custom with underpinnings of
faulty eschatology, which nothing could correct but conversion
followed by education in the doctrine of the Christian hope.

To this point we have been dealing with direct encounters between Christianity and Paganism. They were obstructions to the
acceptance of the Gospel that disappeared with conversion and
Christian education. We now turn to moral problems which came
from the Fijian context after conversion; not problems of becoming Christian but of being Christian.

2. *Indirect Encounters:*

Not all the face-to-face confrontations of the new Christian way of life were direct encounters, calling for *expurgation*
(Anthropologist F. E. Williams' term). There were many cases of
maintenance in which Christianity retained the old Fijian way,
as it were, sanctifying it, or absorbing it into its new selfhood. Thus the structure of the church which emerged in Fiji
was itself utterly Fijian. Many of these were smooth transitions but others did involve the converts in some moral battles.
Social structure itself was a smooth transition. But there were
aspects of the marriage pattern, the rituals of agriculture and
the forms of the dance, for example, which involved value modifications before acceptance. Let us glance very briefly at
these items I have mentioned.

(a) *Social Structure:* Under the head of "Continuities" we have already discussed several aspects of Fijian social organization, which were taken over by the Christian *koinonia* when it was first planted. One was the system of mediation through person and functional role of the herald. Another was the group decision-making pattern, in which long discussion strove for a consensus that would permit corporate action as a result. Decisions passed on a narrow majority (western style) have never been effective in Fiji. The issue comes back year after year and no fixed policy is reached. A good example of this is the church law on drinking yaqona. Some of the later Victorian missionaries persisted in equating it with the western temperance issue, but this was never so in the first generation of Fijian Christianity. We shall return to this when we consider the colonial level. Withholding action until a consensus in the long run may well be the shortest way of solving a problem.

These matters of organizational structure expressed the natural Fijian ways of doing things and the Fijian converts allowed them to continue as the lifestyle with which they were familiar. In those I have just mentioned no moral issues were involved in the organizational procedures--though of course a subject being debated might well be a moral issue. One could also argue, with plenty of supporting data, that the emerging church manifested remarkable structural similarities with the political organization of Fiji itself.

For example, the idea of the assembly (*bose*) of the group for discussion (*veivosaki*) and decision-making (*lewā*) ramified through every level of social life from the household to the nation, exactly as it did through the corresponding levels of the church courts. The tribal structure of such assemblies at different levels, each with its own specified autonomy was taken over by the church at large. The Fijian pattern of separate meetings for homogeneous units, craft groups, work parties, family ceremonials, etc., permitted the missionaries to operate as an integrated group (district meeting, etc.) and to establish a Fijian evangelists' independent advisory committee to discuss social and religious problems of contextualization, and pass on their decisions and opinions to the missionaries. This saved the missionaries from many a bad mistake in matters of custom.

As soon as the Christian community was perceived as a cohesive entity two things were possible. It was expected to meet on its own. It could relate to other persons and groups. The little growing *koinonia* was recognized as a religious group because it was recognizably so: it used the prayer/worship/sacrifice/chant vocabulary of the Fijian religious life and reached out to the Power beyond man.

Then the church organized itself into sub-groups in a truly indigenous manner, developed a hierarchy of leadership roles and discussed public issues among the meetings of the members--all of which reflected the Fijian lifestyle.

The church took over the system of presentation of offerings that came from the pre-Christian way of life. There is nothing western about the *soli vakamisoneri* even today. The annual offerings for the support of the ministry and the emerging ecclesiastical system reflected in style and procedure a pre-Christian presentation of war resources at a military review (*taqa*), or a ceremonial presentation of craft work and food for the rebuilding of a heathen temple. The procedure--i.e., the way in which it was done--was identical. When the Fijians became Christians they remained essentially Fijians. The first western missionaries accepted this as ministry meaningful to the Lord. There were no serious attempts to westernize the church in the pioneering days, and as a result many of these indigenous forms survive to the present day. Even with the literacy program which followed conversion and put a Bible in every convert's hands, it was a Bible in the Fijian language, not an English one. The reading skill was something added to life, building on a language which was already there--not the rejection of one language and the acceptance of another. The grammar and the basic vocabulary continued in use. War and cannibal terminology began to fall into disuse, and the language was enriched by new Christian thought. The semantic change reflected the changing values and lifestyle, but the language is still the language of the Fijian people.

The transition from the pagan to the Christian lifestyle in social organization and language was smooth because they raised no moral issues. There were some social issues, however, that raised moral questions for the convert. Let us move on to them.

(b) *Marriage:* The matter of Christian marriage became a moral encounter when a candidate with more than one wife came up for baptism. A period of instruction followed conversion. The converts were free to worship in the congregation and join in the prayer meetings (i.e., they were adherents), but they did not achieve full member status until after baptism, and this implied a greater degree of maturity in their Christian experience. One of those requirements was a rejection of polygamy. In those early days there were a few converts who enjoyed the worship, bible study and prayer, but kept their wives. But most who turned from paganism to Christianity wanted to go the whole way and became monogamous. There was no fixed time of training for baptism. It varied from a few months to a number of years. More often than not it was the polygamy issue which explains the longer waiting.

The missionaries were probably all in agreement that Christian marriage had to be monogamous; but it is fair to say they had no option in the matter. The requirement for baptism was laid down by the London Committee of the W. M. S. The wide world from Africa to Fiji came under the same legislation despite the different contexts.

Fijian society was not universally polygamous. The multiplicity of wives was limited to the upper classes, who also had concubines. Adult men on a lower level had no wives at all; this was especially so with the warriors. These men lived in male communal houses. Sexually they were "rewarded" by the enslavement and abuse of women captured in war. Their "pay" for military services was cannibal feasting on the captured males and abuse of the females. Many a Christian village suffered this fate.

It was in the chiefly household where wives and serving women were required for domestic and family purposes—although the Fijian family as we know it today was a Christian innovation. Any reference to a pre-Christian Fijian family must thus be confined to one segment of society. Life in the men's communal houses was grim. The most bitter penalty for a misdemeanor possible for a slave of a chief was to be sent to the man's house. Many were abused until they died and then thrown into the cannibal oven.

The reader will understand, then, that the idea of having his own wife and home, however humble, was attractive to most of these warriors. They were no strong advocates of polygamy, and when the Christians supported the idea of monogamy they approved. It meant a fairer distribution of women throughout the whole community. As the wars came to an end, and men were no longer rewarded with the services of captive women, the Christian requirement became more popular among the rank and file.

At the level of the polygynous elite also one needs to reflect on its functional base. There were two undergirding supports of the system. The first of these was again the need for perpetuity of the lineage. The notion of power (*mana*) in the blood of the chief *(dra vakaturaga)* passing down through his offspring was emphatically stated and is still heard in debates on inheritance and authority. The *mana* was said to be transmitted in the blood, stronger in the male than the female, and strongest in the firstborn *(ulumatua)*. The security and prosperity at all social levels depended on the authority and *mana* of the chieftaincy, and the more numerous his offspring the greater the strength of the entire community he ruled. Fijian polygamy was thus validated by the efficacy of the chiefly blood.

Even a chief's child by a slave or concubine had a status higher
than the mother because of the chiefly blood.

Normally a Fijian traditional marriage was a union of persons
in the cross-cousin relationship (*veitavaleni* or *veidavolani*),
which reinforced the tribal whole, preserved inheritance and
consolidated strength and loyalties. However, there was a second support of Fijian elite polygyny.

This was to use the institution for political purposes. Marriages were often purely political, a mark of reconciliation after disagreement, or the termination of a war, or a military alliance, even the symbol of a political friendship or a gesture
of mutual respect. It bound two communities rather than two individuals and secured political assurances, sometimes of a
fairly temporary nature. Such unions held together fairly
loosely and could be terminated when the political expediency
had passed. They were formal mechanisms and ceremonial presentations and left no ill-will. From time to time, a chief used
such "divorce" mechanisms (*veibiu, veisere*) to terminate a marriage which was becoming an embarrassment. The existence of
such a social mechanism made it possible for a chief who became
Christian to send his wives home without dishonoring the marriage and without repercussion, provided he did so with the appropriate formal ceremonies, explanations and exchange gifts.

I know one description in the records of a Lauan chief sending seven of his eight wives home in this way, and subsequently
each of the seven was reported as bettering herself in a monogamous marriage. The great cannibal king, Cakobau, was converted
in 1854 and continued to honor his pagan marriages until 1857,
all this time diligently following the Christian faith, studying
the word, and devout in his prayer life. Ultimately he used
these "divorce" mechanisms and elected to retain only Litia
Samanunu as his Christian wife. She was the most mature Christian of them all, and indeed had been instrumental in his conversion in the first place. These are two of many cases of the
acceptance of monogamy by the Fijian elite without repercussion
from the families of the rejected wives. As the term *veisese*
indicates, it was not really a rejection but a mutual setting
free (*vei* is the reciprocal construction). Occasionally (in the
persecution period when the community was still basically pagan)
such a setting free was an excuse for plundering the Christian
group, but these were not typical.

Nevertheless one wonders what these converts would have done
had their social system not provided them with so convenient an
escape mechanism. If I were to speculate I would suggest that
the wives "set free" were usually from political unions rather

than the cross-cousin marriages--for in Fijian eyes the latter
were "born for each other."

   (c) The Dance and the Chant: People express their emotions and subliminal wants in aesthetic forms, which become psychologically central in their value system. Barnett (1953) has
demonstrated the place of subliminal wants in decision-making
and innovation. Other anthropologists call them "felt needs."
The pre-Christian Fijian expressed these deep feelings in the
dance and chant--as indeed he still does. Both dances and chants
(and they usually went together) came under critical review when
the patterns and morals of the new Christian Fijian way of life
were first emerging.

   We have numerous descriptions of pagan dancing and chanting.
War dances manifestly glorified war and cannibalism, and mocked
at the sexual impotence of captured heroes about to go to the
ovens. The victors, on the other hand, were glorified in terms
of sexual power, and given honorific titles which implied they
were also "lords of sex." Both the mocking (accompanied by abu-
sive jests and acts) and the honorifics were openly sexual and
regionally diversified. Naturally enough the missionaries re-
coiled from these demonstrations.

   The types of dance varied. Some were performed (like their
Hebrew counterparts) by the women going out to meet the home-
coming heroes, others accompanying the victory presentations in
the village, and still others went with the cannibal feasting.
Specific chants accompanied each phase of the cooking and dis-
section of the bodies. Other dances were part of the training
program whereby youths became warriors (rites of passage), and
a special dance honored those who had killed their first victim.
All these had some sexual overtones (at least in the chant, but
often also in the gestures of the dance) because success in war
was related, like sex itself, to the perpetuity or depopulation
of the tribe.

   Even non-war chants and dances might have sexual implications
and lust--sometimes in the wit of the song, sometimes in the
buffoonery of an individual capering around the dancing party
although really quite apart from it; and most frequently in the
rhythmic couplets (quite unrelated to the theme of the chant)
which were repeated (like the Song of Solomon "Daughters of
Jerusalem") between the structural units of the performance.
These couplets, variously known as *dulena, kenai kau,* etc., were
frequently vulgar.

   However, not all Fijian chants and dances were sexy or vulgar.
Some were extremely beautiful and pleasant to the ear. Some were
origin traditions of early tribal migrations, some told how the

ancestors established custom, others were in praise of the beauty
of nature, or nature parables, descriptions of the breaking of
the waves on the reefs, and still others were historical dirges
of epidemics, hurricanes and floods, honorific dirges upon the
death of some great man; or for the commemoration of some technological achievement like the building of a temple, the construction of a canal or the launching of a giant double canoe.
The dance and the chant covered every aspect of the Fijian way
of life and touched on every Fijian subliminal want or felt need.

The dance and chant were so basic for the expression of Fijian feeling that one of the first moral issues faced by the
Christian converts had to be the determination of their attitude
as Christians to the dance and chant. Fortunately this had to
be faced in the 1840s and 1850s. It may have been very differently dealt with in the 1880s and 1890s when the missionaries
were more children of the later Victorian Age. The early missionaries and their Fijian advisors determined that the sexy
performances had to go. The two most vulgar dances, which fea-
tured both war and sex, and tied up with the ancestral religion,
known respectively as *wate* and *dele*, disappeared altogether, and
today even the words have dropped from the Fijian vocabulary and
memory. This was a case of Williams' *expurgation*. But the
parables, the nature songs, the historical dirges, tribal migration songs and honorific dirges one may still find in chant and
dance in Christian assemblies. They still speak deeply to the
Fijian soul. This was Williams' *maintenance*.

But this is more than maintenance or survival. The dance and
chant are currently creative in Fiji. The dedication of a Christian church building frequently features a Fijian chant and/or
dance. The chant of the *Yabaki Drau* (a historical catalogue of
the events of the first Christian century) is used all over Fiji
in Christian worship. I myself once composed an historical chant
for an accompanying dance based on Fijian rhythm and in the Fijian language. It was performed by Fijians at Davuilevu. Three
or four Fijian preachers who expressed their appreciation revealed to me how this form of communication had produced a response on the level of Fijian Christian tradition which penetrated to their subliminal feelings.

Here we have the Christian functional substitute, which is
Williams' *expansion*. However it is more than this because it
shows how a pagan cultural institution may be transformed and
remain functionally creative in its new Christian context.

The anthropologist W. H. R. Rivers was striving for this in
his discussion of the psychological factor in the depopulation
of Melanesia (1923). Barnett talked of "functional equivalents."
One might also point out that as the Fijian form of Christianity

took shape it revealed many affinities with the Hebrew religion of the Bible. Indeed, many of the lyrical passages of Scripture were so aesthetic to the Fijians that scores of them were simply taken over into the Fijian worship service and liturgy. Stories of the acts of God, like the Creation; for dedication commemorations, the building of Solomon's temple, or the description of the New Jerusalem; the more formal code recitals like the Ten Commandments (for liturgical use); the praise passages, like many of the Psalms; and the Old Testament dirges--any of these one may hear in a Christian worship service as a chant, or accompanied by a *vakamololo* in an outside church assembly. (A *vakamololo* is a "dance" performed from a seated posture, the performers sitting in a row, facing the audience. Their movements are confined to bodies, heads and arms and are very rhythmical. The chanting party sits behind the performers and beats one or more drums of different pitch.)

The pre-Christian complex of the dance and chant in pagan Fiji has thus been taken over by the young church (maintenance), purged of sex, cannibalism and war (expurgation), and expanded for purposes of Christian worship and evangelism (expansion). In the maintenance of these aesthetic social institutions we have genuine functional substitutes; and in their expansion the complex is shown to be still dynamic in the Christian context. It is capable of adaptation to the changing requirements of the times, and a good example of effective contextualization in Christian cross-cultural mission.

(d) Theological Conceptualization: I indicated above that the possibility of transforming a pagan context into a Christian one depends on whether or not the thought forms have a capacity for the intellectual conceptualization of a truly Christian but yet indigenous theology. Not all the early missionaries in the Pacific were convinced that this was so. It was, indeed, the theoretical presupposition of those who advocated "civilizing in order to evangelize," a matter on which I have written at length elsewhere and will not discuss here. However, in any discussion on the subject of contextualization, and perhaps best under the head of "indirect encounters," the matter of Fijian thought forms should be raised. Christian dynamic equivalence, and very much more--even conversion itself --depend on the capacity for theological conceptualization. Therefore, in this small unit, I intend raising a few typical Fijian pagan theological concepts and discussing what happened to them in the process of Christianization. I am sorry the section will have to be so brief and the examples so few. It could have been the whole paper.

1. When the westerner, who is deficient in his understanding of sacrificial systems in the first place, begins to

expound the Scriptures he finds the biblical world of sacrifice
too diversified for his western vocabulary. When the first missionaries began translating the Scriptures they found a sacrificial vocabulary in Fiji more diversified even than that of Scripture. They were confronted with a multiplicity of options for
the Scriptural terms and had to enter into complicated theological discussions with their Fijian informants who helped with
translation. The Fijian convert had a capacity for a theology
of sacrifice very much superior to that of the average westerner,
who often stumbles over this theological notion which comes from
a non-western context in any case. One of the prized items in
my collection of Fijian memorabilia is a sermon outline of a
century ago. The preacher was a Fijian. He was preaching on
Christ's sacrifice as a propitiation for our sins. The sermon
comprises a discussion of the character of a pre-Christian sacrifice for sin in old Fiji. He enumerated the significant points
and used his summary as a typology which brought him to the superior sacrifice of Christ. It was worthy of the Letter to the
Hebrews and must have spoken to the Fijian congregation much as
this New Testament letter did to its Hebrew Christian audience.

     2. The notion of salvation from guilt in the Old Testa-
ment Day of Atonement; the theology of the recognition and confession of one's sin, but the hope of escape from its just penalty, shown in such passages as the sending of the scapegoat
into the wilderness, and the person guilty of blood escaping
the avenger by flight to the city of refuge, was not meaningless
to the early Fijian converts. Nor was it without its counterparts in Fijian life. There was, for example, a certain mountain village in Viti Levu where an offender whose offense called
for his death, might run with speed from the avenger and climb
on a great rock. Here the avenger would shake his club in vain.
"You know you are guilty," he would say. "You know the penalty
is death. You know you are saved only because you have stood
on the rock of refuge." People with social mechanisms like that
will have no trouble wrestling with a theology of salvation,
even though the Great Rock is now a Person.

     3. Neither will a people whose whole social organization
is based on a system of heralds or go-betweens, as I have already discussed, have any trouble with a theology of mediation.
The notion of a Father sending forth his Son to declare him is
a totally Fijian way of acting. Neither is there difficulty
with the theology of the Son and the Father being one. He not
only mediates, he represents the Father. He is the Substitute
of the Father and acts with the authority of the Father.   In
Fiji when a high authority sends a substitute, the latter does
not go in his own authority, but in that of the sending authority (his substitute--*sosomi*). The whole complex of biblical
teaching round the word cluster *apostello-apostolos* is meaning-

fully Fijian. With very little instruction the Fijian converts were able to grasp this world of Christian doctrine.

4. The real battle for conversion came, not at these theological levels which came remarkably soon after conversion under instruction and before baptism. The first conversion was a power encounter with the old gods, the spirits and deified ancestors. It was conceptualized in the thought-world of *mana*. This is the thought-world of Joshua at Shechem (Josh. 24) and Elijah at Carmel (1 Kings 18), in Jesus confronting the evil spirits, and the Ephesian experiences of Acts 19:13-20.

The major issue here came to the surface as soon as the missionaries began translating the Scriptures. The terminology of Scripture is power-terminology. Was the pagan concept of *mana* to be taken over? Fijian had two power terms--*mana* and *kaukauwa*--which permitted a differentiation between *exousia* and *dunamis*. Never did the Fijian deny the reality of the evil powers, but he certainly discovered the power above all power (Luke 10:19, Matt. 28:18).

Malinowski pointed out that every word the missionaries had from the vernacular language had originally pagan meanings. Here the risk of faith operates. By the use of *mana*, *kalou*, *masu* and many other such terms, the Christian religion was born in Fiji. Every one of these required a theological transition, but by his Spirit it was achieved.

The danger was that some pagan aspect of thought would be taken over by Christianity and lead to syncretism. This risk was safeguarded against by an emphasis on literacy as an accompaniment of conversion, the provision of a vernacular Bible, the training of preachers to interpret it, and the formation of classes to study it. The Holy Spirit certainly blessed this system. Fiji had the complete New Testament in the language by the twelfth year of the mission--and it was a good translation, and certainly its basic theological vocabulary has stood the test of time. Bible translation, class instruction, hymn-singing and preaching all used this theological terminology so the basic problems of theological expression were all faced in the first decade.

II. *The Colonial Level*

The pre-colonial period of mission in Fiji lasted for about four decades. By this time all the coastal Fijians were Christian and only two pagan tribes remained in the interior. A decade later they too were becoming Christian, evangelized by their own coastal Fijians.

These coastal Fijians were mostly second generation Christians. That is--they had not themselves come out of paganism,
but had been born to Christian parents. They were familiar,
however, with the stories they had heard from their fathers, and
a few of the older generation were still alive. The church was
being carried along by the momentum of forty triumphant years,
but a sudden and dramatic change came with colonial government,
and with the change, a new set of problems or moral confrontations.

The use of the Bible had spread to all corners of Fiji and
although folk still used their various dialects, Bauan was now
known everywhere and became standardized as the Fijian *lingua
franca* for Church and State. With the aid of two missionaries
(Fison and Langham) and a committee of chiefs, the legal department of the new colonial government codified the native laws,
and thereafter they were ruled by their own laws, not those of
the white man. A number of the preacher/teacher trainees of
the church were transferred to the government (they responded
to the invitation) for medical training and this became the beginnings of the Fiji native medical service. The church continued to train teachers for the schools in the Fijian villages.
(They were village schools, not missionary schools, and eventually passed under the control of village committees.) The period of war and cannibalism was over.

Under the new colonial government a great army of white adventurers and land speculators came to Fiji. The import of wine
and spirits rose sharply and brought a new set of social problems.

Unfortunately Cession was followed almost immediately by a
tragic measles epidemic which carried off over forty thousand
Fijians and so physically weakened the race that there followed
a long series of other epidemics--whooping cough, influenza, etc.
By the end of the century the popular idea of political scientists was that the Fijians would die out and the planters of
Fiji would be left without labor. The latter cried out for indentured labor.

Indentured labor came from India. It is a tragic and inhumane story and wrecked the population balance of the country,
for in time the Indians became the greatest racial group in the
population and left the Fijians with a new set of problems which
were not of their own making. Indenture continued for nearly
four decades in spite of the Fijian outcry against it.

Colonial government raised a new set of officials to serve as
"government chiefs" between the district commissioners and the
people. Frequently these were created chiefs, spoke English

well, but had no "birth"--the Fijian criteria for office. On
the other hand, some Fijian customs and chiefly privileges were
strengthened without recognition of the responsibilities they
implied. On the level of civil government there was much confusion which the church did not experience. Nevertheless some of
these matters led to mission clashes with the government. One
of these was related to the ceremonial of missionary gatherings,
and another the nature of Fijian taxation.

The government supported large vested interests rather than
small plantations. The Colonial Sugar Refining Company was established in the mid-1880s and swallowed up most of the plantations, making the planters overseers. This transformed the
economy of the colony and changed the balance of powers in its
control. The Christian mission to the Indians was completely
different from what the Fijians had known. Its patterns came
from India and its missionary values were colonial rather than
traditional. Many of its obstructions had to be removed before
the two churches could move together.

The colonial period lasted for nearly a century. The missionaries were more paternal and more Victorian than the first generation of missionaries had been. The fact that the Fijian
church was able to retain its indigenous components against paternalism and colonialism speaks worlds for its early strength.
It broke out of this "imprisonment" immediately after World
War II and moved towards independence before the colony itself.

The colonial level of our study, then, must be seen as a
period of acculturation, when the Fijians were struggling to
adapt themselves to drastic changes from outside. In many ways
it was a struggle for survival--both for the perpetuity of their
race and the possession of their homeland.

The evangelism which had carried them forward from tribe to
tribe until all Fiji had been won for Christ raised the question:
where do we go from here? The church had answered: to the
islands beyond the horizon. It is very much to the credit of
this young church that she sent her own mission to New Britain
and New Ireland on the first vessel to call after the measles
epidemic, and when the government was setting up a Royal Commission to investigate the decline of Fijian population, these
people should be starting another mission--this time to Papua.
One of the strong continuities of this church has been her missionary spirit.

In the pre-colonial period communications had followed the
coasts and up the rivers. The villages lay along these routes
and the Gospel had also spread along these lines. The colonial
period saw the development of roads and a small railway through

the cane country. These opened up new lines of contact, agricultural areas and markets. They gave the country a new kind of
mobility especially after World War II. From the turn of the
century it had been apparent that Fiji needed a new kind of economic structure with technical and agricultural education. The
mission tried to meet this situation with central educational
institutions. Both technical and agricultural schools appeared
and played a great part in the development of the economy.

Technical education opened the way for many Fijians to train
as housebuilders, boatbuilders and general carpenters. The
district boys' schools taught boys basic carpentry with a minimum set of tools. The aim was to improve the village handyman,
but in reality, when a boy learned to use a saw and square, he
often deserted his village and went to Suva to seek employment
as a carpenter. He joined the new migration to the city. This
process speeded up considerably towards the end of the colonial
period. Suva quadrupled between 1940 and 1960.

The moral problems for the churches in the colonial period
differed vastly from those of the period of penetration into
paganism. They came from historical events and acculturation.
We can only find space to refer to a few of them.

1. *Evangelization of the Fiji Indian:*

I have shown that the colonial period was one of Fijian missionary expansion beyond her own borders--to New Britain and New
Ireland, to Papua, to the Solomons, to North Australia and eventually to the New Guinea Highlands--yet somehow her witness to
the Indian migrants has been slight. How do we explain this?

The first Indian indentured labor reached Fiji in 1879 and
the "trade" continued until 1916. The laborers were to have been
repatriated after a term of service, but ships were unavailable.
The Indians had to sign up for another term or become tenant
farmers (but still dependent on the Company). They had lost
their religious status and caste by coming to Fiji. Even the
family structure was destroyed and only now is the kin structure
reformulating. The first Indians slipped into the country almost unnoticed. Hitherto labor had come from the other Pacific
Islands and the Fijian churches had ministered to it. The Indian
was "just another kind of islander" and the first pastoral care
was supplied by a Fijian missionary just returned from New
Britain. The experiment failed.

Then the Fijian missionaries called on their home Board for a
full-time missionary for Indian work. They received no response.
In the 1890s the Fijian Synod negotiated with the Synod in
Calcutta and obtained the services of an Indian catechist from

the same region as the migrants. He worked for his agreed three years, but his English was very poor and neither his missionary superintendent nor the Chairman knew Hindustani. They just could not communicate. Another unsuccessful appeal was made to the Board and two decades of opportunity were lost. After the turn of the century, a layman, a minister and a missionary sister were established in the Indian work. They were unable to handle their program within the Fijian structures and insisted on being constituted as a separate Synod of their own. Thus were the Fijian and Indian programs recognized as ethnically and socially different, and each proceeded thereafter along its own lines, one retaining its traditional pre-colonial values and the other using models derived from India, a highly institutionalized educational base and a colonial structure.

The saddest thing about this rightful recognition of ethnic and linguistic difference is that it relieved the Fijian churches of a sense of responsibility for the Indian (a feeling which had existed for two decades). The notion of the responsibility of the Fijians to evangelize the Indians did not arise again until very late in the Colonial period. The missionaries to the Fijians were still rather mission-minded than church-minded. Unlike their own predecessors, they still treated their Fijians as children who had a long way to go before they could stand on their feet. Their values were puritanically Victorian and western. They accepted the indigenous cultural ingredient in the Fijian churches because it was too strong for them to change, but they viewed it as backward. The missionaries to the Indians wanted to go their own way, to build schools and other institutions, and often to work in English. They became more and more busy with administration and the reduction in their vernacular outreach can be documented from the records. They built their houses on the hilltops and had servants in the colonial manner.

When I first went down to Fiji the polarity between these two missions shocked me; and even within a committee with representatives from both, their conversation was in terms of "two sides." The Indian and Fijian workers also reflected this polarization. I well remember challenging a Fijian pastor in the early 1940s about the responsibility of his people to evangelize the Indians. His response was immediate, "No! You Europeans brought them here. You evangelize them." However, fifteen years later I heard the same man speak to his colleagues in the Fijian Synod urging them to appoint a Fijian to work among the Indians. This change came during the 1950s, but it was accompanied by strategy changes in both the Indian and Fijian fields. In the mid-1940s the structural organization of the two programs was changed by a new constitution. The European missionary constituency was deprived of its entity and authority; the missionaries were absorbed into their respective Fijian or Indian Synods, and

there outnumbered; and a representative United Synod was created
to develop the unity of the Church at large. Thus were the
ethnic components fully recognized and allowed to be themselves;
but reminded of the greater unity in which they were all one.
This new constitution marked the end of the period of paternalism and prepared the way for full independence. One of the new
blooms to reappear in Fiji since these adjustments is the Fijian
concern for the evangelization of the Indian. When I left Fiji
in 1960 Hindustani was being taught to the Fijian theological
students by an Indian minister.

  2. *The Impact of the Colonial Speculator:*

  Many of the social evils and indulgences of the West which
troubled the Fijian people were introduced by white travelers,
sailors and settlers. For example, in old Fiji, tobacco was
used for delousing the hair. The white man introduced the habit
of smoking in the pre-colonial period. Among my collection of
Fijian material I have a "love song" to Lady Nicotine in the
Macuata dialect.

  However, the influx of western adventurers and speculators
after Cession brought about excessive indulgence in drinking and
smoking so that the health of the Fijian race was threatened,
especially as it had been weakened by the measles epidemic. We
have descriptions of the effect of these habits on Fijians of
both sexes and all ages, including cases of infants with fat
sulukas of Fijian tobacco inhaling until drugged. This became a
moral issue for the Fijian churches especially during the 1890s.

  A series of pamphlets in Fijian on various social and religious issues came from the mission press at Viwa. I have some of
these in my collection of Fijian memorabilia. .One of them is
"Against Tobacco." At the same time the Royal Commission on the
Decrease of Fijian Population was conducting its investigations.
A group of Fijian mothers who had developed the habit were each
given a small piece of tobacco and after a period of use their
milk was tested and found to be poisoned with nicotine which
could be passed on to their infants in this form.

  This same period was marked by revivalism of a severe type.
It differed from the earlier "heaven oriented" evangelism, but
was highly "hell-fire" and served to a generation considered to
have backslidden. It changed the pattern of Fijian preaching
and its influence remained until the 1930s. These late Victorian
missionaries met the violence of the social evils of the day
with violent type of evangelism, brought backsliders to the
penitent form as might have happened in a city mission of the
period.

Now that the backsliders had repented they were urged to be
practical and join an abstinence group known as "the Anti-
Smoking-and-Grog-Drinking Society." Many of them did this, and
it is interesting to see that the areas of Fiji most exploited
by colonial speculators and worked by indentured island labor
were also those where revivalism found its strongest expression
in this abstinence program.

One aspect of "civilized" life which came to the Fijian with
colonial government was taxation. Unfortunately the new government decided that the Fijian should pay his tax with returns
from crops of tobacco. Many Fijians who had taken the pledge of
abstinence regarded it as morally encumbent upon them to refrain
from cultivating the crop or making profit from it. The government officers took exception to this and when the missionaries
supported the Fijian abstainers, the issue became serious and
led to mission/government correspondence. This is a typical
problem of acculturation.

3. *Boy-Girl Problems Under Acculturation:*

Two of the cultural features which disappeared from Fijian
life with the coming of Christianity were the male and female
initiation rites, featuring circumcision and tattooing. They
were associated with the pre-Christian religion and were not
seen at the time to have any basic functional value apart from
the performance itself.

On the contrary they were part of the enculturative process,
rites of passage at the point of transition into manhood and
womanhood where vital education on the facts of life was given.
The ceremonies cut the participants off from the earlier stage
of life, and after a ritualized learning process of transition,
incorporated them back into the communal life at a new level and
with a new understanding of life. What was not sufficiently explored was the character of that learning process, in the inter-
mediate rite of transition. It was here they learned the facts
of life. The church was satisfied with the elimination of the
pagan religious ritual associations, and the substitution of a
harmless visit to the hospital by adolescent boys for the operation of circumcision, which after all was far more hygienic, and
the holding of a simple feast of entry into manhood back in the
village upon their return. It all looked so much better and so
much more Christian. But there were problems for subsequent
generations.

In the process of the historical Christianization the ingredient of sex education, which accompanied the rite, was also
dropped. A boy was now left to pick up his knowledge of the
facts of life as best he could by sharing stories with equally

uneducated boys. With this went all the psychological problems
of "not really knowing whether one knew everything" about sex
and so on.

In the old ceremonies one of the male elders had been always
assigned the role of "educator." He talked to the boys being
circumcised as a group, and they now knew they were truly men,
and knew what men ought to know, because they had been through
it all together. It was the same with the girls, although the
tattooing extended over a longer period of time and was done in
more stages. Their skirts were lengthened with each enlargement of the tattoo design, until finally two little marks on the
face by the mouth indicated one's absolutely full womanhood.

As one goes through the membership roll books one finds a
record here and there of a woman having been disciplined for
being tattooed. It is entered as "a heathen rite," but the fact
that a generation later a woman should feel the need of this reveals a cultural void of some kind. There never was a formal
substitute for sex education. The parents, the minister, or the
school teacher might have done it, but each left it to the other.
It exposed the second generation to unsavory boy/girl specula-
tions or to the temptation to experiment. This is a good example of the danger of the disposal of a ritual without due regard to its true function, and thereby the exposure of a second
generation to a new type of moral problem.

As with sex education, so too with the nature of courtship.
In the olden days a Fijian marriage was arranged by the two
families by correct approaches and responses, the presentation
of mutual gifts, and the giving and accepting of assurances. It
was much more than the union of two persons. Two families were
brought together, families who would, through a network of relationships and obligations, hold the marriage together through
all kinds of marital stress. It was a good system and preserved
the family inheritance. Folk normally courted and married within
certain cultural boundaries. In the early days this was essential. As war disappeared, and enemies became friends, some of
these cultural bonds became less essential, but the range of
choice has always been socially restricted. The missionaries
were happy to leave this aspect of the new Christian way to the
Fijian native ministers, and for a century things ran smoothly.
But the later colonial period brought changes.

First there emerged the new itinerant professions--school
teachers, magistrates, ministers of religion and others--who
were stationed in different parts of the colony and did not locate in their homelands. They mixed with government and mission
leaders--foreigners who married according to their taste and
status. These were the first Fijians who, like their western

friends, married by individual choice. This philosophy hit the
theological students at Davuilevu during the 1950s, and for the
first time these students began seeking the counsel of their
white missionary leaders rather than their own senior Fijian
ministers. This manifestly meant that they wanted a western an-
swer--to marry the girl of their choice regardless of family and
social ties. I well recall a Fijian elder at this time making a
long speech in which, after arguing strongly for the preservation of arranged marriages for Fijians, added that nevertheless
a new pattern was needed for ministers, teachers and magistrates
whose wives had to socialize with westerners in offical positions. It was a requirement which sprang from the colonial context.

The most threatening factor to Fijian marriage in those days
was the increasing migration to the city. There, a Fijian clerk
and typist, say, whose families were far removed and did not
even know of each other, would see the Hollywood version of western marriage, and find it an exciting pattern to follow. Now
here is a marriage utterly without security of any kind, with no
tribal support, and no social mechanisms to hold it together
when stress falls upon it, and no financial undergirdings. If
it is to work it has to do so in the city. By its very nature
the families must cut themselves off from it and do not attend
or support the wedding. For the couple there is no return home
without an atonement. Many have thought it worth an atonement.
But even then there are parental wounds and hurt. Almost all
the Fijian divorces are marriages of this kind. (I checked out
those figures one year when I served as a juvenile delinquent
officer in Suva.) Many times that year I was asked by Fijian
ministers and parents if the Hollywood marriage pattern (and the
courtship that preceded it) was the approved western mode. In
the years immediately following World War II here was the problem of the search for new lifestyle models in a continually
changing situation where ideas from outside and the behavior of
foreigners were being thrust before the people. It was this way
until 1960.

III. *The Post-Colonial Level*

The contours of the post-colonial structures were already
manifest in the closing two decades of the colonial period which
saw a renaissance of Fijian indigenous enthusiasm.

The colonial period--historically the best part of a century
--had seen remarkably few evidences of nationalism. Early in
the period there had been an outburst of nativism (the *Tuka*) in
the highlands of Viti Levu. It was a politico-religious movement in the area still then unconverted to Christianity, and
more an expression against the notion of a foreign government

than anything else. It had many characteristics of a cargo
cult. In the 1930s there had been another movement, *na Guana*,
which the government dealt with by exiling its leader to Rotuma.
There were a few other flutters of nativism, but nothing like
those in other parts of Oceania and especially the more recent
cargo cults of Papua New Guinea. On the whole, Fiji got off
lightly, probably because she offered so much scope for independent Fijian expression and entity in both church and state.

The years of Fijian anomie which followed the measles epidemic and the establishment of colonial rule were marked by a continual decline in Fijian population. Even before the measles
Lorimer Fison had pointed out that Fijian deaths outnumbered the
births. The missionaries kept good statistics and others, like
W. A. Heighway, pressed these figures before government attention. Mrs. Heighway established a women's welfare nursing system. It was indigenous and itinerant and attracted government
attention, and eventually led to an official program. A Royal
Commission was appointed to investigate the Fijian population
decline. Many health regulations were tightened but the race
continued to decline until 1920. Since then the Fijians appear
to have adapted themselves to the acculturating conditions of
life. However, by the end of World War II the Indian population
passed the Fijian and the publication of these figures shocked
the young Fijian leaders. Thereafter many new expressions of
Fijian nationalism appeared.

At the same time the Fijian mission, jointly with the Indian
mission, reorganized with a new constitution, and immediately
there was a renaissance of indigenous Fijian Christianity. The
constitutional structure was worked out in the field regardless
of the feelings of the home Board, which was apprehensive.
Thereafter white missionaries were steadily reduced in number.
The new constitution gave the Fijians a majority vote on everything, even including the stationing of missionaries. Missionaries going on furlough could not return unless invited by the
Fijian Synod. Fijian and Indian affairs were dealt with in
their respective synods and matters of common interest were
designated and dealt with in a united synod. The aim of the
constitution was to transform the mission into a church, dispose
of all western paternalism by eliminating the European Synod altogether and substituting a representative one that would bring
Indian and Fijian together as that was manifestly the structure
of new Fiji. The system operated for seventeen years, exciting
and innovative years. As far as the Fijians were concerned,
they were now autonomous. One by one they took over posts that
had been held by white missionaries. Those of us who remained
were in specialized ministries or in the task of leadership
training.

A Bible School was established to raise the level of candidates for the ministry and to prepare Fijian laymen for church service. Among their extra-curricular activities they presented biblical dramas depicting the circumstances under which the books of the Bible had been written. These were presented in the larger Fijian villages as congregational education.

At the theological institution where Fijian ministers (and a few Indians at times) were trained, a transitional bilateral curriculum was introduced and ran for ten years. A rural church syllabus trained men who would safeguard against too rapid a cut-off from traditional Fiji in the change that was already coming. The academic syllabus trained others for urban and industrial conditions and gave them a foundation for any subsequent degree work they might want to do. By 1960 I (being involved in this program) was satisfied that the men I had seen trained were as competent as Australian missionaries. I felt my time had come to step down and acted on this feeling.

The Youth Department which had been started by a white missionary but had dragged on slowly was handed over to a dynamic Fijian and suddenly it had a new burst of life. Youth camps were held around the islands. Young people began to appear in church committees. The area of church music was charged with musical innovations. A new day was being born.

The Fijian Church passed through a series of centenaries from 1947 onwards, and rediscovered the history of her pioneering period. Historical plays were presented across the country by the Bible School and other groups. The church paper, which had been largely used as an instrument for printing Sunday School lessons, handed this aspect over to the Youth Department and the church paper became more truly a Christian newspaper. This was accompanied by a period of increased vernacular publication--functional material meant to speak to the Fijian context in which the churches were now involved in mission and service. Many of the articles in the paper were reprinted as tracts for free distribution.

When I left Fiji the movement towards full independence was approaching its goal. The new constitution and its seventeen years of practical application provided the leadership required. In 1964 independence came in the church. It was a step ahead of the country at large. Indeed, it was partly the effectiveness of the church independence which convinced the Fijian political leaders that the country itself would be better off as an independent power than as a Crown Colony. This led to a policy of concentrated localization in the colony, until the Dominion of Fiji came into being.

The Contemporary Scene:

The independent Fijian church has now completed the first decade of its history. This year I had the opportunity of revisit-
ing the place and looking at the state of the churches and observing the changes.

I must admit that the country seems far better off as an independent dominion. The development has been considerable. Ag-
riculturally it looks good from the air and from the roads. New
networks of roads reach inland and large tracts of land have
been opened up. Rice fields have replaced the cane in the Rewa
delta. Many small industries have come into being, and the local products in the stores (now supermarkets) show a greater
diversification of industry. Fijian canned tuna stands on the
shelves beside the imported cans and is very much cheaper.
There are more banks and they have many more branches. I stood
in the largest central bank looking over the scene where I remembered an entirely white staff. There were Fijians, Indians,
Chinese--but I saw not one white person.

Next to the complete localization of industry and the end of
the old paternalism, the greatest change is probably the suburbanization of Suva and its environs. Housing areas have been
established and have turned into suburbs. A university has been
established and a number of other academic institutions in the
same area have changed the south side of the peninsula.

I remember the day when folk migrating into Suva from the
rural areas would seek out the area where their fellow tribesmen were squatting and build themselves an unapproved shanty.
This has all gone and proper buildings have taken their place.
They still often have their ethnic character but many now have
cement houses and automobiles. They have good jobs, better
salaries, and are buying city homes rather than thinking of returning in old age to the village. The suburb is a new element
in the Fijian context.

I used to go across the river from Davuilevu to preach at
Nausori. The people would come from Vunimono also. Perhaps
there would be 40 or 50 persons, meeting in an old dilapidated
church, with very little enthusiasm. This year I preached there
in a new building, ornamented with Fijian motifs. There were
two choirs and 400 people crowded into the building. The minister there is one of my old students. Another night I preached
at Raiwaqa, a housing-area suburb of Suva, the congregation
about 250-300, a good choir, and also under another of my ex-
students who had a two-storey cement house with a downstairs
room for small meetings. On another night I preached to 600 at
Nabua in a beautiful new building, with two choirs, and a women's

group serving tea afterwards. Suva is not the only city where
this suburbanization is going on. I spent my last Sunday in
Fiji in the Lautoka area. Lautoka has quite a diversified program and supports two ministers. In the afternoon I went out to
a village which I remembered as quite a small affair. To my
surprise, I found a beautiful new church, filled to capacity--I
calculated "the number per seat x number of seats" and it came
to about 500--under another of my men. He has a strong Rural
Development program operating with government support. He showed
me over their equipment and handwork. It was impressive. The
men work in nearby industrial programs and live in the village.
It is a village but has a suburban mentality.

Another of my old men is located at the international airport. He has a small cause of airport employees and a new church
with a congregation of about 150.

Two decades ago only the central churches of Suva and Lautoka
had big congregations. Village congregations might have aver-
aged about a hundred. The emergence of suburban type churches
is the most obvious change in the first decade of independence.
If it were statistically analyzed, I believe it would indicate a
shift from subsistence farming to wage-earning.

In the outer islands the context is more as it used to be.
Congregations are much as they were--quite alive, but rural rather than suburban. This is what I felt on Vanua Levu.

Many of the activities that accompany these suburban structures have a strong awareness of selfhood. For example, there
is a strong women's group. In the Nausori area, for instance,
women from all the groups meet periodically--about 300 of them--
and wear dresses which indicate their congregational affiliation. Thus while they meet in the unity of a common faith they
are also reminded of the diversity of their representation.

I preached to a community in a place named Caqiri-Nasele. It
was just a swamp in my day, but now it is a suburban settlement
of mixed racial content. There are a good many Indians living
there. Recently the Fijians built a church, a two-storey building; already it is too small and they have architectural problems of enlargement. I preached there to about 400. It was a
totally Fijian service but the steward announced that in the afternoon there would be a service there for Indians in Hindustani.
In this place the choir had innovated with their "robes," elect-
ing to wear capes rather than the hotter garments. After the
service the congregation met together downstairs for the mid-day
meal. In all these places I felt that the church people had a
grip on the ever-changing situation. They were part of the context itself. But it was no melting-pot of cultures. They re-

retained their entity. They were the Fijian component. But
they recognized other components and reached out to them.

During my visit to the country, the Department of Evangelism
had engaged a team of Gospel communicators to give lectures to
Christian workers. I was involved also in this. Workers from
the different components came together in Suva and Lautoka for
the lectures, which had to be given in English. The head of
this department is a Fijian (another of my students), but this
year for the first time the Fijians (who have the majority vote)
elected an Indian as their President.

Another feature of the contemporary scene is the inter-
insular cooperation, which began in the 1950s when Tonga, Samoa
and Fiji moved towards each other in programs relating to theological training and youth work. The W. C. C. sponsored a conference in Samoa and the T. E. F. a consultation on theological
education in the Pacific. The fruit of these programs was the
establishment of the Pacific Theological College, which takes
graduates from the various denominational island training institutions and offers them a bachelor's degree in divinity. This
institution began with the support of sixteen missionary bodies
in the islands. It was intended that the curriculum offer an
island-oriented program. Unfortunately it has turned out to be
more western than intended, but the recent appointment of a national president may correct this matter.

By sending delegates Fiji has participated in numerous conferences (including Lausanne), and by their reporting back to
the churches at home in Fiji, the country is aware of the religious world beyond her shores, and has expressed herself vigor-
ously on public issues which touch the Pacific--as, for example,
the French atomic bombings. I think that the island church of
Fiji fully understands that the world is "one world" and she
cannot live in isolation. This is probably the greatest difference between the pre-colonial and post-colonial levels of contextual analysis.

In the area of the penetrating thrusts of mission at the contemporary level there is still the urgent need of evangelizing
the Indians in the colony. Fiji has her missionaries in the New
Guinea Highlands, in the Solomons and in North Australia; and
she is exploring new fields of university and industrial evangelism. I found the Fijian evangelist of today quite experimen-
tal--for example, running weekly question time evangelism at
lunch-time in an industrial workshop. The Department of Evangelism concluded its recent course of lectures by inviting many
public persons of all races to a monster banquet in the Town
Hall to meet the overseas lecturers and to hear them speak on
the place of the church in Fiji, and of morals in the lives of

public persons. Scores of church groups were involved in that
banquet. The Governor was there, and the press. I should never
have had the audacity to plan that; but one of my graduates
did. And, in passing--the master of ceremonies for that performance was a Fijian woman. How the context has changed in
Fiji!

I hope that in these discussions we do not lose sight of the
fact that we cannot speak of a culture as if it were a static
thing. The context in which our grandfathers worked is not the
same as ours even though we speak virtually the same language
and regard ourselves as of the same culture. This is why I have
handed you a diachronic study of three synchronic levels--a
cultural continuum. Wherever you serve as a missionary, you are
not likely to find yourself at two levels at the same time. The
historical aspect of a contextual analysis is as important as
the cultural. They have to be considered together--to be ethnohistorical. This we have to do to consider the historical
wholeness, but when it comes to my own specific mission I need
to identify two things--the precise culture to which I go, and
the point of time in their cultural history when I go. A context of cannibalism, of population decline, or of suburbanization: each is Fijian, but no Fijian missionary has met all
those three contexts.

The
Willowbank
Report

Report of a Consultation on

GOSPEL AND CULTURE

held at Willowbank, Somerset Bridge, Bermuda

from 6th to 13th January 1978

Sponsored by the Lausanne Theology and Education Group

The Willowbank Report
Contents

INTRODUCTION

The process of communicating the gospel cannot be isolated from the human culture from which it comes, or from that in which it is to be proclaimed. This fact constituted one of the preoccupations of the Lausanne Congress on World Evangelization in July 1974. So the Lausanne Committee's Theology and Education Group convened a consultation on this topic to meet in January 1978. It brought 33 theologians, anthropologists, linguists, missionaries and pastors together from all six continents to study "Gospel and Culture." Co-sponsored by the Lausanne Committee's Strategy Working Group, it had four goals:

1. To develop our understanding of the interrelation of the gospel and culture with special reference to God's revelation, to our interpretation and communication of it, and to the response of the hearers in their conversion, their churches and their life style.

2. To reflect critically on the implications of the communication of the gospel cross-culturally.

3. To identify the tools required for more adequate communication of the gospel.

4. To share the fruits of the consultation with Christian leaders in Church and mission.

This Report reflects the content of 17 written papers circulated in advance, summaries of them and reactions to them made during the Consultation, and many viewpoints expressed in plenary and group discussions.

Our programme for six days was very full, and we worked at high pressure. In consequence, basic methodological questions about the presuppositions and procedures of theology and the social sciences, and about the proper way to relate them to each other, could not be explored; and there were points at which our discussions clearly reflected this fact. Also, many questions which were raised had to be left on one side, and many particular debates had to be foreclosed as we went along. We are conscious, therefore, that what we say is to some extent provisional, and may need to be sharpened and deepened at various points in the light of future work. In addition, we resort to a number of generalizations; more case-studies are needed to see how these relate to specific situations.

Before the Consultation ended, we spent time together working through the draft report and revising it. The final document is a Report, not a Statement or Declaration; so none of us has signed it. But we send it out as a summary of what took place at Willowbank, and we commend it to our fellow Christians throughout the world for study and appropriate action.

1. The Biblical Basis of Culture

"Because man is God's creature, some of his culture is rich in beauty and goodness. Because he is fallen, all of it is tainted with sin and some of it is demonic." (Lausanne Covenant, para. 10)

God created mankind male and female in his own likeness by endowing them with distinctive human faculties--rational, moral, social, creative and spiritual. He also told them to have children, to fill the earth and to subdue it (Gen. 1:26-28). These divine commands are the origin of human culture. For basic to culture are our control of nature (that is, of our environment) and our development of forms of social organisation. Insofar as we use our creative powers to obey God's commands, we glorify God, serve others and fulfill an important part of our destiny on earth.

Now however, we are fallen. All our work is accompanied by sweat and struggle (Gen. 3:17-19), and is disfigured by selfishness. So none of our culture is perfect in truth, beauty or goodness. At the heart of every culture-- whether we identify this heart as religion or world-view--is an element of self-centredness, of man's worship of himself. Therefore a culture cannot be brought under the Lordship of Christ without a radical change of allegiance.

For all that, the affirmation that we are made in God's image still stands (Gen. 9:6; James 3:9), though the divine likeness has been distorted by sin. And still God expects us to exercise stewardship of the earth and of its creatures (Gen. 9:1-3, 7), and in his common grace makes all persons inventive, resourceful and fruitful in their endeavors. Thus, although Genesis 3 records the fall of humanity, and Genesis 4 Cain's murder of Abel, it is Cain's descendants who are described as the cultural innovators, building cities, breeding livestock, and making musical instruments and metal tools (Gen. 4:17-22).

Many of us evangelical Christians have in the past been too negative towards culture. We do not forget the human fallenness and lostness which call for salvation in Christ. Yet we wish to begin this Report with a positive affirmation of human dignity and human cultural achievement. Wherever human beings develop their social organisation, art and science, agriculture and technology, their creativity reflects that of their Creator.

2. A Definition of Culture

Culture is a term which is not easily susceptible of definition. In the broadest sense, it means simply the patterned way in which people do things together. If there is to be any common life and corporate action, there must be agreement, spoken or unspoken, about a great many things. But the term "culture" is not generally used unless the unit concerned is larger than the family, unitary or extended.

Culture implies a measure of homogeneity. But, if the unit is larger than the clan or small tribe, a culture will include within itself a number of subcultures, and subcultures of subcultures, within which a wide variety and diversity is possible. If the variations go beyond a certain limit, a counter-culture will have come into being, and this may prove a destructive process.

Culture holds people together over a span of time. It is received from the past, but not by any process of natural inheritance. It has to be learned afresh by each generation. This takes place broadly by a process of absorption from the social environment, especially in the home. In many societies certain elements of the culture are communicated directly in rites of initiation, and by many other forms of deliberate instruction. Action in accordance with the culture is generally at the subconscious level.

This means that an accepted culture covers everything in human life.

At its centre is a world-view, that is, a general understanding of the nature of the universe and of one's place in it. This may be "religious" (concerning God, or gods and spirits, and of our relation to them), or it may express a "secular" concept of reality, as in a Marxist society.

From this basic world-view flow both standards of judgement or values (of what is good in the sense of desirable, of what is acceptable as in accordance with the general will of the community, and of the contraries) and standards of conduct (concerning relations between individuals, between the sexes and the generations, with the community and with those outside the community).

Culture is closely bound up with language, and is expressed in proverbs, myths, folk tales, and various art forms, which become part of the mental furniture of all members of the group. It governs actions undertaken in community--acts of worship or of general welfare; laws and the administration of law; social activities such as dances and games; smaller units of action such as clubs and societies, associations for an immense variety of common purposes.

Cultures are never static; there is a continuous process of change. But this should be so gradual as to take place within the accepted norms; otherwise the culture is disrupted. The worst penalty that can be inflicted on the rebel is exclusion from the culturally defined social community.

Men and women need a unified existence. Participation in a culture is one of the factors which provide them with a sense of belonging. It gives a sense of security, of identity, of dignity, of being part of a larger whole, and of sharing both in the life of past generations and in the expectancy of society for its own future.

Biblical clues to the understanding of the human culture are found in the threefold dimension of people, land, and history, on which the Old Testament focuses attention. The ethnic, the territorial, and the historical (who, where and whence we are) appear there as the triple source of economic, ecological, social and artistic forms of human life in Israel, of the forms of labour and production, and so of wealth and well-being. This model provides a perspective for interpreting all cultures.

Perhaps we may try to condense these various meanings as follows: Culture is an integrated system of beliefs (about God or reality or ultimate meaning), of values (about what is true, good, beautiful and normative), of customs (how to behave, relate to others, talk, pray, dress, work, play, trade, farm, eat, etc.), and of institutions which express these beliefs, values and customs (government, law courts, temples or churches, family, schools, hospitals, factories, shops, unions, clubs, etc.), which binds a society together and gives it a sense of identity, dignity, security, and continuity.

3. Culture in the Biblical Revelation

God's personal self-disclosure in the Bible was given in terms of the hearers' own culture. So we have asked ourselves what light it throws on our task of cross-cultural communication today.

The biblical writers made critical use of whatever cultural material was available to them for the expression of their message. For example, the Old Testament refers several times to the Babylonian sea monster named "Leviathan," while the form of God's "covenant" with his people resembles the ancient Hittite Suzerain's "treaty" with his vassals. The writers also made incidental use of the conceptual imagery of the "three-tiered" universe, though they did not thereby affirm a a pre-Copernican cosmology. We do something similar when we talk about the sun "rising" and "setting."

Similarly, New Testament language and thought-forms are steeped in both Jewish and Hellenistic cultures, and Paul seems to have drawn from the vocabulary of Greek philosophy. But the process by which the biblical authors borrowed words and images from their cultural milieu, and used them creatively, was controlled by the Holy Spirit so that they purged them of false or evil implications and thus transformed them into vehicles of truth and goodness.

These undoubted facts raise a number of questions with which we have wrestled. We mention five:

(a) *The nature of biblical inspiration.*

Is the biblical author's use of the words and ideas of their own culture incompatible with divine inspiration? No. We have taken note of the different literary genres of Scripture, and of the different forms of the process of inspiration which they imply. For instance, there is a broad distinction in form between the work of the prophets, receiving visions and words of the Lord, and historians and writers of letters. Yet the same Spirit uniquely inspired them all. God used the knowledge, experience and cultural background of the authors (though his revelation constantly transcended these), and in each case the result was the same, namely God's word through human words.

(b) *Form and meaning.*

Every communication has both a meaning (what we want to say) and a form (how we say it). The two--form and meaning-- always belong together, in the Bible as well as in other books and utterances. How then should a message be translated from one language into another?

A literal translation of the form ("formal correspondence") may conceal or distort the meaning. In such cases, the better way is to find in the other language an expression which makes an equivalent impact on the hearers now as did the original. This may involve changing the form in order to preserve the meaning. This is called "dynamic equivalence." Consider, for example, the RSV translation of Rom. 1:17, which states that in the gospel "the righteousness of God is revealed through faith for faith." This gives a word-for-word rendering of the original Greek, that is, a "formal correspondence" translation. But it leaves the meaning of the Greek words "righteousness" and "from faith to faith" unclear. A translation such as TEV--"the gospel reveals how God puts people right with himself: it is through faith from beginning to end"--abandons the principle of one-to-one correspondence between Greek and English words; but it expresses the meaning of the original sentence more adequately. The attempt to produce such a "dynamic equivalence" translation may well bring the translator to a deeper understanding of Scripture, as well as make the text more meaningful to people of another language.

Some of the biblical forms (words, images, metaphors) should be retained, however, because they are important recurring symbols in Scripture (e.g., cross, lamb, or cup). While retaining the form, the translators will try to bring out the meaning. For example, in the TEV rendering of Mark 14:36--"take this cup of suffering away from me"--the form (i.e., the "cup" image) is retained, but the words "of suffering" are added to clarify the meaning.

Writing in Greek, the New Testament authors used words that had a long history in the secular world, but they invested them with Christian meanings, as when John referred to Jesus as "the Logos." It was a perilous procedure, because "logos" had a wide variety of meanings in Greek literature and philosophy, and non-Christian associations doubtlessly clung to the word. So John set the title within a teaching context, affirming that the

Logos was in the beginning, was with God, was God, was the agent of creation, was the light and life of men, and became a human being (John 1:1-14). Similarly, some Indian Christians have taken the risk of borrowing the Sanskrit word "avatar" (descent), used in Hinduism for the so-called "incarnations" of Vishnu, and applied it, with careful explanatory safeguards, to the unique incarnation of God in Jesus Christ. But others have refused to do so, on the ground that no safeguards are adequate to prevent misinterpretation.

(c) The normative nature of Scripture.

The Lausanne Covenant declares that Scripture is "without error in all that it affirms" (para. 2). This lays upon us the serious exegetical task of discerning exactly what Scripture is affirming. The essential meaning of the biblical message must at all costs be retained. Though some of the original forms in which this meaning was expressed may be changed for the sake of cross-cultural communication, we believe that they too have a certain normative quality. For God himself chose them as wholly appropriate vehicles of his revelation. So each fresh formulation and explanation in every generation and culture must be checked for faithfulness by referring back to the original.

(d) The cultural conditioning of Scripture.

We have not been able to devote as much time as we would have liked to the problem of the cultural conditioning of Scripture. We are agreed that some biblical commands (e.g., regarding the veiling of women in public and washing one another's feet) refer to cultural customs now obsolete in many parts of the world. Faced by such texts, we believe the right response is neither a slavishly literal obedience nor an irresponsible disregard, but rather first a critical discernment of the text's inner meaning and then a translation of it into our own culture. For example, the inner meaning of the command to wash each other's feet is that mutual love must express itself in humble service. So in some cultures we may clean each other's shoes instead. We are clear that the purpose of such "cultural transposition" is not to avoid obedience but rather to make it contemporary and authentic.

The controversial question of the status of women was not debated at our Consultation. But we acknowledge the need to search for an understanding which attempts with integrity to do justice to all the biblical teaching, and which sees the relations between men and women as being both rooted in the created order and at the same time wonderfully transformed by the new order which Jesus introduced.

(e) The continuing work of the Holy Spirit.

Does our emphasis on the finality and permanent normativeness of Scripture mean that we think the Holy Spirit has now ceased to operate? No, indeed not. But the nature of his teaching ministry has changed. We believe that his work of "inspiration" is done, in the sense that the canon of Scripture is closed, but that his work of "illumination" continues both in every conversion (e.g., 2 Cor. 4:6) and in the life of the Christian and the church. So we need constantly to pray that he will enlighten the eyes of our hearts so that we may know the fulness of God's purpose for us (Eph. 1:17ff) and may be not timorous but courageous in making decisions and undertaking fresh tasks today.

We have been made aware that the experience of the Holy Spirit revealing the application of God's truth to personal and church life is often less vivid than it should be; we all need a more sensitive openness at this point.

Questions for Discussion

1. The commands of Genesis 1:26-28 are sometimes referred to as "the cultural mandate" which God gave to mankind. How responsibly is it being fulfilled today?
2. In the light of the definition of culture in Section 2, what are the main distinctive elements of your own culture?
3. If you know two languages, make up a sentence in one and then try to find a "dynamic equivalence" translation of it into the other.
4. Give other examples of "cultural transposition" (see 3d), which preserve the biblical text's "inner meaning" but transpose it into your own culture.

4. Understanding God's Word Today

The cultural factor is present not only in God's self-revelation in Scripture, but also in our interpretation of it. To this subject we now turn. All Christians are concerned to understand God's word, but there are different ways of trying to do so.

(a) Traditional approaches

The commonest way is to come straight to the words of the biblical text, and to study them without any awareness that the writer's cultural context differs from the reader's. The reader interprets the text as if it had been written in his own language, culture and time.

We recognize that much Scripture can be read and understood in this way, especially if the translation is good. For God intended his word for ordinary people; it is not to be regarded as the preserve of scholars; the central truths of salvation are plain for all to see; Scripture is "useful for teaching the truth, rebuking error, correcting faults, and giving instruction for right living" (2 Tim. 3:16, TEV); and the Holy Spirit has been given to be our teacher.

The weakness of this "popular" approach, however, is that it does not seek first to understand the text in its original context; and, therefore, it runs the risk of missing the real meaning God intends and of substituting another.

A second approach takes with due seriousness the original historical and cultural context. It seeks also to discover what the text meant in its original language, and how it relates to the rest of Scripture. All this is an essential discipline because God spoke his word to a particular people in a particular context and time. So our understanding of God's message will grow when we probe deeply into these matters.

The weakness of this "historical" approach, however, is that it fails to consider what Scripture may be saying to the contemporary reader. It stops short at the meaning of the Bible in its own time and culture. It is thus liable to analyse the text without applying it, and to acquire academic knowledge without obedience. The interpreter may also tend to exaggerate the possibility of complete objectivity and ignore his or her own cultural presuppositions.

(b) The contextual approach

A third approach begins by combining the positive elements of both the "popular" and the "historical" approaches. From the "historical" it takes the necessity of studying the original context and language, and from the "popular" the necessity of listening to God's word and obeying it. But it goes further than this. It takes seriously the cultural context of the contemporary readers as well as of the biblical text, and recognizes that a dialogue must develop between the two.

It is the need for this dynamic interplay between text and interpreters which we wish to emphasize. Today's readers cannot come to the text in a personal vacuum, and should not try to. Instead, they should come with an awareness of concerns stemming from their cultural background, personal situation, and responsibility to others. These concerns will influence the questions which are put to the Scriptures. What is received back, however, will not be answers only, but more questions. As we address Scripture, Scripture addresses us. We find that our culturally conditioned presuppositions are being challenged and our questions corrected. In fact, we are compelled to reformulate our previous questions and to ask fresh ones. So the living interaction proceeds.

In this process of interaction our knowledge of God and our response to his will are continuously being deepened. The more we come to know him, the greater our responsibility becomes to obey him in our own situation, and the more we respond obediently, the more he makes himself known.

It is this continous growth in knowledge, love and obedience which is the purpose and profit of the "contextual" approach. Out of the context in which his word was originally given, we hear God speaking to us in our contemporary context, and we find it a transforming experience. This process is a kind of upward spiral in which Scripture remains always central and normative.

(c) The learning community

We wish to emphasize that the task of understanding the Scriptures belongs not just to individuals but to the whole Christian community, seen as both a contemporary and a historical fellowship.

There are many ways in which the local or regional church can come to discern God's will in its own culture today. Christ still appoints pastors and teachers in his church. And in answer to expectant prayer he speaks to his people, especially through the preaching of his word in the context of worship. In addition, there is a place for "teaching and admonishing one another" (Col. 3:16) both in group Bible studies and in consulting sister churches, as well as for the quiet listening to the voice of God in the Scriptures, which is an indispensable element in the believer's Christian life.

The church is also a historical fellowship and has received from the past a rich inheritance of Christian theology, liturgy and devotion. No group of believers can disregard this heritage without risking spiritual impoverishment. At the same time, this tradition must not be received uncritically, whether it comes in the form of a set of denominational distinctives or in any other way, but rather be tested by the Scripture it claims to expound. Nor must it be imposed on any church, but rather be made available to those who can use it as a valuable resource material, as a counterbalance to the spirit of independence, and as a link with the universal church.

Thus the Holy Spirit instructs his people through a variety of teachers of both the past and the present. We need each other. It is only "with all the saints" that we can begin to comprehend the full dimensions of God's love (Eph. 3:18,19). The Spirit "illumines the minds of God's people in every culture to perceive its (that is, the Scripture's) truth freshly through their own eyes and thus discloses to the whole church ever more of the many-coloured wisdom of God" (Lausanne Covenant, para. 2, echoing Eph. 3:10).

(d) The silences of Scripture

We have also considered the problem of Scripture silences, that is, those areas of doctrine and ethics on which the Bible has nothing explicit to say. Written in the ancient Jewish and Graeco-Roman world, Scripture does not address itself directly, for example, to Hinduism, Buddhism, or Islam today, or to Marxist socio-economic theory, or modern technology. Nevertheless, we believe it is right for the church guided by the Holy Spirit to search the Scriptures for precedents and principles which will enable it to develop the mind of the Lord Christ and so be able to make authentically Christian decisions. This process will go on most fruitfully within the believing community as it worships God and engages in active obedience in the world. We repeat that Christian obedience is as much a prelude to understanding as a consequence of it.

Questions for Discussion

1. Can you recall any examples of how either of the two "traditional approaches" to Bible reading had led you astray?
2. Choose a well-known text like Matthew 6:24-34 (anxiety and ambition) or Luke 10:25-38 (the Good Samaritan) and use the "contextual approach" in studying it. Let a dialogue develop between you and the text, as you question it and it questions you. Write down the stages of the interaction.
3. Read Sections 3e and 4c, and then discuss practical ways of seeking the guidance of the Holy Spirit today.

5. The Content and Communication of the Gospel

Having thought about God's communication of the gospel to us in Scripture, we now come to the very heart of our concern, our responsibility to communicate it to others, that is, to evangelize. But before we consider the communication of the gospel, we have to consider the content of the gospel which is to be communicated. For "to evangelize is to spread the good news--" (Lausanne Covenant, para. 4). Therefore there can be no evangelism without the evangel.

(a) The Bible and the gospel

The gospel is to be found in the Bible. In fact, there is a sense in which the whole Bible is gospel, from Genesis to Revelation. For its overriding purpose throughout is to bear witness to Christ, to proclaim the good news that he is lifegiver and Lord, and to persuade people to trust in him (e.g., John 5:39,40; 20:31; 2 Tim. 3:15).

The Bible proclaims the gospel story in many forms. The gospel is like a multi-faceted diamond, with different aspects that appeal to different people in different cultures. It has depths we have not fathomed. It defies every attempt to reduce it to a neat formulation.

(b) The heart of the gospel

Nevertheless, it is important to identify what is at the heart of the gospel. We recognize as central the themes of God as Creator, the universality of sin, Jesus Christ as Son of God, Lord of all, and Saviour through his atoning death and risen life, the necessity of conversion, the coming of the Holy Spirit and his transforming power, the fellowship and mission of the Christian church, and the hope of Christ's return.

While these are basic elements of the gospel, it is necessary to add that no theological statement is culture-free. Therefore, all theological formulations must be judged by the Bible itself, which stands above them all. Their value must be judged by their faithfulness to it as well as by the relevance with which they apply its message to their own culture.

In our desire to communicate the gospel effectively, we are often made aware of those elements in it which people dislike. For example, the cross has always been both an offense to the proud and folly to the wise. But Paul did not on that account eliminate it from his message. On the contrary, he continued to proclaim it, with faithfulness and at the risk of persecution, confident that Christ crucified is the wisdom and the power of God. We too, although concerned to contextualize our message and remove from it all unnecessary offense, must resist the temptation to accommodate it to human pride or prejudice. It has been given to us. Our responsibility is not to edit it but to proclaim it.

(c) Cultural barriers to the communication of the gospel

No Christian witness can hope to communicate the gospel if he or she ignores the cultural factor. This is particularly true in the case of missionaries. For they are themselves the product of one culture and go to people who are the products of another. So inevitably they are involved in cross-cultural communication, with all its exciting challenge and exacting demand. Two main problems face them.

Sometimes people resist the gospel not because they think it false but because they perceive it as a threat to their culture, especially the fabric of their society, and their national or tribal solidarity. To some extent this cannot be avoided. Jesus Christ is a disturber as well as a peacemaker. He is Lord, and demands our total allegiance. Thus, some first-century Jews saw the gospel as undermining Judaism and accused Paul of "teaching men everywhere against the people, the law, and this place," i.e., the temple (Acts 21:28). Similarly, some first-century Romans feared for the stability of the state, since in their view the Christian missionaries, by saying that "there is another King, Jesus," were being disloyal to Caesar and advocating customs which it was not lawful for Romans to practise (Acts 16:21; 17:7). Still today Jesus challenges many of the cherished beliefs and customs of every culture and society.

At the same time, there are features of every culture which are not incompatible with the lordship of Christ, and which therefore need not be threatened or discarded, but rather preserved and transformed. Messengers of the gospel need to develop a deep understanding of the local culture, and a genuine appreciation of it. Only then will they be able to perceive whether the resistance is to some unavoidable challenge of Jesus Christ or to some threat to the culture which, whether imaginary or real, is not necessary.

The other problem is that the gospel is often presented to people in alien cultural forms. Then the missionaries are resented and their message rejected because their work is seen not as an attempt to evangelize but as an attempt to impose their own customs and way of life. Where missionaries bring with them foreign ways of thinking and behaving, or attitudes of racial superiority, paternalism, or preoccupation with material things, effective communication will be precluded.

Sometimes these two cultural blunders are committed together, and messengers of the gospel are guilty of a cultural imperialism which both undermines the local culture unnecessarily and seeks to impose an alien culture instead. Some of the missionaries who accompanied the Catholic *conquistadores* of Latin America and the Protestant colonizers of Africa and Asia are historical examples of this double mistake. By contrast, the apostle Paul remains the supreme example of one whom Jesus Christ first stripped of pride in his own cultural privileges (Phil. 3:4-9) and then taught to adapt to the cultures of others, making himself their slave and becoming "all things to all men" in order by all means to save some (1 Cor. 9:19-23).

(d) Cultural sensitivity in communicating the gospel

Sensitive cross-cultural witnesses will not arrive at their sphere of service with a pre-packaged gospel. They must have a clear grasp of the "given" truth of the gospel. But they will fail to communicate successfully if they try to impose this on people without reference to their own cultural situation and that of the people to whom they go. It is only by active, loving engagement with the local people, thinking in their thought patterns, understanding their world-view, listening to their questions, and feeling their burdens, that the whole believing community (of which the missionary is a part) will be able to respond to their need. By common prayer, thought and heart-searching, in dependence on the Holy Spirit, expatriate and local believers may learn together how to present Christ and contextualize the gospel with an equal degree of faithfulness and relevance. We are not claiming that it will be easy, although some Third World cultures have a natural affinity to biblical culture. But we believe that fresh creative understandings do emerge when the Spirit-led believing community is listening and reacting sensitively to both the truth of Scripture and the needs of the world.

(e) Christian witness in the Islamic world

Concern was expressed that insufficient attention had been given at our Consultation to the distinctive problems of the Christian mission in the Islamic world, though there are approximately 600 million Muslims today. On the one hand, a resurgence of Islamic faith and mission is taking place in many lands; on the other hand, there is a new openness to the Gospel in a number of communities which are weakening their ties to traditional Islamic culture.

There is a need to recognize the distinctive features of Islam which provide a unique opportunity for Christian witness. Although there are in Islam elements which are incompatible with the gospel, there are also elements with a degree of what has been called "convertibility." For instance, our Christian understanding of God, expressed in Luther's great cry related to justification, "Let God be God," might well serve as an inclusive definition of Islam. The Islamic faith in divine unity, the emphasis on man's obligation to render God a right worship, and the utter rejection of idolatry could also be regarded as being in line with God's purpose for human life as revealed in Jesus Christ. Contemporary Christian witnesses should learn humbly and expectantly to identify, appreciate and illuminate these and other values. They should also wrestle for the transformation—and, where possible, integration—of all that is relevant in Islamic worship, prayer, fasting, art, architecture, and calligraphy.

All this proceeds only within a realistic appreciation of the present situation of the Islamic countries characterized by technological development and secularization. The social liabilities of new wealth and traditional poverty, the tensions of political independence, and the tragic Palestinian dispersion and frustration--all of these afford areas of relevant Christian witness. The last has given birth to much passionate poetry, one note in which is the paradigm of the suffering Jesus. These and other elements call for a new Christian sensitivity and a real awareness of the habits of introversion under which the church has for so long laboured in the Middle East. Elsewhere, not least in sub-Sahara Africa, attitudes are more flexible and possibilities more fluid.

In order to fulfill more adequately the missionary challenge, fresh attempts are needed to develop ways of association of believers and seekers, if need be outside the traditional church forms. The crux of a lively, evangelizing sense of responsibility towards Muslims will always be the quality of Christian personal and corporate discipleship and the constraining love of Christ.

(f) An expectation of results

Messengers of the gospel who have proved in their own experience that it is "the power of God for salvation" (Rom. 1:16) rightly expect it to be so in the experience of others also. We confess that sometimes, just as a Gentile centurion's faith put to shame the unbelief of Israel in Jesus' day (Matt. 8:10), so today the believing expectancy of Christians in other cultures sometimes shows up the missionary's lack of faith. So we remind ourselves of God's promises through Abraham's posterity to bless all the families of the earth and through the gospel to save those who believe (Gen. 12:1-4; 1 Cor. 1:21). It is on the basis of these and many other promises that we remind all messengers of the gospel, including ourselves, to look to God to save people and to build his church.

At the same time, we do not forget our Lord's warnings of opposition and suffering. Human hearts are hard. People do not always embrace the gospel, even when the communication is blameless in technique and the communicator in character. Our Lord himself was fully at home in the culture in which he preached, yet he and his message were despised and rejected, and his Parable of the Sower seems to warn us that most of the good seed we sow will not bear fruit. There is a mystery here we cannot fathom. "The Spirit blows where he wills" (John 3:8). While seeking to communicate the gospel with care, faithfulness and zeal, we leave the results to God in humility.

Questions for Discussion

1. In Section 5 a and b the Report refuses to give a "neat formulation" of the gospel, but identifies its "heart." Would you want to add to these "central themes," or subtract from them, or amplify them?
2. Clarify the "two cultural blunders" of 5 c. Can you think of examples? How can such mistakes be avoided?
3. Think of the cultural situation of the people you are wanting to win for Christ. What would "cultural sensitivity" mean in your case?

6. Wanted: Humble Messengers of the Gospel!

We believe that the principal key to persuasive Christian communication is to be found in the communicators themselves and what kind of people they are. It should go without saying that they need to be people of Chris-

tian faith, love, and holiness. That is, they must have a personal and growing experience of the transforming power of the Holy Spirit, so that the
image of Jesus Christ is ever more clearly seen in their character and attitudes.

Above all else we desire to see in them, and specially in ourselves, "the
meekness and gentleness of Christ" (2 Cor. 10:1), in other words, the
humble sensitivity of Christ's love. So important do we believe this to be
that we are devoting the whole of this section of our Report to it. Moreover,
since, we have no wish to point the finger at anybody but ourselves, we shall
use the first person plural throughout. First, we give an analysis of Christian humility in a missionary situation, and secondly, we turn to the Incarnation of God in Jesus Christ as the model we desire by his grace to follow.

(a) An analysis of missionary humility

First, there is the humility to acknowledge the problem which culture presents, and not to avoid or over-simplify it. As we have seen, different cultures have strongly influenced the biblical revelation, ourselves, and the
people to whom we go. As a result, we have several personal limitations in
communicating the gospel. For we are prisoners (consciously or unconsciously) of our own culture, and our grasp of the cultures both of the Bible
and of the country in which we serve is very imperfect. It is the interaction
between all these cultures which constitutes the problem of communication;
it humbles all who wrestle with it.

Secondly, there is the humility to take the trouble to understand and appreciate the culture of those to whom we go. It is this desire which leads naturally into that true dialogue "whose purpose is to listen sensitively in order
to understand" (Lausanne Covenant, para. 4). We repent of the ignorance
which assumes that we have all the answers and that our only role is to
teach. We have very much to learn. We repent also of judgemental attitudes. We know we should never condemn or despise another culture, but
rather respect it. We advocate neither the arrogance which imposes our culture on others, nor the syncretism which mixes the gospel with cultural
elements incompatible with it, but rather a humble sharing of the good
news—made possible by the mutal respect of a genuine friendship.

Thirdly, there is the humility to begin our communication where people
actually are and not where we would like them to be. This is what we see
Jesus doing, and we desire to follow his example. Too often we have ignored people's fears and frustrations, their pains and preoccupations, and
their hunger, poverty, deprivation or oppression, in fact their "felt needs,"
and have been too slow to rejoice or to weep with them. We acknowledge
that these "felt needs" may sometimes be symptoms of deeper needs which
are not immediately felt or recognized by the people. A doctor does not necessarily accept a patient's self-diagnosis. Nevertheless, we see the need to
begin where people are, but not to stop there. We accept our responsibility
gently and patiently to lead them on to see themselves, as we see ourselves,
as rebels to whom the gospel directly speaks with a message of pardon and
hope. To begin where people are not is to share an irrelevant message; to
stay where people are and never lead them on to the fulness of God's good
news, is to share a truncated gospel. The humble sensitivity of love will
avoid both errors.

Fourthly, there is the humility to recognize that even the most gifted, dedicated and experienced missionary can seldom communicate the gospel in
another language or culture as effectively as a trained local Christian. This

'fact has been acknowledged in recent years by the Bible Societies, whose policy has changed from publishing translations by missionaries (with help from local people) to training mother-tongue specialists to do the translating. Only local Christians can answer the questions, "God, how would you say this in our language?" and "God, what will obedience to you mean in our culture?" Therefore, whether we are translating the Bible or communicating the gospel, local Christians are indispensable. It is they who must assume the responsibility to contextualize the gospel in their own languages and cultures. Would-be cross-cultural witnesses are not on that account necessarily superfluous; but we shall be welcome only if we are humble enough to see good communication as a team enterprise, in which all believers collaborate as partners.

Fifthly, there is the humility to trust in the Holy Spirit of God, who is always the chief communicator, who alone opens the eyes of the blind and brings people to new birth. "Without his witness, ours is futile" (Lausanne Covenant, para. 14).

(b) The Incarnation as a model for Christian witness

We have met for our Consultation within a few days of Christmas, which might be called the most spectacular instance of cultural identification in the history of mankind, since by his Incarnation the Son became a first-century Galilean Jew.

We have also remembered that Jesus intended his people's mission in the world to be modelled on his own. "As the Father has sent me, even so I send you," he said (John 20:21; cf. 17:18). We have asked ourselves, therefore, about the implications of the Incarnation for all of us. The question is of special concern to cross-cultural witnesses, whatever country they go to, although we have thought particularly of those from the West who serve in the Third World.

Meditating on Philippians 2, we have seen that the self-humbling of Christ began in his mind: "he did not count equality with God a thing to be grasped." So we are commanded to let his mind be in us, and in humility of mind to "count" others better or more important than ourselves. This "mind" or "perspective" of Christ is a recognition of the infinite worth of human beings and of the privilege it is to serve them. Those witnesses who have the mind of Christ will have a profound respect for the people they serve, and for their cultures.

Two verbs then indicate the action to which the mind of Christ led him: "he emptied himself...he humbled himself..." The first speaks of sacrifice (what he renounced) and the second of service, even slavery (how he identified himself with us and put himself at our disposal). We have tried to think what these two actions meant for him, and might mean for cross-cultural witnesses.

We began with his *renunciation*. First, the renunciation of status. "Mild he laid his glory by," we have been singing at Christmas. Because we cannot conceive what his eternal glory was like, it is impossible to grasp the greatness of his self-emptying. But certainly he surrendered the rights, privileges, and powers which he enjoyed as God's Son. "Status" and "status symbols" mean much in the modern world, but are incongruous in missionaries. We believe that wherever missionaries are they should not be in control or work alone, but always with—and preferably under—local Christians who can advise and even direct them. And whatever the missionaries' responsibility may be they should express attitudes "not of domination but of service" (Lausanne Covenant, para. 11).

Next the renunciation of independence. We have looked at Jesus--asking a Samaritan woman for water, living in other people's homes and on other people's money because he had none of his own, being lent a boat, a donkey, an upper room, and even being buried in a borrowed tomb. Similarly, cross-cultural messengers, especially during their first years of service, need to learn dependence on others.

Thirdly, the renunciation of immunity. Jesus exposed himself to temptation, sorrow, limitation, economic need, and pain. So the missionary should expect to become vulnerable to new temptations, dangers and diseases, a strange climate, an unaccustomed loneliness, and possibly death.

Turning from the theme of renunciation to that of *identification,* we have marvelled afresh at the completeness of our Saviour's identification with us, particularly as this is taught in the Letter to the Hebrews. He shared our "flesh and blood," was tempted as we are, learned obedience through his sufferings and tasted death for us (Heb. 2:14-18; 4:15; 5:8). During his public ministry Jesus befriended the poor and the powerless, healed the sick, fed the hungry, touched untouchables, and risked his reputation by associating with those whom society rejected.

The extent to which we identify ourselves with the people to whom we go is a matter of controversy. Certainly it must include mastering their language, immersing ourselves in their culture, learning to think as they think, feel as they feel, do as they do. At the socio-economic level we do not believe that we should "go native," principally because a foreigner's attempt to do this may not be seen as authentic but as play-acting. But neither do we think there should be a conspicuous disparity between our life style and that of the people around us. In between these extremes, we see the possibility of developing a standard of living which expresses the kind of love which cares and shares, and which finds it natural to exchange hospitality with others on a basis of reciprocity, without embarassment. A searching test of identification is how far we feel that we belong to the people, and—still more—how far they feel that we belong to them. Do we participate naturally in days of national or tribal thanksgiving or sorrow? Do we groan with them in the oppression which they suffer and join them in their quest for justice and freedom? If the country is struck by earthquake or engulfed in civil war, is our instinct to stay and suffer with the people we love, or to fly home?

Although Jesus identified himself completely with us, he did not lose his own identity. He remained himself. "He came down from heaven...and was made man" (Nicene Creed); yet in becoming one of us he did not cease to be God. Just so, "Christ's evangelists must humbly seek to empty themselves of all but their personal authenticity" (Lausanne Covenant, para. 10). The Incarnation teaches identification without loss of identity. We believe that true self-sacrifice leads to true self-discovery. In humble service there is abundant joy.

Questions for Discussion

1. If the main key to communication lies in the communicators, what sort of people should they be?

2. Give your own analysis of the humility which all Christian witnesses should have. Where would you put your emphasis?

3. Since the Incarnation involved both "renunciation" and "identification," it was obviously very costly for Jesus. What would be the cost of "incarnation evangelism" today?

7. Conversion and Culture

We have thought of the relations between conversion and culture in two ways. First, what effect does conversion have on the cultural situation of converts, the ways they think and act, and their attitudes to their social environment? Secondly, what effect has our culture had on our own understanding of conversion? Both questions are important. But we want to say at once that elements in our traditional evangelical view of conversion are more cultural than biblical and need to be challenged. Too often we have thought of conversion as a crisis, instead of as a process as well; or we have viewed conversion as a largely private experience, forgetting its consequent public and social responsibilities.

(a) The radical nature of conversion

We are convinced that the radical nature of conversion to Jesus Christ needs to be reaffirmed in the contemporary church. For we are always in danger of trivializing it, as if it were no more than a surface change, and a self-reformation at that. But the New Testament authors write of it as the outward expression of a regeneration or new birth by God's Spirit, a re-creation, and resurrection from spiritual death. The concept of resurrection seems to be particularly important. For the resurrection of Jesus Christ from the dead was the beginning of the new creation of God, and by God's grace through union with Christ we have shared in this resurrection. We have therefore entered the new age and have already tasted its powers and its joys. This is the eschatological dimension of Christian conversion. Conversion is an integral part of the Great Renewal which God has begun, and which will be brought to a triumphant climax when Christ comes in his glory.

Conversion involves as well a break with the past so complete that it is spoken of in terms of death. We have been crucified with Christ. Through his cross we have died to the godless world, its outlook, and its standards. We have also "put off" like a soiled garment the old Adam, our former and fallen humanity. And Jesus warned us that this turning away from the past may involve painful sacrifices, even the loss of family and possessions (e.g., Lk. 14:25ff).

It is vital to keep together these negative and positive aspects of conversion, the death and the resurrection, the putting off of the old and the putting on of the new. For we who died are alive again, but alive now with a new life lived in, for, and under Christ.

(b) The lordship of Jesus Christ

We are clear that the fundamental meaning of conversion is a change of allegiance. Other gods and lords—idolatries every one—previously ruled over us. But now Jesus Christ is Lord. The governing principle of the converted life is that it is lived under the lordship of Christ or (for it comes to the same thing) in the Kingdom of God. His authority over us is total. So this new and liberating allegiance leads inevitably to a reappraisal of every aspect of our lives and in particular of our world-view, our behaviour, and our relationships.

First, our world-view. We are agreed that the heart of every culture is a "religion" of some kind, even if it is an irreligious religion like Marxism.

"Culture is religion made visible" (J.H. Bavinck). And "religion" is a whole cluster of basic beliefs and values, which is the reason why for our purposes we are using "world-view" as an equivalent expression. True conversion to Christ is bound, therefore, to strike at the heart of our cultural inheritance. Jesus Christ insists on dislodging from the centre of our world whatever idol previously reigned there, and occupying the throne himself. This is the radical change of allegiance which constitutes conversion, or at least its beginning. Then once Christ has taken his rightful place, everything else starts shifting. The shock waves flow from the centre to the circumference. The convert has to rethink his or her fundamental convictions. This is *metanoia*, "repentance" viewed as a change of mind, the replacement of "the mind of the flesh" by "the mind of Christ." Of course, the development of an integrated Christian world-view may take a lifetime, but it is there in essence from the start. If it does grow, the explosive consequences cannot be predicted.

Secondly, our behaviour. The lordship of Jesus challenges our moral standards and whole ethical life style. Strictly speaking, this is not "repentance" but rather the "fruit that befits repentance" (Matt. 3:8), the change of conduct which issues from a change of outlook. Both our minds and our wills must submit to the obedience of Christ (cf. 2 Cor. 10:5; Matt. 11:29,30; John 13:13).

Listening to case-studies of conversion we have been impressed by the primacy of love in the new convert's experience. Conversion delivers both from the inversion which is too preoccupied with self to bother about other people and from the fatalism which considers it impossible to help them. Conversion is spurious if it does not liberate us to love.

Thirdly, our relationships. Although the convert should do his utmost to avoid a break with nation, tribe and family, sometimes painful conflicts arise. It is clear also that conversion involves a transfer from one community to another, that is, from fallen humanity to God's new humanity. It happened from the very beginning on the Day of Pentecost: "Save yourselves from this crooked generation," Peter appealed. So those who received his message were baptized into the new society, devoted themselves to the new fellowship, and found that the Lord continued to add to their numbers daily (Acts 2:40-47). At the same time, their "transfer" from one group to another meant rather that they were spiritually distinct than that they were socially segregated. They did not abandon the world. On the contrary, they gained a new commitment to it, and went out into it to witness and to serve.

All of us should cherish great expectations of such radical conversions in our day, involving converts in a new mind, a new way of life, a new community, and a new mission, all under the lordship of Christ. Yet now we feel the need to make several qualifications.

(c) The convert and his culture

Conversion should not "de-culturize" a convert. True, as we have seen, the Lord Jesus now holds his or her allegiance, and everything in the cultural context must come under his Lord's scrutiny. This applies to every culture, not just to those of Hindu, Buddhist, Muslim, or animistic cultures but also to the increasingly materialistic culture of the West. The critique may lead to a collision, as elements of the culture come under the judgement of Christ and have to be rejected. At this point, on the rebound, the convert may try to adopt the evangelist's culture instead; the attempt should be firmly but gently resisted.

The convert should be encouraged to see his or her relation to the past as a combination of rupture and continuity. However much new converts feel they need to renounce for the sake of Christ, they are still the same people with the same heritage and the same family. "Conversion does not unmake; it remakes." It is always tragic, though in some situations it is unavoidable, when a person's conversion to Christ is interpreted by others as treachery to his or her own cultural origins. If possible, in spite of the conflicts with their own culture, new converts should seek to identify with their culture's joys, hopes, pains, and struggles.

Case histories show that converts often pass through three stages: (1) "rejection" (when they see themselves as "new persons in Christ" and repudiate everything associated with their past); (2) "accommodation" (when they discover their ethnic and cultural heritage, with the temptation to compromise the new-found Christian faith in relation to their heritage); and (3) "the re-establishment of identity" (when either the rejection of the past or the accommodation to it may increase, or preferably, they may grow into a balanced self-awareness in Christ and in culture).

(d) The power encounter

"Jesus is Lord" means more than that he is Lord of the individual convert's world-view, standards and relationships, and more even than that he is Lord of culture. It means that he is Lord of the powers, having been exalted by the Father to universal sovereignty, principalities and powers having been made subject to him (1 Peter. 3:22). A number of us, especially those from Asia, Africa, and Latin America, have spoken both of the reality of evil powers and of the necessity to demonstrate the supremacy of Jesus over them. For conversion involves a power encounter. People give their allegiance to Christ when they see that his power is superior to magic and voodoo, the curses and blessings of witch doctors, and the malevolence of evil spirits, and that his salvation is a real liberation from the power of evil and death.

Of course, some are questioning today whether a belief in spirits is compatible with our modern scientific understanding of the universe. We wish to affirm, therefore, against the mechanistic myth on which the typical western world-view rests, the reality of demonic intelligences which are concerned by all means, overt and covert, to discredit Jesus Christ and keep people from coming to him. We think it vital in evangelism in all cultures to teach the reality and hostility of demonic powers, and to proclaim that God has exalted Christ as Lord of all and that Christ, who really does possess all power, however we may fail to acknowledge this, can (as we proclaim him) break through any world-view in any mind to make his lordship known and bring about a radical change of heart and outlook.

We wish to emphasize that the power belongs to Christ. Power in human hands is always dangerous. We have called to mind the recurring theme of Paul's two letters to the Corinthians—that God's power, which is clearly seen in the cross of Christ, operates through human weakness (e.g., 1 Cor. 1:18-2:5; 2 Cor. 4:7; 12:9,10). Worldly people worship power; Christians who have it know its perils. It is better to be weak, for then we are strong. We specially honour the Christian martyrs of recent days (e.g., in East Africa) who have renounced the way of power, and followed the way of the cross.

(e) Individual and group conversions

Conversion should not be conceived as being invariably and only an individual experience, although that has been the pattern of western expectation for many years. On the contrary, the covenant theme of the Old Testament and the household baptisms of the New should lead us to desire, work for, and expect both family and group conversions. Much important research has been undertaken in recent years into "people movements" from both theological and sociological perspectives. Theologically, we recognize the biblical emphasis on the solidarity of each *ethnos,* i.e., nation or people. Sociologically, we recognize that each society is composed of a variety of subgroups, subcultures or homogeneous units. It is evident that people receive the gospel most readily when it is presented to them in a manner which is appropriate—and not alien—to their culture, and when they can respond to it with and among their own people. Different societies have different procedures for making group decisions, e.g., by consensus, by the head of the family, or by a group of elders. We recognize the validity of the corporate dimension of conversion as part of the total process, as well as the necessity for each member of the group ultimately to share in it personally.

(f) Is conversion sudden or gradual?

Conversion is often more gradual than traditional evangelical teaching has allowed. True, this may be only a dispute about words. Justification and regeneration, the one conveying a new status and the other a new life, are works of God and instantaneous, although we are not necessarily aware when they take place. Conversion, on the other hand, is our own action (moved by God's grace) of turning to God in penitence and faith. Although it may include a conscious crisis, it is often slow and sometimes laborious. Seen against the background of the Hebrew and Greek vocabulary, conversion is in essence a turning to God, which continues as all areas of life are brought in increasingly radical ways under the lordship of Christ. Conversion involves the Christian's complete transformation and total renewal in mind and character according to the likeness of Christ (Rom. 12:1,2).

This progress does not always take place, however. We have given some thought to the sad phenomena called "backsliding" (a quiet slipping away from Christ) and "apostasy" (an open repudiation of him). These have a variety of causes. Some people turn away from Christ when they become disenchanted with the church; others capitulate to the pressures of secularism or of their former culture. These facts challenge us both to proclaim a full gospel and to be more conscientious in nurturing converts in the faith and in training them for service.

One member of our Consultation has described his experience in terms of turning first to Christ (receiving his salvation and acknowledging his lordship), secondly to culture (rediscovering his natural origins and identity), and thirdly to the world (accepting the mission on which Christ sends him). We agree that conversion is often a complex experience, and that the biblical language of "turning" is used in different ways and contexts. At the same time, we all emphasize that personal commitment to Jesus Christ is foundational. In him alone we find salvation, new life, and personal identity. Conversion must also result in new attitudes and relationships, and lead to a responsible involvement in our church, our culture, and our world. Finally, conversion is a journey, a pilgrimage, with ever-new challenges, decisions, and returnings to the Lord as the constant point of reference, until he comes.

Questions for Discussion

1. Distinguish between "regeneration" and "conversion" according to the New Testament.
2. "Jesus is Lord." What does this mean for you in your own culture? See Section 7 b and d. What are the elements of your cultural heritage which you feel (a) you must, and (b) you need not, renounce for the sake of Christ?
3. What is sudden and what is (or may be) gradual in Christian conversion?

8. Church and Culture

In the process of church formation, as in the communication and reception of the gospel, the question of culture is vital. If the gospel must be contextualized, so must the church. Indeed, the sub-title of our Consultation has been "the contextualization of Word and Church in a missionary situation."

(a) Older, traditional approaches

During the missionary expansion of the early part of the 19th century, it was generally assumed that churches "on the mission field" would be modelled on churches "at home." The tendency was to produce almost exact replicas. Gothic architecture, prayer book liturgies, clerical dress, musical instruments, hymns and tunes, decision-making processes, synods and committees, superintendents and archdeacons--all were exported and unimaginatively introduced into the new mission-founded churches. It should be added that these patterns were also eagerly adopted by the new Christians, determined not to be at any point behind their western friends, whose habits and ways of worship they had been attentively watching. But all this was based on the false assumptions that the Bible gave specific instructions about such matters and that the home churches' pattern of government, worship, ministry, and life were themselves exemplary.

In reaction to this monocultural export system, pioneer missionary thinkers like Henry Venn and Rufus Anderson in the middle of the last century and Roland Allen earlier in this century popularized the concept of "indigenous" churches, which would be "self-governing, self-supporting and self-propagating." They argued their case well. They pointed out that the policy of the apostle Paul was to plant churches, not to found mission stations. They also added pragmatic arguments to biblical ones, namely that indigeneity was indispensable to the church's growth in maturity and mission. Henry Venn confidently looked forward to the day when missions would hand over all responsibility to national churches, and then what he called "the euthanasia of the mission" would take place. These views gained wide acceptance and were immensely influential.

In our day, however, they are being criticized, not because of the ideal itself, but because of the way it has often been applied. Some missions, for example, have accepted the need for indigenous leadership and have then gone on to recruit and train local leaders, indoctrinating them (the word is harsh but not unfair) in western ways of thought and procedure. These westernized local leaders have then preserved a very western-looking church, and the foreign orientation has persisted, only lightly cloaked by the appearance of indigeneity.

Now, therefore, a more radical concept of indigenous church life needs to be developed, by which each church may discover and express its selfhood as the body of Christ within its own culture.

(b) The dynamic equivalence model

Using the distinctions between "form" and "meaning," and between "formal correspondence" and "dynamic equivalence," which have been developed in translation theory and on which we have commented in Section 3, it is being suggested that an analogy may be drawn between Bible translation and church formation. "Formal correspondence" speaks of a slavish imitation, whether in translating a word into another language or exporting a church model to another culture. Just as a "dynamic equivalence" translation, however, seeks to convey to contemporary readers meanings equivalent to those conveyed to the original readers, by using appropriate cultural forms, so would a "dynamic equivalence" church. It would look in its culture as a good Bible translation looks in its language. It would preserve the essential meanings and functions which the New Testament predicated of the church, but would seek to express these in forms equivalent to the originals but appropriate to the local culture.

We have all found this model helpful and suggestive, and we strongly affirm the ideals it seeks to express. It rightly rejects foreign imports and imitations, and rigid structures. It rightly looks to the New Testament for the principles of church formation, rather than to either tradition or culture, and it equally rightly looks to the local culture for the appropriate forms in which these principles should be expressed. All of us (even those who see limitations in the model) share the vision which it is trying to describe.

Thus, the New Testament indicates that the church is always a worshipping community, "a holy priesthood to offer spiritual sacrifices to God through Jesus Christ" (1 Pet. 2:5), but forms of worship (including the presence or absence of different kinds of liturgy, ceremony, music, colour, drama, etc.) will be developed by the church in keeping with indigenous culture. Similarly, the church is always a witnessing and a serving community, but its methods of evangelism and its programme of social involvement will vary. Again, God desires all churches to have pastoral oversight *(episkopē)*, but forms of government and ministry may differ widely, and the selection, training, ordination, service, dress, payment, and accountability of pastors will be determined by the church to accord with biblical principles and to suit the local culture.

The questions which are being asked about the "dynamic equivalence" model are whether by itself it is large enough and dynamic enough to provide all the guidance which is needed. The analogy between Bible translation and church formation is not exact. In the former the translator controls the work, and when the task is complete it is possible to make a comparison of the two texts. In the latter, however, the original to which an equivalent is being sought is not a detailed text but a series of glimpses of the early church in operation, making the comparison more difficult, and instead of a controlling translator the whole community of faith must be involved. Further, a translator aims at personal objectivity, but when the local church is seeking to relate itself appropriately to the local culture, it finds objectivity almost impossible. In many situations it is caught in "an encounter between two civilizations" (that of its own society and that of the missionaries'). Furthermore, it may have great difficulty in responding to the conflicting voices of the local community. Some clamor for change (in terms of literacy, education, technology, modern medicine, industrialization, etc.), while others insist on the conservation of the old culture and resist the arrival of a new day. It is asked whether the "dynamic equivalence" model is dynamic enough to face this kind of challenge.

The test of this or any other model for helping churches develop appropriately, is whether it can enable God's people to capture in their hearts and minds the grand design of which their church is to be the local expression. Every model presents only a partial picture. Local churches need to rely ultimately on the dynamic pressure of the Living Lord of history. For it is he who will guide his people in every age to develop their church life in such a way as both to obey the instructions he has given in Scripture and to reflect the good elements of their local culture.

(c) The freedom of the church

If each church is to develop creatively in such a way as to find and express itself, it must be free to do so. This is its inalienable right. For each church is God's church. United to Christ, it is a dwelling place of God through his Spirit (Eph. 2:22). Some missions and missionaries have been slow to recognize this, and to accept its implications in the direction of indigenous forms and an every-member ministry. This is one of the many causes which have led to the formation of Independent Churches, notably in Africa, which are seeking new ways of self-expression in terms of local culture.

Although local church leaders have also sometimes impeded indigenous development, the chief blame lies elsewhere. It would not be fair to generalize. The situation has always been diverse. In earlier generations there were missions which never manifested a spirit of domination. In this century some churches have sprung up which have never been under missionary control, having enjoyed self-government from the start. In other cases missions have entirely surrendered their former power, so that some mission-founded churches are now fully autonomous, and many missions now work in genuine partnership with churches.

Yet this is not the whole picture. Other churches are still almost completely inhibited from developing their own identity and programme by policies laid down from afar, by the introduction and continuation of foreign traditions, by the use of expatriate leadership, by alien decision-making processes, and especially by the manipulative use of money. Those who maintain such control may be genuinely unaware of the way in which their actions are regarded and experienced at the other end. They may be felt by the churches concerned to be a tyranny. The fact that this is neither intended nor realized illustrates perfectly how all of us (whether we know it or not) are involved in the culture which has made us what we are. We strongly oppose such "foreignness," wherever it exists, as a serious obstacle to maturity and mission, and a quenching of the Holy Spirit of God.

It was in protest against the continuance of foreign control that a few years ago the call was made to withdraw all missionaries. In this debate some of us want to avoid the word "moratorium" because it has become an emotive term and sometimes betrays a resentment against the very concept of "missionaries." Others of us wish to retain the word in order to emphasize the truth it expresses. To us it means not a rejection of missionary personnel and money in themselves, but only of their misuse in such a way as to suffocate local initiative. We all agree with the statement of the Lausanne Covenant that "a reduction of foreign missionaries and money...may sometimes be necessary to facilitate the national church's growth in self-reliance..." (para. 9).

(d) Power structures and mission

What we have just written is part of a much wider problem, which we have not felt able to ignore. The contemporary world does not consist of isolated atomic societies, but is an interrelated global system of economic, political, technological, and ideological macro-structures, which undoubtedly results in much exploitation and oppression.

What has this got to do with mission? And why do we raise it here? Partly because it is the context within which the gospel must be preached to all nations today. Partly also because nearly all of us either belong to the Third World, or live and work there, or have done so, or have visited some countries in it. So we have seen with our own eyes the poverty of the masses, we feel for them and with them, and we have some understanding that their plight is due in part to an economic system which is controlled mostly by the North Atlantic countries (although others are now also involved). Those of us who are citizens of North American or European countries cannot avoid some feeling of embarrassment and shame, by reason of the oppression in which our countries in various degrees have been involved. Of course, we know that there is oppression in many countries today, and we oppose it everywhere. But now we are talking about ourselves, our own countries, and our responsibility as Christians. Most of the world's missionaries and missionary money come from these countries, often at great personal sacrifice. Yet we have to confess that some missionaries themselves reflect a neo-colonial attitude and even defend it, together with outposts of western power and exploitation such as Southern Africa.

So what should we do? The only honest response is to say that we do not know. Armchair criticism smacks of hypocrisy. We have no ready-made solutions to offer to this worldwide problem. Indeed, we feel victims of the system ourselves. And yet we are also part of it. So we feel able to make only these comments.

First, Jesus himself constantly identified with the poor and weak. We accept the obligation to follow in his footsteps in this matter as in all others. At least by the love which prays and gives we mean to strengthen our solidarity with them.

Jesus did more than identify, however. In his teaching and that of the apostles the corollary of good news to the oppressed was a word of judgement to the oppressor (e.g., Luke 6:24-26; Jas. 5:1-6). We confess that in complex economic situations it is not easy to identify oppressors in order to denounce them without resorting to a shrill rhetoric which neither costs nor accomplishes anything. Nevertheless, we accept that there will be occasions when it is our Christian duty to speak out against injustice in the name of the Lord who is the God of justice as well as of justification. We shall seek from him the courage and wisdom to do so.

Thirdly, this Consultation has expressed its concern about syncretism in Third World churches. But we have not forgotten that western churches fall prey to the same sin. Indeed, perhaps the most insidious form of syncretism in the world today is the attempt to mix a privatized gospel of personal forgiveness with a worldly (even demonic) attitude to wealth and power. We are not guiltless in this matter ourselves. Yet we desire to be integrated Christians for whom Jesus is truly Lord of all. So we who belong to, or come from, the West will examine ourselves and seek to purge ourselves of western-style syncretism. We agree that "the salvation we claim should be transforming us in the totality of our personal and social responsibilities. Faith without works is dead" (Lausanne Covenant, para. 5).

(e) The danger of provincialism

We have emphasized that the church must be allowed to indigenize itself, and to "celebrate, sing and dance" the gospel in its own cultural medium. At the same time, we wish to be alert to the dangers of this process. Some churches in all six continents go beyond a joyful and thankful discovery of their local cultural heritage, and either become boastful and assertive about it (a form of chauvinism) or even absolutize it (a form of idolatry). More common than either of these extremes, however, is "provincialism," that is, such a retreat into their own culture as cuts them adrift from the rest of the church and from the wider world. This is a frequent stance in western churches as well as in the Third World. It denies the God of creation and redemption. It is to proclaim one's freedom, only to enter another bondage. We draw attention to the three major reasons why we think this attitude should be avoided.

First, each church is part of the universal church. The people of God are by his grace a unique multi-racial, multi-national, multi-cultural community. This community is God's new creation, his new humanity, in which Christ has abolished all barriers (see Ephesians 2 and 3). There is therefore no room for racism in the Christian society, or for tribalism—whether in its African form, or in the form of European social classes, or of the Indian caste system. Despite the church's failures, this vision of a supra-ethnic community of love is not a romantic ideal, but a command of the Lord. Therefore, while rejoicing in our cultural inheritance and developing our own indigenous forms, we must always remember that our primary identity as Christians is not in our particular culture but in the one Lord and his one body (Eph. 4:3-6).

Secondly, each church worships the living God of cultural diversity. If we thank him for our cultural heritage, we should thank him for others' also. Our church should never become so culture-bound that visitors from another culture do not feel welcome. Indeed, we believe it is enriching for Christians, if they have the opportunity, to develop a bi-cultural and even a multi-cultural existence, like the apostle Paul who was both a Hebrew of the Hebrews, a master of the Greek language, and a Roman citizen.

Thirdly, each church should enter into a "partnership...in giving and receiving" (Phil. 4:15). No church is, or should try to become, self-sufficient. So churches should develop with each other relationships of prayer, fellowship, interchange of ministry and cooperation. Provided that we share the same central truths (including the supreme lordship of Christ, the authority of the Scriptures, the necessity of conversion, confidence in the power of the Holy Spirit, and the obligations of holiness and witness), we should be outgoing and not timid in seeking fellowship; and we should share our spiritual gifts and ministries, knowledge, skills, experience, and financial resources. The same principle applies to cultures. A church must be free to reject alien cultural forms and develop its own; it should also feel free to borrow from others. This way lies maturity.

One example of this concerns theology. Cross-cultural witnesses must not attempt to impose a ready-made theological tradition on the church in which they serve, either by personal teaching or by literature or by controlling seminary and Bible college curricula. For every theological tradition both contains elements which are biblically questionable and have been ecclesiastically divisive and omits elements which, while they might be of no great consequence in the country where it originated, may be of immense importance in other contexts. At the same time, although missionaries ought not to impose their own tradition on others, they also ought not to deny them access to it (in the form of books, confessions, catechism, liturgies and hymns), since it doubtless represents a rich heritage of faith. Moreover, although the theological controversies of the older churches should not be exported to the younger churches, yet an understanding of the issues, and of the work of the Holy Spirit in the unfolding history of Christian doctrine, should help to protect them from unprofitable repetition of the same battles.

Thus we should seek with equal care to avoid theological imperialism or theological provincialism. A church's theology should be developed by the community of faith out of the Scripture in interaction with other theologies of the past and present, and with the local culture and its needs.

(f) The danger of syncretism

As the church seeks to express its life in local cultural forms, it soon has to face the problem of cultural elements which either are evil or have evil associations. How should the church react to these? Elements which are intrinsically false or evil clearly cannot be assimilated into Christianity without a lapse into syncretism. This is a danger for all churches in all cultures. If the evil is in the association only, however, we believe it is right to seek to "baptize" it into Christ. It is the principle on which William Booth operated when he set Christian words to popular music, asking why the devil should have all the best tunes. Thus many African churches now use drums to summon people to worship, although previously they were unacceptable, as being associated with war dances and mediumistic rites.

Yet this principle raises problems. In a proper reaction against foreigners, an improper flirtation with the demonic element of local culture sometimes takes place. So the church, being first and foremost a servant of Jesus Christ, must learn to scrutinize all culture, both foreign and local, in the light of his lordship and God's revelation. By what guidelines, therefore, does a church accept or reject culture traits in the process of contextualization? How does it prevent or detect and eliminate heresy (wrong teaching) and syncretism (harmful carry-overs from the old way of life)? How does it protect itself from becoming a "folk church" in which church and society are virtually synonymous?

One particular model we have studied is that of the church in Bali, Indonesia, which is now about 40 years old. Its experience has provided the following guidelines:

The believing community first searched the Scriptures and learned from them many important biblical truths. They then observed that other churches (e.g., round the Mediterranean) used architecture to symbolize Christian truth. This was important because the Balinese are very "visual" people and value visible signs. So it was decided, for example, to express their affirmation of faith in the Trinity in a Balinese-style three-tiered roof for their church buildings. The symbol was first considered by the council of elders who, after studying both biblical and cultural factors, recommended it to local congregations.

The detection and elimination of heresy followed a similar pattern. When believers suspected an error in life or teaching, they would report it to an elder, who would take it to the council of elders. Having considered the matter, they in their turn passed their recommendations to the local churches who had the final word.

What was the most important safeguard of the church? To this question the answer was: "we believe that Jesus Christ is Lord and Master of all powers." By preaching his power, "the same yesterday and today and forever," by insisting at all times on the normative nature of the Scriptures, by entrusting elders with the obligation to reflect on Scripture and culture, by breaking down all barriers to fellowship, and by building into structures, catechism, art forms, drama, etc., constant reminders of the exalted position of Jesus Christ, his church has been preserved in truth and holiness.

Sometimes, in different parts of the world, a cultural element may be adopted which deeply disturbs oversensitive consciences, especially those of new converts. This is the problem of the "weaker brother" of whom Paul writes in connection with idol-meats. Since idols were nothing, Paul himself had liberty of conscience to eat these meats. But for the sake of "weaker" Christians with a less well-educated conscience, who would be offended to see him eat, he refrained, at least in specific situations in which such offence might be caused. The principle still applies today. Scripture takes conscience seriously and tells us not to violate it. It needs to be educated in order to become "strong," but while it remains "weak" it must be respected. A strong conscience will give us freedom; but love limits liberty.

(g) The church's influence on culture

We deplore the pessimism which leads some Christians to disapprove of active cultural engagement in the world, and the defeatism which persuades others that they could do no good there anyway and should therefore wait in inactivity for Christ to put things right when he comes. Many historical examples could be given, drawn from different ages and countries, of the powerful influence which—under God—the church has exerted on a prevailing culture, purging, claiming, and beautifying it for Christ. Though all such attempts have had defects, they do not prove the enterprise mistaken.

We prefer, however, to base the church's cultural responsibility on Scripture rather than on history. We have reminded ourselves that our fellow men and women are made in God's image, and that we are commanded to honour, love, and serve them in every sphere of life. To this argument from God's creation we add another from his kingdom which broke into the world through Jesus Christ. All authority belongs to Christ. He is lord of both universe and church. And he has sent us into the world to be its salt and light. As his new community, he expects us to permeate society.

Thus we are to challenge what is evil and affirm what is good; to welcome and seek to promote all that is wholesome and enriching in art, science, technology, agriculture, industry, education, community development and social welfare; to denounce injustice and support the powerless and the oppressed; to spread the good news of Jesus Christ, which is the most liberating and humanizing force in the world; and actively to engage in good works of love. Although, in social and cultural activity as in evangelism, we must leave the results to God, we are confident that he will bless our endeavors and use them to develop in our community a new consciousness of what is "true, noble, right, pure, lovely, and honourable" (Phil. 4:8, TEV). Of course, the church cannot impose Christian standards on an unwilling society, but it can commend them by both argument and example. All this will bring glory to God and greater opportunities of humanness to our fellow human beings whom he made and loves. As the Lausanne Covenant put it, "churches must seek to transform and enrich culture, all for the glory of God" (para. 10).

Nevertheless, naive optimism is as foolish as dark pessimism. In place of both, we seek a sober Christian realism. On the one hand, Jesus Christ reigns. On the other, he has not yet destroyed the forces of evil; they still rampage. So in every culture Christians find themselves in a situation of conflict and often of suffering. We are called to fight against the "cosmic powers of this dark age" (Eph. 6:12, TEV). So we need each other. We must put on all God's armour, and especially the mighty weapon of believing prayer. We also remember the warnings of Christ and his apostles that before the end there will be an unprecedented outbreak of wickedness and violence. Some events and developments in our contemporary world indicate that the spirit of the coming Antichrist is already at work not only in the non-Christian world, but both in our own partially Christianized societies and even in the churches themselves. "We therefore reject as a proud, self-confident dream the notion that man can ever build a utopia on earth" (Lausanne Covenant, para. 15), and as a groundless fantasy that society is going to evolve into perfection.

Instead, while energetically labouring on earth, we look forward with joyful anticipation to the return of Christ, and to the new heavens and new earth in which righteousness will dwell. For then not only will culture be transformed, as the nations bring their glory into the New Jerusalem (Rev. 21:24-26) but the whole creation will be liberated from its present bondage of futility, decay and pain, so as to share the glorious freedom of God's children (Rom. 8:18-25, TEV). Then at last every knee will bow to Christ and every tongue openly proclaim that he is Lord, to the glory of God the Father (Phil. 2:9-11).

Questions for Discussion

1. Is your local church "free" to develop its own selfhood? If not, what forces are hindering it? See Section 8 a-d.
2. Section 8 d has some hard things to say about "power-structures." Do you agree? If so, can you do anything about it?
3. "Provincialism" (8 e) and "syncretism" (8 f) are both mistakes of a church which is trying to express its identity in local cultural forms. Is your church making either mistake? How can they be avoided without repudiating indigenous culture?
4. Should the church in your country be doing more to "transform and enrich" its national culture? If so, in what way?

9. Culture, Christian Ethics and Life Style

Having considered in Section 7 some of the cultural factors in Christian conversion, we come finally to the relations between culture and Christian ethical behaviour. For the new life Christ gives his people is bound to issue in a new life style.

(a) Christ-centredness and Christ-likeness

One of the themes running right through our Consultation has been the supreme Lordship of Jesus Christ. He is Lord of the universe and the church; he is Lord of the individual believer also. We find ourselves gripped by the love of Christ. It hems us in and leaves us no escape. Because we enjoy newness of life through his death for us, we have no alternative (and desire none) but to live for him who died for us and rose again (2 Cor. 5:14,15). Our first loyalty is to him, to seek to please him, to live a life worthy of him, and to obey him. This necessitates the renunciation of all lesser loyalties. So we are forbidden to conform ourselves to this world's standards, that is, to any prevailing culture which fails to honour God, and are commanded instead to be transformed in our conduct by renewed minds which perceive the will of God.

God's will was perfectly obeyed by Jesus. Therefore, "the most outstanding thing about a Christian should not be his culture, but his Christlikeness." As the mid-second century *Letter to Diognetus* put it: "Christians are not distinguished from the rest of mankind by country or by speech or by customs...they follow the customs of the land in clothing and food and other matters of daily life, yet the condition of citizenship which they exhibit is wonderful...In a word, what the soul is in the body, that Christians are in the world."

(b) Moral standards and cultural practices

Culture is never static. It varies both from place to place and from time to time. And throughout the long history of the church in different countries, Christianity has, in some measure, destroyed culture, preserved it, and in the end created a new culture in place of the old. So everywhere Christians need to think seriously about just how their new life in Christ should relate to contemporary culture.

In our Consultation's preliminary papers two rather similar models were set before us. One suggested that there are several categories of customs which need to be distinguished. The first includes those practices which the convert will be expected to renounce immediately as being wholly incompatible with the Christian gospel (e.g., idolatry, the possession of slaves, witchcraft and sorcery, head hunting, blood feuds, ritual prostitution, and all personal discriminations based on race, colour, class or caste). A second category might comprise institutionalized customs which could be tolerated for a while but would be expected to disappear gradually (e.g., systems of caste, slavery, and polygamy). A third category might relate to marriage traditions, especially questions of consanguinity, on which the churches are divided, while into a fourth category would be put the so-called *adiaphora* or "matters indifferent," which relate only to customs and not to morals, and therefore may be preserved without any compromise (e.g., eating and bathing customs, forms of public greeting to the opposite sex, hair and dress styles, etc.).

The second model we have considered distinguishes between "direct" and "indirect" encounters between Christ and culture, which correspond approximately to the first and second categories of the other model. Applied to 19th century Fiji in the case-study presented to us, it was assumed that there would be "direct encounter" with such inhuman practices as cannibalism, widow-strangling, infanticide, and patricide, and that converts would be expected to abandon these customs upon conversion. "Indirect" encounter would take place, however, either when the moral issue was not so clear-cut (e.g., some marriage customs, initiation rites, festivals and musical celebrations involving song, dance and instruments) or when it becomes apparent only after the convert has begun to work out his or her new faith in the applied Christian life. Some of these practices will not need to be discarded, but rather to be purged of unclean elements and invested with Christian meaning. Old customs can be given new symbolism, old dances can celebrate new blessings, and old crafts can serve new purposes. To borrow an expression from the Old Testament, swords can be hammered into ploughs and spears into pruning-knives.

The Lausanne Covenant said: "The Gospel does not presuppose the superiority of any culture to another, but evaluates all cultures according to its own criteria of truth and righteousness, and insists on moral absolutes in every culture" (para. 10). We wish to endorse this, and to emphasize that even in this present age of relativity moral absolutes remain. Indeed, churches which study the Scriptures should not find it difficult to discern what belongs to the first or "direct encounter" category. Scriptural principles under the guidance of the Holy Spirit will also guide them regarding the category of "indirect encounter." An additional test proposed is to ask whether a practice enhances or diminishes human life.

It will be seen that our studies have focussed mainly on situations where younger churches have to take up a moral stance against certain evils. But we have been reminded that the church needs to confront evil in western culture too. In the 20th century West, often more sophisticated but no less horrible examples of the evils which were opposed in 19th century Fiji exist. Parallel to cannibalism is social injustice which "eats" the poor; to widow-strangling, the oppression of women; to infanticide, abortion; to patricide, a criminal neglect of senior citizens; to tribal wars, World Wars I and II; and to ritual prostitution, sexual promiscuity. In considering this parallelism, it is necessary to remember both the added guilt adhering to the nominally Christian nations, and also the courageous Christian protest against such evils, and the immense (though incomplete) successes which have been won in mitigating these evils. Evil takes many forms, but it is universal, and wherever it appears Christians must confront and repudiate it.

(c) The process of cultural change

It is not enough for converts to make a personal renunciation of the evils in their culture; the whole church needs to work for their elimination. Hence, the importance of asking how cultures change under the influence of the gospel. Of course, the evil and the demonic are deeply entrenched in most cultures, and yet Scripture calls for national repentance and reform, and history records numerous cases of cultural change for the better. In fact, in some cases culture is not as resistant to necessary change as it may appear. Great care is needed, however, when seeking to initiate it.

First, "people change as and when they want to." This seems to be axiomatic. Further, they want to change only when they perceive the positive benefits which change will bring them. These will need to be carefully argued and patiently demonstrated, whether Christians are advocating in a developing country the benefits of literacy or the value of clean water, or in a western country the importance of stable marriage and family life.

Secondly, cross-cultural witnesses in the Third World need to have great respect for the in-built mechanisms of social change in general, and for the "correct procedures of innovation" in each particular culture.

Thirdly, it is important to remember that virtually all customs perform important functions within the culture, and that even socially undesirable practices may perform "constructive" functions. That being so, a custom should never be abolished without first discerning its function and then substituting another custom which performs the same function. For example, it may be right to wish to see abolished some of the initiatory rites associated with the circumcision of adolescents and some of the forms of sex education which accompany it. This is not to deny that there is much of value in the processes of initiation; great care must be taken to see that adequate substitutes are provided for the rites and forms of initiation which the Christian conscience would desire to see abolished.

Fourthly, it is essential to recognize that some cultural practices have a theological undergirding. When this is so, the culture will change only when the theology changes. Thus, if widows are killed in order that their husbands may not enter the next world unattended, or if older people are killed before senility overtakes them, in order that in the next world they may be strong enough to fight and hunt, then such killings, because founded on a false eschatology, will be abandoned only when a better alternative, the Christian hope, is accepted in its place.

Questions for Discussion

1. Can "Christ-likeness" be recognized in every culture? What are its ingredients?
2. In your own culture, what would you expect a new convert to renounce immediately?
3. Take some "institutionalized custom" in your country which Christians hope will "disappear gradually" (e.g., polygamy, the caste system, easy divorce, or some form of oppression). What active steps should Christians be taking to work for change?

Conclusion

Our Consultation has left us in no doubt of the pervasive importance of culture. The writing and the reading of the Bible, the presentation of the gospel, conversion, church and conduct---all these are influenced by culture. It is essential, therefore, that all churches contextualize the gospel in order to share it effectively in their own culture. For this task of evangelization, we all know our urgent need of the ministry of the Holy Spirit. He is the Spirit of truth who can teach each church how to relate to the culture which envelops it. He is also the Spirit of love, and love is "the language--which is understood in every culture of man." So may God fill us with his Spirit! Then, speaking the truth in love, we shall grow up into Christ who is the head of the body, to the everlasting glory of God (Eph. 4:15).

NOTE: Unattributed quotations in this report have been drawn from various papers presented at this Consultation.

In Attendance

PARTICIPANTS (Signatories of the Lausanne Covenant and/or committed to its framework and understanding of mission)

Dr. Saphir Athyal, Principal (President) of Union Biblical Seminary Yavatmal, India

Dr. Kwame Bediako, Lecturer in Biblical Studies and Theology, Christian Service College, Kumasi, Ghana

Prof. Dr. Peter P. J. Beyerhaus, Professor of Missiology and Ecumenics, Tubingen University, West Germany

Prof. Robinson Cavalcanti, Professor of Political Science at Recife Federal and Rural Universities of Pernambuco, Brazil

Dr. Chongnahm Cho, President and Professor, Seoul Theological Seminary, Bucheon City, Korea

Dr. Harvie M. Conn, Associate Professor of Missions and Apologetics, Westminster Theological Seminary, Chestnut Hill, Philadelphia, Pennsylvania

Rev. Dr. Orlando E. Costas, Director, Latin American Evangelical Centre for Pastoral Studies (CELEP), San Jose, Costa Rica

Mr. Edward R. Dayton, Director, MARC, Monrovia, California

Cand. theol. Tormod Engelsviken, Teacher of Theology, Fjellhaug School of Missions, Oslo, Norway

Dr. John A. Gration, Associate Professor of Missions, Wheaton Graduate School, Wheaton, Illinois

Dr. Donald R. Jacobs, Director, Mennonite Christian Leadership Foundation

Dr. F.S. Khair-Ullah, Director, Creative Writing Project of M.I.K. Pakistan

Dr. Charles H. Kraft, Professor of Anthropology and African Studies, School of World Mission, Fuller Theological Seminary, Pasadena, California

Rev. Dr. S. Ananda Kumar, Professor of Biblical Studies, Karnataka Theological College, Karnataka State, South India

Dr. Jacob A. Loewen, Translations Consultant for East Central Africa with the United Bible Societies

Dr. I. Howard Marshall, Reader in New Testament Exegesis, University of Aberdeen, Scotland

Dr. I. Wayan Mastra, Chairman of the "Gereja Kristen Protestan di Bali," Indonesia

Mr. Bruce J. Nicholls, Executive Secretary, Theological Commission, World Evangelical Fellowship

Rev. Gottfried Osei-Mensah, Executive Secretary, Lausanne Committee for World Evangelization

Rev. Dr. James I. Packer, Associate Principal, Trinity College, Bristol, England

Dr. C. René Padilla, Director of Ediciones Cereteza, International Fellowship of Evangelical Students

Dr. William E. Pannell, Assistant Professor of Evangelism, Fuller Theological Seminary, Pasadena, California

Rev. Pedro Savage, (Consultation Coordinator), Coordinator, Latin American Theological Fraternity, staff member of Partnership in Mission and of Latin American IFES

Rev. John Stott, (Consultation Chairman), Rector Emeritus, All Soul's Church, Langham Place, London

Dr. Charles R. Taber, Director, Institute of World Studies/Church Growth, Milligan College, Tennessee

Rev. Tite Tienou, Director of Bible School Bobo Dioulasso, Upper Volta, and Executive Secretary of A.E.A.M. Theological Commission

Dr. Alan R. Tippett, Hon. Research Fellow, St. Mark's Library, Canberra, A.C.T. Australia

Rev. Canon James Wong, Anglican Pastor and Coordinator of Asian Leadership Conference on Evangelism, Singapore

CONSULTANTS (in general sympathy with the Lausanne Covenant)

Bishop Kenneth Cragg, Reader in Religious Studies, University of Sussex, and Assistant Bishop of Chichester, England

Rev. Alfred C. Krass, Co-Editor of *The Other Side* magazine

Canon Prof. John Mbiti, Director of the Ecumenical Institute, Bossey, of
the World Council of Churches, Geneva, Switzerland

Bishop Stephen Neill, Resident Scholar, Wycliffe Hall, Oxford, England

VISITOR (contributing to a Consultation committed to the Lausanne
Covenant)

Rev. Louis J. Luzbetak, President, Divine Word College, Epworth, Iowa

Contributors

Stephen Neill, for many years missionary and bishop of the Anglican Communion in South India and East Africa, is the author of
A History of Christian Mission, *Jesus Through Many Eyes*, *Salvation Tomorrow*, and other volumes. He is at present resident
scholar at Wycliffe Hall, Oxford, and is writing a history of
Christianity in India.

I. Howard Marshall is Reader in New Testament Exegesis in the
University of Aberdeen. He is author of *The Gospel of Luke: A
Commentary on the Greek Text*, *I Believe in the Historical Jesus*,
and other volumes.

S. Ananda Kumar is professor of biblical studies, Karnataka Theological College, Karnataka State, South India. He heads a
team involved in village evangelism.

Bruce J. Nicholls is director of the Theological Research and
Communication Institute, New Delhi, India, and executive secre-
tary of the Theological Commission of the World Evangelical
Fellowship.

C. Rene Padilla is director of Ediciones Certeza, Buenos Aires,
Argentina, associated with the International Fellowship of
Evangelical Students. He is editor of *The New Face of Evangeli-
calism*, an international symposium on the Lausanne Covenant.

Charles R. Taber has worked in Central and West Africa, first as
a missionary and later as a United Bible Societies translation
consultant. He is editor of the missiological journal *Gospel
in Context*, and former editor of *Practical Anthropology*, a
pioneer missions journal of applied anthropology.

James I. Packer is associate principal, Trinity College, Bristol, England. He is author of *Knowing God* and *I Want to Be a Christian*.

Jacob A. Loewen has worked for many years with the United Bible Societies in anthropology and linguistics, assisting missionaries engaged in translation of the Bible in South America and Africa. He is author of *Culture and Human Values: Christian Intervention in Anthropological Perspective*.

Donald R. Jacobs is overseas secretary of the Eastern Mennonite Board of Missions and Charities. For many years he was Bishop of the Mennonite Church of East Africa.

Harvie M. Conn is associate professor of missions and apologetics, Westminster Theological Seminary, Philadelphia, Pennsylvania. He is editor of *Theological Perspectives on Church Growth*.

Orlando E. Costas is director of the Latin American Evangelical Center for Pastoral Studies (CELEP), San Jose, Costa Rica. He is author of *The Church and Its Mission: A Shattering Critique from the Third World*.

Kenneth Cragg is reader in religious studies, University of Sussex, and Assistant Bishop of Chichester, England. Known as a specialist in Christian-Muslim relations, he is author of *The Call of the Minaret*, *Christianity in World Perspective*, *The Christian and Other Religions*, and other volumes.

Charles H. Kraft is professor of anthropology and African studies, School of World Mission, Fuller Theological Seminary, Pasadena, California. He is author of a new missions textbook, *Christianity in Culture*.

Alfred C. Krass is a former missionary in Ghana and consultant on evangelism for the United Church Board for World Ministries. A co-editor of *The Other Side* magazine, he is author of *Go . . . and Make Disciples*, and *Five Lanterns at Sundown*.

I. Wayan Mastra is chairman of the *Gereja Kristen Protestan di Bali* (The Bali Protestant Church), Indonesia.

Gottfried Osei-Mensah, a former pastor in Nairobi, Kenya, is executive secretary of the Lausanne Committee for World Evangelization.

Alan R. Tippett is an Honorary Research Fellow, St. Mark's Library, Canberra, A.C.T. Australia. He is author of *People-Movements of Southern Polynesia*, *Solomon Islands Christianity*, and *God, Man and Church Growth*.

About the Editors

JOHN STOTT, rector emeritus of All Souls Church, Langham Place, London, is known for his leadership of the International Congress on World Evangelization, held in 1974 at Lausanne, Switzerland, and for his chairmanship of the committee that drafted the Lausanne Covenant. His informed concern for the critical issues of world mission is attested in the 1975 volume *Christian Mission in the Modern World* (London: Falcon). As chairman of the Lausanne Theology and Education Group, Dr. Stott chaired the 1978 Consultation on Gospel and Culture for which the papers in this present volume were prepared.

ROBERT T. COOTE is director of publications for Partnership in Mission, Abington, Pennsylvania. He was one of several who supported the Lausanne Theology and Education Group in the Coordination and follow-up of the 1978 Consultation on Gospel and Culture. He and Dr. Stott have edited a condensed and popularized version of the Consultation papers, to be released soon by the William B. Eerdmans Publishing Company.

Books by the
William Carey Library

GENERAL

Church Growth Bulletin, Second Consolidated Volume (Sept. 1969–July 1975) edited by Donald McGavran, $7.95x paper, 512 pp.

Evangelical Missions Quarterly, Vols. 7-9, $8.95x cloth, 830 pp.

Evangelical Missions Quarterly, Vols. 10-12, $15.95 cloth, 960 pp.

Evangelicals Face the Future edited by Donald E. Hoke, $6.95 paper, 184 pp.

The Ministry of Development in Evangelical Perspective edited by Robert L. Hancock, $4.95 paper, 128 pp.

Social Action Vs. Evangelism: An Essay on the Contemporary Crisis by William J. Richardson, $1.95x paper, 64 pp.

Word Study Concordance and New Testament edited by Ralph and Roberta Winter, $29.95 cloth, 2-volume set.

STRATEGY OF MISSION

Church Growth and Christian Mission edited by Donald McGavran, $4.95x paper, 256 pp.

Committed Communities: Fresh Streams for World Missions by Charles J. Mellis, $3.95 paper, 160 pp.

The Conciliar-Evangelical Debate: The Crucial Documents, 1964-1976 edited by Donald McGavran, $8.95 paper, 400 pp.

Crucial Dimensions in World Evangelization edited by Arthur F. Glasser et al., $7.95x paper, 512 pp.

Evangelical Missions Tomorrow edited by Wade T. Coggins and Edwin L. Frizen, Jr., $5.95 paper, 208 pp.

The Extension Movement in Theological Education: A Call to the Renewal of the Ministry by F. Ross Kinsler, $6.95 paper, 304 pp.

Here's How: Health Education by Extension by Ronald and Edith Seaton, $3.45 paper, 144 pp.

The Indigenous Church and the Missionary by Melvin L. Hodges, $2.95 paper, 108 pp.

Literacy, Bible Reading, and Church Growth Through the Ages by Morris G. Watkins, $4.95 paper, 240 pp.

Readings in Third World Missions edited by Marlin L. Nelson, $6.95x paper, 304 pp.

AREA AND CASE STUDIES

Christian Mission to Muslims - The Record: Anglican and Reformed Approaches in India and the Near East, 1800-1938 by Lyle L. Vander Werff, $8.95 paper, 384 pp.

The Church in Africa, 1977 edited by Charles R. Taber, $6.95 paper, 224 pp.

Indonesian Revival: Why Two Million Came to Christ by Avery T. Willis, Jr., $5.95 paper, 288 pp.

The Navajos are Coming to Jesus by Thomas Dolaghan and David Scates, $4.95 paper, 192 pp.

People Movements in the Punjab by Frederick and Margaret Stock, $8.95 paper, 388 pp.

Toward Continuous Mission: Strategizing for the Evangelization of Bolivia by W. Douglas Smith, Jr., $4.95 paper, 208 pp.